FIFTH EDITION

AMERICA'S TEACHERS

An Introduction to Education

JOSEPH W. NEWMAN

University of South Alabama

Boston   New York   San Francisco
Mexico City   Montreal   Toronto   London   Madrid   Munich   Paris
Hong Kong   Singapore   Tokyo   Cape Town   Sydney

10/06 AMAZON.3rd (EDU) (Replacement-PD)

Executive Editor and Publisher: Stephen D. Dragin
Editorial Assistant: Meaghan Minnick
Marketing Manager: Tara Kelly
Composition and Prepress Buyer: Andrew Turso
Manufacturing Buyer: Andrew Turso
Editorial-Production Coordinator: Mary Beth Finch
Editorial-Production Service: Stratford Publishing Services
Electronic Composition: Stratford Publishing Services

For related titles and support materials, visit our online catalog at www.ablongman.com

Between the time Website information is gathered and then published, it is not unusual for some sites to have closed. Also, the transcription of URLs can result in unintended typographical errors. The publisher would appreciate notification where these errors occur so that they may be corrected in subsequent editions.

Library of Congress Cataloging-in-Publication Data

Newman, Joseph W.
   America's teachers : an introduction to education / Joseph W. Newman.—5th ed.
      p. cm.
   Includes bibliographical references and index.
   ISBN 0-205-46396-7
      1. Education—United States—History.   2. Teaching—Vocational guidance—
United States.   3. Teachers—United States.   I. Title.

   LA217.2.N5   2006
   370'.973—dc22   2005050927

Printed in the United States of America

10 9 8 7 6 5 4 3 2 1   10   09   08   07   06   05

Photo Credits: 3, 36, 268, Pearson Learning Photo Studio; 73, 150, Pearson Education/PH College; 111 United States National Education Association; 179, The Library of Congress; 190, The Granger Collection; 202, Corbis-Bettmann; 208, Culver Pictures, Inc.; 209, Allyn & Bacon; 225, Lindfors Photography; 238, Larry Downing/ Woodfin Camp and Associates; 243, Bettmann Archive-Corbis; 329 AP/Wide World Photos; 375; Mary Kate Denny/PhotoEdit; 419, Prentice Hall School Division; 437, Tony Freeman/PhotoEdit.

CONTENTS

■ ■ ■ ■ ■ ▬▬▬▬▬▬▬▬▬▬▬▬▬▬▬▬▬▬▬▬▬▬▬▬▬▬▬▬

CHAPTER 3

Learning to Teach and Proving
Your Competence   73

CHAPTER 4

Joining a Teacher Organization and Empowering a Profession   111

CHAPTER 5

Exercising Your Rights and Fulfilling Your Responsibilities   150

PART II   SCHOOLS AND SOCIETY   177

CHAPTER 6

History of American Education   179

CHAPTER 7

Theories of Education   225

CHAPTER 9

Politics of Education   329

PREFACE

Every chapter in this fifth edition of *America's Teachers* contains new material. The book has evolved with every edition, but this one reflects the most extensive revisions yet because of the sweeping changes under way since the passage of the No Child Left Behind Act of 2001 (NCLB). Before I describe how this book has changed, let me explain how it is organized.

The five chapters in Part I are designed to promote informed career decisions. Prospective teachers will investigate the occupation they are considering by examining their motivation and the job market; compensation and evaluation; preparation, licensing, and certification; unions, other organizations, and professionalism; and education law. Part II encourages prospective teachers to explore the relationship between schools and society in four chapters on history, philosophy, sociology, and politics—the foundations of education. The two chapters in Part III offer critical studies of private schooling and educational choice and the effects of standards, assessments, and accountability on the curriculum.

I have updated the research base of every chapter in the book. Prospective teachers will find the latest statistics, Internet boxes and suggested readings, and hundreds of footnotes that, according to some of my colleagues, are almost over the top. I've kept all the documentation. Students say it helps them with their research in other courses.

As I prepared this new edition, I especially enjoyed adding new material on diversity. Chapter 8 on the sociology of education, now the most extensive chapter in the book, has expanded with a fifty-year retrospective on the *Brown* decision, a sharper and more critical analysis of race and whiteness, and more emphasis on Hispanic students. Throughout *America's Teachers* I analyze the impact of school reform on poor, minority, limited English proficient, and disabled students—the "subgroups" that No Child Left Behind calls to our attention. And I pay more attention than NCLB does to gender.

To be sure, the federal law is leaving its mark on the schools. I have rewritten the first half of Chapter 3 around the *highly qualified teacher* provisions of NCLB; the second half analyzes the drive to reform teacher education from the inside, the movement led by the National Council for Accreditation of Teacher Education (NCATE), the Interstate New Teacher Assessment and Support Consortium (INTASC), and the National Board for Professional Teaching Standards (NBPTS). Chapter 2 explains how NCLB, a perfect match for merit pay, is influencing teacher salaries and evaluation. Chapter 4 looks at why the National Education Association (NEA) and the American Federation of Teachers (AFT) have so many reservations about President George W. Bush's education agenda. Chapter 8 investigates the achievement gaps associated with social class, race and ethnicity, English language proficiency, and disability. Chapter 11 pulls together material from throughout the textbook to show how standards, assessments, and accountability may be fundamentally changing teaching and learning. Chapter 9 provides the political context for it all.

Be prepared for a critical discussion. Although this book has a proteacher slant, I constantly push students to consider several points of view on every issue we examine.

I would like to thank the following reviewers, who commented on the drafts of this edition: Susan H. Christian, Patrick Henry Community College; Daniel J. Thompson, Eastern Connecticut State University; Winifred E. Pitts, Southeast Missouri State University; Richard J. Reynolds, Eastern Connecticut State University; Samuel Securro, Jr., Marshall University Graduate College; and Reulan P. Levin, Avila University.

Teaching runs in my family. I dedicate this edition of *America's Teachers* to Wanda Newman, my wife, partner, and best friend. I'm proud to say she's a wonderful teacher.

PART I

TEACHING AS AN OCCUPATION

CHAPTER 1

DECIDING TO TEACH AND FINDING A JOB

When I go home every day, I know that what I do matters to society. I am enriched by the countless students who daily share with me their courage, enthusiasm, talent, sometimes off-the-wall humor, and sheer joy for learning. There isn't a better job anywhere.

—Utah teacher[1]

I hear language and see behavior you wouldn't believe. Not just from a certain group of students—from most of them. When I get on their case, the principal tells me to get used to it. How can I teach in that kind of atmosphere?

—Florida teacher[2]

MOTIVES FOR TEACHING

Talking with prospective teachers about why they want to teach is an excellent way to begin a discussion of teaching as an occupation. On the first day of class, I always ask the students in my introductory education classes to write down their major motive for teaching. Comparing their responses with the results of similar surveys conducted around the nation, I see several clear patterns.

Why do *you* want to be a teacher? Although you probably have several reasons, try to narrow them to your major motive for wanting to teach. Now compare your response with those in Table 1.1. If your motivation centers on *students,* you have plenty of company. With remarkable consistency, about half the prospective teachers in my classes link their desire to teach directly to young people. If *academics*—the love of a particular subject or of learning in general—prompts you to teach, you are also in good company. Approximately one-fifth of the future teachers in my survey give academic reasons as their major motive. Surveys conducted throughout the nation show the same patterns: Student-centered motives top the list, with academic motives running a distant second or third.[3]

Other motives for teaching (and the rounded percentages of my prospective teachers who put them in first place) include *job advantages* (10 percent), the *social value* of teaching (10 percent), and the *influence of other teachers* (5 percent). These patterns, too, are consistent with the results of other surveys. The brief statements

TABLE 1.1   Why Do You Want To Be a Teacher? Motives of Prospective Teachers

1. Students
   "I love children."
   "I like working with young people."
   "I want to help students."
   "I believe I can make a difference in their lives."
2. Academics
   "I enjoy [a particular subject]."
   "I love learning."
3. Job advantages
   "I like having my summers off."
   "My hours as a teacher will match my children's hours in school."
   "Teaching is a good job for people on their way to something else."
4. Social value
   "Teaching is society's most important job."
   "I can improve society by teaching."
5. Influence of other teachers
   "Some of my teachers helped me so much, they made me want to teach."
   "Some of my teachers hurt me so much, they made me want to teach."

Sources: This profile is based on my ongoing survey of prospective teachers at the University of South Alabama and on National Education Association, *Status of the American Public School Teacher 2000–2001* (Washington, DC: NEA, 2003), 69–71; and Susan M. Brookhart and Donald J. Freeman, "Characteristics of Entering Teacher Candidates," *Review of Educational Research* 62 (1992): 37–60.

quoted in Table 1.1 are representative of the ways future teachers summarize their motives.

Considered as a whole, studies of motivation pay future teachers genuine compliments. Teachers are altruistic; they want to help. Most of them enter the occupation with the welfare of others in mind, believing they can make a difference in their students' lives. The prospective teachers I work with are choosing such words as "to make a difference in students' lives" more and more often to explain why they want to teach. They are convinced young people need responsible guidance more than ever before. Table 1.1 also indicates some future teachers have been helped—or, in a few cases, hurt—so much by their own teachers, they feel motivated to go back to the classroom. Some extend their concern for others to society as a whole.

Now notice what the surveys do *not* say. People do not go into teaching for the money—with good reason, as we will see in Chapter 2. Nor do people choose teaching for the prestige. Americans respect teachers, but it is a peculiar respect—the kind accorded to outsiders or people set apart from the mainstream of society.[4]

Perceived Advantages of Teaching

Can we take at face value what prospective teachers say about their motives? Aren't some of their statements too good to be true? Based on my work with future teachers, I am convinced their altruism and idealism are real. But because of what they say outside of class, informally and off the record, I am also convinced the perceived advantages of the occupation pull more people into teaching than the surveys indicate.

Notice the job advantages listed in Table 1.1. Teacher education students often joke, "Teaching has three main benefits: June, July, and August." Of course the summer vacation is attractive, but should it be someone's major reason for wanting to teach? Prospective teachers who admit it is, along with others who are reluctant to confess, should consider that some school districts have already adopted a year-round schedule, and the summer break is closer to ten weeks than to twelve in most districts. Taking graduate and inservice courses during the summer further reduces time off.

So does moonlighting. According to *Status of the American Public School Teacher 2000–2001* (2003), a study from the National Education Association (NEA), 32 percent of America's teachers work a second job. Thirteen percent hold an evening or weekend job outside their school systems during the school year, and 19 percent find outside summer employment. Interestingly, many teachers say they moonlight not for the extra income, but for the contact with adults, something they miss on their day jobs.[5]

Another perceived advantage of teaching is the daily schedule. As more nontraditional students (age twenty-five and older), many of them women, go to college to pursue the degrees they did not obtain when they were younger, more students talk frankly about choosing a career that will allow them to spend time with their own children. As a parent, I can appreciate this motive, but should it be first on a prospective teacher's list? Although the nontraditional students in my classes have generally realistic expectations of the occupation, they often underestimate the time demands teaching will make on their evenings and weekends.[6]

Finally, there is the perception that teaching is a good temporary job for people who have other career and life plans in mind. As students sometimes tell me, "Eventually I want to do something else, but I think I'll teach for a while. After all, teaching is easy to get into and easy to get out of." Actually this is an old notion. Historical studies going back to the colonial era show how some teachers (mostly males) have used the occupation as a stepping-stone to other careers, while others (most of them females) have used it as a way station en route to marriage and family.[7]

Teachers Who Love, Teachers Who Care

Americans view teaching as women's work. The feminization of the occupation began in the mid-1800s when school boards turned increasingly to women to fill teaching positions. Females had two advantages over the males who had dominated the occupation: The character and personality of women were regarded as better suited to working with young children, and women constituted a cheap, reliable labor force. These nineteenth-century perceptions are with us still. Today two out of three secondary school teachers and nine out of ten elementary school teachers are women, and the percentages are even higher in areas of the nation where highly traditional views of sex roles prevail.[8]

"I Love Children."   Prospective teachers often use these words to express their motivation for teaching. Thus we would expect employed teachers to reflect the same sentiment. The evidence, though, is curiously mixed. Contemporary and historical studies of teachers' letters and diaries reveal few discourses on loving children. Instead, teachers discuss how demanding teaching is or focus on matters unrelated to their work. In these letters and diaries, documented in Nancy Hoffman's wonderful book, *Woman's "True" Profession: Voices from the History of Teaching* (2003), teaching comes across as a job, something people do for economic survival. Yet for a century and a half, society has been sending women the message they should teach because they love children. They should want to be teachers—obviously not for the money but for the children. It is almost as if women, trying hard to please by saying what society expects, have repeated "I'm going to teach because I love children" so often they have come to believe it.[9]

Perhaps this discussion is too harsh. Teachers *should* care about students, and the evidence suggests the vast majority of them do. Nel Noddings and other feminist scholars applaud the fact that most teachers, especially those who are women, make caring about students central to their work. When asked why they stick with their demanding jobs, teachers have a ready answer: the students. Responding to ongoing surveys conducted by the NEA and other organizations, an overwhelming majority of teachers talk about students when asked what they like best about their work. Here, happily, is a pattern that has held constant throughout many years of ups and downs in the occupation.[10]

For convincing evidence of how student-centered teachers really are, read almost any issue of *NEA Today*, a magazine for members of the National Education Association (NEA). The "People" section is an especially good place to look. "I always wanted to do something that could make a difference in people's lives," says a California teacher, sounding just like many of my future teachers. "I have one of the greatest jobs in the world." A Michigan teacher with twenty-eight years of experience puts it this way: "I want to make students feel better about themselves when they leave my class than they did when the semester began. . . . Humans are fragile creatures whose egos need stroking and bolstering." A Tennessee teacher explains why she was willing to leave a marketing job with an excellent salary and fringe benefits: "No other profession offers the opportunity to mold dreams and mend broken destinies. I suppose there are just some things an expense account can't begin to cover." A school counselor who was honored as Ms. Wheelchair Colorado believes "it is important for children to realize that people with disabilities can still achieve their goals. Wheelchairs are like glasses. They are tools, not limitations." A California teacher whose career spans six decades, a veteran with "no qualms about using the word love," says the best teachers "exult when children succeed—and bleed when they hurt."[11] As a teacher educator, I only wish the public understood how much teachers care.

"Is Love Really All You Need?"   Admittedly, teaching is no job for people who do not care about young people, but personal concern is not the only quality teachers need. A logician would say caring about students is a necessary but not sufficient qualification for teaching. The job involves an entire range of interpersonal skills, plus much more. Teachers who enter the occupation motivated solely by their good feelings can be bitterly disappointed when students do not return their affection.

Metropolitan Life Surveys of the American Teacher documents the toll teaching takes on the idealism of new teachers. During their first year in the classroom, teachers begin to lose some of their confidence that "all children can learn." During the second year, teacher confidence in student learning slips still further. After spending two years in the classroom, fully half of teachers strongly believe "many children come to school with so many problems that it's difficult for them to be good students."[12]

Let me be blunt. Some students do not want your love. Think twice about becoming a teacher just because you care.

Leaving No Child Behind? Teachers and Culturally Diverse Students

Also reconsider your choice if you believe you will be teaching students whose socioeconomic backgrounds are similar to yours. A demographic profile of prospective teachers shows they are overwhelmingly middle-class white females. The vast majority grew up in suburbs or rural areas and want to return to teach students like themselves. Few want to teach in big cities, where teacher shortages are often acute. As we will see in Chapter 8, the demographic profile of America's public school students is strikingly different. A third of students are in large school districts with enrollments of more than 25,000. Nearly 20 percent of students are growing up in poverty. More than 40 percent—and this figure is steadily increasing—are African American, Hispanic American, Asian American, or Native American.[13]

Each of these minority groups is *underrepresented* in the teaching force; that is, each group makes up a smaller percentage of teachers than it does of students and the general population. Overall, only 15 percent of public school teachers are minorities. Despite the strong demand for minority teachers in almost every teaching field, the number of minority teachers graduating from teacher education programs remains small. As Chapter 3 points out, America's schools are beginning a new century with a student body more multicultural than ever before and a teaching force that, with respect to diversity, is simply not keeping pace. These trends suggest a serious and increasing mismatch between teachers and students.

Future teachers are increasingly unlikely to find jobs teaching Dick-and-Jane kids. Instead, according to the *Education Week* special report *Quality Counts 2003*, many will report for work in "high-poverty, high-minority, and low-achieving schools." *Metropolitan Life Surveys* points out that new teachers assigned to these schools are the teachers most likely to conclude "many students come to school with so many problems that it's difficult for them to be good students." As important as it is to increase the percentage of minorities in the occupation, African American and Hispanic American teachers also experience disappointment and disillusionment. Before their first year of teaching, white teachers are twice as likely as African American and Hispanic American teachers to agree with the above statement about students and their problems. By the end of the first year, African American and Hispanic American teachers are just as likely as their white counterparts to agree.[14]

The editors of *Education Week* dedicated *Quality Counts 2003* to closing the "teacher gap," to finding "well-qualified teachers for those who need them most": the students in the toughest schools. Conceding there is no single, simple solution, *Quality Counts 2003* focuses attention on improving teacher preparation, recruitment, support, salaries, and working conditions—strategies we will examine throughout this textbook.

The No Child Left Behind Act of 2001 (NCLB), which we will also discuss throughout the book, is the driving force behind school reform today. This federal law mandates a *highly qualified teacher* for every student. NCLB also holds teachers accountable for the standardized test scores of all students, including those who are poor, minority, disabled, and limited in English proficiency. Closing the *achievement gap* between these students and others will be, to say the least, a challenge. Are you ready for it?[15]

Teaching as Academic Work

Future teachers not only need to consider the kind of students they will be working with, they also need to think seriously about the kind of work they will be doing. Some prospective teachers, not particularly fond of any academic subject, may gravitate toward elementary, early childhood, or special education, where they believe the emphasis will be on "getting along with the kids." They think much of the school day will be filled with games and activities. The human side of teaching will be fun and rewarding. As for the academic side, surely they will know more than their students. Besides, a number of people—including some teachers and administrators—have told them you don't have to be very smart to be a teacher. They may even have heard being too bright can hurt.

Let me dispel several myths about teaching. In spite of all the publicity about teacher burnout, some people cling to the belief teaching is a fun job. It is not. Getting through to students can certainly be rewarding, but reaching them takes hour after hour of effort. Fun is not the right word. Listen to the counsel of a Florida teacher: "Teaching is work. It is the hardest job there is. Learning is work. We try to make it enjoyable, interesting, exciting, motivating, relevant, palatable, etc. But any way you slice it, it's work."[16]

Notwithstanding the public outcry over academically incompetent teachers, some people believe another myth: Rudimentary literacy is the only academic qualification teachers of the youngest or least able students must have. It is not. This myth, another holdover from the past, finds no support in the research on teacher effectiveness. Nevertheless, it dies hard.

Perhaps such myths appeal to a basic anti-intellectual streak in the American character. When taken to the extreme of "the smarter you are, the worse you will do as a teacher," the mindset has disastrous effects on the occupation. On college campuses, it crops up in the guise of professors who steer bright students away from elementary teaching and toward secondary teaching, or toward college teaching, or out of teaching entirely. In school districts, it appears in the form of administrators and personnel officers who are wary of teacher applicants with excellent grades and test scores because they believe such people will not be patient with slower students. Despite the lack of evidence to support this myth, some districts search diligently for teachers whose academic abilities are mediocre. After all, they reason, these people will probably be less likely to leave teaching for another career.[17]

Education Week devoted its first special report of the new century to the question "Who Should Teach?" According to *Quality Counts 2000,* who *should* teach appears to be quite different from who usually does. When researchers recently tracked the career decisions of college graduates and followed them into the workplace, they found "at every step of the way, the less academically able chose teaching."[18]

Yes, this discussion is harsh. To put things more positively, America has many fine teachers. The best teachers strike a balance between their concern for academics and their concern for students. They do not emphasize one to the exclusion of the other. But today the scales of the occupation are out of balance, tipped heavily toward the concern for students. When recruiting teachers, society in effect asks college students who care about young people to step forward. After academic requirements screen out a few candidates, many of the remainder become teachers.[19]

Suppose society sends a different message: Will people with excellent academic skills please step forward? Of these, the candidates who care about students *and* are able to help them learn can become teachers. To balance the scales in this way will require top-to-bottom reform of teaching as an occupation—major

BOX 1.1

EDUCATION WEEK

Education Week, the "newspaper of record" for K–12 schools, is available online at www.edweek.org. The searchable archives contain every back issue, including the special *Quality Counts* reports. I find *Education Week* more helpful than any other source in keeping this textbook up-to-date. Unfortunately, in 2004 the newspaper's Web site became a pay site.

improvements in teacher salaries and working conditions, as well as in teacher education and licensing.*

Make no mistake about it, these are radical reforms. As we will see in the following chapters, though, the odds they will occur are better today than in earlier years. Despite the many problems we will discuss in the next section and throughout this book, there are good reasons to be cautiously optimistic about teaching as an occupation.

SATISFACTION WITH TEACHING

Ask currently employed teachers how they feel about their jobs. Listen carefully to their answers because they are speaking volumes about teaching as an occupation. Since 1961, the NEA, the nation's largest teacher organization, has asked teachers the ultimate question about job satisfaction: If you could make your decision again, would you teach? The trends in their answers, collected by the NEA at five-year intervals, are reported in Table 1.2.

Throughout the 1960s and into the early 1970s, at least three-fourths of teachers responded they would teach again, with fewer than 15 percent saying they would not. As late as the mid-1970s, more than 60 percent said they would enter the occupation again, while fewer than 20 percent said they would not.

These changes in job satisfaction, though, were an early sign something was going wrong with teaching. The survey conducted in 1980–1981 left no doubt: Only 46 percent of teachers gave their occupation a vote of confidence, while more than a third said they would choose another career.

Some of the most encouraging news in years about teaching is that the four most recent NEA surveys have shown higher levels of satisfaction. Although votes of confidence in the occupation have not returned to the levels of the 1960s and early 1970s, the fifteen-year downward spiral has reversed. The 1986 survey marked the beginning of a turnaround, and the 1991 survey documented further progress. The 1996 survey showed 63 percent of teachers saying they would teach again, a level that dipped slightly, to 60, in 2001.

*Reflecting terminology changes now under way in the occupation (see Chapter 3), I use *license* in this textbook to refer to a state permit to teach. State licensing, traditionally called state certification, attempts to ensure teachers have met minimum standards of competence.

11

**TABLE 1.2   If You Could Make Your Decision Again, Would You Teach?
Teachers' Responses**

RESPONSE	PERCENTAGE OF TEACHERS								
	1961	1966	1971	1976	1981	1986	1991	1996	2001
Certainly/probably would	76	77	74	64	46	49	59	63	60
Chances are about even	13	13	13	18	18	20	19	17	18
Certainly/probably would not	11	9	13	19	36	31	22	20	21

Note: Percentages may not total 100 due to rounding.

Source: National Education Association, *Status of the American Public School Teacher 2000–2001* (Washington, DC: NEA, 2003), Tbl. 51, p. 70. Reprinted with permission of the National Education Association copyright 2003. All rights reserved.

Twenty-one percent insist they would not teach again—a level of dissatisfaction roughly twice as high as during the 1960s and early 1970s. When teachers speak out on the reasons for their dissatisfaction, they highlight several qualities that have become scarce in the public schools, where almost 90 percent of them work. Polls of teachers conducted by Phi Delta Kappa over the last twenty years show teachers believe the main things lacking in the schools are parental interest and support, public financial support, student discipline, and student interest. Compounding these problems, from the teachers' point of view, is the fact that the general public sees things differently. While comparable Phi Delta Kappa/Gallup polls of public attitudes show that Americans readily bring up the lack of money and lack of student discipline as the two biggest problems facing the public schools, poll takers have to prompt people to get their agreement that low parental support and low student interest can "contribute to learning failures."[20]

These problems bother teachers because they are who they are. Most of them, as we have seen, go into teaching because they want to work with students, to help them. Other teachers are attracted to a subject or to the learning process. These teachers, along with others whose motives are equally idealistic, enter the occupation only to discover their work always demands much and often returns little. Teachers care, but they say too few of their students do. It upsets teachers even more that so few parents care. According to a study commissioned by the Sylvan Learning Centers, 95 percent of teachers believe motivating children to learn is the parents' responsibility. Fewer than half of parents agree, and almost three-fourths of parents blame teachers when students fail to get a good academic start in their early school years. That hurts.[21]

Family psychologist and syndicated newspaper columnist John Rosemond touches this sensitive nerve whenever he invites his readers to comment on the dedication of public school teachers. Are most of them "lazy," he asked in a 2004 column, or "self-sacrificing"? Prompted by complaints that teachers sometimes assign homework that requires parental help and then don't grade it, Rosemond concluded that parents and teachers seem to be trading responsibilities: "Parents send undisciplined children to school, expecting teachers to discipline, and teachers send under-educated children home, expecting parents to teach." Rosemond often criticizes parents for doing a poor job of child raising. But when he argues that teacher unions, radical reformers, and tenure are giving teachers bad attitudes and turning them into "slackers," many teachers respond that he's looking for scapegoats and ignoring the real causes of their problems.[22]

What keeps teachers in the occupation then? To put the situation in the most positive and complimentary light possible, many teachers are so strongly committed to their work, they are able to overcome the problems they face. This perseverance is all the more admirable because they rarely receive the praise and recognition they deserve. Another positive but seldom-mentioned factor is that some teachers work in schools with the healthy vital signs other schools lack: supportive parents, adequate financial resources, and interested, well-behaved students.

Burnouts, Dropouts, and the Promise of School Reform

We must also acknowledge a far less pleasant reality: The economic risks of changing careers, combined with teachers' doubts about their ability to succeed in other lines of work, keep many of them on the job. Teachers who remain in spite of their desire to leave are candidates for *burnout*. Typically, they begin by missing a few days of class; then their absences increase. When they report to school, they go through the motions of teaching, but their commitment has gone. They may want to care; they may try to care; yet they cannot. The very quality that brought most of them into teaching, their concern for others, has dissipated. They are physically, mentally, and emotionally exhausted.[23]

Teachers are not the only workers who must cope with burnout, of course. As Thomas Skovholt points out in *The Resilient Practitioner: Burnout Prevention and Self-Care Strategies for Counselors, Therapists, Teachers, and Health Professionals* (2000), people who work in all the helping occupations are highly susceptible to burnout. Helpers have jobs that are stressful by their very nature and working conditions that often aggravate the stress. Fortunately, the workers in some helping occupations are able to manage stress by controlling their jobs, and some helpers have jobs with incentives that encourage people to cope. Other helping occupations, by contrast, leave their workers feeling demoralized and powerless, almost as if the jobs were perversely designed to burn people out.[24]

Doctors and Nurses.   Compare two occupations within the field of health care. Medical doctors and nurses both help the sick, but their jobs differ in several important ways. First, physicians have more *autonomy*, more control over their work. As we will see in Chapter 4, autonomy is the right to make decisions and use judgment. Physicians have a great deal of autonomy—more, in fact, than the members of any other occupation. Being in control helps them manage the stress of their work. But while physicians are in a position to give orders, nurses must take orders. Serving as the buffers between those in control and those who need medical help, nurses experience the frustration that comes from knowing what to do but lacking the authority to do it.[25]

Second, physicians have a greater sense of *self-esteem*. As members of America's most prestigious occupation, they receive a great deal of respect and admiration. Society regards physicians as full professionals but nurses as *semi*professionals. Several steps lower in the health-care hierarchy, nurses feel their work is underrated and underappreciated. They go home feeling far less positive than physicians about their contributions to their patients.[26]

Finally, as everyone knows, physicians earn substantially more than nurses. We do not have to be crass to understand how the *extrinsic rewards* of income go a long way toward encouraging workers to cope with occupational demands. Physicians work hard and receive high monetary rewards; nurses feel they work just as hard, but their incomes are only a fraction as high.

Teachers have more in common with nurses than with physicians. It may sound flattering to call teaching a "noble profession," but teaching, like nursing, is a semiprofession. In fact, teachers have recently become even less like physicians and more like nurses. Teachers have never had the autonomy accorded to full professionals, but beginning in the late 1970s teachers watched their informal control of the classroom slip away. As American education went back to basics by way of standardized testing, teachers lost control over how to teach, how to test, and how to grade. The trend toward regulation accelerated during the 1980s and 1990s, and now schools are marching to the tune of No Child Left Behind, the federal law that has altered the rhythm of classroom life as never before. Mandates of NCLB, as interpreted by state authorities and implemented by local officials, increasingly govern teachers' work, and they must comply whether or not they believe they are acting in the best interest of students. A barrage of public criticism has wounded the self-esteem of teachers. Their salaries are often not high enough to make coping with job stress seem worthwhile. So why try?[27]

Optimistic Scenario.   Chapter 4 points out encouraging signs the tide may be turning, that teachers themselves are trying to take charge of their occupation and move toward professionalism. Empowering teachers and reorganizing workplaces—these are the watchwords of *restructuring,* a school reform movement that began in the late 1980s and peaked during the 1990s. Restructuring put the spotlight on the individual school as a job site and on teachers as the workers with the greatest responsibility for helping students learn. At last, some teachers said, reformers were asking the right question: How can schools change to give teachers the power and support they need to help students?[28]

BOX 1.2

PROFESSIONALISM

As a textbook author, I get more e-mail from students and professors on the question of professionalism than any other issue. Feel free to contact me at jnewman@usouthal.edu

In some schools, in some school districts, and perhaps throughout some states, restructuring moved past the talking stage to produce real improvements. In the early 1990s, teachers in Connecticut, South Carolina, Iowa, Minnesota, Mississippi, New Jersey, and Wisconsin seemed most positive about the success of reform in their respective states. Local teacher organizations throughout the nation, inspired by the success of American Federation of Teacher (AFT) locals in Rochester, Toledo, Cincinnati, and other urban school districts, worked jointly with administrators and school board members on *site-based management* and other experiments in restructuring that promised to empower teachers as never before. We will examine these efforts in Chapter 4.[29]

Gerald Grant and Christine Murray, authors of *Teaching in America: The Slow Revolution* (1999), sketch an optimistic scenario in which social, political, and economic changes work to the benefit of people in the helping semiprofessions. "While doctors are accepting more and more regulation," Grant and Murray suggest, "the schoolteachers and nurses will slowly break out of long-established bureaucratic hierarchies and share more of the autonomy enjoyed by members of the high-status professions."[30] Ongoing women's movements will help narrow gaps in status and earnings. The "slow revolution" of teachers to take charge of their occupation will eventually triumph.

Pessimistic Scenario.   Some teachers find the above scenario hard to believe. As they see the situation, reform has come and gone—or passed them by completely. Restructuring, which never made genuine changes in some states and school districts, is no longer the buzzword among reformers.

Under No Child Left Behind, *standards, assessments,* and *accountability* are all the rage among politicians at every level of government. Even more strongly than during the 1980s, teachers throughout the nation feel high-stakes testing breathing down their necks. As we will find throughout this textbook, they hear almost constant warnings to raise standardized test scores or suffer the consequences. As pressure to "teach the test to meet the standards" erodes autonomy, teachers are growing cynical about school reform.

Many teachers find themselves agreeing with the conclusions of *What Matters Most: Teaching for America's Future* (1996), the report of the National Commission on Teaching and America's Future (NCTAF):

> When it comes to widespread change, we have behaved as though national, state, and district mandates could, like magic wands, transform schools. But all the directives and proclamations are so much fairy dust. . . . On the whole, the school reform movement has ignored the obvious: What teachers know and can do makes the crucial difference in what children learn. . . . School reform cannot succeed unless it focuses on creating conditions in which teachers can teach, and teach well.[31]

These words, written five years before the passage of NCLB, ring even truer today than when they were new.

Grant and Murray realize the slow revolution may not succeed. They outline an alternative scenario, a pessimistic one, in which "tightly engineered" and centralized controls not only increase their grip on K–12 teaching but spread upward to higher education. Another possibility, Grant and Murray suggest, is that nothing much may change, and business as usual will prevail. If either of these sequences of events carries through, teachers will continue to be "treated as functionaries, not as professionals capable of independent judgment."[32] So when the public asks why, after several decades and several waves of school reform, many teachers are still unhappy with their jobs, teachers can still point to their lack of autonomy, self-esteem, and extrinsic rewards.

Teachers who leave the occupation for greener pastures emphasize, again and again, the importance of the factors we are discussing throughout this chapter. Phi Delta Kappa polls of teachers give straight answers to the public's questions. Why do people leave teaching? The number one reason, according to teachers, is the lack of student discipline. This problem took over first place in the mid-1990s. The number two reason is low salaries, which held the top spot for many years. Lack of student interest and lack of parental support are in third and four place, respectively.[33]

The public can also learn a great deal from *Metropolitan Life Surveys* of "teacher dropouts" who have resigned from the occupation. What about teacher stress? Fifty-seven percent of the former teachers say they were under "great stress" in the classroom; only 22 percent find the stress as great in their new careers. Self-esteem? Sixty-four percent say the respect they received as teachers was less than they had expected. Do they miss teaching? Fifty-eight percent say they do, but 83 percent doubt they will ever return to the classroom, because almost all the dropouts are satisfied with their new careers.[34]

When currently employed teachers are polled about their work, their answers are much the same. Sadly, teachers who stick with the occupation echo the complaints of their colleagues who quit. *Metropolitan Life Surveys* show about one-fourth of teachers say they are "very likely" or "fairly likely" to leave within the next five years. Among new teachers, the ones most likely to think seriously about dropping out are those teaching high school, those working in inner-city or urban settings, and those teaching large numbers of poor or minority students. Among all teachers, more than half of those who feel stressed several days a week or more say they have seriously considered quitting.[35]

The good news, though, is that the percentage of all teachers who say they are likely to leave has decreased slightly since the 1980s, as salaries have improved for some teachers, particularly beginners (see Chapter 2). Working conditions have also improved for some teachers, particularly in districts where restructuring has made positive changes.[36]

The Critical Years Ahead

For your sake as a prospective teacher, I am trying to paint a realistic picture of the career you are considering. I prefer to call it realistic rather than negative, because there certainly are positive aspects. In the chapters that follow, we will see the optimistic scenario may well be viable. Teaching could be on the verge of making real progress.

The next few years will be critical. Consider this fact of occupational life: According to the National Center for Education Statistics, the nation needs to hire more than 2 million teachers during the first decade of this century.[37]

The graying of America's teaching force accounts for some of the need. The average age of teachers has reached 44, up from 33 in the mid-1970s, and the average length of teaching experience is now 17 years, more than double the 8 years of the mid-1970s. About one-fourth of those who leave the occupation each year are teachers who reach the end of their career and retire.[38] But quitting before retirement accounts for the other three-fourths of those who leave. As we have seen, teachers drop out for a variety of reasons.

Attrition hits hardest in the earliest stages of their careers: Between 20 and 30 percent of new teachers—some estimates run as high as 40 to 50 percent—quit within their first five years. That fact alone, one of the most sobering I present in this textbook, should make you think carefully about your career choice.[39]

The National Commission on Teaching and America's Future maintains that teacher retention is the "real school staffing problem." The problem is not, as politicians believe, a low supply of new teachers, but rather "high turnover among the teachers who are already there—turnover that is only aggravated by hiring unqualified and underprepared replacements who leave teaching at very high rates." In *No Dream Denied: A Pledge to America's Children* (2003), the NCTAF characterizes teaching as a "revolving door" occupation. Solving *this* problem will require fundamental reform in the schools: improving working conditions, particularly in the worst schools, so teachers can do their work and feel good about it. Otherwise, the door will keep right on spinning.[40]

Before examining the job market in detail, let's look at the big picture. In all, about 6 percent of teachers resign or retire each year, so we can predict that about two-thirds of the teachers who were in the occupation in 2000 will be gone by 2010. Increasing student enrollment, as the next section explains, is also pushing up the demand for teachers. The more than 2 million women and men who become teachers during this decade will be in an excellent position indeed to shape the future of the occupation.

What happens to American education during the critical years ahead may depend on whether parents and other citizens listen to teachers and make long-needed changes in teaching as an occupation. Reg Weaver, president of the NEA, and Edward McElroy, AFT president, constantly remind politicians and the general public that they can no longer afford to ignore teachers' voices. Former NEA President Mary Futrell put it this way: "I think what the teachers are saying and what they are crying out for is that they want to be treated like professionals and want to be paid like professionals." The late Albert Shanker, often at odds with the NEA as head of the rival AFT, in this case heartily agreed: "We have to quit treating teachers like they are hired hands in a factory and start treating them more like partners in a law firm." Otherwise, these leaders caution, the nation will be forced to replace a large number of its teachers with "illiterate baby-sitters."[41] Fair warning.

THE TEACHER JOB MARKET

Your main interest in the job market understandably revolves around your own prospects for employment. Articles in academic journals as well as the popular press offer contradictory views of the odds you face: "Teacher Shortage Worsens." "Teacher Shortage Vanishes." "No One Wants to Be a Teacher." "College Students Show More Interest in Teaching." Whom do you believe?

Always consider the source. Keep in mind that many people have a vested interest in shaping public opinion of the job market. Teacher organizations have been trying their best to convince the nation a major shortage of teachers is just around the corner. Visit the NEA and AFT Web sites, and you're likely to find material of the "Ready or Not: A National Teacher Shortage Looms" variety. The two unions hope that, with teachers in short supply, school systems will compete for their services by raising salaries and improving working conditions. Taxpayers will have to cooperate, of course, and teacher organizations want them to believe better salaries and working conditions offer the only hope for easing the shortage. Obviously, currently employed teachers stand to profit, but if these improvements attract more capable people into the occupation, as the NEA and AFT promise, the entire nation will benefit. These arguments received a great deal of exposure in the mid-to-late 1980s, when a flood of studies and reports on public education helped put the public in the mood to spend more money on schools.

Representing a different point of view are politicians committed to holding down taxes and social spending. They insist throwing money at educational problems will not solve them, adding teachers are better paid and more satisfied than their unions admit. Articles on their Web sites are likely to downplay teacher shortages with such reassurances as "The Sky Is Not Falling!" These politicians say the way to attract more *and* better teachers is to open the occupation to college graduates who have not been trained in traditional teacher education programs. Obviously the politicians have a sharp eye on the bottom line—they want to ease teacher shortages without raising the taxpayers' ante for public education—but their desire to improve the academic quality of the teaching force often seems sincere.

No Child Left Behind has strengthened their point of view, which was already gaining prominence during the 1990s as conservative Republicans increased their control at every level of government. After the election of George W. Bush in 2000, the idea that "highly qualified" teachers can be prepared in a variety of ways, not just in traditional, university-based programs, seemed to catch on across the political spectrum. Now it is the dominant point of view—stronger than ever since Bush's reelection in 2004—with Republicans voicing the idea often and Democrats usually singing the same tune.

I will organize our discussion of the job market around the *demand* for teachers and the *supply* of teachers. In both areas, I will rely heavily on demography, the study of population characteristics and trends.

Baby Boom, Generation X, Generation Y, and Beyond: The Demand for Teachers

Every discussion of the teacher job market must take account of the *baby boom*. Often called the postwar baby boom because it began when World War II ended, this demographic bulge of more than 70,000,000 people continues to throw its weight around in American schools and society. Actually the word *postwar* is misleading, because although the number of births in the United States started to climb in 1946, the peak year for births was 1957, and the number of births remained high through the mid-1960s (see Figure 1.1). Thus the baby boom was a phenomenon that lasted about twenty years. Most of the teachers who will retire in the first two decades of this century are baby boomers, but in this section we are more interested in the impact they had as K–12 students.[42]

The early boomers, the children born from the mid-1940s through the mid-1950s, took American education by surprise. The young people who would come of age in the era of Vietnam, civil rights, and social change strained their schools at the seams. Many of them attended elementary school on double sessions and found high schools and colleges unprepared for their arrival.

The children of the late baby boom, those born from the mid-1950s through the mid-1960s, those who would become young adults during the malaise of the

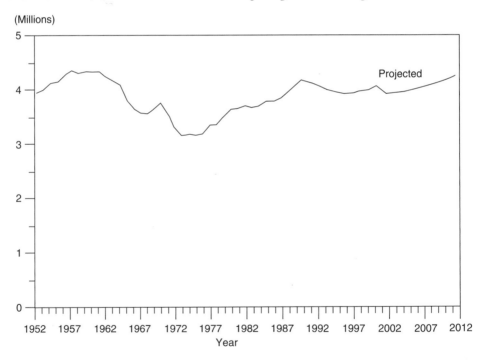

FIGURE 1.1   Births in the United States, with Projections: 1952–2012.

Source: U.S. Department of Education, National Center for Education Statistics, *Projections of Education Statistics to 2012* (2002) [Available: nces.ed.gov/pubs2002/proj2012/figure_01.asp].

1970s, found American education in a better state of physical if not academic readiness. These students strained the schools in other ways. Academic standards fell as drug use and discipline problems increased. School officials breathed a sigh of relief as the last boomers graduated from high school.

Now paying more attention to demography, officials knew the number of births had fallen throughout most of the period between the mid-1960s and the mid-1970s. As the students born during this era made their way through the schools, their much-smaller age cohort picked up the unfortunate label *baby bust*. Understandably, they hoped the label would not stick. What did eventually catch on was *Generation X*, a term the media coined to suggest the group's small numbers and hazy identity. These students saw their schools go back to basics as the national mood grew more conservative in the late seventies and eighties. The oldest students in this group became adults during the Reagan era; their youngest peers graduated from high school in the early nineties. Many of the college students now reading this textbook are Gen Xers.[43]

The demand for teachers rose and fell in response to these trends in student enrollment. As baby boomers entered school and enrollment went through the ceiling, the demand for teachers outstripped the supply. Teacher shortages developed, hitting elementary schools (K–8) during the 1950s and spreading to secondary schools (9–12) during the 1960s. Prospective teachers found excellent employment opportunities throughout this era.[44]

But the favorable job market did not last into the 1970s. Elementary school enrollment peaked in 1969 and then decreased with the baby bust until 1984—fifteen years of virtually unbroken decline. Enrollment in secondary schools reached a peak in 1976 and then decreased until 1990—fourteen years of decline. The total number of students in grades K through 12 decreased from 1972 through 1984. As enrollment dropped, the demand for teachers fell, and the job market soured.

Better Outlook Today.   In 1976 the United States entered the era of the *baby boomlet,* a phenomenon also dubbed the "echo" of the baby boom. At first the nation greeted the echo with little fanfare, but demographers now recognize it as a major trend. The baby boomlet shows up clearly in Figure 1.1. The number of births rose during much of the period between 1976 and 1990, not because of a significant increase in the *fertility rate* (which demographers define as the number of children born per year per 1,000 women) but simply because the baby boomers had entered their prime childbearing years and started families. Their families were often small, but there were so many of them.[45]

Boomlet kids have picked up the label *Generation Y.* Their birth years bridge the Jimmy Carter seventies and the Reagan-Bush eighties. Many grew up during the Clinton era. The youngest have come of age during George W. Bush's presidency, and the oldest were already adults. Some are college students reading this textbook as prospective teachers.

Children born since 1990, when the number of births reached a temporary peak, have yet to receive a label—at least not one that has stuck. Because their entire cohort is growing up in an era of sophisticated electronics, with computers and other high technology woven throughout the fabric of their lives, they are sometimes called the first completely digital generation, or *Generation D.*

Enrollment trends in elementary and secondary schools since 1988 reflect the departure of Generation X, the arrival and departure of Generation Y, and now the arrival of Generation D (see Figure 1.2.). According to *Projections of Education Statistics to 2013* by the National Center for Education Statistics, elementary enrollment rose from 1988 to 2001, fell slightly until 2005, and will rise again through 2013 and beyond. Secondary enrollment will peak in 2007 and then decline slightly for several years. Total K–12 enrollment has been rising since 1988 and is projected to increase through 2013 and thereafter. The overall demand for teachers should remain high.[46]

Even so, trends vary greatly from region to region and state to state. Figure 1.3 shows students coming on strong in the West and South, where enrollment is projected to increase by 13 percent and 4 percent, respectively. The western states that should register the greatest increases, percentage-wise, are Alaska (17 percent) and Hawaii (16 percent), while the southern states with the biggest increases should be Texas (11 percent) and Georgia (7 percent). Different patterns prevail in the

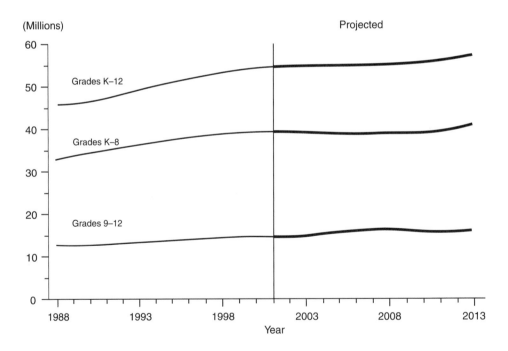

FIGURE 1.2   Enrollment in Elementary and Secondary Schools, with Projections: Fall 1988 to Fall 2013.

Source: U.S. Department of Education, National Center for Education Statistics, *Projections of Education Statistics to 2013* (2003) [Available: nces.ed.gov/programs/projections/figures/figure_02.asp].

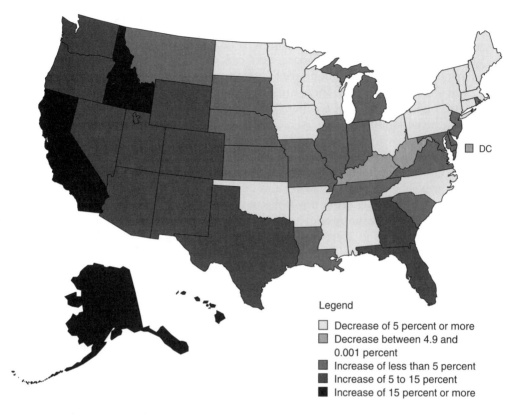

Legend

☐ Decrease of 5 percent or more
▨ Decrease between 4.9 and
    0.001 percent
▨ Increase of less than 5 percent
▨ Increase of 5 to 15 percent
■ Increase of 15 percent or more

■ DC

FIGURE 1.3   Percent Change in K–12 Enrollment in Public Schools, by State: Fall 2001 to Fall 2013.

Source: U.S. Department of Education, National Center for Education Statistics, *Projections of Education Statistics to 2013* (2003) [Available: nces.ed.gov/programs/projections/figures/figure_05.asp].

Midwest and Northeast. Projections call for enrollment to increase by less than 1 percent in the Midwest and to *decrease* by 2 percent in the Northeast. The midwestern states with the greatest percentage increases are expected to be South Dakota (3 percent) and Michigan (2 percent), while the only northeastern states expected to gain enrollment are New Jersey (3 percent) and Rhode Island (2 percent). Notice, though, that within every region except the West, where every state stands to gain, some states will see enrollment increases and others decreases.[47]

■ ■ ■ ■ ■

BOX 1.3

ENROLLMENT PROJECTIONS

To find out more about enrollment projections for the state where you plan to teach, visit the Web site of the National Center for Education Statistics. You can read *Projections of Education Statistics to 2013* online at nces.ed.gov/programs/projections.

A Complex Guessing Game: The Supply of Teachers

The information about teacher supply is far more speculative than the data on teacher demand. While demographers can confidently project elementary and secondary school enrollment well into the century by counting children who have already been born, there are no comparable sources of demographic information on the supply of teachers. A large number of hard-to-estimate variables enter the equation.

First, how many people will *want* to teach between now and, say, the year 2013? The answer hinges on a wide range of social, political, and economic factors, forces at work both inside and outside the occupation. We simply do not know what teacher salaries will be in 2013, for instance, or how attractive those salaries will be in the economy of the new century.

Second, how many people will society *allow* to teach? That answer depends in part on trends in teacher education and licensing. Social, political, and economic variables once again make it impossible to answer precisely.

We can try to answer, though, because we have reliable information on our past answers to such questions. We know that as the baby boom swelled elementary and secondary school enrollments, the news that teaching jobs were available traveled fast. College students responded by preparing to teach in larger numbers. Teacher education, long the most popular program at many colleges and universities, did tremendous business from the mid-fifties through the early seventies. Teacher educators swung the gates open wide in an effort to meet the demand for new teachers, with little concern for standards and selectivity. The public wanted teachers in those classrooms, and teacher educators were more than happy to deliver.

Unfortunately, we overcorrected. As the early baby boomers reached college in the mid-sixties, the gap between teacher supply and demand began to close with astonishing speed. "Major in education and you'll get a job," students were told, and many took the advice. The number of bachelor's degrees in education climbed steadily and peaked in 1972–1973. But recall how elementary school enrollment turned down after 1969 and secondary school enrollment declined after 1976. As these supply-and-demand trends came together, the unhappy result was the teacher surplus of the seventies. Almost overnight, or so it seemed, the job market was flooded with graduates in search of teaching positions that simply were not there.[48]

This news, too, traveled fast, and college students responded by turning away from teacher education. After 1972–1973, the number of bachelor's degrees awarded in education fell steadily for fourteen years. Given the size of the teacher surplus, though, the numbers did not fall nearly fast enough, and many education majors were disappointed when they failed to get a teaching job.[49]

Then the situation changed, once again so rapidly it caught many people off guard. The National Commission on Excellence in Education's *A Nation at Risk* (1983) and the barrage of reports that followed called attention to problems in the schools. Suddenly education was in the news almost every day. School reform became one of the hottest political issues of the 1980s. In state after state, governors and legislators put together reform packages that included pay raises for teachers. At the same time, as we have seen, Gen Xers began pushing up teacher demand. Teacher educators returned to campus in the fall of 1983 to find increasing numbers of freshmen interested in teaching, the first signs of a trend that continued into the 1990s.[50]

Now, in the 2000s, education still makes the news almost daily, and the share of college freshmen who say they want to teach has risen to about 10 percent. One wave of reform after another has kept education in the public eye: first the excellence movement of the 1980s in the wake of *A Nation at Risk,* then the restructuring that began in the late 1980s, and now the drive for state standards, assessments, and accountability. Political polls rank improving the schools as a top national priority. Other polls show teaching running second only to medicine as the career Americans would recommend to a family member. Teaching *leads* medicine, according to the public, as the occupation that benefits society the most.[51]

The message comes through loud and clear. Want to make a difference? Then try teaching.

In spite of our efforts to track the social, political, and economic trends that influence career decisions, predicting the supply of America's teachers remains a complex guessing game. School districts fill more than half their job openings with transfer teachers moving from one school to another (whether within the same district, within the same state, or from one state to another). First-time teachers must compete for jobs not only with transfers but also with former teachers reentering the occupation.[52]

Of the new recruits, most come into the occupation through traditional bachelor's degree programs, and many graduates of these programs are twenty-five and older. A growing number of first-time teachers are entering through master's-level programs and a variety of other alternative routes, which we will examine in Chapter 3. As we will see in the next section of this chapter, politicians have been eyeing every available source of supply—especially alternative routes—hoping to attract enough teachers to avoid or at least minimize a shortage.

The Politics of Teacher Supply and Demand

Shortages: Massive or Spot?   According to the conventional wisdom of the mid-1980s, the nation should now be grappling with a massive shortage of teachers. During the eighties, when report after report told Americans their schools were in trouble, respected commissions such as the Carnegie Forum on Education and the Economy issued dire warnings of an impending shortage. The Carnegie Forum's *A Nation Prepared: Teachers for the 21st Century* (1986) calculated that 23 percent of each college graduating class would have to enter teaching to avoid a major shortage by the early 1990s.[53] Officials of the NEA and AFT dramatized these warnings for the news media. In 1986, former AFT President Shanker predicted the demand for teachers would soon far exceed the supply, creating an "enormous gap." According to Shanker, the nation's schools would soon be searching for "hundreds of thousands of missing teachers."[54]

Looking back with hindsight from the early twenty-first century, we can see a large-scale shortage never materialized. Instead, we see "spot" shortages in particular teaching fields, particular regions of the country, and particular school districts. To generalize, we can say the nation as a whole has been hard-pressed to find enough special education, bilingual education, science, and math teachers; certain states, especially in the West and South, have had a difficult time hiring teachers in many fields; and rural and big-city school districts have also been struggling with shortages in many fields. But these are specific rather than overall imbalances between supply and demand.

So What Happened?   Why did the predictions of massive shortages miss the mark? The answer involves a fascinating case study in the politics of education.

The views of conservative Republican politicians represent one end of the spectrum of opinion on the teacher job market. President George W. Bush calls for opening up the occupation to bright people who know their academic subjects, whether or not they have completed a traditional teacher education program. U.S. Secretary of Education Margaret Spellings, like her predecessor Rod Paige, encourages state school officials to "raise standards" while they "lower barriers." For Spellings and Paige, who helped Bush overhaul teacher education and licensing while he was governor of Texas, raising standards means putting more emphasis on the subject-matter knowledge of prospective teachers. Lowering barriers means cutting back "rigid" licensing requirements that demand, in their view, "excessive numbers" of courses in education.[55]

No Child Left Behind requires states receiving federal Title I funds to insure that all teachers of core academic subjects are highly qualified. To be considered highly qualified, teachers must have

1. a bachelor's degree
2. competency in each core subject they teach, as determined by coursework and/or testing
3. full state licensure.

Each state has a great amount of leeway in defining the second and third requirements, particularly the standards for licensing. Trying to increase the flow of new teachers into the occupation, the president and his two secretaries of education have urged state school officials to take advantage of the flexibility of NCLB and open up "streamlined" alternative licensing programs that can "quickly get talented teachers into the classroom." Under the banner of high qualifications, the federal government is giving states the green light to cut teacher education courses to a bare minimum.[56]

At the other end of the spectrum of opinion are teacher educators who defend traditional training and licensing standards. Arthur E. Wise, president of the National Council for Accreditation of Teacher Education (NCATE), and Linda Darling-Hammond, professor of education at Stanford University and founding executive director of the National Commission on Teaching and America's Future, take the front lines of the defense. Darling-Hammond calls attempts to bypass teacher training and licensing "educational malpractice."[57]

Would society allow bright people who haven't taken all the courses required for a medical school diploma to practice medicine? Of course not, most Americans answer: not even if such people seem genuinely committed to helping people, not even if they want make a mid-career change from, say, biology or pharmacy. Med school is med school—no "streamlined" programs allowed. Shouldn't we be just as careful, then, about the people we allow to teach? As we will see in Chapters 3 and 4, teacher educators beg the question, and society hedges the answer.

Meanwhile, actors in the politics of education take stands at different points along the spectrum of opinion. The NEA and AFT position themselves close to the teacher educators' end of the spectrum. As former NEA President Robert Chase put it, "Americans wouldn't dream of entrusting our homes or our health to an unlicensed professional—or one with fly-by-night training. Yet time and again, we entrust the education of our children to teachers without adequate licensure." Many members of Congress, state governors, and state legislators—whether Republicans or Democrats—locate themselves toward the opposite end of the spectrum. State education officials move back and forth in response to trends in supply and demand.

Bending Standards, Changing Standards, and No Child Left Behind

It is important to place these issues in a larger context. Teacher shortages have been the rule rather than the exception in this century. Politicians and school officials have been willing to bend teacher education and licensing standards to help alleviate the shortages. The plain truth is that academic standards have taken a back seat to market demands. During the 1950s and 1960s, state legislators and state boards of education opened the occupation to large numbers of people with little or no formal training in education. When local school boards exhausted the supply of licensed teachers, state officials simply issued "emergency" licenses that allowed almost any warm body to teach.[58]

What else could we have done? politicians and school officials ask. Raising salaries and improving working conditions would have made the occupation more attractive, and salaries did rise gradually during the sixties. But the main response of the states was putting untrained people into classrooms. State officials also called on licensed teachers to teach out of field—that is, to teach academic subjects outside their areas of expertise—when local school boards ran short of personnel licensed in particular subjects, most frequently science and math.

In some respects, we are now witnessing a replay of the fifties and sixties. Faced with spot shortages in certain regions, school districts, and teaching fields, state officials are once again opening the occupation to large numbers of people with little or no formal preparation for teaching.

No More Emergency Licensing?   But today's situation is different because of No Child Left Behind. NCLB mandates that teachers of all core subjects—the vast majority of elementary, middle, and high school teachers—must be *highly qualified*, which means they must meet full requirements for state licensure. Passed in 2001, NCLB gave the states a 2005–2006 deadline for fully complying with the mandate. On the surface, this reform looks positive and plays well politically because it appears to eliminate emergency licensing.[59]

In reality, some states have simply changed the name of their "emergency" licensing programs to "alternative" licensing programs—with the encouragement and support of the U.S. Department of Education. Under NCLB, states can still hire applicants with no formal teacher preparation and allow them to teach for up to three years while they complete licensing requirements. Some alternative routes, as we will see in Chapter 3, offer an even shorter path into the occupation: Candidates can demonstrate their competence on a series of assessments, "test out" of virtually all education courses, and qualify for a license before they begin teaching.

NCLB also has provisions that appear to eliminate out-of-field teaching, another admirable goal that enjoys strong public support. But just as with the goal of ending emergency licensing, individual states control the standards that determine who is qualified to teach which subjects. Advocates and critics of NCLB agree that out-of-field teaching and emergency licensing—now concealed by new state regulations—are most widespread in poverty-level schools, small schools, and middle schools. Middle schools, widely regarded as the weakest level of American education, play fast and loose with teacher qualifications more often than elementary and high schools, a situation *Quality Counts 2000* calls the "middle school muddle."[60]

The media sometimes call emergency and out-of-field teaching "education's dirty little secret." One of the shadiest parts of the secret is that the least qualified teachers are likely to teach the students with the greatest needs. *Quality Counts 2003* concludes that "few states or districts try to match well-qualified teachers with high-need schools." On the contrary, school officials go to great lengths to disguise the extent of emergency and out-of-field teaching because they have so much trouble staffing the schools where the working conditions are usually the worst.[61]

Alternative Routes.   Well before the passage of NCLB, politicians were trying to ease the shortage of teachers by easing entry into teaching. Former New Jersey Governor Thomas Kean and State Education Commissioner Saul Cooperman led the way in 1984, arguing people with bachelor's degrees in fields other than education, especially the arts and sciences disciplines, can often make excellent teachers. The New Jersey plan, more fully described in Chapter 3, allows people with such credentials to bypass traditional teacher education and move directly into elementary and secondary classrooms as provisional teachers. Now about one-fourth of New Jersey's teachers are entering the occupation by the alternative route. In California and Texas, two other pioneers of alternative licensing, 18 and 24 percent, respectively, of new teachers take a shortcut into teaching.[62]

In all, at least forty-three states and the District of Columbia have opened alternative routes into teaching. Several seem to be competing for the "Easiest Entry into Teaching" award, requiring just a handful of credit hours in education beyond an arts and sciences bachelor's degree for full licensure. Other states, by contrast, require as many as forty-five credit hours in education as part of a complete master's degree program. Here, then, is another reason the teacher shortage has been mild: Politicians have managed the shortage by opening up the occupation, a movement that is still under way as we begin the new century.[63]

Inspired by the ideas of lowering barriers and easing entry, programs such as Teach for America, Transition to Teaching, and Troops to Teachers are playing a role in the new politics of the job market. Teach for America encourages graduates of top-rung public and private colleges to try their hands at teaching, if only en route to careers as doctors, lawyers, or executives. Transition to Teaching appeals to mid-career professionals who are looking for a job with greater personal and social meaning. Troops to Teachers, sponsored by the U.S. Departments of Education and Defense, recruits retirees from the armed forces. All of these programs emphasize a short period of formal training—typically one summer—and the promise of support on the job. School districts facing teacher shortages, particularly for poor and minority students, often turn to these programs.[64]

Whether alternative licensing will eventually crowd out traditional licensing remains to be seen. Constantly shifting political winds combined with social and economic changes make it difficult to forecast how many people will want to teach, how many society will allow to teach, and thus, the job market.

Connecting with a Teaching Position

Job Search Handbook for Educators.   One thing we can do is look at the success prospective teachers are having in their search for jobs. Table 1.3 is a status report on the job market based on research conducted by the American Association for Employment in Education (AAEE). Every year, AAEE surveys teacher placement officers throughout the United States to produce a rank-ordered list of teaching fields based on the balance between teacher supply and demand in each field. This table is a valuable guide to the job market in the nation as a whole.

AAEE publishes an annual *Job Search Handbook for Educators* (see recommended readings at the end of this chapter), a manual that offers advice on everything from putting together a résumé and assembling a portfolio to preparing for an interview and making a good first impression. The *Job Search Handbook* also includes the latest information on teacher supply and demand, listed field by field, as well as region by region. This information is important because, in almost every teaching field, the market varies considerably from one region of the country to another.

Relocating for a Job.   As many prospective teachers view the job market, though, it is not national, regional, or statewide but local. Teachers tend to be less willing than, for instance, lawyers or accountants to move to obtain a job. The

TABLE 1.3   The Job Market for Teachers: Outlook in 2004

TEACHING FIELDS

Considerable Shortage
1. Special education—multicategorical
2. Special education—severe/profound disabilities
3. Physics

Some Shortage
4. Mathematics
5. Bilingual education
6. Special education—mild/moderate disabilities
7. Special education—mental retardation
8. Chemistry
9. Special education—emotional/behavioral disorders
10. Special education—learning disabilities
11. Special education—visual impairments
12. Special education—dual certification (generalist/specialist)
13. Special education—hearing impairments
14. Spanish
15. Special education—early childhood
16. English as a second language
17. Biology
18. Earth/physical science
19. Speech pathology
20. Audiology
21. General science
22. Technology education
23. Administration—superintendency
24. School nursing
25. School psychology
26. Agriculture
27. Computer science

Balanced Supply and Demand
28. Administration—high school principalship
29. Counseling
30. Administration—middle school principalship

31. Administration—elementary school principalship
32. Library science/media technology
33. Occupational therapy
34. Physical therapy
35. School social work
36. Japanese
37. Speech education
38. Reading
39. Home economics/consumer science
40. Instrumental music
41. French
42. Vocal music
43. German
44. Classical languages
45. Curriculum supervision
46. Administration—business management
47. Special education—gifted/talented
48. Administration—human resources
49. General music
50. Elementary education—middle
51. English/language arts
52. Business education
53. Journalism
54. Art/visual education
55. Theater/drama
56. Elementary education—intermediate
57. Driver education/traffic safety

Some Surplus
58. Elementary education—prekindergarten
59. Elementary education—kindergarten
60. Health education
61. Elementary education—primary
62. Social studies
63. Physical education

Considerable Surplus
None

Source: American Association for Employment in Education, *2004 Job Search Handbook for Educators* (Columbus, OH: AAEE, 2003), p. 13. Copyright 2003 by AAEE. Used by permission.

■ ■ ■ ■ ■

BOX 1.4

U.S. DEPARTMENT OF EDUCATION WEB SITE

From Alabama to Wyoming, every state department of eduction has a link at bco102.ed.gov/Programs/EROD/org_list.cfm?category_ID=SEA, a page on the U.S. Department of Education's Web site. Take time to explore other parts of the www.ed.gov site.

financial payoff from a move is less for teachers, and many have family and personal ties that make them reluctant to leave a given area. Teachers who *are* willing to relocate—even within their state—can improve their job prospects dramatically. New York State teachers, for example, can often improve their chances if they are willing to teach in New York City or a rural upstate county rather than in a suburb. Teachers in most other states can follow the same guidelines. In general, the school systems with the greatest difficulty filling vacancies are in central cities and rural areas.[65]

Teachers who want to relocate should find it easier than ever. A good first step is checking to see whether your state is a member of a regional consortium that allows teachers licensed in one state to teach in any other participating state within the region. Teachers who complete preparation programs approved by the National Council for Accreditation of Teacher Education (NCATE) find that many states will honor their licenses if they move. Members of the National Association of State Directors of Teacher Education and Certification (NASDTEC), which includes all fifty states, the District of Columbia, U.S. territories, Department of Defense (DOD) schools, and several Canadian provinces, are beginning to practice "reciprocity" by honoring one another's teaching licenses. The Interstate New Teacher Assessment and Support Consortium (INTASC) is trying to make state-licensing standards more uniform. In the meantime, teachers who qualify for national certificates issued by the National Board of Professional Teaching Standards (NBPTS) probably have the closest thing to a truly "portable" license.[66]

Searching Online.   The Internet can be a powerful resource in your search for a teaching job. Whether you want to move across the country or stay close to home, the Internet can help. In fact, the best way to start a job search is to go online.

As the states begin to take more responsibility for teacher recruitment in the many local school districts inside their boundaries, state departments of education are making their Web sites more helpful to prospective teachers. Almost all provide information on available jobs, and some sites have highly interactive features. An Internet box explains how to reach state departments throughout the United States.

To find out about job availability in a local school district or a particular school, you can go through either a state department of education site or a directory. Two good directories are listed in the following Internet box, "School Directories." Directories also offer a way to locate jobs in private schools.

■ ■ ■ ■ ■

BOX 1.5

SCHOOL DIRECTORIES

Web 66, maintained by the University of Minnesota's College of Education at web66.coled.umn.edu/schools.html, is an International School Web Site Registry. You can use it to locate school districts and schools in the United States and abroad. Yahoo! has anther helpful index, which you can find at dir.yahoo.com/education/K_12/schools

Still another way to locate jobs is by going to the Web sites of teacher employment services. These groups range from university career service offices to commercial employment agencies. The following Internet box, "Search 800 Job Banks!" tells you how to find them.

Recruiting New Teachers, Inc.   As the job market goes high tech, even Madison Avenue gets into the act. "Reach for the Power—Teach" is the slogan of a national advertising campaign sponsored by Recruiting New Teachers, Inc. The toll-free number (800-45-TEACH) flashes on television screens across the nation as viewers learn no other occupation "has this power. The power to wake up young minds. The power to wake up the world. Teachers have that power. Reach for it. Teach." In its first three years of operation, Recruiting New Teachers logged nearly 400,000 calls, one-fourth from minorities and almost one-half from men. Unlike Teach for America, this group is not intent on bending or changing standards to get people into the occupation.[67]

Employment Fairs.   Another way to broaden your job search is to attend a recruitment fair. Florida has pointed the way for other states by holding an annual fair called the Great Florida Teach-In ("Teach Near the Beach!"), which draws large numbers of prospective teachers from the Southeast as well as other regions. In the words of one teacher who attended, "It's great to be wanted for a change. The Florida recruiters made me feel I have an important contribution to make to their state as a teacher." As other states follow Florida's lead, universities and private agencies are also holding recruitment fairs.

AAEE's *2004 Job Search Handbook* lists employment fairs across the nation. Some, such as the Bi-State Education Days in Illinois and Missouri, are regional. Others, like Oregon's, are statewide. Still others, like the Texas Gulf Coast fair, whose motto is "Change Tomorrow—Teach Today!" give prospective teachers a chance to meet representatives of several districts in one geographical area of a state. The largest school district in the nation wants you to know it is looking for candidates who can "Make a Difference . . . Teach New York!" "Sunny Skies, Bright Futures" beckon teachers to the Kern High School District in Bakersfield, California. Colleges and universities, too, sponsor job fairs. And e-fairs, which take place online, are gaining popularity in teaching as in other fields.[68]

■ ■ ■ ■ ■

BOX 1.6

SEARCH 800 JOB BANKS!

The National Teacher Recruitment Clearinghouse, sponsored by Recruiting New Teachers, maintains a Web portal that gives you access to information on thousands of teaching jobs. Go to www.recruitingteachers.org/channels/clearinghouse/jsearch.asp

"Sweetening the Pot."   *Quality Counts 2000* characterizes efforts to attract teachers with enticements and incentives as "Sweetening the Pot." About half the states now offer teacher scholarship and loan forgiveness programs that erase part of a teacher's college loan for every year spent in the elementary or secondary classroom. Worth, on the average, about $5,000 a year, these plans vary greatly. *Quality Counts 2003* brings the encouraging news that seven states— Alabama, California, Idaho, Minnesota, North Carolina, Rhode Island, and Texas—are targeting their programs toward new teachers willing to work in high-need schools.[69]

States as well as local school districts are offering an array of other incentives. Five states—Arkansas, Maryland, Massachusetts, Nevada, and New York— use signing bonuses to attract teachers. California, Connecticut, Florida, Hawaii, Maryland, Mississippi, and North Carolina provide housing assistance. Thirty-four states and the District of Columbia reward veteran teachers financially, most often for attaining certification from the National Board for Professional Teaching Standards. Local school districts throughout the nation use different combinations of these incentives to attract and retain teachers.[70]

Better Late than Never?   This kind of treatment is as welcome as it is overdue. Most teachers have yet to receive it, however, because it is a product of the job market rather than human kindness and goodwill. As I revised this textbook through five editions, I saw the level of consideration shown to teachers rise and fall with the market. During the early and mid-nineties, as it became clear a massive teacher shortage was not in the cards, state and local recruiters scaled back their job fairs, recruitment bonuses, and other concessions. Now, a decade later, *some* education officials are being nicer to teachers because *some* states and districts are having to hustle to hire enough of them.

I agree with Sandra Feldman, former president of the AFT, who said offering enticements and incentives is a great idea, but "you have to do that on top of a basic professional salary in order to get people into the profession in the first place." Feldman added, you also have to offer teachers decent working conditions.[71]

Returning to a market flooded with job seekers would be a giant step backward, but a market in which candidates are sought after and highly prized helped move medicine, law, and other occupations down the road to professionalism. Optimistically, the same thing may happen to teaching.

ACTIVITIES

1. Conduct a survey of teacher motivation. After talking with prospective teachers about their motives, ask currently employed teachers why they chose the occupation. Play the role of a friendly critic in your interviews.

2. Talk with principals and personnel officers about what they look for when they hire teachers. Ask about the relative importance of personal qualities versus academic skills.

3. Interview a variety of currently employed teachers—female and male, experienced and inexperienced, elementary and secondary, urban, suburban, and rural—about job satisfaction. Conduct similar interviews with former teachers and make comparisons.

4. Use the information and suggestions in this chapter to begin your job search. Consider as wide a range of school systems as possible and take advantage of the services provided by your institution's placement office. Browse the Internet for available teaching positions, and if you have the chance to attend a job fair for teachers, do it.

RECOMMENDED READINGS

American Association for Employment in Education. *Job Search Handbook for Educators* (Evanston, IL: AAEE, updated annually). This inexpensive booklet, which may be available from your university's placement office, is the best single guide to the teacher job market.

Grant, Gerald, and Christine E. Murray. *Teaching in America: The Slow Revolution* (Cambridge, MA: Harvard University Press, 1999). One of the most important recent books on teaching, this study draws from the experience of real-world teachers to present an original analysis of how the occupation is evolving.

National Commission on Teaching and America's Future. *No Dream Denied: A Pledge to America's Children* (Washington, DC: The Commission, 2003). This report argues that opening up teaching to almost anybody with a college degree won't work. Genuine reform of the occupation must involve major improvements in teacher preparation, licensing, salaries, and working conditions.

National Education Association. *Status of the American Public School Teacher* (Washington, DC: NEA, released at five-year intervals). Conducted since 1961, these periodic studies offer current information as well as a historical perspective on teaching.

NOTES

1. Quoted in "Who We Are, Why We Teach: A Portrait of the American Teacher," *NEA Today* (September 2003), p. 32.
2. A teacher in my course EDF 515, Multicultural Education, at the University of South Alabama voiced this opinion during fall semester 2004.
3. My ongoing study of teacher motivation, 1977 through the present, includes information on more than 4,000 prospective teachers at the University of South Alabama. Compare the other studies cited as sources for Table 1.1.
4. An excellent study of teachers, their attitudes, and their goals is Gerald Grant and Christine E. Murray's *Teaching in America: The Slow Revolution* (Cambridge, MA: Harvard University Press, 1999). Two landmark studies are Willard Waller's *The Sociology of Teaching* (New York: Wiley, 1932) and Dan C. Lortie's *Schoolteacher: A Sociological Study* (Chicago: University of Chicago Press, 1975).
5. National Education Association, *Status of the American Public School Teacher 2000–2001* (Washington, DC: NEA, 2003), p. 82; Lortie, *Schoolteacher*, pp. 30–37.
6. Lortie, *Schoolteacher*, pp. 31–32.

7. To gain a historical perspective on teaching as an occupation, begin your reading with Willard S. Elsbree's classic, *The American Teacher: Evolution of a Profession in a Democracy* (New York: American Book Company, 1939), and continue with Donald R. Warren, ed., *American Teachers: Histories of a Profession at Work* (New York: Macmillan, 1989).

8. Elsbree, *The American Teacher,* Chap. 17; National Education Association, *Status of the American Public School Teacher 2000–2001,* p. 91.

9. Nancy Hoffman, *Woman's "True" Profession: Voices from the History of Teaching,* rev. 2nd ed. (Cambridge, MA: Harvard Educational Publishing Group, 2003); NEA, *Status of the American Public School Teacher, 2000–2001,* pp. 67–69; Joseph W. Newman, "Reconstructing the World of Southern Teachers," *History of Education Quarterly* 24 (Winter 1984): 585–595.

10. Nel Noddings, *Caring: A Feminine Approach to Ethics and Moral Education,* 2nd ed. (Berkeley, CA: University of California Press, 2003); Louis Harris and Associates, *The Metropolitan Life Survey of the American Teacher, 1984–1995. Old Problems, New Challenges* (New York: Metropolitan Life Insurance Company, 1995), pp. 12–13; Lortie, *Schoolteacher,* Chap. 4.

11. See "Music Makes the Man," *NEA Today* (February 2000), p. 35; Lynn Larson, "Is Self-esteem Oversold?" *NEA Today* (December 1990), p. 31; Rebecca K. Merriman, "What? Leave All This?" *NEA Today* (February 1992), p. 34; "Wheelchairs Are Tools," *NEA Today* (October 1999), p. 39; "Meet: Will Hayes," *NEA Today* (December 1987), p. 11.

12. Louis Harris and Associates, *The Metropolitan Life Survey of the American Teacher, 1992. The Second Year: New Teachers' Expectations and Ideals* (New York: Metropolitan Life Insurance Co., 1992), pp. 7–8.

13. See Figure 3.2 and Table 8.3 in this textbook. Sabrina Hope King, "The Limited Presence of African-American Teachers," *Review of Educational Research* 63 (Summer 1993): 115–149; U.S. Department of Education, National Center for Educational Statistics, *Digest of Educational Statistics, 2002* (2003) [Available: nces.ed.gov/programs/digest/d02/tables/dt088.asp], Tbl. 88.

14. Jennifer Park, "Deciding Factors," *Quality Counts 2003: Ensuring a Highly Qualified Teacher for Every Classroom,* a special report of *Education Week* (January 9, 2003), pp. 17–18; Louis Harris, *The Metropolitan Survey of the American Teacher, 1992,* p. 8.

15. "To Close the Gap, Quality Counts," Executive Summary of *Quality Counts 2003,* p. 7.

16. Ray Rasmussen, "Teaching's Not Fun," *NEA Today* (November 1990), p. 30.

17. National Commission on Teaching and America's Future, *What Matters Most: Teaching for America's Future* (New York: The Commission, 1996), pp. 34–39, 51–52.

18. "Who Should Teach? The States Decide," Executive Summary of *Quality Counts 2000: Who Should Teach?* a special report of *Education Week* (January 13, 2000), p. 9.

19. See Richard J. Murnane, Judith D. Singer, John B. Willett, James J. Kemple, and Randall J. Olsen, *Who Will Teach? Policies That Matter* (Cambridge, MA: Harvard University Press, 1991), and Susan Moore Johnson, *Teachers at Work: Achieving Excellence in Our Schools* (New York: Basic Books, 1990).

20. Carol A. Langdon and Nick Vesper, "The Sixth Phi Delta Kappa Poll of Teachers' Attitudes toward the Public Schools," *Phi Delta Kappan* 81 (April 2000): 609; Lowell C. Rose and Alex M. Gallup, "The 35th Annual Phi Delta Kappa/Gallup Poll of the Public's Attitudes toward the Public Schools," *Phi Delta Kappan* 85 (September 2003): 50.

21. "Parents, Teachers Pass the Buck," *Mobile Register* (September 11, 1996), p. 1D.

22. John Rosemond, "Reader Debate: Are Public School Teachers Slackers?" *Mobile Register* (February 1, 2004), p. 2E.

23. Roland Vandenberghe and A. Michael Huberman, eds. *Understanding and Preventing Teacher Burnout: A Sourcebook of International Research and Practice* (London: Cambridge University Press, 1999); Judy Downs Lombardi, "Do You Have Teacher Burnout?" *Instructor* 104 (January/February 1995): 64–65.

24. Thomas M. Skovholt, *The Resilient Practitioner: Burnout Prevention and Self-Care Strategies for Counselors, Therapists, Teachers, and Health Professionals* (Boston: Allyn & Bacon, 2000).

25. See Wayne M. Sotile and Mary M. Sotile, *The Resilient Physician: Effective Emotional Management for Doctors and Their Organizations* (Washington, DC: American Medical Association, 2001), and Marlene Kramer, *Reality Shock: Why Nurses Leave Nursing* (St. Louis: Mosby, 1974).

26. The classic study of the semiprofessions is Amitai Etzioni's *The Semiprofessions and Their Organizations: Teachers, Nurses, and Social Workers* (New York: Free Press, 1969).

27. Ibid.; Arthur E. Wise, "Legislated Learning Revisited," *Phi Delta Kappan* 69 (January 1988): 329–333; Linda Darling-Hammond, *Beyond the Commission Reports: The Coming Crisis in Teaching* (Santa Monica,

CA: Rand Corp., July 1984), pp. 13–16; Wise, *Legislated Learning: The Bureaucratization of the American Classroom* (Berkeley: University of California Press, 1979).

28. Ann Bradley and Lynn Olson, "The Balance of Power," *Education Week* (February 24, 1993), pp. 9–14; Susan J. Rosenholtz, *Teachers' Workplace: The Social Organization of Schools* (White Plains, NY: Longman, 1989).

29. Carnegie Foundation for the Advancement of Teaching, *The Condition of Teaching*, p. ix; Bradley and Olson, "The Balance of Power," pp. 9–14.

30. Grant and Murray, *Teaching in America*, pp. 231–232.

31. National Commission on Teaching and America's Future, *What Matters Most*, pp. 5–6.

32. Carl Grant, "Teaching in 2020: The Triumph of 'the Slow Revolution'?" *Education Week* (September 15, 1999), p. 46.

33. Langdon, "The Third Phi Delta Kappa Poll of Teachers' Attitudes," p. 246.

34. Louis Harris and Associates, *The Metropolitan Life Survey of Former Teachers in America, 1986* (New York: Metropolitan Life Insurance Company, 1986).

35. Louis Harris, *Metropolitan Life Survey of the American Teacher, 2001: Key Elements of Quality Schools* (New York: Metropolitan Life Insurance Company, 2001), Chap. 6; Louis Harris, *The Metropolitan Life Survey of the American Teacher, 1984–1995*, Chap. 4; Louis Harris, *The Metropolitan Life Survey of the American Teacher, 1992*, pp. 15, 17.

36. Louis Harris, *The Metropolitan Life Survey of the American Teacher, 1984–1995*, Chap. 4; National Education Association, *Status of the American Public School Teacher 2000–2001*, p. 72.

37. U.S. Department of Education, National Center for Education Statistics, *Predicting the Need for Newly Hired Teachers in the U.S. to 2008–09* (1999) [Available: nces.ed.gov/pubs99/1999026.pdf].

38. Estimates and projections based on ibid., pp. 1, 9–12; National Education Association, *Status of the American Public School Teacher*, pp. 22–23, 71; and Jeff Archer, "New Teachers Abandon Field at High Rate," *Education Week* (March 17, 1999), p. 20.

39. Archer, "New Teachers Abandon Field," p. 20; Bess Keller, "Question of Teacher Turnover Sparks Research Interest," *Education Week* (April 30, 2003), p. 8.

40. National Commission on Teaching and America's Future, *No Dream Denied: A Pledge to America's Children* (Washington, DC: The Commission, 2003), p. 6.

41. Quoted in Hellmich, "Teachers Give Up on the Classroom," p. 1.

42. U.S. Department of Education, National Center for Education Statistics, *Projections of Education Statistics to 2005* (Washington, DC: U.S. Government Printing Office, 1995), p. 171.

43. Ibid.

44. U.S. Department of Health, Education, and Welfare, National Center for Education Statistics, *Projections of Education Statistics to 1986–1987* (Washington, DC: U.S. Government Printing Office, 1978), pp. 49–50, 55–60.

45. U.S. Department of Commerce, Bureau of the Census, *Fertility of American Women* (Washington, DC: U.S. Government Printing Office, 1985), pp. 1–7.

46. U.S. Department of Education, National Center for Education Statistics, *Projections of Education Statistics to 2013* (2003) [Available: nces.ed.gov/programs/projections/tables/table_01.asp], Tbl. 1.

47. U.S. Department of Education, *Projections of Education Statistics to 2013* [Available: nces.ed.gov/programs/projections/tables/table_05.asp], Tbl. 5.

48. U.S. Department of Education, *Digest of Education Statistics, 2002* [Available: nces.ed.gov/programs/digest/d02/tables/dt283.asp], Tbl. 283.

49. Ibid.

50. National Commission on Excellence in Education, *A Nation at Risk: The Imperative for Educational Reform* (Washington, DC: U.S. Department of Education, 1983); "Interest in Teaching," *Education Week* (December 4, 1991), p. 7.

51. Lynn Olson, "Finding and Keeping Competent Teachers," *Quality Counts 2000: Who Should Teach?* (January 13, 2000), p. 13; "Perceptions: What Teachers Give to America," *Future Teacher* (Winter/Spring 1999), p. 3.

52. Richard M. Ingersoll, "Teacher Turnover and Teacher Shortages: An Organizational Analysis," *American Educational Research Journal* 38 (Fall 2001): 499–534.

53. Carnegie Forum on Education and the Economy, *A Nation Prepared: Teachers for the 21st Century* (New York: Carnegie Forum, 1986), p. 31.

54. Albert Shanker, "Our Profession, Our Schools: The Case for Fundamental Reform," *American Educator* 10 (Fall 1986): 10–17, 44–45.

55. U.S. Department of Education Press Release, "Paige Releases Report to Congress that Calls for Overhaul of State Teacher Certification Systems" (June 11, 2002) [Available: www.ed.gov.news/pressreleases/2002/06/06112002.html].

56. Ibid.

57. See Linda Darling-Hammond, Ruth Chung, and Fred Frelow, with Heidi Fisher, "Variation in Teacher Preparation: How Well Do Different Pathways Prepare Teachers to Teach?" *Journal of Teacher Education* 53 (September/October 2002) [Available: www.wagner.edu/dept/education/NYC_Teacher_Survey_Study.pdf].

58. Michael W. Sedlak, "'Let Us Go and Buy a School Master': Historical Perspectives on the Hiring of Teachers in the United States, 1750–1980," in Warren, ed., *American Teachers,* Chap. 10; Donald R. Warren, "History and Teacher Education: Learning from Experience," *Educational Researcher* 14 (December 1985): 5–12.

59. U.S. Department of Education, Office of the Under Secretary, *No Child Left Behind: A Toolkit for Teachers* (Washington, DC: USDE, 2003), pp. 19–20.

60. Katherine M. Doherty and Ronald A. Skinner, "State of the States," *Quality Counts 2003* (January 9, 2003), pp. 75–76; Lynn Olson, "Finding and Keeping Competent Teachers," p. 14; Craig D. Jerald and Ulrich Bosser III, "Setting Policies for New Teachers," *Quality Counts 2000* (January 13, 2000), pp. 44–45.

61. Susan E. Ansell and Melissa McCabe, "Off Target," *Quality Counts 2003* (January 9, 2003), pp. 57–58.

62. Saul Cooperman, "The Sky Is Not Falling!" *Education Week* (January 26, 2000), p. 31; C. Emily Feistritzer and David T. Chester, Executive Summary, *Alternative Teacher Certification: A State-by-State Analysis 2003* (2003) [Available: www.ncei.com/2003/executive_summary.htm].

63. Lynn Olson, "Taking a Different Road to Teaching," *Quality Counts 2000* (January 13, 2000), p. 35; Arthur E. Wise and Linda Darling-Hammond, "Alternative Certification Is an Oxymoron," *Education Week* (September 4, 1991), p. 56.

64. Rod Paige, "Remarks at the Education Department's First Annual Teacher Quality Conference" (June 12, 2002) [Available: www.ed.gov/news/speeches/2002/06/061102.html].

65. See Ann Bradley, "States' Uneven Teacher Supply Complicates Staffing of Schools," *Education Week* (March 10, 1999), pp. 1, 10–11.

66. Emily Feistritzer and David T. Chester, *Alternative Teacher Certification: A State-by-State Analysis 2000* (Washington, DC: National Center for Education Information, 2000), p. 40.

67. See *Future Teacher* (Winter/Spring 1999) and Ann Bradley, "Recruitment Ads Said to Uncover Teacher Source," *Education Week* (March 13, 1991), pp. 1, 25.

68. American Association for Employment in Education, *2004 Job Search Handbook for Educators* (Columbus, OH: AAEE, 2003), pp. 41–68.

69. Lynn Olson, "Sweetening the Pot," *Quality Counts 2000* (January 13, 2000), pp. 28–30; Ansell and McCabe, "Off Target," pp. 57–58, 64–65.

70. Ibid.

71. Quoted in Olson, "Sweetening the Pot," p. 33.

CHAPTER 2

EARNING A LIVING AND LIVING WITH EVALUATION

If you have a teacher that is dynamite in a given field, that teacher should be encouraged [with merit pay]. That teacher should receive all the support necessary to shine in that area and to make the whole school shine.
—California teacher

I think the idea sounds wonderful. I just don't know how you can pull it off.
—Missouri teacher[1]

Can you make a decent living as a teacher? "It depends on what you call decent," the students in my classes invariably respond. Although every prospective teacher's answer to this question will be personal and subjective, examining the facts and figures on teacher salaries can make your answer better informed.

This chapter surveys salaries in the past, present, and future, with the future contingent on the success of reforms promising teachers better wages. We will compare salaries of teachers to salaries of workers in other occupations. We will also look at the controversies over *merit pay, accountability,* and *evaluation*—issues that will directly affect your career. The chapter concludes with a discussion of reforms designed not only to raise teacher salaries but also to *restructure* teaching into an occupation with different levels of expertise and responsibility.

Reformers who want to turn teaching into a profession comparable to medicine and law envision a new pay structure that would enable top-level teachers to earn salaries of $75,000 to $100,000. As much as all teachers would welcome that kind of income, not everyone shares the vision of a highly *differentiated* occupation. Reflecting divisions within the teaching force, the National Education Association (NEA) and American Federation of Teachers (AFT) disagree on how to reward teachers and restructure teaching, although the official positions of the two organizations seem to be converging as the new century begins.

Overall, the news about salaries is encouraging. It may even change your mind about how well you can live as a teacher.

TEACHER SALARIES, STATE BY STATE

In the 2003–2004 school year, the average salary of U.S. public school teachers was $46,826. As Table 2.1 indicates, teacher salaries vary considerably around the nation. In thirteen states, the average salary tops $50,000; in two states, the average falls below $35,000. Ranked according to the NEA's regional divisions of the states, salaries tend to be highest in the Far West and Mid East followed by New England, the Great Lakes, the Southeast, the Rocky Mountains, the Southwest, and the Plains (but note the exceptions to this pattern).

Qualified Good News

Now examine the percentages in Table 2.1, figures that show how much teacher salaries changed, in "real" or constant dollars, from 1992–1993 to 2002–2003. Notice that when inflation is taken into account, teachers in the nation as a whole increased their real earnings by 2.6 percent. On the positive side, teachers in eight states, including several that pay salaries far below the national average, are enjoying double-digit percentage gains. Raises that large can make quite a difference in a person's standard of living. On the negative side, eighteen states have allowed teacher salaries to *decrease* in real dollars, eroding hard-won gains of

TABLE 2.1   Average Salaries of All Public School Teachers, 2003–2004, and Percentage Change in Average Salaries, 1992–1993 to 2002–2003 (Constant Dollars)

1. California	$58,287	+10.1	26. Nevada	42,254	−4.0
2. District of Columbia	57,009	+2.8	27. Vermont	42,007	−6.7
3. Connecticut	57,000	−10.3	28. Arizona	41,843	+2.2
4. New Jersey	55,142	−0.6	29. Florida	41,313	+1.2
5. Michigan	54,806	−4.4	30. South Carolina	41,299	+8.2
6. New York	53,482	−7.7	31. Idaho	41,080	+16.5
7. Illinois	52,950	+4.4	32. Tennessee	40,657	+7.3
8. Delaware	52,499	+9.8	33. Texas	40,494	+4.6
9. Rhode Island	52,261	+5.5	34. Kentucky	40,187	−1.8
10. Pennsylvania	52,200	+5.5	35. Nebraska	39,635	+3.3
11. Massachusetts	52,150	+2.9	36. Maine	39,558	−0.2
12. Maryland	51,145	+0.4	37. Iowa	39,432	+1.6
13. Alaska	50,697	−16.6	38. Utah	39,156	+10.1
14. Oregon	49,169	+3.6	39. Alabama	39,133	+11.2
U.S. Average	*46,826*	*+2.6*	40. Wyoming	39,130	+1.2
15. Ohio	46,572	+3.3	41. Kansas	38,883	−9.9
16. Georgia	45,938	+18	42. Arkansas	38,629	+7.8
17. Indiana	45,791	+0.5	43. West Virginia	38,461	−0.5
18. Hawaii	45,479	−4.5	44. Louisiana	38,300	+11.6
19. Washington	45,429	−1.5	45. Missouri	38,006	+ 0.4
20. Minnesota	45,041	−0.1	46. New Mexico	37,624	+9.2
21. Viginia	44,240	+4.8	47. Montana	36,689	+1.4
22. North Carolina	44,076	+15.1	48. Mississippi	35,684	+11.1
23. Colorado	43,669	−0.3	49. North Dakota	35,441	+5.3
24. Wisconsin	43,382	−6.7	50. Oklahoma	34,993	+5.4
25. New Hampshire	42,881	−3.2	51. South Dakota	33,236	+4.6

Source: National Education Association, *Rankings & Estimates: Ranking of the States 2003 and Estimates of School Statistics 2004* (Washington, DC: NEA, 2004), Summary Tbl. G, p. 92, and Tbl. C-14, p. 20. Reprinted with permission of the National Education Association copyright 2004. All rights reserved.

earlier years. Teachers in Alaska, Connecticut, and New York—whose salaries ranked first, second, and third, respectively, in 1999–2000—have sustained the greatest losses.

Nationwide, salary increases have leveled out since the 1980s. Throughout most of that decade, state politicians and local school board members acted positively on teachers' requests for pay raises because inflation had robbed teachers of so much purchasing power during the 1970s. Then the political and economic climate of the 1990s put the brakes on the drive for higher salaries. In the nation as a whole, teacher salary increases since the late 1980s have ranked among the smallest of the last four decades.[2]

But there is more qualified good news. In real dollars, annual teacher salaries are currently higher than they have ever been—for the average American

■ ■ ■ ■ ■

BOX 2.1

INFORMATION ON AVERAGE TEACHER SALARIES

For current figures on average teacher salaries, state by state, visit the NEA Web site at www.nea.org

teacher, some $2,600 higher. Much of the credit for the economic position teachers hold today goes to the educational reforms we will study throughout this book. With the release of *A Nation at Risk* in 1983—followed by a barrage of other reports on the schools—state governors, legislatures, and boards of education went into action. The result was round after round of reform. Two decades later, political interest in school reform is still running high.[3]

Although teachers resent some reforms, such as the standardized test-driven "cookbook" curriculum that takes classroom decisions out of their hands, they find it hard to fault the efforts many states have made to recruit and retain better teachers through better salaries. The job market of the 2000s, characterized by teacher shortages in certain fields and certain geographical areas, could push salaries higher still.

In the era of No Child Left Behind, the emphasis of state school reform is on holding schools accountable through standardized testing and placing a "highly qualifed" teacher in every classroom. As we saw in Chapter 1, NCLB gives the states a great deal of flexibility in determining who is highly qualified. In their efforts to attract an adequate supply of teachers, some states are relaxing teacher education requirements, even as others are raising salaries—two very different approaches.

In the report *No Dream Denied: A Pledge to America's Children* (2003), the National Commission on Teaching and America's Future strongly advocates the latter strategy. The commission cites research showing that higher salaries and better working conditions are essential for transforming teaching into something more than a revolving door occupation. Easing entry standards will only make matters worse.[4]

The NEA and AFT certainly agree. They can rightfully claim part of the credit for higher salaries. Chapter 4 shows how they have lobbied hard in state capitals and negotiated impressive contracts with local school boards. Now the two unions are trying to use teacher shortages and teacher quality as leverage to keep salaries on the incline.

Salaries for New Teachers

Table 2.2 shows 2003–2004 starting salaries for teachers who enter the occupation with a bachelor's degree and no prior experience. The national average is $30,496, but notice the variations. Eight states start beginners at $35,000 or more (better than the average pay of all teachers in Oklahoma and South Dakota),

TABLE 2.2 Average Starting Salaries of Public School Teachers, 2003-2004

1.	Alaska	$38,597	**26.**	Kentucky	$29,790
2.	New Jersey	36,815	**27.**	Ohio	29,790
3.	District of Columbia	36,388	**28.**	Connecticut	29,771
4.	New York	36,387	**29.**	South Carolina	29,590
5.	California	35,919	**30.**	Minnesota	29,515
6.	Illinois	35,627	**31.**	New Mexico	29,020
7.	Hawaii	35,088	**32.**	Missouri	28,973
8.	Georgia	35,005	**33.**	Oklahoma	28,570
9.	Delaware	34,893	**34.**	North Carolina	28,454
10.	Michigan	34,671	**35.**	Wisconsin	28,150
11.	Massachusetts	34,230	**36.**	Utah	28,003
12.	Maryland	33,993	**37.**	Nebraska	27,995
13.	Pennsylvania	33,950	**38.**	Iowa	27,830
14.	Oregon	33,854	**39.**	Kansas	27,714
15.	Nevada	33,198	**40.**	West Virginia	26,692
16.	Colorado	33,089	**41.**	New Hampshire	27,326
17.	Texas	32,894	**42.**	Mississippi	26,956
18.	Virginia	32,420	**43.**	Idaho	26,906
19.	Rhode Island	32,018	**44.**	Wyoming	26,516
20.	Alabama	31,992	**45.**	Vermont	26,048
21.	Florida	31,467	**46.**	Arkansas	25,771
	U.S. Average	30,496	**47.**	Maine	25,419
22.	Louisiana	30,225	**48.**	South Dakota	25,089
23.	Indiana	30,077	**49.**	North Dakota	24,346
24.	Washington	30,050	**50.**	Arizona	24,302
25.	Tennessee	29,974	**51.**	Montana	23,790

Source: American Federation of Teachers, "Teacher Salaries Remain Stagnant," Press Release, July 15, 2004 [Available: www.aft.org/presscenter.releases/2004/071504.htm], Table 2. Used by permission.

while three states pay beginners less than $25,000. Comparing Tables 2.1 and 2.2, you can see that several states rank much higher in beginners' salaries than in salaries of all teachers. Texas, Alabama, and Louisiana are prime examples of states that *front-load* teacher salaries, packing the greatest rewards (relatively speaking) into the first few years.

Because front-loaded salary schedules look good to new teachers, they may help these states avoid teacher shortages—or so their governors, legislatures, and boards of education hope. But these schedules quickly become discouraging as teachers gain experience. Once teachers are in the occupation, front-loading gives them nowhere to go financially. Front-loaded salaries provide poor incentives to make teaching a career.[5]

The patterns and trends in teacher salaries, like those in the teacher job market, are constantly changing. Just as you should investigate job opportunities in your teaching field over as wide a geographic area as possible, you owe it to yourself to conduct the same careful investigation of salaries.

■ ■ ■ ■ ■

BOX 2.2

BEGINNING TEACHER SALARIES

The AFT posts beginning teacher salaries, state by state, at www.aft.org

Other Factors to Consider

Although the information in Tables 2.1 and 2.2 can give you a good start for comparing salary information, you should also take into account state-to-state differences in the cost of living as well as other factors. Housing is the most important cost-of-living variable to consider. As a rule, the cost of buying or renting housing is higher in states ranked near the top of Table 2.1 than in states ranked near the bottom. School officials in low-ranked states often stress cost of living in their recruitment pitches, trying to use affordable housing to compensate for low teacher salaries.

Listen, of course, but be aware that when researchers adjust the rankings in Table 2.1 for cost-of-living differences, the rankings don't change as much as you might think. The majority of the states ranked in the bottom fourth in actual salaries stay in the bottom fourth in adjusted salaries, and most of the top-ranked states stay in the top fourth.[6]

Cost-of-living differences *within* a given state may be more important for you to consider. Housing tends to be more expensive in cities and suburbs than in small towns and rural areas, and the higher salaries in city and suburban school systems may not be enough to offset the difference. The "average" Ohio teacher whose salary is $46,572 may own a home and live quite comfortably in small-town Jackson, while a teacher earning several thousand dollars more in an affluent suburb of Cincinnati or Cleveland may be hard-pressed to make ends meet, much less move out of a rented apartment and make payments on a house or condominium.

AMERICA'S TEACHERS IN 2005:
A DEMOGRAPHIC PROFILE

Who is the "average" teacher? The profile in Figure 2.1 offers some answers. In the United States as a whole, the average teacher is a white woman who is forty-four years old and married. She holds a graduate degree and has fifteen years of teaching experience.

When you ask yourself whether you can make a decent living as a teacher, put yourself in this teacher's shoes—or at least put yourself well into your career. So take another look at Table 2.1 and then answer this question: How would you like to earn the average teacher's salary for the state where you would like to

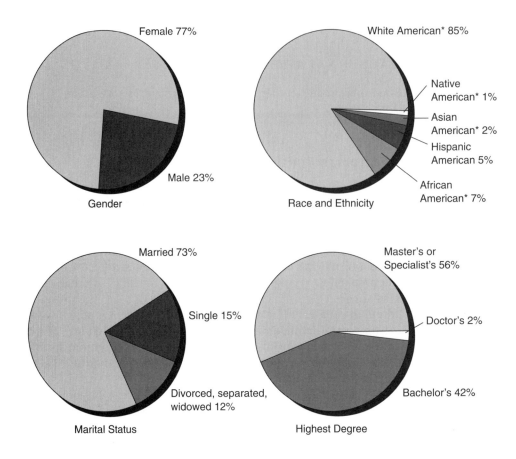

Average Age: 44 years
Teachers with School-Age Children at Home: 38%
Average Number of Children: 2
Married Teachers with Employed Spouses: 91%

*Excludes persons of Hispanic origin

FIGURE 2.1   America's Teachers: 2005.

Sources: Estimates and projections based on U.S. Department of Education, National Center for Education Statistics, *Digest of Education Statistics, 2002* (2003) [Available: nces.ed.gov/programs/digest/d02/tables/dt068.asp], and National Education Association, *Status of the American Public School Teacher 2000–2001* (Washington, DC: NEA, 2003), pp. 5–8, 92–94, 265–267.

teach *after* you have completed a graduate program and spent fifteen years in the classroom?

You should consider that the average teacher has a spouse who contributes to the income of the family. In fact, the average household income for all teachers in 2004 was an estimated $80,000. A household income of $80,000, fifteen years into a teaching career, is certainly a more pleasing prospect than an individual salary of $46,826. With the sum of $80,000 in mind, enjoying a middle-class lifestyle, owning a home, and paying college tuition for the children all seem within reach. If we compare the average U.S. household income of approximately $44,000 in 2004 to the average teacher's household income of $80,000, teachers seem to be doing well indeed.[7]

The first time I discussed household income in my undergraduate classes, my students' reactions took me by surprise. I was being unfairly (and uncharacteristically) positive, they said. Students pointed out household income also includes the moonlighting many teachers do outside the school system (see Chapter 1) as well as the additional duties they take on at school—coaching and summer teaching, for instance. Yes, I admitted, half of all teachers find it necessary to supplement their household income in these ways.[8]

Several students also reminded me, referring to the profile in Figure 2.1, that one of every four teachers is *not* married. It is small consolation to the single teacher who lives on one income that the average teacher has a household income of $80,000. Nor is that figure very comforting to the divorced teacher who is trying to raise several children on one income, even with child support.

So I joined my students and concluded that although it may be helpful to know the average household income of an occupation's members, using household income to make individual salaries seem more acceptable can be deceptive. Prospective teachers who say "teaching provides a good second income" or "I'll never earn much as a teacher, but if I get married I'll be OK financially" are apologizing for their occupation before they ever enter it. This defeatist attitude continues to hold teaching back. Teachers who regard their salaries as secondary may think of their work as secondary—as something less than a "real" career.

"We're teaching for a living, not a hobby," teacher organizations constantly remind politicians and the public. The facts about teaching support this view. In the public school teaching force as a whole, the salaries of male teachers provide 60 percent of the income in their households, while the salaries of female teachers account for more than half their household income. In most teacher households, the income from teaching is primary, not secondary.[9]

Every chapter in Part I of this textbook stresses the point that teaching has the potential to become a full profession, evolving as medicine, law, and a few other occupations have since the early 1900s. For this change to occur, public attitudes toward teaching must change, and the attitudes of teachers themselves must change first.

COMPARING SALARIES IN TEACHING AND OTHER OCCUPATIONS

Income is an important measure of worth in our society, one estimate of how much society values a particular kind of work. How do salaries of teachers compare to those of workers in other occupations?

To begin with some more good news, I can report that during most of the 1980s and into the early 1990s, public school teaching outpaced almost every other occupation in real income growth. Teachers improved their economic position relative to all workers, to government workers, and to white-collar workers. Remember, though, these gains for teachers came after steady losses during the 1970s.[10]

Now for some more bad news: Since the early 1990s, teachers have been losing ground again. The economic boom of the nineties fattened the wallets of private sector workers much more than the purses of teachers and other public employees, and the wage gap is not closing in the economy of the 2000s. The Economic Policy Institute made headlines in 2004 with *How Does Teacher Pay Compare?*, a report that documents trends from 1993 to 2003. Standing teachers shoulder to shoulder with other workers of similar education, experience, and demographic characteristics, the Institute finds teacher salaries falling behind by 15 percent. Moreover, teacher fringe benefits such as health insurance and pensions, which *are* generally good for educators, are not improving relative to the benefits of comparable workers.[11]

When considering the following occupational comparisons, remember that in 2003–2004 the average starting salary of public school teachers was $30,496 and the average salary of all teachers in the public schools was $46,826. Private school teachers, who make up about 10 percent of the nation's teaching force (see Chapter 10), earn considerably less. As a rule, elite independent schools are the only private schools offering salaries comparable to those in public schools.

What Do Other People Earn?

The U.S. Labor Department's *Occupational Outlook Handbook, 2004–05 Edition* provides information we can use to compare salaries. If we begin with *social work*, a female-dominated occupation that society views, like teaching, as semiprofessional, then teaching fares pretty well. Starting salaries for social workers are in the mid-twenties. Average compensation for child, family, and school social workers is $33,150, and the top 10 percent earn more than $54,250.[12]

Turning our attention to *nursing*, another female-dominated semiprofessional field, we find an occupation that has struggled with a shortage of trained workers. Hospitals, medical schools, and medical centers have tried to cope by raising the salary of beginning registered nurses, which has pushed up their starting pay to the mid-thirties. Salaries of all registered nurses average $48,090, with the best-paid 10 percent (including many nurse practitioners and clinical specialists) pulling in wages of more than $69,700.

Compared to business and management, fields in which women now receive about half the bachelor's degrees and 40 percent of the master's degrees, teaching looks less competitive, although it is still in the running. *Accountants* and *auditors* with bachelor's degrees have starting salaries averaging $40,647 and with master's degrees, $42,241. Senior accountants can anticipate earning up to

$61,500. Management accountants can make considerably more: up to $78,750. Directors of accounting and auditing can earn as much as $97,500.

Looking at salaries in scientific and technical occupations—fields in which women remain underrepresented—we can see clearly why there is a shortage of science and math teachers. Quite simply, people with such skills must be willing to make financial sacrifices if they want to teach. *Electrical engineers*, who constitute the largest sector of engineering, go to work with bachelor's degrees for starting salaries of $49,794; with master's degrees, their entry-level salary averages $64,556. The average salary of all electrical engineers is $68,180, and the top 10 percent earn more than $100,980. *Mechanical engineers*, the second-largest sector, start with bachelor's degrees at $48,585 and with master's degrees at $54,565. Their average wages are $62,880, while top salaries exceed $93,430.

Mathematicians have starting salaries of $40,512 and $42,348 with bachelor's and master's degrees, respectively. On the average, mathematicians earn $76,470, and the top 10 percent command $112,780 or more.

In the expanding world of computer technology, we find new graduates with bachelor's degrees going to work for $51,343 in *computer engineering*, $62,806 in *computer science*, low fifties in *management information systems*, and $45,558 in *computer programming*. Wages vary by the type of work, with computer engineers earning an average of $74,040, systems analysts $62,890, and programmers $60,290. One reason these careers are so attractive is that the top 10 percent of workers earn $90,000 and up.

Finally, we turn to the two occupations Americans consider most professional, law and medicine. We can see the substantial financial rewards that accompany high occupational status. More women than ever before are reaping these rewards because women now earn nearly 40 percent of the nation's medical degrees and about 45 percent of its law degrees.

Beginning *attorneys* can anticipate starting out at less than $60,000, although those in private practice average more than $90,000 only six months after graduating from law school. Earnings of all lawyers—in private practice, business, government, and academia—average $90,290, and the sky is literally the limit for the most successful private practitioners.

Physicians work in the occupation with the greatest earning potential. As residents, they receive stipends in the forties, and on entering private practice their incomes climb steeply. *Family practitioners* make an average of $150,267; *pediatricians*, $152,690; *specialists in internal medicine*, $155,530; *psychiatrists*, $163,144; *specialists in obstetrics and gynecology*, $233,061; *general surgeons*, $255,438; and *anesthesiologists*, $306,964.

How Much Will It Cost You to Be a Teacher?

Although you may hope to find greater intrinsic rewards in teaching than in any other career you might choose, you will probably pay for the satisfaction with foregone earnings. Based on the salary gap between teachers and other people of comparable age and education, an *Education Week* report concludes teachers make a tremendous sacrifice. Teachers aged 22 to 28 with bachelor's degrees average $7,894 less per year than comparable workers. As age and education increase, so does the gap. Teachers aged 44 to 50 who hold bachelor's degrees earn $23,655 less annually than their peers, while teachers of the same age but with master's degrees earn $32,511 less.[13]

Telling a story that has become all too familiar, *Teacher Magazine* describes how a young Virginia teacher reluctantly "made a job change that doubled his salary and halved his workweek. He went to work for Bill Gates." The teacher explains he "was looking at trying to start a family and support a family. . . . It was time to cut my losses."[14]

Should teachers have to give up so much to work with young people? Before you answer, please reread the two quotations that open this chapter.

What Lies Ahead?

Barring a drastic reordering of our nation's social and economic priorities, it is hard to foresee a day when teachers command the incomes of doctors or lawyers—or even engineers. Having said that, we should not dismiss the possibility of major improvements in teacher salaries. The pay structures negotiated by unions and school boards in a few local districts now offer top-level salaries in the neighborhood of $85,000. Encouraged by such professionally minded groups as the National Board for Professional Teaching Standards (NBPTS) and National Commission on Teaching and America's Future (NCTAF), these pay plans are new versions of an old idea: merit pay.

Before analyzing the promises and pitfalls of these reforms, we can encourage ourselves with the fact that the most experienced, most highly educated teachers in some school districts are *already* earning $85,000 or more—on traditional salary schedules. Or, we can just as easily discourage ourselves with the fact that, in other districts, teachers with graduate degrees and 30 years in the classroom are making only $35,000—on traditional salary schedules.

TEACHER SALARY SCHEDULES

Tables 2.3, 2.4, and 2.5 illustrate the diversity in teacher pay throughout the United States. As different as the salaries on the three schedules are, they have several key features in common. These schedules, like most in the nation, are based on just two factors: experience and education. The schedules make no distinctions by subject or grade level, nor do they reward teachers according to their competence and performance. On each schedule, a teacher who has five years of classroom experience and a bachelor's degree earns exactly the same salary as every other teacher with five years and a bachelor's degree. Schedules like these give the occupation a sense of predictability and security.

For the first half of the twentieth century, teacher organizations fought for salary schedules with these features. School boards must treat all teachers alike, the organizations insisted: Teacher salaries must be based strictly on experience

TABLE 2.3   **A Teacher Salary Schedule with "Perverse Incentives"**

	TRACK		
STEP	BACHELOR'S	MASTER'S	SPECIALIST'S
1	$26,000	$28,000	$31,500
2	26,200	28,300	31,900
3	26,400	28,600	32,300
4	28,900	32,100	35,800
5	29,100	32,400	36,200
6	29,300	32,700	36,600
7	29,500	33,000	37,000
8	29,700	33,300	37,400
9	29,900	33,600	37,800
10	30,100	33,900	38,200

and education. In district after district, state after state, teacher organizations won these battles, and gradually school boards stopped paying secondary teachers more than elementary, male teachers more than female, and, most recently, white teachers more than black teachers. School boards adopted *single salary schedules* that put teachers with equal experience and education on equal footing.

TABLE 2.4   **A Typical Teacher Salary Sechdule**

	TRACK					
STEP	BACHELOR'S	BACHELOR'S PLUS 20 HOURS	MASTER'S	MASTER'S PLUS 20 HOURS	SPECIALIST'S	DOCTOR'S
1	$31,000	$31,000	$34,000	$34,000	$38,500	$42,000
2	31,300	31,400	35,100	35,700	40,500	44,300
3	31,600	32,300	36,200	36,900	42,500	46,800
4	33,600	34,400	38,400	39,200	45,100	49,600
5	34,100	34,900	39,100	40,000	46,000	50,700
6	34,600	35,400	39,800	40,800	46,900	51,800
7	35,100	35,900	40,500	41,600	47,800	52,900
8	35,600	36,400	41,200	42,400	48,700	54,000
9	36,100	36,900	41,900	43,200	49,600	55,100
10	36,600	37,400	42,600	44,000	50,500	56,200
11		37,900	43,400	44,900	51,500	57,400
12			44,200	45,800	52,500	58,600
13			45,000	46,700	53,500	59,800
14			45,800	47,500	54,500	61,000
15			46,600	48,400	55,500	62,200

Note: Teachers who reach the top of the master's, master's plus 20 hours, specialist's, and doctor's tracks qualify for longevity raises of 3 percent every 2 years.

TABLE 2.5   An Exceptionally Good Teacher Salary Schedule

			TRACK			
STEP	BACHELOR'S	BACHELOR'S PLUS 20 HOURS	MASTER'S	MASTER'S PLUS 20 HOURS	SPECIALIST'S	DOCTOR'S
1	$40,000	$40,000	$46,000	$46,000	$50,000	$54,000
2	40,400	40,700	47,000	47,200	51,500	55,600
3	41,000	41,800	48,500	49,200	53,600	57,800
4	43,000	44,000	51,200	52,000	57,000	61,300
5	43,800	44,800	52,200	53,200	58,400	62,800
6	44,600	45,600	53,200	54,400	59,800	64,300
7	45,400	46,400	54,200	55,600	61,200	64,800
8	46,200	47,200	55,200	56,800	62,600	67,300
9	47,000	49,000	56,200	58,000	64,000	68,800
10	47,800	49,800	57,200	59,200	65,400	70,300
11		50,600	58,400	60,600	66,900	71,900
12			59,600	62,000	67,400	73,500
13			60,800	63,400	68,900	75,100
14			62,000	64,800	70,400	76,700
15			63,200	66,200	71,900	78,300
16				67,600	73,400	80,000
17					74,900	81,700
18					76,400	82,400
19					77,900	84,100
20					78,400	85,800

Note: Teachers who reach the top of the master's, master's plus 20 hours, specialist's, and doctor's tracks qualify for longevity raises of 3 percent every 2 years.

Another battle the organizations won—or hope they've won—is the one over merit pay, the practice of basing salaries on evaluations of competence and performance. Teacher organizations have consistently (and, for the most part, successfully) opposed merit pay, but this old battle keeps breaking out on new fronts.

The operation of single salary schedules like those in Tables 2.3, 2.4, and 2.5 is easy to understand. New teachers with bachelor's degrees start at the first step on the bachelor's track and advance one step per year. When teachers qualify for another track by taking graduate work, they move laterally to the right—they do not return to the first step on the new track. On schedules like Table 2.3, teachers who move through all the tracks and take all the steps reach maximum salary well before retirement—a sad commentary on the view some school boards hold of teaching as a career. For teachers in this situation, an across-the-board raise granted by the state or local board offers the only hope for a higher salary. Schedules like Tables 2.4 and 2.5, though, provide longevity raises for career teachers, as the notes at the bottom of the schedules explain.

A Salary Schedule with "Perverse Incentives"

There are many other differences among the three salary schedules. The schedule in Table 2.3 is the kind that, to be blunt, offers discouragingly low salaries, bottom to top—to beginners with bachelor's degrees, as well as to veterans with graduate degrees. This kind of schedule is standard in states that rank well below average in Tables 2.1 and 2.2. Pointing to states that rank fortieth or below in both tables, we can single out Arkansas, Mississippi, Montana, North Dakota, South Dakota, West Virginia, and Wyoming. But these states are certainly not the only ones that allow this kind of salary schedule to dominate.

One bright spot is that even in the states ranked low in Tables 2.1 and 2.2, better-off suburban and city districts sometimes add enough local revenue to the minimum salary schedule established by the state to offer teachers better wages. To be sure, the lower cost of living in some areas may make this schedule look fairly attractive to some prospective teachers.

Enough apologies and excuses. Let's get real. The schedule in Table 2.3 is full of what economists call "perverse incentives." With its starting salary of $26,000, yearly step raises of $200 to $400, and top salary of $38,200, the schedule gives people strong incentives *not* to become teachers and, even if they do, to leave the occupation after just a few years. Teachers can look forward to a raise exceeding $400 on just three occasions: when they become tenured, which occurs in most states after three years; when they receive a graduate degree; or when the local school board or state legislature grants a cost-of-living raise to all teachers.

Imagine how veteran teachers must feel. After spending a large part of their adult lives in the classroom and going back to school for advanced degrees, they make only a few thousand dollars more than the novice teachers down the hall.

What kind of people does this salary schedule attract? What kind does it keep in the occupation? To be complimentary for now, we can say truly dedicated people, but the next chapter balances this answer with a less flattering one.

A Typical Salary Schedule

The other two schedules offer better prospects. Table 2.4 shows a schedule representative of districts paying average salaries to both beginning and experienced teachers. With its starting point of $31,000 and ratio of about 2 to 1 between its highest and lowest salaries, this schedule is fairly typical for America's teachers.

Salary schedules such as the one in Table 2.4 are often the product of collective bargaining between teacher unions and school boards, a practice we will discuss in Chapter 4. Significantly, collective bargaining is relatively well established in every region but the Southeast. Where bargaining occurs, unions usually negotiate for less compressed schedules that offer relatively good salaries to the experienced teachers who make up most of the organizations' membership. Such schedules give teachers incentives to stick with the occupation and make it a career.

Experienced teachers with graduate degrees can be expensive to school boards, though, and without the pressure of collective bargaining, boards often opt for front-loaded salary schedules. A cold, harsh fact of life makes front-loaded schedules more attractive to some board members than this schedule. Front-loading produces higher rates of teacher turnover, driving out experienced teachers and attracting a steady stream of lower-paid recruits eager to fill the vacancies. What experienced teachers see as a perverse incentive, board members may see as good business.

Fortunately, the salary schedule in Table 2.4 has a fairly respectable high end of $62,200 for teachers with doctorates and $55,500 for teachers with specialist's degrees. Notice this schedule contains more steps and more tracks than the first one we examined. As tenured teachers move down every track except the first two, they are encouraged to find that the later steps bring higher raises than the earlier steps. Notice, too, how the tracks labeled "Plus 20 Hours" provide more immediate incentives for teachers to pursue master's and specialist's degrees because the tracks reward progress toward the degrees.

This salary schedule acknowledges the fact that some classroom teachers are interested in and capable of obtaining doctoral degrees. School officials in districts with salary schedules similar to Table 2.3, by contrast, sometimes justify the lack of a doctoral track by asserting anyone smart enough to earn a doctorate is too smart to be an elementary or secondary school teacher. Considering the salaries in Table 2.3, the officials may have a point.

An Exceptionally Good Salary Schedule

If every teacher worked in a school district with a salary schedule such as the one shown in Table 2.5, this chapter—and probably this whole book—would have a different tone because teaching would be a different occupation. Without question, different would mean better, because we know the small number of districts that actually pay starting salaries of $40,000 and top salaries of $85,000 or more can afford to be more selective in hiring, more careful about granting tenure, and more supportive of people who make teaching their career.

Most such districts have collective bargaining between teacher and school board members, but the emphasis at the bargaining table is on cooperation rather than confrontation. Labor relations specialists call this a "win-win" approach to negotiations. Teachers win, the board wins, and, most important, students win, because all concerned can work together without having to fuss over money.[15]

A visit to a school district with a great salary schedule and the financial resources that make it possible would convince most teachers that although money is not a panacea, it can certainly make a difference. Teachers fortunate enough to work there earn more at the start of their careers than teachers in the nation's poorest districts earn at the end of their careers. At the peak of their careers, these lucky teachers can feel economically competitive with workers in business and industry—even with those in high-tech jobs. The catch, of course, is that most of the districts paying top salaries in the $85,000 range are located in wealthy communities where local support for public education—financial and otherwise—is quite high. These districts are by no means typical. On the other hand, some districts with exceptionally good salary schedules are urban systems with tremendous problems. Such districts try to reward teachers for the very tough work they do, convinced that increasing their investment in teachers is the best way to improve the quality of education for students. A prospective teacher who wanted to visit top-paying districts of both kinds, many within close proximity, could begin a road trip in Massachusetts and drive through Connecticut, New York, and New Jersey; head down into Delaware and Maryland and then across Pennsylvania; check out Illinois and Michigan; and finish the journey in California.

We will take a closer look at school finance in Chapter 9, but obviously it would take quite a commitment from the federal, state, and local governments to put all 3,051,731 of the nation's public school teachers on salary schedules resembling Table 2.5.

Suspend Disbelief for a Moment

Giving America's teachers an across-the-board 30 percent raise would make their average salary more than $60,000. This reform would put the average teacher on a salary schedule almost as good as Table 2.5, and it would give teachers in such low-wage states as Mississippi, Oklahoma, and the Dakotas salaries comparable to those now paid in Ohio, Georgia, Indiana, and Hawaii. The prospect of such a reform is exciting.

How much would it cost? The United States spends about $400 billion annually on public elementary and secondary education, with approximately $145 billion going directly into teachers' paychecks. Considering such additional costs to school systems as retirement, insurance, and Social Security contributions, we can estimate that giving all teachers a 30 percent raise would mean increasing the nation's annual spending for public schools by about $65 billion. Although this reform is too expensive to implement in a single year, it can still serve as a goal for teachers to work toward over several years.[16]

Albert Shanker, former president of the AFT, believed this goal was out of reach and argued the nation would never increase its real spending on public education by such a massive amount. As an alternative, the AFT has been edging warily since the mid-1980s toward the concept of paying much better salaries to some teachers than to others.[17]

Understandably, Shanker bridled at the words *merit pay* because they conjure up bitter memories of bias and favoritism, yet he encouraged the AFT to embrace an updated version of merit pay as part of a plan to make teaching a *differentiated* occupation, one that recognizes and rewards different levels of expertise and responsibility. Shanker's ideas closely paralleled the proposals of the NBPTS and its financial backer, the Carnegie Foundation, which we will examine in the last section of this chapter.

Why has the AFT, a teacher organization that has fought merit pay with do-or-die determination for most of this century, softened its position? And why is the rival union Shanker referred to as the "other organization," the much larger NEA, now giving tentative support to experiments with merit pay?

MERIT PAY: THE BIRTH OF "SOUND AND CHEAP"

Opinion polls show teachers have mixed feelings about merit pay. Until the early 2000s, more than 60 percent consistently said they opposed it, even while the general public supported it by a similar margin. But the situation has become less clear-cut. Politicians and school officials have been trying to change the image of merit pay, and teachers now say they favor certain forms of it—as long as it isn't based on standardized testing. According to a 2003 Public Agenda poll, more than 60 percent of public school teachers now support higher pay for those who "work in tough neighborhoods with low performing students"; those who "consistently work harder, putting in more time and effort than other teachers"; those who "teach difficult classes with hard-to-reach students"; and those who "consistently receive outstanding evaluations by their principals."[18] Almost 60 percent support higher pay for teachers who hold certification from the National Board for Professional Teacher Standards. Newer teachers are more willing than veterans to give these versions of merit pay a try.

But throw student test scores into the equation and the old suspicions return. When pollsters bring up using test scores a basis for merit pay, something many politicians and school officials are ready to do in the climate of accountability created by No Child Left Behind, teacher support drops to 38 percent. Moreover, only 42 percent favor higher salaries in subject fields that are experiencing teacher shortages.[19]

Teachers have every reason to be wary, the NEA insists. The nation's largest teacher union is concerned that teacher acceptance of seemingly positive forms of merit pay will lead them down a dangerous path. Watch the details! the NEA cautions its members, reminding them that merit pay has failed miserably in the past.

Read the handwriting on the wall, the AFT replies. With polls showing strong and increasing public support for merit pay—almost 60 percent of the public, in fact, favor basing it on student achievement—pressure from parents, other taxpayers, and especially the business community may force teachers to live with *some* version of the concept. Trying to cope with what it sees as a new political reality, the AFT has been trying to take the lead and help design the fairest merit pay plans possible, and the NEA is reluctantly going along with the experiments.[20]

At least the two teacher organizations agree on the past. Educational historians have documented the record of merit pay, and a sorry record it is. Forty to 50 percent of the nation's school districts tried merit pay in the World War I era and the 1920s. "Scientific efficiency" was all the rage in business management, and school boards jumped on the bandwagon with a variety of plans to base teachers' salaries on evaluations of their ability and performance. Scientific efficiency as applied to public education was, in theory, an attempt to make the schools "both sound and cheap." Teachers discovered that, in practice, the emphasis was on cheap.[21]

Pyramid Building

A typical merit pay plan entailed arranging a school district's teachers in a pyramid-like hierarchy based on their evaluations. For example, Rank 5 teachers were those judged to be the best; Rank 4 teachers were the next best; and so on down to Rank 1 teachers, who received the worst evaluations. Each rank carried a different salary schedule, with Rank 5 teachers earning the highest salaries and Rank 1 teachers the lowest.[22]

All well and good, some teachers thought. Then, as now, there was undeniable appeal in the principle that the better you are at a job, the greater your rewards should be. But then, as now, there were tremendous difficulties in defining what *better* meant and deciding which teachers fit the description. Relying on two techniques becoming fashionable in business management, school boards required administrators and supervisors to evaluate teachers in the classroom and required teachers to take tests. Neither technique was new in public education. What was different was that under merit pay plans, evaluations and test scores affected salaries for the first time.

Teachers fought back. School boards accustomed to submissive, complacent employees suddenly faced storms of teacher protest. Across the nation, teachers banded together and formed local organizations, sometimes taking the radical step of affiliating with the AFT, the national teacher organization that dared call itself a union. The NEA and state teacher associations, those "professional associations" dominated by administrators and college professors, also expressed reservations about merit pay, albeit more politely than the AFT. But the major battles against merit pay were fought in local school districts by teachers.

Bias and Favoritism

Complaints about classroom evaluations often centered on bias and favoritism. Teachers charged that administrators and supervisors used the evaluations to reward their friends and punish their enemies. Evaluators brought their political views, religious beliefs, and social preferences into the process, teachers claimed. Sometimes an especially controversial evaluation blew up into a newspaper sensation that had the entire community up in arms and taking sides: a Protestant principal's unfavorable evaluation of a Catholic or Jewish teacher, a Democrat's low ranking of a Republican teacher, or a male principal's alleged partiality toward the sharp-looking woman who taught fourth grade. Merit pay could be the perfect topic for community gossip and debate.

The checklist evaluation instruments used during the 1910s and 1920s invited controversy because they were so subjective. Often the evaluator rated teachers on such items as "teacher moves around frequently," "teacher is neat and well groomed," and "teacher has pleasant demeanor." In addition to the fact that such items left room for evaluators to inject their own biases, teachers complained these items had no necessary connection to good teaching. It was possible for students to learn from rumpled, fussy teachers who seldom stirred from their desks as well as from teachers with the traits the checklists favored. The use of such evaluation instruments, slanted toward teachers who dotted their *i*'s and crossed their *t*'s, penalized those who were unconventional but nevertheless commanded the respect of students, parents, and peers.[23]

Teacher Testing

Teacher testing, which we will examine in more detail in Chapter 3, was also controversial. Although it both amuses and irritates the public that the people who give tests to students complain so much when they have to take tests themselves, the consistency of teachers' complaints over the years deserves our attention.

The essence of their criticism has been that many of the questions on teacher tests are irrelevant to the work they do. When school boards in the 1910s and 1920s mandated questions covering the *general knowledge* considered to be the mark of any well-educated person, teachers argued that translating passages from Latin or identifying capitals of foreign countries (yes, such items were frequently on the test) were things most teachers rarely, if ever, had to do. As for *pedagogy*, the art and science of teaching, the complaint was that questions about teaching could not measure the ability to teach. Questions covering the *subject matter* teachers were responsible for—English or math, for instance—were somewhat more acceptable, but teachers often criticized these questions, too, as unrepresentative of the knowledge they actually used in the classroom. There was also controversy over how much English, math, or science the elementary teacher—a generalist—needed to know. Surely not as much as the specialized secondary teacher, but how much?[24]

Tried and Rejected

Administrators and supervisors often joined the protest against merit pay because many of them were as uncomfortable conducting the evaluations as the teachers were being evaluated. Merit ratings proved to be divisive, pitting teachers against administrators and one teacher against another. Running a merit pay system was a bureaucratic nightmare, administrators complained, as a host of new responsibilities competed for time on their already-crowded schedules.

The last straw broke when it became clear many school boards were using merit pay to reduce the budget for salaries. A favorite ploy was refusing to approve any teachers, regardless of their evaluations and test scores, for the highest rank. Sound and cheap? Transparently cheap.

The battles over merit pay were mercifully short in most school districts. Teachers took their case to their local communities, calling on newspaper editors and politicians to help win the sympathy of parents and other citizens. School boards, faced with determined opposition, threw up their hands and decided having a merit pay plan wasn't worth the trouble. Tried and rejected by almost half the nation's school systems, merit pay was a dead issue by the 1930s and 1940s.

THE ACCOUNTABILITY MOVEMENT:
MERIT PAY COMES BACK TO LIFE

If much of the above sounds familiar, it should, because in one sense the arguments over merit pay have changed very little. Merit pay has a habit of reappearing in slightly different incarnations, with each new-and-improved model promising to correct the defects of the older ones. Merit pay revived briefly during the 1950s, died again during the 1960s, and has been trying to stage another comeback since the 1970s as part of the accountability movement. No Child Left Behind has recharged merit pay, giving the concept its biggest boost ever. Merit pay, it seems, just won't go away.

Accountability is a concept with a positive-sounding name and tremendous surface appeal. Who would dare argue that educators should *not* be accountable? Accountability began as a response to the popular perception that the costs of public education have soared while the quality has plummeted. The movement promised taxpayers "more bang for the buck." No more vague promises—school boards found new ways to measure student achievement, and ever since, the pressure has been on teachers to be accountable for how much their students learn.[25]

Accountability has changed the way Americans think about public education. Standardized achievement tests with their aura of scientific respectability have become the accepted means of measuring student achievement. Releasing news about test scores—preferably *rising* test scores—has become the accepted way for school boards to reassure the public that students are learning.

NCLB is turning out to be accountability's ultimate incarnation. Advocates of the federal law can boast it is waging the most effective public relations campaign ever on behalf of accountability. According to critics, however, the campaign is actually an attack on public education. Focusing attention on the low test scores of four demographic subgroups of students—poor, minority, limited English proficienct, and disabled—NCLB puts the blame for low achievement squarely on the schools. That's one-sided and unfair, many teachers say. Throughout this textbook, and especially in Chapters 7 and 11, we will examine the claims and counterclaims in the debate over No Child Left Behind.

In this chapter, the focus is on how the accountability movement is affecting teacher salaries. Well before NCLB, some politicians and school officials wanted to use accountability as the latest twist in merit pay. Why not reward those teachers whose students have the highest achievement? In other words, why not base teacher salaries on student test scores?

The Factory Model of Schooling

From a business management point of view, the above idea sounds great. Follow the logic of a school board member with a background in business. Just as the high-tech assembly-line worker who turns out better silicon chips than other workers deserves a financial pat on the back, so does the teacher who turns out better

■ ■ ■ ■ ■

BOX 2.3

ACCOUNTABILITY UNDER NO CHILD LEFT BEHIND

The U.S. Department of Education explains the federal law's accountability provisions at www.ed.gov/nclb/accountability/schools/accountability.html

students. After all, the board member reasons, a school is like a factory. Educated students are the products of the factory, and teachers, the workers in the factory, must be accountable for the quality of the products. If teachers complain about the subjectivity of classroom evaluations and the irrelevance of teacher tests, then surely they will have no objections to using student test scores as an index of how well they are doing their jobs. What could be more relevant and objective?[26]

Schools are most definitely not like factories, teachers respond—often angrily—because students are not like silicon chips or any other tangible product. Students are human beings, not inanimate objects. The education of a human being is far more complex than the production of a silicon chip. High-tech workers, operating in a sterile environment, have almost complete control over their chips, while teachers have no such environment and no such control. Teachers are responsible for teaching, to be sure, but students are responsible for learning. Countless factors, both inside and outside the school, influence the teaching-learning process.

Teachers have been fighting various versions of the factory model of schooling since before the Civil War, but the model has become more threatening than ever under No Child Left Behind. With political pressure mounting to base merit pay on student test scores, the NEA has drawn the line over the issue. School boards trying to implement such pay plans have faced determined opposition from the big union. The smaller AFT, by contrast, has been less adamant, moving toward a compromise but trying not to alienate its members.

Accountability-Based Merit Pay on Trial

Picture a courtroom with a school district's director of testing on the stand. The director is using the example of a third-grade teacher and her class to explain accountability-based merit pay. "The district administers standardized tests to measure the achievement of the teacher's students at the start of the school year and again at the end of the year," the director testifies. "We attribute the difference between the two sets of test scores—an increase, we hope—to the teacher, even though we know other factors also affect scores. To control some of the other factors, we compare the test scores of this teacher's students with the scores of other students from similar socioeconomic backgrounds."

The testing director concludes, "The teacher gets a merit raise if her students' scores have increased more than the scores of comparable third-grade students. That's the essence of accountability-based merit pay."

Now listen as a witness for the teacher organization, a professor of educational measurement and evaluation, takes the stand. "The fundamental problem with such a plan," the professor begins, "is that the third-grade teacher is not the only influence on her students' test scores, as the previous witness admitted. We can divide the factors affecting test scores into two groups: school influences and nonschool influences. School influences include not just the one teacher but other teachers and also other students, administrators, textbooks, the classroom temperature, and countless other factors, many beyond the teacher's control. The list of nonschool influences is even longer, ranging from parents to peers, from exercise to diet, from magazines to television—virtually all beyond the teacher's control.

"The combined nonschool influences on achievement test scores are two to three times stronger, statistically speaking, than the combined school influences," the professor explains. "Trying to isolate the influence of one teacher as the basis of merit pay is little more than a guessing game."

Value-Added Assessment

This methodology is another gambit in merit pay's comeback bid. Touted as an "accountability revolution" by its supporters, value-added assessment uses methods only slightly different from those discussed in our courtroom drama to try to measure teacher influence on student achievement. The basic procedure is tracking the test scores of individual students to see how much they change over the course of a school year—that is, how much "value" is added that year. William Sanders, the University of Tennessee professor of agricultural statistics who developed the plan, argues that comparing a student's test scores in a given year to her or his past performance helps control for the influence of social class, race and ethnicity, and other socioeconomic factors.[27]

One student's scores don't reveal much about her or his teacher, Sanders admits, but the aggregated scores of all the students in a classroom can say a lot. "If you find that a majority of kids in a particular classroom have flat spots on the growth curve," he explains, "it becomes strong, powerful evidence that something regarding instruction is not happening in that classroom."[28] Over a three-year period, Sanders' plan compares the performance of a teacher's students to the district, state, and national norms (average scores) of students in the same subject and grade level.

Widely used for teacher evaluation in Tennessee as well as Arizona, Colorado, Florida, North Carolina, and Ohio, value-added assessment is attracting attention as a basis for merit pay. The RAND Corporation study *Evaluating Value-Added Models for Teacher Accountability* (2003) gives the methodology a good review. Critics say it has the same fundamental weakness of older accountability plans: Although it professes to control for socioeconomic background, in the end it attributes gains (or losses) in student achievement to the influence of a particular school and, even more specifically, to an individual teacher. What about the far more powerful nonschool influences? Sanders' best answer seems to be that no evaluation system, especially not a new one, is perfect.[29]

■ ■ ■ ■ ■ ■

BOX 2.4

WHAT'S THE VALUE?

Read the RAND Corporation's report on value-added assessment at www.rand.org/pubs/monographs/2004/RAND_MG158.pdf

The opposition of teacher organizations to accountability-based merit pay—adamant opposition up through the mid-1980s—has forced school boards to modify their plans, as we will see in the next section. The NEA still has major reservations about using student test scores to evaluate teachers, while the AFT has indicated a willingness to accept the use of student scores as *one* factor in experimental merit pay plans. Albert Shanker hoped this gamble would pay off for his union and for teaching as an occupation.

School Performance Incentives

The focus of some accountability-based merit pay plans is shifting from individual teachers to whole schools. Once again, trends in business and industry are serving as the blueprints for education. Here is a new, improved factory model of schooling.

Group performance incentives, sometimes called *collective incentives*, give rewards to all the workers at a job site when overall performance improves. Actually the idea is not new—it goes back to the 1930s—but it never really caught on in the United States until other industrial nations, particularly Japan, gained a competitive edge over our country during the 1970s and 1980s. Suddenly General Motors, Ford, and Chrysler paid attention to the way Toyota and Honda ran their automobile plants and treated their autoworkers. As more and more companies, large and small, began to pay attention in the 1980s and 1990s, collective incentives became a buzzword in American business.[30]

Now catching on in public education, group performance incentives are taking the form of *school performance incentives* that reward (or punish) all the teachers in a school when the school's standardized test scores increase (or decrease). School performance incentives, advocates claim, "can encourage teachers to work together by providing them with common goals that can only be reached through common effort. Because their fate is shared, the competitiveness and divisiveness of individual incentive plans [are] avoided."[31]

But accountability-based merit pay presents problems whether it is awarded to individuals or to groups. Above and beyond the statistical problem of separating nonschool influences from school influences, there are obvious human problems involved in rewarding all the teachers in a school when, in virtually every organization, some people work harder than others. In schools with overall test scores that do not qualify for merit pay, there are almost certainly outstanding individual teachers whose excellent work will go unrewarded.

No Child Left Behind: A Perfect Match for Merit Pay

NCLB has made standards, assessment, and accountability the watchwords of public education. As Chapters 7 and 11 explain in more detail, the federal law requires states to establish content and achievement standards, measure students against the standards, and hold local schools and school districts accountable for the results. Student test scores must be *disaggregated* or broken down into *subgroups* based on income, race/ethnicity, proficiency in English, and disability. The goal is for every subgroup of students in every school to score at a *proficient* level by 2014.[32]

A school or school district whose students do not make *adequate yearly progress* (AYP) toward proficiency for two consecutive years is classified as *in need of improvement* and receives intervention ranging from special assistance to sanctions. For a school that fails to bring its scores up, the sanctions can go as far as *reconstitution*— bringing in a new staff of teachers and administrators—or even closure.

NCLB has intensified the climate of reward and punishment in public schools. If students are feeling the pressure, their teachers are feeling even more. This latest version of accountability blames the schools for trying to "hide" the low achievement of children who "slip though the cracks." Under NCLB, the responsibility for improvement falls directly on teachers.

The implications for merit pay are clear. With the rules of the game set up this way, why *not* base teacher salaries on student test scores?

Not surprisingly, virtually all the states and school districts that are experimenting with merit pay acknowledge the influence of No Child Left Behind. Later in this chapter, we will look at several merit pay ventures and examine the approaches they are taking, including value-added assessment and school performance incentives. Some experiments, trying to steer clear of the test-score controversy, are awarding merit pay to teachers based on other criteria: putting in extra time and effort, for instance, or teaching difficult students in tough schools.

BEHAVIORAL EVALUATION OF TEACHERS

Yet another form of teacher evaluation remains in the background of the merit pay debates. It represents a return to the old idea of evaluating teacher performance in the classroom but with a new emphasis on student achievement. This *behavioral* approach to teacher evaluation also plays a role in several of the merit pay plans we will examine in the last section of this chapter.

How Behavioral Evaluation Works

Developed and popularized by the late Madeline Hunter and other researchers, the methodology of behavioral evaluation is disarmingly straightforward. Hunter's influential book *Mastery Teaching* has been released in an updated edition (2004) to meet the demands of NCLB. The basic approach involves breaking down teaching into as many small, discrete behaviors as possible; deciding which behaviors are indicators of effective teaching; observing teachers to determine the degree to which they exhibit these behaviors; evaluating teachers on the basis of the observations; and rewarding teachers accordingly.[33]

Observers—who may be administrators, supervisors, or teachers themselves—are trained to look for the behaviors in the classroom and code them on computer-scanning sheets. As the observers watch a teacher in action during a period of forty-five minutes or so, they repeatedly mark the scanning sheets, "bubbling in" the ovals that correspond to the behaviors they see. For instance, does the teacher "link instructional activity to prior learning"; "conduct lesson or instructional activity at a brisk pace, slowing presentations when necessary for student understanding but avoiding unnecessary slowdowns"; "use student responses to adjust teaching as necessary"; "provide sustaining feedback after an incorrect response by probing, repeating the question, giving a clue, or allowing more time"?[34]

These behaviors are four of the forty-three "effective teaching skills" on the North Carolina Teacher Performance Appraisal Instrument—Revised (TPAI-R). The developers of such systems boast their methodology is "noninferential," that it does not require the evaluator to pass judgment on a behavior, only to recognize the behavior and record the frequency with which it occurs. The actual evaluation comes later, when administrators review the observations and advise teachers how to improve their classroom work. To put things positively, helping teachers improve is the most important purpose of evaluation.[35]

But evaluation also involves the difficult and often unpleasant task of making decisions about salaries, promotions, and careers. Behavioral evaluation systems generate quantitative data; they produce averages, curves, standard deviations, and cutoffs. These systems make evaluation seem scientific and therefore objective. From the administrator's point of view, they have the virtue of shifting the responsibility for tough decisions away from people and toward numbers. If a teacher barely misses the cutoff for a merit raise, the administrator can pinpoint the teacher's problems on the observation sheets: failing to conduct the lesson "briskly" enough, perhaps, or neglecting to "affirm a correct oral response appropriately, and mov[ing] on."[36]

Teacher Likes and Dislikes

Teachers like the behavioral approach because it is specific, letting them know exactly what is expected of them and providing clear pointers on how to change. They dislike it because it is mechanical, pressuring them to teach in a certain way—at least while observers are present—and encouraging game playing.[37]

Teachers are asking critical questions about behavioral evaluation. Standing in front of a mirror at home on the night before an observation, practicing the approved repertoire of behaviors and trying to exhibit as many as possible in forty-five minutes—is that the best way for a teacher to improve? Is it the best

■ ■ ■ ■ ■ ■

BOX 2.5

A SAMPLE BEHAVIORAL EVALUATION INSTRUMENT

Go to www.ncpublicschools.org/evalpsemployees/ to see the North Carolina Teacher Performance Appraisal Instrument—Revised (TPAI-R).

way for a teacher to qualify for a raise or promotion? Consider the goal of making teaching a profession. How would doctors or lawyers react to such an evaluation system? Would anyone dare define the competent practice of medicine or law as a set of forty-three skills?

Effects on the Classroom

We can ask even more critical questions about the effects of behavioral evaluation on classroom instruction. Teachers often make jokes and try to laugh off the effects on their work. "I'll flap my wings, walk in circles, touch my nose, do almost anything else to get a good evaluation," one teacher told me. "Then I'll teach like I want after the principal leaves." But behavioral evaluation may be shaping instruction more than teachers realize.

A study of North Carolina's TPAI suggests as teachers conform to the style of instruction the instrument favors, behavioral evaluation homogenizes their teaching. The forty-three skills on the TPAI reflect a view of teaching as didactic instruction in facts, principles, right answers, and best responses. Not surprisingly, researchers have found teaching characterized by proposing, putting forth, and informing has increased in North Carolina classrooms since adoption of the TPAI. Teaching that involves supposing, speculating, and conjecturing has sharply decreased. Both styles of instruction have their place, of course, but behavioral evaluation, harnessed to a cookbook curriculum that already pressures teachers to "teach the test," may be reducing teaching to an uncritical process of transmitting information.[38]

Some of the most effective teachers educational psychologist Jerome Bruner remembers are those who encouraged him to get beyond the facts—to question, hypothesize, think critically. Bruner recalls how Miss Orcutt, one of his elementary school teachers, made her students marvel at the way water freezes and

> extend[ed] my world of wonder to encompass hers. She was not just informing me! She was, rather, negotiating the world of wonder and possibility. Molecules, solids, liquids, movement were not facts; they were to be used in pondering and imagining. Miss Orcutt was the rarity. She was a human event, not a transmission device.[39]

Unfortunately, behavioral evaluation may be putting teachers like Miss Orcutt on the endangered species list.

PORTFOLIOS: MULTIFACETED
TEACHER EVALUATION

Multifaceted teacher evaluation draws on multiple sources of evidence to produce a complex portrait of a complex art—teaching. *Portfolios,* the heart of multifaceted evaluation, allow teachers to document and reflect on their actual work. Convinced that breaking teaching down into countless minute behaviors can never capture its humane dimensions, such as socialization, civic engagement, and moral and spiritual development, Lee Shulman and other pioneers of multifaceted evaluation turned to portfolios as a more holistic approach.

Today, as computer-based technology becomes increasingly sophisticated, electronic teacher portfolios are making their mark on evaluation. Electronic portfolios take the management and presentation of information to a new level. But will Shulman's broad, humane vision of teaching be lost as portfolios fill up with the very specific documentation, much of it behavioral in nature, required by school districts, state departments of education, and licensing, certification, and accrediting agencies?

"Union of Insufficiencies"

Shulman, president of the Carnegie Foundation for the Advancement of Teaching and former director of the Teacher Assessment Project at Stanford University, admits all teacher evaluation strategies are flawed. As he explains in *The Wisdom of Teaching* (2004), an original goal of his work at Stanford was to form a "union of insufficiencies": a multifaceted evaluation plan capable of rising above the weaknesses of its individual components. Pencil-and-paper testing can provide valuable information about teachers, and so can direct observation. But these methods of assessment offer, at best, narrow views of what teachers do.[40]

Portfolios can paint a more comprehensive picture than any other evaluation strategy, Shulman believes. Portfolios can hold both the "artifacts" of teaching—student papers, lesson plans, teacher-made tests, notes from parents, and the like—and teachers' written reflections on their work. In addition, technology makes it possible to document teaching on videotape or, increasingly, in digital formats. Electronic images of teachers at work can bring the other contents of portfolios to life. Just as photographers and artists compile their best work for others to evaluate, teachers can put their best foot forward with portfolios. In *How to Develop a Professional Portfolio* (2003), Dorothy Campbell and her colleagues explain these and other advantages.[41]

Can portfolios avoid the pitfalls of other evaluation techniques? Shulman and other advocates seem optimistic. Although subjectivity is an inherent feature of portfolios (a strength, advocates say), field tests conducted by the TAP show that trained examiners do not find it difficult to reach a consensus when they evaluate portfolios. Shulman cautions against making scoring rubrics so objective that putting together a portfolio becomes tantamount to taking a "very, very cumbersome multiple choice test." He warns that portfolios can easily be "perverted" and "trivialized" if they are thrown into the arena of high-stakes assessment.[42] Over time, the stakes only get higher, as teachers and prospective teachers have to prove they can meet an increasing array of standards.

Doing the Job Right

Will the benefits for teachers—and students—justify the investment of time and money? Portfolios are time-consuming to assemble, even in the digital formats that teacher education programs increasingly use (see Chapter 3). As the NBPTS has discovered, portfolios are expensive to evaluate if the job is done right.

Portfolio evaluation holds great promise, to be sure, but will we invest the time and money to make it more than another bureaucratic requirement? If we do take portfolio evaluation seriously, will it give teachers the flexibility to emphasize their strengths and show who they really are, or will it work like a cookie cutter and standardize teaching and teacher education to a degree never before possible?

We are looking closely at teacher evaluation because it is so often overlooked in discussions of merit pay. Some of the merit plans we will examine in the next section are admittedly attractive. They offer the hope of pulling the occupation out of a financial rut. But remember: The plans are no better than the evaluation systems they rest on.

THE LATEST VERSIONS OF MERIT PAY

Changing Times

It is surely a sign of changing times when a president of the AFT endorses merit pay. Sandra Feldman has done just that. As a member of The Teaching Commission, Feldman helped craft the report *Teaching at Risk: A Call to Action* (2004), a business-oriented plan for restructuring the occupation, top to bottom. Along with Feldman, the commission's members include Louis Gerstner, the former chief executive officer (CEO) of IBM who organized and chairs the group; Vartan Gregorian, president of the Carnegie Corporation of New York; several other executives from the worlds of business and higher education; and Barbara Bush. Richard Riley, secretary of education in the Bill Clinton administration and former governor of South Carolina, sits on the commission with three other former governors, two big-city public school superintendents, and one public school teacher.[43]

Teaching at Risk calls for higher salaries, across the board, but adds that "simply raising salaries for all teachers will not, by itself, raise student achievement. . . . The Teaching Commission also urges a far-reaching break with tradition: a salary scheme that is commensurate with excellence. That is, paying teachers more for high performance, as measured by fair evaluations and clear evidence of improved student learning."[44]

■ ■ ■ ■ ■

BOX 2.6

THE REPORT OF THE TEACHING COMMISSION

Read *Teaching at Risk* (2004) for yourself on the commission's Web site at www. theteachingcommission.org

It is no surprise that corporate, political, and educational leaders are eager to see merit pay. But the president of the AFT? And what about the commission's lone public school teacher? How many of his colleagues would be willing to support value-added merit pay based on state tests keyed to No Child Left Behind, which is one of the commission's recommendations?[45]

Viewed in a broader context, *Teaching at Risk* is the latest commission report in a series stretching back to the mid-1980s, when two influential studies drew up the blueprints for a teaching profession whose members are paid on their merit: *A Nation Prepared: Teachers for the 21st Century* (1986) by the Carnegie Forum on Education and the Economy, and *Tomorrow's Teachers: A Report of the Holmes Group* (1986) by a consortium of reform-minded research universities. Other links in this chain include reports from the National Board for Professional Teaching Standards and the National Commission on Teaching and America's Future.[46]

The Carnegie Corporation has lent its influence and financial backing to all these commissions. With a vision of corporate professionalism, they all recommend businesslike reforms intended to reshape teaching into a highly differentiated occupation, driven at every level by accountability. The vision is admirable, teachers generally agree, but would the reforms produce real improvement?

Sandra Feldman (who retired from the post of AFT president in 2004) and other AFT leaders still have a bad taste for the words *merit pay*, much preferring *performance-based pay* or another newer, more positive-sounding name. So do many politicians, business and university leaders, and school officials who are trying to reform teacher compensation. In fact, the words *merit pay* don't even appear in *Teaching at Risk*. NEA leaders, by contrast, say the words often and always pejoratively, knowing they can count on a gut-level negative reaction from many teachers.

And yet, as we have seen, solid majorities of teacher seem ready to try certain forms of—shall I call them *quality-based salary incentives*? No, I'm going to stick with merit pay.

Wright Brothers or Alchemists?

Merit pay plans come and go. Experiments that look promising end in disappointment and failure, but advocates of merit pay keep trying. At best, we can liken these advocates to the Wright brothers, who finally built an airplane that could fly after other people had tried and failed for years. At worst, we can compare the

■ ■ ■ ■ ■

BOX 2.7

SEVERAL SPINS ON MERIT PAY

For a positive view, visit the Teacher Compensation Project of the Consortium for Policy Research in Education at the University of Wisconsin, Madison, at www.wcer. wisc.edu/cpre/tcomp/research/denver.asp. You can see the NEA's negative spin at www.nea.org and the AFT's tilt toward the positive at www.aft.org

advocates to the alchemists of old who insisted that, under exactly the right conditions, lead really could turn into gold. Well aware of merit pay's history and how some teachers still regard it as alchemy, recent advocates have experimented with numerous ways of compensating teachers in hopes that at least one will lift off the ground and fly.

To understand and evaluate these plans, we will begin by looking at the *teacher career ladders* that provide a framework for many merit pay programs. Then we will examine several real-world experiments that have tried to make merit pay work.

Teacher Career Ladders

Teachers have long complained that teaching is not a *scaled* or *staged* occupation, that responsibilities and earnings increase relatively little over the course of their careers. Workers in many other occupations feel a satisfying sense of progress as they move through the ranks. Salaries rise and titles change as people get better at their work and take on new duties.

Teachers, though, face the same old routine year after year. Some teachers who want more responsibility and more money become administrators, but not every teacher is suited for administration. Besides, this limited path of career mobility leads many of the best and most ambitious teachers out of the classroom and into the front office, depriving students of contact with excellent instructors. Shouldn't it be possible for talented teachers to stay in the classroom and increase their responsibilities and earnings as their careers progress?

Teaching at Risk answers this question affirmatively: "We need to establish career ladders that give the best teachers incentives to continue teaching and to serve as mentors to young peers, who need guidance and support to become equally successful." Actually, the career ladder movement goes back two decades. The state of Tennessee built the first ladder in the mid-1980s, followed quickly by several other southeastern states. The movement spread to the Midwest and West, and by the late 1980s more than one-third of the states in the nation had career ladders in place or under construction. Eleven state ladders eventually went up, but almost every state eventually pulled them down, usually with complaints about high costs.[47]

Some career ladders built by local school districts, however, are still standing. Innovative districts have sometimes rechristened them *career levels* or *career stages* on a *career continuum*. One of the best-known examples is the Career in Teaching program in Rochester, New York, where local AFT president Adam Urbanski and a succession of superintendents have been conducting a closely watched experiment in school reform.

Moving up the Rungs.   Call them what you will, career ladders usually consist of four or five rungs. Typically, teachers enter the occupation on an *apprentice* rung, where they are evaluated frequently and receive special guidance during their first year. Many career ladders are designed to bring new teachers into closer contact with experienced teachers. Veterans can serve as mentors to novices. Without such planned assistance, new teachers usually have to sink or swim on their own. They complain teacher-education programs do not prepare them well for their first year. They want on-the-job training. Apprenticeships may give teachers a way to pass the lore of their occupation from one generation of practitioners to the next.

After spending three to five years at the apprentice level, teachers who qualify for tenure step up to the *staff* rung of the ladder. Having passed a series of evaluations as apprentices, staff teachers are fully licensed with the job security tenure provides. As Chapter 5 explains, tenured teachers are entitled to continuing employment as long as their evaluations remain satisfactory. On most career ladders, teachers can remain at the staff level indefinitely if they wish. Moving up is voluntary.

The higher rungs may have such titles as (in ascending order) *career level I, career level II,* and *career level III,* with the latter sometimes also designated as *mentor teacher* or *lead teacher.* Teachers must serve a certain period of time at each level—typically five years—before they become eligible to apply for the next, and they must receive favorable evaluations in order to qualify.

Teachers who reach the top two rungs may sign ten- to twelve-month contracts and take on such new responsibilities as working with apprentices, evaluating other teachers, and developing curricula. In some cases, they may teach the equivalent of four periods per day and spend the remaining time on their additional duties.

The quasi-administrative nature of these tasks leads critics to charge career ladders are actually "job ladders" that lure people out of teaching and into administration. The architects of career ladders reply top-rung teachers are just that—teachers—for most of the day. A major goal of the ladders is keeping outstanding teachers in the classroom while allowing them to use their talents and experience in other ways.[48]

Earning Merit Pay on Career Ladders.   Under most plans, a traditional salary schedule remains in place, and climbing the ladder offers teachers a way to earn additional money. Annual incentives can range from a few hundred dollars at career level I to several thousand dollars at career level III. In merit plans that incorporate student test scores, student achievement helps determine the salaries of teachers on every rung of the ladder.

Teacher complaints about career ladders often boil down to a lack of trust in the evaluation system. States and school districts have tried virtually every combination of the evaluation strategies we have studied in this chapter, and none completely satisfies the teachers. Whatever a specific plan involves, teachers voice objections.

The effects of career ladders on teacher morale and collegiality are another target of criticism. Some teachers frankly do not want to make their schools more like factories, corporations, or even law firms. They chose teaching as an occupation precisely because teachers are equals among equals, not climbers on their way past stallers. They like the fact that teachers do not have to joust with one another for slots on a bureaucratic hierarchy. Changing the rules of the game to make teachers compete with one another for salaries and promotions, they argue, weakens the very spirit of cooperation they would like to strengthen.

Recent Experiments: Still Looking for a Better Way to Pay

Is it time for teachers to stop complaining and start helping with salary reform? The Teaching Commission thinks so. "Judgments must be made in every profession about which employees are performing well and which ones are not measuring up," the commission notes, showing its business tilt. "Such determinations are not an exact science, but supervisors are nevertheless expected to use regular evaluations and raises as an incentive to reward performance."

The experiments we will survey in conclusion are applications of concepts we have discussed throughout this chapter. Judge them for yourself as you review the recent history of merit pay.

Houston.   Critics who see merit pay as lead gilded with gold paint point to the failure of the most publicized merit pay experiment of the 1980s, Houston's Second Mile Plan. Initiated in 1979, the Second Mile Plan got a great deal of media attention as a modern pioneer of merit pay because it predated *the* educational reform report of the late twentieth century, *A Nation at Risk* (1983). Houston's teachers could qualify for "bonus stipends" in several different ways, which ranged from teaching in a field with a staff shortage (secondary math or science, for instance) to teaching in a school with better-than-predicted standardized test scores—an early experiment in school performance incentives. On the positive side, more than two-thirds of Houston's teachers took home annual bonuses of up to several thousand dollars. On the negative side, teachers said the plan sent the divisive message that the work of some teachers is more valuable than the work of others. Teacher organizations have argued for years that a high school physics teacher is worth no more and no less than a kindergarten teacher. Teachers also complained about pressure to teach the tests. Faced with teacher opposition, increasing costs, and a downturn in the Texas oil economy, the Houston school board called off the eight-year experiment in 1987.[49]

South Carolina.   South Carolina has also received publicity, positive and negative, for its performance incentive program. Established in 1984 and keyed primarily to student standardized test scores, the program originally gave monetary awards to individual teachers, individual principals, and entire schools. Test scores were rising and public reaction was generally favorable until reports surfaced that some teachers, encouraged by their principals, were resorting to teaching the tests and even outright cheating to reap rewards for themselves and their schools (see Chapter 11). After CBS News aired a *60 Minutes* exposé in 1990 focusing on a teacher who was fired because she gave her students not only the questions but also the answers to a standardized test, South Carolina scaled back the program. Now it offers only group performance incentives to entire schools, and the money must be spent on instructional materials and equipment, not salaries.[50]

Kentucky.   While South Carolina was trimming its program, Kentucky was developing its own school performance incentives. Under the Kentucky plan, schools with standardized test scores and other achievement indicators that improve more than 10 percent over two years receive financial bonuses. Through site-based management councils, teachers themselves originally decided how to allocate the bonuses, and most of the $26 million available in 1995 went into teachers' pockets, as the state legislature intended. Predictably, dissension broke out. Some schools voted to give teachers all the money, others to include staff workers in the bonuses, still others to spend some of the money for instructional purposes. In 1998 the legislature changed its mind and said the bonuses could no longer be used to enhance salaries.[51]

Cincinnati.   The fourth edition of this textbook presented a long discussion of merit pay in Cincinnati and speculated that the proposed plan represented a "breakthrough." The discussion in this edition is much shorter because the plan turned out to be no such thing, although it *did* look promising.

Painstakingly negotiated in the late 1990s and early 2000s by the Cincinnati board of education and the Cincinnati Federation of Teachers, the proposal steered clear of student test scores and focused instead on teacher knowledge and skills. Behavioral evaluation and portfolios were the main evaluation strategies, and teachers were measured against standards aligned with those of the NBPTS and Praxis, the national teacher licensing examination (see Chapter 3). Based on evaluations of their knowledge and skills in four domains—planning and preparing for learning, creating an environment for learning, teaching for learning, and professionalism—teachers would have moved through five career levels—*apprentice, novice, career, advanced,* and *accomplished*—each with its own salary range. Although the new pay plan would eventually have replaced the district's traditional salary schedule, currently employed teachers could have opted to remain on the schedule.[52]

In May 2002, Cincinnati teachers rejected merit pay by a vote of 1,892 to 73. Although they had approved the evaluation portion of the proposal in 2000, teachers had second thoughts about tying the evaluations to their paychecks. Many teachers stated there had not been enough professional development to prepare them to meet the new teaching standards, and some even said the standards had little relevance to their actual work. Some voiced opposition because they feared their salaries would fall under the program.[53]

Denver.   In May 2004, 59 percent of the members of the Denver Classroom Teachers Association approved a merit proposal that combines several features we have discussed in this chapter. Under the Professional Compensation System for Teachers (ProComp), Denver teachers will no longer receive pay increments based on their years of experience. Instead, teachers can qualify for higher salaries in several other ways. From the least to the most controversial, they are: increasing their knowledge and skills in areas related to their classroom work, receiving satisfactory behavioral evaluations, working in high-poverty schools, teaching in subject fields that are experiencing shortages, and raising their students' test scores. Currently employed teachers have seven years to decide whether to stick with the traditional salary schedule or join ProComp, which promises top salaries of $90,000 to the best teachers.[54]

ProComp is trying hard to avoid the pitfalls of earlier merit plans. One of the most attractive aspects of the plan is that it offers teachers a choice of paths to higher salaries. The most controversial path, raising student test scores, is only one option. The ProComp Web site features a salary calculator set up to show teachers how much they might gain (or lose) over the course of their career by selecting different options. At the same time, district and union officials are trying to assure the public that all the paths lead to the "bottom line" of improving student achievement, particularly to the NCLB goal of "clos[ing] the gap between better and poorer performing schools." The president of the teachers association ties the goals together: "ProComp will give teachers more control over their financial destiny while closely aligning their work to the district's goals of improving student learning and attracting, retaining, and rewarding the best teachers."[55]

Developed after several years of piloting, the Denver plan is now the nation's most closely watched experiment in merit pay. NEA officials are certainly paying attention because the Denver Classroom Teachers Association, a NEA local, has moved farther and faster on pay reform than the parent union. Denver's taxpayers are also watching the program because its implementation hinges on their willingness to approve a $25 million property tax increase in November 2005. If the tax levy passes, ProComp will be phased in during 2006 and 2007.

A lack of financial support has recently helped kill several experiments with merit pay, including an Iowa program that also attracted national attention before

---

BOX 2.8

PROCOMP IN DENVER

Explore the well-constructed Web site designed to sell teachers and the public on merit pay in Denver at www.denverprocomp.org

the state legislature cut it back drastically in 2003. "Big-City Districts Scrap Reward-Based Systems of Evaluating Teachers," *Education Week* reported in a 2003 article on the demise of two other merit pay programs in Philadelphia and Baltimore.[56]

But times are changing. Teacher and public attitudes toward merit pay are becoming more positive. Will the Denver version of merit pay prove to be the airplane that finally lifts off the ground, or will it be yet another failed attempt to turn lead into gold?

ACTIVITIES

1. Ask for salary schedules from the school districts where you are most interested in teaching. Compare their schedules with the three representative schedules in this chapter. Inquire about career ladders, school performance incentives, and other forms of merit pay.

2. Talk with several currently employed teachers about merit pay, accountability, evaluation, and other issues discussed in this chapter. Interview retired teachers and compare their opinions.

3. Broaden your interviews to include political officials, particularly local and state school board members, state legislators, and others who have influence on teacher salaries.

RECOMMENDED READINGS

American Federation of Teachers. *Survey and Analysis of Teacher Salary Trends* (Washington, DC: AFT, updated annually). This report, along with the NEA's *Rankings & Estimates* (see note 16) is an excellent fact book on the economic status of America's teachers.

Ingersoll, Richard M. *Who Controls Teachers' Work? Power and Accountability in America's Schools* (Cambridge, MA: Harvard University Press, 2003). Much more critical than the commission report below, this strongly proteacher book analyzes the accountability principles that underlie merit pay and other reforms.

The Teaching Commission. *Teaching at Risk: A Call to Action* (New York: The Commission, 2004). This report exemplifies a stream of school reform that has been trying for twenty years to remake teaching into a profession with businesslike accountability.

NOTES

1. Both quotations are from Public Agenda, *Stand by Me: What Teachers Really Think about Unions, Merit Pay and Other Professional Matters* (New York: Public Agenda, 2003), pp. 24–25.
2. American Federation of Teachers, *Survey and Analysis of Teacher Salary Trends 2002* (Washington, DC: AFT, 2003), Fig. I-5.
3. Ibid., Fig. I-4.
4. National Commission on Teaching and America's Future, *No Dream Denied: A Pledge to America's Children* (Washington, DC: NCTAF, 2003).
5. Catherine Gewertz, "School Chiefs Lead the Way in Pay Trends," *Education Week* (June 23, 2004), pp. 1, 16–21.
6. American Federation of Teachers, *Survey and Analysis of Teacher Salary Trends 2002*, Tbl. I-7.

7. Estimates based on National Education Association, *Status of the American Public School Teacher 2000–2001* (Washington, DC: NEA, 2003), pp. 83–85, and U.S. Department of Commerce, Bureau of the Census, "Three-Year-Average Median Household Income by State: 2001–2003" (2004) [Available: www.census.gov/hhes/income/income03/statemhi.html].

8. NEA, *Status of the American Public School Teacher 2000–2001*, p. 82.

9. Ibid., p. 85.

10. Christy Lynn Wilson, "The Salary Gap," *Quality Counts 2000: Who Should Teach?* a special report of *Education Week* (January 13, 2000), p. 36.

11. Sylvia A. Allegretto, Sean P. Corcoran, and Lawrence Mishel, *How Does Teacher Pay Compare? Methodological Challenges and Answers* (Washington, DC: Economic Policy Institute, 2004).

12. Information in this section is from U.S. Department of Labor, Bureau of Labor Statistics, *Occupational Outlook Handbook, 2004–05 Edition* (2004) [Available: stats.bls.gov/oco/home.htm], and U.S. Department of Education, National Center for Education Statistics, *Digest of Education Statistics, 2002* (2003) [Available: nces.ed.gov/programs/digest/d02/tables/dt255.asp].

13. Wilson, "The Salary Gap," p. 36.

14. Ann Bradley, "If I Were a Rich Man," *Teacher Magazine* (March 2000), p. 14.

15. For more on win-win bargaining, see William A. Streshly and Jerry Franklin, *Preventing and Managing Teacher Strikes* (Lanham, MD: Rowman & Littlefield, 2002).

16. National Education Association, *Rankings and Estimates: Rankings of the States 2003 & Estimates of School Statistics 2004* (Washington, DC: NEA, 2004), p. 66.

17. Albert Shanker, "The Making of a Profession," *American Educator* 9 (Fall 1985): 10–17, 46, 48.

18. Public Agenda, *Stand by Me*, pp. 24–26, 34. For teacher attitudes in earlier years, see Carol A. Langdon, "The Fifth Phi Delta Kappa Poll of Teachers' Attitudes toward the Public Schools," *Phi Delta Kappan* 80 (April 1999): 614; Carol A. Langdon and Nick Vesper, "The Sixth Phi Delta Kappa Poll of Teachers' Attitudes toward the Public Schools," *Phi Delta Kappan* 81 (April 2000): 610.

19. Public Agenda, *Stand by Me*, pp. 25, 34.

20. Public Agenda, *Attitudes about Teaching: Including the Views of Parents, Administrators and the General Public* (New York: Public Agenda, 2004), pp. 22–23.

21. For analysis of merit pay in historical context, see Richard J. Murnane and David K. Cohen, "Merit Pay and the Evaluation Problem: Understanding Why Most Merit Pay Plans Fail and a Few Survive," *Harvard Educational Review* 56 (February 1986): 1–17; Susan M. Johnson, "Merit Pay for Teachers: A Poor Prescription for Reform," *Harvard Educational Review* 54 (May 1984): 175–185; and Raymond E. Callahan, *Education and the Cult of Efficiency: A Study of the Social Forces That Have Shaped the Administration of the Public Schools* (Chicago: University of Chicago Press, 1962), Chap. 5.

22. The discussion in this section is based in part on case studies of the Atlanta Public Schools. See Joseph W. Newman, "A History of the Atlanta Public School Teachers' Association, Local 89 of the American Federation of Teachers, 1919–1956" (Ph.D. diss., Georgia State University, 1978), Chap. 1; and Wayne J. Urban, "Progressive Education in the Urban South: The Reform of the Atlanta Schools, 1914–1918," in Michael H. Ebner and Eugene M. Tobin, eds., *The Age of Urban Reform: New Perspectives on the Progressive Era* (Port Washington, NY: Kennikat Press, 1977), Chap. 9.

23. Arthur C. Boyce, "Methods of Measuring Teachers' Efficiency," *Fourteenth Yearbook of the National Society for the Study of Education,* Part II (Bloomington, IL: Public School Publishing, 1915); Lloyd Young, *The Administration of Merit-Type Teachers' Salary Schedules* (New York: Teachers College, Columbia University, 1933).

24. Arvil Sylvester Barr, "Measurement and Prediction of Teaching Efficiency: Summary of Investigations," *Journal of Experimental Education* 16 (June 1948): 203–283.

25. See Richard M. Ingersoll, *Who Controls Teachers' Work? Power and Accountability in America's Schools* (Cambridge, MA: Harvard University Press, 2003). A highly influential book by the father of the accountability movement is Leon M. Lessinger's *Every Kid a Winner: Accountability in Education* (New York: Simon and Schuster, 1970).

26. The discussion in this section is based on Jason Millman, ed., *Grading Teachers, Grading Schools: Is Student Achievement a Valid Evaluation Measure?* (Thousand Oaks, CA: Corwin Press, 1997), and Donald M. Medley, Homer Coker, and Robert S. Soar, *Measurement-Based Evaluation of Teacher Performance: An Empirical Approach* (White Plains, NY: Longman, 1984), Chap. 3.

27. David Hill, "He's Got Your Number," *Teacher Magazine* (May/June 2000), pp. 42–47.

28. Quoted in ibid., p. 44.

29. Daniel F. McCaffrey, Daniel M. Koretz, J. R. Lockwood, and Laura S. Hamilton, *Evaluating Value-Added Models for Teacher Accountability* (Santa Monica, CA: RAND Corporation, 2003); Hill, "He's Got Your Number," p. 46.

30. Edward E. Lawler, III, *Strategic Pay: Aligning Organizational Strategies and Pay Systems* (San Francisco: Jossey-Bass, 1990).

31. William A. Firestone, "Redesigning Teacher Salary Systems for Educational Reform," *American Educational Research Journal* 31 (Fall 1995): 560–561.

32. The U.S. Department of Education's Executive Summary of the No Child Left Behind Act is available at www.ed.gov/nclb/overview/intro/execsumm.html?exp=0

33. Robin Hunter, *Madeline Hunter's Mastery Teaching: Increasing Instructional Effectiveness in Elementary and Secondary Schools*, updated ed. (Thousand Oaks, CA: Corwin Press, 2004).

34. North Carolina Public Schools, *Public School Employee Evaluation* (2004) [Available: www.ncpublic schools.org/evalpsemployees/].

35. Ibid.

36. Ibid.

37. Noreen B. Garman, "Teachers Ask: Is There Life after Madeline Hunter?" *Phi Delta Kappan* 69 (May 1988): 670–672.

38. Joseph O. Milner, "Suppositional Style and Teacher Evaluation," *Phi Delta Kappan* 72 (February 1991): 464–467. Milner's research provoked a debate on North Carolina's TPAI in *Phi Delta Kappan* 72 (June 1991).

39. Jerome Bruner, *Actual Minds, Possible Worlds* (Cambridge, MA: Harvard University Press, 1990), p. 126.

40. Lee S. Shulman, *The Wisdom of Teaching: Essays on Teaching, Learning, and Learning to Teach* (San Francisco: Jossey-Bass, 2004), Chap. 12.

41. Ibid.; Dorothy M. Campbell, Pamela Bondi Cignetti, Beverly J. Melenwyser, Diana H. Nettles, and Richard M. Wyman, *How to Develop a Professional Portfolio: A Manual for Teachers*, 3rd ed. (Boston: Allyn & Bacon, 2003).

42. Shulman, *The Wisdom of Teaching*, Chap. 14.

43. The Teaching Commission, *Teaching at Risk: A Call to Action* (New York: The Commission, 2004).

44. Ibid., p. 22.

45. Ibid., p. 24.

46. Carnegie Forum on Education and the Economy, *A Nation Prepared: Teachers for the 21st Century. A Report of the Task Force on Teaching as a Profession* (New York: Carnegie Forum, 1986); Holmes Group, *Tomorrow's Teachers: A Report of the Holmes Group* (East Lansing, MI: Holmes Group, 1986).

47. The Teaching Commission, *Teaching at Risk*, p. 24; Lynn M. Cornett, "Lessons from Ten Years of Teacher Improvement Reforms," *Educational Leadership* 52 (February 1995): 29; Southern Regional Education Board, *The 1991 Survey of Incentive Programs and Career Ladders* (Atlanta: SREB, 1991).

48. Firestone, "Redesigning Teacher Salary Systems," pp. 553–560.

49. *The Second Mile Plan* (Houston: Houston Independent School District, n.d.); Elaine Say and Leslie Miller, "The Second Mile Plan: Incentive Pay for Houston Teachers," *Phi Delta Kappan* 64 (December 1982): 270–271.

50. Cornett, "Lessons from Ten Years of Teacher Improvement Reforms."

51. Lonnie Harp, "Ky. Names Schools to Receive Achievement Bonuses," *Education Week* (February 15, 1995), p. 11; Harp, "Ky. Schools Put on the Line in Bonus Budgeting," *Education Week* (April 26, 1995), pp. 1, 9; Ulrich Boser, "Kentucky," *Quality Counts 2000*, p. 118.

52. Julie Blair, "Cincinnati Teachers to Be Paid on Performance," *Education Week* (September 27, 2000), pp. 1, 15.

53. Bess Keller, "Cincinnati Teachers Rebuff Performance Pay," *Education Week* (May 29, 2002), p. 5.

54. Bess Keller, "Teacher Vote on Merit Pay Down to Wire," *Education Week* (March 17, 2004), pp. 1, 22–23, and Keller, "Next Pay-Plan Decision Up to Denver Voters," *Education Week* (March 31, 2004), p. 3.

55. "Professional Compensation System for Teachers (ProComp)" [brochure], Denver Public Schools (2004) [Available: www.denverteachercompensation.org/ProCompBrochure_4-26-04.pdf], p. 1.

56. Karla Scoon Reid, "Iowa's Move toward Pay-for-Performance on Verge of Collapse," *Education Week* (September 10, 2003), pp. 1, 22; "Big-City Districts Scrap Reward-Based Systems of Evaluating Teachers," *Education Week* (October 22, 2003), p. 15.

CHAPTER 3

LEARNING TO TEACH AND PROVING YOUR COMPETENCE

I student taught for a year and did research in the same classroom . . . not with just any teacher who wanted a student teacher to help get stuff done, but a teacher who wanted to help me learn and become a good teacher.

Texas teacher[1]

Education is the only professional field where after people graduate they say they might have been better off without the training.

—Former New York teacher[2]

TEACHER EDUCATION IN THE ERA
OF NO CHILD LEFT BEHIND

Most students who enroll in a teacher education program expecting, reasonably enough, to learn how to teach probably don't realize they have stepped into the middle of a controversy. They soon find out when they read a *Time* or *Newsweek* cover story that is critical of teachers and downright scornful of those who teach teachers, or when they talk to business, engineering, or arts and sciences majors who ask, "What? You're taking education courses? Why would a smart person who has a whole world of options go into teaching?"

As a prospective teacher, you surely have your own answers to such questions, but this chapter will give you a better understanding of why teacher education programs and their graduates generate so much controversy. Just as Chapters 1 and 2 offer hope as well as criticism, this chapter suggests the arguments over teacher education and teacher competency may have a positive outcome. There are signs the occupation may be changing for the better.

The education of America's teachers has always been controversial. In the early years of the nation, before teachers undertook special training, some citizens argued teachers obviously needed help. Teachers lacked both knowledge and skill, a Massachusetts school reformer complained in 1826: They "know nothing, absolutely nothing, of the complicated and difficult duties assigned to them." "Literary and scientific" training, he later suggested, could help people learn what and how to teach.[3]

Not so, others countered. Any intelligent person who had gone to school had already learned "the art of instructing others," and "if intelligence be wanting, no system of instruction can supply its place." Bright people can teach naturally, according to this argument, and dull people who try to teach are just asking for trouble—and dismissal.[4]

We still hear arguments on both sides of this debate. In fact, the opposing positions weave in and out of this chapter as themes.

Challenge.   Although advocates of formal teacher education have generally had the upper hand in the debate, since 2000 the advantage has shifted. The election and reelection of President George W. Bush have given new political clout to critics whose longstanding goal has been cutting back on coursework in teacher education. The *highly qualified teacher* provisions of No Child Left Behind, as we saw in Chapter 1, emphasize knowledge of subject matter and downplay the knowledge and skills specific to teaching. NCLB encourages states to set licensing requirements that make it possible for people to enter the classroom with little formal preparation for working with children.[5]

The news media are focusing public attention on criticism of teacher education, much of it from high-profile people in the Bush administration. U.S. Secretary of Education Margaret Spellings, like former Secretary Rod Paige, speaks out against "artificial" education and licensing requirements that, she claims, discourage bright and talented people from entering the occupation. Lynne Cheney, a senior fellow at the American Enterprise Institute and wife of the vice president, moderated a symposium in June 2003 on the question "Can Schools of Education Be Saved?" The consensus seemed to be no. First Lady Laura Bush is a member of The Teaching Commission, which produced *Teaching at Risk: A Call to Action* (2004), a report that criticizes teacher education programs for a lack of rigor, quality, and accountability: "We must break the cycle in which low-performing students in college become the teachers of low-performing students in public schools."[6]

Response.   Teacher educators and their allies have been busy responding to these challenges. The most vocal and visible spokespersons are Linda Darling-Hammond of Stanford University and Art Wise of the National Council for Accreditation of Teacher Education (NCATE). In such reports as *No Dream Denied: A Pledge to America's Children* (2003), they take the position that schools of education are in the process of reinventing themselves; in fact, they are already graduating a new generation of highly competent teachers. What critics of teacher education seem to want, advocates charge, is to allow just about anybody with a bachelor's degree to walk into the classroom and teach.[7]

Darling-Hammond, Wise, and other advocates are marshaling empirical evidence to show that graduates of teacher education programs are *better* teachers: That is, they are less likely to burn out and quit, they are better equipped to handle discipline problems, and—most important in today's educational and political climate—they can do a better job of raising student test scores. Operating in an education system driven by *standards, assessments, and accountability*, teacher educators are trying to meet the critics on their own terms.[8]

Results.   In this chapter and throughout your own teacher education program, you will see the results of this response taking shape. NCATE, the Interstate New Teacher Assessment and Support Consortium (INTASC), and the National Board for Professional Teaching Standards (NBPTS) are trying to develop a "quality assurance system for the teaching profession": a "coherent system of complementary standards and assessments for preparation, licensing, and certification." Here, advocates believe, is the ammunition teacher education needs to fight back, the strategy it can use to save itself. Here, at last, is accountability.[9]

But will it work? In the second half of this chapter, we will take examine the strengths and weaknesses of this reform movement, one that comes from within teacher education. First we will find out why, as a result of other reforms, there are now several ways—not just one—to enter the occupation.

MULTIPLE ROUTES INTO TEACHING

Although No Child Left Behind has been giving teacher education a run for the money since 2001, new paths into teaching have been opening for twenty-five years. In fact, *traditional undergraduate programs* have been losing their market share of teacher preparation since the era of school reform inspired by the report *A Nation at Risk* (1983). Before the mid-1980s, almost everybody who came into teaching did so in the traditional undergraduate way, with a small number of people entering via a master's degree route. Now the dominance of

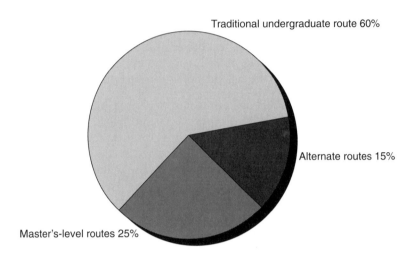

FIGURE 3.1   How New Teachers Enter the Occupation.

Source: Estimates based on C. Emily Feistritzer, *The Making of a Teacher: A Report on Teacher Preparation in the U.S.* [Available: www.teach-now.org/MakingOfATeacher/MOT-1.asp]; "Incentives and Recruitment," *Quality Counts 2000* (January 13, 2000), p. 55.

undergraduate teacher education has been broken, but as Figure 3.1 indicates, about 60 percent of new teachers still follow the traditional path.

A growing number of new teachers are taking other routes into teaching. About 25 percent enter on a *master's-level route*. Depending on the particular program, the graduate path can provide preparation ranging from a compressed version of an undergraduate program to an extensive clinical program designed to be the culmination of a five-year sequence of teacher preparation—the model pioneered by the Holmes Partnership. The remaining 15 percent of new teachers enter the occupation via an *alternate route*. These paths, which vary a great deal in quality, lead in some cases directly into the classroom—a sink-or-swim experience for unprepared novices—and in other cases to on-the-job training under the supervision of a mentor and reinforced by education courses taken after school and on the weekends.[10]

Now we will map these multiple routes. First we will turn to the avenue millions of teachers have taken, a path characterized over the years by more stability than change.

THE TRADITIONAL ROUTE: UNDERGRADUATE TEACHER EDUCATION

At the more than 1,300 American colleges and universities that prepare teachers in undergraduate programs, the curriculum is organized in three main areas:

1. *liberal education* in the arts and sciences

2. the *teaching field* (or *fields*) for which teachers will be responsible in the classroom—the "what" of teaching

3. *professional education* in methods and foundations—the "how" and "why" of teaching.

Although the names and specific content have changed over the years, teacher education programs have consisted of these same three areas for more than a century and a half—since the days of *normal schools*. Normal schools were quasi-secondary institutions that specialized in teacher education from the mid-nineteenth century well into the twentieth. The most successful normal schools transformed themselves first into teachers' colleges, then into colleges, and finally into full-fledged universities.[11]

Pedagogy (an old-fashioned name for the art and science of teaching) struggled to find its place as an academic field in higher education, eventually gaining acceptance because the nation decided it wanted college-educated teachers and, just as important, because colleges wanted the tuition revenue future teachers generated. By the 1920s, teacher education had become the most popular undergraduate major on college and university campuses.

From the days of normal schools to the present, the curriculum for prospective teachers has consisted of liberal education, the teaching field, and professional education, just as arguments have continued over how much emphasis each of the three areas should receive. The debate has usually centered on the trade-off between the first two areas and the third. In 1847, the principal of the State Normal School of Albany, New York, one of the nation's first teacher-training institutions, spoke of the trade-off in terms that have changed little: "To be a teacher, one must first of all also be a scholar. So much stress is now placed on method, and on the theory of teaching, that there is great danger of forgetting the supreme importance of scholarship and culture." Keep the concept of trade-off in mind as we survey each area.[12]

Liberal Education

Liberal education consists of courses in the arts and sciences, the core of any college education. These courses are liberal in the sense that they are designed to liberate the mind from provincial thought and open it to a variety of viewpoints. The arts and sciences transmit a cultural heritage: knowledge educated people deem valuable, organized into such disciplines as history, English, foreign languages, mathematics, biology, and chemistry. These disciplines are more than bodies of knowledge. They represent different ways of knowing. Think for a moment about how differently historians and biologists organize and use knowledge or how differently philosophers and mathematicians solve problems.

Theodore Hesburgh, former president of the University of Notre Dame, suggests liberal education enables people "to think clearly, logically, deeply, and widely"; to express themselves with the same facility; "to evaluate, to have a growing sense of moral purpose and priority"; and "to cope daily with the ambiguities of the human situation."[13] Although the case for liberal education is not primarily vocational, I could argue that of all citizens, teachers have the greatest need in their work for the skills that Hesburgh describes. As the Holmes Group (now the Holmes Partnership) states in *Tomorrow's Teachers* (1986), "Teachers must lead a life of the mind. They must be reflective and thoughtful: persons who seek to understand so they may clarify for others, persons who can go to the heart of the matter."[14]

But Hesburgh, the Holmes Partnership, and other professors and organizations in both education and the arts and sciences recognize that liberal education is imperfect. It, too, cries out for reform. Fragmentation, excessive specialization, poor teaching—prospective teachers encounter these problems far too often in liberal education courses. Professors of the arts and sciences are not always the academic exemplars some of them claim to be. A rivalry has raged for years between education and the arts and sciences. Many teacher educators, battle-weary and defensive, are reluctant to share any more of the teacher education program.[15]

Today, depending on the particular program and institution, liberal education usually accounts for one-third to one-half of the content of undergraduate teacher education. Is that enough? What is the trade-off with the other two areas?

The Teaching Field

This area involves preparation in the subject or subjects prospective teachers will convey to their students. One-fourth to one-third of the courses in teacher education programs are in the teaching field, and that range encompasses even more variation than the fractions suggest. For teachers at every grade level, requirements in the teaching field have changed because of No Child Left Behind.

Consider first the case of prospective high school teachers, who take their teaching field courses in the arts and sciences. Before the passage of NCLB, according to the U.S. Department of Education report *Meeting the Highly Qualified Teachers Challenge* (2002), about two-thirds of high school teachers majored in the arts and sciences—English teachers in the English department, math teachers in the math department, and so forth. A third of high school teachers, however, majored in secondary education, typically trading off three or four semester courses in the teaching field in order to take three or four more courses in education.[16] From the arts and sciences point of view, secondary education majors learned too little about their academic subjects, the "what" of teaching.

NCLB has tilted the playing field toward the arts and sciences. In order to be considered highly qualified, all new high school teachers of *core academic subjects*—English, reading or language arts, history, civics and government, geography, economics, mathematics, science, the arts, and foreign language—must have an arts and sciences major, or the equivalent in coursework, in their teaching field.[17] Taking this much work in the teaching field leaves little room, by comparison, for professional education. From the point of view of many teacher educators, future high school teachers walk into the classroom knowing too little about the "how" and "why" of teaching.

NCLB has also influenced the preparation of middle school teachers, who work in the schools widely regarded as the weakest link in the chain of American education. According to *Meeting the Highly Qualified Teachers Challenge* (2002), only 44 percent of middle school teachers majored in the arts and sciences before NCLB. Federal education officials would like to raise that percentage, but they are running into resistance.[18]

NCLB pressures the states to decide whether middle school students are more like elementary school students or more like high school students and, consequently, whether middle school teachers should be academic generalists or subject-matter specialists. In states that consider the middle grades a part of secondary schooling, NCLB requires that new middle school teachers who teach core academic subjects have the same qualifications as new high school teachers. With few exceptions, they must have an arts and sciences major (or the equivalent) in their teaching field. In states that designate the middle grades part of elementary schooling, middle school teachers can still major in education and meet the less specialized requirements for elementary teachers described below.[19]

Most states are encouraging the latter approach. Their rationale appears to involve filling job openings rather than meeting the developmental needs of young people. *Education Week* describes this situation as the "middle school muddle."[20]

The debate over the value of majoring in arts and sciences versus majoring in education has become especially sensitive in the real world of the schools, because teachers who were employed prior to NCLB have more options for meeting highly qualified requirements than new teachers. The federal law allows each state to develop a "High Objective Uniform State Standard of Evaluation" (HOUSSE), to evaluate the qualifications of experienced teachers. Experienced teachers can meet NCLB requirements through graduate degrees, advanced credentials, and state testing. The states have been extremely flexible with these teachers—too flexible, some say—in order to keep them in their positions.[21]

Elementary education, special education, and physical education deserve special consideration in this discussion. Prospective teachers in these fields earn two-thirds of the bachelor's degrees in education, with elementary majors alone accounting for more than one-third. No Child Left Behind requires that in order for new elementary teachers to be considered highly qualified, they must pass a "rigorous state test" in reading, writing, math, and other basic subjects in the curriculum. New special education and physical education teachers do not have meet highly qualified teacher standards unless they are responsible for teaching a core academic subject, in which case they must pass a state test.[22]

Let's consider where within the university elementary, special, and physical education teachers *should* take their teaching fields. We might argue that prospective elementary teachers, who must be responsible for many subjects, should take a sampler of courses in the arts and sciences. Special education teachers might go to the psychology department, while physical education teachers could concentrate on physiology in the biology department. In some programs, to be sure, these teachers do go to the arts and sciences for at least part of their teaching fields. About 80 percent of them, though, take their teaching fields in the college of education, where they enroll in such courses as Math for

Elementary Teachers, Behavior Modification of Emotionally Conflicted Children, and Sports Physiology.[23]

Many teacher educators argue this practice is both logical and academically sound. They believe teaching field courses designed for teachers and focused on the classroom are more useful than courses designed for arts and sciences majors.

Critics, when they are in a polite mood, argue such courses take future teachers out of the academic mainstream, cutting them off from professors and students who are working in the disciplines. Less politely, critics describe such courses as "Mickey Mouse courses."

Name calling hurts, of course, and it diverts attention from the real questions: How valuable to a second grade teacher is a math course in algebra or number theory? How many professors of biology know or care very much about sports physiology? Do arts and sciences professors understand the academic world in which future elementary, special education, and physical education teachers will work?

Professional Education

This area continues to be the most controversial in teacher education programs. Here *Goofy* joins *Mickey Mouse* in the critics' stock of cartoon-character insults. In the era of No Child Left Behind, officials in the U.S. Department of Education regularly lament the trade-off between "subject-area knowledge" and "courses in pedagogy."[24] A quarter century ago, in a different reform era, *A Nation at Risk* used similar rhetoric: "The teacher-preparation curriculum is weighted heavily with courses in 'educational methods' at the expense of courses in subjects to be taught."[25]

Notice the use of the words *pedagogy* and *methods* as a generic description of everything colleges and departments of education try to do. In fact, the professional education courses that make up one-fourth to one-third of teacher education programs are considerably more varied and complex.

Even the shorthand distinction I make above—"how" courses in methods versus "why" courses in foundations—does not do justice to the array of education courses found in college and university catalogs. Courses in methods of teaching are the most numerous, to be sure, and they are designed to be practical and helpful. In foundations courses, students use such disciplines as history, philosophy, sociology, and political science to study the relationship between school and society. The distinction between methods and foundations courses is clear enough, but other education courses deal with both hows and whys. Courses in evaluation and measurement, among the most technical in teacher education programs, can also raise questions of rationale and purpose, as can courses in educational psychology. Curriculum courses bring together knowledge of how, why, and what. Student teaching, the culmination of teacher education programs, *ideally* puts a prospective teacher's entire repertoire of knowledge and skill to the test.

Ideally is the word that symbolizes the problem with teacher education, according to critics. Teacher education programs abound in wishful thinking, critics charge. Education professors, well meaning but out of touch with elementary and secondary schools, teach courses that run together in a blur. Students waltz in and glide through. Field experiences and student teaching offer a taste of the real world, but after graduation new teachers must literally teach themselves how to teach in order to survive. Even though education professors rarely talk about classroom management and discipline, out in the schools they become the first—often the only—priority. Education courses that seemed fun at best and boring at worst turn out to be useless.[26]

Voicing feelings of frustration verging on bitterness, many experienced teachers give their education courses low marks. Many say the only worthwhile part of their professional education was student teaching.

If the preceding paragraphs seem harsh, I intend them to be. Just as I was honest about teacher satisfaction in Chapter 1 and teacher salaries in Chapter 2, I owe you an objective look at teacher education in this chapter. As the author of a teacher education textbook, I obviously believe professional education is valuable, and we professors of education do have our defenders.

Susan Ohanian, a former third-grade teacher whose writing about educational issues has won her a reputation for pulling no punches, contends

> [T]eachers must stop asking education professors for the whole house. I know plenty of teachers who are disappointed, indignant, and eventually destroyed by the fact that nobody has handed them all four corners. But the best we can expect from any program of courses or training is the jagged edge of one corner. Then it is up to us to read the research and collaborate with the children to find the other three corners.[27]

There are no "stir-and-serve recipes for teaching," Ohanian insists. "We do not need the behaviorist-competency thugs to chart our course." Teachers deserve education courses that are intellectually challenging—and too many are "stupid," she acknowledges—but "much of the training must be self-initiated." Professors of education should open teachers' minds and give them a sense of purpose and direction. Ohanian concludes the only way to learn how to teach is to teach.[28]

MASTER'S-LEVEL ROUTES INTO TEACHING

The Holmes Partnership and Professional Development Schools

The Holmes Partnership promotes clinically based, graduate-level teacher preparation, a model that once seemed poised to take over colleges and departments of education. Dedicated to increasing the intellectual respectability of teacher education by bridging the gap between education and the arts and sciences, the partnership began in the mid-1980s as the Holmes Group, a consortium of teacher education deans and chief academic officers at one hundred major research universities. When the Holmes Group first spoke, people in higher education listened, and politicians soon paid attention too.

Tomorrow's Teachers, the first report of the Holmes Group, appeared in 1986, the same year the Carnegie Forum on Education and the Economy released *A Nation Prepared: Teachers for the Twenty-First Century*. Both reports were responses to *A Nation at Risk*, and both were big hits.[29]

Holmes and Carnegie attracted attention with a controversial proposal that had strong political appeal: closing down undergraduate degree programs in education. Under the new model, bright people with bachelor's degrees in the arts and sciences would apply to a selective master's degree program to learn how to teach. Trying to put a positive spin on things, Holmes argued that teacher education would actually be lengthened to five years rather than cut back to one. With influential institutions such as Ohio State, Columbia, Wisconsin–Madison, UCLA, and Michigan State on board, the Holmes Group looked like a winner.

Drawing analogies to the teaching hospitals that train medical doctors, Holmes proposed that teacher education take place at clinical sites called *professional development schools*. There, in a real-world setting, teacher educators from universities would collaborate with master or mentor teachers from K–12 schools to prepare tomorrow's teachers. Professional development schools would give prospective teachers the chance to put into practice the best available knowledge about teaching rather than mimic the survival strategies of today's teachers.[30]

The Holmes model experienced tremendous initial success. Many (though not all) of its members moved teacher education to the graduate level. More than a dozen state legislatures required all prospective teachers to major in the arts and sciences. Colleges and universities across the nation opened some version of a professional development school.

In the mid-1990s, however, the Holmes agenda stalled. Eliminating bachelor's degree programs in education, the top "cash cows" on many campuses, was a move that even large research universities could not make lightly. Many teacher educators, even in Holmes institutions, became outspoken opponents of the new model, complaining they would be forced to abbreviate or simply eliminate much of the professional education curriculum.

But the Holmes Partnership is still trying. As of 2004, it consists of about seventy-five colleges and universities—now ranging from prestigious research institutions to modest regional ones—each of which has formed a partnership with local school districts and community agencies. A more flexible set of goals has replaced the original emphasis on shutting down undergraduate programs in education. Holmes institutions have a model that is still worthy of consideration.[31]

But teacher education is highly resistant to fundamental reform. Professors of education tend to make cosmetic changes and continue doing business as usual. Consider what has happened to professional development schools. Some institutions, wanting to appear cutting edge, have simply renamed their student teaching sequence an "internship" and rechristened any convenient public school used for student teachers—excuse me, "interns"—a professional development school.

■ ■ ■ ■ ■

BOX 3.1

THE HOLMES PARTNERSHIP

Find out more about the Holmes Partnership at its Web site, www.holmespartnership.org

---

Holmes knows this, of course, and it quite properly brands such imitations "cheap copies" that "threaten to devalue and drive out the real currency."[32] Talking about costs and currency gets us to the heart of the matter. NCATE, the major accrediting body for teacher preparation programs, is trying to set standards for professional development schools. But money—or more precisely, the lack of it—puts limits on what universities and school districts can accomplish.

Professional development schools, done right, are expensive; so are teaching hospitals. Unfortunately, our nation still refuses to invest in teacher education as heavily as it does in medical education. Whenever I leave my university's college of education and walk across campus to the college of medicine, I can easily see the difference money makes.

Alternative Master's Degree Programs

Revamping existing master's degree programs offers an easier, less expensive way to reform teacher education. Many colleges and departments of education have designed alternative master's programs for the large pool of people with bachelor's degrees outside education who want to change careers and give teaching a try.

Alternative master's programs drop the requirement that students must complete an undergraduate program in a particular teaching field—elementary education, for instance, or secondary mathematics—before beginning graduate study in that field. At one university, posters around campus advertise an alternative master's program designed to "prepare almost anyone with almost any college degree to teach in almost any field." That's quite a promise, even if the fine print does admit "certain restrictions."

By their very design, alternative master's programs are a compromise between what teacher educators think they should do and what political pressure compels them to do. But compared to the much shorter routes into teaching we will examine next, graduate programs requiring the equivalent of a full year or more of study (typically stretched out over evenings and weekends to accommodate employed students) at least allow teacher educators to condense their courses, supervise field experiences and student teaching, and hope for the best. Fortunately, alternative master's programs seem to attract students who are experienced in the world of work and committed to helping young people. The dedication and maturity of these prospective teachers may be the programs' greatest assets.

In some respects, the alternative master's programs developed over the last twenty years are an updated version of the master of arts in teaching (MAT)

programs designed to attract arts and sciences graduates during the 1950s and 1960s. In both eras, a new path into teaching opened when teacher shortages threatened. Twenty percent of first-time teachers are now entering the occupation via alternative master's programs, several times more than are entering through clinically based five-year Holmes Partnership programs and far more than the MATs ever attracted.[33] Although the majority of first timers still enter via the traditional undergraduate route, trends in degrees awarded show teacher education slowly shifting away from bachelor's-level preparation and toward master's-level programs.[34]

ALTERNATE ROUTES INTO TEACHING: QUICK AND DIRTY, OR MERELY QUICK?

The opening of "streamlined" alternate routes into teaching is one of the most striking recent developments in the occupation. With the federal government lending its encouragement and support through No Child Left Behind, at least forty-three states and the District of Columbia now offer eased entry to people who already hold a bachelor's degree in a field other than education.

Even the strongest advocates of these programs admit they vary tremendously in quality. The National Center for Education Information (NCEI), a clearinghouse for alternate programs, credits twenty-six states with developing what it considers to be "true alternative routes . . . designed specifically to meet the needs of talented individuals from non-traditional backgrounds who want to teach." The NCEI's *Alternative Certification: A State by State Analysis 2004* explains that at least one program in each of these twenty-six states provides candidates with mentoring and formal instruction in teaching. We might expect these features, which are minimal, to be standard in every alternate route program. They are not. In seventeen states, there are *no* alternate programs that provide both mentoring and formal instruction.[35]

Faced with a 2005–2006 deadline for making teachers of all core subjects highly qualified, at least on paper, some states have been downright sneaky. "I think states will figure out clever ways [to comply]," the director of the Education Commission of the States confessed in 2004. "We all know states are going to game this."[36] As we saw in Chapter 1, some have spruced up and disguised their old emergency licenses, giving them a fresh coat of paint and a new look. Don't be misled by the "alternate route" signs hanging over these formerly unmarked doors into the occupation. The worst of these programs allow applicants to "test out" of all education courses and begin teaching with no formal preparation. Quite literally, these people must teach themselves to teach.[37]

In this section of the chapter, we look to the better end of the alternate route continuum and focus on New Jersey and Texas, two states whose programs the NCEI gives its highest rating: Class A—Exemplary. The programs in New Jersey and Texas, pioneers in the alternate route movement, illustrate some of the better plans in other states (see Internet box).

▪ ▪ ▪ ▪ ▪ ▬▬▬▬▬▬▬▬▬▬▬▬▬▬▬▬▬▬▬▬

BOX 3.2

DO ALTERNATE ROUTES OFFER
QUALITY TEACHER PREPARATION?

Decide for yourself after examining the state-by-state information available from the
National Center for Alternative Certification at www.teach-now.org

The New Jersey Shortcut

New Jersey's Provisional Teacher Program (PTP) gets college-educated people who
want to teach into elementary and secondary classrooms—and gets them there
fast. Originated in 1984 as a response to the threat of teacher shortages, the New
Jersey shortcut was born in the political tradition we examined in Chapter 1.
Historically, state legislatures and boards of education have been more than willing
to bend or alter teacher education and licensing standards to put warm bodies in
front of America's classrooms.[38]

In all fairness, though, the PTP has outgrown its original purpose, and officials in charge of the program say they are trying to staff New Jersey's classrooms
with people who can teach at least as well as traditionally prepared teachers. And
their strategy may be working.

To enter the PTP, applicants for secondary teaching must have a bachelor's
degree with an arts and sciences major in their teaching field, while those who
want to be elementary teachers must have a bachelor's degree in any arts and
sciences major. Since 2004, the PTP has required a grade point average of 2.75.
Secondary applicants must pass the appropriate Praxis II test in their teaching
field; elementary applicants must pass the General Knowledge section of the
Core Battery of the National Teacher Examinations (see the discussion later in
this chapter).

After receiving a provisional teaching license, into the schools the new
teachers go. Before assuming full responsibility in the classroom, they spend their
first month under the supervision of an assigned mentor teacher, who continues
to work with them throughout the school year. After school or on Saturdays, they
take 200 clock hours of coursework in professional education, with university
teacher educators providing some of the instruction. If the provisionals like their
jobs and receive satisfactory evaluations, they become fully licensed teachers at
the end of the year.

Despite dire predictions of failure from teacher educators and teacher unionists, the PTP has managed to survive and iron out some of its early problems. Today
about one-fifth of New Jersey's new teachers are taking the shortcut into the occupation. Alternate-route teachers tend to be older than traditional-route teachers,
and 20 percent are from racial or ethnic minority groups. In addition, their evaluations are comparable to those of traditionally prepared teachers, and their first-year
attrition rates are lower.[39]

Critics of the program point out that some provisional teachers receive less mentoring and formal instruction than they are supposed to. Some mentors are too busy with their own classes to help their novices, it seems, and some of the provisionals are too busy with their demanding new jobs to take their after-school and weekend coursework seriously.

Is the New Jersey shortcut *too* short? Does it expect more than its participants can reasonably deliver in nine months?

The Provisional Teacher Program has served as a model for alternate routes in other states. According to the NCEI, ten other states have developed at least one other Class A—Exemplary program similar to New Jersey's: California, Florida, Georgia, Louisiana, Maryland, Massachusetts, New Mexico, New York, Texas, and Utah. Many more states, as we have seen, have opened New Jersey–like routes the NCEI views as less than exemplary.[40]

The New Jersey shortcut is part of a larger package of teacher education reform. The Garden State now requires *all* of its new teachers to hold a degree in the arts and sciences. Undergraduates preparing to teach can take only twelve semester hours of coursework in education, a restriction that gives a whole new meaning to *traditional* teacher education at the bachelor's level. Moreover, New Jersey now classifies *all* new teachers as provisionals during their first year. Thus, according to school officials, all enter the occupation on relatively equal footing and receive the same support.

The Texas Squeeze Play

The home state of President George W. Bush seems proud of its status as a national model for teacher education reform under No Child Left Behind. As the education governor of Texas, Bush helped opened alternate routes into teaching that NCLB is now promoting in other states.

Governor Bush extended a trail of school reform that had been blazed during the 1980s. In 1986 the Texas legislature abolished bachelor's degree programs in education and prohibited prospective teachers from taking more than eighteen semester hours of professional education. This restriction, fully effective since 1991, marked the first time a state legislature had set maximum rather than minimum requirements for teacher education. Several other states, including New Jersey, followed suit.[41]

Three Alternate Routes.   Now it seems as though Texas is trying to squeeze the responsibility for preparing teachers out of universities and into other institutions. Would-be teachers can still take a trimmed-down university program, but they can also choose from two other alternatives. If they want to teach in Alief, Dallas, Fort Worth, Frenship (Lubbock), Houston, or Pasadena, they can be trained by the district itself, largely on the job and with minimal university coursework. If they apply to one of the Education Service Centers located around the state, they can receive similar training, mostly on the job, though the center.[42]

Applicants to all three alternate programs—university, school district, and service center—must have a bachelor's degree and pass a basic skills test. Before receiving a state license, candidates must also pass Texas Examinations of Educator Standards (TExES), a series of assessments being phased in effective 2004.[43]

Some Texas school districts and service centers use Martin Haberman's Urban Teacher Selection Interview to screen candidates. Haberman, professor of education at the University of Wisconsin, Milwaukee, developed the interview out of his frustration with traditional teacher education programs. Such programs, he claims, simply do not turn out teachers who can survive in the tough world of urban schools. By following the careers of "star" teachers who have proven they can work effectively with poor and minority students, Haberman identified a set of common traits he believes to be keys to their success. His interview is designed to find out whether prospective teachers have these traits, and he claims the interview has a track record of separating potential "stars" from probable "quitters." Haberman strongly supports alternate routes into teaching because, he claims, the best of them bypass "irrelevant" traditional training and give candidates experiential training that actually prepares them to teach.[44]

Learning to Teach on the Job.   All three Texas alternatives are supposed to provide the equivalent of twelve hours of coursework and six hours of internship— with heavy emphasis on the latter. A Texas internship is actually a full-time teaching job, with all the benefits (minus the training costs) and all the responsibilities. As in New Jersey, interns are supposed to work under the supervision of mentors and evaluators from the school district, and they take their coursework after school and on weekends. Wedded to the model of on-the-job training, the Lone Star state is expanding the Texas Beginning Educator Support System (TxBESS), which is supposed to provide support for new teachers throughout their first two years in the classroom.[45]

Notice my use of *supposed to* in the previous paragraph. Critics charge that Texas, like New Jersey, does not deliver all the support and instruction it promises to its alternate route teachers. The overriding goal seems to be getting people into classrooms as quickly and cheaply as possible. Texas continues to have one of the most severe teacher shortages in the nation, and before the passage of NCLB it had almost 15,000 teachers who did not meet licensing standards.[46]

Supporters of the Texas plan, like those in New Jersey, claim the program is improving. Just give it time. District officials say they like "homegrown" teachers who know from personal experience the problems local children face. One-third of alternate route teachers in Texas are minorities, supporters boast, and they account for one-fourth of all new teachers in the state.[47]

Distance Learning.   Offering courses via the Internet is a trend in colleges and universities across the nation. Teacher educators, like other professors, are feeling pressure to go online with distance education courses designed to maximize student access and convenience as well as institutional enrollment and cash flow. Learning to teach by taking Web-based courses could become especially attractive in Texas and other states that have already reduced university-based teacher education to a handful of courses.

A private firm with the name I Teach Texas is offering online programs that lead to alternative certification in Texas. Packaging its content in eleven instructional modules, the company says it will help candidates every step of the way through their programs, including making arrangements for the internship.[48]

Concerns about distance teacher education also apply to Internet courses offered in other divisions of higher education. What is the real driving force behind the programs—student access and convenience or the university balance sheet? What pedagogical features are lost (or gained) when a professor converts a face-to-face course for distance delivery? How effectively can students learn skills as opposed to knowledge over the Internet, even if, as in the Texas program, "the vision of these modules is for the teacher candidate to study and understand various aspects of the teaching discipline and then to translate this knowledge into actual classroom practice"?[49] Such questions are being discussed throughout higher education.

A Tale of Two Occupations

Several times each year, the news media carry the story of someone caught practicing medicine without a license. Usually the ersatz physician has a degree in biology or chemistry and a reassuring bedside manner but no formal training in medicine. The fact that such persons are able to practice successfully for years, completely undetected, casts doubt on the necessity of going to medical school. Shouldn't we allow biologists and chemists to take a few courses in medicine, work with mentors, and see how well they can do as physicians?

Of course not. Most Americans believe medicine is too complex and too important to treat in such a careless way. Medicine is a profession, after all, and we quite rightly insist that professions maintain high standards. Teaching, however, gets no such treatment, as we will find in the rest of this chapter and in Chapter 4.

RAISING THE BAR IN TEACHER EDUCATION

Nostalgia for a Golden Age of Teaching

Americans rediscover the issue of teacher competency every twenty to thirty years, and when they do, the news media join academic journals in tracing the problem back to teacher education. Rallied by the George W. Bush administration under the banner of *highly qualified teachers*, politicians at all levels of government are joining the latest round of rediscovery. Prospective teachers are among the least capable students in colleges and universities, the public hears. Ranked against other undergraduates by their Scholastic Aptitude Test (SAT) and American College Testing (ACT) scores, teacher education students come in near the bottom, ahead only of students majoring in such fields as agriculture and home economics.[50]

Teacher education programs must bear much of the blame, the criticism continues. According to *Meeting the Highly Qualified Teachers Challenge* (2002), teacher educators are "maintaining low academic standards and failing to prepare teachers for the reality of the classroom."[51] *A Nation at Risk* (1983) leveled the very same charges twenty years earlier, during the previous cycle of concern with teacher competency, when it proclaimed "not enough of the academically able students are being attracted to teaching" and "too many teachers are being drawn from the bottom quarter of graduating high-school and college students."[52] How could teacher educators have let the nation down?

A Mythical Past.   Stories in the news media often leave the impression that there was once a golden age of teaching: a time when teachers, if not exactly well paid, were uniformly bright and well educated. Educational historians tell a different story. The mid-to-late 1800s were certainly not golden years. School officials could not afford to be selective in hiring teachers—the problem was finding enough teachers to staff the rapidly growing common schools. At the turn of the twentieth century, the typical elementary teacher was a woman who felt lucky if she had finished high school, much less received any formal training for her work. The typical secondary teacher was a man who had some college credit, a smattering of which may have been in pedagogy. When researchers began administering standardized tests of academic ability during the 1920s and 1930s, their studies showed prospective teachers, many of them enrolled in normal schools and teachers' colleges, ranked low when compared to the full range of college students. In some studies, teachers even ranked below high school seniors. At four-year colleges and universities, "eddies" and "aggies" had to put up with jokes about their shallow interests and weak intellect.[53]

From the nineteenth century to the twenty-first, teacher educators have complained that more prestigious, better-paying occupations were luring bright people away from teaching. Teacher educators documented their complaints in academic journals and books, waiting for the next public discovery of the teacher competency issue. Close on its heels, they knew, would be another round of criticism. The late 1940s and 1950s brought an especially strong media attack, the harshest since muckraking journalists uncovered poor teaching in turn-of-the-twentieth-century schools. The 1950s critics lashed out at teachers and teacher educators, writing such scathing books as *And Madly Teach* (1949) and *Quackery in the Public Schools* (1953). Newspapers, news magazines, radio, and television joined the attack. And since the late 1970s, Americans have taken up the teacher competency issue again.[54]

Women and Minorities.   History is more than cycles and repetition. The social changes of the last four decades have affected teaching as an occupation in ways we are just beginning to understand. In particular, the women's movement and the Civil Rights movement have been powerful influences.

The history of America's teachers is largely women's history, the story of women who have worked hard for little compensation. Since the 1960s, with the reduction of discrimination against women in higher education and in many occupations, teacher education programs have suffered a "brain drain" of bright, career-oriented students. It makes many Americans uncomfortable—even resentful—to realize they can no longer buy teachers of the same quality for the same price, nor even for a higher price. Teaching is a better-paid occupation than ever, but the bright women who once formed a captive employment pool for teaching, nursing, and social work have other options now.[55]

To a degree, the same is true of minorities, especially African Americans. Discrimination placed such severe limits on their opportunities for education and employment in other fields, teaching reaped a bounty of talented people. At the turn of the twentieth century, black teachers in some southern cities had more years of schooling and held higher degrees than their white counterparts. Well into the 1960s, school systems did not have to worry about attracting talented African American college students because after graduation they had so few choices.[56]

The brightest African American college students, like the brightest women, are now going into the full professions. But in contrast to women, the percentage of African American high school students going on to college fell from the late 1960s through the mid-1980s. Although the percentage has now returned to earlier levels, the last few years have been spent merely recouping losses. African American college students are turning away from teaching, to be sure; they are now *less* likely than whites to major in education. Unlike women, though, African Americans are not moving into higher-status fields in sufficient numbers to justify the explanation that teaching's loss is law and medicine's gain.[57]

No, there never was a golden age of teaching, not even when teaching attracted a larger share of the brightest women and minorities. Even then, the overall intellectual quality of the teaching force was not very impressive and teacher competency was a serious concern. It is unfair and inaccurate, however, to paint teachers with a single brush. Teaching has always attracted a wide range of people, some of whom have been among the nation's most intelligent. I hasten to add the public has always gotten better teachers than it has paid for. But the average American teacher, compared with all college students, has ranked low on standardized tests of academic ability as long as there have been standardized tests.

Reforming Teacher Education from the Inside: NCATE, INTASC, and NBPTS

You are preparing to teach at a critical moment in the history of the occupation. As you will see throughout this textbook, powerful pressure for reform is changing teaching from the inside as well as the outside. To conclude this chapter we will examine the internal reform movement that teacher educators themselves are leading. As critics continue to score points with the public, advocates of reform from the inside are trying to save teacher education by frankly acknowledging its shortcomings and working in unison to correct them.

The leaders of this effort want to change the way America regulates the preparation, licensing, and certification of its teachers. Instead of allowing states, colleges, and universities to do things their own way—the loose, decentralized approach we have used since the mid-1800s—advocates want to create, for the first time, a "coherent" national system of standards and assessments for teaching. ·Such a system could be the foundation of a true teaching profession (see Chapter 4), encouraging the occupation to develop along the lines of medicine and law. In fact, teacher education reform could be the "linchpin" of reform for public education as a whole, giving the public the accountability it wants and deserves.[58]

The alternative, advocates maintain, is sticking with the lowest-common-denominator approach in which bad programs drive out good, a non-system riddled with low standards and hobbled by poor performance. No Child Left Behind recognizes these problems, to be sure, but leaves the responsibility for finding solutions in the hands of individual states. The results, as we have seen, have been mixed at best.

Leaders of the internal reform movement believe they can sell their vision to the public by making changes in university-based teacher education programs, conducting empirical research that documents the effects on teaching and learning, and publicizing the results in the news media and the political arena. Changes now under way in your own teacher education program are part of this process.[59]

Three key players in the internal reform movement are NCATE, the national accrediting body for college and university teacher preparation programs; INTASC, a consortium that promotes performance-based licensing at the state level; and NBPTS, the board that offers national certification to accomplished teachers. With the financial and political backing of the Carnegie Corporation (see Chapter 2), these organizations are working together closely, coordinating their efforts with other education groups to develop standards and assessments so attractive that states, colleges, and universities will want to buy into them.

Another key player is the Educational Testing Service (ETS) of Princeton, New Jersey, which produces the Praxis Series of Assessments we will discuss later in this chapter. The ETS publication *Where We Stand on Teacher Quality* (2004) explains how standards and assessments are being *aligned* throughout the continuum of teacher education, licensing, and certification. Computer technology makes it possible to make standards and assessments more uniform—or more "coherent," as NCATE, INTASC, and NBPTS prefer to say—than ever before. As if that were not enough, standards and assessments for teachers are being aligned with standards and assessments for K–12 students. As the president of ETS testified at a recent congressional hearing, "We should connect teacher professional development with teacher preparation standards [and with] student standards, curriculum, and assessments to achieve an aligned system of preparing and supporting new and in-service teachers."[60] Computer technology holds the key.

Will these attempts to reform teacher education from the inside succeed? Do they *deserve* to succeed? The rest of this chapter offers a close look at the new standards and assessments emerging in three areas: literacy skills, the teaching field, and professional education. Just as important, the chapter continues to provide a historical and political context you can use to evaluate the changes for yourself. As you will see, today's internal reform movement must get around roadblocks so formidable they have frustrated earlier attempts at reform.

STANDARDS AND ASSESSMENTS: BREAKING WITH THE PAST

Literacy Skills

Parents know something is wrong when teachers send home notes with grammatical and spelling errors in every other sentence. Students worry when teachers routinely make mistakes in simple arithmetic on the chalkboard. These concerns are legitimate. In teaching, of all occupations, there can be no excuse for weak literacy skills because these skills are the tools of our trade.

Stressing teacher literacy is putting first things first. It seems fitting, then, that the first tests students take when they seek admission to teacher education focus on basic skills in reading, writing, and computing. Unfortunately, teacher literacy tests are slanted toward lower-level skills such as word recognition, punctuation, and simple arithmetic. Moreover, the *cutoff* or *cut scores* prospective teachers must make to pass the tests have traditionally been set very low—in some cases, embarrassingly low.

Why Such Low Cut Scores?   In the process of setting the cutoffs, testing companies *norm* the tests by administering them to various groups—for example, to large samples of eighth graders, tenth graders, twelfth graders, and college freshmen. The average score of each group is that group's *normal score*, or *norm*. Teacher education officials or state board of education members can then decide which norm to use as the cut score for admission to teacher education.[61]

One thing the public has generally overlooked in its latest rediscovery of teacher incompetency is that cut scores for admission to teacher education programs are usually set at the equivalent of tenth- to twelfth-grade norms; that is, the average tenth or twelfth grader could pass the tests.[62]

For obvious reasons, teacher educators and state board members don't go out of their way to publicize the cutoffs but, when pressed, justify them in several ways. First, they want to maintain enrollment in teacher education programs. Raising the cutoffs, they believe, could cause enrollment to fall, worsen the teacher shortage, and put teacher educators out of work. Second, they cannot agree on the exact level of literacy necessary for teaching. Third, they want to be fair to prospective minority teachers, who do not score as well on the tests as prospective white teachers.

Why Not Just Raise the Cut Scores?   "America cannot afford any more teachers who fail a twelfth-grade competency test," the Holmes Group said twenty years ago.[63] But that's easier said than done. If every program moved its cutoff to the equivalent of a college freshman norm, about half of all college freshmen would immediately become ineligible. (Because the norm is the average score of the group being tested, by definition about half the group falls below the norm.) Even more seriously, as many as 80 to 90 percent of all black college freshmen would be ineligible. Teacher educators could boast they had raised standards, but would they have raised the right standards?[64]

Empirical research on the relationship between teachers' literacy test scores and their students' achievement test scores is inconclusive. Some studies show a modest correlation; others do not. Thus some teacher educators argue emphasizing the literacy standard may keep potentially good teachers out of the occupation. The report *Assessment of Diversity in America's Teaching Force* (2004), produced by a broad spectrum of organizations representing teachers and teacher educators, points out that "passing scores alone do not guarantee teachers will be highly effective, nor does failing the tests automatically mean teachers will be ineffective."[65] We can make the same argument about SAT and ACT scores, because research does not show a definite link between the SAT and ACT scores of teachers and the achievement test scores of their students.[66]

Why, then, should teacher education programs turn away students with below-average scores on these tests? Doing so is arbitrary and discriminatory, some professors argue, and can land you in court. In *Tests and Teacher Quality* (2000), a report prepared for the U.S. Department of Education, the National Research Council calls attention to these thorny problems and expresses reservations about teacher testing, especially its impact on minority candidates.[67]

We saw in the last chapter that the entire area of research on measuring teacher influence on student test scores is shot full of holes. Because so many other factors inside and outside of schools outweigh the influence of teachers on student achievement, it is difficult to measure the effect of *any* teacher characteristic or behavior on student test scores. Frankly, this kind of research may never give teacher educators much guidance in setting standards.

As one member of the National Research Council team that produced *Tests and Teacher Quality* explains, literacy assessments and other teacher tests don't predict whether people will be effective teachers any more than driver tests predict whether people will be safe drivers. But society would not even consider eliminating driver tests, of course, because they at least provide a check on basic knowledge and skills. Shouldn't we treat teacher tests the same way?[68]

It often amazes professors in other areas of higher education that teacher educators spend so much time agonizing over standards and grasping for empirical studies to justify every change. Medical schools and law schools do not base their high admission standards on studies showing physicians and lawyers with higher test scores perform better operations and win more cases. Professors of medicine and law do not even conduct such studies. When setting standards, they simply state the obvious: Physicians and lawyers must be highly literate because their jobs demand it.

Surely professors of education can make the same case for teachers. When they have done so in court, they have won, for courts emphasize "job-relatedness": the demonstration of a reasonable relationship between what the test measures and

■ ■ ■ ■ ■

BOX 3.3
FAIRTEST

FairTest, the National Center for Fair and Open Testing, keeps a close watch on standardized employment testing. Find out more about the case against teacher testing at www.fairtest.org and read the Educational Testing Service's defense of employment testing at www.ets.org (click on "Research" to begin exploring the ETS site).

what the job requires. It is only reasonable that people who constantly use literacy skills in their work, people whose jobs involve raising the literacy of others, be highly literate themselves.[69]

The Teaching Field

Tests in the teaching field are less controversial, but they too involve debates over what teachers need to know. We have already seen the disagreements over the teaching fields for elementary, special, and physical education teachers. Consider the difficulty involved in constructing a field test for elementary teachers in, say, mathematics. If the testing company asks classroom teachers, professors of education, and professors of mathematics for advice on the test, these three groups are likely to make different suggestions—especially in math, the subject most elementary teachers like least. The advisers must decide which areas the test will cover, how broad and how deep the coverage will be, and so forth. Then a different group of advisers must repeat the process for every other subject in the curriculum.[70]

Still to come is the highly technical work of actually constructing the test. Item writers compose the questions—a critical job because, in multiple-choice testing, the options listed are the only acceptable answers. An arithmetic problem has only one correct answer, to be sure, but in most academic fields, specialists often disagree over "right" and "wrong" answers. The more you know about literature, for instance, the more likely it is that several answers—or no answers—to a question about a children's story appear to be correct. Thus all standardized tests reflect the "biases" of a variety of people, academic advisers as well as technicians at the testing company. Finally, the company field-tests the questions on a sample of elementary teachers, conducts statistical analyses of the results, and makes revisions in the test. Teacher education officials and state board members, of course, have the ultimate power to determine who passes and who fails because they establish the cutoff scores. Keep in mind that, next to literacy tests, teaching field tests are the most straightforward.[71]

Professional Education

The least straightforward tests, as you must realize by now, are those of professional education. Teacher licensing tests should reflect the *knowledge base* for teaching—what teachers need to know in order to do their work. Actually, the content of teacher education programs and teacher licensing tests shows there are multiple knowledge bases for teaching, which we have called liberal education, the teaching field, and professional education. Rivalries and competition among the knowledge bases are common, and prospective teachers often feel they have been caught in an academic tug-of-war. As if that were not enough, teacher educators continue to disagree over what should constitute the professional knowledge base for teaching—the specialized knowledge that belongs to the occupation alone. Once again the question comes around: What do teachers need to know?

NCATE, the accrediting group that bills itself as the "Standard of Excellence in Teacher Preparation," has made strengthening the knowledge base a top priority. Teacher education programs applying to receive or renew national accreditation must convince NCATE they have given serious thought to the knowledge base, especially the professional education component. NCATE has traditionally allowed a great deal of variation from one institution to another, paying more attention to the process an institution goes through in designing its knowledge base than to the knowledge itself. Teacher educators have long emphasized process over product.[72]

As loose as this approach may seem, it does acknowledge that many teacher educators are engaged in ongoing debates on the knowledge base. Seeing their professors shake hands and agree to disagree, prospective teachers correctly conclude there is no one best way to teach. (Nor is there one best way to teach teachers.) But prospective teachers sometimes wring their hands in confusion when they have to take standardized licensing tests.

Here is the problem they face. The professional education questions on licensing tests have often struck candidates as: (a) obvious; (b) confusing; (c) theoretical; (d) common sense; (e) all of these. The *best* answer, as they say in the testing industry, is *e*. Please understand I am not insulting test makers and teacher educators. I am certainly not insulting prospective teachers. I am only suggesting the lack of consensus about professional education makes testing teachers in that area most difficult.

To dramatize this problem, Linda Darling-Hammond published an analysis of the professional-knowledge section of the National Teacher Examinations (NTE), which were the most widely used teacher tests in the nation until the Educational Testing Service replaced them with the Praxis Series during the 1990s. Examining a sample test provided by ETS, Darling-Hammond found 15 percent of the questions required only "careful reading or knowledge of simple word definitions," another 25 percent called for "agreement with the test's teaching philosophy," which she describes as "liberal" and "highly individualized," and another 15 percent required "agreement with the test's definition of socially or bureaucratically acceptable behavior," which at least one item on the test itself characterized as "nonthreatening."[73]

Overall, according to Darling-Hammond, about 40 percent of the questions had no right answer. One question on techniques of effective teaching, for instance, gave prospective teachers a choice of several answers supported by different bodies of research. Test takers could mark an answer favoring mastery learning or an answer endorsing whole-group instruction. Both of these approaches have support in the research, and both have their advocates among teachers and teacher educators. But ETS counted these answers wrong. Only those who opted for the answer favoring individualized instruction and pacing got the item right.[74]

MOVING INTERNAL REFORM INTO PLACE

Now reformers are trying to clarify the rules of this puzzling game by pushing teacher educators toward a consensus on "what all beginning teachers should know, be like, and be able to do in order to practice responsibly, regardless of the subject matter or grade level being taught."[75] Just as standards developed by such groups as the National Council of Teachers of English and the National Science Teachers Association (see Chapter 4) are shaping tests of the teaching field, NCATE is working with INTASC and NBPTS to develop professional education standards that are becoming the basis for teacher licensing and certification tests. Darling-Hammond, a Stanford University teacher educator with considerable influence, is doing all she can to move the process along.[76]

Under the banner of *performance-based accreditation*, NCATE is for the first time requiring accredited institutions to *prove* that their graduates know what to teach and how to teach it. As we have seen, NCATE, INTASC, and NBPTS have persuaded ETS to align its teacher licensing tests with the emerging pedagogical standards. Institutions that want their graduates to do well on the tests are putting pressure on their professors to teach to the standards, and perhaps—as in K–12 schools—to the tests themselves, despite well-founded doubts that there is one best way to teach (or one best way to teach teachers). NCATE defends the new standards and assessments by insisting they encourage teachers and teacher educators to apply professional knowledge and judgment, not conform to a cookbook.[77]

As the agency boasts in the anniversary retrospective *NCATE at 50* (2004), it has made tremendous strides, with the most impressive progress coming since 1990. Today, for the first time, just over half the nation's 1,300 teacher education programs operate with NCATE's sanction. Although only a handful of states *require* teacher education programs to be accredited, NCATE has signed partnership agreements with 48 states, the District of Columbia, and Puerto Rico that give the agency a powerful voice in program approval. Thirty-nine states have adopted or adapted NCATE standards as their own standards, and 20 states base their own program approval on NCATE's accreditation review process.[78]

NCATE is a political force to be reckoned with. The agency seems determined, in the words of President Wise, to identify a "common body of knowledge that all teachers should know" and to embed that knowledge in teacher licensing tests.[79]

INTASC Standards

The INTASC Model Core Standards provide a template for the development of teacher education and licensing standards across the nation. These ten broad

■ ■ ■ ■ ■

BOX 3.4

NCATE

Visit NCATE online at www.ncate.org to see how performance-based accreditation may be changing your teacher education program.

statements are aligned with the standards NCATE uses to review teacher education programs as well as the standards developed by NBPTS to certify accomplished teachers. Clicking into place in one state after another, the ten INTASC standards are being translated into more specific standards for all the major teaching fields.

Standard 1. The teacher understands the central concepts, tools of inquiry, and structures of the discipline(s) he or she teaches and can create learning experiences that make these aspects of subject matter meaningful for students.

Standard 2. The teacher understands how children learn and develop, and can provide learning opportunities that support their intellectual, social, and personal development.

Standard 3. The teacher understands how students differ in their approaches to learning and creates instructional opportunities that are adapted to diverse learners.

Standard 4. The teacher understands and uses a variety of instructional strategies to encourage students' development of critical thinking, problem solving, and performance skills.

Standard 5. The teacher uses an understanding of individual and group motivation and behavior to create a learning environment that encourages positive social interaction, active engagement in learning, and self-motivation.

Standard 6. The teacher uses knowledge of effective verbal, nonverbal, and media communication techniques to foster active inquiry, collaboration, and supportive interaction in the classroom.

Standard 7. The teacher plans instruction based upon knowledge of subject matter, students, the community, and curriculum goals.

Standard 8. The teacher understands and uses formal and informal assessment strategies to evaluate and ensure the continuous intellectual, social, and physical development of the learner.

Standard 9. The teacher is a reflective practitioner who continually evaluates the effects of his/her choices and action on others (students, parents, and other professionals in the learning community) and who actively seeks out opportunities to grow professionally.

Standard 10. The teacher fosters relationships with school colleagues, parents, and agencies in the larger community to support students' learning and well-being.[80]

INTASC breaks down each standard into knowledge, disposition, and performance components. Under *Standard 3,* relating to diverse learners, for instance, there are five statements of what teachers should know, five statements of the dispositions they should hold, and seven statements of what they should be able to do. Here is an example in each area:

Knowledge: The teacher understands how students' learning is influenced by individual experiences, talents, and prior learning, as well as language, culture family, and community values.

Dispositions: The teacher is sensitive to community and cultural norms.

Performances: The teacher brings multiple perspectives to the discussion of subject matter, including attention to students' personal, family, and community experiences and cultural norms.[81]

Portfolio Assessment

Portfolio assessment seems tailor-made for INTASC standards and other performance-based standards. As we saw in Chapter 2, the contents of portfolios can include written statements and reflections on your work; such "artifacts" of your teaching as student papers, lesson plans, and teacher-made tests; even electronic images of your classroom performance.[82] You could use a portfolio to show how you meet the knowledge, disposition, and performance substandards we just discussed under **Standard 3**, diverse learners.

More and more teacher education programs are requiring their students to assemble an electronic portfolio, or *e-portfolio*, in some cases on a rewritable disk (CD-RW) but increasingly on the Internet. Commercial service providers are developing flexible Web sites that are preloaded with a wide menu of teacher education, licensing, and certification standards. Teacher educators select the standards adopted by their state for their particular programs and courses. As prospective teachers move through the preparation program, they construct an e-portfolio documenting how they meet the standards. Regarding knowledge of how "language, culture, family, and community values" affect learning, for instance, what could you include from the introductory course you are taking right now?

Some candidates use the electronic portfolio in the job application process and then take it into their first teaching position, where they add the documentation the state and local school district require for evaluation. Student test score data go into the portfolio at this point. Later, teachers are able to adapt the contents, bulked up considerably with several years of data, if they apply to the NBPTS for national certification. *How to Develop a Professional Portfolio* (2003) by Dorothy M. Campbell and her colleagues is an excellent guidebook.[83]

The Praxis Series of Assessments

The Educational Testing Service claims its new-and-improved teacher testing package is the vanguard of a "new generation of teacher assessments." The largest testing

■ ■ ■ ■ ■

BOX 3.5

E-PORTFOLIOS IN TEACHER EDUCATION

Visit the University of Wisconsin–Whitewater's College of Education online at academics.uww.edu/coe/e_folio/ to see how future teachers meet NCATE and state standards using e-portfolios.

corporation in the world, ETS also produces the SAT, Graduate Record Examinations (GRE), and numerous other standardized tests. According to ETS, the Praxis Series for beginning teachers offers more sensitivity to cultural and racial differences, less reliance on what test takers cynically call the "multiple-guess" format, and a better picture of what teacher candidates can actually do. The pencil-and-paper NTE, introduced in 1940, changed little in its lifetime. The Praxis Series, parts of which rely on computer technology, claims to be state of the art and adaptable.[84]

Praxis allows state school officials to choose from a menu of assessments to design a testing program for the teachers in their jurisdiction. The next section goes through the menu, taken from the Praxis Web site.

Praxis I: Academic Skills Assessments measures basic literacy skills in reading, writing, and mathematics. Typically administered during a prospective teacher's sophomore year in college (or later for students in nontraditional programs), Praxis I is the most widely used test for admission to teacher education programs.

Praxis II: Subject Assessments, given when the candidate nears completion of the teacher education program, measures knowledge in more than 120 teaching fields. Praxis II also offers tests of Principles of Learning and Teaching that call on candidates to apply what they have learned in professional education courses.

Praxis III: Classroom Performance Assessments, administered early in a new teacher's career (usually the first year), is an evaluation of teaching skills. States and school districts use these assessments primarily for licensure.

Candidates take Praxis I in one of two formats, and the differences between the two illustrate how technology is changing standardized testing. Candidates who take Praxis I the traditional way use the Pre-Professional Skills Test, which requires them to sit for a series of pencil-and-paper assessments involving multiple-choice questions and an essay. Candidates who take the computer-based tests answer computer-delivered questions.

Computer-based tests are *adaptive*, which means the computer considers a candidate's answers to all previous questions in selecting the next question. As ETS explains on the Praxis Web site, a "computer-adaptive test is precision-tailored to your ability level." The computer stops asking questions in math, for instance, when candidates score high enough in that area to meet state requirements. Candidates demonstrate their proficiency in writing by composing an

■ ■ ■ ■ ■

> **BOX 3.6**
> **PRAXIS**
>
> A variety of information on Praxis is available from ETS at www.teachingandlearning.
> org, a Web site that allows you to download a booklet on each test, locate state-by-
> state requirements, and register online for the assessments.

essay at the word processor. According to ETS, computer-based assessments are the wave of the future in standardized testing.

Praxis II assesses knowledge of the teaching field with multiple-choice questions and constructed-response questions. The latter questions offer exciting possibilities, because they call on candidates to create their own answers instead of picking them from a list in a–b–c–d–e fashion. Constructed-response questions often appear on licensing examinations in medicine, law, and other full professions (see Chapter 4), where the emphasis, as Darling-Hammond explains, "is not primarily on finding the 'right' answer but is on the candidate's ability to apply knowledge and judgment in professionally acceptable ways."[85] Imagine the possibilities if ETS keeps moving away from multiple choice.

As Praxis II evolves, ETS is indeed trying to emphasize applications of knowledge and judgment. A prospective social studies teacher may be asked to write an essay integrating history, geography, economics, and political science. A foreign language teacher may have to demonstrate competence in listening or speaking. A music teacher may answer questions on theory and submit a performance tape as well. An elementary teacher may have to show proficiency in several academic subjects. ETS customizes Praxis II to the requirements of the state where the candidate is applying for a license to teach.

The Praxis III assessment of teaching skill involves classroom evaluations conducted by state and local school officials. As we have seen, many controversies cloud the history of performance evaluation. Hoping to break through the clouds, ETS has field-testing interviews, work samples, videotapes, and other assessment strategies. Such evidence, Lee Shulman suggests in Chapter 2, can become part of an evaluation portfolio.

National Board Certification for Accomplished Teachers

While the Praxis Series is designed for the preparation and licensing of new teachers, the National Board for Professional Teaching Standards regards board certification as a "way for the teaching profession to define and recognize highly accomplished practice. A certificate awarded by the National Board attests that a teacher has been judged by his or her peers as one who meets high and rigorous professional standards." According to NBPTS, board certification "is the highest honor the teaching profession has to bestow."[86] NBPTS is a nonprofit, nongovernmental, nonpartisan organization headed by a board of directors, the majority of whom are classroom teachers.

The board's central policy statement is *What Teachers Should Know and Be Able to Do*, originally adopted in 1989 and now available online. This document sets forth five core propositions that, in the board's judgment, describe accomplished teaching:

> Proposition 1. Teachers are committed to students and their learning.
>
> Proposition 2. Teachers know the subjects they teach and how to teach those subjects to students.
>
> Proposition 3. Teachers are responsible for managing and monitoring student learning.
>
> Proposition 4. Teachers think systematically about their practice and learn from experience.
>
> Proposition 5. Teachers are members of learning communities.[87]

Ever mindful of public relations, NBPTS goes to great lengths to demonstrate that these propositions are more than nice-sounding words—that teachers who have these qualities really are superior teachers. In *Moving Education Forward through National Board Certification* (2003), a publication intended for politicians and the general public, the board breaks down each proposition into "What this means . . . What it looks like in the classroom . . . What research shows." In trying to describe teacher commitment (Proposition 1), for instance, the board notes that

> teachers must know many things about the particular students they teach: Alex has a stutter, Maria loves science fiction, Toby is anxious about mathematics, Marcus is captivated by jazz. Accomplished teachers also know much more— whom their students go home to every night, how they have previously performed on standardized tests, what sparks their interest. This kind of specific understanding is constantly used in deciding how to best tailor instruction.[88]

The board supports these easy-to-understand explanations with citations of empirical research.

Committees dominated by classroom teachers are using the five core propositions to develop detailed standards for more than thirty teaching fields organized by four developmental levels: early childhood, middle childhood, early adolescence, and adolescence and young adulthood. Teachers can apply to the board for either a generalist certificate (early childhood/generalist, for instance) or a subject-specific certificate (early adolescence/science, for instance). By 2004, standards for twenty-four fields were in place.

Teacher-dominated committees are also confronting the problem of how to apply the standards to identify superior teachers. Convinced, like ETS, that multiple-choice testing can do only part of the job, NBPTS uses a variety of other assessment strategies. Candidates work throughout the school year to compile a portfolio that includes a videotape of their work in the classroom, lesson plans, examples of their students' work, and reflective essays. Candidates also take a computer-based assessment of their knowledge in the content area, six exercises of up to 30 minutes each designed by classroom teachers in the specific teaching field. In all, candidates spend 200 to 400 hours applying for certification.[89]

The process is demanding, not only of candidates but of those who develop and administer the system. Classroom teachers who have been trained as assessors are responsible for evaluating the portfolios and computer-based exercises. Evaluating each candidate's materials can take many hours—up to twenty-three, in fact, during the board's early years—and even then the assessors sometimes feel they are getting only glimpses of candidates' work. Because paying the assessors is expensive, NBPTS charges each candidate a fee of $2,300, a sum that 37 states subsidize in some way.

I am dwelling on time and money to emphasize a point I make throughout this textbook: Doing things right is rarely easy. Unfortunately, Americans consistently look for the easy way out when it comes to public education. Linda Darling-Hammond observes that every time educators have tried to take the far more difficult path to fundamental reform, their work has been "killed by an underinvestment in teacher knowledge and school capacity."[90] NBPTS hopes to break the pattern.

National board certification is open to all teachers with a bachelor's degree who have taught successfully and held a state license for three years. As of 2004, more than 40,000 teachers have qualified for NBPTS certification—30,000 of them since 2000. Almost every state recognizes board certification in its licensure structure and rewards the accomplishment with a bonus or salary increase.[91]

It is encouraging that *teachers themselves*—two words I use often in the next chapter—are taking the lead in developing the first national system of teacher certification. Medicine, law, and other full professions have long recognized the value of national board certification, a process of peer recognition that extends above and beyond state licensing.

Optimistically speaking, teaching may now be where medicine was in the 1870s—just beginning to develop a professional knowledge base that *actually works*. In medicine, it took several decades for the new scientific knowledge base to prove its worth. Only then, in the early 1900s, were medical educators and the American Medical Association able to drive out quacks and improve medical practice. Only then could they use examinations based on scientific medicine to raise standards.[92]

Teaching is still an occupation in search of a specialized knowledge base. Giving teachers a major role in finding it, as NBPTS has, is a great step forward. But before any group can develop fair assessments, teachers and teacher educators must reach a consensus on how to evaluate answers on tests and performance in the classroom; in our haste to move ahead, we cannot take shortcuts, however intense the political pressure may be.

Are NCATE, INTASC, and NBPTS rushing things? If they are, a teach-by-the-numbers approach will lock into place, and the occupation will splinter into teachers who go along with it and teachers who see through it and reject it.

■ ■ ■ ■ ■ ▬▬▬▬▬▬▬▬▬▬▬▬▬▬▬▬▬▬▬▬▬▬▬▬▬▬▬▬▬▬▬▬▬

BOX 3.7

NATIONAL BOARD CERTIFICATION

Find out how the state where you plan to teach supports and recognizes national board certification and learn more about the assessment process, including sample test items and activities, at www.nbpts.org

TEACHER TESTING AND MINORITY TEACHERS

A Precarious Situation

Fairness to minority teachers is one of the most difficult issues in teacher testing. The issue is part of a larger question: How can America's schools attract qualified minority teachers? Organizations across the political spectrum recognize the urgent need to find answers. Journals feature articles with titles as alarming as "Teacher Competency Whitewash: How One High-Stakes Test Eliminates Diversity from the Teaching Force" and as positive as "The Power of Their Presence: Minority Group Teachers and Schooling."[93]

Even if there is room for hope, there is broad agreement that the current situation is precarious. At a time when the percentage of elementary and secondary minority students is rapidly increasing (see Chapter 8), the percentage of minority teachers is clearly not keeping pace (Chapter 2). As Figure 3.2 indicates, Hispanic Americans, African Americans, Asian Americans, and Native Americans are all *underrepresented* in the teaching force. Each group makes up a smaller percentage of teachers than it does of students (and of the nation's population as well).

Consider African Americans as a case in point. The percentage of students who are black has risen for several decades and now stands at 17 percent. The percentage of black teachers, by contrast, has vacillated between 7 and 8 percent since the 1970s. Moving into the 2000s, some research suggests the percentage of African American teachers has stabilized at about 7 percent, while other studies show a decline. In either case, African Americans are *increasingly* underrepresented in the teaching force.[94]

Different patterns prevail for other minority groups. In contrast to African Americans, the percentage of teachers who are Hispanic or Asian American appears to be increasing, a positive development considering the steady increases in Hispanic and Asian American students. But notice the wide teacher-student gaps that persist for both groups. Although Figure 3.2 does not show the details, Native Americans are also underrepresented in teaching. They account for just over 1 percent of students and just under 1 percent of teachers.[95]

What can be done to attract more minority teachers? Almost everyone agrees that making teaching a more rewarding occupation, intrinsically and extrinsically, will help. But will it be possible to recruit minorities while simultaneously raising

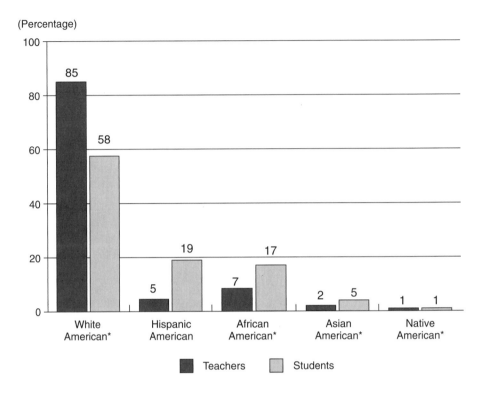

(Percentage)

*Excludes persons of Hispanic origin

FIGURE 3.2   Race and Ethnicity of Public School Teachers and Students: 2005.

Sources: U.S. Department of Education, National Center for Education Statistics, *Digest of Education Statistics, 2002* (2003) [Available: nces.ed.gov/programs/digest/d02/tables/dt068asp], and National Education Association, *Status of the American Public School Teacher 2000–2001* (Washington, DC: NEA, 2003), pp. 5–8, 92–94, 265–267. See Table 8.3 for documentation on students.

the bar with new standards and assessments? As Chapter 8 points out, Hispanic, African, and Native Americans continue to attend and graduate from college at much lower rates than whites and Asians. Wide gaps in college entrance exam scores persist between the racial and ethnic groups. According to data on the SAT released by FairTest in 2004, Hispanics are 150 points behind whites, blacks are 200 points behind, and Native Americans are 90 points behind. Asians are 25 points ahead of whites.[96]

Thus it is not surprising that, with the exception of Asian Americans, teacher testing hits prospective teachers who are minorities harder than those who are white. According to *Tests and Teaching Quality* (2000), during the mid-to-late 1990s the white passing rate on both Praxis I and Praxis II was about 90 percent, while passing rates for African and Hispanic Americans ranged from 46 percent to 77 percent. *Assessment of Diversity in America's Teaching Force* (2004) documents similar gaps in the 2000s.[97]

Tests and Teaching Quality expresses great concern over the situation: "With repeated retaking, black and Hispanic candidates' pass rates approach those of whites, but the differences are still substantial, and it is not certain how many candidates drop out of the pool after failing the test for the first time."[98]

In states with large minority populations, teacher testing has brought forth bitter accusations. Teacher testing is a racist ploy, some educators contend—the latest chapter in a long record of discrimination. No, others reply, it is a necessary step in improving the occupation—the real ploy is using the race issue to block higher standards.

A Way Out?

Teacher education must find a way out of this dilemma, even if doing so proves to be difficult and expensive, as it certainly will. Listen to the counsel of Patricia A. Graham, former dean of the Graduate School of Education at Harvard:

> The problem cannot be solved simply by raising the cutoff scores on tests, by ignoring the tests, by calling them racially biased, or by declaring them inappropriate for future teachers. The tests may contribute to the problem, but they are not central. The central problem is that blacks in the U.S. are not getting as good an education as whites are—and the education that whites are getting is not good enough.[99]

Thus Graham's major recommendation is improving elementary and secondary education.

Graham also insists the nation needs to invest more money and imagination in attracting bright minority college students to teaching. Noting the influx into teaching of people who are dissatisfied with their present jobs, she calls for the recruitment of more minorities at mid-career or even later. She specifically mentions government workers and military retirees.[100]

These are just the kind of people who are now taking nontraditional routes into teaching. From my perspective as a teacher educator, one of the strongest arguments in favor of the new programs is they may be able to attract more minorities into the occupation.

Educating the Emerging Majority (2000), a report from the Alliance for Equity in Higher Education, seconds most of the points Graham makes but focuses more closely on improving traditional teacher education programs for the new century. One positive trend, the report notes, is that minority enrollment in teacher education programs has risen to approximately 15 percent. Colleges and universities that enroll a high proportion of minority students have a key role to play in sustaining this trend because they prepare nearly half the minority students who graduate from teacher education programs. But such institutions have been chronically underfunded. Another mark on the negative side of the ledger is the trend toward judging teacher education programs by "onerous single pass-rate measures": that is, by how well their students do on teacher tests.[101]

What do teachers need to know? What should they be able to do? Will standards and assessments produce better teachers, or are they keeping capable and deserving people out of the occupation? I hope reading this chapter has helped you appreciate how complex these questions really are. If there are easy answers out there, I have yet to find them.

ACTIVITIES

1. Invite several professors of education and professors of arts and sciences into your class for a panel discussion of reform in teacher education, especially the influence of No Child Left Behind and the efforts to reform teacher education from the inside.

2. Talk with a public school administrator and an administrator in your college or university's teacher education program about the effects of standards and assessments on the quality of the teaching force. Be sure to discuss admission and licensing tests and their effects on minority teachers.

3. Ask currently employed teachers for their views on the issues in this chapter, especially the strengths and weaknesses of teacher education programs.

RECOMMENDED READINGS

Campbell, Dorothy M., Pamela Bondi Cignetti, Beverly J. Melenwyser, Diana H. Nettles, and Richard M. Wyman. *How to Develop a Professional Portfolio: A Manual for Teachers*, 3rd ed. (Boston: Allyn & Bacon, 2003). Here is a practical guide to the standards-based portfolios many teacher education programs and some school districts are requiring.

National Collaborative on Diversity in America's Teaching Force. *Assessment of Diversity in America's Teaching Force: A Call to Action* (Washington, DC: National Education Association, 2004). The authors of this report argue that in our national quest for highly qualified teachers under the direction of No Child Left Behind, we are marginalizing diversity issues that should be "central to the quality equation in teaching."

National Commission on Teaching and America's Future. *No Dream Denied: A Pledge to America's Children* (Washington, DC: The Commission, 2003). The commission explains how internal reform of teacher education must be connected to fundamental reform in other areas of the occupation, particularly to better working conditions.

U.S. Department of Education, Office of Postsecondary Education. *Meeting the Highly Qualified Teachers Challenge: The Secretary's Annual Report on Teacher Quality* (Washington, DC: U.S. Department of Education, 2002). The 2002 edition of this annual report offers especially pointed criticism of traditional teacher education programs and strong support for alternative routes.

NOTES

1. Quoted in Public Agenda, *Stand by Me: What Teachers Really Think about Unions, Merit Pay and Other Professional Matters* (New York: Public Agenda, 2003), p. 30.
2. The former New York teacher is the late Albert Shanker, former president of the American Federation of Teachers, quoted in "Why Teachers Fail," *Newsweek* (September 24, 1984), p. 64.

3. James G. Carter, *Essays on Popular Education* (1826) and *Outline of an Institution for the Education of Teachers* (1866), in David B. Tyack, ed., *Turning Points in American Educational History* (Waltham, MA: Blaisdell, 1967), pp. 153, 428.

4. Report of the Committee on Education of the Massachusetts House of Representatives (1840), in Rush Welter, ed., *American Writings on Popular Education: The Nineteenth Century* (Indianapolis: Bobbs-Merrill, 1971), p. 94.

5. U.S. Department of Education, Office of the Under Secretary, *No Child Left Behind: A Toolkit for Teachers* (Washington, DC: USDE, 2003), pp. 19–20.

6. U.S. Department of Education Press Release, "Paige Releases Report to Congress that Calls for Overhaul of State Teacher Certification Systems" (June 11, 2002) [Available: www.ed.gov.news/pressreleases/2002/06/06112002.html]; American Enterprise Institute for Public Policy Research, "Can Education Schools Be Saved?" (2003) [Available: www.aei.org/events/eventID.316,filter./event_detail.asp]; The Teaching Commission, *Teaching at Risk: A Call to Action* (New York: The Commission, 2004), p. 33.

7. National Commission on Teaching and America's Future, *No Dream Denied: A Pledge to America's Children* (Washington, DC: The Commission, 2003).

8. Linda Darling-Hammond, "Research and Rhetoric on Teacher Certification: A Response to 'Teacher Certification Reconsidered,'" *Education Policy Analysis Archives* 10 (September 6, 2002) [Available: epaa.asu.edu/epaa/v10n36.html].

9. National Council for Accreditation of Teacher Education, "NCATE's Role in a Quality Assurance System for the Teaching Profession" (2004) [Available: www.ncate.org/ncate/ncatrole.htm].

10. C. Emily Feistritzer, *The Making of a Teacher: A Report on Teacher Preparation in the U.S.* (2003) [Available: www.teach-now.org/MakingOfATeacher/MOT-1.asp]; National Commission on Excellence in Education, *A Nation at Risk: The Imperative for Educational Reform* (Washington, DC: U.S. Department of Education, 1983).

11. See Jurgen Herbst, *And Sadly Teach: Teacher Education and Professionalization in American Culture* (Madison, WI: University of Wisconsin Press, 1989), and Donald R. Warren, *American Teachers: Histories of a Profession at Work* (New York: Macmillan, 1989).

12. David Page, *Theory and Practice of Teaching: Or, the Motives and Methods of Good School-Keeping* (1849), in Tyack, *Turning Points in American Educational History*, p. 412.

13. Theodore M. Hesburgh, "The Future of Liberal Education," *Change* 13 (April 1981): 38–39.

14. Holmes Group, *Tomorrow's Teachers: A Report of the Holmes Group* (East Lansing, MI: Holmes Group, 1986), p. 47.

15. See Sander L. Gilman, *The Fortunes of the Humanities: Thoughts for after the Year 2000* (Stanford, CA: Stanford University Press, 2000). I base my estimates of the amount of coursework allocated to each area of teacher education on an examination of college and university bulletins.

16. U.S. Department of Education, Office of Postsecondary Education, *Meeting the Highly Qualified Teachers Challenge: The Secretary's Annual Report on Teacher Quality* (2002) [Available: www.ed.gov/about/reports/annual/teachprep/2002title-ii-report.pdf], Tbl. 1.

17. U.S. Department of Education, *No Child Left Behind*, pp. 12, 20. Although the federal law provides for exceptions based on "rigorous state testing," virtually all undergraduate teacher education programs now require the full arts and sciences major or its equivalent in coursework.

18. U.S. Department of Education, *Meeting the Highly Qualified Teachers Challenge*, Tbl. 1.

19. U.S. Department of Education, *No Child Left Behind*, p. 23.

20. Craig D. Jerald and Ulrich Bosser, "Setting Policies for New Teachers," *Quality Counts 2000* (January 13, 2000), p. 44.

21. U. S. Department of Education, *No Child Left Behind*, pp. 12–13; Bess Keller, "'Qualified' Teachers: A Victory on Paper?" *Education Week* (December 8, 2004), pp. S8–S9.

22. U.S. Department of Education, *No Child Left Behind*, pp. 21–22.

23. Diane Ravitch, "Lesson Plans for Teachers," *Washington Post* (August 10, 1998), p. A17.

24. U.S. Department of Education, *Meeting the Highly Qualified Teachers Challenge*, p. 11.

25. National Commission on Excellence in Education, *A Nation at Risk*, p. 22.

26. To sample the vast critical literature on teacher education, start with the studies cited in the notes above and then read the well-balanced "inside" critique by two professors of education, Geraldine Joncich Clifford and James W. Guthrie, *Ed School: A Brief for Professional Education* (Chicago: University of Chicago Press, 1988). Two classic studies from the 1960s are James Bryant Conant, *The Education of*

American Teachers (New York: McGraw-Hill, 1963), and James Koerner, *The Miseducation of American Teachers* (Boston: Houghton Mifflin, 1963).

27. Susan Ohanian, "On Stir-and-Serve Recipes for Teaching," *Phi Delta Kappan* 66 (June 1985): 701.

28. Ibid., pp. 697, 699–700.

29. Holmes Group, *Tomorrow's Teachers*; Carnegie Forum on Education and the Economy, *A Nation Prepared: Teachers for the 21st Century* (New York: Carnegie Forum, 1986).

30. Holmes Group, *Tomorrow's Schools: Principles for the Design of Professional Development Schools* (East Lansing, MI: Holmes Group, 1990).

31. See Holmes Partnership, "Goals" and "Member List" (2004) [Available: www.holmespartnership.org].

32. Holmes Group, *Tomorrow's Schools of Education: A Report from the Holmes Group* (East Lansing, MI: Holmes Group, 1995), p. 79.

33. U.S. Department of Education, National Center for Education Statistics, *Digest of Education Statistics, 2003* (2004) [Available: nces.ed.gov/programs/digest/d03/tables/dt283.asp], Tbl. 283.

34. C. Emily Feistritzer, *Alternative Teacher Certification: A State-by-State Analysis 2004* (2004) [Available: www.teach-now.org/frmOverviewOfATC1.asp], Overview.

35. Ibid., Introduction.

36. Michael A. Allen quoted in Keller, "'Qualified' Teachers," p. S9.

37. Bess Keller, "Rigor Disputed in Standards for Teachers," *Education Week* (January 14, 2004), pp. 1, 14.

38. The discussion in this section is based on National Center for Alternative Certification, "New Jersey" (2004) [Available: www.teach-now.org/states/newjersey/frmProg_ProvisionalTeacher.asp].

39. See Leo Klagholz, *Growing Better Teachers in the Garden State: New Jersey's "Alternate Route" to Teacher Certification* (2000) [Available: www.edexcellence.net/foundation/publication/publication.cfm?id= 13&pubsubid=26#26].

40. Feistritzer, *Alternative Teacher Certification*, Introduction.

41. Lynn Olson, "Colleges of Education Coming under Attack as Weak Link in the Drive to Improve Nation's Schools," *Education Week* (December 12, 1990), pp. 13, 25.

42. Texas State Board for Educator Certification, "How to Become a Teacher in Texas" (2004) [Available: www.sbec.state.tx.us/SBECOnline/certinfo/becometeacher.asp].

43. Texas State Board for Educator Certification, "Texas Examinations of Educator Standards" (2004) [Available: www.texes.nesinc.com].

44. Martin Haberman, *Star Teachers of Children in Poverty* (West Lafayette, IN: Kappa Delta Pi, 1995).

45. National Center for Alternative Certification, "Texas" (2004) [Available: www.teach-now.org/states/ texas/frmProg_AltCert.asp]

46. "Loopholes for Bypassing Minimum Requirements," *Quality Counts 2000* (January 13, 2000), pp. 52–53.

47. Feistritzer, *Alternative Teacher Certification*, Overview.

48. I Teach Texas, "Syllabus" (2004) [Available: www.iteachtexas.com/Syllabus.cfm].

49. Ibid.

50. For the latest round of criticism, see U.S. Department of Education, *Meeting the Highly Qualified Teachers Challenge*, Chaps. 1–3. For the preceding round, see W. Timothy Weaver's "In Search of Quality: The Need for Talent in Teaching," *Phi Delta Kappan* 61 (September 1979): 29–32, 46, and Victor S. Vance and Phillip C. Schlechty's "The Distribution of Academic Ability in the Teaching Force: Policy Implications," *Phi Delta Kappan* 64 (September 1982): 22–27. For criticism in the popular press, see "Teachers Are in Trouble," *Newsweek* (April 27, 1981), pp. 78–79, 81, 83–84.

51. U.S. Department of Education, *Meeting the Highly Qualified Teachers Challenge*, p. 15.

52. National Commission on Excellence in Education, *A Nation at Risk*, p. 22.

53. These points are highlighted in several chapters of Donald R. Warren's edited volume *American Teachers: Histories of a Profession at Work* (New York: Macmillan, 1989).

54. Mortimer Smith, *And Madly Teach* (Chicago: Regnery, 1949); Albert Lynd, *Quackery in the Public Schools* (Boston: Little, Brown, 1953).

55. Weaver, "In Search of Quality"; Vance and Schlechty, "The Distribution of Academic Ability"; Michael Sedlak and Steven Schlossman, *Who Will Teach? Historical Perspectives on the Changing Appeal of Teaching as a Profession* (Santa Monica, CA: RAND Corp., November 1986).

56. Joseph W. Newman, "Reconstructing the World of Southern Teachers," *History of Education Quarterly* 24 (Winter 1984): 585–595.

57. U.S. Department of Education, National Center for Education Statistics, *Digest of Education Statistics, 2003* (2004) [Available: nces.ed.gov/programs/digest/d03/tables/dt185.asp], Tbls. 185, 271; U.S. Department of Education, National Center for Education Statistics, *The Condition of Education, 1995* (Washington: U.S. Government Printing Office, 1995), p. 333; Patrica Albjerg Graham, "Black Teachers: A Drastically Scarce Resource," *Phi Delta Kappan* 68 (April 1987): 598–605.

58. National Council for Accreditation of Teacher Education, "NCATE's Role in a Quality Assurance System for the Teaching Profession."

59. See, for example, Linda Darling-Hammond and Peter Youngs, "Defining 'Highly Qualified Teachers': What Does 'Scientifically Based Research' Actually Tell Us?" *Educational Researcher* 31 (December 2002): 13–25.

60. Educational Testing Service, *Where We Stand on Teacher Quality: An Issue Paper from ETS* (Princeton, NJ: ETS, 2004), p. 5.

61. Robert M. Thorndike, *Measurement and Evaluation in Psychology and Education*, 7th ed. (Upper Saddle River, NJ: Prentice-Hall, 2004), Chap. 3.

62. U.S. Department of Education, *Meeting the Highly Qualified Teachers Challenge*, pp. 23–25.

63. Holmes Group, *Tomorrow's Teachers*, p. 4.

64. See Carnegie Forum, *A Nation Prepared*, pp. 79–87.

65. National Collaborative on Diversity in the Teaching Force, *Assessment of Diversity in America's Teaching Force: A Call to Action* (Washington, DC: NEA, 2004), p. 8.

66. Philip C. Schlechty and Victor S. Vance, "Institutional Responses to the Quality/Quantity Issue in Teacher Testing," *Phi Delta Kappan* 65 (October 1983): 101; Vance and Schlechty, "The Distribution of Academic Ability in the Teaching Force," *Phi Delta Kappan* 65 (October 1983): 25, 27.

67. Committee on Assessment and Teacher Quality, Board on Testing and Assessment, National Research Council, *Tests and Teacher Quality: Interim Report* (2000) [Available: www.nap.edu/openbook/0309069467/html/index.html].

68. Ann Bradley, "National Research Panel Tepid over Tests for Licensing Teachers," *Education Week* (March 15, 2000), pp. 1, 16.

69. Louis Fischer, David Schimmel, and Cynthia Kelly, *Teachers and the Law*, 5th ed. (New York: Addison Wesley Longman, 1999), pp. 355–356.

70. National Research Council, *Tests and Teacher Quality*, pp. 13–15.

71. Ibid. David Owen and Marilyn Doerr critique multiple-choice testing in *None of the Above: The Truth Behind the SATs* (Lanham, MD: Rowman & Littlefield, 1999).

72. Karen Diegmueller, "Revamped NCATE Post Highs, Lows in Tides of Teacher-Education Reform," *Education Week* (February 26, 1992), pp. 1, 12–13, 15.

73. Linda Darling-Hammond, "Teaching Knowledge: How Do We Test It?" *American Educator* 10 (Fall 1986): 18–21, 46.

74. Ibid.

75. Interstate New Teacher Assessment and Support Consortium, "What INTASC Has Accomplished So Far" (2004) [Available: www.ccsso.org/projects/Interstate_New_Teacher_Assessment_and_Support_Consortium].

76. See Arthur E. Wise, "Performance-Based Accreditation: Reform in Action," *Quality Teaching* 9 (Spring 2000): 1–2.

77. National Council for Accreditation of Teacher Education, *Professional Standards for the Accreditation of Schools, Colleges, and Departments of Education: 2002 Edition* (Washington, DC: NCATE, 2002), Chap. 2.

78. National Council for Accreditation of Teacher Education, *NCATE at 50: Continuous Growth, Renewal, and Reform* (2004) [Available: www.ncate.org/pubs/15YearsofGrowth.pdf].

79. Wise, "Performance-Based Accreditation," p. 2.

80. Interstate New Teacher Assessment and Support Consortium, *Model Standards for Beginning Teacher Licensing, Assessment and Development: A Resource for State Dialogue* (Washington, DC: INTASC, 1992), pp. 14–34.

81. Ibid., pp. 18–19.

82. Lee S. Shulman, *The Wisdom of Teaching: Essays on Teaching, Learning, and Learning to Teach* (San Francisco: Jossey-Bass, 2004), Chaps. 12, 14.

83. Dorothy M. Campbell, Pamela Bondi Cignetti, Beverly J. Melenwyser, Diana H. Nettles, and Richard M. Wyman, *How to Develop a Professional Portfolio: A Manual for Teacher*s, 3rd ed. (Boston: Allyn & Bacon, 2003).

84. Educational Testing Service, "Praxis Test Development" (2004) [Available: www.ets.org/praxis/prxfaq. html#testdev]; Educational Testing Service, *Working Papers toward a New Generation of Teacher Assessments* (Princeton, NJ: ETS, 1990).

85. Linda Darling-Hammond, Arthur E. Wise, and Stephen P. Klein, *A License to Teach: Building a Profession for 21st-Century Schools* (Boulder, CO: Westview, 1995), p. 9.

86. National Board for Professional Teaching Standards, "Candidate Resource Center" (2004) [Available: www.nbpts.org/candidates/index.cfm#1].

87. National Board for Professional Teaching Standards, *What Teachers Should Know and Be Able to Do* (1989) [Available: www.nbpts.org/pdf/coreprops.pdf].

88. National Board for Professional Teaching Standards, *Moving Education Forward through National Board Certification* (2003) [Available: http://www.nbpts.org/pdf/04_moving_ed_forward.pdf], p. 4.

89. National Board for Professional Teaching Standards, "Candidate Resource Center."

90. Quoted in Ann Bradley, "Building a Profession," *Teacher Magazine* (August 1995), pp. 1, 12–13.

91. National Board for Professional Teaching Standards, "Quick Facts" (2004) [Available: www.nbpts.org/ pdf/quickfacts.pdf].

92. For an insightful essay comparing the development of professionalism in medicine and teaching, see William R. Johnson, "Empowering Practitioners: Holmes, Carnegie, and the Lessons of the Past," *History of Education Quarterly* 27 (Summer 1987): 221–240.

93. Rona F. Flippo and Julie G. Caniff, "Teacher Competency Whitewash: How One High-Stakes Test Eliminates Diversity from the Teaching Force," *Connection* (Fall 2000): 28–31; Alice Quiocho and Francisco Rios, "The Power of Their Presence: Minority Teachers and Schooling," *Review of Educational Research* 70 (Winter 2000): 485–528.

94. U.S. Department of Education, National Center for Education Statistics, *Digest of Education Statistics, 2002* (2003) [Available: nces.ed.gov/programs/digest/d02/tables/dt068asp], and National Education Association, *Status of the American Public School Teacher 2000–2001* (Washington, DC: NEA, 2003), pp. 5–8, 92–94, 265–267. See Table 8.3 for documentation on students.

95. Ibid.

96. FairTest, "2004 College Bound Seniors Test Scores: SAT" (2004) [Available: http://www.fairtest.org/ nattest/SAT%20Scoresn%202004%20Chart.pdf].

97. National Research Council, *Tests and Teaching Quality*, p. 17; National Collaborative on Diversity in the Teaching Force, *Assessment of Diversity in America's Teaching Force*, p. 8.

98. National Research Council, *Tests and Teaching Quality*, p. 17.

99. Graham, "Black Teachers," p. 601.

100. Graham, "Black Teachers," pp. 603–604.

101. Institute for Higher Education Policy, *Educating the Emerging Majority: The Role of Minority-Serving Colleges & Universities in Confronting America's Teacher Crisis* (2000) [Available: www.ihep.com/alliance/reports/htm].

CHAPTER 4

JOINING A TEACHER ORGANIZATION AND EMPOWERING A PROFESSION

Unions are the most democratic of all organizations. . . . Those who are put off by [teacher unions' political endorsements] need to remember that those unions are concerned only with those policies and ideologies that support public education. That is their business and, from everything I can see, they know it well.

New York teacher[1]

I'm in the [teacher union] and basically just paying to it for the insurance thing. I teach out in a pretty small district. . . . We've never seen [a union representative] in there as far as doing anything.

Texas teacher[2]

111

In the first three chapters, I tried to paint a realistic picture of teaching as an occupation. As you can see, the picture is not exactly rosy. America's teachers have their share of problems. The idealism and commitment new teachers bring to their work can vanish in the face of low salaries, poor working conditions, public doubts about teacher competency, and lingering questions about teacher education.

As I keep pointing out, a realistic assessment of the occupation does not have to be a hopeless assessment. Taking an honest look at their mutual problems encourages many teachers to seek solutions by working together in teacher organizations.

One of the first decisions you will make as a public school teacher is whether to join one of the two major organizations: the National Education Association (NEA) or the American Federation of Teachers (AFT). This chapter opens with a comparison of the two and continues with a discussion of their strategies. Both the NEA and the AFT are unions that use *collective bargaining* and *political action* in their efforts to upgrade teaching as an occupation, and therein lies one of the great controversies of public education.

If you talk with people about the NEA and AFT, you will find few teachers (or other informed citizens, for that matter) have neutral opinions, because these organizations have a clear vision of what they want and they pursue that vision aggressively. In major election years—and particularly during presidential campaigns—teacher organizations receive a great deal of national media attention, positive as well as negative. Academic researchers are paying more attention to these organizations, and the conclusions of their studies are anything but neutral. One recent book carries the positive subtitle *Fighting for Better Schools and Social Justice*, while another lashes out with *How the Teacher Unions Are Destroying American Education*.[3]

In 2004, U.S. Secretary of Education Rod Paige touched off a sharp confrontation when he branded the NEA a "terrorist organization" because of its outspoken opposition to No Child Left Behind. As the NEA called for Paige's resignation, a war of words broke out, with Paige the main target. The superintendent of a large California school district sent the secretary a letter explaining that "a member of al-Qaida hijacks an airliner and flies a plane into the World Trade Center killing thousands of innocent people. That is a terrorist. Teachers throughout America who raise legitimate questions about the many untenable components of No Child Left Behind are not 'terrorists.'" Paige apologized for his "inappropriate choice of words" but stood by the substance of his criticism.[4]

Whoa. Whatever happened to Miss Brooks and Mr. Chips—or Mr. Holland, for that matter?

The NEA and AFT have helped shatter the image of teachers as self-sacrificing servants. They would like to replace this image with one of teachers as competent professionals. No popular media characters have completely captured that image because teachers are still in the process of creating it.

Bringing the professional teacher to life requires a complete restructuring of the occupation, which is exactly what the AFT and NEA are trying to do. They do not use the word *professional* lightly. Rallying around the concept of a *new unionism*, they want to win for teachers the rights and responsibilities society currently reserves for physicians, lawyers, and members of a few other occupations. To some, making teaching a profession represents the best hope for improving the public schools; to others, it is educational heresy. We will explore why the goal of professionalism is so controversial and why it has eluded teachers for so long.

We will also look at teacher organizations that claim to be more professional precisely because they are *not* unions. Competing for members with the NEA and AFT, these groups say they are less interested in teacher power, less adversarial in their relations with the education power structure, and less partisan in the political arena.

This chapter closes with an Internet box of still other associations teachers can join. These groups are organized around teaching fields and academic specializations, and they too have roles to play in the drive to make teaching a profession.

NEA AND AFT

Throughout most of this century, the NEA and AFT have been in competition to organize America's teachers. Until the 1960s, the two groups were very different. The NEA was a large, mild-mannered professional association that was better at collecting information, issuing reports, and talking about teachers' problems than taking action to solve them. The AFT was a small, scrappy union that was trying hard but making little progress toward improving teachers' salaries, benefits, and working conditions.

Things changed during the 1960s and 1970s as the long-standing rivalry between the two intensified. The AFT's militant tactics began to make sense to more teachers, its membership figures soared, and the NEA's "tea-sipping ways" seemed behind the times. Since then, the organizations have become more alike—that is, the NEA has become militant, too—but several key differences remain, enough to keep the two from merging.[5]

Before we look at how the organizations differ, it is important to note how much they have in common. Today the AFT and NEA are unions whose major goals are increasing the economic security of public school teachers and improving their working conditions. Both groups pursue these goals by looking after teachers' interests in the political arena and, in most states, by representing teachers in collective-bargaining sessions with school boards. Both are also professional associations that take stands on a variety of issues affecting students, teachers, and public education generally, issues ranging from the curriculum to teacher education to the federal budget. Convinced a stronger teacher voice in all educational decisions can only improve the schools, both groups believe in teacher power. Above all, the AFT and NEA say they are trying to make public school teaching a true profession.

Four Key Differences

The similarities just mentioned conceal important differences between the organizations in size, geographical strength, official positions on major issues, and labor relations. We will look at each difference in turn.

Size.   The NEA has more than 2,700,000 members, the AFT more than 1,300,000. Figure 4.1 shows how the two groups have grown while organizing America's public school teachers. The NEA, now the largest union/employee organization/professional association of any kind in the world, argues its size gives

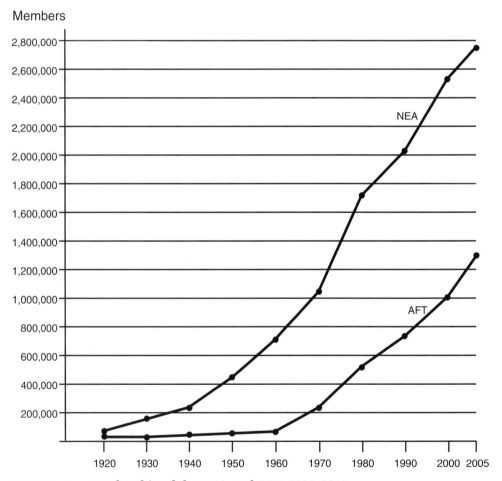

FIGURE 4.1   Membership of the NEA and AFT: 1920–2005.

Source: National Education Association, *NEA Handbook, 1999–2000* (Washington, DC: NEA, 1999), p. 179; Marjorie Murphy, *Blackboard Unions: The AFT & the NEA, 1900-1980* (Ithaca, NY: Cornell University Press, 1990), p. 227. Current membership figures are available at www.nea.org and www.aft.org

it more clout. Delegates to its recent conventions have boasted "We're One in One Hundred," meaning nearly one in every one hundred Americans is a NEA member. The AFT points to its dramatic recent growth—it is more than twenty times larger today than in 1960—and claims to represent the wave of the future. Although both organizations recruit members from outside the ranks of teachers, encouraging paraprofessionals, support personnel, college professors, and others in the education field to join, more than 70 percent of the members in both are classroom teachers. Overall, the NEA has organized about 60 percent of America's public school teachers, the AFT about 25 percent.[6]

Geographical Strength.   Whether you join the AFT or NEA (or neither) may depend on where you teach. The AFT is essentially a big-city union, while the NEA dominates in suburbs, small towns, and rural areas. The AFT, as a member of the American Federation of Labor–Congress of Industrial Organizations (AFL-CIO), the umbrella labor organization in the United States, has always been most successful where the labor movement is strongest and best established—in such major cities as New York, Chicago, Pittsburgh, Cleveland, Detroit, and St. Louis. Even though the AFT now has about 3,000 local affiliates or *locals* (a good union word) and forty-three state federations, there are so few members in some school districts—indeed, in some entire states—the organization has virtually no power in these districts.

The NEA, by contrast, has state-level associations in every state and about 13,000 local affiliates, most of which now call themselves locals. The NEA boasts of its grassroots strength throughout the United States, proud of having brought together in one organization more than half the nation's highly diverse public school teaching force.

Doing so has not been easy. While the AFT has always required teachers to become local, state (if possible), and national members, the NEA has required "unified" membership only since the 1970s. Some of the NEA's state and local associations are well over a century old, and many teachers maintain stronger loyalties to their state and local associations than to the national. Some NEA members try to distance themselves from the national association, complaining the NEA's politics are "too liberal" or its policies "too militant." The unified NEA is powerful, to be sure, but the diversity it is so proud of can be a source of weakness as well as strength.[7]

Official Positions on Major Issues.   Although both organizations make policy democratically—delegates elected in the locals come together in national summer conventions to confer, debate, and vote—for the last thirty-five years the NEA has been more willing than the AFT to take a stand on broad social and political issues that, while not strictly educational, have an impact on the schools. These human and civil rights issues range from family planning to gun control to gay and lesbian rights. Many of the NEA's stands are considered liberal, which is ironic because the NEA has historically had the reputation of a moderate-to-conservative association while the AFT has been the liberal-to-radical union.

Before the 1960s, for instance, the NEA dragged its feet on race relations. It did not merge with the all-black American Teachers Association (ATA) until 1966, and some of the NEA's state and local affiliates in the South remained segregated until the late seventies. The AFT, on the other hand, went on record in support of desegregation well before the landmark *Brown* decision (1954) and required its locals to desegregate in 1956. Standing history on its head, today's NEA is one of the nation's strongest advocates of minority rights, including affirmative action, while the AFT carefully positions itself in the middle of the road or, in some cases, just to the right of the center line.[8]

On the other hand, some of the NEA's positions on controversial social issues do not turn out to be as radical as its critics portray them. Often accused of having a "prohomosexual agenda," the NEA has in fact struggled to take a stand on sexual orientation that reflects the diverse views of its members, some of whom are religious conservatives. For years the NEA has stood for protecting students and school employees from discrimination and abuse regardless of their sexual orientation. This position differs little from the AFT's, but the NEA catches more political flack.[9]

Although the two organizations agree far more often than they disagree on education issues—and it is important to remember that fact—several important differences have emerged since the 1970s. As we saw in the last two chapters, the NEA has tried harder to swim against the tide of conservatism that has swept the nation and its schools, while the AFT has been more willing to go with the flow. Although both groups say they are opposed to merit pay, the NEA has dug in its heels and opposed virtually every move away from traditional salary schedules, while the AFT has been more willing to experiment with merit pay in updated and renamed versions.

AFT past president Sandra Feldman is a member of The Teaching Commission, which produced *Teaching at Risk* (2004). The report made several proposals for salary reform including pay based on student test scores. NEA President Reg Weaver, who was *not* a member of the report commission, responded in a *USA Today* column that such documents are "simplistic" and full of "flashy, cure-all remedies." Weaver argued that "proposals to pay some teachers more than others do nothing to motivate all teachers and simply create a competitive environment."[10]

Which organization is more in touch with America's teachers? Consider the 2003 Public Agenda poll we reviewed in Chapter 2. Teachers have been moderating their views on merit pay, and a sizable majority—more than 60 percent—now seem willing to accept certain kinds, particularly those that reward teachers for working in tough schools and with difficult students. But more than 60 percent of teachers remain opposed to using standardized test scores as a factor in their pay.[11]

Regarding standards, assessments, and accountability, the NEA has been sharply critical, claiming these measures hurt the very students they are supposed to help: poor, minority, limited English proficiency, and disabled. The AFT has been more accepting of such reforms, although the federation does admit testing can be overdone.

Not surprisingly, the two organizations take somewhat different positions on the No Child Left Behind Act of 2001, the most powerful force behind standards, assessment, and accountability today. Whenever I visit the two unions' Web sites, as I often did while revising this chapter during the presidential election year of 2004, I can see clear differences on NCLB. I can also see a fundamental similarity.

The material on the NEA's Web site is overwhelmingly critical, repeatedly referring to the federal program as the "so-called No Child Left Behind law." It "needs fixing before expanding," according to Reg Weaver, because "teachers and parents find the current law's use of one-size-fits-all tests to determine whether a school is labeled as failing to be a major flaw."[12]

The material on the AFT's Web site strikes a more conciliatory tone. "The legislation—though far from perfect—embraced a number of positive measures the AFT has long championed, particularly accountability for the progress of all students and high standards around core academic subjects. . . . The AFT remains firmly committed to NCLB's goals and supportive of the framework." Then, accompanied by frequent reassurances that the AFT is willing to work with politicians to get things right, the union offers a point-by-point critique of NCLB's funding and implementation. The content of the AFT's review is as negative as the NEA's. But the tone is more cordial.[13]

Trying to be fair to both groups, we can say the AFT has taken a front seat on the bandwagon of standards, assessments, and accountability—albeit with reservations about NCLB—while the NEA is still reluctant to climb aboard. The NEA continues to take a skeptical (some would say obstructionist) view of many educational reforms, while the AFT takes a hopeful (some would say opportunistic) view.

Both organizations are highly conscious of their public image. With all the talk about families and values in political conversations, both groups are going to great lengths to prove they are in step with parents and average citizens, whom they like to call "stakeholders" in public education.

The AFT's outreach to families revolves around *Helping Your Child*, a series of booklets that emphasize discipline, hard work, and cooperation between home and school. The theme of helping children meet high standards runs through the series, which the union copublishes with the U.S. Department of Education.[14]

The NEA offers families similar guidance, but with less praise for standards and accountability and more emphasis on such basics as getting off to a good start in the school year and keeping up with homework. The *Parent's Guide* series, which is jointly published with the National PTA, covers issues ranging from increasing scientific literacy to "raising ready readers." One booklet coaches parents on overcoming the limitations of current testing programs.[15]

The NEA and AFT are trying to reinvent themselves. As we will see later, leaders of both talk glowingly about a new unionism that tones down militance, plays up cooperation, and recasts the organizations as advocates of teacher quality and student achievement. Beneath the nice-sounding words, though, important differences remain on major issues.

Relations with the Labor Movement. These relations are significant enough to deserve separate consideration as a fourth difference between the NEA and the AFT. Since its founding in 1957 as the National Teachers' Association, the NEA has been quite status conscious, billing itself as "professional" in an attempt to distinguish teachers from mere "workers." Until recently, the NEA steered clear of organized labor.

The AFT, by contrast, has been affiliated with the American Federation of Labor since shortly after the AFT's founding in 1916. The AFT has always insisted teachers are workers who aspire to be professionals. According to the AFT, joining a union and expressing solidarity with other workers does not make teachers less professional. Teachers and other workers can find strength in numbers in their mutual quest for better salaries, benefits, and working conditions, and the labor movement can support teachers as they try to gain the same control over their occupation that physicians and lawyers have over theirs.

Until the 1960s, as Figure 4.1 suggests, few teachers paid much attention to the AFT's calls to unionize. The NEA deliberately and effectively exploited antilabor sentiment, telling teachers they would be stooping to the level of blue-collar workers if they joined the AFT, "that labor union." Even after the NEA itself began using the tactics of organized labor, the association was reluctant to sew the union label into its jacket. Frankly, many NEA members are still uncomfortable with the label, especially those who live where organized labor is unpopular.[16]

But today's NEA *is* a union, recognized as such by the U.S. Department of Labor. The NEA is also a member of the Coalition of American Public Employees (CAPE), an organization whose major goal is winning collective bargaining rights for all public employees. Thus the NEA has, in a sense, joined the labor movement, but it refuses to join the AFL-CIO, arguing doing so would compromise its independence. The AFT, for its part, refuses to leave the AFL-CIO, and this difference has frustrated efforts to merge the NEA and AFT.[17]

The most recent setback came in the summer of 1998, when NEA convention delegates rejected a set of merger guidelines. In addition to the long-standing AFL-CIO stumbling block, NEA members raised objections to voting procedures, term limits for officers, and guarantees of minority representation proposed for the unified organization.[18]

Still, the prospects of an eventual merger look good. Delegates to the AFT's 1998 convention voted overwhelmingly to merge, and 85 percent of the NEA's delegates said they supported the merger in principle. Presidents of both organizations remained committed.

Since then, some of the action has shifted to the state level. After the two unions' affiliates in several states, including New Mexico, Pennsylvania, and Wisconsin, agreed not to raid each other's bargaining territory, the AFT and NEA declared a nationwide moratorium on raiding in 2001. State affiliates of the two organizations in Florida, Minnesota, and Montana have actually merged.[19]

Now the unions have agreed to form a "new partnership," *NEAFT*, whose blended initials may be the harbinger of a full merger in the future. Based on an agreement ratified in 2001, NEAFT encourages cooperation on matters ranging from public relations to political lobbying. The combined strength of the two unions is formidable indeed. As a researcher who studies teacher unionism puts it, "If you were in a legislature, and two lobbyists from the NEA and AFT came in, and they were arm-in-arm, you'd probably pay closer attention."[20]

NEAFT is trying to live up to its promise. After beginning on an emotional note by establishing a September 11 Fund to assist families of teachers who died or lost relatives in the terrorist attacks, the new partnership has brought together state and local affiliates to work for such causes as opposing private school vouchers, protesting budget cuts, and getting out the vote for endorsed political candidates.

Labor, Management, and Gender

The list of differences between the NEA and the AFT was once much longer. One difference that has lost much of its significance is the NEA's willingness to admit school administrators as members.

Throughout most of the NEA's history, its administrative members, although only a small fraction of the association's total, aligned themselves with the even smaller group of college professors and effectively ran the show. As Wayne Urban explains in *Gender, Race, and the National Education Association* (2001), the organization's internal structure virtually duplicated the larger structure of public education: A few administrators, mostly males, held sway over a large number of teachers, mostly females. The men who ran the NEA were the same men who ran the public schools. Most teachers joined the association not because they wanted to but because their superintendents and principals said to. Until power began to shift away from administrators in the 1960s, the NEA was not truly a *teacher* organization.[21]

Since then, classroom teachers have taken control of the NEA. As the organization has grown militant on *bread-and-butter issues*—another good union term encompassing salaries, benefits, and working conditions—many administrators have grown uneasy and left. Most of those who remain play minor roles.

This changing of the guard has been a source of much amusement to the AFT, which classroom teachers have always controlled. Some of the key leaders of the early AFT were women with a strong commitment to feminist causes, from voting rights to social and economic equality. Their struggle to make the voice of teachers heard in education was part of the larger struggle to make the voice of women heard in society. Although men eventually displaced women in the federation's leadership, the AFT, like other unions, has always drawn a line between workers and managers, insisting their outlook, interests, and work are fundamentally different. According to the AFT, teachers cannot be expected to stand up for their rights in an organization controlled by their bosses.[22]

Only recently has the NEA come around to this adversarial, labor-versus-management point of view, and some members still find it hard to accept. In many rural and small-town school districts, administrators still encourage teachers to join "our professional association, the NEA." In these districts, administrators and teachers enjoy a comfortable if paternalistic relationship, and teacher militancy is something that takes place only in the newspapers. The point to remember is that although the days are gone when administrators dominated the NEA and required teachers to join, rural and small-town school districts are still a world apart from Chicago and New York.

What Membership Means

Joining the AFT or NEA means different things in different districts. In some, it is a statement of militant professionalism; in others, an expression of concern with bread-and-butter issues; in others, a means of self-protection; in still others, just the thing to do. As a new teacher, you should find out what each organization stands for in your state and district. If both groups are viable and actively competing for members, find out what one can do for you that the other cannot. You will probably discover both are proud, and rightly so, of what they have won for teachers through local, state, and national political activity. Ask what they have done about salaries, class sizes, preparation periods, noninstructional duties, and other matters that will affect you daily as a teacher.

As you listen to their recruitment pitches, you will find both organizations offer their members a wide range of services. The NEA publishes *NEA Today, NEA Now, Tomorrow's Teachers* (a magazine for student members), and several other periodicals. The AFT's list includes *American Teacher* and *American Educator*. Some issues of these publications are available online, and the AFT sends out a weekly e-mail newsletter, *Inside AFT*. Although the NEA is more involved in research and publication at the national level, members of both groups receive a variety of materials from state and local organizations. State and local newsletters often contain information of immediate concern to teachers: job market news, recent court decisions, the status of education bills in the state legislature, activities in the local schools.

Both national unions and many of their state and local affiliates are online. The NEA and AFT maintain Web sites ranked among the best and most visited education pages on the Internet. Designed to be useful to the general public as well as teachers, the union sites offer access to a wide variety of information—from the latest figures on teacher salaries to previews of upcoming school-related television programs to politically charged press releases—as well as links to other education sites. The strong proteacher and prounion slant to virtually all the content should be a noticeable change from the media coverage you are used to.

Both organizations offer their members life and supplemental health insurance and, more important, liability insurance and legal services for protection in lawsuits arising from job-related activities. One of the first things a teacher hears from NEA and AFT *building reps*—teachers who serve as the unions' on-site, front-line contacts—is likely to be, "You'll wish you were a member if a student has an accident in your classroom and you get sued." As we will see in Chapter 5, that message is fair warning, but it sometimes puts off teachers who think such things happen only to other people.

Both organizations will tell you their combined local, state, and national dues, which usually run between $400 and $500 per year, are a sound investment. Ask for specific ways the investment pays dividends.

What Teachers Think of Their Unions

You may be surprised that 85 percent of public school teachers are members of either the NEA or AFT. That percentage is impressive, to be sure, but what does it

> ■ ■ ■ ■ ■
>
> **BOX 4.1**
>
> **AFT AND NEA WEB SITES**
>
> Visit and compare the AFT and NEA sites at www.aft.org and www.nea.org and click on the links to their affiliates in the state and local school district where you hope to find your first teaching position.

really mean? Based on my ongoing research as well as years of conversations with teachers and future teachers, I am convinced that although teachers certainly don't glamorize their unions, just as surely they wouldn't want to do without them. Fundamentally, teachers look to the NEA and AFT for protection.

A 2003 Public Agenda report on teacher attitudes toward their organizations carries the apt title *Stand by Me*. In the words of the report's directors, "Teachers often feel vulnerable to a wide range of dangers—unfair charges from parents and students, bureaucratic machinations and favoritism, simpleminded educational 'solutions' and cost-cutting. Their union is their ally, one they can count on." More than 80 percent of teachers believe that without the union's protection, they would be vulnerable to administrative and political abuse. More than 80 percent believe that without collective bargaining, which we will discuss next, teacher salaries and working conditions would deteriorate. Seventy-seven percent worry that in the face of unfair accusations by students of parents, without the union they "would have nowhere to turn."[23]

At the same time, most teachers keep busy with their classroom work and deal with the union only when they need to. Two-thirds say they "aren't involved or engaged with their local union, other than receiving mailings and notices." For most teachers, membership is a practical matter, not an ideological commitment.[24]

Accordingly, NEA and AFT building reps stress bread, butter, and security, often sharing their peers' skepticism toward loftier reform issues. Keep your head down, do your work, and the union will protect you if somebody gets on your case. That's not glamorous advice, but most teachers will tell you it's realistic.

COLLECTIVE BARGAINING

Seated on one side of a long table are representatives of the teachers in a school district. Facing them across the table are representatives of the board of education. At issue is the master contract for the district's teachers, a thick document of more than one hundred pages, and today the discussion is focused on the starting salary for new teachers. Reminding the board of teacher shortages, stressing the importance of attracting capable people to the occupation, the teacher representatives ask for a raise of $1,000. The board representatives reply they are well aware of the supply-and-demand situation, but they are also aware of the tight budget.

A thousand dollars? Ridiculous. No way. Two hundred would be more like it. The negotiations wear on into the evening and into the days and nights that follow. No one is completely satisfied with the compromise raise of $450, but both sides feel pressured to work through the rest of the contract, which spells out teacher salaries, benefits, working conditions, and grievance procedures in great detail.

Most of America's public school teachers bargain with their school boards in sessions similar to this one. More than forty states have laws guaranteeing public school teachers the right to bargain collectively with their school boards. Some state laws outline a collective bargaining process borrowed directly from labor-management relations. Teacher representatives and board representatives try to reach agreement on the terms of a contract, and if they are unable to agree, there are provisions for resolving the impasse. Other states specify a milder form of bargaining that requires boards to "meet and confer" with teachers. Here board members must listen to teachers in a formal session, but the boards retain the decision-making power. A few states have no laws on collective bargaining in the public schools, but some local boards in these states negotiate with teachers on a limited basis.[25]

AFT Points the Way

The AFT pioneered collective bargaining in public education. Its success with the practice not only helped the federation grow but pushed the rival NEA toward unionism.

In the late 1950s, the AFT mounted an organizing campaign in New York City schools in an effort to get the union moving again. At the time, New York's 50,000 teachers were splintered into a bewildering array of organizations according to their subjects and grade levels. The AFT's strategy, engineered by former high school teacher Al Shanker and other experienced union leaders, was to hit hard on bread-and-butter issues common to all teachers, bring them together in a single unit, and win the right to bargain as a group with the board of education.[26]

After a bitter struggle punctuated by a one-day strike in November 1960, the board agreed to a collective bargaining election. In 1961, New York's teachers endorsed bargaining by a 3-to-1 margin and voted to be represented by AFT Local 2, the United Federation of Teachers. Local 2 won the right to bargain for the city's entire teaching force.

The AFT's victory went into the record books as a turning point in the history of teacher organizations. Teacher militancy spread quickly, first to other big cities and then beyond. During the 1960s and 1970s, the AFT grew four times as fast as the NEA. Shanker went on to be elected president of the AFT in 1974, an office he held until his death in 1997. Shanker became one of public education's elder statespeople, more influential than any individual NEA president.[27]

The NEA had no choice but to take notice. After first trying to dismiss the AFT's militancy as "unprofessional," the larger group gradually followed suit.[28]

Today both organizations believe collective bargaining, combined with political action, offers the best hope for improving salaries, benefits, and working conditions. Both groups regard the combination of bargaining and politics as the best strategy for professionalizing public school teaching.

How Bargaining Works

The mechanics of collective bargaining are not hard to understand. First, the teachers in a school system choose a union to represent them. Usually, teachers vote by secret ballot; in other cases, they fill out authorization cards, or the locals competing for representation submit membership lists. The union that wins the support of the majority of teachers becomes the exclusive bargaining agent for all teachers in the system. (Some states allow the school board to negotiate with more than one local representing teachers, but this procedure is rare because it is time consuming and divisive.) The exclusive bargaining agent has the obligation to represent every teacher fairly—a tall order because some teachers may be members of a rival union and others of no union. Most states have regulations to make sure the bargaining union takes the interests of both members and non-members into account.[29]

In more than half the states, *agency shop* or *fair share* contracts may require teachers who are not members of the bargaining union to pay the local a service fee, generally the same amount as union dues. This fee reimburses the local for its work as the teachers' bargaining agent. But that amounts to compulsory union-ism, some teachers charge, claiming these regulations run roughshod over their freedom of choice and force them, in effect, to join the union whether they want to or not. Prounionists reply that because the local is obligated to negotiate on behalf of all teachers, and because nonmembers and members alike reap the ben-efits won through bargaining, all teachers should share the costs.[30]

Although the U.S. Supreme Court has ruled agency shop regulations consti-tutional, several groups are waging an ongoing battle against them. Leading the opposition are the Concerned Educators against Forced Unionism, a branch of the National Right to Work Committee, and two organizations billing themselves as "more professional" alternatives to the NEA and AFT: the Association of American Educators and the National Association of Professional Educators. Later in this chapter we will look at these and other nonunion teacher organizations.

Once teachers have selected their bargaining agent, the union and the school board choose negotiating teams. In small school districts, a team of

---

BOX 4.2

AN ANTIUNION POINT OF VIEW

For a distinctly antiunion point of view on collective bargaining and other issues dis-cussed in this chapter, visit the National Right to Work Committee at www.nrtw.org and the Education Policy Institute at www.educationpolicy.org

teachers (often the union officers) sits down at the table and talks directly with members of the board. In some districts, administrators are part of the board's team; in others, administrators have their own unions. As unions and boards become more sophisticated with collective bargaining, they usually seek the advice of lawyers specializing in labor-management relations. The larger the school district, the more likely both sides are to call in more outside help, with unions looking to their state and national offices and boards looking to their state and national associations. Both sides may also employ professional negotiators.

More often than not, the bargaining process is long and slow. Occasional flashes of insight and humor lighten up the tedious deliberations. The process usually results in a new contract all board members and all teachers have the right to examine and ratify. If the two sides reach an impasse, most states have laws that outline steps for breaking the deadlock.

What Bargaining Covers

Although the scope of collective bargaining varies considerably from district to district and state to state, salaries, benefits, and working conditions are always the bottom line. Traditionally, bread-and-butter issues have been the *only* line. Some union leaders still stick to these issues because they know many *rank-and-file* (yet another union term) teachers want their bargaining agent to deliver the economic goods, period. Other leaders with broader goals envision the day when collective bargaining will give teachers a voice in virtually every policy decision in the public schools, from the content of the curriculum to teacher evaluation plans.

As we will see later in this chapter, the vision of these leaders is becoming a reality in some school districts. The eyes of teacher unionists throughout the nation are on the contracts negotiated in Rochester, Cincinnati, Toledo, Denver, Minneapolis, Montgomery County (Maryland), and other urban systems. These contracts empower teachers with some of the rights and responsibilities recommended by the National Commission on Teaching and America's Future (NCTAF) and National Board for Professional Teaching Standards (NBPTS).

Collective bargaining is entering a new phase as teachers press toward a new unionism. In the near future, all the cards may be face up on the table as teachers, administrators, and school board members share power voluntarily in win-win bargaining, which emphasizes cooperation rather than confrontation.[31]

To teachers in school districts that do not bargain at all, this vision can seem remote indeed. Rochester, New York, and Raleigh, North Carolina, are two different worlds. Tough political battles lie ahead for teacher unionists who want to expand the scope of negotiations and extend bargaining rights to more teachers. The AFT and NEA support federal legislation that would allow every public school teacher in the nation to bargain. Opponents counter such a law would violate states' rights and hand over control of public education to teacher unions. On balance, collective bargaining seems likely to stay, expand, and eventually involve teacher unions and school boards throughout the nation in the process of give and take.

Teacher Strikes

Unions, bargaining, and strikes run together in the public's mind. When students return to school every fall, the news media run stories about teacher strikes, usually playing up those staged by AFT locals in big-city systems. "Do Chicago teachers strike every year?" one of my students asked me recently (and quite seriously). As many people see the situation, unions strike when they cannot get their way at the bargaining table, causing employers and often the public to suffer.

This analysis overlooks the fact that teachers who do not have collective bargaining rights also go on strike. A rash of teacher strikes broke out during the years of rapid inflation following World War II, well before the rise of collective bargaining in public education, and some strikes still occur in school systems that do not bargain. In fact, teachers in such systems say requiring board members to sit down, listen, and negotiate may prevent strikes. To be sure, the AFT made its breakthrough in the 1960s by bargaining, threatening to strike, and, in some cases, carrying out its threats—but bargaining is not the cause of strikes.[32]

Instead, teacher frustration with low salaries and poor working conditions, aggravated by a sense of powerlessness, made teachers turn to collective bargaining in the first place and to strikes as a last resort. The state of the economy plays a leading role. Teacher strikes reached an all-time high during the double-digit inflation of the late 1970s and early 1980s, when increases in the cost of living far outstripped increases in teacher salaries. In 1979–1980 alone, AFT affiliates staged 34 strikes and NEA affiliates struck 208 times. Ten years later, with lower inflation and better raises, teacher strikes decreased to fewer than one hundred per year, with most called by the NEA. The conservative national mood of the Reagan years, which spawned a get-tough-with-unions attitude, also made teachers less willing to strike.[33]

The situation has changed several times since then with the ups and downs of the economy. The early 1990s ushered in another era of labor unrest in the teaching force. As state and local governments reduced spending on public education, many teachers saw their salaries and working conditions absorbing a disproportionate share of the cutbacks. Strikes increased again, although the yearly totals were less than half those of the 1979–1980 peak. From the mid-1990s through the mid-2000s, teacher strikes have been occurring at one-tenth the peak rate—and most recently, even less often.[34]

During the economic slowdown of the last few years, teacher salaries have been able to keep pace with increases in the cost of living, and teacher strikes have become relatively rare events. It is a commentary on the times that *Preventing and Managing Teacher Strikes* (2002), one of the only recent books on the subject, has less to say about strikes themselves than about bargaining fairly with teachers to keep strikes from ever occurring.[35]

Given the 15,000 local school districts in the United States, even the 242 strikes of 1979–1980 could hardly be called a runaway problem. Teachers, like other public employees, are aware of how much is at stake when they strike.

Risky under any circumstances, strikes are literally desperate measures. Although the trend in state law is toward giving teachers a limited right to strike, in about half the states teacher strikes are still against the law, and the U.S. Supreme Court has ruled school boards can fire teachers who engage in illegal strikes. Judges can levy fines against unions and individual teachers who strike illegally. In rare instances, striking teachers can find themselves in jail. Strikes can also alienate parents and the general public. Beyond these problems, teachers face an ethical question when they strike: Can they justify denying students the opportunity to learn?[36]

Rest assured teachers who decide to strike think seriously about these issues. Striking teachers gamble the school board will not fire them in large numbers because of the difficulty in finding replacements. In some cases, teachers are willing to take the risk because they have community support. Conditions are so bad in some school districts, parents and other citizens side with teachers against the board. Other unions sometimes lend their support, especially if an AFT local is on strike.

Ethically, some teachers believe short-term losses for students are outweighed by long-term gains for the school district as a whole. As the AFT and NEA like to point out, better salaries and benefits attract better teachers, and improving teachers' working conditions also improves students' learning conditions. If school boards force teachers to strike to reach those goals, the unions reason, then so be it.[37]

Political Action

Less dangerous and almost as controversial, political action is a strategy teachers use to attain the same goals. As we will see in Chapters 6 and 9, this nation's public schools have always been involved in politics. Tax revenues support the schools, public officials govern the schools, and teachers compete for a share of power and influence.

When administrators controlled the NEA, the association engaged in dignified political activity, lobbying Congress for federal aid for education and other measures. The NEA's state affiliates worked quietly with legislatures and school boards to secure tenure laws, retirement benefits, and health and sick leave provisions.[38]

The AFT also lobbied Congress, and some of its locals were deeply involved in city and state politics. Leaders of the more powerful AFT locals—Chicago, New York, and Atlanta—mastered the political arts only to encounter opposition from the public and their own members. Many citizens argued, and some teachers agreed, that it is undignified and unprofessional for teacher organizations to engage in politics if that means such things as supporting candidates for office and taking stands on political issues.[39]

But for more than three decades, the AFT and NEA have done exactly that. Undignified? Not unless the entire way we govern ourselves in the United States is undignified, teacher unionists answer. Politics is the name of the game, and during the 1970s, teachers looked around and saw the members of almost every organized occupational group playing it. Some groups—physicians, lawyers, farmers, manufacturers—had been playing seriously and successfully for years.

Unprofessional? Quite the contrary, say the unionists, because teachers are using politics to win more control over their occupation, and control is the very essence of professionalism.[40]

Today it is difficult to find a professional association or union more active in United States politics than the NEA or the AFT. At all three levels of government—federal, state, and local—teacher organizations operate with clout and sophistication. In 1976, the NEA broke long years of official silence on presidential elections by endorsing the Democratic ticket of Jimmy Carter and Walter Mondale. Since then, candidates for the Democratic presidential nomination have eagerly courted both the NEA and the AFT. The two organizations now maintain a high profile in races for the U.S. Senate and House of Representatives. Candidates for state office, from governors to legislators, come under the unions' political scrutiny. So do aspiring local politicians, from mayors to school board members.

PACs

The NEA and AFT have set up political action committees (PACs) to raise money through teachers' voluntary contributions. Together, the teacher PACs now collect more than $10 million to be spent on federal campaigns during a two-year presidential election cycle, with the NEA PAC typically outraising the AFT's Committee on Political Education (COPE) by about 2 to 1. The NEA may have the larger war chest, but both organizations are able to make contributions of as much as $10,000 to the Senate and House candidates they endorse. In support of their choices, both unions send out e-mails, operate telephone banks, and run media ads. Moreover, both groups encourage their members—85 percent of all public school teachers, remember—to get involved in politics on a personal level by contacting elected officials, volunteering to work in campaigns, registering voters, and turning out at the polls on election day.[41]

This level of political activity is high enough to get the candidates' attention, to say the least. The NEA and AFT believe endorsements, contributions, and direct member involvement make elected officials more likely to act in the interest of teachers. Considering the competition teachers face in their quest for power and influence, both organizations have matured politically in an amazingly short time. Even though corporate PACs outspend labor PACs by 3 to 1, the NEA and AFT's PACs rank among the top 25 in the nation in spending on federal elections.[42]

State and local NEA and AFT PACs also raise substantial sums, enabling the unions to have clout in state, city, and county governments. In agricultural states, for instance, organized teachers often do battle with the farm bureau and forestry association over school taxes, while in industrial states, teacher unions may square off against manufacturers' and bankers' associations.

Who Gets Endorsed

Most of the candidates teacher organizations endorse are moderate-to-liberal Democrats, because such politicians tend to be prounion and willing to "invest in public education," which is a nice way of saying they are willing to spend more money on the schools. The AFT and NEA have stuck with Democratic presidential tickets despite their losses to Republicans in the 1980, 1984, 1988, 2000, and 2004 elections. Republicans George H. Bush and Bob Dole made a point of *not* seeking teacher union support during the 1988 and 1992 campaigns. Dole, in fact, went out of his way to attack the two organizations. Democrat Bill Clinton, by contrast, pursued and won the unions' endorsements in 1992 and 1996 on his way to winning both elections.

The presidential campaigns of the 2000s have been different stories. Although the NEA and AFT, just as expected, endorsed Al Gore in 2000 and John Kerry in 2004, George W. Bush rarely attacked the unions and tried instead to attract the votes of individual teachers. Even though No Child Left Behind has been a hard sell to America's teachers—and Rod Paige's "terrorist" remark made matters worse—education proved to be a less important issue in the 2004 campaign than in 2000. Kerry promised more federal funding, to be sure, but muted his criticism of NCLB while Bush pushed standards, assessments, and accountability. Bush defeated Kerry with 51 percent of the vote.[43]

Beyond the presidency, Republican victories in congressional elections since 1994 have stung both unions. Living with GOP control of both the House and the Senate has been difficult for teacher unions as well as other groups that traditionally support the Democratic Party. Rethinking their strategies, the NEA and AFT are now reminding the public of their officially bipartisan stance. The AFT is advertising its willingness to work with Republicans and, as we have seen, cooperating with the U.S. Department of Education in publishing guidebooks for parents. The NEA, despite its harder-edged politics, has been a visible presence at the last three Republican conventions. During the 2004 convention, the NEA held a luncheon for Republican members of Congress, reminding them that the organization was endorsing sixteen Republicans seeking House or Senate seats—a big increase over the one endorsed in 1996.[44]

Numbers do tell the story. Twenty-five NEA members were delegates to the 2004 Republican convention; 275 were delegates to the Democratic convention. On balance, both teacher organizations are still pinning their hopes on Democrats.

America's teachers have diverse political views and party affiliations, of course, and polls suggest almost as many teachers vote for Republican presidential candidates as for Democratic candidates. But bread-and-butter issues are critically important factors in political endorsements, just as they are in collective bargaining. Faced with a choice between a Republican committed to holding down taxes and spending and a Democrat less adamant about taxes and more willing to increase spending, the NEA and AFT have little difficulty choosing the latter.

The unions regard the Republican Party's support for private school vouchers (Chapter 10) as a threat to public education as an institution. The defeat of well-financed voucher initiatives in several states is one of the NEA and AFT's most gratifying successes in the politics of the 2000s.

Teacher Power and Grassroots Politics

Both organizations are digging in at the grassroots level, paying more attention than ever to local school board, state school board, state legislative, and gubernatorial races. AFT and NEA locals invite candidates to screening sessions in which teachers ask point-blank questions: How will you vote on teacher salary increases? On raising retirement benefits? Where do you stand on agency shop regulations? On raising state taxes? Based on the candidates' answers, teachers vote whether or not to make an endorsement in the various races and then decide how much to contribute to each endorsed candidate.

After attending one such session, I was impressed by how forceful the teachers were and how polite the candidates, in this case would-be state legislators, were. After the candidates left, a frank discussion took place, the teachers voted, and the treasurer of the local association sat down to write out checks of several hundred dollars each. Weren't teachers simply buying politicians? I asked several members. They replied the candidates were "making the rounds. Last night they went to the chamber of commerce; tomorrow night they'll be at the bar association; next week they'll visit the labor council and farm bureau. Why should teachers sit on the sidelines when everybody else is playing the game?"

Teacher organizations see political action and collective bargaining as complementary strategies. Both are roads to power. Teachers exercise power indirectly by endorsing political candidates and lobbying in Congress and state legislatures. Teachers wield power directly when they bargain with school boards. Both strategies are controversial because they give power to a group that historically has had little.

NONUNION ALTERNATIVES TO THE NEA AND AFT

Some public school teachers who belong to neither the AFT nor the NEA hold membership in a nonunion teacher organization. Rejecting the militance and politics of the two unions, these groups describe their orientation as more *professional*—a concept we will examine closely to conclude this chapter. State-level associations such as the Arizona Professional Educators, Professional Association of Georgia Educators, and Professional Educators of Illinois provide an alternative in about half the states. At the national level, the Association of American Educators (AAE) and National Association of Professional Educators (NAPE) offer membership to nonunion teachers whether or not they decide to join a state organization. Yet another national group, the Coalition of Independent Education Associations (CIEA), serves as a coordinator for the state organizations.[45]

Most nonunion teacher associations date back to the 1980s and 1990s, when they organized to provide liability insurance, legal services, and other support to public school teachers who have ideological reasons for not joining the NEA or AFT. As the AAE puts it, these groups offer the alternative of "Professionalism and Protection . . . without the Politics."[46]

BOX 4.3

THE THREE LARGEST NONUNION TEACHER ORGANIZATIONS

Visit the Association of Texas Professional Educators at www.atpe.org, the Professional Association of Georgia Educators at www.pageinc.org, and the Missouri State Teachers Association at www.msta.org

---

Elaborating on this slogan, the AAE and other such organizations explain they are less adversarial in their relations with school officials and less partisan in the political arena. From their point of view, collective bargaining is inappropriate, taking positions on broad social issues is unwise, and striking is out of the question. At the same time, they say they are more concerned with children and more accepting of public control of public schools, by which they mean citizen control exercised through local school boards.

Teacher power is not on their agenda. Teacher professionalism is, even though the AFT and NEA insist that making nice and going along won't ever get teachers to the goal. Interestingly enough, the Association of Texas Professional Educators—the nation's largest independent teacher organization—is flexing its muscles and getting involved in politics, but with a far more conservative agenda than the NEA and AFT's affiliates in the Lone Star State.[47]

Most teachers who join nonunion organizations are socially and politically conservative. Some seem nostalgic for the kind of association the NEA was before the 1960s. Some may want to create a public school counterpart of the National Catholic Educational Association or National Association of Catholic School Teachers, neither of which is comparable to the AFT or NEA. If private schools can get along without unions, some teachers reason, so can public schools.

Although reliable membership figures are hard to come by, the growth of nonunion organizations for public school teachers seems to have slowed during the 2000s. Independent teacher associations in Texas, Georgia, and Missouri now claim more membership than either the NEA's or AFT's affiliates in their respective states, but this success seems to be due to particular political circumstances, such as protracted antiunion campaigns waged by politicians and school officials. Across the nation, the union share of the public school teaching force is holding constant.[48]

With both union and nonunion teachers claiming to be professional, and with each camp accusing the other of selling out, we need to consider several questions: What are the characteristics of a profession? To what degree does teaching have those characteristics? Can the teacher power strategies of collective bargaining and political action make teaching more professional?

A TEACHING PROFESSION?

Because the word *profession* has such a nice ring, people use it in a variety of ways. The question "What is your profession?" may simply mean "What kind of work do you do?" Some people use *professional* in an attempt to add status and prestige to an occupation. Thus we hear of professional entertainers and professional secretaries. To other people, a professional is anyone who excels in a particular occupation—a highly professional mechanic or salesperson, for instance.

If we apply more stringent criteria, only a few occupations qualify as professions. Medicine, law, and theology—the oldest and most familiar—were originally called the learned professions. Dentistry, architecture, and engineering are among the other occupations that have established themselves as professions.

Developments in medicine and law over the last 150 years have set the modern standards for professionalism, but only since 1900 have physicians and attorneys become fully professional, organizing and controlling their occupations in ways that distinguish them from other types of work. Based on comparative studies of many occupations, sociologists have developed a set of characteristics to define the professions. They have paid particular attention to medicine, often referring to it as the "prototype" profession because medicine exhibits the characteristics to a greater degree than any other occupation.[49]

We can distill the discussion of professionalism in the sociological literature to a set of three major characteristics:

1. A profession performs a unique, essential social service.
2. A profession has a defined, respected knowledge base.
3. A profession has autonomy.

Throughout this book I avoid referring to teaching as a profession. I call it an occupation. My choice of words does not reflect a lack of respect for teaching—I respect it immensely—but rather the fact that teaching does not possess the characteristics of professionalism to the extent medicine, law, and several other occupations do. Teaching does, though, exhibit the characteristics to a greater degree than most lines of work, prompting people to call teaching, along with nursing and social work, a *semiprofession* or, more optimistically, an *emerging profession.*[50]

Terminology is important. I am careful with my choice of words because I want them to remind you teachers must make fundamental changes in their occupation if they want to make it more professional.

Our discussion of professionalism pulls together many of the main issues from the preceding chapters, touching on supply and demand, salaries, teacher competency, and teacher education. The key to professionalism is the role teachers themselves must play. Physicians and attorneys moved their occupations along the road to professionalism by taking collective action through the American Medical Association (AMA) and American Bar Association (ABA). As we saw earlier in this chapter, some teachers believe they can professionalize their occupation by working together through the NEA, the AFT, or a merged organization.

A Unique, Essential Social Service

The first characteristic of a profession suggests society regards some work as so vital—healing the sick is the best example—that members of one occupation get exclusive rights to perform the work. Society allows the profession to "corner the market," in other words, to ensure the service is available at a high level of quality. Society must regard the service as essential, and it must be convinced only the members of the profession can render the service to acceptable standards. Otherwise, society will not grant a monopoly for performing the service.[51]

Certainly Americans believe teaching young people is an essential task, and society has given one occupational group, public school teachers, a monopoly of sorts in public education. However, as we saw in Chapters 1 and 3, most states have been willing to overlook teacher education and licensing standards and allow people to teach with emergency licenses or, in some cases, with no licenses at all.

Although No Child Left Behind appears to eliminate such backdoor practices by mandating that teachers of all core subjects be highly qualified—and fully licensed—by 2005–2006, some states have simply redesignated their "emergency" licenses as "alternative" licenses. States can still hire people with *no* formal teacher education and put them into classrooms while they complete licensing requirements, and some states even allow candidates to "test out" of almost every education course.[52] The National Commission on Teaching and America's Future (NCTAF) puts it bluntly in *No Dream Deferred* (2003): "Loopholes can make licensing a mockery."[53]

Most states still look the other way when it comes to private school teachers, who make up about 10 percent of the nation's teaching force. In most states, private school teachers do not have to meet state education and licensing standards. This situation opens a loophole without parallel in medicine, law, and most other professions. As we will see in Chapter 10, there are some good arguments against state regulation of private schools and their teachers. On the other hand, our society would not tolerate two classes of physicians—one licensed by the state, the other unlicensed, but both doing the same work—because we regard medicine as so important we cannot entrust it to unlicensed practitioners.

But teaching? Many people believe almost anyone can do it. Parents teach their children, after all, and most people have taught on the job, in church, or in a similar situation. Can teaching be so complex only one occupational group, people with a state license based on an approved teacher education program, can perform the service?

Many Americans answer no. Teacher education doesn't have the best reputation in the world, and state officials have shown they will do almost anything to get warm bodies in front of classrooms when teacher shortages hit. Such factors make it difficult to argue one group should have exclusive rights to teach in the public schools, much less that the regulations governing public schools should extend to private schools. As the NCTAF laments in *What Matters Most: Teachers for America's Future* (1996), "States pay more attention to the qualifications of veterinarians treating the nation's cats and dogs than to those of teachers educating the nation's children and youth."[54]

Although public school teachers and private school teachers will probably never become one professional group, promising developments related to the first characteristic of professionalism are under way. In the last chapter, I expressed cautious optimism about teacher education and licensing for public school teachers. Higher standards are sending the message that not just anyone can teach. The recommendations of the NCTAF and National Board for Professional Teaching Standards (NBPTS) dovetail with those of the National Council for Accreditation of Teacher Education (NCATE) and Interstate New Teacher Assessment and Support Consortium (INTASC). Higher standards for educating, licensing, and certifying teachers hold great promise. They deserve a fair trial.

But the danger, as Chapters 1 and 3 point out, is that states will ignore these recommendations and use the leeway NCLB has given them to open up even more "streamlined" routes into the occupation for people with little or no formal teacher education. If "lower barriers," to use the language of NCLB, produce an adequate supply of new teachers, why go to the extra trouble and expense of higher standards?

Citizens do get mixed messages. Not just anyone can teach, to be sure, yet, on the other hand, the job requires little or no specialized training. Perhaps anyone who is intelligent and liberally educated can teach. Back we go to the nineteenth-century debates over teacher education.

A Defined, Respected Knowledge Base

America's continuing uncertainty about these issues relates also to the second characteristic of a profession: a defined, respected knowledge base. Professionals have expertise not shared by the general public. People recognize a body of knowledge called "the law" exists, for instance, and they recognize attorneys as experts in the law. Professionals acquire their knowledge in specialized training programs, usually in graduate-level university programs. Bar examinations for lawyers, like similar examinations in other professions, assure the public that professionals are in command of their knowledge before they enter practice.[55]

Teaching does not fare well on this characteristic. The controversy over teacher education haunts the occupation here, too. Inside and outside of universities, there is little agreement on the knowledge teachers must master. One of the most damaging aspects of the controversy, as we have seen, is that teachers themselves belittle their training in education. Once they begin teaching, they tend to ignore their training and just wing it. Teachers say they learn much more on the job than from their undergraduate and graduate education courses.

Now for some tough questions: When will the body of knowledge about teaching become strong enough to change people's minds? What, exactly, is the role of the NBPTS, NCATE, and INTASC in defining the knowledge base? What is the role of the Praxis Series of Assessments, developed by the Educational Testing Service as the long-awaited successor to the National Teacher Examinations? When the smoke clears and all the new standards and assessments fall into alignment, will they be useful to teachers themselves?

Medicine developed a knowledge base that actually worked *before* devising tests to measure it. In teaching, we are putting the cart before the horse if we expect national organizations and testing companies to devise tests before we have agreed on what works and what doesn't. The consensus on knowledge must come first; then tests can follow. It is encouraging that teachers themselves have the strongest voice on the NBPTS, which concerns itself with national certification, but so far teachers have had less influence in developing the new standards and assessments for teacher education and licensing.

Autonomy

Teachers themselves: I use these words often in this discussion because they hold the key to professionalism in teaching. Autonomy, the third characteristic of a profession, is the right the members of an occupation have to make their own decisions and use their own judgment. The members themselves are in charge. Professionals have two kinds of autonomy: individual and group.

As *individuals,* professionals have the right to perform their work as they see fit, based on knowledge acquired through specialized training. Physicians, for example, enjoy a wide range of autonomy in their daily work. Society trusts them to make one decision after another as they diagnose their patients' illnesses and prescribe appropriate treatments. Physicians may turn to their colleagues for help and advice, but they do not have to check with a boss or supervisor before they act.[56]

As a *group,* physicians control their occupation through a network of state and national boards that set standards for medical education, licensing, and practice. Group autonomy is a relatively recent development in medicine. Although the AMA was founded in 1846, it took the organization three-quarters of a century to win physicians the right to regulate themselves. In the late 1800s, medical education was notoriously poor. Licensing was a sham. "Quacks" were an embarrassment to competent physicians and a danger to people seeking medical care.[57]

Then a series of developments turned the occupation around. Over several decades, scientific medicine gradually won acceptance among physicians. Because scientific medicine worked, prospective physicians became willing to attend university medical schools to learn how to practice. This revolution in knowledge and training was already under way when the Carnegie Foundation for the Advancement of Teaching published *Medical Education in the United States and Canada* in 1910. Popularly known as the Flexner Report, this study was a call to continue upgrading the occupation. The Flexner Report capped—not caused—the trend toward scientific medicine.[58]

The report's greatest value was as a political document because the AMA was able to use it to convince Congress and the state legislatures that physicians should control their occupation. Give physicians the right to regulate themselves, the AMA promised, and they will give the nation better medical care. The AMA fought and won its political battles. Medicine became a self-regulating profession with the AMA as its major professional association. And along the way, the AMA also became one of the nation's most effective "unions," highly successful at safeguarding its members' interests.

The lesson for teachers is that although there are good reasons to be optimistic about the prospects for professionalism, teachers have a long way to go in their quest for autonomy. Consider this old saying among teachers: "I may have to follow school board policies and take orders from the principal, but when I close the classroom door, I'm in charge." To a degree, this statement is true—or rather was true. Until the late 1970s, teachers did have a fair amount of individual autonomy in the workplace, at least informally. Teachers were able to use methods they thought appropriate, administer tests they had designed, and grade students using their best judgment. Being able to work with relatively little direct supervision, escaping bureaucracy by closing the door, was one of the most attractive features of the occupation.

The back-to-basics movement changed the situation drastically, ushering in a regimen of standardized teaching, testing, and grading. From the start of the movement to the present era of No Child Left Behind, teachers have felt increasing pressure from their bosses, school board members and school administrators, to teach objective by objective, straight from the cookbook. As we will find in Chapter 11, the cookbook—often called an instructional pacing guide—tells teachers what to teach, how to teach it, when to teach it, and which tests to use to measure how much students have learned about it. As one teacher recently joked with me, "The pacing guide tells me everything but when to go to the restroom, and that will probably be covered in next year's edition."

The sad truth is that teachers have lost rather than gained individual autonomy. Backed into a corner, teachers in some school systems are fighting back with collective bargaining, trying to carve out areas where they can use their judgment. Local unions now find themselves having to negotiate for a stronger teacher voice in student grading and other decisions that once rested entirely with teachers themselves.

Teachers have never had much group autonomy, which is another way of saying they have never won the right to control their occupation. One reason is that most teachers are public employees, paid with public money, while most physicians and lawyers are in private practice, paid by their clients on a fee-for-service basis. (Predictably, as the public pays a larger share of the nation's medical bills, physicians rail against creeping government restrictions on their autonomy.) The public tries to regulate what it pays for, to be sure, but something more fundamental is involved in public education: a long tradition of state and local governance, grounded in the belief citizens should control "their" schools (see Chapter 9). Given this tradition, we must face the fact that teachers will never have the group autonomy of physicians or lawyers.

REACHING FOR PROFESSIONALISM

From Job Control to Quality Control

As teacher organizations are quick to point out, though, the public regulates every profession to some degree. The task that lies ahead, as the AFT and NEA see the situation, is finding a way to balance public power and teacher power.

But how? In the intriguingly titled book *United Mind Workers* (1997), Charles Kerchner, Julia Koppich, and Joseph Weeres explain how large-scale trends in labor relations and technology could help transform teacher unionism for the better. As the U.S. economy shifts from industrial to postindustrial and a "knowledge society" emerges, workers in every occupation find their lives changing. Education in particular seems caught in a crossfire of change, and teachers—"mind workers"—feel the stress. Old ways of organizing schools, although highly resistant to reform, are breaking down. The challenge is for teachers themselves to seize the moment, restructure their work, and take charge of their occupation.[59]

The central argument of *United Mind Workers* is that teacher organizations must now shift their focus from job control to quality control. "Organized teachers would gain unbeatable influence," the authors suggest, by saying to the public:

We will take joint custody of reform.

We will evaluate ourselves and hold ourselves to high, and public, professional standards.

We will come to understand our students' lives and advocate for them before we advocate for ourselves.[60]

TURN.   Some teachers are serious about translating these words into action. The Teacher Union Reform Network (TURN) is a coalition of more than twenty-five AFT and NEA locals committed to transforming teacher unionism. Its members include the AFT affiliates in Albuquerque, Boston, Cincinnati, Douglas County (CO), Hammond (IN), Minneapolis, New York City, Pittsburgh, Poway (CA), Rochester, and Toledo; the NEA affiliates in Bellevue (WA), Cambridge (MA), Columbus (OH), Denver, Memphis, Montgomery County (MD), Portland (OR), San Diego, San Juan (CA), Seattle, Syracuse, and Westerly (RI); and the merged AFT/NEA locals in Dade County (FL), Los Angeles, Pinellas (FL), and San Francisco. By negotiating changes in contracts and then tackling far more difficult changes in school culture, these teacher organizations are trying to show the way for other locals.[61]

Adam Urbanski, cofounder of TURN and president of the Rochester Teachers Association, often talks about the "cultural change" that must occur before a new unionism can take hold. Teacher organizations must more clearly recognize their responsibilities to students, families, and society, Urbanski says, as well as to "public education as a vital element of our democracy. What unites these responsibilities is our commitment to help all children learn."[62]

The foundation of this reorientation must be "teachers themselves," who "must accept responsibility for change and see themselves as agents rather than

■ ■ ■ ■ ■

BOX 4.4
TURN

Find out more about TURN and link to some of the nation's most progressive local teacher organizations at www.turnexchange.net/index.htm

mere targets of reform." Urbanski argues that "unions and union leaders must expand their view of themselves to include the role of leaders of reform."[63]

Urbanski and other advocates of a new teacher unionism are calling for nothing less than a complete transformation in occupational culture. Teachers have traditionally been reactive instead of proactive in school reform, as we have seen. They have looked to their unions for protection and security more often than leadership and innovation. Union leaders have played defense rather than offense.

How much is the culture of teaching changing? And where? Gerald Grant and Christine Murray, the authors of *Teaching in America* (1999) we met in Chapter 1, answer the first question by describing a "slow revolution" in teaching, one in which teachers are gradually taking charge of their occupation. In the optimistic scenario Grant and Murray sketch, the slow revolution will eventually enable teachers to transform their occupation from a semiprofession into a profession.[64] But the authors readily acknowledge what the first four chapters of this textbook document: The revolution has been more successful in some states and school districts than others.

If we want to be pessimistic, we can cite the attitudes documented in the 2003 Public Agenda poll *Stand by Me* as evidence that most of America's teachers still have a limited view of their unions, looking to them almost exclusively for protection and advocacy on bread-and-butter issues. Unions have yet to register with most teachers as leaders of reform. Nor do teachers themselves, as we saw in Chapter 1, have much faith in reform generally.

Yet here and there we can see hopeful signs. The changes you may see in teaching over the course of your career will depend on the politics of education where you teach. One important factor may well be whether the AFT or the NEA is more powerful in your locale. Although the national leaders of both organizations have shaken hands over reinventing unionism, the goals and strategies of their state and local affiliates vary tremendously. Remember, the NEA is the more recent convert to the new unionism, and its state and local leaders generally take a more cautious approach to occupational reform, particularly to such sticky issues as peer review, career ladders, and merit pay. The case studies that follow will help you understand these differences.

Professional Standards Boards: A Case Study

Both the NEA and AFT would like teachers to have more autonomy in setting standards for teacher education and licensing. No surprise there. But in typical fashion, the two unions are pursuing the goal differently.

State by State.   The NEA has been using its greater clout in state politics to push for *state professional standards boards,* commissions with the authority to set standards for educating and licensing teachers and, in some cases, to impose sanctions on teachers for misconduct. These boards include classroom teachers as voting members. Although state boards of education already consult with teachers on such matters, the NEA looks forward to the day when teachers themselves can actually vote on the standards rather than merely give advice.

The NEA's ultimate goal is to have a professional standards board in every state, with teachers holding a majority of votes on each. Beginning in the late 1960s, California, Oregon, Minnesota, and a few other states established professional standards boards, but for years no state was willing to give teachers a controlling voice.[65]

The breakthrough the NEA was working for came in 1987, when the Nevada legislature created a nine-person board, with teachers holding four of the seats, a school counselor or psychologist holding the fifth, and the remaining seats occupied by two administrators, a dean of education, and a state board of education member. Because teacher organizations represent school counselors and psychologists, the NEA proudly hailed the Nevada board as the nation's first "teacher-dominated" professional standards board.[66]

The NEA, encouraged by this victory, has stepped up its campaign in other states. In 1989, the Iowa legislature established a professional standards board, with teachers holding the largest bloc (although not quite a majority) of seats. That same year, the Minnesota legislature redesigned its professional standards board to put teachers in the majority. Georgia created an autonomous teacher-dominated board in 1991. Indiana followed in 1992. In all, seventeen states have now established an autonomous professional standards board, and twelve more have an advisory board that can make recommendations. The NEA's state affiliates, sometimes in concert with the AFT, are pressing for boards in other states.[67]

Professional standards boards attracted national attention in 1996 when the NCTAF released the report *What Matters Most.* The commission rated all the states on their "attention to teacher quality" using such criteria as the percentage of teachers who are fully licensed and the percentage teaching in their field of study. Minnesota came out on top, in part because the teachers who dominate its state professional standards board have tried to hold the line on licensing standards and make it hard for local school officials to relax standards when teacher shortages occur. Kentucky and Iowa, the states ranked second and third, respectively, also have professional standards boards that have been willing to take firm stands on teacher education and licensing. Are these boards acting professionally, as the commission believes, or selfishly, as some critics charge?[68]

No Child Left Behind has added a new political twist to this question. The federal law has become the driving force behind reform in teacher education and licensing, and it is overshadowing the work of professional standards boards by skewing the definition of "highly qualified" teachers away from teaching skill and toward knowledge of subject matter. Some professional standards boards find themselves struggling with state politicians and school officials who seem determined to lower barriers rather than raise standards. We will return to this issue near the conclusion of this chapter.

NBPTS.   Teachers also hold a majority of the seats on the National Board for Professional Teaching Standards. Although this board does not have the power to set standards nationwide, it hopes the national certificates it issues will become prestigious enough to make the states want to follow its lead. The AFT lost little time throwing its support behind the national board, on which the AFT has a better chance of holding its own with the NEA than on the state boards the NEA is sure to dominate. The NEA hesitated, expressing reservation after reservation before finally warming up to the NBPTS.[69]

The different approaches of the two unions are not necessarily in conflict because most professions have national *and* state standards boards. In fact, the work of the NBPTS and state standards boards can be complementary, as the NEA now recognizes.

The NBPTS makes a distinction between *licensing* and *certification,* and in this book I follow the national board's lead. Long recognized in most professions, the distinction between licensing and certification is finally gaining recognition in teaching. Physicians, for instance, receive licenses to practice medicine from individual state boards, and those who wish to can seek certification in medical specialties from national boards. Using this model, state and national boards may be able to work together in education. The NBPTS would like state standards boards to be responsible for licensing teachers—for setting standards to govern how teachers enter and advance in the occupation based on education and experience. The NBPTS hopes to be responsible for certifying teachers—for setting standards to recognize teachers whose performance is outstanding.[70]

Opposition to Teacher Autonomy.   Although the prospects of teacher empowerment are exciting, the opposition is already out of the box. Some resistance comes from school board members and school administrators. In Nevada, the bill creating the teacher-dominated professional standards board passed the legislature with only one dissenting vote, despite the efforts of the state board of education, state department of education, and local school boards to defeat it. The executive secretary of the Nevada Association of School Boards stated bluntly, "These are not doctors, lawyers, accountants, and engineers. These are public employees, working in the public sector, and much public benefit is lost with them having total control." Unable to block the establishment of the professional standards board, opponents did persuade the Nevada legislature to give the state board of education veto power in certain areas. Opposition is running high in other states as well.[71]

Opponents charge teacher autonomy breaks the administrative chain of command within school systems and reduces the power of the state and local boards that represent the public. The charge is accurate. Instead of trying to deny it, teacher organizations will have to counter that changing the balance of power in public education is desirable. They must argue, as physicians did, that teachers can improve the quality of their services if they have more autonomy.

In order to convince the public, teachers must begin to set standards of performance for their occupation. Unlike the NEA's existing Code of Ethics for the Education Profession and the AFT's Bill of Rights, two documents that sit on the shelf collecting dust, the performance standards must be specific, and teachers themselves must enforce the standards. The Carnegie Corporation says more accountability—specifically, some form of merit pay based on student achievement—must go hand in hand with more autonomy. As we saw in Chapter 2, a series of commission reports stretching from *A Nation Prepared* (1986) to *Teaching at Risk* (2003) has promoted a Carnegie-inspired and Carnegie-funded vision of corporate professionalism. The NBPTS and NCTAF are major links in this chain of reform, which is designed to reshape teaching into a highly differentiated occupation. Advocates believe such *proactive* reforms offer the best hope of overcoming opposition to teacher autonomy.[72]

But Chapter 2 also points out how teacher are *reacting* to NCLB, the latest and most powerful incarnation of accountability. Because teacher organizations have balked at holding teachers accountable for student test scores—and with good reason, as we have seen—accountability will be a bitter pill to swallow. The AFT and NEA have both mounted opposition to NCLB, but the AFT is more willing to participate in merit pay experiments. AFT leaders are convinced the pressure for merit pay is not going to go away.

Broadening the definition of accountability to include factors other than student test scores may make the pill more palatable. The new accountability may involve peer review, for instance. Teachers evaluating teachers, another Carnegie recommendation, would be a major step toward professionalism, but peer review is also controversial. Some teachers are as reluctant to take on the responsibility as some administrators and board members are to share it.

The New Unionism in Rochester: A Case Study

Notice how every change we consider leads to several others. We are talking about a complete realignment of teaching as an occupation, and more—a complete overhaul of America's schools. The situation is certainly not hopeless. Since the late 1980s, some local teacher organizations have been negotiating experimental versions of the Carnegie recommendations with their school boards, tying together salaries, evaluation, and autonomy. *Restructuring* became the watchword of school reform during the late 1980s and remained so into the 1990s.[73]

AFT locals jumped off to an early lead in the race to restructure, attracting media attention with the innovative contracts they negotiated in Rochester, Toledo, Cincinnati, Pittsburgh, Miami-Dade, and other large urban school systems. Shanker and the AFT gave their locals the green light, encouraging them to take calculated risks and shake free of some of the traditional contract restrictions in labor-management relations.

The NEA, by contrast, moved slowly and cautiously at first. Major changes almost always involve risks, so the NEA says it is only wise to look before leaping. Having looked and seen its rival moving ahead, the NEA brags of its own leadership in fundamental school reform. But the NEA's affiliates, as we have noted, remain more wary of change—the willingness of the Denver Classroom Teachers Association to try merit pay is a notable exception—while the AFT's affiliates are more willing to push the envelope.

Maybe the AFT and NEA should not merge. Maybe their differences in style and approach offer teachers valuable alternatives. In the case of restructuring, different approaches have probably been desirable, because restructuring can involve virtually every aspect of schooling.

Now, in the 2000s, restructuring is no longer the watchword of school reform. In many school districts that bought into restructuring, the changes turned out to be cosmetic. Teacher committees and "Building Leadership Teams" met regularly but soon found they had little real power. Parent involvement came across as a public relations ploy. Then, as NCLB crowded out almost every kind of reform except for standards, assessments, and accountability, restructuring became just another buzzword in most school districts, further reinforcing teacher cynicism about the possibility that some reforms could actually be helpful.

In Rochester and a few other big-city school systems, though, restructuring has produced real changes, and the district is still trying to sort them out and decide which to keep and which to discard. As you read the following case study, you can decide for yourself how much hope teachers should pin on school reform.

In the Public Eye.   For the last twenty years, Rochester has been home to one of the nation's most closely watched experiments in school reform. Working toward the twin goals of better education for students and more professionalism for teachers, the Rochester Teachers Association and Rochester City Schools have assumed joint custody of reform. Leading the teachers union throughout the experiment has been local president Adam Urbanski, who as a vice-president of the AFT has also directed the Teacher Union Reform Network. Urbanski has dealt, usually cooperatively but sometimes not, with a succession of city superintendents.[74]

For twenty years, Rochester's public schools have faced the same problems as other large urban systems: low student achievement and low teacher morale, high student dropout rates and high teacher burnout rates. Over the course of the experiment, the percentage of students living in poverty and the percentage who are racial or ethnic minorities have increased from 70 to 90 percent. The population of Rochester and its suburbs, while changing in the same direction, remains predominantly middle class and white. Eighty percent of the city's teachers are white. Fewer than 20 percent of the city's taxpayers and voters have children in the public schools.

The experiment in reform began in 1987 with a "revolutionary" contract negotiated by Urbanski and Superintendent Peter McWalters, who became friends as well as colleagues as they worked together in a textbook example of win-win bargaining. At a time when restructuring was the going thing in school reform nationwide, Rochester tried to strike a new balance between teacher responsibilities and administrative responsibilities. Planning committees were formed in every school, with the principal as chair and teachers as the majority of members.

This part of the experiment, like most similar efforts around the nation, has yielded mixed results. Administrators have jealously guarded their turf, and teachers have complained about taking on extra work on top of their already demanding jobs. On the other hand, administrators have gradually become more willing to share certain responsibilities with lead and mentor teachers, as we will see in the next section.

Career in Teaching Program.   The most distinctive and generally most successful part of the Rochester experiment has been the effort to build professionalism through the Career in Teaching (CIT) Program. A teacher career ladder with four rungs—intern, resident teacher, professional teacher, and lead teacher—has been in place for two decades, offering higher salaries and greater responsibilities. When the ladder first went up, Rochester could boast that it paid teachers better than any other big-city district in the nation. Salaries have slipped considerably since then, however, as a result of on-again, off-again taxpayer support.

Teacher evaluation has been the most critical—and most controversial—component of the CIT. *Accountability* has taken on different meanings as the experiment has evolved. Initially, the union and school board agreed to define accountability broadly as system-wide commitment to meeting student needs. Since the early 1990s, as citizen activists have pushed for more emphasis on measurable results, the definition has narrowed to statistical indicators such as dropout rates, graduation rates, and standardized test scores. Just as in the rest of the nation, test scores have emerged from the mix as *the* measure of teacher accountability. And Rochester's teachers, like their colleagues elsewhere, have objected to what they see as an obsession with testing, especially when a politician or school official suggests using student scores as a factor in teacher pay.

Looking for other ways to evaluate teachers and hold them accountable, the district tried portfolios during the early 1990s. Teachers voted down a sophisticated if complicated plan for awarding performance raises based on portfolios keyed to professional practice standards. Despite assistance from Lee Shulman, the evaluation guru we met in Chapter 2, the district finally gave up after several portfolio trials met teacher resistance. Today Rochester uses a traditional behavioral evaluation model based on thirty-minute observations by principals. A more innovative approach, the Performance Appraisal Review for Teachers (PART), is available to tenured teachers as an option. PART involves projects that allow teachers to show how they assess student achievement and tailor their instructional methods to enhance learning.

Another CIT innovation is the Mentor/Intern Program that pairs mentors, who are carefully selected from the ranks of the district's lead teachers, with first-year teachers. Mentoring provides nurture and support that are all too rare in teaching. In Rochester, the program has increased the five-year retention rate of new teachers to 86 percent, an impressive improvement over the 65 percent rate before the program began. The CIT also provides peer support for struggling teachers and peer intervention for those who are having serious problems.

▪ ▪ ▪ ▪ ▪

BOX 4.5

**ROCHESTER TEACHERS ASSOCIATION
AND ROCHESTER CITY SCHOOL DISTRICT**

Look inside the world of big-city teachers involved in an experiment with school reform at www.rochesterteachers.com and www.rcsdk12.org, and notice the different perspectives presented by the two Web sites.

The Mentor/Intern Program gives teachers a voice in the tenure and retention decisions that administrators make by themselves in other school districts.

"Real Change Is Real Hard."   The process of collective bargaining puts the spotlight on different views and opinions, and the differences have often been glaring during the Rochester experiment. From the mid-1990s through the early 2000s, Rochester's district superintendent was Clifford Janey, an African American who has since become superintendent of schools in the District of Columbia. Janey's strong business orientation often clashed with Urbanski's strongly prolabor outlook. The stage was set for confrontation when Janey proposed a pay-for-performance plan for teachers—a merit pay plan keyed to student test scores—and sought help from the business community in promoting it. A bitter fight ensued, and teachers won.

But Rochester's teachers realize standardized testing won't go away any more than merit pay will. Having agreed for twenty years that teacher pay should be based on competence and responsibility, not just education and experience, the union and school board now feel more accountability than ever because of No Child Left Behind. The public sees constant reminders of the test scores of Rochester's poor and minority students, scores that are still lagging after twenty years of school reform. "Real change is real hard," Urbanski confesses.

But there are bright spots. Test scores of some student subgroups are rising in some Rochester schools, although supporters and detractors of NCLB disagree on why. Is it genuinely improved achievement? More skillful teaching of the test? A combination of the two? The Career in Teaching program continues to get positive reviews for improving the work lives of teachers who serve in very demanding schools. The report *Developing Careers, Building a Profession* (2002) from the National Commission on Teaching and America's Future praises the CIT and especially the Mentor/Intern Program.[75]

PROFESSIONALISM, FEMINISM, AND UNIONISM

Even in districts and states with fewer challenges, teachers will have to get past two major roadblocks on their way to professionalism. One roadblock is antifeminism. Our discussion in the first three chapters highlights the perception of teaching as women's work. To the degree some people still view women as second class and subordinate, teachers, along with nurses and social workers, will run into resistance in their bid for professional status. Today this opposition is rarely expressed openly, although it occasionally slips out in such remarks as "After all, most teachers are only working for a second income" or "Women are naturals at teaching kids in the classroom, but they could care less about running a school district."

The other roadblock, antiunionism, may be even more formidable. Antiunionism is a factor to be reckoned with inside as well as outside the occupation. On the inside, some teachers who join the NEA or AFT strictly for self-protection do so reluctantly and with great reservations. Unions are too political, too bureaucratic, too adversarial, they believe. Unions have no interest in what goes on inside the classroom. Unions don't care about quality. *Stand by Me* (2003) confirms that younger teachers are more likely than their older colleagues to hold these attitudes. And even though teachers come to appreciate their unions more the longer they remain in the occupation, the AFT and NEA are worried about the future of unionism after the present cohort of leaders retires and a new generation inherits the associations. Is the success of nonunion organizations in a few states the harbinger of a national trend?[76]

Outside the ranks of teachers, union-bashing critics often charge teacher organizations with using professionalism selfishly to make life easy for their members. Teachers are coming out the winners, critics claim, with students, parents, and the general public the losers. Here is an updated version of the old "featherbedding" charge critics have historically leveled at unions in every occupation.

Consider again the example of professional standards boards—state boards as well as the NBPTS. There is little doubt the NEA and AFT will use their influence on the boards to set teacher education and licensing standards high enough to restrict the supply of new teachers, a move that could drive up teacher salaries. Moreover, the organizations give every indication their members will oppose relaxing the standards in response to teacher shortages. Just like the teachers on the Minnesota, Kentucky, and Iowa professional standards boards, they will insist that if school boards want qualified teachers, the only way to attract them is by offering better salaries, benefits, and working conditions.[77] Self-serving, critics say.

The NEA and AFT counter by claiming what is good for teachers is good for public education. They argue that although all professional associations try to take care of their own members, ultimately they have the interests of their clients at heart. Certainly physicians were thinking about themselves when they restricted access to their occupation. By making medicine a highly selective occupation, physicians ensured those who got in a comfortable living.

But they were also thinking about the public. When shortages of physicians develop today, state medical boards do not allow people with partial or no medical education to fill in, even on an emergency basis. Instead, the profession maintains its standards, fees for medical care rise, medicine becomes even more attractive to young people, and a greater supply of licensed, fully trained physicians eventually meets the need. The AMA claims what the public loses in short-term convenience

■ ■ ■ ■ ■

BOX 4.6

ORGANIZATIONS IN THE TEACHING FIELDS

Organizations other than the NEA, AFT, and nonunion associations have roles to play in teacher professionalization. These groups try to meet their members' needs through publications, conferences, in-service training, and the like. They are organized to serve teachers in particular teaching fields and a academic specializations.

American Alliance for Health, Physical Education, Recreation, and Dance www.aahpherd.org

American Council on the Teaching of Foreign Languages www.actfl.org

Association for Career and Technical Education www.avaonline.org

Association for Education Communications and Technology www.aect.org

Council for Exceptional Children www.cec.sped.org

International Reading Association www.reading.org

Music Teachers National Association www.mtna.org

National Art Education Association www.naea-reston.org

National Association for the Education of Young Children www.naeyc.org

National Council for the Social Studies www.ncss.org

National Council of Teachers of English www.ncte.org

National Council of Teachers of Mathematics www.nctm.org

National Science Teachers Association www.nsta.org

it gains in long-term quality. Don't Americans deserve the same quality in public education, the AFT and NEA ask?[78]

Yes, but trying to answer that question sends us back to others we have already considered. Can we justify giving one occupational group exclusive rights to teach in public schools? Is the knowledge base for teaching strong enough to support an emerging profession? Is the public ready to trust teachers and their organizations with more autonomy?

The questions are old, but some of the answers are new. For two decades now, people have been taking the questions seriously because teacher organizations, respected study commissions, and some public officials are serious about making teaching a profession. Part of your job will be helping to find new answers if you take your place among America's teachers in the twenty-first century.

ACTIVITIES

1. Invite representatives of the NEA and AFT to speak to your class about their organizations' similarities and differences. Press them on what the differences really mean at the local level. Ask how they feel about No Child Left Behind.

2. Talk with people who hold a variety of opinions about teacher organizations. Begin with classroom teachers, then expand your interviews to include school administrators, school board

members, parents, labor and business leaders, politicians, officials of the Democratic and Republican parties, and reporters.

3. Attend a collective-bargaining session and a teacher organization's screening session for political candidates.

4. Discuss the concept of professionalism with representatives of the medical association and bar association in your community. Ask them to trace any parallels they see between the professionalization of their occupations and teaching.

RECOMMENDED READINGS

Brimelow, Peter. *The Worm in the Apple: How the Teacher Unions Are Destroying American Education* (New York: HarperCollins, 2003). Brimelow, a true believer in the idea that free-market forces can improve education, will force you to think despite his needlessly mean-spirited tone.

Kerchner, Charles Taylor, Julia E. Koppich, and Joseph G. Weeres. *United Mind Workers: Unions and Teaching in the Knowledge Society* (San Francisco: Jossey-Bass, 1997). "This is a book about teacher unions, not as they are, but as they might be," the authors explain as they chart a course for the new unionism.

Murphy, Marjorie. *Blackboard Unions: The AFT and the NEA, 1900–1980* (Ithaca, NY: Cornell University Press, 1990). A history of teacher unionism as a movement, this study provides an especially good account of the AFT's early years and the NEA's recent transformation into a union.

Peterson, Bob, and Michael Charney, eds. *Transforming Teacher Unions: Fighting for Better Schools and Social Justice* (Milwaukee: Rethinking Schools, 1999). The editors, both of them classroom teachers and union activists, have assembled a set of very readable essays on how unions can help reform schools using an agenda of equity and social justice.

Public Agenda. *Stand by Me: What Teachers Really Think about Unions, Merit Pay and Other Professional Matters* (New York: Public Agenda, 2003). Cited in several chapters of this textbook, this in-depth opinion poll with thoughtful commentary offers a look at unions through teachers' eyes.

Urban, Wayne J. *Why Teachers Organized* (Detroit: Wayne State University Press, 1982). Urban paints a realistic, sympathetic portrait of teachers striving for economic improvement and job security.

NOTES

1. Mark Vona, "Why the Union Endorses," *New York Teacher* (June 2, 2004) [Available: www.nysut.org/newyorkteacher/2003-2004/040602opinion.html].

2. Quoted in Public Agenda, *Stand by Me: What Teachers Really Think about Unions, Merit Pay and Other Professional Matters* (New York: Public Agenda, 2003), p. 18.

3. Bob Peterson and Michael Charney, eds., *Transforming Teacher Unions: Fighting for Better Schools and Social Justice* (Milwaukee: Rethinking Schools, 1999); Peter Brimelow, *The Worm in the Apple: How the Teacher Unions Are Destroying American Education* (New York: HarperCollins, 2003).

4. Erik W. Robelen, "Furor Lingers over Paige's Union Remark," *Education Week* (March 3, 2004), pp. 18–22.

5. For a critical historical study of the two organizations, see Marjorie Murphy's *Blackboard Unions: The AFT and the NEA, 1900–1980* (Ithaca, NY: Cornell University Press, 1990). William Edward Eaton's *The American Federation of Teachers, 1916–1961* (Carbondale, IL: Southern Illinois University Press, 1975) remains the classic account of the AFT. Wayne J. Urban's new history of the NEA is *Gender, Race, and the National Education Association: Professionalism and Its Limits* (New York: Routledge and Falmer, 2000).

6. The two organizations' Web sites—www.nea.org and www.aft.org—provided much of the information for my discussion of their differences. The most recent edition of the *NEA Handbook* (Washington, DC: NEA) and recent issues of the AFT's *American Teacher* magazine are also valuable sources.

7. For a history of the state and local associations that provided the foundation for the NEA's rise to power, see Willard S. Elsbree, *The American Teacher: Evolution of a Profession in a Democracy* (New York: American Book Company, 1939).

8. Michael John Schultz, Jr., *The National Education Association and the Black Teacher: The Integration of a Professional Organization* (Coral Gables, FL: University of Miami Press, 1970); Eaton, *The American Federation of Teachers,* pp. 159–160.

9. Jeff Archer, "NEA: Local Schools Must Address Safety of Gays," *Education Week* (February 20, 2002), p. 3.

10. The Teaching Commission, *Teaching at Risk: A Call to Action* (New York: The Commission, 2004); Reg Weaver, "Solution Isn't That Simple," *USA Today* (June 27, 2004) [Available: www.nea.org/columns/rw040627.html].

11. Public Agenda, *Stand by Me: What Teachers Really Think about Unions, Merit Pay and Other Professional Matters* (New York: Public Agenda, 2003), pp. 24–26.

12. Reg Weaver, "Educators Give Bush 'Incomplete,'" (September 3, 2004) [Available: www.nea.org/newsreleases/2004/nr040903.html].

13. American Federation of Teachers, "No Child Left Behind (NCLB) Act" (2004) [Available: www.aft.org/topics/nclb/index.htm].

14. American Federation of Teachers, "Just for Parents" (2004) [Available: www.aft.org].

15. National Education Association, "Help for Parents: NEA Resources" (2004) [Available: www.nea.org/parents/nearesources-parents.html].

16. Murphy, *Blackboard Unions,* Chap. 11.

17. Ibid., p. 255.

18. Jeff Archer and Ann Bradley, "Despite National Defeat, NEA and AFT Work toward Mergers in States," *Education Week* (August 5, 1998), 1, 18, 20.

19. Jeff Archer, "Unions Cement Partnership to Work on Range of Projects," *Education Week* (August 8, 2001), p. 9; Ann Bradley, "Teachers' Unions to Merge in Two More States," *Education Week* (April 5, 2000), p. 3.

20. Archer, "Unions Cement Partnership," p. 9.

21. Wayne J. Urban, *Gender, Race, and the National Education Association: Professionalism and Its Limitations* (New York: Taylor & Francis, 2001); Urban, *Why Teachers Organized* (Detroit: Wayne State University Press, 1982), Chap. 5.

22. Murphy, *Blackboard Unions,* Chap. 4.

23. Public Agenda, *Stand by Me,* p. 17.

24. Ibid., p. 18.

25. Louis Fischer, David Schimmel, and Leslie R. Stellman, *Teachers and the Law,* 6th ed. (Boston: Allyn & Bacon, 2003), Chap. 4.

26. Eaton, *The American Federation of Teachers,* pp. 161–166; Stephen Cole, *The Unionization of Teachers: A Case Study of the UFT* (New York: Praeger, 1969).

27. See David Hill, "The Education of Al Shanker," *Teacher Magazine* (February 1996), pp. 22–29, and Dickson A. Mungazi, *Where He Stands: Albert Shanker of the American Federation of Teachers* (Westport, CT: Greenwood, 1995).

28. Anthony M. Cresswell and Michael J. Murphy, with Charles T. Kerchner, *Teachers, Unions, and Collective Bargaining in Public Education* (Berkeley, CA: McCutchan, 1980), Chaps. 3–4.

29. Helpful sources of information on the mechanics of bargaining include Roy J. Lewicki, Bruce Barry, David M. Saunders, and John W. Minton, *Essentials of Negotiation,* 3rd ed. (Columbus, OH: McGraw-Hill, 2003); Cresswell and Murphy, *Teachers, Unions, and Collective Bargaining;* and William G. Webster, Sr., *Effective Collective Bargaining in Public Education* (Ames, IA: Iowa State University Press, 1985).

30. Fischer, Schimmel, and Stellman, *Teachers and the Law,* pp. 49–50.

31. Tom Mooney, "Raising Professional Standards," in Peterson and Charney, eds., *Transforming Teacher Unions,* pp. 31–32.

32. Cresswell and Murphy, *Teachers, Unions, and Collective Bargaining,* p. 81.

33. "Teacher Strikes," *Education Week* (September 24, 1984), p. 4.

34. Karen Diegmueller, "Teachers' Strikes Up 36% Amid Signs of Growing Tension," *Education Week* (September 18, 1991), p. 5; Joanna Richardson, "Fewer Teachers Out on Strike This Year Than in Recent Past," *Education Week* (September 7, 1994), p. 18; Ann Zehr, "Philadelphia Strike Reaches End; Others Go On," *Education Week* (September 24, 2003), p. 5.

35. William A. Streshly and Jerry Franklin, *Preventing and Managing Teacher Strikes* (Lanham, MD: Rowman & Littlefield, 2002).

36. Fischer, Schimmel, and Stellman, *Teachers and the Law*, pp. 55–56.

37. A. Wilson, "To Strike or Not to Strike?" *Learning* (October/November 1995), pp. 13–15; Cresswell and Murphy, *Teachers, Unions, and Collective Bargaining*, pp. 341–364.

38. Urban, *Why Teachers Organized*, Chaps. 2–6, discusses the early political involvement of the NEA, AFT, and local teacher organizations in Chicago, New York, and Atlanta.

39. For a case study of political action in one city, see Joseph W. Newman, "A History of the Atlanta Public School Teachers Association, Local 89 of the American Federation of Teachers, 1919–1956" (Ph.D. diss., Georgia State University, 1978).

40. Martin R. Berube, *Teacher Politics: The Influence of Unions* (Westport, CT: Greenwood Press, 1988).

41. Bess Keller, "Teachers' Union Shifts into Campaign Gear," *Education Week* (July 14, 2004), p. 5.

42. Jeff Archer, "Unions Pull Out Stops for Education," *Education Week* (November 1, 2000), p. 31.

43. Erik W. Robelen, "Kerry Aiming for the Center on Education," *Education Week* (August 11, 2004), pp. 1, 34–35.

44. Sean Cavanagh and Michelle R. Davis, "Teachers and Republicans Seek Common Ground in N.Y.C.," *Education Week* (September 8, 2004), p. 36.

45. Association of American Educators, "About Us" (2004) [Available: www.aaeteachers.org/aboutus.htm].

46. Ibid. See also Kentucky Association of Professional Educators, "What Sets Independent Educators Apart?" (2004) [Available: kentuckyteachers.org/page16.shtml].

47. Association of Texas Professional Educators, "ATPE Political Action Committee" (2004) [Available: www.atpe.org/LegisAdv/pac.htm].

48. Charlene K. Haar and Myron Lieberman, *NEA/AFT Membership: The Critical Issues* (Washington, DC: Education Policy Institute, 2000) [Available: www.educationpolicy.org/EPIseries/membership-bklt.htm].

49. See Eliot Freidson, *Professionalism Reborn: Theory, Prophecy, and Policy* (Chicago: University of Chicago Press, 1994); Andrew Abbott, *The System of Professions: An Essay on the Division of Expert Labor* (Chicago: University of Chicago Press, 1988).

50. See Amitai Etzioni, *The Semiprofessions and Their Organizations: Teachers, Nurses, and Social Workers* (New York: Free Press, 1969), and Nigel Malin, *Professionalism, Boundaries, and Workplace* (New York: Routledge, 2000). An often-cited study of teaching is Myron Lieberman's *Education as a Profession* (Englewood Cliffs, NJ: Prentice Hall, 1956).

51. Abbott, *The System of Professions*.

52. U.S. Department of Education, Office of the Under Secretary, *No Child Left Behind: A Toolkit for Teachers* (Washington, DC: USDE, 2003), pp. 19–20.

53. National Commission on Teaching and America's Future, *No Dream Deferred: A Pledge to America's Children* (Washington, DC: The Commission, 2003), p. 23.

54. National Commission on Teaching and America's Future, *What Matters Most: Teaching and America's Future* (New York: The Commission, 1996), p. 15.

55. Ibid., pp. 4–6.

56. Ibid., pp. 6–12.

57. Paul Starr, *The Social Transformation of American Medicine: The Rise of a Sovereign Profession and the Making of a Vast Industry* (New York: Basic Books, 1982); Kenneth M. Ludmerer, *Learning to Heal: The Development of American Medical Education* (New York: Basic Books, 1988); Morris Fishbein, *A History of the American Medical Association, 1847–1947* (Philadelphia: Saunders, 1947).

58. Abraham Flexner, *Medical Education in the United States and Canada* (New York: Carnegie Foundation for the Advancement of Teaching, 1910). For an excellent discussion of these issues, see William R. Johnson, "Empowering Practitioners: Holmes, Carnegie, and the Lessons of History," *History of Education Quarterly* 27 (Summer 1987): 221–240.

59. Charles Taylor Kerchner, Julia E. Koppich, and Joseph G. Weeres, *United Mind Workers: Unions and Teaching in the Knowledge Society* (San Francisco: Jossey-Bass, 1997).

60. Ibid., p. 196.

61. Teacher Education Reform Network, "TURN Locals" (2004) [Available: www.turnexchange.net/web/members.htm].

62. Teacher Education Reform Network, "Mission Statement" (2004) [Available: www.turnexchange.net/about.htm].

63. Adam Urbanski and Roger Erskine, "School Reform, TURN, and Teacher Compensation," *Phi Delta Kappan* 81 (January 2000): 367.

64. Gerald Grant and Christine E. Murray, *Teaching in America: The Slow Revolution* (Cambridge, MA: Harvard University Press, 1999).

65. Marilyn Scannell and Judith Wain, "New Models for State Licensing of Professional Educators," *Phi Delta Kappan* 78 (November 1996): 211–214.

66. Blake Rodman, "Nevada Creates 'Teacher Dominated' Licensing Board," *Education Week* (August 4, 1987), p. 7.

67. Arthur E. Wise, "On Teacher Quality: A Hard-Won System Begins to Pay Off," *Education Week* (May 19, 1999), pp. 68, 45; National Commission on Teaching and America's Future, *No Dream Deferred*, p. 24.

68. National Commission on Teaching and America's Future, *What Matters Most*, pp. 146–147.

69. Blake Rodman, "N.E.A. Pursues Its Plan"; Ann Bradley, "N.E.A. Assails Board's Policy on Prerequisites for Certification," *Education Week* (January 17, 1990), pp. 1, 11.

70. See the "central policy statement" of the National Board for Professional Teaching Standards, *What Teachers Should Know and Be Able to Do* [Available: www.nbpts.org/nbpts/standards].

71. Rodman, "Nevada Creates 'Teacher-Dominated' Licensing Board."

72. Carnegie Forum on Education and the Economy, *A Nation Prepared: Teachers for the 21st Century. A Report of the Task Force on Teaching as a Profession* (New York: Carnegie Forum, 1986); The Teaching Commission, *Teaching at Risk: A Call to Action* (New York: The Commission, 2004).

73. John J. Lane and Edgar G. Epps, eds., *Restructuring the Schools: Problems and Prospects* (Berkeley, CA: McCutchan, 1992).

74. This case study is based on Grant and Murray, *Teaching in America*, Chap. 7; Christine E. Murray, "Teaching as a Profession: The Rochester Case in Historical Perspective," *Harvard Educational Review* 62 (Winter 1992): 494–518; and Julia Koppich, Carla Asher, and Charles Kerchner, *Developing Careers, Building a Profession: The Rochester Career in Teaching Plan* (New York: National Commission on Teaching and America's Future, 2002).

75. Koppich, Asher, and Kerchner, *Developing Careers, Building a Profession*.

76. Public Agenda, *Stand by Me*, pp. 17–19, 33–35. Christine E. Murray, "Exploring the 'New' Unionism," paper presented to the Special Interest Group on Teachers' Work and Teachers' Unions, American Educational Research Association, New Orleans (April 25, 2000).

77. See Linda Darling-Hammond, Arthur E. Wise, and Stephen P. Klein, *A License to Teach: Building a Profession for the 21st Century* (Boulder, CO: Westview, 1995).

78. Arthur E. Wise, "A Case for Trusting Teachers to Regulate Their Profession," *Education Week* (October 8, 1986), p. 24; Wise, "States Must Create Teaching Standards Boards," *Education Week* (January 11, 1989), p. 48.

CHAPTER 5

EXERCISING YOUR RIGHTS AND FULFILLING YOUR RESPONSIBILITIES

Tenure makes it impossible to fire a bad teacher. Everybody knows that.
—Alabama teacher[1]

I've watched our principal now for the last three years take an awful lot of heat. We have gotten rid of two totally incompetent, very divisive teachers and are now dealing with another. I'm sympathetic, because I'm one of the many that's affected by the poor job that's being done there.
—Missouri teacher[2]

Teachers need to know where they stand with the law. Teachers who know their legal rights and responsibilities can put some of their doubts and fears to rest. No, the law is not so complex it is impossible to understand. No, there isn't a lawyer lurking around every corner, waiting to file suit against you. Much of the legal paranoia teachers share with other Americans is simply a fear of the unknown. By the time you reach the end of this chapter, I hope you will feel a sense of relief from knowing more about your rights and responsibilities in three areas: *employment, liability,* and *expression.*

On the other hand, becoming more familiar with school law should also give you a greater sense of caution. When we discuss employment, for instance, you will see teacher tenure is not the ironclad guarantee to a lifetime job it is reputed to be. In the area of liability, one of the issues we will examine is the teacher and AIDS, and you may be surprised to learn what your responsibilities are concerning students who have the disease. When we discuss expression, you will find that although academic freedom protects teachers, the protection has limits.

Throughout this chapter, you will see the law is a double-edged sword. It gives teachers rights to exercise. It also gives them responsibilities to fulfill.

This chapter is not the only one that involves school law. Collective bargaining, teacher testing, merit pay—these are only three of the issues in the preceding chapters that illustrate the influence of law on teaching as an occupation. In Part II, the spotlight is on students more often than teachers, and the law helps illuminate such issues as school desegregation, bilingual education, and gender equity. The focus of Chapter 9 is the political arena in which the law originates. The debates we will examine in Part III also involve legal questions. Who should control the curriculum? Should the government regulate private schools? Every chapter in *America's Teachers* shows the influence of school law.

EMPLOYMENT

Contracts

When you get your first teaching job, you will sign a *contract* with a local school board. A contract is a legally binding agreement, a statement of the rights and responsibilities of both parties, the teacher and the board. A contract typically specifies such things as salary, grade level or subject area, and length of school day and school year. A contract also obligates the teacher and the board to follow state school laws, state board of education policies, and local board regulations. In school districts with collective bargaining, the contract binds both parties to the master contract the teacher organization and the board have negotiated. Most teachers sign annual contracts, although some work under continuing contracts that remain in effect until either party gives notice of intent to change the agreement.[3]

Read your contract carefully. You may want to discuss it with an official of the local teacher organization, because lawyers retained by the organization have almost certainly scrutinized the document, just as the school board's attorneys have.

Tenure

In most states, teachers have the protection of *tenure*, which is a status of protected employment granted to teachers after satisfactory service during a probationary period. While teachers are on probation (typically for three years), it is easy for school boards to dismiss them. After teachers receive tenure, dismissal is difficult. Our discussion of tenure will emphasize the nature of the protection it affords.

Tenure laws are controversial, and they are coming under attack in states and school districts throughout the nation. Does tenure protect good teaching? Or shield incompetence? It is impossible to understand the pros and cons of tenure without knowing its history.

Public school teachers campaigned for the passage of tenure laws in the early 1900s, stressing their need for protection from "petty political and social attacks." That teachers were vulnerable is a real understatement. State school laws allowed local boards to fire teachers at will by simply not renewing their contracts. Teachers lost their jobs because of administrative whim, political patronage, social prejudice, and religious intolerance. In most states, dismissed teachers received neither a statement of the charges against them nor an opportunity to defend themselves at a hearing. They were simply out of work and out of luck.[4]

Teacher organizations took the case for tenure to the public and the state legislatures. Flagrant miscarriages of justice often tipped the balance of opinion in the teachers' favor: teachers who were dismissed for having the "wrong" religion or supporting the "wrong" political party; those who were fired for discussing a controversial issue from several points of view rather than just the "right" one; those who lost their jobs because they smoked or drank in public (or even in private). Citing examples like these to dramatize the case for tenure, teachers argued they deserved the same kind of protection from arbitrary dismissal that civil service laws gave to other government employees.

After the District of Columbia passed a teacher tenure law in 1906 and New Jersey followed suit three years later, the quest for job security gradually spread across the nation. Supported by the NEA, AFT, and independent state teacher organizations, teachers in city school systems led the tenure campaigns. By 1937, seventeen states had passed some form of tenure legislation. Most of the early tenure laws applied just to urban teachers, but during the 1940s and 1950s, state legislatures extended tenure to rural teachers as well.

Think of tenure laws as a bargain struck between teachers and local school boards. Tenure allows the boards to dismiss teachers for almost any reason during the probationary period, but after that the boards must have a very good reason. As part of the bargain, tenure laws leave teachers vulnerable while they are on probation. They are literally on trial.

The future teachers in my classes often feel uneasy when they learn school boards can dismiss an untenured teacher simply by not offering a new contract. In most states, the untenured teacher is entitled to no explanation and no hearing—and, of course, no further employment. I remind my students that this sense of insecurity is exactly what *all* teachers, twenty-five-year veterans and beginners, felt without tenure. Even untenured teachers who can prove their dismissal violates federal or state law because it was based on race or sex, for example, can win back their jobs if they are willing to go to court. All teachers, tenured or not, enjoy a wide range of rights under the U.S. Constitution, especially the First Amendment with its guarantee of free speech and the Fourteenth Amendment with its guarantee of due process and equal protection of the laws.

Dismissal

Tenure does not give absolute job security to any teacher. It does, however, put the burden on the school board to prove a tenured teacher unfit for further employment. In most states, the local board must prove a tenured teacher guilty of one of the "three *i*'s": incompetence, insubordination, or immorality. Some states add the *u* of unprofessional conduct or even broader grounds, such as "good and just cause."

Incompetence is the inability to perform the job the contract calls for. To prove a teacher incompetent, school officials must show a pattern of behavior, a clear record of failure. In dismissal cases that reach the court system, charges of incompetence most often center on a teacher's inability to maintain classroom discipline. As we saw in Chapter 3, incompetence can also be the inability to speak or write grammatically, or it can be a lack of subject-matter knowledge. Incompetence can stem from a physical or mental condition—impaired hearing or mental illness—that renders the teacher incapable of effective work. The mere existence of a disability is not proof of incompetence. The board must produce evidence the teacher cannot perform adequately. In most dismissal cases, teachers face charges of not one but several kinds of incompetence—a "collapse of performance."[5]

Insubordination is the willful violation of reasonable rules or the deliberate defiance of school officials. A reasonable rule, according to the courts, is one that officials have the authority to issue, that is clear enough to be understood, and that does not violate a teacher's constitutional rights. In cases involving alleged defiance of school officials, the courts often look for a pattern of behavior rather than a single incident. When a tenured teacher consistently refuses to comply with reasonable requests from a principal or supervisor, for instance, the courts are likely to rule in favor of dismissal.[6]

Although definitions of *immorality* vary from community to community and change from time to time, the courts have narrowed the range of immoral conduct that can deprive tenured teachers of their jobs. In general, the conduct must interfere with a teacher's effectiveness before it can become grounds for dismissal. In *Morrison v. State Board of Education* (1969), a landmark case involving a gay teacher, the California Supreme Court ruled "an individual can be removed from the teaching profession only upon a showing that his retention in the profession poses a significant danger of harm to either students, school employees, or others who might be affected by his actions as a teacher." The courts usually distinguish between public and private conduct, and they usually protect what adults do in private. But when a teacher's private conduct becomes a matter of public controversy that spills over into the classroom and impairs his or her effectiveness, the courts generally support dismissal. Moreover, immoral conduct involving teachers and their students—a sexual relationship, for instance, or the use of alcohol or other drugs—is a sure ticket out of the occupation. We will return to the issues of lifestyle and other forms of personal expression in the last section of this chapter.[7]

Another category of immorality in teacher tenure law is *sexual harassment*, which is defined as "any type of sexual behavior or advance that is *unwanted* or *unwelcomed*." In *School Law and the Public Schools* (2005), Nathan Essex points out that harassment can take the form of verbal behavior, such as sexual comments; nonverbal behavior, such as facial expressions or gestures; sexual coercion based on the difference in power between the teacher and the victim; and unwanted touching. Regardless of whom a teacher harasses—a student, another teacher, a staff member, or anyone else—sexual harassment constitutes grounds for dismissal, and victims can also sue for damages under Title VII or Title IX of the Civil Rights Act of 1964.[8]

The term *unprofessional conduct* is disturbingly vague, yet the courts have sometimes upheld the dismissal of tenured teachers on these and other broad grounds. The courts have reasoned that because society entrusts teachers with the important responsibility of working with young people, which calls into play numerous personal qualities ranging from "cleanliness" to "wisdom and propriety," school boards must have considerable discretion to determine who is fit for the task. In some cases, the courts have interpreted unprofessional to mean immoral; in other cases, unprofessional has been construed as unethical. The latter interpretation presents special problems because teaching's two most prominent statements of ethics, the NEA's Code of Ethics and the AFT's Bill of Rights, have no legal standing. Even so, the courts have upheld the dismissal of teachers who use their classrooms for activities other than teaching, such as urging students to support a particular political candidate. The courts have also allowed the dismissal of "uncooperative" teachers. *Unprofessional conduct* and similar phrases are the catchalls of tenure law.[9]

In addition to the three *i*'s and the *u*, tenured teachers can lose their jobs as a result of reduction in force, or "riffing." When enrollment in a school district falls sharply, when a district decides to reorganize its curriculum for economic reasons, or when a financial crisis makes severe budget cuts necessary, school boards can dismiss tenured as well as untenured teachers. Seniority usually dictates which jobs go first. Although riffing has been relatively rare, it posed a threat to teachers during the tax- and budget-cutting era of the late 1970s and early 1980s, and it made a comeback in the uncertain economic times of the early 1990s.[10]

Due Process

Teachers have the same right to *due process* that the Fourteenth Amendment guarantees to all citizens. Because of the Fourteenth Amendment, no state can "deprive any person of life, liberty, or property, without due process of law." Tenure gives teachers a "property interest" in their jobs, the U.S. Supreme Court ruled in *Board of Regents v. Roth* (1972), because tenure gives them a "legitimate claim of entitlement" to continuing employment. In a sense, tenured teachers *own* their jobs. If attempts to dismiss teachers damage their reputation or reduce their chances of finding other employment, teachers may also have a "liberty interest" in their positions.[11]

When school boards try to deprive teachers of jobs in which, because of tenure, they have property or liberty interests, teachers can exercise their rights to due process. In *Goldberg v. Kelly* (1970) and other cases, the U.S. Supreme Court has ruled due process rights include a statement of charges, sufficient time to prepare a defense, a hearing before a fair tribunal (usually the local school board), representation by legal counsel, the opportunity to present evidence and cross-examine witnesses, a transcript of the hearing, and appeal of adverse rulings.[12]

"Ever Try to Flunk a Bad Teacher?" This article in the July 20, 1998, issue of *Time* suggests—and none too subtly—that trying to dismiss a tenured teacher can be expensive and time consuming. Considered by itself, this fact of life in public schools makes tenure unpopular with many Americans. Attacks on tenure are increasing in both frequency and bitterness as a climate of downsizing and anti-unionism spills over from the business world. A prime example is *The Excuse Factory: How Employment Law Is Paralyzing the American Workplace* (1997). This book is part of conservative writer Walter Olson's ongoing campaign to discredit teacher tenure along with employment safeguards in other lines of work.[13]

Taking aim directly at teachers in *The New York Times* and other popular media, Olson praises the "anti-tenure momentum" he sees in state capitals. Indeed, the momentum that built in Oregon, South Dakota, New York, Florida, and other states during the 1990s carried through into the twenty-first century as Georgia eliminated tenure in 2001, joining Texas and Mississippi on the list of states with no tenure laws. More typically, other state legislatures have been streamlining the hearing and appeal process, a change the NEA and AFT find easier to accept.[14]

"Revise Teacher Tenure Law and Give Students a Break," an editorial in the *Detroit News* (January 11, 2004), reflects the sentiment that keeps the antitenure campaign rolling.[15] Articles and editorials in *U.S. News & World Report* and other popular magazines carry the same message. Tenure and due process rights have gone too far, and as a result, "bad teaching is not only tolerated but often safeguarded to an extent that leaves principals gnashing their teeth and parents in despair." School boards can anticipate steep legal expenses in dismissal proceedings, costs that can climb to several hundred thousand dollars in exceptional cases. To be sure, the NEA and AFT usually pay the legal fees of their tenured members whose jobs come under

■ ■ ■ ■ ■

BOX 5.1

"TENURE MAKES THIS 'MISSION IMPOSSIBLE'"

Some of the sharpest criticism of teacher tenure comes from activist organizations on the political right. Read the Eagle Forum's viewpoint at www.eagleforum.org/educate/1998/dec98/teachers.html

■ ■ ■ ■ ■

BOX 5.2

"TEACHER VS. TEACHER? NO WAY!"

Former NEA President Bob Chase explained why teacher unions now support peer assistance and review on the NEA's Web site at www.nea.org/neatoday/9711/presview.html

fire. Without question, teacher organizations make it more difficult for school boards to dismiss tenured teachers.[16]

Trying to refocus public attention on larger historical and constitutional issues, the NEA and AFT are attempting to show why such a degree of job security is necessary. As Keith Geiger, former president of the NEA, explains, "Tenure doesn't protect incompetent teachers; it protects competent teachers from unfair practices and dismissals." Union officials remind the public that teachers, like all citizens, are innocent until proven guilty.[17]

Local school boards win most of the dismissal cases that go to court—a fact tenure critics often neglect to point out—yet very few cases even reach the hearing stage before a local board. Unwilling to spend time and money on dismissal proceedings, many administrators and board members simply tolerate tenured teachers they know to be unfit for the classroom. Parents become incensed, and rightly so, when principals claim their hands are tied because of tenure laws. Some principals transfer unfit teachers from school to school—a game called "pass the turkey" or the "dance of the lemons" in the literature on tenure.[18]

Other principals take more constructive approaches. One is remediation: trying to help teachers improve. Assistance from other teachers often proves helpful, which makes the peer evaluation and peer intervention programs we considered in Chapters 2 and 4 seem very promising. It is encouraging that the NEA and AFT are showing more willingness than ever to help police the ranks of the occupation.[19]

If remediation fails, the principal can try confrontation. After observing an inadequate teacher and compiling a thick folder of evidence, the principal can confront the teacher with stacks of evaluation forms, dated observations, complaints from parents, and so forth. The object is to convince the teacher that resignation is a better option than a dismissal hearing and possible court battle. And if confrontation fails, the principal can take the folder of evidence to a superior and press for a dismissal hearing.[20]

Cutting through all the rhetoric about tenure as a shield for incompetence, we can see administrators have options. They can do *something*. As North Carolina's former state superintendent of schools candidly admitted, "Tenure itself may not be the barrier—the barrier in many instances may be the unwillingness of school leaders to confront unpleasant tasks associated with dealing with performance problems."[21] The laws outline grounds for dismissal, and it is the responsibility of administrators, admittedly an unpleasant and demanding one, to see unfit teachers do not remain in the classroom. It's a tough job, but somebody has to do it.

LIABILITY

A student falls in the classroom and breaks an arm. Several students come to school showing signs of child abuse and neglect. Parents confide in a teacher that their child has tested positive for HIV, the virus that causes AIDS. Despite a teacher's best efforts, some students learn very little. What are the rights and responsibilities of teachers in each of these situations? Can teachers be sued and held liable for failing to fulfill their responsibilities? In the excellent guidebook *Teachers and the Law* (2003), Louis Fischer, David Schimmel, and Leslie Stellman provide some answers.

Injuries to Students

According to Fischer, Schimmel, and Stellman, a student who is hurt while under a teacher's care must prove four things in order to hold the teacher liable for the injury:

1. The teacher had a duty to be careful not to injure the student and to protect the student from being injured.
2. The teacher failed to use due care.
3. The teacher's carelessness caused the injury.
4. The student sustained provable damages.[22]

In most injury cases that go to court, there is little question the teacher had a duty to care for the student, and there is little question the student sustained monetary damages. There may be questions about the cause of the injury. But the real dispute usually centers on the second requirement. Did the teacher fail in her or his duty of care and thereby act in a negligent manner?

The courts place great emphasis on the concept of *reasonable care,* "the degree of care a teacher of ordinary prudence" would exercise.[23] Take the example of a student who falls and breaks an arm in a teacher's classroom. Court proceedings would probably revolve around several key questions. Was the teacher in the room at the time of the injury? Unless the teacher had an excellent reason not to be, his or her absence in itself could increase the chances of being found liable. Could the teacher have foreseen the accident? Could the teacher have taken steps to prevent the accident? If the accident happened unpredictably—if the student simply lost balance and fell—the teacher would probably have little to worry about in court. But if the student slipped on water, for instance, or tripped over a wire, there would be further questions about whether the teacher had made a reasonable effort to remove the hazards or keep the students away. Did the student fall while running? If so, did the teacher make a reasonable effort to stop the running? Questions like these help the court decide whether the teacher was negligent.

The teacher's attorney would certainly want at least one more question answered: Did the student's own negligence contribute to the injury? Depending on the age and maturity of the student, an affirmative answer could partially or completely clear the teacher. Depending on state laws, a judge or jury could compare the negligence of the teacher with that of the student and award damages accordingly.[24]

Teachers should know they can be held liable for injuries occurring outside as well as inside the classroom. Teachers who provide transportation for students to field trips, athletic events, debate tournaments, and the like are taking a risk, and the permission slips, waivers, and covenants not to sue that parents sign usually do not protect teachers from negligence suits. Regardless of what the piece of paper says, the courts generally allow an injured student to sue.[25]

Teachers can reduce their risk with liability insurance. They should find out how much coverage (if any) they have through their school district's policy. Does the policy cover teachers in the classroom? Does it protect them while they are supervising extracurricular activities? Does it cover transporting students in a private automobile? A major benefit of membership in the AFT or NEA is being able to buy low-cost liability insurance designed especially for teachers. While it is possible to be overinsured, it is wise for a teacher to have personal liability insurance to supplement whatever protection the district's policy provides.

Abused and Neglected Children

The National Child Abuse Prevention and Treatment Act of 1974 (P.L. 93-247) defines child abuse and neglect as

> physical or mental injury, sexual abuse or exploitation, negligent treatment, or maltreatment of a child under the age of eighteen or the age specified under the child protection law of the state in question, by a person who is responsible for the child's welfare, under circumstances which indicate that the child's health or welfare is harmed or threatened thereby.[26]

According to estimates from the National Center on Child Abuse Prevention Research, more than three million children are abused or neglected each year. Reports of abuse and neglect have increased between 30 and 40 percent since the late 1980s, when intensive studies and record keeping began. Most cases still go unreported. Looking just at sexual abuse, Prevent Child Abuse America estimates that "at least 20% of American women and 5–16% of American men experienced some form of sexual abuse as children." Many researchers believe the vast majority of sexual abuse cases are not reported. Teachers at every grade level should be alert to abuse and neglect.[27]

Statistics only hint at the human dimensions of the problem, but at least they can put teachers on notice they are *likely* to have abused and neglected children in their classrooms. Studies commissioned by Prevent Child Abuse America find 37 percent of American parents report insulting or cursing at their children within a twelve-month period. Fifty percent of parents report neglecting their children emotionally, with 60 percent of those parents admitting the neglect occurs "almost every day." The top four problems caseworkers discover in abusive and neglectful families are substance abuse, poverty and financial strain, poor parenting skills, and domestic violence.[28]

■ ■ ■ ■ ■

BOX 5.3

PREVENT CHILD ABUSE AMERICA

To get more information on child abuse and neglect, visit the Web site of Prevent Child Abuse America at www.preventchildabuse.org

Neglect and abuse can haunt their victims throughout their lives. Adults who suffered maltreatment as children are more likely to become addicted to alcohol and other drugs, more likely to spend time in prison, and—most tragically—more likely to become abusive and neglectful parents themselves.[29]

The laws of every state require teachers to report suspected cases of child abuse and neglect. Every state grants teachers who make such reports immunity from civil and criminal suits. State laws vary in their requirements, and you should become familiar with the laws where you teach. Most states require an oral report to an administrator followed by a written statement. Let me stress the law will protect teachers who act in good faith. Teachers should not hesitate to file a report if they believe a student is a victim of abuse or neglect. In most states teachers can be fined or imprisoned if they do *not* make the report, and in some states they can be sued for negligence.[30]

Table 5.1 presents some of the physical and behavioral indicators of abuse and neglect. The table lists some of the more common indicators, but it is not exhaustive, nor are the categories mutually exclusive. Physical abuse and sexual abuse, for instance, can be so traumatic they produce some of the indicators shown under emotional abuse. Please keep in mind that these indicators only suggest the possibility of abuse or neglect. They do not prove anything improper has occurred.

A teacher who sees a student exhibit several of these indicators over a period of time should think seriously about why the indicators are present. As in other areas of the law, the *reasonable person* standard applies: Under similar circumstances, would a reasonable person suspect abuse or neglect? If your answer is yes, you should make a report. Remember, the law will protect you if you act in good faith. Please do not be blind to the problem.[31]

The Teacher and AIDS/HIV

How schools should respond to Acquired Immune Deficiency Syndrome (AIDS) is an important issue. Almost every state mandates some form of AIDS education, and many teachers—certainly not just high school biology teachers—have a role in providing students information about the disease.[32]

Because of the highly charged controversies surrounding AIDS, some states and local school boards issue detailed teaching guides that tell teachers what to say, what not to say, and how to answer student questions. Should a teacher

TABLE 5.1   Indicators of Child Abuse and Neglect

PHYSICAL INDICATORS	BEHAVIORAL INDICATORS
Physical Abuse and Neglect	
Bruises, welts, cuts, fractures, or burns	Complaints about harsh treatment
Pain	Poor school attendance
Unattended medical or dental problems	Chronic fatigue, listlessness, or drowsiness
Lagging physical development	Sudden behavioral changes
Hunger	Fear of going home
Poor hygiene	Running away from home
Inappropriate dress	Use of alcohol or other drugs
Emotional Abuse and Neglect	
Speech disorders	Habit disorders (biting, sucking, or rocking)
	Conduct disorders (destructive or antisocial behavior)
Neurotic traits (obsession, compulsion, or inhibited play)	
Lagging mental and emotional development	
	Suicide attempts
Sexual Abuse	
Stained or bloody underclothes	Unusual or sophisticated sexual knowledge or behavior
Difficulty walking or sitting	
Pain, itching, bruises, or bleeding in genital or anal area	Withdrawal
	Frequent fantasies
Sexually transmitted diseases	Very childish or very adult behavior
Pregnancy	

Sources: Prevent Child Abuse America, "Recognize the Warning Signs" (2002) [Available: www.preventchildabuse.org/help/recognize_warning_signs.html]; Dennis L. Cates, Marc A. Markell, and Sherrie Bettenhausen, "At Risk for Abuse: A Teacher's Guide for Recognizing and Reporting Child Abuse," *Preventing School Failure* (Winter 1995): 7; Louis Fischer, David Schimmel, and Leslie R. Stellman, *Teachers and the Law,* 6th ed. (Boston: Allyn and Bacon, 2003), pp. 97–98.

mention the word *condom* to a class of fifth graders, or should the teacher suggest only sexual abstinence? In how much detail should a teacher describe the sexual acts that can transmit the disease? AIDS guidelines vary from state to state and district to district, and they raise academic freedom issues we will consider in the last section of this chapter. Teachers should be familiar with the state and local AIDS policies applicable to them.[33]

Of greater emotional as well as legal concern for teachers is the issue of how to deal with students who have contracted the Human Immunodeficiency Virus (HIV), which causes AIDS. What should a teacher do after learning a student has tested positive? Many teachers are concerned they could be sued for negligence for not reporting a student with the virus or, on the other hand, sued for invasion of privacy or infliction of emotional distress for making a report.

Medical facts about AIDS shape judicial opinion. An excellent source of medical information for teachers as well as students is the brochure *AIDS and HIV: Are You at Risk?* (2003) from the Centers for Disease Control and Prevention (CDC). All teachers should know people contract HIV in two main ways: having unprotected sexual intercourse (vaginal, anal, and possibly oral) and sharing hypodermic needles. HIV can also be transmitted through transfusions of contaminated blood and by contact between mother and child during pregnancy, during birth, and possibly through breast-feeding. One of the few positive things about HIV is that it is difficult to contract; people do not become infected through casual contact. It should be most encouraging to teachers that there are no documented cases in which a student has contracted the virus through ordinary activity in the classroom.[34]

Teachers should also know that AIDS is progressive and, at present, incurable, even though people can live for years with the disease. HIV carriers may not realize they have been infected for up to ten years or even longer—until the first symptoms of an impaired immune system appear. Based on a classification system developed by the Centers for Disease Control and Prevention, people infected with HIV are considered to have AIDS when certain T-lymphocyte cell counts in their blood fall below a specified level, indicating suppressed immunity. Physicians also look for the presence of AIDS-indicator diseases such as lymphoma and recurrent pneumonia. More than half of all persons who have been diagnosed with AIDS have died.[35]

According to the CDC, reported cases of AIDS decreased or remained stable during the late 1990s and into the early 2000s, as did reported deaths from AIDS. In 2002, however, reported cases of AIDS reversed this trend and registered their first increase since 1992. Seventy-four percent of those diagnosed with AIDS from 1998 through 2002 were male, reflecting a long-established pattern, although the number of reported cases increased among females and decreased among males. Males were most often exposed through homosexual contact and females through heterosexual contact. The incidence of AIDS increased among African Americans—by far, the hardest hit racial/ethnic group—and also among Asian Americans and Native Americans. Although AIDS decreased among young children, it increased sharply among teenagers.[36]

HIV trends are often forerunners of trends in AIDS. Reported cases of HIV infection increased from 1998 to 2002, which could signal a continuing upswing in AIDS. Males accounted for 71 percent of the new HIV cases. The number of diagnoses increased among males, who tended to contract HIV through gay sex, and remained stable among females, who were usually exposed through heterosexual activity. Whites, Hispanic Americans, and Asian Americans showed increases in reported cases of HIV. Within the K–12 age cohort, the trends were a decrease among young children and an increase among teenagers.[37]

Which students are at the greatest risk? The National Commission on AIDS offers this thought-provoking answer: "HIV infection is not about who you are,

■ ■ ■ ■ ■

BOX 5.4

CDC

For the latest information on AIDS/HIV, visit the Centers for Disease Control and Prevention online at www.cdc.gov/hiv

but rather about what you do."[38] The message hits home with me. While I was revising this section for the third edition of *America's Teachers,* my community was trying to come to grips with a morning newspaper headline that read, "Small Town Rocked by Big-City Problem: HIV." A clean-cut 18-year-old football player in a private school located just outside my metropolitan area tested HIV-positive. His neighbors, residents of a rural county that had almost no experience with AIDS, found themselves "struggling with a dose of modern reality."[39] The reality, according to the National Commission on AIDS, is *any* person from *any* background who engages in unprotected sex or injects drugs runs the risk of contracting HIV.

Nevertheless, the commission has developed the category "youth in high-risk situations" to call attention to the social and economic context of AIDS. The high-risk category includes young people who

> have hemophilia or other coagulation diseases, have run away or been rejected by their family, are homeless, are incarcerated, use alcohol and other drugs or are the sexual partners of those who do, have dropped out of school or attend school only sporadically, are gay, lesbian, or bisexual, are survivors of sexual abuse, or have recently immigrated to the United States. The list must also include some larger categories, such as certain racial/ethnic groups (including African American and Hispanic/Latino youth in most inner cities and Native American youth), young women, and youth in smaller and rural communities.[40]

Based on medical evidence, the courts are generally ruling that students who have AIDS can come to school. Judges are applying to HIV carriers Section 504 of the Rehabilitation Act of 1973:

> No otherwise handicapped individual in the United States . . . shall, solely by reason of his handicap, be excluded from participation in, be denied the benefits of, or be subjected to discrimination under any program or activity receiving Federal financial assistance.[41]

Students who test HIV-positive are also protected by P.L. 94–142, enacted in 1975 as the Education of All Handicapped Children Act (see Chapter 9) and now retitled the Individuals with Disabilities Education Act (IDEA).[42]

The courts sometimes allow school districts to isolate or exclude, on a case-by-case basis, student HIV carriers whose condition or behavior—biting or drooling, for instance—*might* pose a "significant risk" to others. The word *might* is appropriate because, again, HIV is difficult to contract. The CDC brochure *HIV and Its Transmission* (2003) offers the reassurance that "contact with saliva, tears, or sweat has never been shown to result in transmission of HIV." It bears repeating that there are no documented cases in which a student has passed the virus to a classmate through casual contact.[43]

Section 504 of the Rehabilitation Act of 1973 also covers teachers who test HIV-positive. Unless a school district can show their condition impairs their performance in the classroom, teachers cannot be dismissed because they have contracted the virus. The courts have stressed there is no medical evidence of "any appreciable risk of transmitting the AIDS virus under the circumstances likely to occur in the ordinary school setting."[44]

Who needs to know when a student with AIDS/HIV comes to school? To answer this question, the courts have to weigh the student's right to privacy against the public's right to information. The verdict is clear. The student's right to privacy, which is protected by the Family Educational Rights and Privacy Act (1974) and the Education of All Handicapped Children Act (1975), prevails. These federal laws allow the release of medical information on a student to qualified persons—to a teacher, principal, or school nurse, for example—only to protect health and safety. In the absence of a threat to health and safety, information on a student's medical condition is strictly confidential.[45]

In light of the legal obligations to educate and protect all students, many school districts form special teams to make case-by-case decisions about students who have contracted HIV. Such teams often consist of a student's doctor, a doctor representing the school board, a public health officer, the school nurse, and the student's teacher(s). After reviewing information on the student's medical condition and behavior, the team makes a recommendation to the superintendent on whether the student should remain in school and whether anyone else needs to know he or she carries the virus.[46]

What school systems try to avoid is the public uproar that can occur if a student's condition becomes widely known. A teacher who breaches a parent's confidence and leaks information about an infected student can start a chain of events that can force the student out of school—the law and the courts notwithstanding. In addition to inviting a lawsuit, the teacher's action can discourage other parents and students from coming forward with information about the illness.[47]

Many school districts have developed policies on how teachers should report AIDS cases. Find out whether your district has a policy and, if so, what it provides. In the absence of a clear policy, a confidential report to the principal is probably the teacher's safest course of action.

AIDS policies in school districts, like court decisions on the disease, are relatively new and still evolving. One of the greatest challenges is convincing students the disease can strike heterosexuals and females—not just gay males. The Internet box on page 162 and the Recommended Readings at the end of the chapter list several good sources of information, including a catalog of education and prevention materials from the CDC National AIDS Clearinghouse.[48]

Educational Malpractice

Malpractice suits against physicians are common. The soaring cost of malpractice insurance is prompting some physicians to raise their fees, change their specialties, even leave the profession. Teachers face the same kinds of lawsuits, although far less often. Some parents have argued that just as teachers can be held liable for physical injuries to students under their care, they should also be liable for mental injuries—that is, for educational malpractice. Two precedent-setting cases raise issues teachers need to consider, issues we have examined in a different light in other chapters.

The most famous case, *Peter W. v. San Francisco Unified School District* (1976), involved a young man who sued the San Francisco public schools because he graduated from high school with only a fifth-grade reading level. Peter produced evidence in court that his IQ scores were at least average and that teachers and administrators had informed his mother on numerous occasions he was making adequate progress in school. Peter claimed the school system had acted negligently by giving him inadequate teachers, assigning him to inappropriate reading groups, and socially promoting him from one grade to the next. The system's negligence had damaged him, he charged, by reducing his chances of finding a job.[49]

When weighing Peter's claim of negligence, the judge considered the lack of an agreed-on knowledge base in education, an issue we discussed in Chapters 3 and 4. By what standard could he find the school system negligent, the judge wondered, when the "science of pedagogy itself is fraught with different and conflicting theories of how or what should be taught?"[50]

The judge ran into a further problem when he looked for a link between teacher behavior and student achievement. He concluded student achievement is "influenced by a host of factors which affect the pupil subjectively, from outside the teaching process," such factors as the home, the media, and an assortment of "physical, neurological, emotional, cultural, [and] environmental" forces. How could anyone isolate the influence of teachers—indeed, of schools—and hold them responsible for a student's reading ability? This question, of course, is one we asked about teacher evaluation in Chapter 2.[51]

The judge rejected Peter's claim, adding that a ruling in the student's favor would encourage countless other lawsuits of the same kind and place an impossible burden on schools and society. Peter W.'s lawsuit was an attempt to force accountability with a vengeance, and the judge turned it back.

Another case, *Hoffman v. Board of Education of the City of New York* (1979), appeared to have a better chance of succeeding. Danny Hoffman entered kindergarten with a severe speech defect. Scoring seventy-four on an IQ test emphasizing verbal skills, Danny was placed in a class for mentally disabled students. Even though the school psychologist who administered the test recommended retesting within two years, stating the child "obviously understands more than he is able to communicate," the school system never retested Danny. He graduated from high school after spending eleven years in classes for mentally disabled students.[52]

At age eighteen, Danny took an intelligence test required by the Social Security Administration. Because he scored in the normal range, he lost both his Social

Security benefits and his eligibility for rehabilitation training. At that point, Danny sued the New York public schools for negligence. He charged the school system with a serious error, a mistake that had damaged him intellectually and psychologically. A lower court ruled in Danny's favor, awarding him $750,000 (later reduced to $500,000) in damages. The lower court regarded *Hoffman*, unlike *Peter W.*, as a case of clearcut malpractice.[53]

The New York Court of Appeals reversed the decision. By a 4-to-3 margin, the justices ruled the courts cannot second-guess schools on academic matters. A court of law is not the appropriate place to question the "professional judgment of educators," the majority wrote. Instead, students and parents who are unhappy with educational decisions can use the educational appeals process provided by state school laws.[54]

Peter W. and *Hoffman* established precedents other courts have followed, with very few exceptions, in educational malpractice suits from the 1980s through the 2000s. But will the precedents remain in place? The mounting pressure for accountability and the increasing willingness of courts to question the judgment of physicians, lawyers, and other professionals may yet make it possible for educational malpractice suits to succeed.[55]

EXPRESSION

Academic Freedom

Academic freedom for teachers is grounded in the First Amendment, which guarantees teachers, along with all other citizens, the right to free speech. Teachers argue that because their jobs involve working with knowledge and testing ideas, they need special protection as they experiment, question, and criticize. Democracy demands free teaching, teachers insist.

But the courts have not always recognized the concept of academic freedom. Although the First Amendment went into effect in 1791 as part of the Bill of Rights, only since 1900 have elementary and secondary school teachers won a degree of protection for their academic work in the classroom. Even college professors, who work with older students and are responsible for generating new knowledge, have faced an uphill struggle for academic freedom. During the twentieth century, teachers at all levels of education won major victories, but the courts have made it clear academic freedom is far from absolute.

Banned Books and Controversial Teaching Methods.   Despite the protection of tenure laws, teachers still come under fire for assigning controversial readings and discussing controversial issues. Consider the case of Alabama teacher Marilyn Parducci, who had her eleventh-grade English class read Kurt Vonnegut, Jr.'s, comic satire "Welcome to the Monkey House." After several students and parents complained, the teacher's superiors told her to stop using the story, which they branded "literary garbage." The teacher refused. Defending the literary value of the work, she continued to discuss it in the classroom. The school district fired her for insubordination.[56]

The lawsuit the teacher initiated to get her job back led to a precedent-setting court decision, *Parducci v. Rutland* (1970). The federal district judge who heard the case observed academic freedom, while "fundamental to a democratic society," does have limits. Trying to define some of the limits, the judge considered two major questions. Had the school district shown the assignment was inappropriate for the age group or grade level? Had the district shown the assignment interfered with discipline or disrupted the educational process? On both counts, the judge weighed the evidence and answered no. Thus he ruled in favor of the teacher, stating her dismissal had been "an unwarranted invasion of her First Amendment right to academic freedom."[57]

Such controversies rarely cost teachers their jobs, although they often cost books their place in the classroom or in the library. Citizen complaints about books are increasing, and few teachers or librarians seem to be as willing as Marilyn Parducci to stand their ground and defend their choices. One or two parental complaints may be enough to make a teacher change an assignment or a librarian remove a book from the shelf. Even worse, from the standpoint of academic freedom, is the subtle form of censorship known as *prior restraint,* which occurs when teachers or librarians never assign or never order certain books for fear of causing controversy, even though they believe the books have educational value.[58]

School boards have the right to ban textbooks and library books, the courts have held. But board members must base their decisions on legitimate educational reasons, not on their disagreement with social, political, or religious ideas.[59]

A school board can ban one of Phyllis Reynolds Naylor's *Alice* books, a book from the Harry Potter series by J. K. Rowling, John Steinbeck's *Of Mice and Men,* Michael Bellesiles's *Arming America: The Origins of a National Gun Culture,* or *Fallen Angels* by Walter Dean Myers if the board can make a reasonable case that the content of the book is educationally inappropriate for a particular age group or grade level. These five titles were, in fact, the most frequently challenged in the nation in 2003. Every year the American Library Association cosponsors Banned Books Week to call attention to the ongoing controversy. But make no mistake about it: Even if teachers disagree with the justification school board members present for banning a book, the board can prevail as long as it couches its arguments in legitimate educational concerns.[60]

When refereeing such disputes, judges distinguish between what they regard as unlawful and what they regard as unwise. In a recent Florida case, a panel of judges who admitted they sided with teachers on the educational merits of two literary classics, Chaucer's "The Miller's Tale" and Aristophanes' *Lysistrata,* still allowed a local school board to ban the works because the board presented a justification related to legitimate educational concerns. The members argued the classics were too "explicit" and "vulgar" for high school students, and the judges accepted the justification as questionable but constitutional. The point—not an easy one for advocates of teacher power to accept—is that the ultimate authority to make educational decisions about the curriculum rests with school board members, not teachers.[61]

■ ■ ■ ■ ■

BOX 5.5

INTELLECTUAL FREEDOM TOOLKITS

The American Library Association offers a series of toolkits to combat censorship and other restraints on intellectual freedom. The toolkits, along with several complete chapters from the association's *Intellectual Freedom Manual*, are available at www. ala.org/ala/oif/iftoolkits/intellectual.htm

On the other hand, a board cannot ban books about teenage pregnancy, gay and lesbian rights, the wars in Vietnam and Iraq, the Islamic faith, the occult, or any other topic just because the board objects to the social, political, or religious ideas in the books. Teachers who believe in the educational merits of books that generate controversy will have to find evidence that board members are trying to keep ideas away from students.[62]

As Supreme Court Justice Thomas Brennan stated in *Texas v. Johnson*, "If there is a bedrock principle underlying the First Amendment, it is that the Government may not prohibit the expression of an idea simply because society finds the idea itself offensive or disagreeable."[63] With the American Library Association's *Intellectual Freedom Manual* (see Recommended Readings at the end of this chapter) as a reference, teachers can stand their ground.

Many school districts have developed procedures to resolve disputes over contested books. If a dispute goes to court, the school board must show a legitimate educational reason for its decision to ban a book. Denying students access to controversial ideas is not a legitimate educational reason.[64]

In all cases regarding controversial issues in the classroom, the courts emphasize relevance to the curriculum. In general, the courts have found teachers who deal with controversial topics that are a logical part of the subject at hand—a lecture on racism in an American history class, for instance, or a discussion of human reproduction in a biology class—to be operating within the limits of academic freedom. Yet the limits stretch only so far. A teacher who continually injects politics into a math class is probably out of bounds, and anything a teacher does that substantially disrupts the class may not be protected by academic freedom.[65]

The courts generally protect teachers who use controversial teaching methods, if they can produce reasonable evidence that other members of the occupation consider the techniques valid. Remember, though, state and local school boards clearly have the right to determine the content of the curriculum and prescribe particular teaching techniques. The cookbook curriculum I discuss in this book as a threat to autonomy may be unwise, or so many teachers think, but it is legal. Regarding the example of AIDS instruction we discussed earlier, school systems have the right to control what teachers say about the disease. Teachers should check their instructional guides before they utter the words *safe sex*.[66]

Although the emphasis throughout this chapter is on the legal rights and responsibilities of teachers, you should know the courts have also defined rights of expression for students. Two U.S. Supreme Court cases set the precedents. In *Tinker v. Des Moines Independent School District* (1969), the court ruled neither students nor teachers "shed their constitutional rights to freedom of speech or expression at the schoolhouse gate." At issue was the right of students to wear black armbands to protest the Vietnam War. The court viewed the wearing of armbands as "symbolic speech" and ruled students have the right to this and other kinds of speech at school. But just as in some of the teacher cases we just reviewed, the court pointed out students do not have absolute freedom to express themselves. Educators can limit any student action that "materially disrupts classwork or involves substantial disorder or invasion of the rights of others."[67]

Even expression that is not disruptive or invasive can be regulated, the Supreme Court held in *Hazelwood School District v. Kuhlmeier* (1988). Here the issue was freedom of speech in a school-sponsored student newspaper, and the court ruled educators can ban certain forms of student expression as long as they have "legitimate pedagogical concerns." The examples the court used to illustrate legitimate pedagogical concerns ran the gamut from poor grammar to vulgarity and profanity to advocacy of drugs, alcohol, and irresponsible sex. Educators cannot restrict "underground" publications that are not sponsored by the school, however, unless the publications cause a substantial disruption or infringe on the rights of others.[68]

Teaching about Sexual Orientation.   Courts, legislatures, and school boards are just now setting limits on teachers' freedom to discuss issues of sexual orientation. Can a biology teacher give students information on the incidence of homosexuality in the general population? Can a social studies teacher talk about discrimination against gays and lesbians in the workplace? The answer to both questions is probably *yes*, at least for middle and high school students, if the teacher can provide the instruction without substantially disrupting the class.

But can a teacher urge students not to discriminate against gays and lesbians, just as a teacher might encourage students not to discriminate against African Americans and Jewish Americans? Here the answer is hazy. Lawsuits are still working their way through the courts, and for now the answer varies from state to state and even community to community.

At a time when sexual orientation is being discussed more openly than ever, public schools have become a major battleground for gay and lesbian rights. Lining up on one side are such groups as the American Civil Liberties Union, People for the American Way, and gay rights organizations. These groups see the battle as a struggle for tolerance and respect as well as academic freedom. On the other side are the Christian Coalition, its state and local chapters, and similar organizations. These groups view homosexuality as an aberration, a sin—a threat to traditional family values.

State and local school systems are coming under intense pressure to take sides. So far, at least seven states—California, Connecticut, Minnesota, New Jersey, Vermont, Washington, and Wisconsin—plus the District of Columbia have followed the lead of Massachusetts and revised their school codes to prohibit discrimination based on sexual orientation, and a number of local school districts throughout the nation have taken the same step. The trend is clearly in their direction.[69]

Yet other state and local school systems, following the lead of Colorado and Virginia, have chosen the opposite road, in some cases excluding gays and lesbians from the protection of antidiscrimination laws, in other cases forbidding teachers from saying anything positive about homosexuality. The U.S. Supreme Court slowed down this latter movement in 1996, when it declared Colorado's ban on laws that protect homosexuals from discrimination unconstitutional. Meanwhile, the NEA, AFT, Association for Supervision and Curriculum Development (ASCD), and other large education groups are angering conservatives because the organizations generally view teaching about sexual orientation as a matter of academic freedom and human diginity.[70]

Consider the controversy over *Just the Facts About Sexual Orientation and Youth: A Primer for Principals, Educators and School Personnel*, a booklet mailed in late 1999 to the superintendents of all 15,000 of the nation's school districts. Prepared by a coalition of education, health, and mental health organizations including the NEA, AFT, American Psychological Association, and American Academy of Pediatrics, the publication offers "factual" (from the coalition's point of view) information on the development of sexual orientation and criticizes reparative therapy, transformational ministries, and other attempts to "convert" gay and lesbian students. Because homosexuality is not a mental disorder, the booklet argues, it does not need to be "cured."[71]

As soon as the booklet reached school district mailboxes the arguments began. The Family Research Council contends teaching students to accept homosexuality violates the religious faith of students who have learned in church and at home that homosexuality is sinful. Conservative syndicated columnist Mona Charen regards the publication as yet another attempt by homosexuals to gain not just acceptance but affirmation.[72]

The tide of public and legal opinion seems to be turning in favor of gay and lesbian rights. One sign is that the National School Boards Association, hardly a radical organization (see Chapter 9), now recommends *Just the Facts About Sexual Orientation and Youth* on its Web site. A related sign is the gradual acceptance of Gay-Straight Alliances in more than 1,200 high schools. These clubs, which teachers can join or sponsor, work on behalf of students whose sexual orientation makes them the target of bullying and other forms of harassment. The trend

BOX 5.6

SEXUAL ORIENTATION

Read the booklet *Just the Facts About Sexual Orientation and Youth* online at www.apa.org/pi/lgbc/facts.pdf

emerging from recent court decisions is that under the federal Equal Access Act (1984), school officials must accord such organizations the same rights and recognition that other clubs enjoy.[73]

Summarizing this section on academic expression, we can see the courts have ruled that academic freedom is fundamental to a democratic society, but they have also placed limits on the concept. When deciding where to draw the lines, the courts consider such factors as the age and grade level of students, effects on discipline and the educational process, relevance to the curriculum, the judgment of other educators, and state and local curriculum requirements.

Right of Public Dissent

With the rise of teacher unionism and the push for teacher power, teachers are more likely than ever to express their disagreement with administrators and school board members. Are teachers protected when they go public with their criticism?

In *Pickering v. Board of Education* (1968), the U.S. Supreme Court considered a suit brought by Marvin Pickering, a tenured Illinois high school teacher who lost his job because of a critical, sarcastic letter he wrote to the editor of a local newspaper. In it, Pickering took his superintendent and school board to task on the sensitive issue of school finance. He faulted his superiors for the way they raised and spent money, accusing them of shortchanging academics to enrich athletics. He also criticized the "totalitarianism" that stifled teacher dissent in the schools. The school board fired Pickering, claiming he had damaged the reputations of his superiors and impeded the efficient operation of the school's system. Pickering filed suit to regain his job, arguing the First Amendment protected his right to speak out.[74]

Although a state court upheld the dismissal, the U.S. Supreme Court ordered Pickering reinstated. Several points in the decision deserve our attention. Most important, the Supreme Court upheld the teacher's right to make public statements on matters of public concern. Obviously, said the justices, school finance is a public concern. They pointed out

> free and open debate is vital to informed decision making by the electorate. Teachers are, as a class, the members of a community most likely to have informed and definite opinions as to how funds allocated to the operation of the schools should be spent. Accordingly, it is essential that they be able to speak out freely on such questions without fear of retaliatory dismissal.[75]

Even though Pickering made several erroneous statements in his letter, the court found no evidence he did so intentionally. Nor did the court find evidence his letter had harmed anyone's reputation or interfered with the operation of the school system.

The court did place limits on the teacher's right of public dissent, implying that if his criticism had disrupted his working relationship with an immediate superior—a principal or assistant principal, for example—the dismissal might have been justified. The court also observed that the need for confidentiality—the need to safeguard the privacy of a student's records, for instance—could override a teacher's right to speak out on a matter of public concern.[76]

The most important limitation on public dissent came in another Supreme Court decision, *Connick v. Meyers* (1983). The court held that "when a public employee speaks not as a citizen upon matters of public concern, but instead as an employee upon matters only of personal interest," the courts cannot interfere with personnel decisions. According to this decision, not everything that goes on inside a school is a matter of public concern.[77]

In a later Florida case, a federal judge ruled a teacher who had criticized teacher-assignment policies, including the long-controversial practice of assigning coaches to social studies classes, had not raised a legitimate public concern. Instead, the teacher was simply disgruntled over "internal school policies." School finance is a public concern; job assignments, according to the judge, are not. The judge observed that "in the wake of *Connick,* the federal courts have substantially broadened the employer's rights to control employee speech activities that *relate to his employment.*"[78]

Teachers can publicly criticize their school systems, but only if their dissent involves a matter of public concern. Teachers can speak out within their systems on any educational issue, but even then they must be wary of causing disruptions and upsetting working relationships.

Other Forms of Expression

Now our focus expands to encompass broader forms of expression, such matters as personal appearance, political activities, and private life. As I pointed out in the discussion of tenure and dismissal, the courts have established the general principle that a teacher's behavior must impair effectiveness in the classroom before the behavior can become grounds for dismissal.

Hair, Clothes, and Earrings.   Decisions are constantly evolving, though, and a prime example of how they change with the times is the matter of personal appearance. When long hair, beards, and mustaches were popular during the 1960s and 1970s, the courts often came to the defense of male teachers who wore the styles. Viewing grooming as a symbolic expression that is protected by the First Amendment, the courts tended to put the burden on the school system to prove the hair disrupted the classroom.

In more recent cases, the burden of proof has shifted to the teacher. Unless the teacher can prove that a school system's grooming regulations are irrational or unreasonable, judges are increasingly allowing the regulations to stand. Early twenty-first-century teachers who sport shaved heads or green hair may be forced to choose between their hairstyles and their jobs.[79]

Courts are giving teachers even less leeway in dress. Rejecting arguments that clothing is symbolic expression, judges have validated regulations requiring male teachers to wear coats and ties and female teachers to wear skirts longer than minis. Clear precedents are lacking on whether the courts will protect articles of religious clothing—a Jewish teacher's yarmulke, for instance—or clothing that marks racial or ethnic pride, such as an African American teacher's dashiki.[80]

As for male earrings, we can look to court decisions that have allowed school districts to ban them for students. We can surmise that officials can probably prohibit earrings for male teachers as well, especially if the officials couch their regulations in terms of upholding "local community standards" and promoting a "positive educational environment."[81]

Political Activities.   The courts have sent mixed signals on political involvement. Reversing earlier decisions, the U.S. Supreme Court has made it clear teachers cannot be dismissed because of their membership in radical organizations. Teachers can belong to the Communist Party or Ku Klux Klan, for example, and still retain their jobs. If teachers show they intend to further the illegal aims of an organization, however, they can be fired. Regarding participation in political activities, the courts have held teachers, like all citizens, can vote, contribute to political candidates, express opinions on political issues, and display bumper stickers. But as public employees, how far can teachers go? Can teachers, like federal employees, be prohibited from managing political campaigns and playing other key roles? The NEA and AFT encourage their members to get involved in partisan politics, yet several recent court decisions have upheld political restrictions on teachers—even restrictions limiting their First Amendment rights—on the grounds that the state has a compelling interest in controlling political influence in the public schools.[82]

The courts have rendered conflicting decisions on whether teachers have to resign if they are elected to public office and, indeed, whether they can run for office without resigning. This issue has become quite controversial in some states. Is it a conflict of interest for teachers to serve in a state legislature, where they cast votes on education bills that directly affect their jobs? The answer may be yes in one state and no in the state next door. Look for more litigation on political activity as teachers continue to push for power.[83]

Back to Lifestyle.   Finally, there are the lifestyle issues we discussed earlier in this chapter. The landmark decision in this area of expression is *Morrison,* which protected the rights of a gay teacher. Again, the critical issue is the degree to which teachers' private lives affect their work. Marc Morrison kept his job, but the courts have upheld the dismissal of other gay and lesbian teachers when students, parents, and colleagues protested their continued employment. Decisions affecting unmarried teachers who become pregnant or simply live with someone of the opposite sex are also mixed. The courts consider the circumstances of each case, sometimes affirming and sometimes rejecting the teacher's right to remain in the occupation.[84]

The Supreme Court's landmark ruling in *Lawrence v. Texas* (2003), although not about public school employees, should make it more difficult for school boards to fire teachers for their sexual behavior away from work. In eloquent words, the majority opinion stated that two gay men were "entitled to respect for their private lives. The state cannot demean their existence or control their destiny by making their private sexual conduct a crime. . . . It is a promise of the Constitution that there is a realm of personal liberty which the government may not enter."[85]

ACTIVITIES

1. Talk with several principals about the legal issues surrounding teacher tenure, especially the dismissal of unfit teachers. Interview several officers of a teacher organization and compare the responses.

2. Start your own information file on child abuse, neglect, and AIDS/HIV. Education journals run many stories on these vital issues, often emphasizing legal aspects. Write to state and local boards of education for policies that will apply to you as a teacher.

3. Where do you stand on the expression issues in this chapter? Stage a classroom debate on academic freedom, public criticism of school system policies, or a teacher's right to lead an unconventional lifestyle.

RECOMMENDED READINGS

American Library Association, Office of Intellectual Freedom. *Intellectual Freedom Manual*, 6th ed. (Chicago: ALA, 2001). This guide offers valuable suggestions to educators who want to protect their academic freedom.

Crosson-Tower, Cynthia. *Understanding Child Abuse and Neglect*, 5th ed. (Boston: Allyn and Bacon, 2001). Comprehensive and sensitively written, this definitive book is useful to teachers, social workers, psychologists, and parents.

Fischer, Louis, David Schimmel, and Leslie R. Stellman. *Teachers and the Law*, 6th ed. (Boston: Allyn and Bacon, 2003). The authors give straightforward, plain-English answers to teachers' questions about the law.

Zirkel, Perry A. "De Jure," a monthly column in *Phi Delta Kappan*. Zirkel covers a wide range of issues in school law, including the teacher-focused concerns discussed in this chapter.

NOTES

1. A teacher in my course EDF 515, Multicultural Education, at the University of South Alabama made this statement during fall semester 2004.

2. Quoted in Public Agenda, *Stand by Me: What Teachers Really Think about Unions, Merit Pay and Other Professional Matters* (New York: Public Agenda, 2003), p. 21.

3. Louis Fischer, David Schimmel, and Leslie R. Stellman, *Teachers and the Law*, 6th ed. (Boston: Allyn and Bacon, 2003), Chap. 2.

4. For the history of teacher tenure, see National Education Association, *The Problem of Teacher Tenure*, Research Bulletin, vol. II, no. 5 (Washington, DC: NEA, 1924); Cecil Winfield Scott, *Indefinite Teacher Tenure: A Critical Study of the Historical, Legal, Operative, and Comparative Aspects* (New York: Bureau of Publications, Teachers College, Columbia University, 1934); and Commission on Educational

Reconstruction, American Federation of Teachers, *Organizing the Teaching Profession* (Glencoe, IL: Free Press, 1955), Chap. 4.

5. Edwin M. Bridges, *The Incompetent Teacher: Managerial Responses,* rev. ed. (New York: Routledge/Falmer, 2004); Fischer, Schimmel, and Stellman, *Teachers and the Law,* pp. 37–38.

6. Fischer, Schimmel, and Stellman, *Teachers and the Law,* pp. 36–37.

7. *Morrison v. State Board of Education,* 461 P.2d 375 (Cal. 1969); Fischer, Schimmel, and Stellman, *Teachers and the Law,* pp. 38–39.

8. Nathan L. Essex, *School Law and the Public Schools: A Practical Guide for Educational Leaders,* 3rd ed. (Boston: Allyn and Bacon, 2005), pp. 234–238.

9. Fischer, Schimmel, and Stellman, *Teachers and the Law,* p. 39.

10. Ibid., pp. 39–41.

11. *Board of Regents v. Roth,* 408 U.S. 577, 572 (1972).

12. *Goldberg v. Kelly,* 397 U.S. 254 (1970).

13. Andrew Goldstein, "Ever Try to Flunk a Bad Teacher?" *Time* (July 20, 1998); Walter K. Olson, *The Excuse Factory: How Employment Law Is Paralyzing the American Workplace* (New York: The Free Press, 1997).

14. Walter Olson, "Time to Get Off the Tenure Track," *New York Times* (July 8, 1997); Michael D. Simpson, "NEA Examines the Rights of Nontenured Teachers," *NEA Today* (May 2001) [Available: www.nea.org/neatoday/0105/rights.html].

15. "Revise Teacher Tenure Law and Give Students a Break," *Detroit News* (January 11, 2004) [Available: www.detnews.com/2004/editorial/0401/12/a12-32026.htm].

16. Thomas Toch, Robin M. Bennefield, Dana Hawkins, and Penny Loeb, "Why Teachers Don't Teach," *U.S. News & World Report* (February 26, 1996), p. 65.

17. Toch et al., "Why Teachers Don't Teach," p. 65.

18. Edwin M. Bridges, *Managing the Incompetent Teacher,* 2d ed. (Eugene, OR: ERIC Clearinghouse on Educational Management, 1990).

19. See "Teacher vs. Teacher? Nonsense," NEA President Bob Chase's opinion piece in *Education Week* (October 22, 1997), pp. 26, 29.

20. One of the guidebooks available to help principals and other administrators is Alexander D. Platt, Caroline E. Tripp, Wayne R. Ogden, and Robert G. Fraser, *The Skillful Leader: Confronting Mediocre Teaching* (Acton, MA: Research for Better Teaching, 2000).

21. Quoted in Ann Bradley, "Confronting a Tough Issue: Teacher Tenure," *Quality Counts '99,* a supplement to *Education Week* (January 11, 1999), p. 48.

22. Fischer, Schimmel, and Stellman, *Teachers and the Law,* p. 59.

23. Ibid., p. 60.

24. Ibid., pp. 59–61.

25. Ibid., pp. 61–62, 66–67.

26. National Child Abuse Prevention and Treatment Act of 1974 (P.L. 93-247), quoted in Fischer, Schimmel, and Stellman, *Teachers and the Law,* pp. 94–95.

27. National Center on Child Abuse Prevention Research, *Current Trends in Child Abuse Prevention, Reporting, and Fatalities: The 1999 Annual Fifty State Survey* (2001) [Available: www.preventchildabuse.org/learn_more/research_docs/1999_50_survey.pdf], p. 7; Prevent Child Abuse America, *Fact Sheet: Sexual Abuse of Children* (Chicago: PCAA, n.d.).

28. Public Knowledge LLC, *Discipline and Development: A Meta-Analysis of Public Perceptions of Parents, Parenting, Child Development and Child Abuse* (2003) [Available: www.preventchildabuse.org/learn_more/research_docs/meta%20final.pdf]; Deborah Daro, *Public Opinion and Behaviors Regarding Child Abuse Prevention: 1999 Report* (1999) [Available: www.preventchildabuse.org/learn_more/research_docs/1999_survey.pdf].

29. Patrick F. Guyton, "Sex Abuse: A Trauma That Lasts a Lifetime," *Mobile Register* (February 13, 2000), p. 1D, 3D. An excellent book that focuses on the social context is Cynthia Crosson-Tower's *Understanding Child Abuse,* 5th ed. (Boston: Allyn and Bacon, 2001).

30. Dennis L. Cates, Marc A. Markell, and Sherrie Bettenhausen, "At Risk for Abuse: A Teacher's Guide for Recognizing and Reporting Child Neglect and Abuse," *Preventing School Failure* (Winter 1995), 6; Fischer, Schimmel, and Stellman, *Teachers and the Law,* Chap. 7.

31. Fischer, Schimmel, and Stellman, *Teachers and the Law,* p. 96.

32. See Nancy D. Brener, Janet L. Collins, Laura Kann, and Meg L. Small, "Assessment of Practices in School-Based HIV/AIDS Education," *Journal of Health Education Supplement* 30 (September/October 1999): S28–S33, and Clark Robenstine, "HIV/AIDS Education for Adolescents: School Policy and Practice," *The Clearing House* 67 (March/April 1994): 229–232.

33. National Commission on Acquired Immune Deficiency Syndrome, *Preventing HIV/AIDS in Adolescents* (Washington, DC: NCAIDS, 1993).

34. Centers for Disease Control and Prevention, *AIDS and HIV: Are You at Risk?* (2003) [Available: www.cdc.gov/hiv/pubs/brochure/atrisk.htm]. The *HIV/AIDS Surveillance Reports* compiled by the Centers for Disease Control and Prevention, Public Health Service, U.S. Department of Health and Human Services, show no cases of transmission through ordinary contact in the classroom.

35. Centers for Disease Control and Prevention, *1993 Revised Classification System for HIV Infection and Expanded Surveillance Case Definition for AIDS among Adolescents and Adults,* MMWR 1992, 41, RR–17 (Atlanta: CDC, 1993); "AIDS Cases Up in Alabama," *Mobile Register* (April 19, 1996), p. 10-A.

36. Centers for Disease Control and Prevention, *HIV/AIDS Surveillance Report 2002* (2002), pp. 5–8 [Available: www.cdc.gov/hiv/stats/hasr1402/2002SurveillanceReport.pdf].

37. Ibid.

38. National Commission on Acquired Immune Deficiency Syndrome, *Preventing HIV/AIDS in Adolescents,* p. 6.

39. J. C. Zoghby, "Small Town Rocked by Big-City Problem: HIV," *Mobile Register* (April 23, 1996), p. 1.

40. National Commission on Acquired Immune Deficiency Syndrome, *Preventing HIV/AIDS in Adolescents,* p. 6.

41. Rehabilitation Act of 1973, Section 504, quoted in Cathy Allen Broadwell and John L. Strope, Jr., "Students with AIDS," *West's Education Law Reporter* 49 (January 5, 1989), p. 110.

42. Fischer, Schimmel, and Stellman, *Teachers and the Law,* p. 364. For further information see Centers for Disease Control and Prevention, *The Americans with Disabilities Act* (Rockville, MD: CDC National AIDS Clearinghouse, 1996).

43. Centers for Disease Control and Prevention, *HIV and Its Transmission* (2003) [Available: www.cdc.gov/hiv/pubs/facts/transmission.htm].

44. *Chalk v. U.S. District Court,* 840 F.2d 701 (9th Cir. 1988). See also Fischer, Schimmel, and Stellman, *Teachers and the Law,* p. 326, and Centers for Disease Control and Prevention, *HIV/AIDS and Employees* (Rockville, MD: CDC National AIDS Clearinghouse, 1996).

45. Fischer, Schimmel, and Stellman, *Teachers and the Law,* pp. 67–68, 364; Debra Viadero, "AIDS in Schools: Compassion vs. 'The Public's Right to Know,'" *Education Week* (January 20, 1988), pp. 1, 26; Broadwell and Strope, "Students with AIDS."

46. Ibid., p. 26.

47. Ibid.

48. "AIDS Cases Up in Alabama," p. 10-A.

49. *Peter W. v. San Francisco Unified School District,* 131 Cal. Rptr. 854 (Cal. App. 1976).

50. Ibid.

51. Ibid.

52. *Hoffman v. Board of Education of the City of New York,* 64 A.D.2d 369, 410 N.Y.S.2d 99 (1978).

53. Ibid.

54. *Hoffman v. Board of Education of the City of New York,* 49 N.Y.2d 317, 424 N.Y.S.2d 376 (1979).

55. For a discussion of two exceptions to the precedents, see Fischer, Schimmel, and Stellman, *Teachers and the Law,* pp. 69–70.

56. *Parducci v. Rutland,* 316 F. Supp. 352 (N. D. Ala. 1970).

57. Ibid.

58. See Henry Reichman, *Censorship and Selection: Issues and Answers for Schools,* 3rd ed. (Chicago: American Library Association, 2001), and International Reading Association, *Censorship: A Threat to Reading, Learning, and Thinking* (Newark, DE: IRA, 1994).

59. Eugene C. Bjorklun, "School Book Censorship and the First Amendment," *Educational Forum* 55 (Fall 1990): 37–48.

60. American Library Association, *Challenged and Banned Books* (2004) [Available: www.ala.org/ala/oif/bannedbooksweek/challengedbanned/challengedbanned.htm]; Fischer, Schimmel, and Stellman, *Teachers and the Law,* pp. 136–137.

61. *Virgil v. School Board of Columbia County, Florida,* 862 F.2d 1517 (11th Cir. 1989).

62. Bjorklun, "School Book Censorship"; Fischer, Schimmel, and Stellman, *Teachers and the Law,* p. 137.

63. *Texas v. Johnson*, 491 U.S. 397 (1989).
64. Ibid.
65. Fischer, Schimmel, and Stellman, *Teachers and the Law,* pp. 134–141.
66. Ibid., pp. 141–144.
67. *Tinker v. Des Moines Independent School District,* 393 U.S. 503 (1969).
68. *Hazelwood School District v. Kuhlmeier,* 484 U.S. 260 (1988).
69. Karla Scoon Reid, "Ky. Protests Highlight Increasing Visiblity of Gay-Straight Clubs," *Education Week* (November 27, 2002), p. 11; Lisa Fine, "Ore. Rejects Proposal to Restrict What Schools Teach about Gays," *Education Week* (November 15, 2000), p. 24.
70. Justin Bergman, "Virginia's Anti-Gay Law Has Many Threatening to Leave," *Mobile Register* (May 26, 2004), p. 10A; "Colorado Amendment on Gays Rejected," *Mobile Register* (May 21, 1996), p. 8A.
71. Just the Facts Coalition, *Just the Facts About Sexual Orientation and Youth* (n.p.: The Coalition, 1999) [Available: www.nea.org/achievement/gayfacts.pdf].
72. Kathleen Kennedy Manzo, "Group Issues 'Facts' on Gay Youths," *Education Week* (December 1, 1999), p. 11; Mona Charen, "Gay Community Seeking 'Affirmation' through Public Schools," *Mobile Register* (January 26, 2000), p. 14A.
73. Scoon, "Ky. Protests," p. 11; Darcia Harris Bowman, "High School Students Stay Silent to Protest Mistreatment of Gays," *Education Week* (April 17, 2002), p. 10; Fischer, Schimmel, and Stellman, *Teachers and the Law,* pp. 203–205.
74. *Pickering v. Board of Education,* 225 N.E.2d 1 (1967), 391 U.S. 563 (1968).
75. *Pickering v. Board of Education,* 391 U.S. 563 (1968).
76. Ibid.
77. *Connick v. Myers,* 461 U.S. 138 (1983).
78. *Ferrara v. Mills,* 596 F. Supp. 1069 (S.D. Fla. 1984), 761 F.2d 1508 (11th Cir. 1986). Emphasis in the original.
79. Fischer, Schimmel, and Stellman, *Teachers and the Law,* pp. 404–406.
80. Ibid., pp. 406–407, 174–175.
81. Ibid., p. 419.
82. Ibid., pp. 210–213.
83. Ibid.
84. Ibid., pp. 265–277, 284–286.
85. *Lawrence v. Texas,* 123 S.Ct. 2472 (2003).

PART II

SCHOOLS AND SOCIETY

CHAPTER 6

HISTORY OF
AMERICAN EDUCATION

LOOKING FORWARD, LOOKING BACK

The late Lawrence Cremin of Teachers College, Columbia University, one of the most distinguished educational historians of the twentieth century, observed that "reform movements are notoriously ahistorical in outlook. They look forward rather than back, and when they do need a history, they frequently prefer the fashioning of ideal ancestors to the acknowledgment of mortals."[1]

I hope you have already noticed how I try to encourage an awareness of history in every chapter of *America's Teachers,* particularly when the discussion turns to proposals for educational reform. Merit pay comes from a long line of very mortal ancestors, as we have seen. So does standardized testing. So do efforts to accommodate cultural diversity in schools. And so it is with most of the other reforms being promoted today.

Despite promoters' claims to the contrary, few educational wheels are brand new. Most have been reinvented. Sold to the public as innovations, they are more like retreaded and recycled tires. This chapter, focused entirely on the history of American education, should help you build a framework for the historical analysis I present throughout the textbook.

DEBATES AND PATTERNS

Here I use debates and patterns to introduce the history of American education. The debates you will hear took place before the Civil War and at the turn of the twentieth century, yet they have a surprisingly contemporary ring. The patterns you will see have appeared over the course of the twentieth century and are still shaping the schools. All historians try to avoid reading the present into the past— they call that the sin of "presentism"—but most historians believe studying the past can help us live better in the present.

I have tried to capture the excitement of educational history by focusing on debates that occurred during two eras of educational reform. In both periods the future of the schools—indeed, the fate of the nation—hung in the balance as citizens debated fundamental questions about education: Whose children should go to school? What kinds of schools should they attend? What should they study? Who should control the schools?

Debates over these issues were especially heated in the mid-nineteenth century and at the turn of the twentieth century. Looking back, it is easy to see why. Both eras were periods when the United States itself was changing rapidly, times when many people were convinced they could improve the nation if only they could channel change in a constructive way. In both eras, reformers who wanted to change the schools took their place alongside reformers with plans to remake other social institutions. And in both eras, citizens spoke out freely for and against the proposals for reform.

After listening to the debates, we will turn our attention to twentieth-century patterns of education. We will examine four patterns: the competition for control of the schools, the local/state/federal balance of power, the quest for equal educational opportunities, and trends in the curriculum. Some historians argue these patterns show more stability than change, claiming the basic structure and purposes of American education changed relatively little during the 1900s. Other historians disagree, contending the growing strength of teacher organizations and the development of the cookbook curriculum (two examples discussed in earlier chapters) are fundamental changes—major breaks with the past. Whichever point of view you eventually accept, understanding historical patterns can help you separate genuinely new ideas on the reform agenda from the retreaded tires that are sure to roll by during your teaching career.

To understand why historians disagree, you need to realize history is not a literal record of the past. History is an *interpretation* of the past. History reflects the spirit of the times in which it is written—how historians view their own era influences how they view the past. Historians select from the past those ideas and events that seem significant to them and then interpret what they have selected through the lens of their own experience. Although they do not deliberately distort the past, historians readily acknowledge they "cannot jump out of [their] intellectual skin."[2]

As you read this chapter, please understand that you are reading interpretations of the past. I have included debates to expose you to different points of view, but you should be aware that as I wrote the chapter, I constantly had to decide which debates to include and which to omit, how to present opposing positions on the issues, and so forth. In other words, this chapter is interpretive from beginning to end.

I want to challenge you to judge the past for yourself as you read. Be critical and think of different interpretations. The factors of social class, race, ethnicity, and gender exert a powerful influence on how people derive meaning from their experiences. The belief that reality is constructed in people's minds and therefore varies from one person to another is known as *constructivism*. In this spirit, ask yourself how your own background and experiences are shaping your reactions to what you read. I hope this chapter helps you see the personal side of historical debate, the clash of opinion *in* the past as well as *about* the past.

COMMON SCHOOL REFORM IN HISTORICAL CONTEXT

During the three decades before the Civil War, public education as we know it began to take shape. Americans built statewide public school systems—*common school systems*, they were originally called. Controlled to some degree by the state governments, common schools were different from the various kinds of locally controlled schools Americans were familiar with. Common schools, according to the reformers who advocated them, would be common to all children; they would teach a common political creed; and they would instill a common morality based on nonsectarian religion.

Until the 1960s, most educational historians gave common school reform rave reviews. *Celebrationist* historians who wrote in the early 1900s were hard-pressed to criticize it at all. *Liberal* historians writing from the 1920s to the present have generally viewed the common schools crusades as noble, if imperfectly conducted.

Since the 1960s, though, the clash of historical interpretation has intensified. *Revisionist* historians have accused school reformers of running roughshod over the values and interests of certain groups—poor people, religious minorities, political dissenters—in the drive to bring schooling under state control. *Neoconservative* historians have come to the reformers' defense, contending revisionists have exaggerated the drawbacks and downplayed the benefits of common schools. Now *multiple-perspective* historians are trying to portray the complexity of the past with more subtlety, revealing the many and sometimes conflicting motives people had for favoring or opposing common school reform.

These contrasting historical interpretations recall the educational debates that occurred before the Civil War. In order to understand the debates, we need to be familiar with the locally controlled schools common school reformers wanted to replace.

Informal and Formal Education among Native and European Americans

We also need to understand the difference between the *formal education* that takes place primarily in schools and the *informal education* provided by the family and other social agencies. Historian Bernard Bailyn urges us to think of education broadly as the "entire process by which a culture transmits itself across the generations."[3] So conceived, education involves much more than schooling. Historically, informal education has been the stronger influence on most people's lives because families, religions, workplaces, and communities have done most of the educating.

Informal education took place in North America for centuries before Europeans arrived. The indigenous peoples who had inhabited the continent since 15,000 B.C. relied on the family and the tribe to educate their children. Although customs varied, there was a common emphasis in Native American education on survival skills and cultural heritage—on spirituality in particular. The process of cultural transmission was woven into virtually every activity that involved young people. Teaching by example, storytelling, and inducting young people into adulthood through rites of passage helped Native Americas transmit their culture from one generation to the next.[4]

When Europeans began to colonize North America during the 1500s and 1600s, they too relied on informal education provided by the family, community, and church. For most Europeans—whether English, Spanish, French, or Dutch—schools ranked several places down the list in importance, just as in the Old World. Soon, though, the colonists began relying more on formal education, using schools as another way to reproduce the cultural patterns they brought over from

Europe. They looked to schools to provide an additional margin of assurance that their traditions would not be lost in the New World. With an ethnocentric attitude toward indigenous peoples and their well-established civilizations, colonists sometimes forced Native American children to attend school in an effort to eradicate their culture.

During the colonial era, then, transplanted European families gradually relinquished some of their educational responsibilities to schools, which took their place as a key institution within the community. Today, several hundred years later, schools have become so well established, so ingrained in our thinking as *the* place for education, we have to remind ourselves that much teaching and learning still go on outside their walls.

District Schools, Academies, and Other Schools

If you had been able to tour the new nation in the late 1700s and early 1800s, you would have seen a great deal of variation in education. In New England, where traditions of schooling were strongest, *district schools* dotted the countryside well before the American Revolution. Massachusetts led the way in 1642 with legislation requiring parents and guardians to make sure their children could read, and that legislation was followed by a 1647 act requiring every town of fifty or more families to appoint a reading and writing teacher.[5]

The religious and political influence of the Puritans on these developments was unmistakable. The Puritans believed universal literacy would prevent the development of a pauper class, enable citizens to understand the law, and—most important—save souls. The 1647 school act was known as the "Old Deluder Satan Law" because it was intended to help people resist the wiles of the devil himself.[6]

The "New England model" of district schools grew out of this heritage. New England towns and townships were, on the average, six miles square. By the mid-1700s, most of them contained several population centers or villages. As population growth continued, the towns gradually delegated control over the schools to the individual villages, which began to function as school districts. This decentralized model of schooling took local control of education to the extreme. The citizens of each village set their own school taxes and, through a committee of selectmen, hired the teacher (usually a man), established the length of the school year, and determined the course of study.[7]

The one-room district school took in boys and girls ranging in age from five to fifteen. Their attendance, limited by weather, distance, and farm work, was irregular. Literacy, morality, and religion were the heart of the curriculum, with memorization and recitation the dominant pedagogy. The teacher rarely stayed in one school for more than a session or two. For the children of the wealthiest New Englanders, tutors offered an alternative to the district school. The sons of the elite could then enroll in a *Latin grammar school,* a private school with a classical orientation.

District schools moved west after the Revolution with the passage of the Northwest Ordinances of 1785 and 1787. These laws, which governed the settlement of the territory west of the Allegheny Mountains, laid out land in townships six miles square, with each township divided into thirty-six sections, each one mile square. The sixteenth section, which fell close to the center of the township, was set aside for education and often became the site of a district school. Other acts of Congress applied the sixteenth-section principle to the settlement of territory outside the Old Northwest. In this way the decentralized New England model came to many of the states admitted to the new nation. District schools were scattered throughout the Midwest by 1850 and across the Great Plains and Far West during and after the Civil War.

District schools were never as popular in the South, even in the newer southern states that entered the union with sixteenth-section lands earmarked for education. In the antebellum South, a different model of education prevailed. The children of the wealthy had their tutors and private schools; "middling" whites attended academies (which we will discuss next), denominational schools, or the few district schools; poor whites received little or no formal education; and in most states, African slaves were prohibited by law from learning to read and write.[8]

In the Middle Atlantic states—New York, New Jersey, Pennsylvania, and Delaware—yet another model of schooling developed. Here differences in ethnicity, language, and religion drew people into a variety of denominational schools, among them Dutch Reformed, Quaker, Jewish, and Roman Catholic. District schools and academies were more numerous in the Middle Atlantic region than in the South, but the pull of private religious education was strong.

Academies offered schooling to students who were at least middling in social status—or had aspirations to be. Billing themselves as more practical than the Latin grammar schools, academies took in students aged fourteen to twenty-five. The education academies provided was supposed to be both "ornamental" and "useful," as Benjamin Franklin explained in his 1749 proposal for an academy in Philadelphia. Franklin outlined plans for a school that would place more emphasis on English grammar, composition, and public speaking than on Latin and Greek. History, mathematics, and science—subjects to which Latin grammar schools paid little attention—would be prominent in the curriculum. Carpentry, printing, farming, and other practical skills would also have a place. Such a course of study, Franklin argued, would prepare students to get ahead in life.[9]

But the academies that grew increasingly popular throughout the nation in the first half of the nineteenth century rarely had so practical a slant. Ironically, Franklin's proposal led to the establishment of a school that evolved into the University of Pennsylvania, an elite, classically oriented institution. Parents wanted their children to get ahead, to be sure, but most parents believed an education in the classics was the key to social mobility. Thus the academies stressed practicality in moderation, careful not to steer too far away from the subjects that were the mark of middle- and upper-class culture.[10]

From our twenty-first-century vantage point, academies were a curious blend of "public" and "private." Typically, academies held public charters and received public funds, yet they also charged tuition and were governed by private boards of trustees. Academies also blurred the line we draw between high schools and colleges. Most academies were more like the former; a few were more like the latter. Indeed, academies were sometimes called "people's colleges." Academies were usually coeducational, although some, like Emma Willard's Troy Female Seminary and Mary Lyon's Mount Holyoke Seminary, were exclusively for females. Such institutions made their reputations by offering women educational opportunities unavailable elsewhere. The popularity of academies grew rapidly between the Revolution and the Civil War.[11]

Enlightenment Ideology, the Republican Spirit, and Early Plans for "Systems of Education"

In the early years of the nation Americans attended a variety of locally controlled schools. Such figures as Benjamin Franklin, Noah Webster, Benjamin Rush, George Washington, Thomas Jefferson, and James Madison spoke out in support of, as Jefferson put it, the "general diffusion of knowledge." Drawing on the Enlightenment ideology that reason is the guide to knowledge and progress is not only possible but inevitable, these leaders advanced a variety of different plans to take formal education to the masses. The republican spirit of the new nation included the belief that schooling had a crucial *political* role to play in promoting nationalism, patriotism, and balance between freedom and order. Most Americans were in agreement that schooling was a good thing and that the nation needed more of it.[12]

But this broad consensus concealed fundamental disagreements over the purposes and control of schooling. Jefferson, Rush, and Webster, for instance, differed over whether schools should impose order and virtue on students (Rush's and Webster's position) or simply cultivate the inborn reason and moral sense that students bring to school (Jefferson's position). Clearly, they also disagreed over the nature of human beings. Moreover, Rush advocated giving tax revenue to schools controlled by different religious groups, something Jefferson and Webster could not support.

All sorts of proposals for "systems of education" came forth in the early republic. During the late 1700s, the prime time for such plans, Jefferson and Rush drew up detailed blueprints for statewide school systems—Jefferson's for Virginia and Rush's for Pennsylvania. Webster outlined his views in essays, in the widely used "blue-backed" *American Spelling Book* and *American Dictionary of the English Language*, and as a member of the Massachusetts legislature during the early 1800s. But all these proposals, along with countless others from less influential figures, made little headway. For more than half a century after the Revolution, Americans saw little need to involve the state governments in schooling.

The Impact of Modernization

But the nation was changing. By the 1830s, three major trends were under way, exerting their strongest influence on New England and the Middle Atlantic states. Urbanization, industrialization, and immigration—historians call them the forces of *modernization*—were altering the way Americans felt about their nation and its schools.[13]

These three trends were closely related. A worldwide movement of people from the farm to the city had begun, prompted by changes in agriculture and accelerated by the lure of factory jobs. Many of those who swelled the population of cities like Boston, New York, and Philadelphia had been born in the rural areas of the nation, but many others were newly arrived from abroad. Immigration from Ireland and Germany was heavy in the three decades before the Civil War, bringing to the United States large numbers of people whose language was not English and whose religion was not Protestant. These immigrants seemed especially "foreign" to Americans of British descent.

The entire process of modernization threatened many people because the traditional community controls that worked well in small towns and rural areas seemed to break down in industrial cities. Agrarian communities were usually homogeneous, composed of people with similar backgrounds and beliefs. Out in the country, family, church, and neighbors kept people in line. Everybody knew everybody else's business. In the heterogeneous cities, by contrast, people could and did go their own way. The social and economic distance between rich and poor seemed to widen. The popular press constantly reminded the public of the consequences of urban poverty, playing up sensationalized accounts of crime and degradation: men turning to strong drink, women turning to prostitution, and children working in factories or roaming the streets at all hours. To some citizens, it seemed the cities were already out of control and the entire nation would soon be in danger. Something had to be done.

The Urge to Reform.   Out of this ferment came an upsurge of reform, a remarkable variety of movements that had in common the urge to perfect and control the modernizing society. Urbanization, industrialization, and immigration held out the promise of great rewards, not the least of them economic development—thus the drive to perfect society. But the forces of modernization also exacted a frightening toll that was painfully obvious on city streets—thus the quest for control. Temperance crusaders, prison reformers, advocates of women's rights, pacifists, abolitionists, and many others worked to win popular support for their causes, sometimes competing and sometimes cooperating. Often an individual reformer worked for several causes simultaneously or moved from one to another over the course of a lifetime.[14]

School reformers mounted an educational crusade, often quoting scripture to prove the changes they sought were the most fundamental: "Train up a child in the way he should go: and when he is old, he will not depart from it" (Proverbs 22: 6). Pay the schoolmaster today, they exhorted, or pay the jailer tomorrow. The common school movements of the antebellum era were one piece in an elaborate mosaic of reform.

Before the pace of modernization quickened in the 1830s, some Americans were already finding fault with district schools. Even in Massachusetts, which prided itself as the nation's educational leader, decentralization had yielded a patchwork of schools that varied tremendously from one district to the next. The lack of uniformity was evident in many ways, including the quality of teachers. It troubled Massachusetts educator and legislator James G. Carter that his state had established no qualifications for teaching. The selectmen of each district, usually advised by local clergy, hired whomever they pleased. The result, as we saw in the introduction to Chapter 3, was often the employment of teachers "who [knew] nothing, absolutely nothing, of the complicated and difficult duties assigned to them"—or so Carter claimed. With an eye toward raising standards and eventually enforcing them statewide, in 1826 he proposed a network of state colleges to train teachers.[15]

But Carter had more on his mind, as the following warning on the perils of decentralization indicates:

> If the policy of the legislature, in regard to free schools, for the last twenty years be not changed, the institution, which has been the glory of New England will, in twenty years more, be extinct. If the State continue to relieve themselves of the trouble of providing for the instruction of the whole people, and to shift the responsibility upon the towns, and the towns upon the districts, and the districts upon individuals, each will take care of himself and his own family as he is able, and as he appreciates the blessing of a good education. The rich will, as a class, have much better instruction than they now have, while the poor will have much worse or none at all. The academies and private schools will be carried to much greater perfection than they have been, while the public free schools will become stationary or retrograde.[16]

Carter's basic argument was that the state could no longer afford to entrust something as vital as schooling to the whims of local people. He envisioned schools less stratified by social class and accessible, at least at the lower levels, to rich and poor alike. Girls as well as boys would attend. Reaching this goal, he insisted, would require some degree of state control.

In time, the Massachusetts legislature responded favorably to Carter's pleas. The first public *normal school* (teacher-training institution) in the state as well as the nation opened in Lexington in 1839. But Carter had already won his greatest victory in 1837 with the creation of a state board of education, also the first in the nation, and the appointment of Horace Mann as its secretary. Mann, who would soon be called the *father of public education* in the United States, set out on a twelve-year crusade to establish common schools throughout Massachusetts.

Gradually other states followed suit. In 1838, Connecticut established a state board of education with Henry Barnard as its secretary, and during the 1840s and 1850s, common school movements appeared in almost every state. Even the South had its common school reformers, although before the Civil War the movement was not very successful outside a few southern cities.[17]

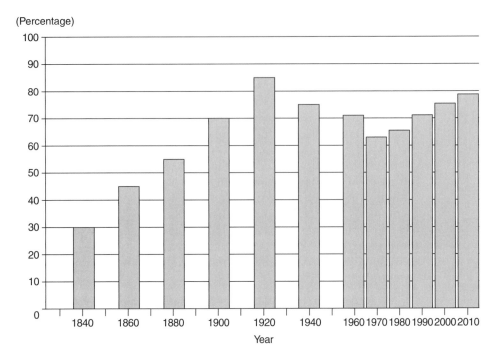

(Percentage)

FIGURE 6.1   Women Teachers: 1840–2010.

Sources: Percentages for 1840 are author's estimates based on Willard S. Elsbree, *The American Teacher: Evolution of a Profession in a Democracy* (New York: American Book Company, 1939), Chap. 17. Percentages for 1880–2000 are from U.S. Department of Education, National Center for Education Statistics, *Digest of Education Statistics, 2002* (2003) [Available: nces.ed.gov/pubs2003/2003060.pdf], Tbls. 36, 68, 70. Percentage for 2010 is author's estimate.

Goals of Common School Reform.   These reformers were ambitious. They wanted to provide at least three years of tax-supported schooling for every white child in the nation. In the cities, they usually set their sights higher, proposing grammar schools and high schools for students who wished to go beyond the primary level. Reformers wanted to upgrade teaching by setting standards for training and hiring teachers, who increasingly were young women (see Figure 6.1 as well as Chapters 1 and 3). Centralizing some of the control of schooling at the state level was the key to reaching the other goals, reformers were convinced, because they found how hard it was to rely on the power of persuasion alone.[18]

Even though Carter, Mann, Barnard, and other reformers were tireless promoters, collecting statistics, publishing reports and journals, and traveling from community to community to drum up interest in common schools, they obtained mixed results at first. But they were persistent, and they knew how to play the game of state politics. Some of them were lawyers, former holders of other political offices, or veterans of other reform crusades. Horace Mann was all of these: an attorney and former legislator who numbered temperance, prison and asylum reform, and abolition among his many causes.[19]

Battles over centralization would continue throughout the nineteenth century, even longer in the South, but state legislatures gradually gave state boards of education the ultimate political weapon: the power of the purse. With the passage of statewide school taxes, state boards could withhold funds from local districts to force compliance with state standards.[20]

Still, the reformers found some things very resistant to change: teacher behavior, for instance. It was one matter for reformers to convince state legislators to set standards for training and hiring teachers; it was quite another to persuade teachers to change how they taught.

Barbara Finkelstein's study *Governing the Young* (1989) reveals that despite the reformers' best efforts to upgrade the teaching force, teacher behavior changed very little. Teachers saw themselves as intellectual overseers and drillmasters, and they were set in their ways. Largely rejecting the child-centered pedagogies of the day, paying little heed to the reformers' goals of developing critical intelligence and self-discipline in students, teachers were content to enforce rote work and instill the dominant values of their local communities. Carter, Mann, Barnard, and other common school crusaders became the first in a long series of reformers to discover how difficult it is to make changes in the day-in, day-out routine of teaching and learning.[21]

DEBATES OVER COMMON SCHOOL REFORM

Common school campaigns peaked in intensity during the 1840s and 1850s. Feelings ran high in legislative chambers, courthouses, town halls, and lyceums across the nation as citizens debated educational issues. When reformers stood up to argue district schools were not reaching many children, a typical reply was local people could simply increase their financial support and improve the schools, making them more attractive to all students. To the argument that many teachers were unqualified, the reply came that better wages would attract better teachers—if the people really wanted them. As we saw in Chapter 3, opponents often added that training in pedagogy was useless. The existing district schools had no inherent weaknesses, opponents of common schooling suggested. It was the responsibility of local citizens to strengthen the schools as they saw fit. State-regulated common schools and normal schools were totally unnecessary.[22]

As the debates unfolded, it became clear the reformers were using the word *common* not in the sense of "ordinary" or "only for the poor" but in three more inclusive ways. Common schools would be common to all children; they would teach a common political creed; and they would instill a common morality based on nonsectarian religion.[23]

Interestingly, outside the South most of the opponents conceded the desirability of the first kind of commonality, although we know few advocates on either side envisioned racially integrated schools. The relatively small number of

Horace Mann (1796–1859)

African Americans who lived outside the South usually went to school, but rarely with whites. Even so, conceding the importance of schooling for all children weakened the opponents' case when the discussion turned to "laggard" districts where people seemed to care little about providing schools of any sort. In those instances, Mann and other reformers argued, the best interests of both the children and the nation compelled the state to step in.[24]

The political, moral, and religious dimensions of commonality drew sharp attacks, even though the reformers tried to walk a tightrope in hopes of avoiding controversy. Orestes Brownson, editor of *The Boston Quarterly Review*, did his best to shake the tightrope in his critique of Mann's *Second Annual Report of the [Massachusetts] Board of Education* in 1839. Brownson wrote:

> Education, then, must be religious and . . . political. Neither religion nor politics can be excluded. Indeed, all education that is worth anything is either religious or political and fits us for discharging our duties either as simple human beings or as members of society.[25]

Building on this premise, Brownson posed the dilemma America's public schools have always faced. If they exclude politics and religion, some people will regard the education they provide as worthless. If politics and religion are included, some people will take offense.

Politics

Orestes Brownson was a Democrat. Before the Civil War, his party supported schooling for all citizens but often opposed common schools. State governments should leave local schools in the hands of local people, Democrats said. Common school reformers were more likely to be Whigs. Their party advocated an active role for the states as well as the federal government in securing internal improvements for the nation. In Massachusetts and other states, the common school crusade was dividing people along traditional party lines.

Turning his attention to the common political creed Mann, a prominent Whig, wanted to teach in the schools, Brownson dryly observed:

> Establish, then, your Whig board of education; place on it a single Democrat, to save appearances; enable this board to establish normal schools and through them to educate all the children of the commonwealth, authorize them to publish common-school libraries, to select all the books used in school, and thus to determine all the doctrines which our children shall imbibe, and what will be the result? We have then given to some half a dozen Whigs the responsible office of forming the political faith and conscience of the whole community.[26]

Mann and the common schoolers would admit nothing of the sort. They rejected the idea that teachers had to avoid discussing politics and government entirely or else offend students by taking sides on partisan issues. As Mann put it,

> Surely, between these extremes, there must be a medium not difficult to be found. . . . Those articles in the creed of republicanism, which are accepted by all, believed in by all, and which form the common basis of our political faith, shall be taught to all. But when the teacher, in the course of his lessons or lectures on the fundamental law, arrives at a controverted text, he is either to read it without comment or remark; or, at most, he is only to say that the passage is the subject of disputation, and that the schoolroom is neither the tribunal to adjudicate, nor the forum to discuss it.[27]

The common schoolers were able to walk the tightrope in arguments over the political aspects of commonality. Most Americans seemed content with the "middle course" Mann suggested, involving *controlled* political discussion. To be sure, since Mann's day a variety of groups from across the political spectrum have objected that their views were not getting a fair hearing in the public schools, but the protests have never convinced large numbers of Americans to abandon the schools.

Morality and Religion

The common schoolers fell off the tightrope in their quest for a common morality based on nonsectarian religion. For most nineteenth-century Americans, religion and morality were firmly linked. Few people entertained the thought that common schools could inculcate morality without also inculcating religion. In the context of the times, morality divorced from religion was no morality at all.

But in an increasingly heterogeneous nation, where Catholics, Jews, people of other non-Protestant faiths, and people of no religious faith were becoming more numerous every year, how could the schools provide a common moral and religious education?

Mann naively believed the answer lay in removing specific religious doctrine from the schools while retaining a common, nonsectarian creed as the basis for moral education. The nonsectarian creed he had in mind, however, was not a distillation of principles from religions around the world. Even though Mann was a Unitarian, he centered his faith on Christ, and he was well aware that most Americans thought of themselves as Christians. Thus *nonsectarian* came to mean "nondenominational Christian" in the language of Horace Mann and most other leaders of the common school movement.[28]

Once again, Mann believed he had found a middle course, a compromise. How could anyone object to moral lessons based on nondenominational Christianity? Mann expressed it this way:

> In this age of the world, it seems to me that no student of history, or observer of mankind, can be hostile to the precepts and the doctrines of the Christian religion, or opposed to any institutions which expound and exemplify them.[29]

Orestes Brownson found the compromise unacceptable. He spoke for many opponents of common schooling when he said:

> The board assure[s] us Christianity shall be insisted on so far, and only so far, as it is common to all sects. This, if it mean anything, means nothing at all. All who attempt to proceed on the principle here laid down will find their Christianity ending in nothingness. Much may be taught in general, but nothing in particular. No sect will be satisfied; all sects will be dissatisfied. For it is not enough that my children are not educated in a belief contrary to my own; I would have them educated to believe what I hold to be important truth.[30]

Brownson was a Roman Catholic. Like other members of his faith, he rejected moral instruction based on general Christian principles as watered-down and meaningless; some Catholics even branded it "godless," calling instead for moral instruction grounded explicitly in the doctrines of Catholicism. Would such instruction be possible in common schools regulated by the state? No, but it would be possible in district schools that left decisions on moral and religious education in the hands of local citizens. Many Catholics and a small number of Protestants took this position along with Brownson.

In effect, the content of moral and religious education would be subject to majority rule in each district. In Catholic districts, Catholicism would prevail in the schools; in Methodist districts, Methodism would dominate; and so on. Those who were unhappy with the schools in their district could open parochial schools and receive public funds to support them, a widely accepted practice before the rise of common schools.

Brownson's vision of publicly funded sectarian schools clashed with Mann's vision of moral and religious commonality. Sectarian schools were divisive, Mann argued. He was relieved that most Protestants seemed content to teach their children specific religious principles at home and in church. Protestants generally accepted common schools that based moral instruction on what was called nonsectarian religion. Catholics, though, continued to protest, not only in Massachusetts but also wherever they were a significant religious minority. Mann became alarmed as other disputes over commonality broke out, making the possibility of compromise seem increasingly remote.[31]

We have already seen how common schoolers construed "nonsectarian religion" as "nondenominational Christianity." Catholics took the argument a step further, charging "nondenominational Christianity," as put into practice in the common schools, was really "nondenominational Protestantism." Daily reading of the King James version of the Bible, "without note or comment," was standard practice in common schools. The practice was fast being written into law as state legislatures and state boards of education began to regulate the schools. Catholics objected that they used another translation of the Bible, the Douay version, and contended it was dangerous to read the scriptures without commentary—students might interpret them incorrectly without guidance. The common schools were filled with Protestantism, they further complained. Many textbooks were replete with slurs against Catholics in general and Irish immigrants in particular. Protestant teachers and students often ridiculed Catholic students. How could Catholic parents send their children to such schools?

The most publicized battle over these issues occurred in New York City during the 1830s and 1840s. Trustees of the Public School Society were determined to increase Catholic enrollment, for they were convinced Catholic children, especially those of recent immigrants, needed common schooling to fit into society; otherwise, they might grow up as unsocialized outsiders. The trustees offered to edit some of the offensive passages from the textbooks, but they would not budge on reading the King James Bible without explication. After Catholics rejected the offer and petitioned for public funds to support their parochial schools, a statewide political controversy erupted. In 1842, the legislature intervened to make New York City part of the state's common school system, at the same time banning the use of public funds to support sectarian religious instruction.[32]

Although similar battles would be fought in other places, the confrontation between Protestants and Catholics in New York City set two precedents. In state

---

BOX 6.1

ANTI-CATHOLICISM AND SCHOOLING

The Catholic League offers a distinctive viewpoint on "Anti-Catholicism and the History of Catholic School Funding" at www.catholicleague.org/research/schoolfunding.htm

after state, legislatures withdrew financial support from sectarian education, and in city after city, Catholics withdrew into their own schools.[33]

THE TRIUMPH OF COMMON SCHOOLS

By the outbreak of the Civil War, common school reformers could sense they had turned a corner. The failure to enlist Catholics in the school crusades had been a setback, to be sure, but there had been many victories. The idea of commonality had spread west and south as state legislatures committed themselves to the goals of tax-supported primary schooling for all white children, higher standards for training and hiring teachers, and a degree of centralized control vested in state boards of education. Even in the South, common schools were a reality in some cities, and southern legislatures were trying to translate the commitment they had made on paper into actual schools for the rural South. Thus the framework to support statewide school systems was either in place or under construction throughout most of the nation.

For fifty years after the Civil War, educators kept busy building, reinforcing, and expanding the systems. Two trends illustrate their progress.

Compulsory Attendance Laws

The passage of compulsory school attendance laws, which appeared first in Massachusetts in 1852, quickened after the war. By 1900, the laws were on the books in thirty states; by 1910, in forty states; and by 1918, in every state. Enforcement of the laws, haphazard at best before the turn of the century, became serious as state governments tightened their reins of control. Enrollment in elementary school became a near-universal experience for Americans, with more than 90 percent of the 5-to-13-year-old age group attending school for at least a few years.[34]

Public High Schools

A parallel development was the rise of public high schools. It should come as no surprise that Massachusetts led the way, opening Boston English High School in 1821, with other New England states, the Middle Atlantic states, and then the rest of the nation gradually following.

Nineteenth-century public high schools present a paradox to educational historians. The institutions seem at once democratic and elitist. In *The Origins of the American High School* (1995), William J. Reese presents a multiple-perspective history that helps us understand the social complexities of secondary education.[35]

With regard to gender, for instance, public high schools were in many ways egalitarian, as Reese and other historians have shown. The schools gave girls a chance to compete on relatively equal footing with boys, and the girls competed well. In a pattern that lasted into the early twentieth century, girls outnumbered and often outperformed boys in high school. Because jobs outside the home were less accessible to girls than to boys, girls stayed in school longer. Girls seemed to enjoy the intellectual challenge of advanced study. With the exception of those taking normal courses in city high schools to prepare for work as teachers, girls tended to view secondary education as an academic pursuit instead of a pathway to a job.[36]

With respect to social class and race, public high schools were highly exclusive. As late as 1890, only 6 percent of the eligible age group in the nation enrolled in high school (see Table 6.1), with 4 percent in public schools and 2 percent in private schools. Almost all the students were white. Public secondary education had a narrow appeal in the nineteenth century, primarily to middle-class whites who lived in cities. The wealthy, the poor, and the rural, in fact, sometimes challenged the right of governments to levy taxes for public high schools, arguing the few families who wanted secondary education for their children should pay for it themselves. And if it was hard enough, as Reese shows, to sell taxpayers on the idea of paying for public secondary education for the white middle classes, it was impossible to get wide support for "helping the most despised youth," African Americans.[37]

A landmark decision of the Michigan Supreme Court in the *Kalamazoo* case (1874) handed public educators yet another victory over their critics, legally establishing a place for high schools as one rung on an educational ladder extending from primary schools through colleges and universities. The *Kalamazoo* decision

TABLE 6.1   High School Attendance and Graduation: 1890–2010

YEAR	PERCENTAGE OF ELIGIBLE AGE GROUP ATTENDING	PERCENTAGE OF ELIGIBLE AGE GROUP GRADUATING
1890	6	4
1900	10	6
1910	14	9
1920	31	17
1930	51	29
1940	73	51
1950	76	59
1960	83	70
1970	92	77
1980	90	71
1990	93	74
2000	93	70
2010	93	72

Source: U.S. Department of Education, National Center for Education Statistics, *Digest of Education Statistics, 2002* (2003) [Available: nces.ed.gov/pubs2003/2003060.pdf], Tbls. 56, 103. Percentage for 2010 is author's estimate.

strengthened the framework of public school systems and readied them for unprecedented expansion in the early twentieth century.[38]

Judging by enrollment figures and similar statistics, we can readily agree with the editors of *Education Week* that public schools were "opening the doors." Elementary schools soon bulged at the seams, and by 1920, almost one-third of the eligible age group was enrolled in secondary education in public high schools. As Table 6.1 indicates, more students also graduated from high school.[39]

Yet many young people fortunate enough to get in the front door of the public high school still left before they earned a diploma. Biases against poor and minority students remained powerful, while educational opportunities for females improved in some ways but deteriorated in others as the twentieth century unfolded (see Chapter 8). Looking back on the century, *Education Week* concludes that "while access has been assured, questions remain about the quality of schooling and the value of a diploma."[40]

PROGRESSIVE SCHOOL REFORM
IN HISTORICAL CONTEXT

Once the students got to school, what were educators supposed to do with them? This question goes to the heart of school reform during the *progressive era,* as historians call the period from the election of President William McKinley in 1896 through the U.S. entry into World War I in 1917. During these years, public schools changed in several lasting ways. Arguing schools should meet the needs of an increasingly heterogeneous student body, educators diversified the curriculum and broadened the schools' responsibilities. Increasingly, students took different courses and different programs depending on their abilities and "probable destinies" in life. Schools assumed more responsibility for the students' health and home life, for instance, and for the work they would do after graduation.[41]

One of the major legacies of progressive school reform is the strong link it forged between going to school and getting a job. Nineteenth-century educators had felt some pressure to make schools relevant to work, but in the early twentieth century, educators became job brokers. Now their goal was fitting students into vocational slots—very narrow slots, in some cases, and very early determined. Schools sorted and selected students as never before. Ability grouping and tracking, ostensibly based on academic talent and individual goals, divided students along social lines as well. Wealthy kids here, middle-class kids there, working-class kids over there. Boys here, girls there. Blacks here, whites there—with subdivisions, of course, for various white ethnic groups.[42]

Historians differ in their interpretations of progressive school reform. To those writing in the early twentieth century, some of whom were reformers themselves, the diversified curriculum and new responsibilities the schools assumed were in the best interest of students as well as society. Liberal historians, regarding progressive reform as basically well intended, have nevertheless argued certain reforms—vocational tracks and low-ability classes, for instance—often harmed the very students they were designed to help. Revisionists have said they know why. The thrust of progressive reform was *not* to help students, especially those on the lower rungs of the social ladder, but to serve the interests of corporate capitalism. Neoconservatives have defended corporate capitalism, of course, but they, too, have been critical of public educators for fragmenting the curriculum and taking on too many social and economic responsibilities. Now multiple-perspective historians are urging us to look beyond caricatured portraits of reformers, supporters, and opponents to see how ordinary people have made their influence felt in the schools.

David Labaree offers a fresh interpretation of the sorting-and-selecting process by emphasizing the role schools play in the "credentials race." Since the late 1800s, Americans have increasingly viewed education as a "private good" rather than a "public good," Labaree contends, and "from this perspective, the point of seeking an education is to gain a competitive advantage over other people by acquiring a badge of merit—an educational credential—that will distinguish the owner from the rest of the pack."[43] The results, he argues, can be seen in our hierarchical educational system, one that "promotes opportunity for some by preserving disadvantage for others."[44]

How to Succeed in School without Really Learning, Labaree's 1997 book, hits the nail on the head. Schools tell students in no uncertain terms that outdoing one another in the quest for grades, credits, degrees, and other credentials is more important than actually learning something. Because middle-class families are the ones whose consumer-oriented demands created this kind of system in the first place, it is not surprising that middle-class students take home the best prizes in the education game.

Keep different interpretations in mind as you read about progressive school reform. What do you think of Labaree's, for instance?

Our major concern in this chapter is with how progressive reforms affected immigrant and African American children. Educators believed these children confronted the schools with special problems. How should the schools respond? The debates in the next section, focused on the cultural theories of *assimilation, pluralism,* and *separation,* suggest some of the strategies educators considered. At the end of this chapter as well as in Chapter 7, we will take a closer look at the curricular changes that began during the progressive era. And Chapter 8 further explores the reform legacy we have just discussed: the stratification of schools by social class.

Modernization Accelerates

Even though the reform movements that occurred during the progressive era were quite diverse, the popular belief that the nation could take charge of its affairs and move forward gave the era a degree of unity. The need for reform seemed great because the forces of modernization—urbanization, industrialization, and immigration—were once again in high gear, confronting the nation with problems and opportunities similar to those pre–Civil War reformers had faced.

But now the stakes seemed even higher. In 1860, only 20 percent of Americans lived in cities. By 1920, that figure had climbed to 51 percent, with more than five million people crowded into New York City and more than two million into Chicago. Industrialization continued to fuel the growth of urban America, but Horace Mann and his contemporaries, certainly no strangers to change, could hardly have anticipated the pace and scale of industrial development after the Civil War: the rapid growth of big business, the extreme concentration of wealth in the hands of the most successful capitalists, and the flight of workers into labor unions.[45]

Many of the workers who took jobs in steel mills, meat-packing plants, garment factories, and other industrial settings were immigrants. The "new" immigration that occurred after 1870 made the "old" immigration seem mild by comparison. In the largest mass movement of people in history, approximately twenty-eight million men, women, and children arrived in the United States from 1870 through 1920. Figure 6.2 shows that by the turn of the twentieth century, immigrants made up almost 15 percent of the population. From the 1890s through the 1920s, in fact, one-third of all the people in the nation were either foreign-born or children of the foreign-born.

Beyond their sheer numbers, more than half the newcomers were from Central, Eastern, and Southern Europe, bringing with them a host of differences in language, religion, food, work habits, and other cultural traits. To people who

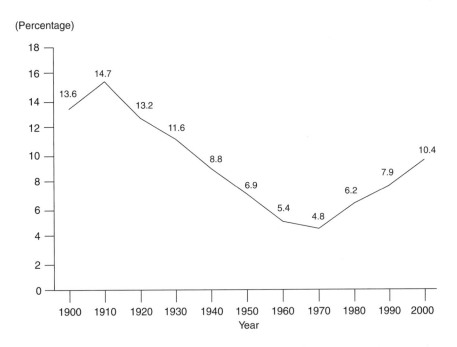

FIGURE 6.2   Percentage of the U.S. Population That Was Foreign-born: 1900–2000

Source: U.S. Department of Commerce, Bureau of the Census, *Profile of the Foreign-Born Population in the United States: 2000* (2001) [Available: www.census.gov/prod/2002pubs/p23-206.pdf], p. 9.

had already put down their roots in this country, these new immigrants seemed even more alien than the old Irish and German immigrants.[46]

Just as in the decades before the Civil War, calls for change went out as Americans decided something had to be done. The resulting reforms show *progressive* could mean different things in different contexts. Some reforms were designed to improve the lot of ordinary people: housing regulations to clean up the squalor of tenements, food and drug acts to ensure standards of purity, and labor legislation to establish a reasonable work day and to get children out of the labor force. Other progressive reforms betrayed a lack of faith in ordinary people. Immigrants were greeted with laws designed to minimize their influence on the nation, and African Americans lost rather than gained rights during the period. Today, almost a century later, some of these reforms appear quite liberal, others profoundly conservative, still others a curious mixture.[47]

Liberal and Conservative School Reformers

School reform during the progressive era was just as complex. John Dewey stands out as the major educational theorist of the era. The theory he and his followers developed became known as *progressivism.* Social worker Jane Addams and African American sociologist W. E. B. Du Bois were among the liberal reformers who were concerned, like Dewey, with social justice and social service. In this chapter we will call Addams and Du Bois to the podium to present the case for liberal reform. In the next chapter, we will pay closer attention to Dewey. Conservative reformers, represented here by school administrator and historian Ellwood P. Cubberley and African American leader Booker T. Washington, had a different set of priorities, an agenda centered on social order and business efficiency.

Conservatives outnumbered liberals and often held positions that gave them more direct influence on the schools. Moreover, most of the teachers, administrators, and school board members who were responsible for putting educational reforms into practice on the front lines took an eclectic yet fundamentally conservative approach, paying lip service to the ideas of a Dewey, perhaps, but acting more like a Cubberley in their day-to-day work.[48]

Ordinary People: Students, Parents, Teachers, and Others

Since the 1980s, historians have paid more attention to the ways ordinary people—students, parents, teachers, and others—influenced school reform. Multiple-perspective history reveals that ordinary people did not just stand by passively and let things happen to them. They stood up and made things happen their way.

Four multiple-perspective studies capture this phenomenon especially well. In *Power and the Promise of School Reform* (1986), William J. Reese describes the "grass-roots" efforts of women's groups, parent-teacher coalitions, labor unions, socialists, and others to reshape schools during the progressive era. Voicing a variety of local concerns, these groups often won compromises and concessions from more powerful business interests. *Outside In* (1989) presents Paula S. Fass's argument that European immigrants, African Americans, women, and Catholics—cultural "outsiders" at the turn of the century—transformed American education as they moved through the schools. The education system we know today is the result of a tug of war between liberalism and conservatism as the schools came to grips with diversity. In *The Education of Blacks in the South, 1860–1935* (1988), James D. Anderson portrays African Americans as active agents in their own education, people working to take charge of their lives and advance themselves. Their burning desire to learn threatened whites because blacks were often able to use schools to resist racial and class oppression. And Jeffrey Mirel's book *The Rise and Fall of an Urban School System: Detroit, 1907-81* (1993) is a fine example of how a historian can give fair play to the voices of diverse people with different agendas and at the same time allow the historian's own voice (in Mirel's case, neoconservative) to be heard.[49]

As you read the debates in the next section, keep in mind the complexities and contradictions of school reform. The process of reform involved much more than prominent people speaking while ordinary people listened.

DEBATES OVER PROGRESSIVE SCHOOL REFORM

Nowhere is the complexity of reform more clearly illustrated than in the debates over the schooling of immigrant and African American children, debates strikingly similar to those we hear today. Two cultural theories dominated the debates.

According to the theory of *assimilation*, it was the duty of the schools to fit children into society by washing out cultural differences and ironing in values and behaviors that conformed to Anglo-American ways. Here was the idea of the *melting pot* as most Americans understood it—a crucible that would melt away the immigrants' cultural differences.

According to the theory of *separation*, by contrast, certain cultural groups were so different that their children were better off attending separate schools, an experience that prepared them to reside in separate neighborhoods, hold separate jobs, and lead separate lives as adults. Members of these groups were not candidates for the melting pot because they were regarded as too different to assimilate—incurably inferior.

The schools, taking their cues from the rest of the nation, used these theories to develop two distinct educational agendas: schools to promote assimilation for immigrant children and schools to foster separation for African American children. Also singled out for separation were Mexican Americans and Native Americans, with California adding Asian American children to the list of those schooled separately.[50]

In *The American People and Their Education: A Social History* (2003), Richard Altenbaugh discusses the varieties of separation that were imposed on different racial and ethnic groups. The segregation that Mexican Americans experienced closely paralleled the segregation of African Americans. During the progressive era, the separation of these two groups in schooling and in other walks of life gained the full force of law. For Native American children, progressive era policies reinforced the federal government's longstanding goal of eradicating tribal culture by sending Indian children to boarding schools. State and local governments often segregated Asian America students, whose numbers were small and geographically concentrated, and the federal government passed immigration restrictions to insure that the Asian population remained small.[51]

Assimilation for Immigrant Children

Ellwood Cubberley stated the case for immigrant assimilation in the textbooks he wrote for teacher education courses. Cubberley, who rose quickly through the ranks of teachers and administrators to become dean of education at Stanford University, was one of the most prominent education professors of his day as well as a leading historian. His textbooks went into numerous editions, influencing several generations of American educators. Had you decided to become a teacher sixty or seventy years ago, your introduction to education might well have been a course taught with one of Cubberley's books.[52]

In the well-thumbed volume from which I took the following quotation, the administrator who originally owned the book underlined and annotated Cubberley's views on the new immigrants:

> These Southern and Eastern Europeans were of a very different type from the North and West Europeans who preceded them. Largely illiterate, docile, often lacking in initiative, and almost wholly without the Anglo-Saxon conceptions of righteousness, liberty, law, order, public decency, and government, their coming has served to dilute tremendously our national stock and to weaken and corrupt our political life. . . . They have created serious problems in housing and living, moral and sanitary conditions, and honest and decent government, while popular education has everywhere been made more difficult by their presence. The result has been that in many sections of our country foreign manners, customs, observances, and language have tended to supplant native ways and the English speech, while the so-called "melting pot" has had more than it could handle. The new peoples, and especially those from the South and East of Europe, have come so fast that we have been unable to absorb and assimilate them, and our national life, for the past quarter of a century, has been afflicted with a serious case of racial indigestion.[53]

Nevertheless, Cubberley looked to the future with characteristically progressive optimism. If immigrant children would only attend public schools rather than "foreign-language parochial schools," Cubberley opined as he gestured toward the Catholic and Lutheran churches, they would begin to lay aside their Old World culture and pick up American ways. The diversified public school curriculum, he believed, offered vocational courses that would help immigrant children make a contribution to society. The process of *Americanization* might take two or three generations to complete, but Cubberley felt sure the public schools, "our greatest agency for unifying the diverse elements of our population," were up to the task.[54]

Children in an urban public school, circa 1900.

Since Cubberley's day, historians have analyzed the experiences of immigrant groups with less condescension and more sensitivity to the complexities involved in becoming American. The Americanization process varied greatly from group to group and individual to individual. Some immigrant groups were eager to assimilate, while others resisted. Some groups supported public schools, while others, as Cubberley indicated, rejected public education and sent their children to private schools. The picture becomes even more complex when we realize generalizations about a particular group do not apply to every individual within the group.

Even so, historians writing since the 1960s have added tremendously to our understanding of immigrants and their schooling. The children of Eastern European Jews, for instance, usually attended public schools and did remarkably well. Historians attribute their success to such factors as their urban origins—they were acclimated to city life before they ever came to the United States—and their respect for formal education, which was deeply embedded in their religion and other aspects of their culture. Most Eastern and Southern Europeans who were not Jewish were Roman Catholic, and they generally fared less well in public schools. Southern Italians, for example, experienced culture shock in American cities. They usually came from the rural areas of their homeland, where they viewed extended schooling as a luxury for the rich and a threat to the authority of the family.[55]

At the turn of the twentieth century, about half of all Roman Catholic children attended parochial schools, which offered a kinder, gentler form of Americanization: acculturation in American ways tempered by respect for Old World traditions. Among the factors influencing a Catholic family's choice between public and parochial schooling were the ethnic group the family belonged to, the strength of the family's attachment to ethnic traditions, the intensity of the family's religious faith, and the level of anti-Catholic prejudice in the local community. Catholic educators, as might be expected, disagreed in the strongest possible terms with Cubberley's negative assessment of their schools. Culturally as well as academically, Catholic educators contended, their schools did a superior job. This debate is still going on, and you will hear a more detailed and contemporary version in Chapter 10.[56]

■ ■ ■ ■ ■

BOX 6.2

IMMIGRATION HISTORY RESEARCH CENTER

Housed at the University of Minnesota, the Immigration History Research Center maintains a Web page at www.ihrc.umn.edu/ which you can visit to investigate the role of schooling in the immigrant experience.

The Middle Course of Pluralism

Most public educators agreed with Cubberley. A strong consensus supported the policies of assimilation he advocated. Two liberal reformers who dissented, though, were Jane Addams and John Dewey, both of whom tried to chart a middle course between assimilation and separation. Certainly it would be undesirable if each immigrant group went its own way, turning inward and never learning what it means to be American. Such separation would fragment the nation, they acknowledged. But total assimilation would also be unwise, they insisted, for already it was driving a wedge between immigrant parents and their children, depriving the immigrants as well as other Americans of a valuable cultural heritage.

■ ■ ■ ■ ■

BOX 6.3

IMMIGRANTS AND ROMAN CATHOLIC SCHOOLS

To find out how Catholic schools helped successive waves of immigrants adjust to American life in the most ethnically diverse city in the South, read "A History of the Archdiocese of New Orleans" at www.archdiocese-no.org/history

The middle course Addams and Dewey were seeking eventually became known as *pluralism*. According to this theory, every person is expected to learn the common culture—which in this nation consists of the English language, American history, and the American political system, among many other things—but other cultures are not only tolerated but encouraged. As Addams told the National Education Association in 1908:

> [T]he schools ought to do more to connect these children with the best things of the past, to make them realize something of the beauty and charm of the language, the history, and the traditions which their parents represent. . . . If the body of teachers in our great cities could take hold of the immigrant colonies, could bring out of them their handicrafts and occupations, their traditions, their folk songs and folk lore, the beautiful stories which every immigrant colony is ready to tell and translate; could get the children to bring these things into school as the material from which culture is made and the material upon which culture is based, they would discover by comparison that which they give them now is a poor meretricious and vulgar thing. Give these children a chance to utilize the historic and industrial material which they see about them and they will begin to have a sense of ease in America, a first consciousness of being at home. I believe if these people are welcomed upon the basis of the resources which they represent and the contributions which they bring, it may come to pass that these schools which deal with immigrants will find that they have a wealth of cultural and industrial material which will make the schools in other neighborhoods positively envious.[57]

Addams's commitment to pluralism was based on her experience as a social worker and leader of the settlement house movement. In 1889, she founded Hull House in Chicago to encourage contact between privileged women (like Addams herself) and poor people, believing both could profit from the exchange. Mutual respect was the cornerstone of her philosophy. Addams envisioned settlement houses as community centers offering educational, social, and recreational programs. She hoped they would serve as models for public schools and other public agencies.[58]

A few public educators who shared Addams's pluralistic outlook started pioneer programs in what we now call *multicultural education*. Leonard Covello, who immigrated with his parents from Southern Italy at the turn of the century, experienced cultural dislocation as a student in the New York City public schools. Feeling strong pressure to turn his back on Italy if he wanted to succeed in America—a teacher even changed his name from the original Leonard*o* Cov*i*ello—the young man complied, only to have second thoughts about assimilation after he graduated from college and began a career in education.[59]

■ ■ ■ ■ ■

BOX 6.4

JANE ADDAMS AND HULL HOUSE

Take an online tour of Hull House at www.uic.edu/jaddams/hull/hull_house.html and see how it served as a social and educational center. This Web site is rich with information on Addams and her work as a reformer.

Covello devoted the rest of his life to promoting pluralism. As a teacher in the New York City system, Covello worked with Italian students and parents to build pride in their heritage. When he became a principal, Covello turned a high school enrolling twenty-five different ethnic groups into the kind of community center Addams envisioned. Ordinary people from ethnic neighborhoods—the largest groups were Italian, Puerto Rican, and African—helped shape the new school. Students performed plays in Italian and Spanish. Parents spoke out in advisory meetings conducted in several languages. The curriculum upheld racial and ethnic tolerance.[60]

Such schools were rare. To Addams's disappointment, most public educators found little they wanted to emulate either at Hull House or at schools like Covello's because most educators saw little they wanted to save in immigrant cultures. Instead, their emphasis was on preparing immigrants for the workforce. Addams was alarmed that the vocational programs many immigrant children were tracked into led to dull, repetitive jobs that, she predicted, would produce alienation and drug abuse.

In Addams's day, as today, the issue of language was especially sensitive. Why should public schools encourage the use of any language but English, critics wanted to know. Hadn't the schools always used English as the only medium of instruction?

Conveniently ignored in most of the debates was the history of bilingual public schools in such cities as Cincinnati, Cleveland, Indianapolis, St. Louis, New Orleans, and San Francisco, some of which were using languages other than English as a medium of instruction before the Civil War. Responding to parents who wished to preserve their ethnic culture, some public schools offered bilingual instruction, usually in German and English, as late as World War I, when antiforeign sentiment forced the programs to close. Although bilingual public schools were the exception, not the rule, they set an early precedent for a pluralistic approach to public education, an approach that became more popular in the 1960s and thereafter (see Chapter 8).[61]

Separation for African American Children

If immigrants were thrown into the melting pot and expected to climb out, completely assimilated, within a few generations, African Americans got no such treatment. Some immigrants were enthusiastic supporters of assimilationist public schools, as we have seen, while others chose private schools. Africans, with few exceptions, did not have the choice. In parts of the nation, most notably the rural South, they were lucky if they could go to school at all. As the progressive era opened in 1896, the U.S. Supreme Court handed down its decision in the *Plessy v. Ferguson* case, which placed the stamp of judicial approval on the "separate but equal" doctrine. *Plessy* gave a Louisiana railroad company the right to segregate African American passengers in train cars that were clearly separate and supposedly equal, and the decision quickly became the legal basis for segregation in other walks of life, including public education.

■ ■ ■ ■ ■

BOX 6.5

BILINGUAL EDUCATION

"Speaking of Learning: Bilingual Education," a multimedia examination of the roots of the ongoing controversy over language, is available on the Public Broadcasting System (PBS) Web site for the series "School: The Story of American Public Education." Visit at www.pbs.org/kcet/publicschool/roots_in_history/bilingual.html

The result was a steady deterioration in the quality of education for African Americans as a bad situation became worse. In the South, where more than 90 percent of African Americans lived, the gaps in financial and physical resources between white schools and black schools widened. At the end of Reconstruction in 1877, the South spent $1.50 to $2.00 per white student for every dollar spent per black student, a ratio of almost 2 to 1. By the end of the progressive era, the ratio increased to perhaps 4 to 1. These figures estimate regional averages; we know the gap was wider, appallingly wider, in many rural systems, and some historians put the overall ratio of white to black expenditures as high as 15 to 1. Whatever the exact figures, it is obvious that "separate but equal" really meant "separate and unequal."[62]

The worst situation was in the South, but elsewhere racial attitudes hardened as lines were drawn to separate blacks and whites, either by law (as in the South) or by custom (as in most of the nation). Race riots and lynchings left ugly scars across the face of the country. In an era often remembered for social progress and uplift, African Americans found their educational rights eroding along with their voting rights, property rights, and other civil rights.

African Americans fought back, as we can tell by listening to the debates over their education during the progressive era. The most important debate was between Booker T. Washington and W. E. B. Du Bois, two leaders whose social and educational views were as different as their backgrounds.[63]

Washington, born in Virginia just before the Civil War, literally worked his way *Up from Slavery*, as he explained in his aptly titled autobiography. The education he received at Hampton Institute, an industrial school for African Americans in Virginia, convinced him hard work, practical training, and cooperation with whites were the keys to success for blacks. He put his ideas into practice as head of Tuskegee Institute in Alabama, building the school from the ground up as a national model for the education of African teachers, farmers, and other workers. Washington soon became the best-known and most influential African American of his day.[64]

Du Bois, born in Massachusetts just after the Civil War, attended integrated public schools, graduated from all-black Fisk University in Nashville, studied abroad at the University of Berlin, and capped his education at Harvard University, where he became the first African in the nation to earn a Ph.D. As a professor at Atlanta University and later as a leader of the National Association for the

■ ■ ■ ■ ■

BOX 6.6

SEGREGATION AND INEQUALITY

"I look history straight in the eye, and call it like it is," declares John Hope Franklin. For an interactive "biographical conversation" with Franklin, who grew up in segregation, faced down discrimination, and went on to become a distinguished historian, go to the University of North Carolina Public Television Web site at www.unctv.org/biocon/jhfranklin/index.html

Advancement of Colored People (NAACP), Du Bois spoke out sharply against all forms of racial discrimination. He pushed for equal access to schools at every level, but his heart was in higher education, which he hoped would prepare the "talented tenth"—the most gifted 10 percent of young African Americans—to become the leaders of their race.[65]

Washington Advocates Industrial Education.   While Du Bois was considered radical and outspoken for the times, Washington was so popular he was often invited to address white audiences, a distinction few other blacks could claim. By the 1890s, Washington was already in demand on the lecture circuit, but his 1895 speech at the Cotton States and International Exposition in Atlanta cemented his reputation as "the spokesman for his race."

On this occasion, the audience consisted of whites and blacks, seated in separate sections. Washington's thesis was the two races would have to cooperate in order to move the South forward economically. But he carefully distinguished between economic and social progress. With words chosen to admonish blacks and reassure whites, Washington said:

> The wisest of my race understand that the agitation of questions of social equality is the extremest folly, and that progress in the enjoyment of all the privileges that will come to us must be the result of severe and constant struggle, rather than of artificial forcing. . . . The opportunity to earn a dollar in a factory just now is worth infinitely more than the opportunity to spend a dollar in an opera house.[66]

Delivering the line that would prove to be the most quoted in the speech, Washington held his hand high: "In all things that are purely social we can be as separate as the fingers, yet one as the hand in all things essential to mutual progress." Thus Washington struck the conservative chords of social order and business efficiency.[67]

Despite his reference to factory work, the *industrial education* Washington advocated for African Americans did not emphasize preparation for city jobs in plants and machine shops. Instead, the accent was on rural life, because Washington believed blacks could make their greatest contribution in farming and farm-related crafts. Moreover, he used the word *industrial* much as we use *industrious* today, stressing such values as efficiency, punctuality, thrift, obedience, and cleanliness

*Booker T. Washington
(1856–1915)*

more than specific job skills. Above all, he urged African Americans to adopt the proper attitudes toward work and their place in the economic order. As he cautioned in the Atlanta speech:

> Our greatest danger is, that in the great leap from slavery to freedom, we may overlook the fact that the masses of us are to live by the production of our hands, and fail to keep in mind that we shall prosper in proportion as we learn to dignify and glorify common labor and put brains and skill into the common occupations in life, shall prosper in proportion as we learn to draw the line between the superficial and the substantial, the ornamental gewgaws of life and the useful. No race can prosper till it learns that there is as much dignity in tilling a field as in writing a poem. It is at the bottom of life we must begin, and not at the top.[68]

Industrial education worked its way into African American schools at every level. In some elementary schools, it threatened to crowd academic studies into a corner, and as the small number of black students who were able to continue their formal education discovered, industrial education was firmly entrenched in high schools and colleges as well.[69]

Du Bois: Political Power, Civil Rights, and Higher Education.   It angered Du Bois that the ideas Washington articulated were so widely accepted. Few blacks and fewer whites paid attention as Du Bois and other activists outlined dissenting points of view. Ellwood P. Cubberley's teacher education textbooks, for instance, contained words of praise for Washington and industrial education with no mention of the alternatives. As Cubberley explained matter-of-factly to future teachers and administrators, the black's "peculiar mental makeup and character have made his vocational and industrial education almost a necessity." These words hit college-educated African Americans like a slap in the face.[70]

In the early 1900s, Du Bois established himself as Washington's most vocal critic. As a professor at Atlanta University, Du Bois knew firsthand how difficult it was to raise money for African American colleges and universities with a strong academic orientation. Northern philanthropists were sending money South, to be

W. E. B. Du Bois
(1868–1963)

sure, but Washington's endorsement of industrial education carried so much weight that Tuskegee, Hampton, and similar schools were receiving the lion's share. Atlanta, Fisk, and other institutions with more traditional academic programs found it difficult to compete. Adding insult to injury, white philanthropists sometimes required them to develop industrial programs as a condition for receiving financial support.

Du Bois believed "progress in human affairs is more often a pull than a push, a surging forward of the exceptional man, and the lifting of his duller brethren slowly and painfully to his vantage ground." How could the black race produce the professionals and leaders it needed when the deck seemed to be stacked against academic programs?[71]

In his book *The Souls of Black Folk* (1903), Du Bois grappled with that question and went considerably further, offering a pointed critique of Washington's overall approach to black–white relations. Calling Washington's 1895 speech the "Atlanta Compromise" and referring to him with more than a hint of sarcasm as "the most distinguished Southerner since Jefferson Davis," president of the Confederate States of America, Du Bois charged Washington had asked African Americans to trade their political power, civil rights, and higher education for "industrial education, the accumulation of wealth, and the conciliation of the South." They had made the bargain, Du Bois noted, and three things had occurred:

1. The disfranchisement of the Negro.
2. The legal creation of a distinct status of civil inferiority for the Negro.
3. The steady withdrawal of aid from institutions for the higher training of the Negro.

> These movements are not, to be sure, direct results of Mr. Washington's teaching; but his propaganda has, without a shadow of a doubt, helped their speedier accomplishment. . . . And thus Mr. Washington faces the triple paradox of his career:
>
> 1. He is striving nobly to make Negro artisans businessmen and property owners; but it is utterly impossible, under modern competitive methods, for workingmen and property owners to defend their rights and exist without the right of suffrage.
> 2. He insists on thrift and self-respect, but at the same time counsels a silent submission to civic inferiority such as is bound to sap the manhood of any race in the long run.
> 3. He advocates common-schooling and industrial training, and depreciates institutions of higher learning; but neither the Negro common schools, nor Tuskegee itself, could remain open a day were it not for teachers trained in Negro colleges, or trained by their graduates.[72]

Although Du Bois's ideas may sound more acceptable than Washington's to our modern ears, we must remember to judge both men by the standards of their times rather than ours. By all accounts, both were sincere and well intended, and both saw education as resistance to oppression.

Washington was not trying to sell African Americans short—he was trying to make the best of a miserable situation. In fact, historical evidence has come to light showing how Washington worked behind the scenes to support civil rights litigation he could not afford to endorse in public.

By the same token, Du Bois was not the elitist his blunt statement on "the exceptional man" and "his duller brethren" might suggest. Most of the African American college students he taught came from poverty. Du Bois saw what they could achieve when given the opportunity, and he refused to compromise their future. His work with the NAACP helped pave the way for the modern Civil Rights movement.[73]

PROGRESSIVE SCHOOL REFORM IN PERSPECTIVE

When progressive reformers, liberal and conservative, stepped back to survey what they had accomplished, conservatives could see more reasons to be pleased. Assimilation and separation were well established in educational theory and practice. Pluralism was so undeveloped and unrefined it had yet to be named.

To be sure, all school reformers could point with pride to shared victories. Public schools were virtually everywhere, with centralized, statewide systems in place even in the South. The passage and enforcement of compulsory attendance laws was filling the schools with unprecedented numbers of students. More than 90 percent of children aged five to thirteen were in school, as we have seen, and more students were continuing their formal education through high school. Reflecting the growing consensus that the schools had to assume new social and economic responsibilities to meet the needs of a diverse student body, the diversified curriculum was rapidly winning acceptance. Another victory virtually all educational reformers could celebrate was the trend toward more specialized training for teachers. Colleges and universities were adding departments of pedagogy during the progressive era, state teachers colleges were emerging, and state normal schools and high school normal programs were in their heyday. In an era that fell in love with statistics, the facts and figures on the schools looked good.

Liberal reformers could take heart that a new theory of education, *progressivism,* was receiving a great deal of rhetorical support, especially among professors of education and school administrators. Because progressivism was so closely associated with John Dewey, the leading liberal reformer, liberals had high hopes that progressivism would eventually usher in a new era of social service and social justice in the schools.[74]

Imagine their disappointment when, in the years after World War I, the nation took a conservative turn and "returned to normalcy." The spirit of liberal reform was a dead letter as far as the schools were concerned, but professors of education continued to preach, and administrators increasingly encouraged teachers to practice, "progressive" methods of classroom instruction. By the 1920s, the methodology had been dubbed *progressive education.*[75]

■ ■ ■ ■ ■

BOX 6.7

STANDARDIZED TESTING

The Web site of the PBS series "School: The Story of American Public Education" offers a multimedia historical look at "Measuring Up: Tests, Curriculum, and Standards" at www.pbs.org/kcet/publicschool/roots_in_history/testing.html

Liberals were also disappointed that the academic discipline of psychology, which many progressive educators were turning to in their quest to make teaching and learning more scientific, was becoming another justification for the new status quo. As intelligence testing became widespread in the schools during the 1920s, educators gathered evidence that seemed to support what they were already doing: placing immigrant children, African American children, and poor children generally in low-ability classes and vocational programs.[76]

And so it was the form but not the substance of progressivism that influenced the schools after the war, the rhetoric but not the spirit. At the end of this chapter and throughout the next one, we will examine the controversy over how much the schools changed as a result of progressive influence, whether or not they improved, and who deserves the credit—or the blame.[77]

TWENTIETH-CENTURY PATTERNS OF EDUCATION

We can now look back on the twentieth century and identify major trends in the schools. Because many of the chapters in this book provide historical perspectives on the issues they examine, the purpose of this section is to outline broad patterns to help structure the analysis presented elsewhere. Four patterns stand out as especially important: competition among school board members, administrators, and teachers for control of the schools; the changing balance of educational power among the local, state, and federal levels of government; the quest for equal educational opportunities; and trends in the curriculum.

Competition for Control of the Schools

This first pattern has roots in the progressive era. "Get the schools out of politics" was the rallying cry of conservative reformers who charged local school boards with inefficiency and corruption.

The problem, they said, was that school boards in major cities had too many members with too many different points of view to do business efficiently. The boards were packed with "petty local politicos" elected from the various wards (political subdivisions) of the city. According to the reformers, such board members lacked a vision of what was good for the system as a whole—they were interested only in the schools in their own wards, and, to make matters worse, some of them were on the take, soliciting bribes, kickbacks, and payoffs. The reformers' solution: smaller school boards with members elected or appointed at-large, with each member representing the city as a whole rather than an individual ward.[78]

The trend toward smaller boards with at-large members swept the nation during the progressive era, spreading from major cities into other school systems. One result was the appearance on local boards of more people the reformers liked to call "the better sort"—successful businesspeople and professionals, mostly upper-middle and upper class—and a sharp drop in the number of members with lower socioeconomic status.

A closely related trend was the rise to power of "professional" school administrators. As enrollments increased and the management of school systems became ever more complex, local board members gladly turned over more responsibility to superintendents and their growing administrative staffs. "Let the experts manage the schools" was another popular slogan during the progressive era, signaling a shift of power away from board members and toward upper-level administrators. As the twentieth century wore on, local superintendents consolidated their power, claiming only experienced educators with advanced degrees from university departments of educational administration had the expertise necessary to run the schools. A self-conscious class of "professional" educators was emerging.[79]

Teachers felt lost in the shuffle. In some respects, they had felt more comfortable before progressive reform. Many teachers had known the board member who represented their ward—a shopkeeper from the neighborhood, perhaps. The smaller, at-large board seemed remote, aloof—a group of elites. The worst development from the teachers' point of view was the attempt to apply the "sound and cheap" principles of scientific management to the schools. Merit pay and promotions based on evaluations by administrators and supervisors posed the greatest threat, as we saw in Chapter 2.

In 1920, as Figure 6.1 shows, 86 percent of America's teachers were women. Just when the numerical dominance of women in the occupation was greater than at any time before or since, women were losing power in the school system hierarchy. In the late nineteenth century, most elementary school principals had been women. During the twentieth century, women watched these administrative positions go increasingly to "school men," as male educators like to be called to set themselves apart. High school principalships had always belonged to men. David Tyack describes the situation bluntly:

> Hierarchical organization of the schools and the male chauvinism of the larger society fit as hand to glove. The system required subordination; women were generally subordinate to men; the employment of women as teachers thus augmented the authority of the largely male administrative leadership.[80]

In the early decades of this century, teachers organized to protect their interests and improve their economic security. Their early organizations were local groups responding to local problems. Teacher organizations gave women the

■ ■ ■ ■ ■

BOX 6.8

TEACHERS ORGANIZE

For a deeper understanding of how and why teachers organized, explore the history of the American Federation of Teachers at www.aft.org/history/Index.html

opportunity to lead, but these groups, too, were often dominated by school men. With the NEA in the hands of college professors and administrators, some local teacher organizations affiliated with the AFT, a small, struggling union.[81]

From the 1920s through the 1950s, teachers had to strain to make their voices heard in school system policy, even when they combined their voices and spoke through an AFT local. The situation has changed since the 1960s. The AFT led the way by showing how collective bargaining can amplify the teachers' voice. After scoring organizing victories in New York City and several other large systems, the AFT became a power to be reckoned with. In short order, the NEA also became a teacher union, a national giant with strength in every state and in most local school systems. For the first time, teachers had a collective voice in educational policy making at all three levels of government, and the voice of female teachers was stronger than ever.

As we saw in Chapter 4, the new power of teacher organizations is highly controversial. Supporters say teachers are beginning at last to act like professionals rather than employees; detractors say just the opposite is true.

The Local/State/Federal Balance

The increasingly complex politics of teacher organizations add their own weight to the educational balance of power among the local, state, and federal levels of government, the second pattern of twentieth-century education we will consider. Recall the debates over the merits of local versus state control of public education, the tension between the idea that citizens should be able to run their local schools as they see fit and the idea that a degree of centralized control is necessary to ensure minimum standards of education. Notwithstanding the statewide standards promoted by school reformers, local school boards still enjoyed a great deal of autonomy at the turn of the century because the regulations state legislatures and state boards of education imposed left plenty of discretion at the local level.

As the century unfolded, the states gradually tightened their reins of control, often in response to controversies and shortcomings in local school districts. Several examples illustrate the trend. Complaints about the content of textbooks—just as in Horace Mann's day—led to more power for state textbook committees. But local school officials were usually able to choose from several titles on the state-approved list or, in some states, simply to ignore the list. Arbitrary dismissals of teachers triggered the passage of state tenure laws, often after successful campaigns by teacher organizations. But local boards could still fire probationary teachers without stating a reason, and administrators could make life miserable for tenured teachers who violated local mores.

Financial problems also enhanced state control. During the Great Depression, thousands of local school districts declared insolvency and closed. Faced with already wide gaps in spending between rich systems and poor systems within virtually every state, legislatures stepped in to provide relief, mandating minimum levels of local support as a condition for receiving state aid. Lawsuits from citizens and advocacy groups led to a still greater state role in school finance beginning in the 1960s. As Chapter 9 points out, the latest round of litigation is pushing many states closer than ever toward equalizing expenditures from one district to the next.

Financial problems were also behind the trend toward consolidation of local school systems. In 1900, there were approximately 150,000 independent school districts in the United States; today there are about 15,000. State legislatures justified consolidation on the grounds of economic and academic efficiency—more programs could be offered to more students at lower cost—but local people complained their control over the schools was slipping away.[82]

Such complaints are not new. Most of them would seem familiar to Horace Mann. What would strike him as novel is the federal government's growing involvement in public education during the twentieth century. Even a Whig like Mann, an advocate of active government, never envisioned public education as a major item on the federal list of "internal improvements." But in 1917, the federal government made its first annual appropriations to secondary schools through the Smith-Hughes Act, which was designed to promote vocational education. For the next few decades, the federal role was focused, with Congress trying hard not to step on state and local toes. A series of federal relief acts aided schools during the Depression, the 1944 G.I. Bill helped veterans further their education, and the 1958 National Defense Education Act (NDEA) entered the schools in the space race.

The real breakthrough came during the 1960s and 1970s, when the federal government began to target most of its assistance toward students whose education had been a low priority in state and local school systems: poor, minority, disabled, and female students. Judicial activism in the federal courts complemented the high profile Congress maintained in public education, and Lyndon Johnson said he wanted to go down in history as an "education president."

We will take a closer look at federal involvement in other chapters, especially Chapter 9, but here it is important to note the mixed reviews the new federal role received. Once again debates over centralized control, this time control at the federal level, broke out across the nation, and during the 1980s, Ronald Reagan capitalized on a strong backlash as he cut federal involvement in education.

Part of the backlash reflected the general distrust Americans have always had of central government, though part of it was based on the newer and more specific concern that the federal government was paying too much attention to certain groups of students—poor, minority, disabled, and female—and promoting their advancement at the expense of the rest. This development was an ironic reversal of the situation during the first half of the twentieth century, when members of these same groups criticized the federal government for its lack of interest in their plight.[83]

The Quest for Equal Educational Opportunities

As we examine the third pattern of twentieth-century education, we will consider African Americans as a case in point. Since the 1920s, the NAACP and other organizations working on behalf of African Americans have put legal pressure on public schools and colleges, seeking better treatment for black students and teachers. The results were disappointing at first. Southern states continued to spend several times as much money on white as on black children, and in other regions, particularly in large industrial cities, schools became more segregated instead of less. In the late 1930s, the tide began to turn as African Americans won court decisions that eventually led to equal salaries for black and white teachers.[84]

Other litigation began the long process of desegregation. The major victory came with the U.S. Supreme Court's landmark decision in *Brown v. Board of Education of Topeka* (1954). The court unanimously overturned *Plessy v. Ferguson* (1896) for elementary and secondary schools, declaring "in the field of public education the doctrine of 'separate but equal' has no place." As James Patterson explains in his book *Brown v. Board of Education: A Civil Rights Milestone and Its Troubled Legacy* (2001), the struggle to translate the court's words into action continues today.[85]

The modern Civil Rights movement that gathered strength in the post-*Brown* era not only helped improve educational opportunities for African Americans but also inspired other Americans to press for better education for their children. During the 1960s and 1970s, Mexican Americans, Asian Americans, and Native Americans pressed for better schooling using a variety of strategies. For Mexican Americans, the years 1965 to 1975 were marked by militancy on the issues of segregation and language but followed by a time of retrenchment, especially on segregation. Many Asian Americans walked the path of assimilation toward the nation's educational and economic mainstream, although the degree of success they found varied from one Asian ethnic group to another. Under the banner of self-determination, Native Americans insisted on taking charge of their own schooling, which remained segregated for those who attended the reservation. The Civil Rights movement also encouraged women, the disabled, and the poor to mount campaigns for better education.[86]

The schools responded in a variety of ways, often by developing special programs with federal funds. The development of special education, the renewed interest in bilingual instruction, and the growth of multicultural education led to arguments reminiscent of earlier debates over assimilation, separation, and pluralism. Despite the backlash against federal involvement in education during the 1980s, educators continued to show concern—at least rhetorical concern—for students labeled "at risk." In Chapters 8 and 9, we will analyze the current status of the quest for equal educational opportunities.

Historians are reassessing how much the quest has actually accomplished: What has been gained and what has been lost in the process of school desegregation, for instance? *Brown* is more than fifty years old, and historians are trying to answer the difficult questions it has raised. Vanessa Siddle Walker argues in *Their Highest Potential: An African American Community in the Segregated South* (1996) that black students could attain excellence despite segregation when black communities gave them the support they needed. Has desegregation weakened such support? Siddle Walker thinks so. Peter Irons takes a different position in *Jim Crow's Children: The Broken Promise of the* Brown *Decision* (2002), blaming federal courts for backing down in the face of resistance and not pushing desegregation far enough. Would more pressure have worked? Irons says yes. James Patterson's recent book, mentioned previously, does an excellent job of weighing evidence and balancing interpretations before arriving at a position of qualified support for *Brown*.[87]

Trends in the Curriculum

The final twentieth-century pattern is a fascinating study of the relationship between educational theory and educational practice. Historians enjoy investigating the evolution of the *formal* curriculum, the one discussed in teacher education courses and written down in school board policies. Usually the historical analysis focuses on major studies and reports that have influenced the curriculum. To show how the curriculum has changed during this century, historians often begin by describing the nineteenth-century curriculum as subject-centered, revolving around a set of academic subjects said to strengthen the mind in the same way physical exercise strengthens the muscles. The report most often cited to illustrate this "mental discipline" approach came from the NEA: the *Report of the Committee of Ten on Secondary School Studies* (1893).[88]

The NEA's ten-member study committee, dominated by college presidents, argued the best way to prepare students for life was to discipline their minds with the academic subjects that would also prepare them for college—and this at a time when only 6 percent of the eligible age group went to high school and only 2 percent went on to college. Although the committee recommended several alternatives to the then-fashionable concentration on Latin and Greek, it affirmed the idea that schools should challenge *all* high school students with a subject-centered curriculum, and it suggested elementary schools take a similar approach.

This point of view came under attack in the twentieth century, but two subject-centered theories of education, *essentialism* and *perennialism*, continued to

■ ■ ■ ■ ■ ▬▬▬▬▬▬▬▬▬▬▬▬▬▬▬▬▬▬▬▬▬▬▬▬▬▬▬▬▬▬▬▬▬▬▬▬

BOX 6.9

THE FIFTIETH ANNIVERSARY OF *BROWN*

Purdue University, like many other institutions, celebrated the golden anniversary of the *Brown* decision throughout 2004. For an excellent retrospective as well as useful links, go to the Purdue Web site www.purdue.edu/oop/brown

influence the schools. I will argue in Chapters 7 and 10 that essentialism (its most recent incarnation is the standards, assessments, and accountability movement) has had more influence on educational practice than any other theory.

But at times during this century, there has been a strong pull away from a curriculum centered on subjects and a push toward a curriculum that attempts to balance academic content, social needs, and student interests. The report historians usually cite to illustrate this trend also came from the NEA, but this report appeared at the end of the progressive era, twenty-five years after the Committee of Ten: the *Cardinal Principles of Secondary Education* (1918). The study group that produced the report, the Commission on the Reorganization of Secondary Education, was dominated by high school principals and professors of education who urged the development of a diversified, more flexible curriculum with different programs designed to prepare *all* students for *all* aspects of life.[89]

By 1918, almost one-third of the eligible age group was going to high school, and the NEA's commission envisioned a time when almost all students would attend. (By 1930, as Table 6.1 indicates, half the age group was in high school, and today the figure exceeds 95 percent.) To meet the needs of a heterogeneous student body, the NEA commission recommended educators reorganize and supplement the traditional academic subjects in order to pay more attention to such areas as health, leisure, and vocation.[90]

The *Cardinal Principles* reflect *progressivism,* the modern theory of education developed primarily by John Dewey and his followers. But as we will see in the next chapter, Dewey was often unhappy with what happened when progressivism was translated into practice in the schools.

Describing twentieth-century changes in the curriculum as an ongoing battle between mental discipline and the *Cardinal Principles* or as a contest between traditional and modern theories of education allows historians to simplify an immensely complicated process and explain it in understandable terms. Now historians are beginning to investigate what teachers actually did with the formal curriculum. We know progressivism was popular in teacher education programs by 1920, but how and when did the progressive methods that teachers and administrators learned about actually work their way into elementary and secondary classrooms? How much did teachers change the formal curriculum after they shut the classroom door? Our answers to such questions are tentative at best.[91]

■ ■ ■ ■ ■ ▬▬▬▬▬▬▬▬▬▬▬▬▬▬▬▬▬▬▬▬▬▬▬▬▬▬▬▬▬▬▬▬▬▬▬▬▬

BOX 6.10

THE COMMITTEE OF TEN AND THE CARDINAL PRINCIPLES

See "Liberal Education and American Schooling," a dissertation by Thomas McCambridge (1997), which is available online at www.ditext.com/mcam/disser.html. Chapters 2 and 3 are especially relevant to our discussion of twentieth-century curriculum trends.

Larry Cuban's book *How Teachers Taught* (1993) is forcing historians to rethink their standard explanations, because Cuban has discovered more constancy than change in twentieth-century classrooms. Using photographs, textbooks, tests, recollections of teachers and students, and other sources that historians often neglected, Cuban argues teacher-centered instruction, in which the teacher stands up front and spends most of the time talking to the whole class, has remained dominant throughout this century.[92]

Even though progressives have urged teachers to become more student-centered by letting students exercise more responsibility and by teaching them individually or in small groups, most teachers have not changed. Cuban estimates that since 1900, approximately two-thirds of America's teachers, including over 90 percent of high school teachers, have stuck firmly to teacher-centered instruction. About 25 percent of teachers have tried a few student-centered techniques, developing "hybrids" that blended with their routine. Only 5 to 10 percent have been true believers in student-centered instruction. Like their nineteenth-century counterparts, twentieth-century teachers have resisted pressure to alter their style.[93]

Why so little change? According to Cuban, the organizational structure of schools and the occupational culture of teaching work against change. The structure of schools requires teachers to maintain order, cover a body of material, and show evidence students have learned. Quite simply, teacher-centered instruction helps teachers get the job done. Student-centered instruction, on the other hand, is risky. It reduces the authority of teachers. It disrupts the quiet routine. From the teachers' point of view, more freedom for students may or may not result in more learning. Most teachers prefer to settle for tried-and-true methods rather than invest their time and energy—scarce commodities—in an experiment.[94]

Have teaching methods really changed so little since the days of the NEA's Committee of Ten? Before accepting or rejecting Cuban's arguments, you need to become familiar with philosophies and theories of education because they offer a way of thinking about teaching and learning that complements the historical analysis in this chapter.

ACTIVITIES

1. Now that you have read this chapter, think about your own interpretation of American educational history. Is your interpretation celebrationist, liberal, revisionist, neoconservative, or multiple perspective?

2. Debate some of the issues in this chapter with friends whose interpretations of history differ from yours.

3. Conduct an oral history project. Interview older citizens with diverse social and educational backgrounds about their school experiences.

4. Compile a history of an older elementary or secondary school to see the local effects of national educational trends. Oral history, microfilmed newspaper accounts, and school system records are some of the sources you may be able to use.

RECOMMENDED READINGS

Cremin, Lawrence A. *The Transformation of the School: Progressivism in American Education, 1876–1957* (New York: Knopf, 1961). Cremin's study remains the best introduction to the progressive impulse in education.

Kaestle, Carl F. *Pillars of the Republic: Common Schools and American Society, 1780–1860* (New York: Hill & Wang, 1983). The definitive work on common schools, this study has clear themes and rich detail.

Labaree, David F. *How to Succeed in School without Really Learning: The Credentials Race in American Education* (New Haven, CT: Yale University Press, 1997). This very readable book uses historical case studies to examine the idea that getting ahead is the main reason for going to school.

Patterson, James T. *Brown v. Board of Education: A Civil Rights Milestone and Its Troubled Legacy* (New York: Oxford University Press, 2001). Prize-winning historian Patterson puts the *Brown* decision into perspective for a popular audience.

Urban, Wayne J., and Jennings L. Wagoner, Jr. *American Education: A History*, 3rd ed. (New York: McGraw Hill, 2004). Here is a well-balanced history that draws on tried-and-true studies as well as the best recent scholarship in the field.

NOTES

1. Lawrence A. Cremin quoted in Sandra Reeves, "A Nation and Its Schools Come of Age," *Education Week* (January 27, 1999), p. 24.
2. Robert Allen Skotheim, ed., *The Historian and the Climate of Opinion* (Reading, MA: Addison-Wesley, 1969), p. 2.
3. Bernard Bailyn, *Education in the Forming of American Society: Needs and Opportunities for Study* (Chapel Hill, NC: University of North Carolina Press, 1960), p. 14.
4. The discussion in this section is based on Wayne J. Urban and Jennings L. Wagoner, Jr., *American Education: A History*, 3rd ed. (Boston: McGraw-Hill, 2004), Chaps. 1–2. For a more extensive account, see Margaret Connell Szasz, *Indian Education in the American Colonies, 1607–1783* (Albuquerque: University of New Mexico Press, 1988).
5. Two important studies of the colonial era are Bailyn's *Education in the Forming of American Society*, which called attention to the importance of educational agencies other than schools, and Lawrence A. Cremin's *American Education: The Colonial Experience, 1607–1783* (New York: Harper & Row, 1970).
6. Urban and Wagoner, *American Education: A History*, Chap. 2.
7. One of the best accounts of district schools is Robert L. Church and Michael W. Sedlak's *Education in the United States: An Interpretive History* (New York: Free Press, 1976), Chap. 1.
8. On the distinctiveness of the South, see John Hardin Best, "Education in the Forming of the American South," *History of Education Quarterly* 36 (Spring 1996): 39–51. This essay is reprinted in a volume that further explores the distinctiveness issue: Wayne J. Urban, ed., *Essays in Twentieth-Century Southern Education: Exceptionalism and Its Limits* (New York: Garland, 1999).
9. Albert Henry Smith, ed., *The Writings of Benjamin Franklin*, vol. 3 (New York: Macmillan, 1904–1907), pp. 395–421.
10. Church and Sedlak, *Education in the United States*, Chap. 2.
11. Joel H. Spring, *The American School, 1642–1993*, 3rd ed. (New York: McGraw-Hill, 1994), pp. 16–21; H. Warren Button and Eugene F. Provenzo, Jr., *History of Education and Culture in America*, 2nd ed. (Englewood Cliffs, NJ: Prentice Hall, 1988), pp. 85–90.
12. Urban and Wagoner, *American Education*, Chap. 3.
13. Two important studies of modernization and its effects are Clinton Rossiter's *The American Quest, 1790–1860: An Emerging Nation in Search of Identity, Unity, and Modernity* (New York: Harcourt Brace Jovanovich, 1971), and Robert H. Wiebe's *The Segmented Society: An Introduction to the Meaning of America* (New York: Oxford University Press, 1975).
14. An old but still useful study emphasizing the "humanitarian" aspects of the various reform crusades is Alice Felt Tyler's *Freedom's Ferment: Phases of American Social History from the Colonial Period to the Outbreak of the Civil War* (Minneapolis: University of Minnesota Press, 1944).

15. James G. Carter, *Essays on Popular Education* . . . (1826), in David Tyack, ed., *Turning Points in American Educational History* (Waltham, MA: Blaisdell, 1967), p. 153.
16. Ibid., p. 155.
17. An excellent study of the movements is Carl F. Kaestle's *Pillars of the Republic: Common Schools and American Society, 1780–1860* (New York: Hill & Wang, 1983). For a study of the South, see Joseph W. Newman, "Antebellum School Reform in the Port Cities of the Deep South," in David N. Plank and Rick Ginsberg, eds., *Southern Cities, Southern Schools: Public Education in the Urban South* (Westport, CT: Greenwood Press, 1990), Chap. 1.
18. Church and Sedlak, *Education in the United States,* Chap. 3.
19. Ibid. See also Joseph W. Newman, "Mann, Horace (1796–1859)," in J. J. Chambliss, ed., *Philosophy of Education: An Encyclopedia* (New York: Garland, 1996), pp. 379–381; Jonathan Messerli, *Horace Mann: A Biography* (New York: Knopf, 1972), and Edith Nye MacMullen, *In the Cause of True Education: Henry Barnard and the Nineteenth-Century School Reform* (New Haven, CT: Yale University Press, 1991).
20. Church and Sedlak, *Education in the United States,* Chap. 3.
21. Barbara Finkelstein, *Governing the Young: Teacher Behavior in Popular Primary Schools in Nineteenth-Century United States* (New York: Falmer Press, 1989).
22. A typical defense of district schools came from the Committee on Education of the Massachusetts House of Representatives in 1840, reprinted in Rush Welter, ed., *American Writings on Popular Education: The Nineteenth Century* (Indianapolis: Bobbs-Merrill, 1971), pp. 85–96.
23. Spring discusses various aspects of commonality in *The American School,* Chap. 4.
24. Urban and Wagoner, *American Education,* pp. 114–115.
25. Orestes Brownson, *The Boston Quarterly Review* (October 1839), in Michael B. Katz, ed., *School Reform: Past and Present* (Boston: Little, Brown, 1971), p. 280.
26. Ibid., p. 281.
27. Horace Mann, *Twelfth Annual Report of the [Massachusetts] Board of Education* (1848), in Lawrence A. Cremin, ed., *The Republic and the School: Horace Mann on the Education of Free Men* (New York: Bureau of Publications, Teachers College, Columbia University, 1957), p. 97.
28. Joseph W. Newman, "Morality, Religion, and the Public Schools' Quest for Commonality," *Review Journal of Philosophy and Social Science* 4 (Winter 1980): 18–32.
29. Mann, *Twelfth Annual Report,* p. 102.
30. Brownson, *The Boston Quarterly Review* (1839), in Katz, *School Reform,* pp. 280–281.
31. R. Freeman Butts, *Public Education in the United States: From Revolution to Reform* (New York: Holt, Rinehart & Winston, 1978), pp. 114–120.
32. Two studies of the confrontation in New York are Carl F. Kaestle's *The Evolution of an Urban School System: New York City, 1750–1850* (Cambridge, MA: Harvard University Press, 1973), pp. 145–158, and Diane Ravitch's *The Great School Wars: New York City, 1805–1973* (New York: Basic Books, 1974), pp. 3–79.
33. An excellent recent history of how the line was drawn between public and private education is Timothy Walch's *Parish School: American Catholic Parochial Education from Colonial Times to the Present* (New York: Crossroad Publishing Company, 1996), Chaps. 1–4.
34. Butts, *Public Education,* p. 181; U.S. Department of Education, National Center for Education Statistics, *Digest of Education Statistics, 1995* (Washington, DC: U.S. Government Printing Office, 1995), pp. 50, 68.
35. William J. Reese, *The Origins of the American High School* (New Haven, CT: Yale University Press, 1995).
36. Ibid., pp. 207, 222–230. See also David Tyack and Elizabeth Hansot, *Learning Together: A History of Coeducation in American Public Schools* (New Haven, CT: Yale University Press, 1990), and John L. Rury, *Education and Women's Work: Female Schooling and the Division of Labor in Urban America, 1870–1930* (Albany, NY: State University of New York Press, 1991).
37. Reese, *Origins of the American High School,* p. 232. Enrollment data are from U.S. Department of Education, *Digest of Education Statistics, 1995,* p. 68.
38. *Stuart et al. v. School District No. 1 of Kalamazoo* (1874). Edward A. Krug has written the classic histories of secondary education: *The Shaping of the American High School, 1880–1920* (New York: Harper & Row, 1964) and *The Shaping of the American High School, 1920–1941* (Madison, WI: University of Wisconsin Press, 1972).
39. "Opening the Doors," *Education Week* (January 27, 1999), p. 1.
40. Ibid.

41. To appreciate the variety of historical interpretations of these reforms, see David L. Angus and Jeffrey E. Mirel, *The Failed Promise of the American High School, 1890–1995* (New York: Teachers College Press, 1999); Herbert M. Kliebard, *The Struggle for the American Curriculum, 1893–1958* (New York: Routledge, 1994); and Cremin, *Transformation of the School.*

42. See Herbert M. Kliebard, *Schooled to Work: Vocationalism and the American Curriculum, 1876–1946* (New York: Teachers College Press, 1999); Harvey Kantor and David B. Tyack, eds., *Work, Youth, and Schooling: Historical Perspectives on Vocationalism in American Education* (Stanford, CA: Stanford University Press, 1982); and Rury, *Education and Women's Work.*

43. David F. Labaree, *How to Succeed in School without Really Learning: The Credentials Race in American Education* (New Haven, CT: Yale University Press, 1997), p. 2. Also see Labaree, *The Making of an American High School: The Credentials Market and the Central High School of Philadelphia, 1838–1939* (New Haven, CT: Yale University Press, 1988).

44. Labaree, *How to Succeed in School*, p. 262.

45. Robert H. Wiebe, *The Search for Order, 1877–1920* (New York: Hill & Wang, 1967), provides an excellent historical context, emphasizing the impact of modernization.

46. Joel Perlmann, *Ethnic Differences: Schooling and Social Structure among the Irish, Italians, Jews & Blacks in an American City, 1880–1935* (New York: Cambridge University Press, 1988).

47. John D. Buenker, *Urban Liberalism and Progressive Reform* (New York: Scribner, 1973); Gabriel Kolko, *The Triumph of Conservatism: A Re-Interpretation of American History, 1900–1916* (New York: Free Press of Glencoe, 1963).

48. Alan Ryan, *John Dewey and the High Tide of American Liberalism* (New York: Norton, 1997); Church and Sedlak, *Education in the United States*, Chap. 9.

49. William J. Reese, *Power and the Promise of School Reform: Grass-Roots Movements during the Progressive Era* (Boston: Routledge & Kegan Paul, 1986); Paula S. Fass, *Outside In: Minorities and the Transformation of American Education* (New York: Oxford University Press, 1989); James D. Anderson, *The Education of Blacks in the South, 1860–1935* (Chapel Hill, NC: University of North Carolina Press, 1988); Jeffrey Mirel, *The Rise and Fall of an Urban School System: Detroit, 1907–81* (Ann Arbor, MI: University of Michigan Press, 1993).

50. Raymond A. Mohl, "Cultural Assimilation versus Cultural Pluralism," *Educational Forum* 45 (March 1981): 323–332.

51. Richard J. Altenbaugh, *The American People and Their Education: A Social History* (Upper Saddle River, NJ: Merrill Prentice Hall, 2003), Chap. 8.

52. Joseph W. Newman, "Ellwood P. Cubberley," in Richard J. Altenbaugh, ed., *Historical Dictionary of American Education* (Westport, CT: Greenwood Press, 1999), pp. 104–105; Newman, "Ellwood P. Cubberley: Architect of the New Educational Hierarchy," *Teaching Education* 4 (Spring 1992): 161–168.

53. Ellwood P. Cubberley, *Public Education in the United States: A Study and Interpretation of American Educational History* (Cambridge, MA: Houghton Mifflin, 1919), pp. 485–486.

54. Ibid., p. 489. For excellent studies of the tension between ethnic identity and Americanization, see Fass, *Outside In*, and Maxine Schwartz Seller, *To Seek America: A History of Ethnic Life in the United States* (Englewood, NJ: Jerome S. Ozer, 1988).

55. For insightful discussions of the immigrant–school relationship, see Urban and Wagoner, *American Education*, pp. 202–205, and David B. Tyack, *The One Best System: A History of American Urban Education* (Cambridge, MA: Harvard University Press, 1974), pp. 229–255.

56. Joseph W. Newman, "Comparing Private Schools and Public Schools in the 20th Century: History, Demography, and the Debate over Choice," *Educational Foundations* 9 (Summer 1995): 8–10.

57. Jane Addams,"The Public School and the Immigrant Child" (1908), in Daniel Calhoun, ed., *The Educating of Americans: A Documentary History* (Boston: Houghton Mifflin, 1969), pp. 421–423.

58. Ellen Condliffe Lagemann, ed., *Jane Addams on Education* (New York: Teachers College Press, 1985).

59. Covello describes his experiences in the autobiographical *The Heart Is the Teacher* (New York: McGraw-Hill, 1958), rereleased in 1970 as *The Teacher in the Urban Community.*

60. Tyack, *The One Best System*, pp. 239–240.

61. Ibid., pp. 106–109.

62. Anderson, *The Education of Blacks*, Chap. 5; Louis R. Harlan, *Separate and Unequal: Public School Campaigns and Racism in the Southern Seaboard States, 1901–1915* (Chapel Hill, NC: University of North Carolina

Press, 1958), pp. 255–256. See also Horace Mann Bond, *The Education of the Negro in the American Social Order* (Englewood Cliffs, NJ: Prentice Hall, 1934), and Henry Allen Bullock, *A History of Negro Education in the South: From 1619 to the Present* (Cambridge, MA: Harvard University Press, 1967).

63. Anderson, *The Education of Blacks*, pp. 65, 77, 102–109.
64. Booker T. Washington, *Up from Slavery* (New York: Doubleday, 1901).
65. W. E. B. Du Bois, *The Autobiography of W. E. B. Du Bois: A Soliloquy on Viewing My Life from the Last Decade of Its First Century* (New York: International Publishers, 1968).
66. Booker T. Washington, "Address . . . [on] September 18, 1895," in Calhoun, *The Educating of Americans*, p. 351.
67. Ibid., p. 350.
68. Ibid.
69. Donald Spivey, *Schooling for the New Slavery: Black Industrial Education, 1868–1915* (Westport, CT: Greenwood Press, 1978).
70. Cubberley, *Public Education*, p. 744.
71. W. E. B. Du Bois, *The Souls of Black Folk* (Chicago: A. C. McClurg, 1903), Chap. 6.
72. Ibid., Chap. 3.
73. See Louis R. Harlan, *Booker T. Washington: The Making of a Black Leader, 1856–1901* (New York: Oxford University Press, 1972), and *Booker T. Washington: The Wizard of Tuskegee, 1901–1915* (New York: Oxford University Press, 1983).
74. For the histories of several genuinely progressive schools, see Susan F. Semel and Alan R. Sadovnik, eds., *"Schools of Tomorrow, Schools of Today": What Happened to Progressive Education?* (New York: Peter Lang, 1999).
75. Lawrence A. Cremin, *The Transformation of the School: Progressivism in American Education* (New York: Knopf, 1961).
76. Erwin V. Johanningmeier, *Americans and Their Schools* (Prospect Heights, IL: Waveland Press, 1985), Chap. 13.
77. Arthur Zilversmit, *Changing Schools: Progressive Education Theory and Practice, 1930–1960* (Chicago: University of Chicago Press, 1993).
78. Joseph M. Cronin, *The Control of Urban Schools: Perspectives on the Power of Educational Reformers* (New York: Free Press, 1973).
79. Raymond E. Callahan, *Education and the Cult of Efficiency: A Study of the Social Forces That Have Shaped the Administration of the Public Schools* (Chicago: University of Chicago Press, 1962); David Tyack and Elizabeth Hansot, *Managers of Virtue: Public School Leadership in America, 1820–1980* (New York: Basic Books, 1982); William Edward Eaton, ed., *Shaping the Superintendency: A Reexamination of Callahan and the Cult of Efficiency* (New York: Teachers College Press, 1990).
80. Tyack, *The One Best System*, p. 60.
81. Wayne J. Urban, *Why Teachers Organized* (Detroit: Wayne State University Press, 1982); Marjorie Murphy, *Blackboard Unions: The AFT and the NEA, 1900–1980* (Ithaca, NY: Cornell University Press, 1990).
82. Educational historians need to pay more attention to relations between the local and state levels. One study that does provide some historical perspective is Frederick M. Wirt and Michael W. Kirst's *Schools in Conflict: The Politics of Education* (Berkeley, CA: McCutchan, 1982).
83. Joel Spring, *The Sorting Machine Revisited: National Educational Policy since 1945*, rev. ed. (White Plains, NY: Longman Publishers USA, 1989); Henry J. Perkinson, *The Imperfect Panacea: American Faith in Education*, 4th ed. (New York: 1995), Chaps. 6–7; Frank J. Munger and Richard F. Fenno, Jr., *National Politics and Federal Aid to Education* (Syracuse, NY: Syracuse University Press, 1962); Hugh Davis Graham, *The Uncertain Triumph: Federal Education Policy in the Kennedy and Johnson Years* (Chapel Hill, NC: University of North Carolina Press, 1974).
84. Meyer Weinberg, *A Chance to Learn: The History of Race and Education in the United States* (London: Cambridge University Press, 1977).
85. James T. Patterson, *Brown v. Board of Education: A Civil Rights Milestone and Its Troubled Legacy* (New York: Oxford University Press, 2001); Richard Kluger, *Simple Justice: The History of Brown v. Board of Education and Black America's Struggle for Equality* (New York: Knopf, 1976).
86. Altenbaugh, *The American People and Their Education*, Chaps. 8, 10.

87. Vanessa Siddle Walker, *Their Highest Potential: An African American Community in the Segregated South* (Chapel Hill: University of North Carolina Press, 1996); Peter H. Irons, *Jim Crow's Children: The Broken Promise of the* Brown *Decision* (New York: Viking, 2002); Patterson, *Brown v. Board of Education.*

88. *Report of the Committee of Ten on Secondary School Studies* (Washington, DC: National Education Association, 1893).

89. Commission on the Reorganization of Secondary Education, *Cardinal Principles of Secondary Education* (Washington, DC: U.S. Government Printing Office, 1918).

90. U.S. Department of Education, *Digest of Education Statistics, 1995,* p. 68.

91. The best historical studies of the curriculum are Kliebard's *The Struggle for the American Curriculum, 1893–1958* and Edward A. Krug's two-volume set *The Shaping of the American High School, 1880–1920* and *The Shaping of the American High School, 1920–1941.*

92. Larry Cuban, *How Teachers Taught: Constancy and Change in American Classrooms, 1890–1990,* 2nd ed. (New York: Teachers College Press, 1993).

93. Ibid., Chap. 8.

94. Ibid.

CHAPTER 7

THEORIES OF EDUCATION

"WHY" QUESTIONS

Every chapter in this book asks "why" questions, questions of rationale and purpose, but this chapter digs deepest into human experience for answers. Here we will use the discipline of philosophy to study schools and society. Most introduction to education textbooks challenge prospective teachers to personalize educational philosophy by developing their own, a request that seems reasonable enough. As we go about our careers and lives, we have all too little time to ask "why" questions, and thus we may never see the values and assumptions underlying what we do and what we believe. One value of philosophy, then, is it requires us to pause and reflect on deeply personal matters.

But as much as philosophy has helped me understand myself and my teaching, it has given me even more guidance as I have tried to make sense of the changes I have seen in education during my lifetime. Studied in conjunction with history, philosophy has helped me analyze controversies that seem to reappear, albeit in slightly different guises, with surprising regularity. For instance, why do Americans keep sending their schools back to basics every few years? What is back? What is basic? What are the alternatives? Although I cannot guarantee you will have all the answers after you read this chapter, you will have some of them. Just understanding the questions is a step forward.[1]

FOUR THEORIES: AN OVERVIEW

We will study four educational theories that apply philosophy to education. *Perennialism* and *essentialism*, the two traditional theories, dominated education almost unchallenged until a hundred years ago. Since then, the modern theory of *progressivism* has emerged as a competitor. Looking back on the twentieth century, we will see an especially lively tug-of-war between essentialism and progressivism. *Critical theory*, a politically charged version of progressivism, has developed since the mid-1970s as a postmodern theory of education.

Out in the schools, it is difficult to find any of the four theories in pure form. When theory goes into practice, some things change in translation. Most teachers are eclectic, blending this theory with that and alternating the mix from time to time. In this chapter we will examine educational theory alongside educational practice, pointing out discrepancies between what the theorists say and what actually goes on in the schools.

The questions educational theory deals with are less sweeping than, What is real? How do we know? and What is of value? Nevertheless, the concerns of educational theory are far reaching. Each theory tries to answer four basic questions:

1. What is the purpose of education?
2. What is the content of the school curriculum?
3. What is the place of students?
4. What is the role of teachers?

Now we will see how perennialism, essentialism, progressivism, and critical theory answer the questions.

PERENNIALISM

Perennial means "everlasting." This theory of education emphasizes knowledge that has endured. Perennialism itself has stood the test of time. It is an old educational theory that shaped the development of European universities and dominated U.S. higher education until the late nineteenth century. Perennialism exerts a continuing influence through the work of Robert M. Hutchins, former president and chancellor of the University of Chicago, and Mortimer J. Adler, for many years the preeminent philosopher at Hutchins's university. Adler's followers have been leading a revival of interest in perennialism since the early 1980s.

Hutchins presented a succinct rationale for perennialism in his book *The Higher Learning in America* (1936): "Education implies teaching. Teaching implies knowledge. Knowledge is truth. Truth is everywhere the same. Hence, education should be everywhere the same." The education perennialists advocate focuses on both intellect and character, on enlightenment as well as goodness. Perennialists believe a careful study of our cultural heritage reveals more agreement than disagreement on the four basic questions. Intent on passing time-honored concepts from one generation to the next, perennialists look for continuities in human existence.[2]

Perennialists stress the authority relationship in teaching and learning. If teachers are knowledgeable people of good character, as perennialists insist they must be, then they should not hesitate to take command in the classroom. Students are incompletely formed human beings; they should not come to school expecting to dictate the terms of their education because they have less knowledge and maturity than the adults they will be working with. The very idea of a "student voice" in a "democratic classroom"! Students may question ideas, of course—perennialists require them to think critically—but they must never challenge their teachers' authority.

The Great Books

Critics have joked that perennialists won't even read books written after 1900, much less use them in school. The joke exaggerates the point, but the charge is just accurate enough to irritate perennialists. In fact, they do like modern works, though they are more comfortable with those that have stood the test of time. During the 1930s, Robert Hutchins, Mortimer Adler, and other perennialists tried to revive classical tradition in higher education with a curriculum based on the "great books of Western civilization." They assembled a set of books ranging from Plato's *Republic* to the Bible to the U.S. Constitution to Einstein's *On the Electrodynamics of Moving Bodies,* works that in their judgment represent the best of Western civilization.[3]

A great book, they argued, is one that accomplishes just what it sets out to do. It does not need to be rewritten. A great book is always contemporary. It does not need to be reinterpreted. A great book can be read by almost anyone. A great book helps people develop standards of taste and judgment.

Unfortunately, many of the debates over perennialism as an educational theory have been little more than arguments over the books on Hutchins's and Adler's shelf. Why did they choose this book but not that one? Do Asian, African, and other non-Western cultures have adequate representation? What about modern fiction? Can very young students understand the books? These arguments, still flying back and forth between great-books fans and great-books critics, have settled nothing.

The Paideia Proposal

Adler, whose long and distinguished career included chairing the board of editors of *Encyclopaedia Britannica*, began the task of revitalizing perennialism with the publication of *The Paideia Proposal* (1982). As one school reform package after another hit the table during the early 1980s, the Paideia Proposal managed to attract its share of attention and more, due partly to its comprehensive nature and partly to Adler's tireless work as a promoter. Although he died in 2001 at age 98, two different groups of his disciples are carrying the campaign for perennialism into the twenty-first century.[4]

Make no mistake about it. The Paideia Proposal is far-reaching. No longer concerned with a particular set of books, Adler instead proposed a particular kind of education for all students: schooling that is the same for everybody, with no tracking and virtually no electives. For twelve years, all students pursue the same curriculum, which Adler organized into "three distinct modes of teaching and learning."[5]

He called the first mode *acquisition of knowledge*. Using didactic methods, teachers acquaint students with fundamental knowledge in three subject-matter areas: language, literature, and fine arts; mathematics and natural sciences; and history, geography, and social sciences.

The second mode of teaching and learning is *development of skill*. Here teachers act like "coaches" who help students learn to *do;* that is, they help students acquire the basic skills of reading, writing, speaking, listening, observing, measuring, estimating, and calculating. Students get their only elective in this area: their choice of a second language.

Enlargement of understanding, the third mode, goes to the heart of perennialism by emphasizing ideas and values. Teachers conduct seminars in which they use not didactics and coaching but the Socratic method of questioning and discussing. Students study not textbooks but books and art forms, original works that represent the best of human endeavor. The Socratic seminars are turning out to be the most widely adopted of all the Paideia reforms.

Adler Takes on the Critics.   Adler enjoyed responding to criticisms of *The Paideia Proposal* and its two companion volumes, *Paideia Problems and Possibilities* (1983) and *The Paideia Program* (1984).[6] Until he stepped back from the front lines in his early nineties, he seemed to like nothing better than a rousing debate over educational reform. I once had the privilege of seeing him in action at an academic conference as, with obvious relish, he took on a roomful of friendly and not-so-friendly critics.

"You are an elitist, just as perennialists have always been," one critic charged. "Your proposal sounds like the curriculum of an exclusive prep school 'back East.'" "*You* are the elitist," Adler replied. "I am trying to make education in the United States truly democratic by giving all students the high-quality schooling that has been reserved for a privileged few."[7]

"You are trying to educate children as if they were all alike, when actually they are all different," another critic stated. "There is infinite variety in human beings. One child may be a rose, so to speak, while another may be a tulip and still another a violet. Just as roses, tulips, and violets require different amounts of light, water, and heat to thrive, so, too, do children need different kinds of education."

"Your analogy is fundamentally flawed," Adler shot back, with more than a hint of irritation. "The plants you named are members of different species. All human beings are members of the same species. Children are inherently alike, and all deserve the same excellent education."

Somewhat more cautiously, another critic stood up and said, "But students do differ in their academic abilities. Let's face it. Some are smarter than others. The curriculum you advocate may suit the academically gifted, but it is inappropriate for below-average or even average students."

Smiling now, Adler replied, "Certainly some people have a greater capacity for learning than others. Some of us are large buckets who can hold a great deal; some of us are medium-sized; some of us are small buckets with small capacities. The mistake educators make is pouring different liquids into the different sizes. The large buckets often get wine, the excellent education offered in the best public and private schools. The medium-sized buckets get water, an education of lesser quality. Perhaps the greatest tragedy is the small buckets usually get dirty water: make-work courses, vocational training, a curriculum that is admittedly third class. We in the Paideia Group want to pour the same wine into all buckets, irrespective of size. We want to educate all students up to their capacity."

Adler seemed less confident fielding questions about teachers and teacher education. Given prevailing salaries and working conditions, can this nation attract the moral, intelligent people needed to make the Paideia Proposal work? Given the kind of education students receive in the vast majority of public and private schools today, is it reasonable to expect these students to become the kind of teachers Adler wanted? Even if all prospective teachers receive a liberal arts education in college, as Adler demanded, will they be able to bring perennialism to life in the classroom? Adler admitted finding favorable answers to these questions would not be easy, but he insisted we try: "An ideal—even a difficult one—excites everyone's imagination. To say it cannot be done is to beg the question. We've got to try it."[8]

Perennialism in the Real World.   It is hard not to admire Adler for trying, but it is also hard to imagine perennialism succeeding on a large scale in the United States. Although Adler defended himself well, easily deflecting charges of elitism, in the end he found it impossible to counter the socioeconomic biases that run so deep in the history of American education. Simply stated, public educators have consistently given up on certain children, poor and minority students in particular. Perennialists have tended to wall themselves off in private schools with carefully selected students, proudly cultivating the very image of elitism Adler tried to dispel. And, to tell the truth, we have to admit that not everybody is sold on the power of great books and great ideas. Not everybody *wants* a perennialist education.

All of which helps explain why perennialism in its latest incarnation has not exactly taken the nation by storm. A quarter century after the publication of *The*

██ ██ ██ ██ ██ ▬▬▬▬▬▬▬▬▬▬▬▬▬▬▬▬▬▬▬▬▬▬▬▬▬▬▬▬▬▬▬▬▬▬

BOX 7.1

THE PAIDEIA PROGRAM AND PAIDEIA SCHOOLS

Find out more by visiting the National Paideia Center at www.paideia.org and the Paideia Group at www.hometown.aol.com/paideiapgi/page/index.htm

Paideia Proposal, the reforms it sets forth may still be an "idea whose time has not yet come." Estimates put the number of Paideia-inspired schools in the nation at only a few hundred. Moreover, no school is completely faithful to the vision the proposal outlines—most have adopted only parts or limited the program to large-bucket students—but Adler always praised even small steps in the right direction.[9]

Meanwhile, Adler's followers have broken into at least two camps. The National Paideia Center, housed at the School of Education of the University of North Carolina, has helped more schools develop Paideia-style programs. The Paideia Group, less visible on the landscape of educational reform, maintained closer ties to Adler and hews more closely to his personal views.

Adler harbored no illusions that reform would be easy. Although he felt more optimistic as his life and career drew to a close than when he began teaching in the 1930s, he cautioned there is "no quick fix." In fact, Adler admitted the reforms in *The Paideia Proposal* might take "the better part of two generations to achieve." While some advocates of essentialism, the educational theory we will examine next, are promoting reform by the cookbook—step by step, to the letter, and right into the oven—Adler held out for reform that is more gradual, complex, and fundamental.[10]

Known for skewering his critics, Adler often rebuked educators and politicians for not "fully understand[ing] the shape of an adequate reform or all the obstacles to be overcome in achieving it." One of Adler's favorite essentialist targets was the equally sharp-tongued William J. Bennett, secretary of education during the second term of the Reagan administration. According to Adler, Bennett sells the quick fix. Bennett is one of today's leading spokespersons for essentialism, and Adler held him partially responsible for the educational excesses of our nation's most recent back-to-basics movement, especially the "uncritical, almost superstitious" faith in testing, testing, testing (see Chapter 11). Bennett and other essentialists—including Chester E. Finn, Jr., Diane Ravitch, and E. D. Hirsch, Jr.—are more than happy to defend themselves, and you should weigh the arguments on all sides as you read the next section.[11]

ESSENTIALISM

Of all the theories of education, essentialism has had the greatest influence on U.S. elementary and secondary schools. Its popularity may wax and wane, but essentialism never fades away entirely. It is like a durable undercoat of paint.

Educational reformers may cover it temporarily with other theories, but when times and fashions change, essentialism reappears. Essentialists sometimes say their theory is what remains when we peel away the "fads and frills" of American education. To go back to basics is to go back to essentials, although it is becoming increasingly difficult to get a consensus on what is essential and what is not.

Although the term *essentialism* was not coined until the 1930s, when traditional educators were organizing to do battle with progressive educators, the principles of essentialism dominated the district schools and common schools of nineteenth-century America. The twentieth century witnessed a struggle between essentialists and progressives (whose ideas we will study next), with the former having more influence on daily practice in the schools and the latter having a stronger voice in teacher education programs. Now, in the first decade of the twenty-first century, essentialism has become so firmly entrenched in schools that teacher educators—whether they like essentialism or not—are falling into line and preparing their students for a "real world" dominated by standards, assessments, and accountability.

Comparing Essentialism and Perennialism

As traditional theories of education, essentialism and perennialism have a lot in common. Advocates of both theories dismiss the criticism that "Some students can't handle your curriculum" with a terse "Certainly they can—all but the very small percentage of students who have severe mental deficiencies." Advocates of both are comfortable with the image of students as receptacles or containers for teachers to pour knowledge into. Getting filled to the brim can be exciting, they hasten to add. Both theories are conservative in a cultural sense because both emphasize passing a cultural inheritance from one generation to the next.

There are also important differences between essentialism and perennialism. The essentialist curriculum is less wedded to the classics. It is likely to contain more modern literature, for instance, and to feature more knowledge and skills of recent vintage—computer science and word processing. Notwithstanding Adler's attempts to avoid debates over the great books in promoting the Paideia Proposal, most perennialists do have a preference for older, tried-and-true works, and even though Adler said he found a place for the manual arts in his curriculum, perennialist schools are not exactly rushing to add courses in cooking and auto repair. Essentialists, on the other hand, have long favored industrial arts courses in theory, although in practice they tend to look the other way when only the less academically talented students sign up.

Essentialism has a stronger vocational emphasis. In theory, essentialists and perennialists both say there is more to life than getting and holding a job, but in practice essentialists are more likely to try to sell students on the value of academic subjects in the job market: "You'll need this math course if you want to work in a high-tech company." This strand of essentialism has grown especially strong since the early 1980s, when business leaders began promoting school reform as the key to making the United States more productive and competitive in the world economy. Perennialists realize almost everyone has to work, yet they believe too much emphasis on job preparation inevitably tracks small-bucket students into vocational courses, robbing them of a first-rate education.

The most important practical difference between essentialism and perennialism may be that essentialists have more faith in standardized testing. To a greater degree than the advocates of any other educational theory, essentialists see standardized testing as a yardstick of student progress, a quality-control check on teachers, a guarantee of accountability for the taxpaying public. Perennialists, by contrast, join progressives in arguing standardized testing has been so overdone, it has corrupted the entire teaching-learning process.

During the twentieth century, essentialism surged forward three times, in each case capitalizing on recurring public beliefs that the schools have become too soft and too involved in social engineering. In the late 1930s, William Bagley led the essentialist crusade. During the 1950s, the "academic critics"—a group of essentialist professors of the arts and sciences—launched their attacks. And from the late 1970s to the present, essentialist banners have been flying again. During its most recent revival, essentialism has inspired such reforms as minimum competency testing; the "excellence in education" campaign outlined in *A Nation at Risk* (1983); the America 2000 and Goals 2000 programs of former Presidents George H. Bush and Bill Clinton, respectively; and the state standards, assessments, and accountability movement that began in the mid-1990s and gained tremendous political clout from George W. Bush's signature education program, the No Child Left Behind Act of 2001 (NCLB).

William C. Bagley and the 1930s

William C. Bagley, a professor of education at Teachers College, Columbia University, emerged during the 1930s as the most prominent and articulate spokesperson for essentialism. Faced with the social upheaval of the Great Depression, Bagley looked to the schools to provide stability in the midst of change. Above all, he argued, the schools should equip students with the basic academic skills they need to survive in society and continue their education. He complained that many students were graduating from high school "essentially illiterate." Tracing such problems back to the elementary schools, Bagley called for a renewed emphasis on reading, writing, and arithmetic. If essentialism stands for nothing else, it stands for mastery of the 3Rs.[12]

But essentialism stands for much more, Bagley continued. The schools must conserve and transmit our cultural heritage. "An effective democracy demands a community of culture," he maintained. "Educationally this means that each generation must share a common core of ideas, meanings, understandings, and ideals, representing the most precious elements of the human heritage."[13] Like many traditional educators, Bagley downplayed differences of opinion on the content of the curriculum. "There can be little question as to the essentials," he asserted, urging a program of history, geography, health, science, the fine arts, and the industrial arts, supported by continuing instruction in the 3Rs.[14]

Schools must also stress morality, Bagley insisted. Cornerstone values such as honesty and respect for other people's property are as essential to the orderly operation of schools as they are to the very existence of society. So are obedience, discipline, and hard work. Much learning is simply not fun, Bagley argued, and students should not come to school expecting to have a good time every day. Essentialists talk so much about the importance of work, they sometimes appear to believe in work for its own sake. Essentialist teachers want to wear the mantle of authority in the classroom, insisting on order and making no apologies for instilling traditional values in students.

The Academic Critics of the 1950s

The academic critics were articulate, colorful, and for the most part bitter in their attacks on American education. The titles of their books tell much of the story: Arthur E. Bestor's *Educational Wastelands: The Retreat from Learning in Our Public Schools* (1953) and *The Restoration of Learning* (1955) were the perfect complements to Mortimer Smith's *And Madly Teach* (1949) and *The Diminished Mind: A Study of Planned Mediocrity in Our Public Schools* (1954). James B. Conant offered less biting criticism in *Education and Liberty: The Role of Schools in a Modern Democracy* (1953) and *The American High School Today* (1959).[15]

Whether their tone was vicious or gentle, the academic critics agreed on key points. The public schools, by embracing a progressive theory of education that made them responsible for meeting every need of every student, had strayed from their central purpose: providing intellectual training in the basic skills and academic disciplines. This change harmed all students, the critics maintained, but gifted students suffered the most. The schools had abandoned their Jeffersonian mission of identifying bright students, whatever their backgrounds, and preparing them to lead the nation.

The academic critics found no difficulty casting villains for their drama. Leading the list was philosopher John Dewey, often called the father of progressivism, followed by professors of education who were infecting teachers with modern educational theory. Teacher education was the biggest joke on college campuses, yet state licensing standards were written so only people trained in colleges and departments of education could become teachers.

Arthur Bestor and Mortimer Smith, as professors of history, leaned heavily on the liberal arts in their proposals for reform. In 1956, they helped organize the Council for Basic Education, which is still one of the most prominent voices of essentialism.

James Conant, trained in chemistry, appreciated the liberal arts but placed more emphasis on science and math. After the Soviet Union put *Sputnik I* into orbit in 1957, Conant's ideas became tremendously popular. Fed up with progressive pedagogy, Americans turned to the schools to help the nation win the space race. Congress passed the National Defense Education Act (NDEA) in 1958; math, science, and foreign language teachers suddenly found themselves in great demand; and students across the nation found out what it meant to build a science project. Essentialism was in the driver's seat.

Many Americans look back on the late fifties and early sixties with a kind of *Happy Days* nostalgia, recalling the era as a time of academic excellence. To be sure, the schools were excellent for some students in some schools. If you were lucky enough to live in a well-off suburban district and were fortunate enough to be in the college preparatory track, you probably did receive a rigorous, academically demanding education, particularly in the mathematically and scientifically oriented subjects that were in vogue.

Excellence was not uniformly distributed. Within those same suburban districts it was business as usual for students in the lower-ability groups, especially for those in the vocational tracks. Essentialism probably did bring more academic rigor to the students caught in the middle—those in the general track—although their program continued to be less demanding than the college prep curriculum. Moreover, academic excellence was hard to reach in the nation's poorest school systems, even with the federal government's financial assistance.

It is also questionable that the new math, new science, and new social studies deserved the label of excellence. If we take the word of the students, teachers, and parents who struggled with them, they were academic disasters. Arts and sciences professors do not like to be reminded they led the schools down the "new" paths, only to beat a hasty retreat when the innovations flopped.

Back to Basics through Behavioral Essentialism: The 1970s through the Early 2000s

Since the mid-1970s, going back to basics has been all the rage. To people who have studied the history and philosophy of American education, much of the rhetoric of recent school reform has a familiar ring. There are echoes of William Bagley in the calls for old-fashioned morality and discipline in the classroom. Charges that the schools became soft and affective in the mid-1960s as they tried to engineer a racially integrated society recall the academic critics of the 1950s. Once again it has become fashionable to poke fun at teacher education, much to the delight of the Council for Basic Education and other essentialist organizations.

James Conant would surely approve of the renewed emphasis on science, math, and technical subjects, although the educational race is now more economic than military. While the Soviet Union was falling apart during the 1980s and 1990s, Japan and West Germany with their high-tech economies became our main rivals. Now, in the early 2000s, our students must compete with those in India, Ireland, and other nations that are cashing in on information economy jobs that American corporations are outsourcing. Whatever the economic problems we face at a given moment, essentialists line up first to make the schools part of the solution.[16]

Public pressure on the schools to stress the 3Rs—"Teach our children reading, writing, and arithmetic if you teach them nothing else"—also seems familiar. Although the pressure has varied in intensity over the years, it has always been a force to be reckoned with. More thoughtful essentialists have tried to remind the public that basic skills are just the beginning of formal education, advice that seems more timely than ever in an information-based economy. But when theory meets practice, essentialism has been so fixed on basic skills that some students received drill in the 3Rs and hardly anything else. It has always been easy for essentialist college professors to blame parents, teachers, and administrators for corrupting the theory in this way, but the corruption has occurred nevertheless. It is widespread today.

The Marriage of Behaviorism and Essentialism.   What makes the latest back-to-basics movement different is that behavioral psychology is influencing the schools to a far greater degree than ever before, as educators are combining behaviorism and essentialism in powerful new ways. We will return to this issue in Chapter 11, but here it is important to note how *behavioral essentialism* emphasizes observable, measurable results.

The marriage of behaviorism and essentialism has produced standardized tests designed to offer the public "scientific proof" that students are learning. In response to the public outcry for more basics and higher test scores, the curriculum for most students has narrowed. Educators have deemphasized music, art, health, and physical education—and, in some cases, even science and social studies—because these subjects are not basic enough, particularly for elementary school students. Given the difficulty of measuring higher-level academic skills with multiple-choice/true-false tests, the curriculum has tilted, even in middle and secondary schools, toward lower-level skills. In math classes, most students spend far more time practicing computation than solving application problems. In history, they memorize lists of battles and generals rather than analyze issues and trends.

As behavioral essentialism swept the schools in the late 1970s and early 1980s, scores on tests of lower-level skills rose. The public was impressed. Most teachers knew better.

From *A Nation at Risk* to No Child Left Behind.   Some prominent essentialists, to their credit, were as skeptical as the teachers. *A Nation at Risk*, the 1983 report that still shapes debates over educational reform, was essentialist to the core. Prepared by the Reagan administration's National Commission on Excellence in Education, the report curtly rejected the obsession with minimum competency testing and lower-level skills. It proposed instead a curriculum built on Five New Basics, all of them to be taught with a higher-level emphasis. Four years of English, three years of mathematics, three years of science, three years of social studies, and one-half year of computer science should be the minimum requirements for *all* high school students, the commission urged. Foreign language was the sixth basic for college-bound students, and the report also gave a nod of approval to fine arts and performing arts.[17]

With its references to "the essentials of a strong curriculum" and their role in preserving "the mind and spirit of our culture," *A Nation at Risk* tried to pull essentialism out of its behavioral rut. Unfortunately, the attempt was not very successful because the report had its share of inconsistencies and contradictions. On the one hand, it tried to be egalitarian by insisting on a higher-level curriculum for all students. On the other, it deliberately evoked nostalgia for the schools of the late

1950s and early 1960s, conveniently ignoring the grossly unequal educational opportunities that characterized the era. Along the same lines, the cold-war and *Sputnik* rhetoric was so strong in the report, which called on science and math to ride to the rescue of America once again, that teachers of other subjects wondered how they would fare under this Conant-like version of essentialism.

Even the attack on minimum-competency testing and the lower-level mediocrity it promotes struck some teachers as halfhearted. The report turned right around and recommended the development of a "nationwide (but not federal) system of state and local standardized tests," a proposal Presidents George H. Bush and Bill Clinton would both push in the 1990s. Teachers, who were already under pressure to teach to numerous existing national, state, and local tests, were not encouraged.[18]

Now, some twenty-five years after *A Nation at Risk*, we are in the era of No Child Left Behind. Although President George W. Bush and U.S. Secretaries of Education Margaret Spellings and Rod Paige have touted NCLB as the "law that ushered in a new era," the act is actually an extension of essentialist reforms that have been under way for thirty years. NCLB requires states receiving federal Title I funds to develop content and achievement standards in all core subjects at every grade level; to assess the basic skills of all students annually in grades 3 through 8 and at least once in grades 10 through 12; and to hold individual schools and districts accountable for making *adequate yearly progress* (AYP). Although these requirements are extensive, some states were putting similar regulations into place during the 1990s, well before NCLB. The federal law's focus on *disaggregating* (breaking down) achievement data and raising the test scores of *subgroups* of students—poor, minority, limited English proficient, and disabled—adds a new feature to this latest version of behavioral essentialism.[19]

The pileup of test upon test upon test is reaching critical proportions—and still drawing mixed reviews. Behavioral essentialism finds strong supporters among politicians at every level of government and especially in state capitals; strong critics who include classroom teachers as well as the progressive reformers we will meet later in this chapter; and a large group of parents, students, teachers, and other citizens who simply accept behavioral essentialism as business as usual in school. For now, the political support is powerful enough to sustain the movement.

To be sure, No Child Left Behind has been controversial in some states and school districts. The state legislatures of Arizona, Hawaii, New Hampshire, New Mexico, Utah, Vermont, and Virginia have protested the costs and regulations of the federal law, sometimes even threatening to give up their Title I funding and opt out of the program. During the 2004 political campaign, John Kerry and other Democrats voiced criticism of NCLB. Significantly, though, most of the controversy has revolved around how much money states have to spend to comply with federal mandates rather than what behavioral essentialism is doing to teaching and learning.[20]

Judged by its own criteria—standardized test scores—behavioral essentialism has hardly been a resounding success. Scores on tests of higher-level skills

■　■　■　■　■

BOX 7.2

EMPOWER AMERICA

Explore Empower America's Web site at www.empower.org to see how William Bennett fits essentialist education under the umbrella of conservative politics.

have declined throughout the reign of back to basics, as we will see in Chapter 11, and some of the lower-level test scores that were rising twenty-five years ago have stagnated or fallen.

Can the latest version of the get-tough curriculum deliver what essentialists have long promised? Of course it can, say the advocates we will study next, academicians who are providing an intellectual justification for the political push toward essentialism.

Contemporary Essentialists

Some of essentialism's best proponents are conservative scholars who shuttle back and forth between positions in universities, the federal government, foundations, and think tanks. Rising to prominence during the 1980s, William Bennett, Diane Ravitch, and Chester Finn continue to use their visibility in the media to advance the cause of traditional education. Americans who follow current events are more likely to know their names, perhaps even catch them on television talk shows, than any of the perennialists or progressives we discuss in this chapter. The jet set of traditional education, Bennett, Ravitch, and Finn shuttle between conferences, consultancies, and speaking engagements.

William Bennett.   One of the most colorful characters on both the educational and the political scene, his impressive résumé traces his career as a university professor, chair of the National Endowment for the Humanities, U.S. secretary of education under President Reagan, director of the Office of National Drug Control Policy under President George H. Bush, fellow at the Heritage Foundation, and codirector of Empower America.

Students should *know* things when they get out of school, he argues with disarming simplicity. In *The De-Valuing of America* (1992), he looks back on his federal service and summarizes the lessons he learned: "Students should finish high school knowing not just the 'method' or 'process' of science or history; they should actually know some science and history. . . . They should know that for every action there is an equal and opposite reaction, and they should know who said 'I am the state' and who said 'I have a dream.' . . . They should know where the Amazon flows, and what the First Amendment means."[21] Bennett is a strong advocate of what he considers to be the common culture of the United States: the democratic ethic, work ethic, and Judeo-Christian ethic.

Ever since the publication of *The Book of Virtues: A Treasury of Great Moral Stories* (1993), Bennett has redoubled his efforts to stake out the high ground in what he sees as a battle for the very heart and soul of the nation.[22] "I'm convinced that efforts aimed at improving people's lives that don't have a moral and spiritual dimension are a waste of time,"[23] he insists, taking a firm stand against moral relativism and in favor of *virtues,* a set of fundamental character traits he believes most Americans respect. This approach obviously strikes a chord with many members of the reading public. *The Book of Virtues* went to the top of the best-seller lists, sold more than two million copies, and put Bennett back in the media spotlight.[24]

Devoting a chapter to each of ten virtues—self-discipline, compassion, responsibility, friendship, work, courage, perseverance, honesty, loyalty, and faith—Bennett's book is an anthology of stories, poems, essays, and other works intended to help students build *moral literacy* (a concept related to the *cultural literacy* we will discuss briefly in this section and extensively in Chapter 11). School children once knew "great moral stories" by heart, Bennett contends: the stories of William Tell and his son, of George Washington and the cherry tree. But, succumbing to moral relativism, we stopped teaching them during the 1960s.

Today many adults seem hungry for such sustenance again, and Bennett wants to make sure children partake from an early age. The 831 pages of *The Book of Virtues* span classical and modern literature, even if Bennett acknowledges the emphasis on older, tried-and-true works. From Cicero to Winston Churchill, from the First Book of Kings to Martin Luther King, Jr., from the "Boy Who Cried Wolf" to the "Battle Hymn of the Republic," the selections can transport readers to a "different time and place," Bennett claims, "a time when there was little doubt that children are essentially moral and spiritual beings and that the central task of education is virtue."[25]

Bennett hopes a reemphasis on virtue can help stem the tide of drugs, teen pregnancy, child abuse, divorce, and related problems in contemporary America. He

William J. Bennett
(1943–)

is encouraged that school districts around the nation are starting *moral education* and *character education* programs, sometimes using selections from *The Book of Virtues* as required reading. To critics who say this medicine seems weak, given the severity of the problems, Bennett counters the remedy is strong because it goes to the heart of the matter, to the fundamentals: "Children must have at their disposal a stock of examples illustrating what we see to be right and wrong, good and bad. . . . What is morally right and wrong can indeed be known and promoted."[26]

Bennett is an excellent promoter, and he has followed up the success of *The Book of Virtues* with a series of books targeted to different age groups: *The Children's Book of Virtues* (1995), *The Book of Virtues for Young People* (1995), *The Moral Compass: Stories for a Life's Journey* (1995), and *Virtues Collection* (1996). Other books in the series include *The Broken Hearth: Reversing the Moral Collapse of the American Family* (2001), which is addressed to parents, and *Why We Fight: Moral Clarity and the War on Terrorism* (2003), an attempt to place the attacks of 9/11 and the aftermath in a moral context. Blending his traditionalist background with cyber-age technology, Bennett is now promoting K12 Inc., an online, for-profit venture dedicated to making morally grounded "classical" education more widely available.[27]

Next to the best-selling *Book of Virtues*, Bennett's most widely read book is *The Educated Child: A Parent's Guide from Preschool through Eighth Grade* (2000). Coauthored with Chester E. Finn, Jr., whom you will meet in the next section, and John T. E. Cribb, Jr., this self-help book promises concerned parents it will "deliver what you need to take control." Several key principles run through the pages of this thick volume, which the authors wrote as a resource, guide, and reference.[28]

Every principle puts parents "squarely at the center." As the "first and most important teachers," they are ultimately in charge of their children's education. They must stay involved to insure the quality of that education, because "American schools are underperforming." Common sense and instinct can tell parents a great deal: that discipline is important, for instance, and that the factual content of education, not the process of education, is the real bottom line. Television does more harm than good. Parents should keep it turned off during the school week. Parents can help reform American education, but they must be ready to take on "the blob," the education establishment that includes government bureaucracies, teacher unions, the PTA, and other special-interest groups.[29]

The Educated Child is an attempt to put a plain-talking, politically conservative, consumer-friendly face on essentialism. Subject by subject and grade by grade, Bennett, Finn, and Cribb outline a K–8 curriculum focused on the basics and illustrated with examples from the Core Knowledge Sequence developed by E. D. Hirsch, another essentialist you will meet in the next section and again in Chapter 11. As contemporary essentialists often say, "Aim high, expect much and children will prosper."[30]

Chester Finn and Diane Ravitch.   Both Finn and Ravitch are helping Bennett carry on the essentialist campaign. Finn, now a fellow at the Manhattan Institute and president of the Thomas B. Fordham Foundation, served as assistant secretary of education under Bennett during Reagan's second term. Ravitch, now a research professor at New York University and senior fellow at the Brookings Institution, left Teachers College, Columbia University, to become assistant secretary of education during the George H. Bush administration. Having founded the Educational Excellence Network, Finn and Ravitch brought to Washington their credentials as defenders of traditionalism. Both continue to advise conservative policymakers on education issues. Both are ardent advocates of the humanities, and Ravitch is a well-known neoconservative historian (see Chapter 6).

Ravitch and Finn captured national attention in 1987 with their book *What Do Our 17-Year-Olds Know?,* which announced that America's students are ignorant of the most basic factual knowledge. In the tradition of Bagley, Bestor, and Bennett, essentialists update and recycle this criticism during every back-to-basics movement. Ravitch and Finn focused their concern on history and literature. What do students know about the Civil War, for instance? The Great Depression? Shakespeare? Faulkner? Based on the results of a test administered by the National Assessment of Educational Progress (NAEP), their answer was "not much."[31]

The timing of this announcement was perfect. E. D. Hirsch, an English professor at the University of Virginia, had just made the best-seller lists in 1987 with *Cultural Literacy: What Every American Needs to Know.* Perennialist Allan Bloom released *The Closing of the American Mind,* a biting critique of higher education, that same year. Ravitch, Finn, Hirsch, and Bloom all stress the importance of passing a cultural heritage from one generation to the next, and their books have touched off a debate over the role of the schools in increasing cultural literacy. Hirsch delves into these arguments in *The Schools We Need and Why We Don't Have Them* (1996). He outlines his Core Knowledge Sequence in *Books to Build On: A Grade-by-Grade Resource for Teachers and Parents* (1996) and *Realms of Gold* (2000), a multivolume set of readers.[32]

Since the 1990s, Ravitch and Finn have been in the front ranks of the campaign to set standards for every academic subject at every grade level. They originally pushed for national standards, but as we will find in Chapter 11, unexpectedly strong political resistance deflected the standards movement to the state level, where reform-minded governors and state legislators harnessed the movement to accountability through standardized testing. Ravitch and Finn had mixed feelings about the crazy quilt of reforms that went into place, because

■ ■ ■ ■ ■ ▬▬

BOX 7.3

THE THOMAS B. FORDHAM FOUNDATION

The Thomas B. Fordham Foundation web site at www.edexcellence.net supplies intellectual ammunition for those who are convinced, like essentialists Finn and Ravitch, that "America's children are America's future. Unfortunately, our education system is short-changing them."

standards and tests varied tremendously from one state to another. No Child Left Behind ushered in an era of greater uniformity, something the two essentialists have welcomed. As we will see in Chapter 11, they have become advocates of teaching to the test—focusing instruction on the specific content of standardized tests—because they believe the strategy enhances learning and reassures the public with rising test scores.[33]

Two decades after asking how much America's students know, Ravitch and Finn are still answering "not much." But as Ravitch says, "What we're trying to do is difficult and takes time. It's too soon to say we tried it, and it failed. This is just part of the agony of change."[34]

A book Finn published in 1991 remains the best guide for citizens who want to support the cause of essentialist reform. *We Must Take Charge* is the political companion to *The Educated Child*. Using military imagery, Finn argues that the essentialist battle for the schools is America's best hope for averting catastrophe. The nation is still at risk, he warns, urging "civilians" outside "the blob" to get angry, alarmed, and armed. Among the contemporary essentialists we discuss in this section, Finn is the truest believer in the power of standardized testing to promote positive change in schools. For civilians who are looking for a campaign guide to test-driven school reform, *We Must Take Charge* is the ultimate field manual.[35]

As the new century begins, Finn and Ravitch are searching for alternatives to mainstream public education. Although Finn's heart has always been in private education, Ravitch counted herself until recently among the defenders of public schooling. Now both argue that private schools and charter schools, which are experimental schools funded with public money, offer certain students their only chance to get a decent education.

Ravitch presents herself as an advocate for all children, particularly poor and minority children. *Left Back: A Century of Failed School Reforms* (2000) is a history full of accusations that progressive reform has been especially harmful to poor and minority students, while *New Schools for a New Century: The Redesign of Urban Education* (1999) and *City Schools: Lessons from New York* (2000) offer her insights on how to move forward with a reform agenda that reaches outside the established system. Often citing essentialist William Bagley as one of her heroes, Ravitch accuses progressives of dumbing down schools in pursuit of pedagogical fads and social engineering. She attacks censors on the political right and especially the political left in *The Language Police: How Pressure Groups Restrict What Students Learn* (2003).[36]

Finn, a longtime advocate of vouchers that give students public money to attend private schools, is now promoting charter schools. His book *Charter Schools in Action: Renewing Public Education* (2000) advances the idea that good schools will drive out bad and, in the process, actually strengthen public education. To Finn and other essentialists, competition is not only a fact of life, it is an almost unquestioned good thing. In Chapter 10 we will take a close look at these issues and others relating to private schools and charter schools.[37]

So there you have the case for essentialism as presented by some of its best contemporary advocates. Let me remind you that this theory of education is the one that dominates the vast majority of America's schools, public and private. Be prepared to deal with essentialism, especially the behavioral variety, when you get your first teaching job.

I have found that many teachers who share the essentialist commitment to such goals as stressing basic academic skills, transmitting a cultural heritage, reemphasizing moral education, and making public education more competitive nevertheless express serious reservations about holding teachers and schools increasingly accountable through standardized testing. Haven't we had enough of that, teachers ask? Of course we have, say advocates of progressivism, whose theory of education we will examine next.

PROGRESSIVISM

John Dewey, School Furniture, and Democracy

While he was a professor at the University of Chicago during the 1890s, John Dewey went shopping for school furniture. He had just started a laboratory school at the university with a group of parents who were unhappy with the traditional education their children were receiving. Now the problem was finding suitable desks and chairs, and none of the school supply stores in Chicago had what he was looking for.

Finally one dealer made a remark that struck Dewey as so insightful he included it in his book *The School and Society* (1899): "I am afraid we have not what you want. You want something at which the children may work; these are all for listening."[38]

For Dewey, that comment got to the essence of the traditional classroom, "with its rows of ugly desks placed in geometrical order, crowded together so that there shall be as little moving room as possible, desks almost all of the same size." Listening is the only educational activity that can take place in such a setting, Dewey claimed, "because simply studying lessons out of a book is only another kind of listening; it marks the dependency of one mind upon another. The attitude of listening means, comparatively speaking, passivity, absorption; . . . the child is to take in as much as possible in the least possible time."[39]

An old joke in colleges of education is that Dewey wanted the words "Here Lies the Man Who Convinced Americans to Unbolt School Desks from the Floor" chiseled on his tombstone. Funny or not, the joke does point out the symbolic importance of something as ordinary as school furniture. Dewey looked into traditional classrooms and saw passivity, rigidity, and uniformity locked into place. Teachers, the dispensers of knowledge, took their places at the front. Students, the receivers of knowledge, sat in their places at the rear.

Like many observers, Dewey saw similarities between classrooms and factories, but unlike many, Dewey did not approve of what the similarities suggest. Schools should not be places where adult "supervisors" give orders while child "employees" grudgingly sit and listen, their minds often a thousand miles away. Instead, schools should be places where adults serve as guides and advisers to

John Dewey
(1859–1952)

students who are actively involved in their education, doing things that are interesting to them as well as important to society.

Given a world in which change is the central feature, education must help people adapt. Dewey rejected the kind of education traditionalists prefer, an education based on truths passed from one generation to the next, an education students absorb. Dewey called instead for an education based on what works for the present generation, an education students *experience* as they interact with the environment. Students are not receptacles or buckets, Dewey argued. They are organisms. They need to be active. They learn best by doing.

Dewey's theory of education came to be known as *progressivism*, because it developed during the progressive era in American history. As we saw in the last chapter, a spirit of reform was in the air at the beginning of the twentieth century. Because Dewey was a liberal reformer, progressivism in education has always been linked to liberalism.

The linkage is less direct than it may seem because most of the people who translated educational theory into practice—teachers, administrators, school board members—were moderates and conservatives. It took time for Dewey's progressivism to work its way into teachers colleges and from there into the schools, and when *progressive education* did appear in classrooms, it was often difficult to recognize the original ideas. Beyond the social and political differences that separated theorists and practitioners, Dewey's writing was dense, ponderous, and easily misinterpreted. Few educators read his work carefully, and those who did disagreed over how to use his ideas in the classroom.[40]

Throughout his long life, which spanned the Civil War and the atomic age, Dewey kept claiming his ideas had been misquoted, misunderstood, and misapplied in the schools. We should be sympathetic, but only to a point. After all, Dewey insisted that the ultimate test of a theory is the difference the theory makes in practice. Just as we saw that perennialists, despite Hutchins's and Adler's egalitarian rhetoric, have reserved their brand of education for a few students in a few schools, and that educators have consistently corrupted essentialism, denying its full benefits to many students despite the good intentions of Bagley, Bestor, and Bennett, we must evaluate progressivism in the same way, judging not only theory but practice.[41]

Dewey based his educational theory on his view of democracy. As he explained in his best-known book, *Democracy and Education* (1916), democracy is more than a form of government. It is a way of life. The essence of democracy is people working together cooperatively to find solutions to common problems. The schools in a democratic society bear a great responsibility because they must help give people the problem-solving skills that they need to make democracy work. Dewey was very much the liberal progressive in his belief that ordinary people can contribute to society if schools help them to do so. He went even further: Unless America's schools equip *all* students to solve problems, democracy cannot survive.[42]

Children, Society, and Their Problems

But which problems should the schools focus on? According to Dewey, there are two sources from which problems can be selected: children and society. Students can suggest problems they are having, and society is full of problems crying out for solutions. Unfortunately, Dewey continued, the traditional curriculum does justice to neither. A collection of facts and skills pigeonholed into academic subjects, the curriculum may make sense to college-educated adults, but it is remote from children's experience and out of touch with pressing social problems.

Dewey versus the Traditionalists.   Imagine how Dewey's ideas must have sounded at the turn of the century. They were nothing short of heresy to traditionalists. What? Ask the *children?* But they're too immature to make suggestions about their education. Furthermore, why bring the problems of society into the classroom? Shouldn't schools keep a safe distance from society, striving to be above politics, beyond controversy, and apart from the unpleasant realities of life?

Dewey replied to traditionalists in several ways. Hadn't they noticed the bored looks on children's faces? To the degree that schools ignore problems that concern students, schools are meaningless to students. Hadn't traditionalists noticed how difficult it was to move the nation forward, even in a progressive era? To the degree that schools ignore problems that beset society, schools are useless to society. Moreover, in *The Child and the Curriculum* (1902) and later works, Dewey urged traditionalists to recognize that student problems and social problems are identical. The questions even the youngest children ask—Do others like me? Should I share my toys? What makes automobiles run? Why are vegetables better for me than candy?—are scaled-down versions of the questions society asks. Students do not come to school to get ready for life. They are already alive. Education is not preparation for life. It *is* life.[43]

Miniature Societies.   Dewey wanted schools to be miniature societies, "embryonic communities" that simplify, purify, and integrate culture. In his laboratory school at the University of Chicago, students engaged in such "real-life activities" as gardening, weaving, woodworking, and metalworking. Because everyone has to eat, Dewey and his fellow teachers found it easy to build on the natural interest children have in food. As students worked in the school garden, they began to understand, often for the first time, where food comes from and how important it is to any society. With student interest presumably running high, resourceful teachers provided gentle guidance as students investigated how food production has changed over the years, why some nations have more food than others, how seeds germinate—the possibilities were endless. Science, geography, history, and other academic subjects were no longer the center of the curriculum. Instead, the curriculum was at once child-centered and society-centered, with subject matter brought into play as necessary to study particular problems or issues.

In 1904, Dewey moved from the University of Chicago to Columbia University in New York City, where his reputation grew steadily. Although he concentrated more on philosophy than education after the publication of *Democracy and Education* in 1916, Dewey soon became the nation's preeminent educational theorist. He developed a strong following among the faculty of Columbia's Teachers College, attracting a group of dedicated professors who spread his ideas—more precisely, their interpretation of his ideas—to numerous teachers and administrators.

As Teachers College established itself as the top school of education in the country, Dewey and his followers were in an influential position indeed. During the 1920s, 1930s, and 1940s, they were the pacesetters in educational theory.

Progressivism in the Classroom

How much educational practice changed as a result of progessive influence is a hard question to answer, as Larry Cuban's book *How Teachers Taught* suggests (see Chapter 6). As early as World War I, there were signs of growing interest in progressivism. In 1918, the Commission on the Reorganization of Secondary Education, a committee of the National Education Association, issued what would prove to be one of the most significant educational reports of this century. Titled *Cardinal Principles of Secondary Education*, the report called on secondary educators to broaden their aims, to do more than offer a relatively small group of students a traditional academic curriculum. The report encouraged schools to prepare *all* students for *all* aspects of life. The cardinal principles were an ambitious statement of the schools' responsibilities for seven broad areas of life: health, command of fundamental processes (basic academic skills), worthy home membership, vocation, civic education, worthy use of leisure, and ethical character.[44]

William H. Kilpatrick and the Project Method.   Despite warnings that the schools were asking for more than they could handle, progressivism gained ground. Another breakthrough came in that same year when William Heard Kilpatrick, a Teachers College professor who had studied under Dewey, published "The Project Method." This article was Kilpatrick's attempt to translate Dewey's ideas into a set of practical guidelines for teachers. *Foundations of Method* (1925), Kilpatrick's elaboration on the article, became *the* methods textbook in many teacher education programs.

Education should revolve around "wholehearted purposeful activity in a social situation," Kilpatrick declared. Using the problems and questions students brought to school as a point of departure, teachers could help students design projects that taught social lessons and conveyed academic content as well. If students were curious about buying and selling, they could set up a store in the classroom. Using play money, they could learn to make change. The thoughtful teacher could stock the shelves with items chosen to stimulate further learning. Buying a cotton shirt could get a student interested in where cotton is grown and how clothes are made. The student who spent money too quickly would have to face the realities of budgeting. If another student turned into a loan shark, the teacher could help the class decide how to handle the situation.[45]

Kilpatrick's project method seemed easy to understand and easy to use in the classroom—deceptively easy, as it turned out. Almost immediately distortions appeared, and the popular press had a field day with progressive education. By some accounts, a few teachers simply turned things over to the students. With "What do you want to do today, kids?" as their major question, these teachers provided little guidance. Other teachers were willing to be more directive but found it difficult to come up with a steady stream of projects that did justice to children, society, and subject matter. Teacher educators and curriculum specialists rushed in with preplanned projects that laid out virtually everything in advance—stimulation, problems and questions, subject-matter content, probable outcomes, new interests—but spontaneity and student motivation suffered.

Criticisms, Distortions, and Success Stories.   Journalists of the 1920s sniped away at child-centered private schools that seemed to lack structure of any kind, at least to the casual observer. Why, the children sang, danced, and made pottery all day! They read books and did arithmetic only when they wanted to. And so the caricatures went. Journalists who were aware of the Progressive Education Association, organized in 1919 with an accent on child-centered private education, could lampoon the first two principles on the association's charter, "freedom to develop naturally" and "interest the motive of all work." "Scientific study of pupil development," another principle, somehow received less attention in the press.[46]

To many citizens and some teachers, progressivism became little more than a set of slogans: Learning by doing. Educating the whole child. Teaching students, not subjects.

Dewey, Kilpatrick, and other theorists spoke out against the distortions of progressivism in the schools and the distortions of the distortions in the press. The image of progressivism as totally permissive was especially irritating to Dewey. "The child does not know best," he reminded his supporters and detractors alike. Trusting students to make intelligent decisions with little or no adult guidance "is really stupid. For it attempts the impossible, which is always stupid; and it misconceives the conditions of independent thinking." Nor did Dewey agree with his Teachers College followers on all matters. Tired of seeing progressivism reduced to playing store, Dewey cautioned against projects so trivial they miseducated students. Kilpatrick's method was only one alternative, he pointed out.[47]

Whereas Kilpatrick seemed almost ready to discard the entire subject-matter curriculum and replace it with a series of projects, Dewey wanted to make academic subjects more responsive to the needs of students and society. If the curriculum began with the experiences of students, as the students gained maturity they could delve into subject matter in a rigorous way that might even please the traditionalists. Dewey's scientific method of problem solving was structured and systematic. He also believed there was a time and place for didactic instruction—for a teacher to stand at the chalkboard and show students how to work a math problem, for instance—and a time and place for students to memorize and practice their multiplication tables. In other words, Dewey was no pedagogical anarchist.[48]

Visiting and studying early progressive schools reassured Dewey they were indeed the "schools of to-morrow"—models of what education could be, perhaps even *would* be, in the future. Chicago was home to the Francis W. Parker School and the University of Chicago Laboratory School established by Dewey himself. In New York City he spent time at several well-known institutions, including the Lincoln School of Teachers College, Columbia University, the City and Country School, and the Dalton School. These urban, elite private schools were some of progressivism's most impressive showcases. But progressive education could also work with ordinary students in public schools, as it did in the factory town of Gary, Indiana, as well as in such out-of-the-way places as Fairhope, Alabama, where the highly experimental and child-centered School of Organic Education operated as a publicly subsidized community school. Shrugging off essentialist jibes, all these schools had genuine success stories to tell.[49]

Organic School founder Marietta Johnson and other progressive educators shared Dewey's hope that their collective vision of the "new education" would

■ ■ ■ ■ ■ ▬▬

BOX 7.4

PROGRESSIVE SCHOOLS

Go online to visit the Marietta Johnson Museum and experience the Organic School in its prime years at www.mariettajohnson.org and read more about the progressive "platoon schools" of Gary, Indiana, in "A Blueprint for Change" (April 21, 1999) by David Hoff at www.edweek.org/1999/32gary.h18

soon shine in public schools across the nation. Although that never quite happened, progressivism has been successful enough to keep its light burning in the eyes of devotees.

It troubled Dewey that much of what passed as progressive education had only tenuous connections to social reform. Before World War I, progressivism in education had been part and parcel of the larger reform movements. After the war, progressive education went its own way, enjoying its greatest popularity in private schools such as those we just discussed. During the 1930s, though, as the nation faced the Great Depression and the rise of totalitarian governments abroad, Dewey was encouraged as progressive education became more society centered. This version of progressivism made more headway in public schools. It was impossible for educators to ignore unemployment, breadlines, and fascism, and progressive education offered a way to infuse social issues into the curriculum.

The social studies, which progressive educators had developed during the 1920s as an interdisciplinary, problem-centered subject, enjoyed an upswing in popularity. Students took field trips and studied problems in their own communities. Kilpatrick's project method seemed ideally suited to this kind of progressivism because students and teachers could design their projects around studies of city and county governments, housing conditions, New Deal public works programs, and the like.

Social Reconstructionism

A politically focused form of society-centered progressivism called *social reconstructionism* also developed during the 1930s. Inspired in part by Dewey's reaction against the permissiveness and lack of social concern in child-centered progressivism, social reconstructionists went to another extreme with their desire to use the schools to engineer a new society.

George S. Counts, a Teachers College professor, galvanized the annual meeting of the Progressive Education Association in 1932 with his speech "Dare Progressive Education Be Progressive?" Calling on teachers to become leaders of social change, Counts urged them to take stands on controversial social issues and prepare students for the emerging society. Teachers should increase their power by joining teacher unions and casting their lot with the labor movement and other forward-looking groups. Counts's book *Dare the School Build a New Social Order?* (1932) became the charter document of reconstructionism.[50]

Counts, Kilpatrick, and several of their colleagues at Teachers College, most notably Harold Rugg and John Childs, joined other professors in education and the arts and sciences to publish *The Social Frontier*, a journal that served as the voice of reconstructionism. Dewey, a regular contributor to the journal, was at the center of all this activity, even though he occasionally rebuked his followers for their naïve faith in the power of schools to change society.

Social reconstructionism, a fusion of progressive pedagogy and left-of-center politics, had little direct influence on the schools. Even though the nation became more liberal during the 1930s, most educators and school board members simply did not share the reconstructionists' vision of an emerging society that, if not exactly socialist, was clearly collectivist. Predictably, reconstructionism drew the fire of people who were educationally conservative, politically conservative, or both. A series of social studies textbooks produced by Harold Rugg fell victim to a censorship campaign in the late 1930s and 1940s, and conservative critics have cited the social reconstructionists' writings as evidence of a left-wing conspiracy to control the schools.[51]

Life Adjustment

By the time the academic critics launched their attack in the 1950s, progressive education had undergone a name change. Now the dominant strain of progressivism was called *life adjustment* education. More than the name had changed. Dewey's ideas could hardly be recognized. On a rhetorical level, to be sure, life adjustment incorporated elements of both child-centered and society-centered pedagogy, but in theory and practice it departed from Dewey's progressivism at almost every turn.

The rationale for life adjustment was schools were not preparing large numbers of students for the realities of modern life, particularly the world of work. There were well-developed programs for the 20 percent of students who were college bound and the 20 percent who were in the vocational track, but what were the schools doing for the majority, the 60 percent in the middle? Surely these students did not need a rigorous academic program, the life adjusters asserted, and just as surely they did not belong in wood shop or metal shop.[52]

What they did need was training in good habits that would pay off on almost any job; help with their immediate personal problems as well as the ones they would face as adults; advice on how to spend their leisure time, which was predicted to be more plentiful in the years after World War II; and preparation for good citizenship. Students in the general track soon found themselves in such courses as Developing an Effective Personality, Marriage and the Family, and Metropolitan Living. Designed to focus and integrate the curriculum, courses revolving around class discussions and field trips became quite popular.

John Dewey turned ninety as life adjustment education hit its stride and the academic critics mounted their attack. Although he wrote little about education in his last years, it is easy to imagine his disappointment with what was passing for progressivism in education. Perhaps he held his peace because he found himself agreeing with the critics on many points.

Certainly the basic assumption of life adjustment education, that only students who were headed for college needed a curriculum with substantial academic content, made Dewey recoil. He knew vocational educators were the theorists and strongest advocates of life adjustment, which surely made him suspicious. Dewey parted company with vocational educators in the early 1900s when he realized they wanted to give job skills to a few students—the academic castoffs, most of them poor and minority students—while he wanted to give all students the chance to work with their hands and sample a variety of occupations.

Now a vocational mentality was limiting the education of another group of students, those in the large general track; essentialists were getting the credit for saving the schools; and Dewey was getting the blame.

Blame It on Progressivism: 1960s and 1970s Bashing

Spectator Sport.   Dewey died in 1952, but today it is fashionable in some circles to blame progressivism for everything that went wrong in the schools from the mid-1960s through the mid-1970s. William Bennett, Diane Ravitch, Chester Finn, and E. D. Hirsch have turned 1960s and 1970s bashing into an essentialist spectator sport, and Education Secretary Margaret Spellings, like Rod Paige before her, is joining the fun. Whenever progressivism shows signs of stirring and reviving, essentialists point to progressivism as the culprit that messed up America's schools.

Surely the nation doesn't want to go down *that* road again. As Finn puts it, beware the slippery slope! As Bennett says, don't give those dopey ideas another chance!

When students demanded more relevant courses during the 1960s and 1970s, educators responded by making things easy and elective, encouraging students to pick and choose their way through a cafeteria-style curriculum that included science-fiction English courses, values clarification social studies courses, and consumer math courses. Even the brightest students sometimes steered clear of foreign languages, advanced math and science, and other demanding courses while teachers, parents, and other adults stood by and watched. Essentialists chalk it up as another failed experiment in progressive education. Compensatory education, school integration, and affirmative action are, to essentialists, the social engineering legacy of progressivism.

Essentialists who are conservative Christians go even further. During the 1960s and 1970s, as the United States underwent a moral revolution that brought sex, drugs, and rock and roll into the schools, to some people it seemed the schools themselves were to blame. Didn't John Dewey say values are relative? Hasn't he had a lot of influence on education? Don't some teachers practice values clarification? As we will find in Chapter 10, affirmative answers to such questions provide conservative Christians all the evidence they need to implicate progressivism (and often existentialism, too) in a secular humanist conspiracy.

No one expresses the moral and academic indignation of essentialists better than Bennett. Just look at what happened when liberals led America astray during the 1960s and 1970s, he says: "We neglected and denied much of the best in American education. We simply stopped doing the right things. We allowed an assault on intellectual and moral standards. . . . We experienced the worst education decline in our history." Bennett voices the desire to return to better days, to set things straight—the same desire he articulated as director of President George H. Bush's antidrug program.[53]

Politics and Labels.   In the educational politics of the 1980s and early 1990s, Bennett and other officials of the Reagan and George H. Bush administrations tried to lay claim to essentialism as the conservative (and therefore Republican) theory of education, labeling progressivism as the liberal (and therefore Democratic) approach. All is fair in politics, of course, but we should be wary of such neat labels. They are not a good fit for the two theories as they have been practiced in recent school reform.

During this most recent back-to-basics movement, people with diverse political views and party affiliations have jumped on the essentialist bandwagon. As *Education Week* puts it, "Entering the new century, no other school reform can match its size, speed, and momentum."[54] Politicians of both parties and at all levels of government are on board the bandwagon, rolling merrily along together. No Child Left Behind passed with strong bipartisan support in 2001, and although some of the law's provisions have drawn political fire, essentialism itself hasn't lost momentum.

Which educational issue do George H. Bush, Bill Clinton, and George W. Bush most strongly agree on? The best answer, as test writers like to say, is standards, assessments, and accountability. All three presidents favor state-mandated curricula monitored by regular standardized testing—in short, behavioral essentialism. These prominent national politicians have plenty of lesser-known company in state capitals and local school board offices throughout the country.

So who speaks up for progressivism? To answer the question we must look outside the ranks of politicians, their essentialist allies in newspaper editorial offices and corporate board rooms, and the educators who are following their lead.

Where to Find Progressivism: Don't Spend Time in State Curriculum Guides

In the first edition of *America's Teachers* (1990), I concluded this discussion of progressivism on a pessimistic note. Progressivism was out of step with current educational theory and practice, I wrote. By the time I revised the book for the second edition (1994), I sensed behavioral essentialism was losing support and educators were searching for something to replace it. I went so far as to suggest progressivism might make a modest comeback. In the third edition (1998) I took a position somewhere between my 1990 pessimism and my 1994 optimism.

Now I'm back to square one. The fourth (2002) and fifth (2006) editions of *America's Teachers*, like the first, have come on the scene at a time when public school policy makers are under the spell of behavioral essentialism. Specifying in minute detail what students *should* know and finding out through standardized testing how much they *do* know make sense to politicians just now. Chapters 2, 9, and 11 point out how powerfully their faith in standards and accountability is shaping educational policy in fifty state capitals and influencing teaching and learning in more than 2,500,000 classrooms.

If you pick up a copy of a state curriculum guide in your teaching field and look for evidence of progressive influence, you're not likely to find much. But you can find it in other places. Progressivism is still alive in some classrooms. It's still on the agenda of some school reformers. Read on.

Why Do These Kids Love School?   "I'm talking about schools that have high standards—incredibly high standards, in fact—but standards that are met through mutual trust and mutual respect." Tom Peters, author of the best-selling series of *Excellence* books for businesspeople, uses these words to introduce "Why Do These Kids Love School?" (1990), a program originally telecast on PBS and now available on videotape from media retailers. After nodding to Dewey and taking viewers on a tour of a private school that practices an almost pure strain of child-centered progressivism, the program surveys variations on the progressive theme in nine public schools.[55]

Viewers see Central Park East Elementary School in Harlem, New York, a school that proves, according to the April 2000 issue of *Education Week*, that "disadvantaged kids . . . can thrive in small schools with offerings as rich as those of elite private schools."[56] Founded in 1974 by Deborah Meier, Central Park East has become the nation's best-known progressive public school. Another stop on the video tour is a magnet school in Lowell, Massachusetts, that functions as a "microsociety" in which students run the political and economic system. (*Time* magazine sang the praises of this school to an even larger audience.) An alternative school in Jackson, Mississippi, encourages students of different abilities to work as a group and assist one another—a strategy known as *cooperative learning* (see Chapter 8). By stressing high standards and associating such schools with "excellence," the producers of "Why Do These Kids Love School?" hope to deflect 1960s and 1970s bashing and give progressivism a chance.[57]

The video introduced Deborah Meier to a national audience. After spending twenty years at Central Park East, Meier retired from the New York City Public Schools but soon opened another highly successful public school in Boston, the Mission Hill School. Her books *The Power of Their Ideas: Lessons for America from a Small School in Harlem* (1996) and *In Schools We Trust: Creating Communities of Learning in an Era of Testing and Standardization* (2003) explain her belief in small schools driven from the inside by intellect and peer review rather than from the outside by legal mandates. In the next section of this chapter you will meet another reformer whose progressive vision, like Meier's, is credible because it has stood the test of the real world.[58]

Theodore Sizer.   "The nation's most famous school reformer," according to *Teacher Magazine*, is a good listener.[59] During the 1980s, while *A Nation at Risk* and other essentialist reports were telling teachers how to do their jobs better, Sizer was paying attention while teachers explained why their jobs are so difficult. Along with John Goodlad and the late Ernest Boyer, former president of the Carnegie Foundation for the Advancement of Teaching, Sizer has tried to offer teachers hope and encouragment, carefully avoiding the Here's-what-you-must-do-first posture

■ ■ ■ ■ ■

BOX 7.5

VISIT DEBORAH MEIER'S MISSION HILL SCHOOL

Using video as well as text, the school's Web site at www.missionhillschool.org/index.php offers a look inside classrooms that revolve around democratic teaching and learning.

teachers find so irritating in education professors, school administrators, and school reformers. Sizer should know, because he has in fact played all three of these roles.

To Sizer, Goodlad, and Boyer, the "Work Harder! Reach Higher! Do More!" advice of essentialism seemed simplistic and unrealistic given the conditions teachers and students face every day. Sizer's *Horace's Compromise* (1984), Goodlad's *A Place Called School* (1984), and Boyer's *High School* (1983) proposed fundamental changes in the occupation of teaching, the organization of schools, and the relationship between students and teachers. Based on thousands of hours of classroom observation, these studies predicted the nose-to-the-grindstone essentialist remedy would not work.[60]

Sizer followed up on that prediction in *Horace's School* (1992), a work of "nonfiction fiction" that reintroduces Horace Smith, the frustrated high school teacher who was the subject of Sizer's 1984 book. Forced by his working conditions to compromise his ideals, Horace wondered in the early 1980s whether the reforms getting under way then would help him and his students. Sadly, Sizer reports the promise of better education through school reform has never come true.[61]

Horace still has to compromise. He still has too many students to teach. He still has to cover too many topics in too little depth. He still has to fragment his work into fifty-two-minute bites of sound and sight punctuated by bells and class changes. Horace's students are still compromising, too, bargaining informally with their teachers for "the least hassle," learning how to adjust their standards downward as they move through the system.

Horace's School presents reform proposals that contrast with the "more of the same" reforms of the 1980s. At Franklin High School, the model school Sizer envisions, students and staff are divided into more manageable, largely self-contained units called "houses." Each teacher is responsible for no more than eighty students. The curriculum is organized into three areas: math/science, history/philosophy, and the arts. Faculty members work together in multidisciplinary teams. All share responsibility for teaching oral and written expression, inquiry techniques, and study skills.

Franklin High's teachers have reached consensus on what high school graduates should be capable of doing, and they have designed student "exhibitions," a type of *performance assessment* (see Chapter 11), to replace "seat time" as the basis for awarding diplomas. Unlike pencil-and-paper tests, which typically give students one shot at telling what they know, exhibitions take place over an extended

■ ■ ■ ■ ■ ▬▬▬▬▬▬▬▬▬▬▬▬▬▬▬▬▬▬▬▬▬▬▬▬▬▬▬▬▬▬▬▬▬▬▬▬▬▬▬

BOX 7.6

COALITION OF ESSENTIAL SCHOOLS

Visit the Coalition of Essential Schools Web site at www.essentialschools.org and be sure to investigate how successful progressive schools work by clicking on "Ten by Ten," a set of ten schools exemplifying the Ten Common Principles of the coalition.

time period to let students show what they can do. While some exhibitions involve formal expression in words and numbers—writing an essay or solving a set of problems, for instance—others are as varied as drawing a map, composing a piece of music, or demonstrating the skills acquired in a community service job. Students keep their work in *portfolios* that are open to inspection by parents, teachers, and state officials.

Granting more autonomy to individual schools and individual teachers is the key to successful reform, Sizer maintains. Regarding external regulation, his motto is "The least imposition is the best imposition." At Franklin High, standardized testing is limited to periodic assessments of reading, writing, and basic math. Anything more is not only unnecessary but counterproductive, Sizer argues, criticizing proposals to create a national curriculum driven by national tests.

Yet Franklin High does not shirk accountability, he insists. Student portfolios, test results, site visits, and annual reports to the community provide all the information anyone could need to judge the school's effectiveness.

These ideas have a track record of success, Sizer points out. They are working right now in schools across the nation. Sizer chairs the Coalition of Essential Schools, a group of over a thousand schools that are field-testing reform in more than thirty-eight states. The proposals in *Horace's School* are based on the experiences of the coalition. Deborah Meier's Mission Hill School is a member of Sizer's coalition, and the two reformers have coauthored a book with Nancy Faust Sizer titled *Keeping School: Lessons to Families from Principals of Two Small Schools* (2004). "Essential Schools" may be a traditional-sounding name, but the progressive theory of education they are putting into practice would hearten Dewey.[62]

Still, Sizer feels unsure about when—or whether—Horace Smith will be able to make a better set of compromises. "I fear," Sizer confesses, "that the preferred alternative to careful rethinking will be continued pushing, prodding, testing, and protesting our largely mindless, egregiously expensive, and notably unproductive current system. It is not a pretty prospect." "And yet," he concludes, "there are glimmers of hope."[63]

Sizer explores this theme in the final volume of the Horace trilogy, *Horace's Hope: What Works for the American High School* (1996). Although people who read all three books will find more pessimism in this volume than in the preceding two, Sizer's faith triumphs in the end. His faith is all the more impressive because Sizer first forces his readers to confront, just as he has, the spotty record of school reform. In the opening chapter of *Horace's Hope,* Sizer returns to several schools he visited thirteen years earlier, when reform seemed promising. The title of the chapter reflects his disappointment with what has transpired: "A Story Where Nothing Happens."[64]

But Sizer, like Horace, is stubbornly determined to keep the faith. By suggesting "nothing happens" in the first chapter, Sizer turns the small victories he describes in the rest of the book into hopeful signs of genuine renewal. "No one said it was going to be easy," he confides to a reporter for *Teacher Magazine.* "I mean, it's easy to say that schools should be for educating and not sorting kids, but it involves a radical shift in attitudes. You can't just say track them, bring out the bell curve, or whatever. It's going to take time."[65]

Yes it is. I hope you are forming your own opinions of the prospects of fundamental reform. In the chapters that follow, we will continue our study of the social and political forces shaping the schools.

Sizer's latest work shows he is still a good listener and still a keen observer of social and political forces. But now he is focusing his attention on *moral* forces, specifically on the moral influence we teachers exert on our students. (My writing in this section reflects Sizer's inclusive first-person-plural style.) *The Students Are Watching* (1999), coauthored with his wife Nancy Faust Sizer, reminds teachers we "have a profound moral contract with our students."[66] For all their apparent inattention to what we say and do, students learn from us all the time. And what they learn goes well beyond the formal curriculum.

The Sizers politely distance themselves from essentialists who believe moral education should revolve around a collection of "impressive nouns" (ten virtues in William Bennett's case), such powerful words as *honesty, responsibility,* and *loyalty.* Nouns can represent worthy goals of life, the Sizers readily admit, but to young people just starting out, nouns can seem so remote and abstract they come across as little more than rhetoric.

Taking a different approach, the Sizers build their version of moral education around six verbs: modeling, grappling, bluffing, sorting, shoving, and fearing. These verbs represent actions young people constantly observe in their teachers and other adults. Day in and day out, students see teachers *modeling* behaviors that may or may not reflect the values we claim to hold; *grappling* with problems that, whether we admit it or not, have no easy solutions; *bluffing,* or "misleading others by means of an artful demeanor"; *sorting* young people in ways that are sometimes in their best interest and sometimes not; *shoving,* or "going where you are not invited," a practice that can be either helpful or harmful; and *fearing,* which can either freeze or energize people. Drawing on Zen Buddhism, the Sizers suggest verbs represent the journey of life, while nouns describe the destination.[67]

When students see teachers act in certain ways and schools function in certain ways "as a matter of *habit,*" the lessons taught and learned are powerful indeed. The Sizers offer this advice to those who want to be positive influences on young people's lives: First, look in the mirror.[68]

Alfie Kohn.   The provocative question "Is Progressive Education Dead?" ties together a series of articles in the April 2000 issue of *Teacher Magazine*. According to Alfie Kohn and other progressive "gurus" profiled in the series, the answer is a clear no. Kohn, who may be emerging as the Theodore Sizer of the early twenty-first century, believes our nation is "facing what I think can be called, without fear of hyperbole, an educational emergency."[69] The cause of the emergency, Kohn argues, is essentialism gone mad—essentialism in its latest incarnation as back to basics and testing, testing, testing—which he dubs the "Tougher Standards movement." Kohn is convinced progressivism offers the best way to stop the madness and end the emergency.

Although he is too young to remember much about the sixties, a decade that left its mark on Sizer, Meier, Jonathan Kozol, and other progressives, Kohn obviously enjoys playing the role of gadfly, radical, and provocateur. In the many speeches he gives around the nation, he challenges students, parents, and teachers to rise up and protest "testing frenzy." Teachers understand even better than parents and students, he notes, how accountability based on standardized tests (see Chapter 2) can corrupt teaching and learning. If teachers become more willing to stand up, speak out, and tell the truth, if they can somehow find the courage to resist, then they can derail the Tougher Standards movement.

A central-office administrator I know was almost converted on the spot when she heard Kohn deliver a keynote address urging teachers to mount the barricades and revolt. "It was all I could do to keep from yelling, 'YES!'" she later told me, "but there I was, sitting beside my superintendent, . . ." Kohn looks forward to the day when more teachers will take the risk and "go out on a limb" like the teachers in Massachusetts who have joined their students to boycott that state's test-driven standards movement. He gives them all the encouragement he can in *The Case against Standardized Testing: Raising the Scores, Ruining the School*s (2000).[70]

Kohn's books put a fresh face on the Deweyan tradition. Like his speeches, his books are by turns passionate, funny, sarcastic, and insightful. *No Contest* (1992) presents, as its subtitle explains, *The Case against Competition*. *Punished by Rewards* (1999) continues in the same vein, documenting *The Trouble with Gold Stars, Incentive Plans, A's, Praise, and Other Bribes*. A good sampler of his writing is *What Does It Mean to be Educated? and More Essays on Standards, Grading, and Other Follies* (2004).[71]

Kohn's most comprehensive work is *The Schools Our Children Deserve: Moving beyond Traditional Classrooms and "Tougher Standards"* (1999). Here he identifies five

■ ■ ■ ■ ■

BOX 7.7

ALFIE KOHN

For future Teachers interested in joining the revolution and getting beyond what Kohn calls the "bunch o' facts" model of instruction, his Web site at www.alfiekohn. org can help show the way.

fatal flaws in the academic toughness campaign that is sweeping vitually every state:

1. a preoccupation with achievement, which Kohn says diverts attention from the proper focus, learning;
2. "Old School" teaching that treats students as inanimate objects into which skills and knowledge can be poured;
3. an obsession with standardized testing;
4. top-down coercion of too-specific requirements;
5. the assumption that harder is better, with the corollary that "if something isn't working well . . . then insisting on more of the same will surely solve the problem."[72]

Ready for a state-mandated test? Then consider the following situation described in *The Schools Our Children Deserve*.

> Abigail is given plenty of worksheets to complete in class as well as a substantial amount of homework. She studies to get good grades, and her school is proud of its high standardized test scores. Outstanding students are publicly recognized by the use of honor rolls, awards assemblies, and bumper stickers. Abigail's teacher, a charismatic lecturer, is clearly in control of the class: students raise their hands and wait patiently to be recognized. The teacher prepares detailed lesson plans well ahead of time, uses the latest textbooks, and gives regular quizzes to make sure kids stay on track.

"What's wrong with this picture?" Kohn asks. If you can justify his true-believer-in-progressivism answer, "Just about everything," you pass the test.[73]

CRITICAL THEORY

Here is a theory of education designed to "empower the powerless and transform existing social inequalities and injustices."[74] Through the work of Henry A. Giroux, Stanley Aronowitz, Peter McLaren, Joe Kincheloe, Shirley Steinberg, and other radical scholars, critical theory is reaching a small audience inside colleges of education. The very accessible writing of Jonathan Kozol is taking critical theory to larger popular audiences.

Critical theory is a contemporary extension of social reconstructionism. Beginning with the premise that "men and women are essentially unfree and inhabit a world rife with contradictions and asymmetries of power and privilege,"[75] critical theorists resolve to help students and teachers escape oppression. Since the mid-1970s, they have tried to fuse progressive pedagogy and radical politics, acknowledging the influence of Dewey, Counts, and other society-centered progressives.

But critical theorists say their twin goals of empowering individuals and transforming society are more explicitly political than the goals of Dewey and his colleagues because critical theorists claim they have developed a better under-standing of the link between knowledge and power. They contend that what is regarded as worthy of study in school—indeed, the very concept of "knowledge" itself—privileges some students and penalizes others.[76]

To understand their argument, we must see how critical theory in colleges of education fits into the movement in higher education toward *postmodern criticism.* University scholars in a variety of academic disciplines have grown more sensitive to the influence of class, race, ethnicity, and gender. Postmodernists argue these cultural factors strongly affect how people derive meaning from their experiences, a belief I mentioned in the last chapter's discussion of *constructivism.* Postmodernists deny that people can ever perceive reality objectively because every perception is an interpretation shaped by prior experience. Thus they contend that women and men, for instance, see things differently because they construct reality differently in their minds.

Traditional academic scholarship glosses over such differences, holding up men as the standard and depicting reality from masculine points of view. History, as it comes across in school, is primarily an account written by men about men. Literature is primarily a text of men's feelings and perceptions. Thus, postmod-ernists contend, what passes for knowledge in school marginalizes women. Patti Lather argues this case convincingly in *Getting Smart: Feminist Research and Pedagogy with/in the Postmodern* (1991). In similar ways, knowledge as traditionally defined marginalizes poor people and members of racial and ethnic minorities.[77]

Interrogating the Canon

Critical theorists in colleges of education, along with their postmodern counter-parts in departments of history, English, and other academic disciplines, are trying to listen to the voices of marginalized groups. To help students hear these voices, critical theorists are urging educators to "interrogate the *canon,*" the body of knowledge deemed worthy of serious study.

Critical theorists were not the first scholars to make this demand. Well before the mid-1970s, scholars were debating the contents of the canon, arguing over which works to put in and which to leave out. Critical theorists and other postmodernists, though, are now questioning "the priority of canonicity itself." Critical theorists want each school's students and teachers to negotiate the con-tent of the curriculum, to select the knowledge that can help empower the partic-ular people in that particular situation.[78]

"The curriculum can best inspire learning only when school knowledge builds upon the tacit knowledge derived from the cultural resources that students already possess," Aronowitz and Giroux argue in *Postmodern Education* (1991). It becomes the teachers' job to relate traditional academic subjects to projects stu-dents and teachers have jointly chosen. Such projects might center on "rap music, sports, the Civil War, neighborhoods, youth in society, race relations, sexuality, or almost anything else."[79]

■ ■ ■ ■ ■

BOX 7.8

CRITICAL PEDAGOGY ON THE WEB

This University of Iowa site is a wonderful resource on critical theory in education, providing clear explanations of difficult concepts and well-annotated links on such topics as feminism, postmodernism, race and postcolonialism, and sexuality and queer theory. Go to mingo.info-science.uiowa.edu/~stevens/critped/index.htm

In the postmodern high school, students and teachers are free to negotiate virtually every aspect of education. "There are no requirements imposed from above," Aronowitz and Giroux point out. Here is a pedagogy designed to be as different as possible from the essentialism of Bennett and company. Critical theory is progressivism pushed to the limit.[80]

"Whiteness" and Other Paradigm Shifts

Critical scholarship causes *paradigm shifts:* fundamental changes in the ways researchers conceptualize issues, based on new paths of intellectual inquiry. Patti Lather and other feminists have contributed to paradigm shifts in gender studies. In studies of race and ethnicity, critical theorists are developing the new paradigm of *whiteness*. Instead of looking at race and ethnicity in traditional ways and focusing on, for instance, how the white majority in the United States has oppressed minorities, critical theorists are examining what it means to be white: how whiteness offers advantages to those who are included within its boundaries.

As Chapter 8 points out, the very definitions of race and ethnicity are open to question. Mainstream news media are paying close attention to the debates raging in academia, and articles such as Darryl Fears' "Hue and Cry on 'Whiteness Studies'" in the *Washington Post* (June 20, 2003) are taking the debate nationwide. A cornerstone of the new whiteness paradigm is that race is not a physical reality but a social construct, only a few hundred years old, invented by Europeans and European Americans to preserve their own power while denying it to others.[81]

This kind of inquiry leads critical scholars to pose a whole new set of questions. How have conceptions of race evolved in different parts of the world and in different cultures? How are conceptions of race changing today? In what sense are "white Americans . . . so accustomed to being part of a privileged majority they do not see themselves as part of a race?"[82] The edited volume *White Reign: Deploying Whiteness in America* (1999) is a good introduction to these issues and their educational implications.[83]

Paradigms are shifting in studies of social class as well. Stanley Aronowitz argues in *How Class Works: Power and Social Movement* (2004) that we should consider class less in terms of socioeconomic stratification—the traditional view—and more as the "power of social groups to make a difference." Groups that occupy a variety of social and economic positions can become "ruling classes" by struggling to change the social order, Aronowitz explains. He offers the examples of the labor and feminist movements, both of which have increased the power of teachers. Yet many teachers have resisted identifying with such movements.[84]

Language, Accessibility, and Barbie Dolls

Not only are the critical theorists' ideas radical, their language can be difficult and even impossible. When pressed on this complaint, critical theorists tend to reply they are leaving "lite" writing and "popcorn imagery" to others, thank you. Some of them feel they must create a new language so they can "deconstruct and challenge dominant relations of power and knowledge legitimated through traditional forms of discourse."[85]

Since the early 1990s, critical theorists have gradually faced the fact that readers who cannot understand their words cannot get their message. As a result, their writing has become somewhat more accessible. The transformation in the writing of Giroux, perhaps the most prominent critical theorist, signals his desire to communicate with a broader audience. He has even authored a "fastback" (short paperback) for Phi Delta Kappa, the education honor society: *Corporate Culture and the Attack on Higher Education and Public Schooling* (1999). Although Peter McLaren still employs a bizarre, stream-of-conscious style in some of his work, he has written a plain-English introduction to critical theory in *Life in Schools* (2002). The popular books of Jonathan Kozol, which we will review in the last section of this chapter, are giving critical theory its broadest exposure.[86]

Critical theorists may be at their best analyzing the impact on education of corporate culture, popular culture, and especially the media. As they constantly remind us, education takes place outside schools as well as inside. McLaren's *Rethinking Media Literacy: A Critical Pedagogy of Representations* (1995) and *Revolutionary Multiculturalism: Pedagogies of Dissent for the New Millennium* (1997) offer valuable insights for those who are ready to dig deep. Giroux explores the manufacture and sale of pop culture in *Channel Surfing: Racism, the Media, and the Destruction of Today's Youth* (1998) and *The Mouse that Roared: Disney and the End of Innocence* (2001). Joanne Pagano takes a critical look at media influences on young people in *Adolescent Culture, Knowledge and Gender in Contemporary Film and Music* (2004).[87]

The liveliest, most accessible, and often most humorous critical theory can be found in books written or edited by Joe Kincheloe. In *The Sign of the Burger: McDonald's and the Culture of Power* (2002), Kincheloe proves Giroux isn't the only critical theorist with the nerve to dissect an American icon, and Kincheloe does his work with a much lighter touch. Shirley Steinberg, Kincheloe's wife and collaborator, is equally deft with her essays on Barbie, "the bitch who has everything." *Kinderculture: The Corporate Construction of Childhood* (1997) is their edited collection of essays on fast food, dolls, professional wrestling, Beavis and Butt-Head, and other mass-marketed influences on children's lives.[88]

A serious message shines through the "Oh, wow, we're radical now!" fun the writers are obviously having. Corporate America, motivated by the bottom line of profit, manipulates children, perpetuates stereotypes, and reinforces injustices of race, ethnicity, class, and gender. In the postmodern era, childhood comes prefabricated—packaged for easy consumption.

Despite their goal of reaching a wide audience, critical theorists still pride themselves on being outside the mainstream. While essentialist William Bennett waves the American flag in *Why We Fight: Moral Clarity and the War on Terrorism* (2003), Kincheloe approaches the post-9/11 world entirely differently in *The Miseducation of the West: How Schools and the Media Distort Our Understanding of the Islamic World* (2004). Relishing their role as dark horses and outsiders, critical theorists make other progressives look less radical to Americans searching for educational alternatives.[89]

Taking It to the Masses: Jonathan Kozol

Of all the scholarly studies of education released during the 1990s, the one that continues to attract the most public attention is Jonathan Kozol's *Savage Inequalities* (1991). Kozol first captured a national audience in 1967 with *Death at an Early Age* (1967), an account of his inner-city teaching career with poor African American children. With *Savage Inequalities,* he has once again moved the social reform agenda of progressivism to center stage.[90]

Kozol, winner of the National Education Association's Friend of Education Award in 1992, is trying to restart a conversation very few people wanted to have during the 1980s. He wants to talk about inequality and segregation. The reforms of the 1980s never reached schools like those Kozol visited in East St. Louis, Chicago, San Antonio, New York, Camden, and Washington, DC. Making a mockery of the *Brown* decision, these schools remain separate and *un*equal. Urban schools for the minority poor are miserable by any standards, Kozol insists, but instead of dwelling on test scores, dropout rates, and other quantitative indicators, he shows us overcrowded classrooms, dangerous hallways, and filthy conditions. These schools are "extraordinarily unhappy places," he says, far worse than any schools he saw during the 1960s.[91]

Kozol lets us hear the voices of those trapped inside—teachers, parents, and especially students. A fifth grader in Washington, DC, says that if her school somehow got more money, she would want to "make it a beautiful clean building. Make it pretty. Way it is, I feel ashamed." These students realize suburban schools are vastly different, and they are resentful.[92]

Voices from the suburbs surrounding the central cities also speak in *Savage Inequalities.* These voices, mostly those of middle-class whites, boast their public schools exemplify "what is possible when citizens want to achieve the best for their children." In a self-congratulatory mood, a community magazine published in Chicago's wealthy New Trier suburb applauds its schools by observing that "a supportive attitude on the part of families . . . translates into a willingness to pay" for quality. Suburban Americans would not allow *their* children even to walk past the inner-city schools Kozol visited, much less try to learn there. Yet these same Americans believe higher graduation requirements, more standardized testing, and more homework can make the schools good enough for *other people's* children.[93]

Kozol believes in desegregation, as do most of the minority students he interviews, but the main reform he advocates is financial: spending at least as much on urban schools as on suburban schools. Kozol indicts America's school finance system, which by relying on local property taxes enables wealthier school districts to raise far more money. As we will see in Chapter 9, lawsuits are under way throughout the nation to try to reduce the spending gap between rich and poor districts. But Kozol's disquieting conclusion is better-off Americans will continue to resist equalization because "they are fighting for the right to guarantee their children the inheritance of an ascendant role in our society."

> There is a deep-seated reverence for fair play in the United States, and in many areas of life we see the consequences in a genuine distaste for loaded dice; but this is not the case in education, health care, or inheritance of wealth. In these elemental areas we want the game to be unfair and we have made it so; and it will likely so remain.[94]

Kozol's words hit home. Written to reach the widest possible audience, *Savage Inequalities* spells out a message much more accessible and only slightly milder than the work of Henry Giroux, Stanley Aronowitz, Peter McLaren, Joe Kincheloe, and other critical theorists. Kozol is taking critical theory to the masses.

Kozol hopes the national exposure he is receiving will help his latest books, *Amazing Grace* (1995) and *Ordinary Resurrections* (2000), touch people's consciences—or, as he increasingly chooses to express it, their souls. While *Savage Inequalities* and *Death at an Early Age* focus on schooling, and his 1988 book *Rachel and Her Children* presents the plight of the homeless, *Amazing Grace* casts a wider net that tries to encompass the entire lives of the urban poor. Housing, medical care, police protection, employment, religion, and education all take their place in a hostile landscape peopled by drug dealers, junkies, prostitutes, arsonists—along with good, decent children and adults. In *Ordinary Resurrections*, Kozol refocuses his attention on young children and their teachers, producing a touching book that, if less overtly political than his other works, is more personal and hopeful.[95]

The subtitle of *Amazing Grace* is *The Lives of Children and the Conscience of a Nation*, which reflects both the scope of the work and the goal of its author. By

■ ■ ■ ■ ■

BOX 7.9

AN INTERVIEW WITH JONATHAN KOZOL

To find out how Kozol's background and personal experiences have shaped his writing, read an interview with him in *Technos Quarterly* at www.technos.net/tq_07/3kozol.htm

writing a disturbing account that brings readers face to face with the residents of the Mott Haven neighborhood in New York City's South Bronx—the poorest congressional district in the United States—Kozol hopes to go over the heads of policy makers to reach ordinary Americans. Readers meet Alice Washington, her son David, the children of P.S. 69, and the pastor of the Episcopal church that tries to provide them all a "safe sanctuary." After watching people die from drugs, AIDS, fires, and shootings, only the coldest reader can walk away from the book unaffected.

"The question is whether we want to be one society or two," Kozol insists. The residents of Mott Haven

> are living in a place where no white person would ever want to live. And it is not enough to fix a single part of it. Educators could talk forever about restructuring, decentralizing, recentralizing. . . . You can debate all these things forever. But virtually no one in education will speak of the abiding cancer of our society. Do you mean restructured ghetto schools? Decentralized ghetto schools? Ghetto schools with ghetto choices for ghetto parents? The ghetto itself is a permanent cancer on the body of America that goes unquestioned.[96]

Ordinary Resurrections finds Kozol back in Mott Haven but in a different frame of mind. Readers looking for an uplifting, even spiritual view of elementary school students and their teachers should be able to find it in this book, subtitled *Children in the Years of Hope.* Although Kozol cannot help but be critical of the socioeconomic circumstances that trap the people of Mott Haven, he manages to transcend poverty and other negative factors to celebrate children running through sprinklers and cooling off, children finding joy in dance and song, and adults allowing themselves the same childish pleasures.

Kozol allows his admiration for teachers to show, again and again. "Teaching children of this age, when it's done right, is more than craft," he muses; "it's also partly ministry and partly poetry."[97]

ACTIVITIES

1. Visit the central office of a local school district and ask for a copy of the district's philosophy of education (sometimes called a statement of goals and purposes). Compare it with the philosophies and theories in this chapter. Try to obtain an earlier statement of goals from the same district and analyze the changes. Can you see the influence of No Child Left Behind?

2. Interview currently employed teachers who represent a variety of philosophies and theories.

3. Talk with retired teachers about swings of the educational pendulum and how one educational theory may have displaced another during their careers.

4. Observe in a public or private school that seems to be dominated by a theory of education different from yours.

RECOMMENDED READINGS

Adler, Mortimer J. *The Paideia Proposal: An Educational Manifesto* (New York: Macmillan, 1982). This book, assisted by its two companion volumes (see note 9), has breathed new life into perennialism.

Bennett, William J., Chester E. Finn, Jr., and John T. E. Cribb, Jr. *The Educated Child: A Parent's Guide from Preschool through Eighth Grade* (New York: Simon & Schuster, 2000). This book uses examples from E. D. Hirsch, Jr.'s, Core Knowledge Sequence to help parents evaluate schools and demand an essentialist education for their young children.

Kozol, Jonathan. *Amazing Grace: The Lives of Children and the Conscience of a Nation* (New York: Crown Publishers, 1995). Critical theory written for a popular audience, this book puts the highly charged message of the best-seller *Savage Inequalities* (see note 90) into an even broader social context.

Sizer, Theodore R., Deborah Meier, and Nancy Faust Sizer. *Keeping School: Letters to Parents from Principals of Two Small Schools* (Boston: Beacon Press, 2004). The *Horace* series (see notes 60–61, 64) and *The Students Are Watching* (note 66) remain excellent, but this more recent book is full of practical wisdom and guidance that teachers will appreciate as much as parents.

NOTES

1. An excellent anthology designed to help teachers use philosophy is Ronald F. Reed, ed., *Philosophical Documents in Education*, 2nd ed. (New York: Addison Wesley Longman, 1999).

2. Robert M. Hutchins, *The Higher Learning in America* (New Haven, CT: Yale University Press, 1936), p. 66.

3. Robert M. Hutchins, *Great Books: The Foundation of a Liberal Education* (New York: Simon & Schuster, 1954). See also the excellent discussion in Christopher J. Lucas, *Foundations of Education: Schooling and the Social Order* (Englewood Cliffs, NJ: Prentice Hall, 1984), Chap. 3.

4. Terry Roberts, "His Life a Reminder of Our Humanity," *Education Week* (September 5, 2001), pp. 61, 63.

5. Mortimer J. Adler, *The Paideia Proposal: An Educational Manifesto* (New York: Macmillan, 1982).

6. See Mortimer J. Adler's *Paideia Problems and Possibilities* (New York: Macmillan, 1983) and *The Paideia Program: An Educational Syllabus* (New York: Macmillan, 1984).

7. Based on my notes and recollections, I have reconstructed exchanges that took place at the annual meeting of the American Educational Studies Association, Milwaukee, WI, November 4, 1983.

8. "Quality, Not Just Quantity," *Time* (September 6, 1982), p. 59.

9. See Terry Roberts, "The Paideia Movement: An Idea Whose Time Has Come?" *Education Week* (February 26, 1997), pp. 36, 39, and Debra Viadero, "Early Star, Paideia Has Had Its Ups and Downs," *Education Week* (February 17, 1993), pp. 1, 12–13.

10. Mortimer J. Adler, *Reforming Education: The Opening of the American Mind*, ed. Geraldine Van Doren (New York: Macmillan, 1988), p. 314.

11. Ibid., pp. 312, 314.

12. Two key documents of the early essentialist movement are William C. Bagley, *Education and Emergent Man* (New York: Ronald Press, 1934), and Bagley, "An Essentialist's Platform for the Advancement of American Education," *Educational Administration and Supervision* 24 (April 1938): 241–256. Lucas analyzes essentialism in *Foundations of Education*, Chap. 2.

13. Bagley, "An Essentialist's Platform," p. 253.

14. William C. Bagley, "The Case for Essentialism in Education," *Journal of the National Education Association* (October 1941): 202.

15. Arthur E. Bestor, *Educational Wastelands: The Retreat from Learning in Our Public Schools* (Urbana, IL: University of Illinois Press, 1953); Bestor, *The Restoration of Learning* (New York: Knopf, 1955); Mortimer Smith, *And Madly Teach* (Chicago: Regnery, 1949); Smith, *The Diminished Mind: A Study of Planned Mediocrity in Our Public Schools* (Chicago: Regnery, 1954); James B. Conant, *Education and Liberty: The Role of Schools in a Modern Democracy* (Cambridge, MA: Harvard University Press, 1953); Conant, *The American High School Today* (New York: McGraw-Hill, 1959).

16. See Jyoti Thottam, "Is Your Job Going Abroad?" *Time* (March 1, 2004), pp. 27–36.

17. National Commission on Excellence in Education, *A Nation at Risk: The Imperative for Educational Reform* (Washington, DC: U.S. Government Printing Office, 1983).

18. Ibid.

19. U.S. Department of Education, *No Child Left Behind: A Toolkit for Teachers* (Washington, DC: USDE, 2003), pp. 3–5.

20. "States Rebel against New Education Law," *Mobile Register* (February 18, 2004), p. 7A; David J. Hoff, "Chiefs to Help States Figure Costs of ESEA," *Education Week* (February 18, 2004), p. 31.

21. William J. Bennett, *The De-Valuing of America: The Fight for Our Culture and Our Children* (New York: Summit Books, 1992), p. 61.

22. William J. Bennett, ed., *The Book of Virtues: A Treasury of Great Moral Stories* (New York: Simon & Schuster, 1993).

23. Interview with William J. Bennett by Peter Ross Range, *Modern Maturity* 38 (March–April 1995): 28.

24. See Dan Goodgame, "The Chairman of Virtue Inc.," *Time* (September 16, 1996), pp. 46–49.

25. Bennett, *The Book of Virtues*, p. 14.

26. Ibid., p. 12.

27. William J. Bennett, ed., *The Children's Book of Virtues* (New York: Simon & Schuster, 1995); Bennett, *The Book of Virtues for Young People* (Morristown, NJ: Silver-Burdett, 1995); Bennett, *The Moral Compass: Stories for a Life's Journey* (New York: Simon & Schuster, 1995); Bennett, *Virtues Collection* (New York: Simon & Schuster, 1996); Bennett, *The Broken Hearth: Reversing the Moral Collapse of the American Family* (New York: Doubleday, 2001); Bennett, *Why We Fight: Moral Clarity and the War on Terrorism* (New York: Simon & Schuster, 2003); David J. Hoff and Michelle R. Davis, "Federal Grant Involving Bennett's K12 Inc. Questioned," *Education Week* (July 28, 2004), pp. 1, 24–25.

28. William J. Bennett, Chester E. Finn, Jr., and John T. E. Cribb, Jr., *The Educated Child: A Parent's Guide from Preschool through Eighth Grade* (New York: Simon & Schuster, 2000).

29. Ibid., pp. 18–19, 628.

30. Ibid., p. 19.

31. Diane Ravitch and Chester E. Finn, Jr., *What Do Our 17-Year-Olds Know?: A Report on the First National Assessment of History and Literature* (New York: Harper & Row, 1987).

32. E. D. Hirsch, Jr., *Cultural Literacy: What Every American Needs to Know* (Boston: Houghton Mifflin, 1987); Allan Bloom, *The Closing of the American Mind* (New York: Simon & Schuster, 1987); Hirsch, *The Schools We Need and Why We Don't Have Them* (New York: Doubleday, 1996); Hirsch and John Holdren, *Books to Build On: A Grade-by-Grade Resource for Teachers and Parents* (New York: Delta, 1996); Michael J. Marshall and Hirsch, eds., *Realms of Gold: Core Knowledge Readers* (Charlottesville, VA: Core Knowledge Foundation, 2000).

33. See Lynn Olson, "Worries of a Standards 'Backlash' Grow," *Education Week* (April 5, 2000), pp. 1, 12–13, and Diane Ravitch, ed., *Debating the Future of American Education: Do We Need National Standards and Assessments?* (Washington, DC: Brookings Institution, 1995).

34. Quoted in Olson, "Worries of a Standards 'Backlash' Grow," p. 13.

35. Chester E. Finn, Jr., *We Must Take Charge: Our Schools and Our Future* (New York: Free Press, 1991).

36. Diane Ravitch, *Left Back: A Century of Failed School Reform* (New York: Simon & Schuster, 2000); Ravitch, *New Schools for a New Century: The Redesign of Urban Education* (New Haven, CT: Yale University Press, 1999); Ravitch, *City Schools: Lessons from New York* (Baltimore: Johns Hopkins University Press, 2000); Ravitch, *The Language Police: How Pressure Groups Restrict What Children Learn* (New York: Alfred A. Knopf, 2003).

37. Chester E. Finn, Jr., Bruno V. Manno, and Gregg Vanourek, *Charter Schools in Action: Renewing Public Education* (Princeton, NJ: Princeton University Press, 2000).

38. John Dewey, *The School and Society* (Chicago: University of Chicago Press, 1899 [1927]), p. 32.

39. Ibid.

40. The classic study of the movement is Lawrence A. Cremin's *The Transformation of the School: Progressivism in American Education, 1876–1957* (New York: Knopf, 1961). Also useful are Arthur Zilversmit, *Changing Schools: Progressive Education Theory and Practice, 1930–1960* (Chicago: University of Chicago Press, 1993); Henry J. Perkinson, *The Imperfect Panacea: American Faith in Education*, 4th ed. (New York: McGraw-Hill, 1995), Chaps. 4 and 6; and Lucas, *Foundations of Education*, Chap. 6.

41. See Larry A. Hickman, "Dewey, John (1859–1952)," in J. J. Chambliss, ed., *Philosophy of Education: An Encyclopedia* (New York: Garland, 1996), pp. 146–153.

42. John Dewey, *Democracy and Education: An Introduction to the Philosophy of Education* (New York: Macmillan, 1916). Also see Robert B. Westbrook, *John Dewey and American Democracy* (Ithaca, NY: Cornell University Press, 1991).

43. John Dewey, *The Child and the Curriculum* (Chicago: University of Chicago Press, 1902).

44. Commission on the Reorganization of Secondary Education, *Cardinal Principles of Secondary Education,* Bulletin No. 35 (Washington, DC: U.S. Government Printing Office, 1918).

45. William H. Kilpatrick, "The Project Method," *Teachers College Record* 19 (September 1918): 319–335; Kilpatrick, *Foundations of Method* (New York: Macmillan, 1925).

46. See Patricia A. Graham, *Progressive Education: From Arcade to Academe. A History of the Progressive Education Association, 1919–1955* (New York: Teachers College Press, 1967).

47. John Dewey, *Art and Experience* (New York: Capricorn Books, 1934), pp. 32, 40.

48. Dewey published many of his criticisms of progressive education in *Experience and Education* (New York: Macmillan, 1938).

49. John and Evelyn Dewey, *Schools of To-Morrow* (New York: E. P. Dutton, 1915). For a then-and-now look at some of the schools Dewey visited as well as a study of several modern progressive schools, see Susan F. Semel and Alan R. Sadovnik, eds., *"Schools of Tomorrow," Schools of Today: What Happened to Progressive Education?* (New York: Peter Lang, 1999).

50. George S. Counts, *Dare the School Build a New Social Order?* (New York: John Day, 1932).

51. C. A. Bowers, *The Progressive Educator and the Depression: The Radical Years* (New York: Random House, 1969). Theodore Brameld of Boston University became the major voice of social reconstructionism in the 1950s and 1960s. See his books *Toward a Reconstructed Philosophy of Education* (New York: Holt, Rinehart & Winston, 1956) and *Education for the Emerging Age* (New York: Harper & Row, 1965).

52. Lucas, *Foundations of Education,* pp. 183–185; Cremin, *The Transformation of the School,* pp. 332–338.

53. William J. Bennett, *Our Country and Our Children: Improving America's Schools and Affirming the Common Culture* (New York: Touchstone, 1989), pp. 9–10.

54. Drew Lindsay, "Call to Arms," *Education Week* (April 2000), p. 26.

55. "Why Do These Kids Love School?" produced by Dorothy Fadiman and KTEH–TV (San Jose, CA: Concentric Media, 1990). Mary Anne Raywid describes the video in "Why Do These Kids Love School?" *Phi Delta Kappan* 73 (April 1992): 631–633. See Tom Peters, *Heart and Soul of Excellence* (New York: Random House Value, 1997).

56. Lindsay, "Call to Arms," p. 26.

57. Kevin Fedarko, "Can I Copy Your Homework—And Represent You in Court?" *Time* (September 21, 1992), pp. 52–53.

58. Deborah Meier, *The Power of Their Ideas: Lessons for America from a Small School in Harlem* (Boston: Beacon Press, 1996); Meier, *In Schools We Trust: Creating Communities of Learning in an Era of Testing and Standardization* (Boston: Beacon Press, 2002).

59. David Ruenzel, "The Essential Ted Sizer," *Teacher Magazine* (October 1996), p. 33.

60. Theodore R. Sizer, *Horace's Compromise: The Dilemma of the American High School* (Boston: Houghton Mifflin, 1984); Ernest L. Boyer, *High School: A Report on Secondary Education in America* (New York: Harper & Row, 1983); John I. Goodlad, *A Place Called School: Prospects for the Future* (New York: McGraw-Hill, 1984).

61. Theodore R. Sizer, *Horace's School: Redesigning the American High School* (Boston: Houghton Mifflin, 1992).

62. Theodore R. Sizer, Deborah Meier, and Nancy Faust Sizer, *Keeping School: Letters to Parents from Principals of Two Small Schools* (Boston: Beacon Press, 2004).

63. Sizer, *Horace's School,* p. 197.

64. Theodore R. Sizer, *Horace's Hope: What Works for the American High School* (Boston: Houghton Mifflin, 1996).

65. Quoted in Ruenzel, "The Essential Ted Sizer," p. 38.

66. Theodore R. Sizer and Nancy Faust Sizer, *The Students Are Watching: Schools and the Moral Construct* (Boston: Beacon Press, 1999), p. xviii.

67. The Sizers devote a chapter of *The Students Are Watching* to each verb. The quotations are from pp. 43 and 82, respectively.

68. Sizer and Sizer, *The Students Are Watching,* p. 116.

69. Lindsay, "Call to Arms," p. 26.

70. Ibid; Alfie Kohn, *The Case against Standardized Testing: Raising the Scores, Ruining the Schools* (Boston: Beacon Press, 2004).

71. Alfie Kohn, *No Contest: The Case against Competition* (Boston: Houghton Mifflin, 1992); Kohn, *Punished by Rewards: The Trouble with Gold Stars, Incentive Plans, A's, Praise, and Other Bribes* (Boston: Houghton Mifflin, 1999); Kohn, *What Does It Mean to be Educated? and More Essays on Standards, Grading, and Other Follies* (Boston: Beacon Press, 2004).

72. Alfie Kohn, *The Schools Our Children Deserve: Moving Beyond Traditional Classrooms and "Tougher Standards"* (Boston: Houghton Mifflin, 1999), pp. 21–22.

73. Ibid., p. 1.

74. Peter McLaren, *Life in Schools: An Introduction to Critical Pedagogy in the Foundations of Education,* 4th ed. (Boston: Allyn and Bacon, 2002), p. 168.

75. Ibid., p. 175.

76. Stanley Aronowitz and Henry A. Giroux, *Education Under Seige: The Conservative, Liberal, and Radical Debate over Schooling* (South Hadley, MA: Bergin & Garvey, 1985).

77. Patti Lather, *Getting Smart: Feminist Research and Pedagogy with/in the Postmodern* (New York: Routledge, 1991).

78. Stanley Aronowitz and Henry A. Giroux, *Postmodern Education: Politics, Culture, and Social Criticism* (Minneapolis: University of Minnesota Press, 1991), p. 17.

79. Ibid., p. 15.

80. Ibid., p. 21.

81. Darryl Fears, "Hue and Cry on 'Whiteness Studies': An Academic Field's Take on Race Stirs Interest and Anger," *Washington Post* (June 20, 2003), p. A01.

82. Ibid.

83. Joe L. Kincheloe, Shirley R. Steinberg, Nelson M. Rodriguez, and Ronald E. Chennault, eds., *White Reign: Deploying Whiteness in America* (New York: Palgrave Macmillan, 1999).

84. Stanley Aronowitz, *How Class Works: Power and Social Movement* (New Haven, CT: Yale University Press, 2004), pp. 1–2.

85. Aronowitz and Giroux, *Postmodern Education*, pp. 90–91.

86. Henry A. Giroux, *Corporate Culture and the Attack on Higher Education and Public Schooling* (Bloomington, IN: Phi Delta Kappa Educational Foundation, 1999); Peter McLaren, *Life In Schools.*

87. Peter McLaren, *Rethinking Media Literacy: A Critical Pedagogy of Representations* (New York: Peter Lang, 1995), and *Revolutionary Multiculturalism: Pedagogies of Dissent for the New Millennium* (Boulder, CO: Westview Press, 1997); Henry A. Giroux, *Channel Surfing: Racism, the Media, and the Destruction of Today's Youth* (New York: St. Martin's Press, 1998), and *The Mouse that Roared: Disney and the End of Innocence* (Lanham, MD: Rowman & Littlefield, 2001); Joanne Pagano, *Adolescent Culture, Knowledge and Gender in Contemporary Film and Music* (London: RoutledgeFalmer, 2004).

88. Joe L. Kincheloe, *The Sign of the Burger: McDonald's and the Culture of Power* (Philadelphia: Temple University Press, 2002); Shirley R. Steinberg and Joe L. Kincheloe, eds., *Kinderculture: The Corporate Construction of Childhood* (Boulder, CO: WestviewPress, 1997).

89. William Bennett, *Why We Fight: Moral Clarity and the War on Terrorism;* Joe L. Kincheloe, *The Miseducation of the West: How Schools and the Media Distort Our Understanding of the Islamic World* (Westport, CT: Greenwood, 2004).

90. Jonathan Kozol, *Savage Inequalities: Children in America's Schools* (New York: Crown, 1991); Kozol, *Death at an Early Age: The Destruction of the Hearts and Minds of Negro Children in the Boston Public Schools* (Boston: Houghton Mifflin, 1967).

91. Kozol, *Savage Inequalities*, p. 5.

92. Ibid., p. 181.

93. Ibid., pp. 66–67.

94. Ibid., p. 223.

95. Jonathan Kozol, *Ordinary Resurrections: Children in the Years of Hope* (New York: Crown Publishers, 2000); *Amazing Grace: The Lives of Children and the Conscience of a Nation* (New York: Crown Publishers, 1995); *Rachel and Her Children: Homeless Families in America* (New York: Crown Publishers, 1988).

96. Lonnie Harp, "Soul Searching," *Education Week* (October 11, 1995), pp. 28–29.

97. Kozol, *Ordinary Resurrections*, p. 277.

CHAPTER 8

SOCIOLOGY
OF EDUCATION

Sociologists study people in groups. The discipline of sociology is valuable to teachers and other educators because it enables us to see patterns in human behavior, patterns we could easily overlook because so many individuals demand our attention in school. Without minimizing the importance of individuals, sociology helps us realize how behavior reflects the positions people occupy in society.

In other words, we can better understand schooling if we think of it as more than just a steady stream of individuals pouring through an institution. We need to step back, consider the individuals as members of social groups, and sort out the patterns in their behavior.

One of the first lessons I learned as a teacher was that *social class, race, ethnicity,* and *gender* have a powerful effect on the process of education. I found, to be blunt, that even in the schools of a nation that prides itself on equality of opportunity, some students are more equal than others.

As pleasant as it would be to pretend schools take in students from diverse social backgrounds and give them all the same chance to succeed, that simply does not happen. Students who are members of some social groups come to school with advantages, and schools are organized in ways that help them maintain their advantages. Other students arrive with two strikes against them, socially speaking, and schools often throw the third strike.

No Child Left Behind is calling public attention to these unpleasant facts of educational life. I often criticize the federal law in this textbook, but I must give credit where it is due: NCLB is forcing educators to confront the very inequities we discuss in this chapter. The prospective teachers in my introduction to education classes admit NCLB makes them uncomfortable. Some of them say they find it difficult to face the achievement gaps that appear when test score data are broken down by subgroups of students.

"It's embarrassing," one future teacher recently wrote on her course evaluation. "It's hard for me to discuss race and class because some of the people in our class graduated from high schools with low test scores, and now they're going to be teachers. Think about how they must feel when we talk about their schools."

This chapter does raise sensitive issues—exactly the kind you'll deal with every day if you become a teacher. In the opening section, we look at social class differences in families and peer groups, differences that affect how well students do in school. One way schools respond to these differences is by separating students into *ability groups* and *tracks,* a process that brands many working-class students as second-class citizens. The next section surveys race and ethnicity, focusing on African American, Hispanic American, Asian American, and Native American students. At the heart of the chapter is a study of *desegregation, bilingual education,* and *nonstandard dialects of English,* an analysis of strategies designed to increase educational opportunities in our multicultural nation. The concluding section on gender—to which, unfortunately, NCLB pays little attention—focuses on both girls and boys, but the emphasis is on how females are the second sex in school, just as they are in society.

As you read this chapter, keep in mind the demographic changes we have discussed in earlier chapters, trends our nation's newspapers, news magazines, and other popular media are tracking closely. In *America's Children: Key National Indicators of Well-Being* (2004) and other U.S. government reports, we can see how the trends are affecting education. Remember that almost one in five students comes to school from a family living in poverty, and the child poverty rate is increasing. Remember that more than one-third of the nation's students are Hispanic American, African American, Asian American, or Native American. The public schools of the District of Columbia and six states—Hawaii, California, New Mexico, Texas, Mississippi, and Louisiana—are already "majority minority." In seven more states—New York, South Carolina, Nevada, Georgia, Florida, Maryland, and Arizona—minority students make up more than 45 percent of public school enrollment.[1]

Consider, too, how families are changing. Since the mid-1980s, more than half of American families have contained no children. Only one-third of today's families reflect the traditional profile of a father, mother, and two or more children. Families with a wage-earning father, homemaking mother, and at least two children are rare: Only 7 percent of families fit that description. Although the percentage of students who do not live with two parents has stabilized since the mid-1990s, it remains high. Twenty-three percent of students now live with their mothers, 5 percent with their fathers, and 4 percent with neither of their parents. Almost half of America's students will live in such circumstances before reaching their eighteenth birthday.[2]

The trend toward single-parent and no-parent families illustrates how interwoven the factors of class, race, ethnicity, and gender are. African American and Hispanic American students are far more likely than other students to grow up in single- or no-parent homes. Thirty-six percent of Hispanic American children and a startling 65 percent of African American children are now living with either one parent or no parents, compared to 23 percent of white children. Furthermore, most single- or no-parent families are headed by a woman, and female-headed households are more than twice as likely as male-headed households to be living in poverty. Thirty-two percent of African American children, 28 percent of Hispanic American children, and 9 percent of white children are growing up in poverty.[3]

Although I have organized this chapter into separate sections on class, race and ethnicity, and gender, life is not so easily subdivided. As you read, you should constantly look for connections and relationships. You will see them often in the classroom.

SOCIAL CLASS

Many Americans like to believe the United States is relatively free of the rigid social stratification we criticize in other nations, but our country, too, has social classes, a class structure that influences education more than we may care to admit. While we can take pride in our efforts to educate children from all socio-economic backgrounds, we should be concerned that once students get to school, their backgrounds can play a powerful role in their success—or lack of it.

The American Social Structure

Based on studies conducted since the 1920s, sociologists have determined that the United States has a five-tiered class structure. In *Society and Education* (1996), Daniel U. Levine and Rayna F. Levine describe the social structure as follows:

Upper class	three percent of the population—people with substantial wealth that is usually inherited.
Upper-middle class	twenty-two percent of the population, including professionals, executives, managers, and more successful small-business owners and farmers.

Lower-middle class	thirty-four percent of the population, composed of white-collar workers (such as clerks, salespeople, and teachers), small-business owners and farmers, and better-paid skilled blue-collar workers.
Upper-working class	twenty-eight percent of the population, composed of skilled and semi-skilled blue-collar workers (such as craftspeople and assembly-line workers).
Lower-working class	thirteen percent of the population, ranging from unskilled manual workers (the "working poor") to the chronically unemployed.

Sociologists use such factors as income, occupation, education, and housing to place people on the social class hierarchy. The size of the classes and the rigidity of their boundaries vary considerably throughout the country. As a rule, the larger the community, the wider the extremes of poverty and wealth and the sharper the separation of classes.[4]

Sorting and Selecting in School

Patterns from the Past.   For as long as sociologists have studied social class, they have been intrigued with its effects on education. George Counts, the social reconstructionist we met in the last chapter, was one of the first researchers to document how schools sort and select students by their social backgrounds. In *The Selective Character of American Secondary Education* (1922), Counts showed children from more privileged backgrounds were not only more likely to attend high school but also more likely to take the schools' most prestigious academic courses. In *Middletown* (1929), a portrait of life in a medium-sized midwestern city, Robert and Helen Lynd found that although parents from every social class said they believed in the importance of formal education, students from higher-status families enjoyed school more and stayed in school longer.[5]

Research conducted throughout the nation added details to the picture. As we saw in Chapters 6 and 7, educators diversified the curriculum during the twentieth century, developing different programs in their quest to "meet the needs" of students from different socioeconomic backgrounds. This trend, relatively new when Counts and the Lynds undertook their research, soon swept the country. Other sociologists documented the results of the trend: The schools became stratified by social class. In the influential study *Who Shall Be Educated* (1944), which involved research in the South, the Midwest, and New England, W. Lloyd Warner and his associates used the metaphor of a sorting machine to depict educational stratification:

> The educational system may be thought of as an enormous, complicated machine for sorting and ticketing and routing children through life. Young children are fed in at one end to a moving belt which conveys them past all sorts of inspecting

TABLE 8.1   Social Class and Tracking: Elmtown High School in the 1940s

	PERCENTAGE OF STUDENTS IN TRACK		
SOCIAL CLASS	COLLEGE PREPARATORY	GENERAL	COMMERCIAL
Upper and upper-middle	64	36	0
Lower-middle	27	51	21
Upper-working	9	58	33
Lower-working	4	58	38

Source: Adapted from August B. Hollingshead, *Elmtown's Youth* (New York: Wiley, 1949), p. 462.

stations. One large group is almost immediately brushed off into a bin labeled "nonreaders," "first grade repeaters," or "opportunity class" where they stay for eight or ten years and are then released through a chute to the outside world to become "hewers of wood and drawers of water." The great body of children move ahead on the main belt, losing a few here and there who are "kept back" for repeated inspection.[6]

Warner concluded the machine does provide upward mobility for a few working-class students, but it also "keep[s] down many people who try for higher places."[7]

A study that brought the picture into even sharper focus appeared in the post–World War II era. *Elmtown's Youth* (1949) by August B. Hollingshead became a classic because it highlighted patterns that appeared again and again in later research. In Elmtown High, a small-town school in the Midwest, Hollingshead found a startling correspondence between the socioeconomic status of students and their academic program or *track*. As Table 8.1 shows, nearly two-thirds of the upper- and upper-middle-class students were enrolled in the college preparatory program, and the rest were in the general track. These higher-status students shunned the commercial track. By contrast, more than one-third of the working-class students were in the commercial program, and fewer than 10 percent were in the college prep track. Placement of lower-middle-class students fell between these two extremes.[8]

Contemporary Patterns.   While it might be comforting to dismiss this phenomenon as a relic from the past, we cannot. The percentages have changed, but the patterns remain the same. Based on recent studies and reports, my estimates of tracking in the year 2005 are in Table 8.2. Compare them to tracking at Elmtown High during the 1940s. Notice that with the exception of the most privileged students, whose placement has changed little, higher percentages of students from up and down the social hierarchy are in the college prep track. This trend reflects the increased popularity of higher education generally and the attempt to open college doors to students from lower socioeconomic backgrounds.

TABLE 8.2   Social Class and Tracking: Public High Schools, 2005

SOCIAL CLASS	PERCENTAGE OF STUDENTS IN TRACK		
	COLLEGE PREPARATORY	GENERAL	"TRACK THREE"
Upper and upper-middle	70	30	0
Lower-middle	50	40	10
Upper-working	35	50	15
Lower-working	25	55	20

Sources: Estimates and projections based on U.S. Department of Education, National Center for Education Statistics, *Digest of Education Statistics 2003* (2004) [Available: http://nces.ed.gov/programs/digest/d03/tables/dt137.asp], Tbl. 37; U.S. Department of Education, National Center for Education Statistics, *The Condition of Education 2003* (2004) [Available: nces.ed.gov/programs/coe/2003/section4/indicator24.asp#info], Indicator 24; U.S. Department of Education, National Center for Education Statistics, *Youth Indicators, 1996: Trends in the Well-Being of American Youth* (1996) [Available: http://nces.ed.gov/pubs98/yi/y9626a.asp], Indicator 26.

Since the release of *A Nation at Risk* (1983), the rise of the New Basics curriculum that purports to challenge all students, and most recently the development of state standards and high-stakes tests for promotion and graduation (see Chapter 11), the college prep and general tracks have grown at the expense of "track three." My choice of words to describe the least prestigious track reflects the ambivalence educators have always felt about it. Over the years the track has worn such labels as *commercial, business, vocational, basic, remedial,* and *alternative.* Now it is trying on such new labels as *school-to-work, tech prep,* and *career.* But by any other name, track three is still track three, and people usually think "low status" whatever they call it.[9]

As Table 8.2 indicates, the relationship between social class and academic placement remains strong in public high schools. Similar patterns of stratification by social class appear in public middle schools that track students. Advocates of private education, especially Roman Catholic education, say their schools are less stratified by social class because they practice less tracking. We will examine their claims in Chapter 10.

Eight decades of research show social class correlates with almost every conceivable outcome of formal education, including grades, standardized test scores, and participation in extracurricular activities. The higher your social class, the more likely you are to graduate from high school and attend college. The lower your social class, the more likely you are to drop out of school.[10]

But Why?   Now comes the hard part, because it is much easier to describe something than to explain it. At the outset, we need to realize that although statistics allow us to make generalizations about group behavior, individuals within those groups may act quite differently. Some working-class students do great work in school, just as some wealthy students blow it off. Moreover, the fact that social class *correlates* with many outcomes of schooling does not necessarily mean social class *causes* success or failure. Other factors may be responsible. But in a nation committed to equal opportunity, the strong statistical relationship between social class and so much of what goes on in school should make educators take the "why" question seriously.

Families, Peer Groups, and Schools

Sociologists have traditionally explained the influence of social class on education by analyzing the role of families, peer groups, and the schools themselves. Prospective teachers have traditionally studied the sociology of education in textbooks like the one you're reading now. But they've often forgotten what they learned—sometimes dismissing it as impractical—only to find themselves struggling later when they come face to face with social class issues in their own classrooms.

Former teacher and administrator Ruby Payne is trying to bridge this gap with her books and staff development workshops. A growing national phenomenon, Payne interprets the sociology of poverty through her quarter century of educational experience and presents an approach to teaching poor students that teachers themselves find credible. School districts across the nation are contracting with her to provide "Ruby Payne Training," and you may well learn more about her strategies in a methods course in your teacher education program. The best single volume of her work is *A Framework for Understanding Poverty* (2003).[11]

Now we will consider families, peer groups, and schools in turn. The discussion draws on Payne's work as well as many other sources.

Families. Beyond the obvious fact that more affluent parents can give their children more of the things money can buy—books, magazines, toys, trips, and such—social class affects family life in several important ways. Linguistic studies show working-class families often raise their children with a language system significantly different from the one used in school. Everyone speaks a dialect, as linguists point out, but some working-class dialects are very different from the "official" dialect of the school. Payne calls attention to two *registers* of the English language: *formal* and *casual*.

> In the formal register, the pattern is to get straight to the point. In casual register, the pattern is to go around and around and finally get to the point. For students who have no access to formal register, educators become frustrated with the tendency . . . to meander almost endlessly through a topic.[12]

Furthermore, linguists have found that working-class parents are less likely than middle- and upper-class parents to carry on extended conversations with their children and less likely to answer their children's questions as if they were talking with other adults.[13]

Later in this chapter we will look at a case study of Black English Vernacular or *Ebonics*, a dialect of English that has been stigmatized more than other dialects because most of the people who use it are not only poor but members of a historically oppressed minority group. Going beyond differences in dialect, we will also examine the controversy over how to teach the growing number of working-class students whose primary language is not English.

Regarding disciplinary practices, working-class families tend to stress obedience based on respect for authority—"You'll clean up your room because I'm your mother and I told you to"—while middle- and upper-class parents are more likely to encourage obedience by cajoling and reasoning with their children—"Please straighten your room so you can find things more easily next time." Ruby Payne explains that "in poverty, discipline is about penance and forgiveness, not necessarily change," yet change is one of the most fundamental outcomes of going to school. Corporal punishment occurs more frequently in working-class homes, where many parents believe a certain amount of physical discipline is a good thing on principle. Middle- and upper-class parents tend to use corporal punishment sparingly, in exceptional situations.[14]

We would be wrong to conclude working-class parents love their children less—fortunately, love does not recognize social class boundaries—just as we would be mistaken to apply the generalizations about any social class to all its members. But we would be blind to conclude working-class children, as a group, come to school well prepared for what they will encounter. Such children often see school as an unfamiliar game with strange players and crazy rules.[15]

Sociologists speak of the mismatch between the world working-class children know at home and the world they discover at school. Some students adapt. Many do not.

Peer Groups.   Working-class peer groups can hinder the transition more than they help. Here we must avoid stereotyping working-class students as rebels who reject school and all it represents and more privileged students as serious scholars with a deep respect for learning. Students from every social class care more about clothes, music, cars, sports, and friends than the academic subjects they are taking. Friends are especially important. By adolescence, they are the number one influence in students' lives.

Still, there are differences among the social classes. Simply put, middle- and upper-class students are usually more willing to *play the game*. Typically, they take the courses and make the grades necessary to keep their parents off their backs, participate in a few extracurricular activities, and get into some sort of college. Among their friends, attitudes toward teachers and academic subjects may be quite cynical, but there is peer pressure to keep enough of the rules to stay in the game.[16]

One of the first lessons I learned as a new teacher was that working-class students often feel peer pressure *not* to play the game. In schools where working-class students are accustomed to wearing the label of losers, stepping out of character and doing well can be embarrassing—an open invitation to peer ridicule.

In *Equality and Achievement* (2004), Cornelius Riordan describes the *oppositional culture* of working-class peer groups, a culture that becomes even more intense when the students are not only poor but also African American or Hispanic American. Critical theorists (Chapter 7) say working-class students who conform to peer pressure and refuse to play the game are *resisting* schooling.[17]

Gangs: Peer Resistance in the Extreme.   The peer group most dreaded by adults, gangs capitalize on their outlaw image to glamorize attitudes and behaviors directly opposed to those the school sanctions. Gang members get points from their peers for doing drugs and having sex at school, vandalizing school property, and intimidating teachers and "straight" students. As part of their rejection of the larger society, gangs despise virtually everything the school stands for.[18]

Mike Knox, a gang specialist on the Houston police force, explains how gangs attract

> kids looking for security, a sense of belonging, and social acceptance. They view themselves as failures, but they really want to be successes. So they reorganize their beliefs. In their mind, failing to succeed within the system is the key to success. What's good becomes bad, what's bad becomes good.[19]

Gangs have their strongest appeal to working-class students who live in central cities, which in today's society are filled with African Americans, Hispanic Americans, and Asian Americans. But gangs are also organizing in suburbs, small towns, and rural areas, where their members are more likely to be white students from more privileged backgrounds. In addition, more females are joining gangs. Notice once again the interaction of several social factors: class, race, ethnicity, and now gender.[20]

Breaking Rank (2002) is the fictionalized but fact-based story of a young white gang member, Baby, who finds himself in honors classes despite his worst efforts. Baby's gang, the Clan, does "nothing" in school.

> Literally nothing. The remedial classes were rife with Clan because their grades were a resounding baseline; no one in the Clan ever lifted a pencil in class except to draw pictures that no teacher ever got to see. No Clan member answered questions. Not one of them ever opened a book. The Clan just sat. Hour after hour. It nearly drove the teachers out of their minds.[21]

I recommend this book to prospective teachers who want to understand the pressures that students feel from all sides when they try to break away from a gang.

To counter gang influence, educators are trying strategies ranging from the "crackdown"—symbolized by Joe Clark, the baseball bat–wielding principal popularized in the film *Lean on Me*—to working with youth-service agencies such as the YMCA and YWCA, Boy Scouts and Girl Scouts, and Boys and Girls Clubs of America. Jesse Jackson's People United to Save Humanity (PUSH) is leading the antigang campaign in several big cities. These efforts sometimes succeed in pushing gangs out of individual schools, but what gangs embody in the extreme—resistance to schooling and other conventional socialization—may be growing.

How Safe Are Schools?   Violence sometimes breaks out in schools we would hardly consider gang turf. The kind of violence symbolized by the shootings at Columbine High School in Littleton, Colorado, a mainstream American school in most respects, has raised questions about how safe schools really are. The answers are mostly positive. The U.S. Departments of Education and Justice have been keeping up with trends in school safety since well before tragedies occurred at Columbine and several other schools during the late 1990s and early 2000s. The government reports *Indicators of School Crime and Safety* reassure us that schools, at least when compared to other places where students spend time, are safe.

The report for 2004, which focuses on students aged 12 to 18 in middle and high schools, finds that they are more than three times as likely to become victims of serious crimes while they are away from school than while they are at school. The overall rate of nonfatal victimization of students at school—a crime category that includes rape, sexual assault, robbery, and aggravated assault—*fell by half* from 1992 to 2002. Moreover, only 1 percent of all young people's deaths by murder and one-third of 1 percent of all youth suicides take place at school.[22]

Rates for some school crimes, unfortunately, have not decreased. From 1993 to 2003, the percentage of high school students threatened or injured by a weapon at school fluctuated between 7 and 9 percent. The percentage of students who were bullied increased from 5 percent in 1999 to 8 percent in 2001 and has fluctuated since then. We will take a closer look at bullying and other forms of harassment later in this chapter. In what some people consider an extreme response to school violence, many school districts have passed *zero tolerance* policies that mandate suspension or expulsion for any offense involving a weapon or, in some districts, drugs.[23]

On balance, young people say they feel safer at school than they did several years ago. The media have made Americans more aware of school safety statistics since the Columbine incident, often pointing out that other indicators on young people look relatively good, too. It appears that young people's use of alcohol, marijuana, and other drugs is now on the downswing after increasing through the late 1990s.[24]

But all the words of reassurance in the world leave unanswered questions about the causes of the worst school violence, the mass murders that capture public attention. Most of these shootings have taken place in middle-class, predominantly white schools, and the criminals have turned out to be male students from seemingly ordinary American families. Speculations on the causes range from easy access to guns to negligent parents; from hate group propaganda to the conflicting demands society puts on males; from exposure to violence in the media to peer ridicule and rejection.[25]

We can be thankful that the Columbine shootings are exceptional. Very few American students see their classmates gunned down at school, and most do not consume a steady diet of violence and hate.

Every student, though, has stories to tell about families and peers, factors we will continue to examine as we discuss social class. In the final section of this chapter we will discuss the powerful influence of gender.

Ability Grouping and Tracking

As a new high school English teacher, I noticed that every time I gave one working-class student a good grade, his friends gave him a hard time. So I tried to get around the situation by telling him his grades privately. This strategy worked fairly well for him, but it failed with most of his peers. By the end of the year, I was still trying to reach working-class students, and now I wish someone like Ruby Payne had been around to advise me on strategies. But even as a young teacher, I realized my classroom methods were not the only things that needed to change.

Of course not, critical theorists say. Working-class students are the ones who usually put up the strongest resistance to schooling because they see the very structure of schools working against their best interests. Like other students, they hear the constantly repeated message that success in school will lead to success in life: "Want to get a good job? Then do a good job in school."

Yeah, right. Working-class students are more likely than other students to scoff at the message because as they watch the educational sorting machine crank out winners and losers, they can see their chances of success slipping away—from a very early age.

The Sorting Machine in Action.   Ability grouping and tracking, key components of the sorting machine, must bear some of the responsibility for turning off working-class students. *Ability grouping* places students of similar ability together for instruction in particular *subjects*—forming separate groups for fast, average, and slow readers, for instance. Although research on the academic effectiveness of ability grouping is mixed, with as much evidence unfavorable to the practice as favorable, many teachers believe some grouping is necessary, especially in schools with students whose academic skills vary considerably. How else, teachers ask, can we do justice to twenty-five or thirty students reading on several different levels?

One answer is that differences in academic ability are relatively small when children first enter school. The studies most favorable to ability grouping show it offers slight advantages to students in the top groups. Their achievement tends to be almost as high in ungrouped classrooms. The studies least favorable to ability grouping show it does significant harm to the achievement of the students in the bottom groups. Far from narrowing the academic differences children bring to kindergarten and the first grade, ability grouping appears to widen them. I will return to these issues at the end of this section.[26]

Jeannie Oakes, whose books *Keeping Track* (1985), *Multiplying Inequalities* (1990), and *Becoming Good American Schools* (2002) are calling attention to the inequalities of ability grouping, has concluded that without ability grouping in the elementary grades, middle and high school teachers would have much easier jobs.

Oakes and other researchers suggest a number of alternatives to ability grouping. In *cooperative learning,* one of the more popular alternatives, teachers form learning teams composed of students with different abilities. Students work cooperatively rather than competitively. Teachers assign grades based on individual progress. Oakes and other advocates argue cooperative learning benefits students of all abilities, and it seems to be especially helpful in keeping slower students from falling farther and farther behind.[27]

With ability grouping, by contrast, students grow apart academically as they grow older, and the conventional wisdom among educators is that by middle school or high school something more than ability grouping is not only desirable but essential. That something more is *tracking,* which involves placing students in different *programs,* often called college preparatory, general, and vocational. Some schools have developed *sub*programs to sort out students within the main three tracks: advanced-placement college prep, regular college prep; high general, low general; regular vocational, remedial vocational. As a result of tracking, some students take four years of math and four years of science while others take only two of each (and, before the educational reforms of the 1980s, only *one* of each). Some students learn a foreign language, while others pass time in study hall. Some write essays, while others doodle on worksheets.[28]

Researchers draw vivid pictures of how tracking can fragment a school into several different schools serving different social groups. In the aptly titled study *Dividing Classes* (2003), Ellen Brantlinger shows how middle-class families use tracking and other practices to pass their relatively privileged status from parent to child. In "What Happens to a Dream Deferred" (2003), Linda Darling-Hammond shows how, in a nation whose African American, Hispanic American, and Native American families tend to be poorer than others, students from these families tend to wind up in lower tracks.[29] As we will see later in this chapter, tracking also helps push girls and boys down different career paths.

Gatekeepers and Self-Fulfilling Prophecies.   Not surprisingly, students who take a less demanding curriculum do less well on standardized tests. Research conducted by the testing companies that produce the Scholastic Aptitude Test (SAT) and American College Testing (ACT) Program shows students who do not complete a core curriculum in high school (four years of English and at least three years each of mathematics, social studies, and science) score significantly lower on college entrance examinations than students who take the core. In particular, algebra, geometry, laboratory sciences, and foreign languages seem to be "gatekeepers" for college.[30]

To put things positively, research suggests students from lower socioeconomic backgrounds have a lot to gain from getting out of lower tracks and into programs with higher standards and expectations. Put negatively, the best way for educators to ensure working-class students will never have a serious chance at jobs and careers requiring a college degree is to encourage or simply allow them to take the easy way out of middle and high school.

Take a walk through a tracked school and see for yourself. Lower-track students get an education that differs not just in the quantity and quality of

■ ■ ■ ■ ■

BOX 8.1

A CORE FOR ALL

You can find more information on the benefits of a core curriculum for all students at the Web sites of the ACT, www.act.org, and the College Board, www.collegeboard.com

academic courses but also in the *climate* of instruction. Lower-track students believe their teachers are less concerned with academic skills than with their willingness to take orders and follow directions. Students in lower-track classes are less likely than others to have friends who want to go to college. Perhaps most seriously, tracking lowers the self-esteem of students in the least prestigious programs. Well aware they are the outcasts of the school, lower-track students band together in peer groups that guard their losers' image as if it were a badge of honor. Here is *self-fulfilling prophecy* at its worst: lower-track students living down to our expectations.[31]

Some of Ruby Payne's most practical advice is on how to "sell" students on academic achievement. To most students growing up in *generational poverty,* which is chronic poverty passed from one generation to the next, the standard teacher lines "You're going to need this information on the job" or "You'll want this course on your transcript to get into college" mean nothing, especially when the teacher and students do not have a positive relationship. Payne suggests selling students on the power that comes with knowledge: "This course will make you smarter, so you can defend yourself better." "This information will keep people from cheating you." "Learning how to talk this way will make people respect you."[32]

The College Board makes the same point in a different way. Helping students raise their aspirations increases the probability they will choose to attend college. Among students who expect to complete a bachelor's degree program, low-income students are almost as likely as high-income students to enroll in college. At every income level, the College Board concludes, "students who want to get a college degree, and know which courses will lead them toward that goal, go to college."[33]

Creating a Culture of Detracking

Why Is It So Hard?   Since the mid-1980s, the tide of academic opinion has been turning against ability grouping and tracking. After evaluating studies such as those we have just reviewed, groups as diverse as the Carnegie Foundation, the National Education Association, and the National Governor's Association have gone on record in favor of less grouping and tracking. Collecting evidence on local schools where such reforms are under way, Jeannie Oakes has found that a "*culture of detracking* is more important than the specific alternative or implementation strategy chosen."[34]

Still, creating that culture is "unsettling" and "extraordinarily difficult,"[35] Oakes reported in 1992, early in her study of sixteen schools that were trying out different kinds of detracking. Now, reflecting on her research in *Becoming Good American Schools*, she acknowledges even more readily how enormous the task is.

Historically, Americans have rarely questioned a set of interlocking assumptions about academic success, social class, and jobs. For the last one hundred years, as working-class children have come to school in larger numbers and stayed there longer, educators have voiced the assumptions in a variety of ways to justify ability grouping and tracking. Stated bluntly, the assumptions are:

1. Many children lack both the ability and the interest necessary to succeed in school.
2. These children come disproportionately from the lower social classes.
3. They are probably destined for jobs that involve working with their hands rather than their heads.
4. Therefore, they need little or no academic training beyond the 3Rs.

These assumptions have withstood challenges from educational theorists of all persuasions—perennialists, essentialists, and progressives. Most of the school reforms of the last two decades have the unmistakable ring of essentialism in their calls for more academic work for all students, but given the deeply ingrained assumption that many students are incapable of academic success, exactly what their work will consist of remains to be seen.

Let's Be Honest.   Allow me to ask a critical question: As tougher state standards and high-stakes tests push more working-class students into algebra and geometry, chemistry and physics, Spanish and French, are they going to end up in "special" sections that stress what teachers call *skill-n-drill* instruction? If you become a teacher, you can help shape the answer. The challenge you face will be to make schooling more than a reflection of your students' social backgrounds, more than an assumption about their future roles in the labor force.

Based on my own experience as well as Oakes' ongoing research, I want to add a corollary to the four assumptions above, an argument I often hear as a let's-be-honest defense of ability grouping and tracking. Mixing students from the lower social classes with those from more privileged backgrounds, this argument runs, will harm the more privileged students. Socially, the harm is often expressed as discomfort from having to associate with people who are so different. "Oil and water don't mix," several teachers informed me recently in a graduate course. Academically, the harm can come across as harshly as this teacher's statement to Oakes' research team: When concepts have to be explained over and over in class, "the top kids get screwed."[36]

So add up the beliefs we've just discussed: Many poor kids are neither able nor willing to learn. They don't need a fancy education. They don't mix with better-off kids. They slow teachers down. The sum of these beliefs explains the real resistance to detracking.

RACE AND ETHNICITY

Defining a "Sense of Peoplehood" in a Multicultural Nation

It's hard to miss the media coverage of our nation's changing racial and ethnic makeup. Flurries of news stories and op-ed pieces appear whenever the U.S. Census Bureau releases demographic data. The September 18, 2000, issue of *Newsweek* featured a cover on "Redefining Race in America" and no fewer than nine stories spanning the country from Silicon Valley to Birmingham, analyzing issues from intermarriage to changing conceptions of "whiteness." When the Census Bureau confirmed that Hispanics had displaced African Americans as the nation's largest minority, editorialists wrote about "Unspoken Conflicts of Blacks and Latinos." Population projections released in 2004 prompted such articles as "Census: Half of U.S. Will Be Minorities by 2050."[37]

For teachers who live where racial and ethnic shifts are well under way, cultural diversity already wears a personal face. Other teachers—and future teachers—need to get ready for the changes they will experience during their careers.

Although people often use *race* and *ethnicity* interchangeably, the words are not synonymous. By definition, race is based on *physical* characteristics such as skin color and hair texture, while ethnicity is based on *cultural* factors such as language, religion, and nationality. The concept of race has evolved over several hundred years and now denotes three major groups: white (Caucasoid), black (Negroid), and yellow (Mongoloid). Ethnicity, a much newer concept, is a *sense of peoplehood*, an identity that holds a cultural group together within a race or, less commonly, across races. In our nation, Irish Americans are one well-known ethnic group, and Hispanic Americans are another. In this textbook I use the concepts of race and ethnicity because both continue to be helpful in describing our nation's diversity.[38]

For several decades, though, the definition and even existence of race have been under question. As a prospective teacher, you need to be aware of the controversy.

Is Race Real? Historians and anthropologists tell us that the idea of race emerged during the 1600s and 1700s as Europeans explored and attempted to colonize the world. From the outset, race was a concept Europeans constructed to distinguish themselves from other peoples and establish their supremacy over them. During the late nineteenth and early twentieth centuries, university professors in Europe and the United States refined the concept of race, stamping it with scientific approval and helping to shape public consciousness.[39]

Without fail, white scholars assigned whites to the top of the racial hierarchy, but debates raged over how to draw boundaries between the races and how to place cultural groups within a race, particularly within the white race. Which cultural groups should be considered white? Which characteristics made some groups whiter than others? During the first half of the twentieth century, the search for allegedly scientific answers to such questions led to labeling some groups genetically superior and others inferior.

As the twentieth century unfolded, race manifested itself in ways that revealed its cultural loading. Newspaper stories as late as the World War II era, for instance, referred to the English race, the German race, and the Japanese race—classifications based on nationality—as well as to the Jewish race, a classification based on religion and other cultural factors. Using race in these ways edged the concept closer to the modern concept of ethnicity, which began to enter public consciousness during the 1960s.

Clearly, race is a social construction that has evolved over time, and now scholars are questioning whether it has any value as a scientific concept. Anthropologists and biologists know human beings are members of a single species that appears to have originated in Africa and spread across the world. Evidence from fossils and DNA suggests that living in different environmental conditions produced the physical and cultural differences we see today. Genetically, there are greater differences *within* each race than *between* the races. Weighing all the evidence, anthropologists and biologists are concluding that race is "real," but in a social rather than biological sense.

Public opinion in the United States may be moving gradually toward this view, in part because of immigration. Many Hispanic immigrants, for instance, see skin color as a continuum without distinct lines of separation. They see ethnic shades of brown and red that are more subtle than the standard racial categories of white, black, and yellow. In addition, intermarriage across racial and ethnic lines is producing children with less rigid views. One of the prospective teachers in my class recently described her ancestry as Filipino, Mexican, and French and then asked us how she should classify herself racially and ethnically.

Ethnicity as Cultural Identity.   Before answering her question, let's think again of ethnicity as a sense of peoplehood.[40] The members of an ethnic group have a shared identity based on a common history and a sense of common destiny. Members of the group often share a language, religion, and other cultural traditions, and they often have common geographical origins. In the United States, many ethnic groups identify themselves by the nation from which their ancestors came. Thus, in addition to Irish Americans, we have German Americans, Chinese Americans, Swedish Americans, Italian Americans, Polish Americans, Vietnamese Americans, and a host of others. Native Americans, the people who inhabited North America before Europeans and Africans came to the continent, constitute an ethnic group with hundreds of tribal subdivisions.[41]

Other ethnic groups in the United States emphasize nongeographical factors as the basis of their identity. Jewish Americans stress the religion of Judaism, while Hispanic Americans are unified by the Spanish language. As these two groups illustrate, though, the members of a group may view their ethnicity in different ways. Many American Jews put less emphasis on religion than on shared historical experience and a sense of common destiny. The words *Hispanic* and *Latino* are too general for some Americans, who may prefer the more specific ethnic identification of such names as Mexican American, Puerto Rican, and Cuban American.

Muslim Americans are an ethnic group that is receiving a great deal of attention, unfavorable as well as favorable. Sharing the Islamic faith and often the Arabic language, Muslims have come to the United States from the Middle East as well as Asia, Africa, Europe, and other parts of the world. They can be of any race. Although they account for only a fraction of a percent of the nation's population, Muslims are one of our best-educated ethnic groups: Almost 60 percent are college graduates.[42]

The strength of ethnic ties also varies from group to group and person to person. The sense of peoplehood is usually stronger within groups of lower socioeconomic status. As people climb the ladder of success, they tend to think of themselves less as members of an ethnic group and more as members of a social class. Ethnic identity may also be weaker in large groups with a long period of U.S. residence. Americans whose roots lie primarily in England outnumber German Americans to form the largest "ancestral group" in the nation. Yet English Americans—sometimes called white Anglo-Saxon Protestants, or WASPs, a name some of them do not appreciate—generally do not think of themselves as ethnic at all.[43]

The prospective teacher I mentioned earlier started a good discussion in my class with her question about how to classify herself. As we talked about Table 8.3 and the five major racial and ethnic classifications the U.S. Census Bureau uses, I pointed out that a small but growing number of Americans say they either don't fit into any single category or reject all the categories. The 2000 census offered these people several new categories, including "two or more races" and "some

TABLE 8.3   Racial and Ethnic Distribution of U.S. Population and Public School Enrollment: 2000, 2005, 2010, 2030, 2050

GROUP	PERCENTAGE OF U.S. POPULATION					PERCENTAGE OF PUBLIC SCHOOL ENROLLMENT				
	2000	2005	2010	2030	2050	2000	2005	2010	2030	2050
White American*	69	67	65	58	50	61	58	56	49	40
Hispanic American	13	14	16	20	25	17	19	21	26	32
African American*	13	13	13	14	15	17	17	17	18	19
Asian American*	4	4	5	6	8	4	5	5	6	8
Native American*	1	1	1	2	2	1	1	1	2	2

Note: Some columns do not total 100 due to rounding.

*Excludes person of Hispanic origin.

Sources: Estimates and projections based on U.S. Department of Commerce, Bureau of the Census, "Projected Population of the United States, by Race and Hispanic Origin: 2000 to 2050" (2004) [Available: www.census.gov/ipc/www/usinterimproj/natprojtab01a.pdf], Tbl. 1a; Federal Intragency Forum on Child and Family Statistics, *America's Children: Key Indicators of Well-Being 2004* (2004) [Available: www.childstates.gov/ac2004/tables/pop3.asp], Tbl. POP3.

other race." "I checked both of those blocks," my Filipino-Mexican-French student said, "because most of the time I think of myself as just an American."

The New Immigration and Other Demographic Trends.   Still, since the mid-1960s, the United States has experienced an upsurge of ethnic consciousness, and a new wave of immigration is increasing the nation's ethnic and racial diversity. About half these new immigrants are from Latin America, with more arriving from Mexico than any other country in the world; about 30 percent are from Asia; and the rest are from Europe and elsewhere. In absolute numbers, the immigration now under way is likely to surpass the immigration that occurred from 1870 to 1920, which historians regard as the largest mass movement of people in history. Twenty-eight million people came to the United States during those fifty years, as we saw in Chapter 6, but the more than 23 million who immigrated in the forty years from 1960 to 2000 arrived at an even faster pace. Although the pace of immigration slowed during the late 1990s, between 600,000 and 1 million newcomers are still arriving every year.[44]

The demographic data in Table 8.3 suggest why racial and ethnic changes are such strong forces in American society and why educators are finally taking the need for multicultural education seriously. Notice that while the percentage of students who are white is decreasing, the percentage who are African or Native American is increasing. The percentage of Hispanic and Asian American students is increasing *substantially.*

These trends are projected to continue well into the century. According to the U.S. Census Bureau, whites will account for only 58 percent of the total population in 2030 and barely 50 percent in 2050. If so, public school enrollment in the nation as a whole will become "minority majority" around 2030. These trends, as you can see, will eventually change the very meaning of *minority* and *majority* in America.[45]

Researchers say recent immigrants are experiencing the "best of times and the worst of times." Teachers see plenty of both in their classrooms, and their faculty-lounge stories about immigrants range from spectacular success to bitter failure. In fact, immigrant students do account for a disproportionate share of both valedictorians and dropouts. The principal of an elementary school in culturally diverse Broward County, Florida, the fifth-largest school district in the nation, insists on taking an optimistic view of her situation: "Foreign-born parents have the most middle-class values I've seen in ages. If you call them to come in, they're there."[46]

Hispanic American Students

Hispanics are a diverse, rapidly growing group. As Table 8.3 indicates, they have just overtaken African Americans as the largest minority group in both the general population and the public schools. Actually Hispanics are several groups, unified culturally by the Spanish language and often the Roman Catholic faith but historically distinct.[47]

Mexican Americans, some 60 percent of all Hispanics in the United States, have a long history in the Southwest. By the early 1600s, Spaniards had settled much of the land in the present states of California, New Mexico, Arizona, Colorado, and Texas. For 250 years, the Spanish language and Catholic faith were dominant in this large territory.

The U.S. victory in the Mexican–American War (1846–1848) officially established a different culture, English-speaking and Protestant. Public schools and Catholic schools stressed conformity to the English (more recently called Anglo) culture, but the goal was usually separation rather than assimilation. Heavy legal and illegal immigration from Mexico to the United States at the turn of the twentieth century, during World War II, and especially since the 1960s has produced a modern Mexican American population that is heavily concentrated in the Southwest, highly urbanized, largely working-class, and increasingly segregated.[48]

Puerto Rico became a U.S. territory at the end of the Spanish–American War in 1898 and a commonwealth in 1952. Excluding the population of the island itself, about 10 percent of Hispanics in the United States are Puerto Ricans. The poorest of American Hispanics, many Puerto Ricans travel back and forth between the island and the mainland, their circular migrations tied to the availability of jobs. Puerto Ricans are also the most segregated Hispanics. Typically, their children attend highly segregated schools in New York and other central cities.

Cuban Americans are the most prosperous Hispanics in the United States. Most have come to this nation since Fidel Castro's rise to power in the late 1950s. Many professionals and businesspeople left the island during the 1960s and 1970s, to be joined later by much poorer refugees. Now approximately 4 percent of Hispanic Americans, Cubans are heavily concentrated in the Miami–Dade County area of Florida.

Recent immigrants from Central and South America account for some 12 percent of Hispanic Americans. Often overlooked in academic research on the nation's Hispanic population, these people are culturally and economically heterogeneous. Many are political refugees from such countries as El Salvador, Guatemala, Nicaragua, and Colombia, and many are settling in Los Angeles and New York City.

Remember that Hispanics are an ethnic group, not a racial group. Table 8.3, which paints a useful but simplified picture, puts all Hispanics into one category. If we ask Hispanics who they are, a more complex portrait emerges. Ethnically, most Hispanics have a sense of peoplehood strongly related to their country of origin. Mexican Americans and Cuban Americans, for instance, are often rivals because of their cultural, economic, and political differences. Racially, about half of Hispanics consider themselves white, but almost as many think of themselves as brown—a color that falls between the lines of the standard three-race classification. Still other Hispanics regard their race as red, yellow, or black. It will be fascinating to see how these identities evolve as Hispanics find their way in a nation in which assimilation, separation, and pluralism are the options.[49]

The statistical indicators on Hispanic American students are, at best, mixed. As immigrants continue to arrive in the United State and go to work at the bottom of the ladder, average Hispanic family income remains low—comparable to that of African Americans but less than two-thirds that of whites. Sixty-six percent of

Hispanic young adults have graduated from high school, well below the 91 percent of whites who have finished. Another large differential persists in higher education, where among 25-to-29-year-olds, 34 percent of whites but only 10 percent of Hispanics are college graduates.[50]

Figures 8.1 and 8.2 illustrate the racial and ethnic achievement gaps that are a source of great concern. The gaps shown in eighth grade reading and math are typical of those in other grade levels and subjects. On the one hand, long-term trends are positive: Hispanics, like other minorities, have increased their test scores relative to whites since the 1970s (see Chapter 11). On the other hand, large gaps in achievement remain, and the short-term trend in reading is not encouraging.

One in ten Hispanic students comes to school as an English Language Learner (ELL) with limited proficiency in English. How to help these students is a controversial issue, as we will see later in this chapter. The desire of many Hispanics for bilingual education strikes some Americans as logical and pluralistic and others as dangerous and separatist.

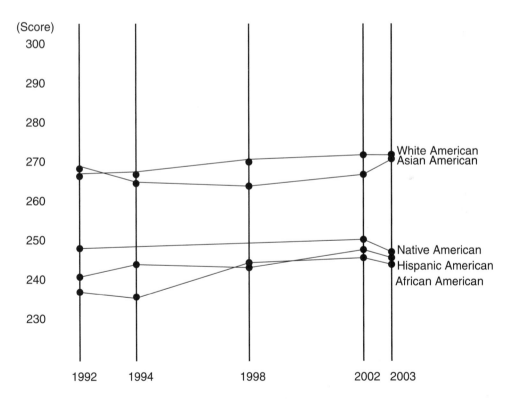

FIGURE 8.1   The Achievement Gap in Reading: NAEP Scores of Eighth-Grade Students by Race/Ethnicity, 1992–2003.

Source: U.S. Department of Education, National Center for Education Statistics, "Reading 2003 Major Results" (2003) [Available: nces.ed.gov/ nationsreportcard/reading/results2003/raceethnicity.asp].

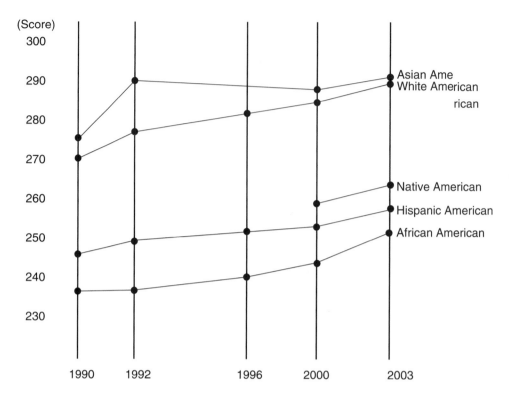

FIGURE 8.2   The Achievement Gap in Mathematics: NAEP Scores of Eighth-Grade Students by Race/Ethnicity, 1990–2003.

Source: U.S. Department of Education, National Center for Education Statistics, "Mathematics 2003 Major Results" (2003) [Available: nces.ed.gov/nationsreportcard/mathematics/results2003/raceethnicity.asp].

African American Students

As Chapter 6 suggests, African Americans have a unique history. Africans began arriving in the North American colonies as involuntary immigrants in the early 1600s. During 250 years of slavery, African labor built up the colonies that became the southern states, while African culture influenced the entire nation more deeply than most whites realized—or were willing to admit. After the Civil War, the promise of freedom and equality for African Americans proved false. In the South, where more than 90 percent of blacks lived, whites imposed a "new slavery" at the turn of the twentieth century, turning to legally sanctioned segregation in an effort to keep blacks subservient. African Americans created a separate society behind the wall of segregation, using education to advance themselves and resist white oppression.[51]

School desegregation, the subject of this chapter's next section, is one of the most important issues in African American history. Separate schools were clearly unequal; black people looked to desegregation as the major strategy for equalizing educational opportunities. By winning the legal right to attend formerly all-white schools, moreover, modern civil rights leaders hoped to build up enough momentum to break down segregation in other walks of life. But the goals that seemed so clear and simple during the 1950s and 1960s have turned cloudy and complex in the last three decades. Today, the desirability of desegregation itself seems questionable to some African Americans.

One reason is that African Americans have not shared equally in the benefits of desegregation and other social policies. On the one hand, almost half of African Americans are now middle class. The average income of black married couples has climbed to almost 90 percent of what white married couples earn. On the other hand, the average income of all black families is only about 60 percent of white family income. Young African American males growing up poor face especially tough obstacles.[52]

Not surprisingly, the educational indicators on African Americans are also mixed. Figures 8.1 and 8.2 illustrate the achievement gaps that black students are struggling to close. Eighty-six percent of blacks aged 18 to 24 have completed high school, which is close to the 91 percent figure for whites, but only 18 percent of blacks aged 25 to 29 are college graduates, compared to 34 percent of whites.[53]

Educators are beginning to confront a problem that affects African, Hispanic, and Native American students: the disproportionate percentages of these students who are classified as disabled. In special education classes throughout the nation, the overrepresentation of students from all three groups, and especially blacks, is striking. Compared to white students, blacks are three times as likely to be classified as mentally retarded, twice as likely to be classified as emotionally disturbed, and nearly one and a half times as likely to be classified as learning disabled. In some states, the overrepresentation is even greater.[54]

Alabama made national education news in 2000 with the landmark consent decree in the *Lee v. Macon* desegregation case, which orders revisions in the criteria used to place students in special education classes. Teachers and other educators must be careful, the decree states, not to mistake language, dialect, and other aspects of culture for indicators of disabilities (see Internet box). No Child Left Behind, which holds schools accountable for the standardized test scores of subgroups of students, including disabled students, is focusing further attention on this complex issue (Chapter 9).[55]

BOX 8.2

OVERREPRESENTATION OF AFRICAN AMERICAN STUDENTS IN SPECIAL EDUCATION

Learn about the steps you can take as a teacher to help solve this problem. A guidebook from the Council for Exceptional Children and National Alliance of Black School Educators is available at www.cec.sped.org/law_res/doc/resources/files/AddressingOverRep.pdf

Asian American Students

The Asian population in the United States is growing five times faster than the general population, almost doubling between 1980 and 1990 and projected to double again between 2000 and 2030. Chinese are the largest Asian American ethnic group, followed by Filipinos, Japanese, Asian Indians, Koreans, Vietnamese, and more than seventy smaller groups including Laotians, Thai, and Cambodians. Asians are concentrated in urban areas within a few states. Approximately 40 percent of Asian Americans live in California, where they represent 10 percent of the population, and another 30 percent live in New York, Illinois, Texas, and Hawaii.[56]

Asian Americans are so diverse, the "model minority" stereotype conceals as much as it reveals. In fact, some researchers describe the academic achievement of Asian students as an inverted normal curve with large numbers of high achievers and low achievers and relatively few students in the middle. Four family-related factors influence where individual students fall on the curve: socioeconomic status, length of U.S. residence, level of education before immigrating, and proficiency in English.[57]

Chinese, Filipino, and Japanese students are often from families who have lived in the United States since the 1800s or early 1900s. Along with Koreans and Asian Indians, these students are usually middle class. In fact, the educational and economic attainment of well-established Asian American families is much higher than that of the general population. Unfortunately, the grandparents in some of these families can recall overt anti-Asian discrimination through the World War II era and more subtle discrimination since.

Vietnamese, Laotian, Thai, Cambodian, and other Southeast Asian students are usually from families who immigrated after 1975 to escape political repression. With the exception of professional families who fled Vietnam in 1975 and 1976, most of these families arrived in the United States poor, speaking little English. More than 15 percent of Southeast Asian students in the United States have limited proficiency in English, double the 7 percent rate for all Asian American students.

Desegregation is not a major issue for Asian Americans. Although they were segregated by law in California at the turn of the twentieth century, today the average Asian student attends a schools where whites are almost a majority.

Bilingual education is a major issue. Asian Americans often disagree with Hispanics on what kind of education is best for students whose native language is not English.

The statistical indicators on Asian American students are impressive, as Figures 8.1 and 8.2 suggest. Although there is considerable variation among Asian ethnic groups, composite test results rank Asian students first in the nation in math, and they are not far behind whites in reading. Asians are less likely to drop out of high school and more likely to finish college than any other students. Influencing these educational indicators is an important economic indicator: Among the major racial and ethnic groups we are discussing, Asian Americans have the highest family income.[58]

Native American Students

Descendants of America's indigenous peoples face educational problems unlike those of any other group. Alternately romanticized, denigrated, and ignored, Native Americans are probably the least understood of the groups discussed here.[59]

Deprived of most of their land and forced onto reservations during the nineteenth century, Native Americans encountered powerful forces of assimilation in schools operated by missionary societies, philanthropic groups, and the federal Bureau of Indian Affairs. White educators tried to eradicate the culture of hundreds of tribes by stressing U.S. patriotism, banning native languages, and teaching students allegedly "superior" ways of farming and housekeeping.[60]

Even though these policies produced miserable results, they continued into the second half of the twentieth century. Much native culture disappeared, to be sure, but few Native Americans assimilated. As late as 1950, half were still living on reservations in grinding poverty.

Native Americans began a struggle to control their own education during the 1960s and 1970s. Today reservation schools are centers of tribal culture. But three-fourths of Native Americans now live off the reservations, where economic opportunities are greater but opportunities to regain their culture are fewer.

As Tsianaina Lomawaima, author of "Educating Native Americans" (1999), reminds us, "Not all native people are the same. . . . Each native community is distinguished by its own language, customs, religion, economy, historical circumstances, and environment."[61] Today the U.S. government recognizes more than 500 tribes and estimates another 250 native groups have yet to gain federal recognition. The largest tribes are the Cherokee, Navajo, Chippewa, Sioux, and Choctaw.[62]

Although the Native American population has grown since the 1950s, it still accounts for only 1 percent of the nation's total population and public school enrollment. The dire problems Native Americans face do not attract the attention they deserve. Among the four minority groups we have profiled, Native Americans have the highest dropout rates and the lowest college completion rates. Nine percent come to school with limited proficiency in English.[63]

FIFTY YEARS AFTER *BROWN*: DESEGREGATION OR *RE*SEGREGATION?

In 2004, the United States marked the fiftieth anniversary of the U.S. Supreme Court decision in *Brown v. Board of Education of Topeka*. Media attention made it hard to miss the occasion. Readers of *Time, Newsweek, U.S. News & World Report*, and other popular magazines could choose from a year-long series of reports and featured articles. City and county newspapers ran stories that played up the many local celebrations of *Brown* that took place not just in the South but all over the country. With the electronic media joining in, *Brown* was in the spotlight.[64]

By the end of the year, though, I could sense the anniversary had left little lasting impression on most Americans. For one thing, much of the attention seemed to focus not on the effects of segregation itself, which was the major concern of the

Supreme Court, but on how minority students are doing in schools today *despite* continuing segregation. If we can't all go to school together, the question seems to have become, can we at least make one segregated school as good as another? This shift in focus, while understandable in the current educational and political climate, made the coverage of *Brown* seem less distinctive, blending it into countless other stories on how to raise standardized test scores in the face of long odds.

Bringing together students from diverse backgrounds through the process of school desegregation is no longer the front-burner issue it once was. It's not that students, parents, and teachers have stopped paying attention to the racial and ethnic makeup of the schools. They're still paying close attention, just as virtually all Americans continue to keep an eye on race and ethnicity in their neighborhoods. It's that desegregation as a policy issue has grown cold. Politicians and school officials rarely touch it, and that seems to be fine with most Americans. Meanwhile, public schools are *re*segregating. That, too, seems fine to most Americans.

Has the nation all but given up on school desegregation? As you read this section, you'll discover how complex this question is.

Historical Perspective

When the U.S. Supreme Court issued its decision in *Brown*, the court framed its ruling as the answer to a related question: Can segregated schools ever be equal? In the wake of *Plessy v. Ferguson* (1896), African Americans had no more than the rhetorical equality suggested by the words *separate but equal.* The rhetoric bore no resemblance to reality. Black schools were inferior to white schools, and it was impossible to pretend otherwise. There were obvious differences in such tangible factors as physical facilities, courses of study, pupil-teacher ratios, teacher salaries, and overall expenditures per student. These inequalities, although greatest in the South, existed throughout the nation. By the 1950s, some school boards were narrowing—but by no means completely closing—the gaps between black and white schools, hoping to avoid or at least postpone a Supreme Court mandate for desegregation.[65]

When that mandate finally came on May 17, 1954, the court used language so clear and direct, even supporters of desegregation were startled. Can segregated schools ever be equal? The answer was a unanimous *no*. The justices cited social science evidence to support their conclusion that even when expenditures and other tangible factors are equal, segregated schools are psychologically damaging to African American students. Thus the court declared "separate educational facilities are inherently unequal"—an unequivocal answer.[66]

Brown represented such a direct confrontation with established educational practice that the court did not issue an enforcement decree for a full year. When it called for desegregation "with all deliberate speed" in 1955 and ordered lower courts to supervise the process, opponents of desegregation seized on the word *deliberate* and proceeded to drag their feet.

In the South, massive resistance blocked the way as governors vowed "segregation forever" and state legislatures stalled for time. Lengthy legal battles ensued. Battles also raged out of court as riots and other violent acts sometimes made it necessary for federal troops to escort African American children into newly desegregated schools. Taking massive resistance to the extreme, Prince Edward County, Virginia, simply closed its public schools from 1959 through 1964 to avoid desegregation. Confrontations of the same kind accompanied the desegregation of colleges and universities.

But the quest for desegregated education drew strength from the Reverend Martin Luther King, Jr., and the larger Civil Rights movement, constant legal pressure from the NAACP, and after 1960, all three branches of the federal government. The major breakthrough came with the passage and enforcement of the Civil Rights Act of 1964. Title VI of the act gave federal officials the power to cut off federal funds to school systems refusing to desegregate. Other federal legislation passed in the mid-1960s made school systems throughout the nation, and especially in the South, increasingly dependent on federal funding. The Civil Rights Act, national in scope but admittedly aimed at the South, was a powerful weapon indeed.[67]

Federal pressure produced remarkable results—in some parts of the United States. Table 8.4 shows public schools in the South, the *most* segregated in the nation for African Americans as late as 1968, became the nation's *least* segregated only four years later. They remained so through the early 1990s.

Now compare the trends in other regions. The greatest contrast is between the South and the Northeast. Notice that although northeastern public schools were the nation's *least* segregated for African Americans in 1968, they became *more* segregated while southern schools were moving in the opposite direction.

TABLE 8.4 Segregation of African American Students by Region: 1968–2001

	PERCENTAGE OF STUDENTS IN 90–100% MINORITY SCHOOLS								
REGION	**1968**	**1972**	**1976**	**1980**	**1984**	**1988**	**1992**	**1996**	**2001**
South	78	25	22	23	24	24	27	28	31
Border	60	55	43	37	37	NA	33	37	42
Northeast	43	47	51	49	47	48	50	51	51
Midwest	58	57	51	44	44	42	39	43	47
West	51	43	36	34	29	NA	26	28	30
U.S. Average	64	39	36	33	33	NA	34	35	38

NA = not available.

Sources: Gary Orfield and Chungmei Lee, Brown *at 50: King's Dream or* Plessy's Nightmare? (2004) [Available: www.civilrightsproject.harvard.edu/research/reseg04/brown50.pdf], Tbl. 8; Gary Orfield and John T. Yun, *Resegregation in America's Schools* (1999) [Available: www.law.harvard.edu/groups/civilrights/publications/resegregation99html], Tbl. 9; Gary Orfield and Franklin Monfort, *Are American Schools Resegregating in the Reagan Era?* (Chicago: National School Desegregation Project, University of Chicago, 1987), pp. 313–314, 392; and Gary Orfield, *Public School Desegregation in the United States, 1968–1980* (Washington, DC: Joint Center for Political Studies, 1983), p. 4.

Today the Northeast has the nation's *most* segregated public schools. But as Table 8.4 reveals, the schools in every region have been resegregating. For the first time since the *Brown* decision, the trend is clearly away from desegregation. Why?

De Facto versus De Jure

To answer this question we must distinguish between two types of segregation: de jure and de facto. *De jure* means "by law." De jure segregation is the result of legislation, policy, or official action: a state law or local school board policy requiring black students and white students to attend separate schools, for instance, or a public official's statements supporting segregation. Because laws, policies, and officials mandated segregation in every southern state, the eyes of the nation were on the South after the *Brown* decision. But de jure school segregation also existed in the border states and in school districts scattered throughout every region of the nation—the one in Topeka, Kansas, the Brown family sued, for example. During the 1950s and 1960s, this kind of segregation was obvious and relatively easy to prove in court. It was a smoking gun.

Vestiges of de jure segregation remain today, but in guises more subtle and more difficult to document. De jure segregation may take the form of a principal who quietly discourages black students from requesting voluntary transfers to a predominantly white school or a school board that opens new schools with attendance zones that increase segregation within the district. In a precedent-setting 1987 decision involving Yonkers, New York, a federal court of appeals ruled de jure segregation can even take the form of a city government that locates public housing projects in a way that promotes residential segregation.[68]

Most segregation in the United States today, though, is *de facto*, which means "in fact." De facto school segregation is largely the result of segregated neighborhoods. The "fact" is that most Americans still choose to live among people of their own race. Such segregation is sometimes called voluntary, which is an accurate description only to the degree people can choose housing without encountering racial discrimination—and can afford housing of their choice.

Trends in the Courts. Although the line between de facto and de jure can be fine, as the examples in the preceding paragraph suggest, the Supreme Court and lower courts have tried since *Brown* to distinguish between the two types of segregation. In the early 1990s, the Supreme Court reviewed the progress of desegregation in Oklahoma City, the Atlanta suburb of DeKalb County, and Kansas City, Missouri, school districts that had been under court order to reduce de jure segregation. The court let all three districts off the hook, allowing them to cut back on busing, magnet schools, and other desegregation strategies once they convinced the court they were no longer practicing de jure discrimination.[69]

As the use of busing and magnet schools to maintain desegregation decreases, segregation can increase. And it usually does. According to *Resegregation in American Schools* (1999), a report from Harvard University's Civil Rights Project, the Supreme Court decisions in the three cases from the early 1990s have given the green light to resegregation. Among the school districts that have subsequently gone to court to phase out their desegregation plans are Buffalo; Minneapolis; Cleveland; Wilmington, Delaware; Davidson County (Nashville), Tennessee; Mobile, Alabama; Broward (Fort Lauderdale) and Duval (Jacksonville) Counties, Florida; Clark County (Las Vegas); San Jose; and Seattle.[70]

Trends in Neighborhoods.   The distinction between de facto and de jure helps explain why public schools in the Northeast are more segregated today than they were in the 1950s. This change reflects demographic trends in the large urban areas of the Northeast. Since the end of World War II, many working-class whites have grown more prosperous, joined the middle class, and abandoned the central cities. For these families, moving up in social status has meant moving out to the suburbs. Close on their heels have been middle-class African American and Hispanic American families. Providing yet another example of the intertwining of class, race, and ethnicity, many urban neighborhoods that were once white are now African American or Hispanic American—and very poor. In addition, many of the whites who remain in northeastern central cities today send their children to private schools, although the influence of this factor on school resegregation is small compared to the influence of suburbanization.[71]

The Northeast is not unique. These same demographic trends have altered the racial composition of urban school districts throughout the nation. In Chicago, Houston, and Los Angeles no less than New York, Philadelphia, and Boston, minority students who are poor are now in the majority. In fact, these students constitute the majority in every one of the twenty-five largest school districts in the United States.[72]

Although large central-city districts have the most segregated public schools in the nation, high levels of segregation can also be found in the suburbs surrounding large metropolitan areas as well as in smaller central-city districts. Rural and small-town districts, by contrast, are the least segregated, offering the greatest opportunities for students from different racial and ethnic background to go to school together.[73]

Brown *at 50* (2004), another report from the Harvard Civil Rights Project, allows us to trace different patterns of segregation for different racial and ethnic groups. The average Asian American and Native American students go to schools where 45 percent of the students are white. The average African American and Hispanic American students, by contrast, attend schools where only about 30 percent of their classmates are white. As we have seen, the segregation of African American students has been increasing since the late 1980s. For Hispanic American students, segregation has been rising since the 1960s, particularly in the region with the largest share of Hispanic Americans, the West. There, Hispanic students are more segregated than black students are in the region where they are most numerous, the South. Given the tremendous growth of the Hispanic American population, demographers predict steady increases in the segregation of Hispanic students.[74]

Which students are *most* segregated? Whites. The average white student goes to a school where 79 percent of the student body is white.[75]

■ ■ ■ ■ ■

BOX 8.3

RESEGREGATION

Read the full report on *Resegregation in American Schools* at www.law.harvard.edu/groups/civilrights/publications/resegregation99.html

Academic, Social, and Economic Effects of Desegregation

Turning our attention to the effects of school desegregation, we face a controversial question: Does desegregation improve the academic achievement of minority students? How we answer the question depends on whose research we accept.

One problem is some researchers have approached the question with their minds already made up, obviously looking for evidence to support their ideological biases. Another problem is researchers have studied the academic effects of desegregation using so many different methodologies and research designs, it is difficult to compare studies and draw conclusions. Despite these problems, answers are emerging from almost four decades of research on the question.

The basic answer is *yes*. Desegregation has a positive effect on the academic achievement of minority students. (Almost all the research has focused on African American students, although the few studies on Hispanic American students show the same pattern.) Janet Ward Schofield, senior scientist in the Learning Research and Development Center at the University of Pittsburgh, is the author of the most extensive analysis to date of the hundreds of studies on the subject. After sifting through mountains of wheat and chaff, Schofield concludes in "Maximizing the Benefits of a Diverse Student Body: Lessons from School Desegregation Research" (2001) that the most positive academic impact is on the reading skills of African American students.[76]

The research Schofield cites most often in her review is the work of Robert L. Crain of Teachers College, Columbia University, who emerged as one of the most prominent desegregation specialists in the nation during the 1980s. Crain and his associates offer several explanations for why desegregation improves achievement. Desegregation produces the greatest academic benefits when it begins early, with young children. The most rapid gains in achievement occur in the early primary grades, and they can total a full grade level by graduation. Moreover, the achievement of African American students is highest in schools that are predominantly white and middle class, but where blacks are at least 20 percent of the student body.[77]

Like many other researchers, Crain attributes the gains for African Americans less to the "whiteness" of their classmates than to the resources and standards available in middle-class settings. Schools oriented toward middle-class students usually have better teachers and more demanding programs, characteristics benefiting *all* students.

"This relationship is absolutely central to explaining the different educational experiences and outcomes of the schools," the authors of Brown *at 50* and *Resegregation in American Schools* agree. "A great many of the educational characteristics of schools attributed to race are actually related to poverty."[78] The average white student goes to a school where fewer than 20 percent of the students are poor, the report notes, while the average black and Hispanic students attend schools where more than 40 percent of their classmates are poor.[79]

But what about the white students? How does segregation affect them? As long as I have been a teacher and teacher educator, I have heard white parents argue against desegregation in the same way people argue against detracking: It will harm their children's academic achievement. Schofield's review of research may help put these fears to rest. Study after study shows no negative impact on white achievement.[80]

Although achievement usually takes center stage in discussions of desegregation's impact, its long-term social and economic benefits may be even more important. In "The Effects of School Desegregation" (2001), Jomills Henry Braddock II and Tamela McNulty Eitle review mounting evidence that desegregated schools are helping to desegregate society. African American students who graduate from desegregated schools are more likely to attend desegregated colleges and universities, live in desegregated neighborhoods, and hold jobs in desegregated workplaces. Desegregation makes black and white students alike more comfortable with racial and ethnic diversity.[81]

As Robert Crain explains in a *Time* magazine cover story, the "great barrier to black social and economic mobility is isolation from the opportunities and networks of the middle class." School desegregation, Crain contends, can improve the "life chances" of minority students by helping them get past the barrier and break out of the isolation. Hopeful words, to be sure, but right there on the cover of the magazine was a reminder of the trend of the day: "Back to Segregation."[82]

Busing

Public opinion polls on school desegregation show Americans of virtually all racial and ethnic groups are overwhelmingly for it. Eighty-seven percent of Americans think the *Brown* decision was right. Mention busing, though, and the polls swing dramatically in the opposite direction. Many Americans jump at the word and quickly voice their disapproval of busing as a desegregation strategy.[83]

Gary Orfield, director of the Harvard Civil Rights Project, says we can't have one without the other. We can't have desegregated schools, on a significant scale, without busing. Take another look at Table 8.4, which is based on Orfield's research. Why is segregation increasing again? According to both supporters and opponents of busing, one of the main reasons is that judges, following precedents established in the early 1990s in the Supreme Court's Oklahoma City, DeKalb County, and Kansas City decisions, are allowing school districts to reduce or eliminate busing for desegregation. Given the demographic trends we have examined, abandoning busing as a desegregation tool is leaving increasing numbers of minority students, most of whom are also poor, isolated in central city schools.

Like Jonathan Kozol in *Savage Inequalities* (1991), Orfield wants to touch people's consciences. He believes Americans do not fully understand the choices they are making about desegregation—or, more precisely, the choices judges and school officials are making for us when they reject busing. In fact, Orfield points to opinion polls showing that when people are given a clear choice between segregation or busing, about half of whites and 80 percent of African Americans and Hispanic Americans choose busing. Among parents whose children have actually been bused for desegregation, 64 percent of whites and 63 percent of blacks rate the experience "very satisfactory."[84]

Orfield is one of the few nationally prominent figures who not only supports desegregation—that's still easy—but actively advocates busing as a necessary strategy. Increasingly, that takes real courage. In his most recent studies, Orfield acknowledges he's swimming upstream.

Magnet Schools

What seems to bother future teachers as well as other Americans most about busing for desegregation is its involuntary nature. Court orders from federal judges often trigger resentment. Americans dislike riding school buses past their neighborhood schools, although the concept of neighborhood differs greatly from cities to suburbs to rural areas.

Magnet schools are designed to overcome both objections. Sometimes referred to as schools so good, students volunteer to attend them, magnet schools offer special programs to attract students from throughout a school district. New York City's School of Performing Arts and the Bronx High School of Science are two well-known examples, although they were established long before the term *magnet school* came into vogue. Magnet schools started during the 1970s and 1980s usually have *voluntary* desegregation—an alternative to court-ordered busing—as their major goal.

In addition to regular academic programs, magnet schools offer specializations not available elsewhere in a school district. One school may specialize in communications and mass media, another in health professions, another in foreign languages, still another in commercial art. For more traditional students, back-to-basics magnet schools featuring strict discipline and dress codes have proved popular in some districts.

The consensus is magnet schools can be a good supplementary desegregation strategy, but by themselves they probably cannot make a significant statistical dent in big-city segregation. They do offer the attractive prospect of positive, voluntary desegregation. As the idea of educational choice continues to gain acceptance (see Chapter 10), magnet schools are becoming a key component in the public school choice plans some districts and states are adopting. The Supreme Court decisions of the early 1990s, though, may have handed magnet schools a setback.[85]

A major disadvantage of magnet schools is that they can increase segregation by social class even as they decrease segregation by race and ethnicity. In some school districts, magnet schools have filled up with middle-class students, leaving working-class students stranded in neighborhood schools most people regard as second-class.[86]

Neo-*Plessy* Thinking? Effective Schools Research and No Child Left Behind

The last twenty-five years have not been prime time for school desegregation. Even though public opinion polls show support for desegregation in principle, the political climate has been chilly. Are Americans ready to settle for an updated version of *Plessy v. Ferguson*?

Consider the record of the last four presidents. The Reagan administration sought the dismissal of desegregation cases in several hundred school districts throughout the nation, sending the clear message multiracial and multiethnic classrooms are not a top educational priority. The George H. Bush administration virtually ignored desegregation in elementary and secondary schools. President Clinton, while more attentive to minority needs than his two immediate predecessors, showed little interest in desegregation as a way to improve schools. Under President George W. Bush, scant interest has turned into indifference mixed with hostility. Former Attorney General John Ashcroft came to his position with a track record of opposition to court-ordered desegregation in St. Louis and Kansas City. Bush's first secretary of education, African American Rod Paige, often voiced his commitment to raising minority achievement—but by means of standards, assessments, and accountability, *not* desegregation. Education Secretary Margaret Spellings is taking a similar approach.

During all four presidential administrations, educators have turned increasingly to *effective schools* research to guide policy. Effective schools advocates say it is time to pay less attention to the racial composition of schools and more attention to their academic quality. Defining effective schools as those in which minority and poor students make high scores on standardized tests, researchers have found such schools tend to have the following characteristics: teachers with high standards, a principal with strong skills in instructional management, an orderly but not oppressive climate, a clear set of goals, strong emphasis on basic skills, a high percentage of time on task, frequent evaluation of student progress, and close ties between home and school. Whether segregated or desegregated, schools with these characteristics can be effective, advocates insist.[87]

With minor modifications, effective schools research has become the framework for No Child Left Behind. Given highly qualified teachers, strong principals, rigorous testing, and accountability for results, all students can learn—no matter what the socioeconomic makeup of their schools. That core belief is an article of faith for supporters of NCLB.

"Let's Get 'Separate but Equal' Right This Time."   Is that an unstated agenda of NCLB? Supporters say we must stop dreaming and start facing reality.

However much we would like students of different races and ethnic groups to attend school together, the harsh fact is that demographics and politics have left many students in segregated schools. We must educate these students as best we can. For some students, there may even be advantages to segregated schooling.[88]

Although the arguments in the preceding paragraph strike me as neo-*Plessy* thinking, I am aware of demographic and political trends. We have already seen that if present trends continue, many students who are minority and poor—particularly those concentrated in large urban school districts—will remain in segregated schools.

Critics of desegregation say its advocates paint an idealized picture of its benefits. To be sure, desegregation does not always occur under the conditions advocates would like. Tracking, for instance, can defeat the purposes of desegregation by creating vastly different programs and expectations for different students within the same school. If minorities go to a desegregated school only to be grouped together in the lower tracks, their academic gains are likely to be minimal. Unfortunately, this kind of resegregation occurs frequently as a second-generation desegregation problem. Enrollment statistics may show a school is desegregated, while a walk through the halls may reveal that almost every classroom is highly segregated.[89]

Under these circumstances, critics charge, desegregation may backfire by reinforcing stereotypes. Minorities may lose self-esteem and come to resent whites for dominating the academic side of schooling. Whites may feel superior and look down on minorities.

Gains and Losses.   As we saw in Chapter 6, historians are contributing to the critical conversation on desegregation. A theme in many historical studies of desegregation is *loss of community*. When black students attended segregated schools, black teachers and administrators were able to give them crucial support by drawing on resources from throughout the community—parents, neighbors, ministers, businesspeople. Whether in rural areas or big cities, black people knew and helped one another. Since the 1950s, desegregation has contributed to the weakening of this network, so that most of today's black students find themselves cut off from a positive adult community of any kind. This recounting of life before and after *Brown*, admittedly tinged with nostalgia, dominated many of the academic panels and community forums held during the anniversary year of 2004.[90]

Desegregation has produced both gains and losses, to be sure, and you owe it to yourself to consider both. Gary Orfield surveys the era of No Child Left Behind and sees some of the gains slipping away.

> Future historians will doubtless be incredulous that so much of the energy in this period was devoted to dismantling desegregation where it was a clear success and to developing ways to harshly sanction segregated minority schools. Yet this is what is happening as our states publish required lists of "failing" schools, which all too often are schools segregated by race and poverty.[91]

How can we stand by and let it happen, Orfield asks, when we know better?

John Obgu and Bill Cosby: The Black Community Must Take More Responsibility

Coinciding with the fiftieth anniversary of *Brown*, two prominent African Americans added a highly personal dimension to the debate over the causes of the minority-white achievement gap. In *Black American Students in an Affluent Suburb: A Study of Academic Disengagement* (2003), anthropologist John Ogbu argued that black parents don't do enough to help their children succeed in school. Black parents turn over too much responsibility to teachers; they don't supervise homework closely enough; they don't get involved at school. As a result, African American children grow up without understanding the "strong connection between school success and self-betterment." Black students eventually *disengage* from academic achievement. "They do not work hard," Obgu bluntly concluded.[92]

Entertainer Bill Cosby delivered a pop version of the same message to the NAACP in May 2004. "What the hell good is *Brown v. the Board of Education* if nobody wants it?" he asked, accusing young black people of "squandering the gains of the civil rights movement."[93] Cosby, who holds a doctorate in education, continued the public scolding in a series of speeches over the rest of the year. The man known as "America's favorite father" since his television days as Dr. Heathcliff Huxtable criticized black parents for not keeping up with their children's schoolwork and for managing them "with a cell phone." "My call is for more, tighter reins," he stated. "Know what your children are doing." Cosby unloaded on black students for speaking nonstandard English, which he said shows how little they value their education.[94]

"Acting White."   Ogbu, who died while the news media were taking Cosby's rebuke to a national audience, conducted research throughout his career on how families, peer groups, and cultural traditions within the black community shape the attitudes and behaviors that black students bring to school. In a series of studies with anthropologist Signithia Fordham, Ogbu pointed out how black students face strong pressure *not* to do well in school because many African American peer groups view academic success as "acting white." Blacks who study and make good grades are seen as "Oreos": like the cookie, black on the outside, white on the inside. With racial pride centered on contemporary African rap and hip-hop culture, acting white is the last thing black students want to do. Therefore, they "put the brakes on" their learning.[95]

Debates over this research show how closely race, class, and gender are intertwined. Some researchers argue that peer pressure against academic achievement is a phenomenon primarily of class rather than of race, that middle-class African Americans are far less likely than working-class African Americans to hold the attitude that "playing school is a white thing." Other researchers interject the influence of gender, claiming African American males face much stronger peer pressure than females to hold back in school.[96]

The influence of desegregation is just as controversial. Advocates say desegregation gives African American students greater incentives to succeed by exposing them to a wider range of peers and role models. Critics say just the opposite is true. In desegregated schools, pressure on black students not to succeed is even stronger because white students and teachers often treat blacks as outsiders, rejecting them along with their culture.

A line of research started by sociologist Claude M. Steele suggests black students grow anxious about fulfilling stereotypes of poor academic performance, a phenomenon he calls "performance threat." After a series of negative experiences with high-stakes standardized testing, for instance, black students may "disidentify" with testing and convince themselves it has no importance to their future. Other researchers have found African American males experience the strongest performance threats, especially in middle and high school. Many young black men may disidentify entirely with the academic side of schooling and turn elsewhere for their self-esteem.[97]

Sensitive Issues.   While acknowledging the role of gender, Obgu believed he had identified cultural patterns within the black community that cut across social class lines. For Ogbu, the primary issue was race, not class. Even in places like Shaker Heights, Ohio, the affluent suburb of Cleveland where Ogbu did the research for his last study, black students are underachievers compared to their white peers. Yet both groups come from privileged families and attend the same desegregated schools. Ogbu was determined to find out why, realizing the answers would be sensitive.

Critics have accused both Ogbu and Cosby of "blaming the victim," telling whites exactly what they want to hear. Harsher critics even lump together Obgu and Cosby with Abigail Thernstrom and Stephen Thernstrom, white neoconservatives whose book *No Excuses: Closing the Racial Gap in Learning* (2003) considers biological as well as cultural factors responsible for the achievement gap.[98] Cosby shrugs off the criticism with "Come at me all you want."[99]

Afrocentric Schools

Looking for a way out of what they term a "desperate situation," some African Americans are founding private schools to help students build racial identity and self-esteem. While "public schools are agents of the social order," the director of the Council of Independent Black Institutions states, "African-centered independent schools are not limited in responsibility to reproduce the status quo in social and power relations." Most of the several hundred such schools have an *Afrocentric curriculum* that presents every subject from an African point of view.[100]

While the movement toward black private schools is growing, other African Americans are looking to public schools for the same kind of alternative. The decision of school boards in Atlanta, Cleveland, Detroit, Kansas City, Milwaukee, Oakland, New York City, and the District of Columbia to establish Afrocentric schools has made the national news and sparked national controversy since the early 1990s. Afrocentric *charter schools*, which are publicly funded experimental schools (see Chapter 10), have also opened in several cities. What has often attracted the most attention is not the Afrocentric curriculum but the desire of some schools to concentrate on male students.[101]

As the mass media have pointed out repeatedly, more African American males are in jail than in college. They are disciplined, suspended, and expelled far more often than other students; they are overrepresented in remedial and special education classes and underrepresented in top ability groups and tracks. To some African American educators, this situation cries out for public schools that provide black male role models, special programs to involve parents, and "cultural innoculation" against negative racial stereotypes.[102]

Legal challenges based on Title IX (see the discussion later in this chapter) have opened all Afrocentric public schools to students of both sexes. Some schools are running parallel programs for males and females. Although the schools are also open to students of any race or ethnic group, their cultural goals and their location in segregated school districts virtually ensure an all-black student body.[103]

Are Afrocentric schools promoting resegregation? Not at all, their advocates say, pointing to the widespread segregation that already exists in public and private schools. Many African Americans are isolated in lower academic tracks and one-race schools that "condemn students to a lifetime of segregation by sending them out into the world unprepared, untrained, and marginally literate." Confronting this harsh reality, educators in Afrocentric schools have resolved to turn segregation against itself by preparing "academically competent and self-confident individuals" who can thrive in a pluralistic society.[104]

These schools, advocates hope, can offer an antidote to the biases that hold so many African American students back, biases that seem to have strengthened since *The Bell Curve: Intelligence and Class Structure in American Life* climbed to the top of the best-seller lists in 1994. This book resurrected the old arguments that heredity has a much stronger influence than environment on intelligence and that whites, as a group, are intellectually superior to blacks. Despite the preponderance of evidence to the contrary, these arguments seem to resurface and make new converts in every generation.[105]

And so we come full circle to the question the Supreme Court considered in *Brown*: Can segregated schools ever be equal? Although the Court answered with an unqualified *no* in 1954, African American educator and activist W. E. B. Du Bois expressed mixed feelings the following year. The *Brown* decision posed a "cruel dilemma" to African Americans, he observed. Acknowledging the promise of academic and social gains, Du Bois nevertheless predicted cultural losses as racial identity and heritage slipped away. Now the question is whether African Americans can use segregation itself to fulfill the promise and restore the losses.[106]

CULTURE WARS OVER LANGUAGE AND DIALECT

Bilingual Education

Washing Culture Out, Ironing Culture In.   It may strike you as incongruous that inside a single public school, you can walk down one hall and find teachers working hard to wash Spanish out of one group of students, usually in classes stigmatized as remedial. Based on judgments about their language and other aspects of their culture, these students are at a disproportionate risk of being misclassified as disabled.[107] Walk down another hall, and you can find teachers trying just as hard to iron Spanish into another group of students, usually in college prep classes.

Welcome to the culture war over bilingualism and bilingual education. In a nation where conservatives and liberals agree that more students should learn foreign languages in school, sharp differences of opinion arise on how to educate the more than 3 million students who speak a language other than English at home and have difficulty speaking English at school. School officials classify these students as *English Language Learners* (ELLs). According to a 2004 *Issue Brief* from the National Center for Education Statistics, they are 7 percent of all public school students. They represent 3 percent of the enrollment in the Midwest, 4 percent in the Northeast, 5 percent in the South, and 16 percent in the West. In every region, the percentage of ELLs is increasing. These young people find their education caught up in conflicts over assimilation, pluralism, and separation.[108]

If we listen carefully to the debate over bilingual education, we may be able to hear the voices of ordinary people, of students and parents who live in homes where English is not often spoken. Most of these families are Hispanic. Many of the rest are Asian, although literally hundreds of languages other than English are spoken in homes throughout the United States.[109]

Based on opinion polls of Hispanic Americans, bilingualism is not an artificial cause promoted by politicians and activists. It is the genuine desire of the vast majority of Hispanics. Thus the pressure Hispanics have brought to bear on educators for bilingual schooling reflects a strong preference for bicultural living.[110]

It is more difficult to generalize about Asian Americans. On the one hand, they are less likely to ask schools to help maintain their native languages. Well-established Asian families with long residence in the United States often have assimilationist attitudes on language. Recently arrived families—Vietnamese, Cambodians, Laotians, and others—seem most concerned that their children learn English. On the other hand, many of the new immigrants are trying to maintain ethnic culture in their homes, community centers, and houses of worship, because evidence is mounting that their children's loss of native language is weakening the family structure. As we will see in a moment, different models of second-language instruction can accommodate these different desires.[111]

These subtleties may be lost on Americans who see Asians as the model minority and Hispanics as a self-seeking group. Some Americans react with alarm to the Hispanic call for pluralism in schools and society. To some, it seems Hispanics are asking not for pluralism but for segregation.

Predictably, a backlash against bilingualism developed during the 1980s and seems to be strengthening in the 2000s. California, where approximately one-third of Hispanic Americans live and where more than half of all public school students are minorities, became the first state whose voters declared English the official language and the second state to amend its constitution accordingly. Other states have followed. More than thirty-five state legislatures have debated the official language issue, and more than twenty have passed an English-only law.

BOX 8.4

THE ENGLISH-ONLY MOVEMENT

For more information on the English-only movement and the campaign against bilingual education, visit English First online at www.englishfirst.org, and then look at the other side of the coin at the Language Policy Web Site & Emporium at ourworld.compuserve.com/homepages/JWCRAWFORD

English First, U.S. English, and other political action groups are leading a campaign to make English the official language of the nation. The campaign is directed specifically against bilingual ballots and bilingual education.[112]

As Chapter 6 indicates, bilingual education in the United States has a long but little-known history. In recent times, bilingualism became a hot issue after Congress passed the Bilingual Education Act of 1968. Responding to the complaints of Mexican American parents in Texas, Congress resolved that students whose primary language is not English need some form of special assistance in school. James Crawford provides a fascinating political history of these developments in *Educating English Learners* (2004).[113]

The Supreme Court's decision in *Lau v. Nichols* (1974), which involved not Hispanics but Chinese in San Francisco, affirmed the principle that school districts must do *something* to help. The court prohibited the policy of *submersion,* which simply puts ELL students into regular classrooms and forces them to sink or swim with no special assistance in their native language. Standard practice in public schools for immigrants at the turn of the century, submersion remains the unofficial standard in some school systems today, *Lau* notwithstanding.

Although the Supreme Court left a great deal of leeway for educators to decide how to help ELLs, the other two branches of the federal government have favored particular approaches. Federal policy on bilingual education has changed as the political winds have shifted in Washington.

Four Models of Second-Language Instruction.   Since the 1970s, with Congress and a succession of presidents trying to shape language policy, attention has focused on four models of second-language instruction: immersion, English as a Second Language (ESL), transitional bilingual, and bilingual/bicultural maintenance. The models differ in the amount of emphasis placed on English.

In the *immersion* model, teachers who may or may not know the students' native language provide instruction in the regular academic subjects. Teachers always speak in English—usually a slow, simplified version—and encourage students to use English. This model, which in some school districts borders on submersion, is popular with state and local school districts because it does not require teachers who are trained and certified in bilingual education. You may recall the shortage of such teachers from Chapter 1.

The *English as a Second Language* model can be used alone or as a supplement to any of the other models. ESL typically involves "pull-out" instruction in which students practice reading, writing, and speaking English part of the day and attend regular classes the rest of the day. Students whose English skills are weak may spend all day with their ESL teachers, studying English as well as other subjects. Chapter 1 also points out the shortage of trained and certified ESL teachers.

The *transitional bilingual* model is designed to ease the transition from the native language into English. Teachers who are bilingual instruct students in their native language to keep them from falling behind in their regular academic subjects while they are learning English. Students in transitional bilingual classes usually speak the same native language, and they are encouraged to move into classes conducted in English as soon as they can—but usually not soon enough to satisfy critics of bilingual education.

Although the immersion, ESL, and transitional bilingual models employ very different methods, they have the same goal: developing skills in English as quickly as possible, ideally during the early elementary grades. Under all three models, second-language instruction ends when the students reach a specified level of English proficiency. Asian Americans generally prefer these models, especially immersion and ESL.

The fourth model, *bilingual/bicultural maintenance,* is the most controversial because it has a different goal: developing and increasing proficiency in both English and another language. In every grade, students take some classes taught in their native language, ideally by trained and certified bilingual teachers, and some classes taught in English. The curriculum may highlight the students' ethnic culture through a program of multicultural education. Some bilingual/bicultural maintenance programs use a *two-way* or *dual* approach that brings together English-speaking students and ELL students from several different language backgrounds. In this case, the model relies on team teaching by instructors with different language specializations.

Even though the immersion and ESL models have been more widely used, the transitional and bilingual/bicultural maintenance models have drawn more criticism from English First and similar groups. Critics charge that the two bilingual education models—especially the bilingual/bicultural maintenance model—turn out students who speak two languages poorly, students unprepared to compete in an English-dominant culture. Defenders of bilingual education reply that many programs work well, urging educators to acknowledge the bilingual or even Spanish-dominant subculture most Hispanic Americans live in.

Recent research on Mexican American students suggests those who become fluent in English but maintain their ethnic culture, including the Spanish language, become most successful in the United States. Students who abandon their home language and other aspects of culture often discover, too late, that "assimilation can be hazardous to your health."[114]

Bilingual Politics and No Child Left Behind.   The controversy over bilingual education has heated up since the late 1990s. California voters passed a 1998 initiative that severely limits bilingual education, and Arizona voters followed suit with a similar initiative in 2000. Both laws mandate "intensive one-year English immersion" for ELL students, although it is possible for parents to request waivers so students can receive bilingual services. In both California and Arizona, the percentage of students enrolled in bilingual education has dropped from 33 to 11. Leaders of the anti-bilingual education drive in these two states are trying to export their campaign to other states.[115]

The provisions of No Child Left Behind may make that strategy unnecessary. Under the federal law, English Language Learners are one of the four subgroups of students whose standardized test scores come under close scrutiny. NCLB requires states to develop English language proficiency standards for ELLs along with assessments to track their progress. In addition, ELLs must meet adequate yearly progress (AYP) goals on all the other tests mandated by NCLB, although they can take these tests in their native language during their first three years in U.S. schools.[116]

Faced with this kind of pressure, state and local school officials are enrolling increasing numbers of students in ESL, which is clearly the program of choice in the 2000s. Evidence is mixed on the effectiveness of ESL compared to the other three models of language instruction. Based on a 2004 meta-analysis of thirty years of studies, Johns Hopkins researcher Robert Slavin concludes that teaching students to read in both English and their native language is superior to English-only methods. But as we might expect, critics of bilingual education cite other evidence for support, and in today's educational and political climate, any program with "bilingual" in its name is suspect.[117]

Nonstandard English: Black English and Other Dialects

I grew up in a working-class white community in the suburbs of Atlanta where most of my friends spoke nonstandard dialects of English. My parents, better educated than most in the neighborhood, spoke a dialect that was closer to the one in dictionaries and grammar books. I thought some of my friends sounded a little different when they talked about "vine-ripe maters" and "french-fried taters," when they played poker and drew "two pair," or when they said they had "already did" something a few days ago.

I remember adjusting my speech to fit in with my friends, and I never thought much about the underlying issues until I went to college and majored in English. Soon I learned a *dialect* is a cultural variation of a language, a variation reflecting social class, race, ethnicity, and geography, among other factors. Because some dialects are closer than others to the *standard English* that is supposed to be used in school, some students have an easier time than others speaking and writing by the official rules. As a new teacher, I immediately noticed the wide range of dialects students (and teachers) used. I also became aware of the controversy surrounding one dialect in particular: black English.

The controversy is alive and well in the 2000s. In the speeches Bill Cosby made during the *Brown* anniversary, for instance, he referred scornfully to low-income black students who hang out "on the corner and they can't speak

English. I can't even talk the way these people talk: 'Why you ain't,' 'Where you is' . . . and I blamed the kid until I heard the mother talk. And then I heard the father talk."[118]

Now that's harsh. No wonder some African Americans who agree with Cosby's basic message of responsibility don't appreciate the condescending tone that seemed to come through in this particular criticism.

Cosby explained that the well-publicized debate over black English in the Oakland, California, public schools helped shape his attitude. The Oakland board of education stirred up a whirlwind during the 1996–1997 school year with its resolution instructing the superintendent to "devise a program to improve the English-language acquisition and application skills of African-American students."[119] The reaction to the Oakland resolution has been not only negative—some of it has been downright spiteful. What may be the low point came in *Time* magazine's op-ed piece "Ebonics According to Buckwheat" (January 13, 1997), which featured a photo of the *Our Gang* character wearing suspenders and a straw hat, flashing a pearly-toothed smile, and saying, "Here I Is!"[120]

As prominent people from across the political and educational spectrum lined up in the media to take turns kicking the resolution, it was hard at first to find anyone willing to defend the Oakland board's position. What had the board done to deserve such a mean rebuke?[121]

The resolution, drafted by a task force of African American teachers, administrators, and community members, advanced three main propositions. First, the board recognized *Ebonics* (a term that combines *ebony* and *phonics* to suggest "black sounds") not as a dialect of English but as a separate language. Second, the board recommended teachers learn more about how African American students speak and write. Third, the board called for instructing African American students "both in their primary language and in English." The windstorm of criticism that descended on Oakland almost drowned out the board's clearly stated goal: helping the students master standard English.[122]

Systematic Differences.   With the goal of mastering standard English in mind—and it hardly seems radical—the recommendation that teachers learn more about the language characteristics of their students seems only reasonable. Teachers who have a better understanding of how their students speak and write outside of school are in a better position to help them learn standard English in school. Such teachers can use what linguists call *contrastive analysis,* a technique that involves pointing out to students the differences between

> "he late" and "he is late"
> "he be late" and "he is usually late"
> "three dollar" and "three dollars"
> "dat" and "that"
> "skreet" and "street."

In each of these examples, the two terms carry the same meaning, but notice how differently black English and standard English express the meaning. The first

■ ■ ■ ■ ■

BOX 8.5

CENTER FOR APPLIED LINGUISTICS

The Center for Applied Linguistics maintains a Web site full of information on language issues, including several pages on bilingual and bidialectal education, at www.cal.org

three examples illustrate grammatical differences; the last two illustrate differences in pronunciation.[123]

These differences are *systematic*. They occur again and again, forming patterns teachers and students can identify and discuss. Linguists trace the roots of such differences to the west coast of Africa, the region where the ancestors of most African Americans lived before they were abducted and sold into slavery. The way verbs were used in West African languages influences the way many African Americans use verbs today. The rules that governed the formation of plural nouns in West Africa still show up in the way many African Americans form plurals. The pronunciations that were characteristic of West African languages can be heard in black speech today.[124]

Linguists have documented these differences for several decades. Following the publication of J. L. Dillard's breakthrough study *Black English* (1973), scholars have built a solid base of knowledge on the subject.[125]

Language or Dialect?   Linguists disagree over whether African American speech and writing are distinctive enough to constitute a separate language. Most linguists take the position that they are not. Instead, African American patterns constitute a nonstandard dialect of English. Black English differs significantly from standard English, to be sure, but so do the dialects many white students learn at home.[126]

Teachers across the nation are gradually becoming more aware of dialect research. Since the 1980s, California has offered its teachers linguistic training through the Standard English Proficiency program. Other states have similar programs. In some teacher education programs, teachers learn how to help their students understand the distinction between "home talk" and "school talk" and then extend their understanding to other settings. People talk differently in different situations, teachers can explain. What is appropriate at a party may not be appropriate on a job interview. A radio DJ may use standard English on the air but talk in black English among friends. Linguists call the ability to choose the dialect that suits the situation *code-shifting* or *code-switching*.

Unfortunately, by using the exotic-sounding name Ebonics and sprinkling its resolution with such phrases as "Pan-African Communication Behaviors" and "West and Niger-Congo African languages," the Oakland board made its resolution an inviting target. Far worse, the board's suggestion that "African Language Systems are genetically based" sounded like an echo of *The Bell Curve*.[127]

The wording of the resolution also allowed people to misinterpret what the board meant by "instructing African American children both in their primary language and in English." Using black English in contrastive analysis, as I explained previously, is a tried-and-true strategy. But the public, egged on by the media, cracked jokes about teachers talking like Buckwheat. That was not what the board had in mind, as it later explained in a clarification of its resolution.

The board has never lost sight of its goal of helping students master standard English. Today, a decade after the big controversy, a plan that seems less radical is in place. Reading instruction revolves around phonics, a traditional approach favored by essentialist educators and highly compatible with contrastive analysis. The Oakland approach to reading is also culturally sensitive: Teachers use "repetition, recitation, relationships, ritual, and rhythm," techniques proven to work with African American students. In staff development sessions, teachers study the history of black English and learn to appreciate it as different from, not inferior to, standard English. The goal remains the same as in the original resolution: helping students bridge the gap between the two dialects.[128]

Other Voices.   Now that the noise of this culture war has died down a bit—remarks like Cosby's notwithstanding—we can listen to calmer, quieter voices. It is important to consider the social context in Oakland. African Americans make up more than half the students in the school district, and they lag behind every other racial and ethnic group in grades and test scores. The African American educators and community leaders who drafted the Oakland resolution were trying to make the public aware of the language difficulties black students face—difficulties in some ways tougher than those faced by students who qualify for bilingual education programs. Although some educators look down on Spanish and Vietnamese and seem determined to wash them out of students' lives, at least they recognize Spanish and Vietnamese as languages.[129]

The same educators usually hold even more negative attitudes toward black English and refuse to acknowledge it as a systematic means of communication. Instead, they put down black English as slang, jive, loose talk, street talk—a "mass of random errors committed by Blacks trying to speak English."[130]

The Skin That We Speak: Thoughts on Language and Culture in the Classroom (2003), edited by Lisa Delpit and Joanne Dowdy of Georgia State University, contains several essays that claim the controversy over black English is actually a power struggle involving the very attitudes discussed above, attitudes that serve to keep black Americans "in their place."[131] From my experience as a teacher and teacher educator, I can tell you white teachers are much more likely to label black English as inferior than they are to pin the same label on nonstandard white dialects. It's the black kids who *really* need to change how they talk and write, these teachers say. To be fair, I must say I have heard black teachers say the same thing. These attitudes, which reflect unconscious as well as conscious racial preferences, are one of the factors in the overclassification of black students as having a disability.[132]

The Oakland resolution was an attempt to call attention to deep-seated problems most Americans wish would simply go away. Why do African American students want to keep talking like Buckwheat? Why do teachers want to encourage them? Even join them? Framing the questions that way, as most media critics have, is a good way to ensure the problems will not only remain but worsen.

GENDER

Are Schools *Still* Shortchanging Girls?

Future teachers often seem less interested in discussing gender than social class, race, and ethnicity. Young women may react with amazement or even amusement to the suggestion that in the twenty-first century, male and female students receive different treatment in school. "No one ever put me down for being a girl. I took the courses I wanted to take and participated in whatever activities and sports I chose," one of my students said recently. Many male prospective teachers have the same attitude: "No, I don't think I had any advantages or disadvantages in school because of my sex."

If an older student brings up the discrimination she (or, less often, he) faced in school, the rest of the class smiles and sighs with relief, grateful things have changed so much. To many future teachers, unequal treatment based on sex is a thing of the past, a quaint relic from another age.

Unfortunately, it lives on. A series of reports from the American Association of University Women (AAUW), one of the strongest advocacy groups for women, surveys the playing field and finds it is still not level, despite encouraging progress in education and the workplace. That's why I still paraphrase the title of the most influential AAUW report, *How Schools Shortchange Girls* (1992), for the subheading of this section in our textbook. In powerful language, this study urges educators to consider gender on a par with social class, race, and ethnicity.

> There is clear evidence that the educational system is not meeting girls' needs. Girls and boys enter school roughly equal in measured ability. On some measures of school readiness, girls are ahead of boys. Twelve years later, girls have fallen behind their male classmates in key areas such as high-level mathematics and measures of self-esteem.[133]

How Schools Shortchange Girls continues to attract attention. Several of its authors speak to audiences throughout the nation, and they never fail to get a reaction when they point out that "girls are the only group in our society that begins school ahead and ends up behind."[134]

Gender Gaps: Where Schools Still Fail Our Children (1998) is AAUW's follow-up to its 1992 report. Like the earlier one, this report synthesizes more than a thousand studies.[135] Acknowledging progress in some areas—girls are taking more upper-level science and math courses, for instance, and more Advanced Placement courses in biology, English, and foreign languages—*Gender Gaps* claims schools are still giving girls short change in technology, "the new 'boys' club' in our nation's public schools. While boys program and problem solve with computers, girls use computers for word processing, the [new] version of typing."[136]

The AAUW is especially concerned that girls are less likely than boys to find the new computer technology "user friendly." In *Gender Gaps* as well as *Tech-Savvy: Educating Girls in the New Computer Age* (2000), the AAUW points out girls use computers at home less often than boys and enroll less often in advanced computer science and graphics courses. Girls find it hard to identify with the mostly male role models featured in computer software.[137]

These reports, some of which can be downloaded for free on the AAUW's Web site (see Internet box), are having the desired effect: They are shaking up the system. They may be shaking too hard, in fact, because they are provoking counterarguments and even a backlash.

Several studies released since the mid-1990s argue that girls have closed most of the gender gaps with boys and are doing just fine in school. A report issued by the U.S. Department of Education under the Bush administration, *Trends in Educational Equity of Girls and Women: 2004*, makes exactly that claim, painting a much rosier picture of the situation for girls than the 2000 edition of the same report issued during the Clinton administration. Some studies, such as Christine Sommers's *The War against Boys* (2000), take politics and ideology even farther and contend that misguided feminists are running the public schools, harming boys as they go out of their way to help girls.[138]

Few of the future teachers in my classes share the latter view. But now more often than ever before in my career as a teacher educator, I hear evidence of a gender backlash from students who say, "Hey, enough is enough. It's the *guys* who are worse off in school. They're the ones having the hardest time."

Aware of these feelings, the AAUW is asking all sides to tone down the rhetoric. *Beyond the Gender Wars: A Conversation about Girls, Boys, and Education* (2001) is the AAUW's call to abandon the us-versus-them mindset that pits females against males and assumes one gender can win only if the other loses. After all, girls and boys face similar if not identical problems in school.[139]

The AAUW's *Hostile Hallways: Bullying, Teasing, and Sexual Harassment in School* (2001), points out that almost as many boys (79 percent) as girls (83 percent) experience harassment in schools, even though girls take it more seriously and are more upset by it. Boys are more likely to be teased about their sexuality and challenged to prove their toughness, while girls are more likely to get suggestive comments, unwelcome touches, and overtly sexual advances. Focusing on both sexes, the report suggests ways educators can reduce harassment and help all students.[140]

■ ■ ■ ■ ■

BOX 8.6

AAUW REPORTS ON GENDER

Read more about all the AAUW reports cited in this chapter plus many others at www.aauw.org/research/all.cfm, which includes executive summaries and teacher resource guides for some of the reports.

Before we declare a truce in the gender wars, however, we need to examine more evidence on how much things have really changed for males and females. Gender researchers David Sadker and the late Myra Sadker have asked hundreds of students the following question: "Suppose you woke up tomorrow and found you were a member of the other sex. How would your life be different?" Over the years, the answers have been surprisingly consistent. Students of both sexes readily admit boys have it better than girls. Boys don't have to worry much about their appearance, the students say, but girls must be concerned with attractiveness and neatness or risk rejection. Boys can participate in a wider range of activities and choose among more careers, the students continue. Girls have to watch their behavior more carefully—they have to be "nicer" than boys. The students are also aware girls have to be more concerned with their safety. In fact, the physical vulnerability of girls, particularly as it relates to the changes girls go through as they mature sexually, is something students of both sexes see as a problem. In short, America's students see many disadvantages to being female and many advantages to being male.[141]

Gender-Role Socialization

When confronted with such studies, prospective teachers tend to place the blame on the home: "Students must pick up those attitudes from their parents. Teachers would never favor one sex over the other."

Of course, there is abundant evidence many parents still raise boys and girls differently. Males begin life as the preferred sex. By a ratio of more than 2 to 1, both future mothers and future fathers express their preference for boys. Some studies show mothers tend to be physically and emotionally closer to their daughters, expecting them to need more attention and nurturance. Fathers tend to be rougher and more physical with their sons, and boys receive more encouragement from both parents to be independent.[142]

Parents are more tolerant of girls than of boys who show cross-sex behavior. Parents usually put up with girls who act like tomboys because they believe they will "grow out" of the role when they reach adolescence. Not so for boys who get labeled as sissies. Their parents worry they will never change, and fathers can be especially harsh with sons who show traits and interests society stereotypes as feminine. Boys eventually get the message: Whatever girls do, you must not do. These patterns of socialization help explain why, in the Sadkers's ongoing "suppose you woke up" research, 95 percent of the boys are hard pressed to think of any advantages to being a girl.[143]

The labels *tomboy* and *sissy,* most often used by adults to describe children, are mild compared to *queer* and *fag,* words young people throw at one another to insult, ridicule, and hurt. This kind of sexual harassment, *Hostile Hallways* points out, is increasing. The fear of being labeled homosexual by their peers heightens as children grow older, so that by adolescence it ranks as one of the worst things that can happen to them. Imagine the conflicted feelings of students who realize they are gay or lesbian. As we saw in Chapter 5, the issue of sexual orientation is so sensitive, some states forbid teachers to say anything positive about homosexuality. And most teachers, frankly, are happy to steer clear of the issue.[144]

But even in areas that are far less controversial, teachers often say gender-role socialization is beyond their control because so much of it takes place outside of schools. Consider toys and games, for instance. Although it is now acceptable (in some cases, even fashionable) for girls to play with hammers and trucks, many stores continue to advertise and display boys' toys and girls' toys. Doctors' kits and tool boxes are for one gender; nurses' kits and kitchen sets are for the other. With toys going increasingly high tech, more girls are wondering along with the AAUW, "Why do they make the cool toys as if they're for boys?" The games children play also vary by gender, with girls' games more likely to take place indoors and more likely to emphasize cooperation over competition. Families, peer groups, the media, churches—all these institutions, as teachers are quick to tell you, play major roles in showing and telling children what society considers "proper" masculine and feminine behavior.[145]

I can understand why future teachers look outside the schools for the origins of gender-role socialization. Still, it is all too easy to overlook how schools reinforce stereotypes students have learned elsewhere.

Gender Bias in Textbooks

Numerous studies conducted during the 1970s documented the gender bias in textbooks. One influential study of elementary school readers showed the books featured two and one-half to three times as many males as females and portrayed males in almost six times as many occupational roles. In what some researchers have called the "cult of the apron," the books rarely showed women working outside the home, even though a few women were, of course, nurses, secretaries, or teachers. Studies of secondary school textbooks uncovered the same patterns. Social studies books rarely mentioned women; literature texts presented few selections by female authors; science texts downplayed the contributions of women; math books featured males more frequently than females in word problems; and so forth through the other subjects.[146]

In "Gender Bias" (2004), Sadker and Sadker point out that after women's groups brought pressure to bear on publishers, textbooks began to change, but not as much as many educators think. A 1980s study of elementary school readers found that while the overall ratio of males to females had narrowed, it was still nearly 2 to 1. Compared to older texts, the books used in the 2000s present more career options for both sexes, but males hold up to 80 percent of all the careers. Publishers have also modified secondary school texts, though often in cosmetic ways. Token females, like token racial and ethnic minorities, are now on prominent display, but males remain dominant.[147]

The *Statistical Abstract of the United States, 2004–2005* and other U.S. government reports show how unrealistic such portrayals are in a nation where females make up 51 percent of the population and almost half the labor force. More than 70 percent of adult women—and more than 80 percent of women with college degrees—are employed outside the home, and more than 90 percent of women work outside the home at some time during their lives. But while women are moving into managerial positions and into the professions of law, medicine, and dentistry, men are not showing the same interest in fields women have traditionally dominated. Ninety-seven percent of secretaries and 90 percent of registered nurses are still women. Most women who work outside the home are in *pink-collar* jobs that pay low salaries, which helps explain why women still earn less than men with the same level of education. Even among younger workers aged twenty-five to thirty-four, female high school graduates earn only 73 percent of their male peers' salaries, while women with bachelor's degrees take home 78 percent of what comparable men earn.[148]

Few textbooks reflect these realities, even though new stereotypes may be replacing old ones. The irony of the situation is that some conservative groups are now charging textbooks have changed too much, to the point of promoting nontraditional and antifamily lifestyles. Often the evidence is a book's favorable portrayal of a female auto mechanic, a male nurse, or another stereotype-breaking character. Feminists, citing the continuing gap between the overall percentages of males and females in textbooks and the continuing masculine dominance of occupational roles, counter they have not changed enough.

Such disputes can become quite heated because both sides know textbooks and other instructional materials do indeed affect the way students view the world. Research on multicultural education shows that what children read in school can reinforce gender as well as class, racial, and ethnic biases. Conversely, more favorable portrayals of nondominant groups can transmit more favorable attitudes to students. When curriculum committees meet to review books and school boards meet to adopt books (see Chapter 5), the stakes are high.[149]

Unequal Treatment in the Classroom

In the "suppose you woke up" survey we examined earlier, the students agreed that, in general, people treat boys better than girls. Other researchers, though, have found one major exception to this pattern. Students of both sexes perceive girls get treated better than boys in school. The consensus is teachers like girls more and pick on boys more. The students therefore conclude girls have the advantage. The students' perceptions are right, but their conclusion is wrong.[150]

Girls *do* behave in ways teachers like and reward. In the classroom, girls tend to be quieter and more cooperative than boys. Girls depend more on their teachers and identify more closely with them. In the year 2006, 77 percent of all teachers (and more than 90 percent of elementary school teachers) are female. Some researchers describe the typical classroom as a feminized environment in which girls feel comfortable and at ease.[151]

Boys react to the classroom differently. Trained in the home to be more active and independent, boys often rebel against the routine of silence, seat work, and conformity. A few rebel so strongly, they refuse to learn, which is one basis for the complaint that feminism is running rampant in today's schools. We will return to this charge later in the chapter.

Most boys learn to channel their activity in ways that can work to their advantage and give them the academic edge over girls. Empirical studies of classroom interaction show boys quickly master the art of getting their teachers' attention. Boys are eight times as likely as girls to shout out answers, and teachers—male as well as female—usually play along and acknowledge the boys' participation. Strikingly, teachers are more likely to reprimand girls for calling or yelling out in class, often with a comment like "Please raise your hand if you want to answer." Overall, boys dominate classroom discussion by a ratio of three to one over girls.[152]

In the Sadkers' book *Failing at Fairness: How America's Schools Cheat Girls* (1994), a fascinating chapter titled "Missing in Interaction" points out how teachers spend more of their time interacting with boys. Research indicates the quality of interaction also differs, with boys more likely than girls to receive specific directions, praise, and criticism: "Draw the picture like this" as opposed to "Mm-hmm" or "Okay." Few teachers realize they teach this way, but videotapes of classes reveal the underlying patterns of interaction. Such behavior is slow to change precisely because it is unconscious and unintentional.[153]

Closing the Gender Gaps

Title IX.   Some things have changed, though, and we can credit some of the progress schools have made toward sex equity to Title IX of the Education Amendments of 1972. Title IX states:

> No person in the United States shall, on the basis of sex, be excluded from participation in, be denied the benefits of, or be subjected to discrimination under any educational program or activity receiving federal financial assistance.

As Louis Fischer, David Schimmel, and Leslie R. Stellman point out in *Teachers and the Law* (2003), Title IX protects both students and employees. It has helped open up courses, activities, and jobs once officially or unofficially closed to one sex or the other. In part as a result of Title IX, boys now take homemaking and consumer courses and girls are enrolled in industrial arts and agriculture classes. Title IX has made a tremendous difference in athletic programs, putting the pressure on sometimes-reluctant schools to provide equal opportunities for female and male athletes. Title IX has helped female teachers move into administrative positions once controlled by the "good old boy" network.[154]

No legislation is a panacea. While more and more females are participating in school athletics, budgets are still tilted toward male sports. Homemaking and consumer classes are still feminine turf, despite the enrollment of more boys, while boys continue to dominate electronics and auto repair. And despite the fact that more than half the teachers taking school administration courses at universities are women, two out of three school principals and nine out of ten district superintendents are still men. In 2004, the National Women's Law Center charged that, under the Bush administration, the U.S. Department of Education has declined to investigate complaints that women are still being excluded from jobs and educational opportunities in traditionally male fields.[155]

Real Progress.   In some areas, though, females are making extraordinary progress. Some of the most encouraging news is girls are closing the gender gap in high school math and science course taking. Not too many years ago, it was unusual to find girls enrolled in upper-level math classes. But since the early 1990s, according to *Trends in Educational Equity of Girls and Women: 2004* girls have overtaken boys in algebra, geometry, trigonometry, and precalculus enrollments and closed fast in calculus. As for first-year science courses, girls are now more likely than boys to take every major subject but physics.[156]

Gender gaps are also closing in higher education, although males continue to dominate quantitative and scientific majors. In engineering, to cite the field with the greatest disparity, 77 percent of the bachelor's degrees still go to men— although 99 percent went to men in 1970. Women now take a majority of the bachelor's degrees in biological and life sciences, but men still claim about 60 percent of the degrees in physical sciences and 70 percent of those in computer and information sciences. In mathematics, where women currently receive 48 percent of bachelor's degrees, the gender gap narrowed during the 1970s and early 1980s but has closed little since then.[157]

Single-Sex Schooling?   On balance, this news is encouraging. But it could be even better, some educators say, if single-sex schooling were more widely available. Once the norm in public as well as private education, especially at the high school level, separate schooling for girls and boys lost popularity during the twentieth century. By the 1980s, it had become extinct in public education, and only a small number of single-sex private schools remained. The decline occurred in higher education as well.[158]

But the private girls' schools and women's colleges that survived never gave up their cause, and since the 1990s Americans have been paying closer attention to their claims. In single-sex schools, advocates say, girls can learn without trying to compete with boys or worrying about what they think. Single-sex schooling can offset the decline in self-esteem and academic interest that occurs in many girls during adolescence. Teachers can talk more frankly about the problems girls face. Girls can learn leadership skills. Overall, advocates contend, graduates of all-girl private schools are better prepared for college and the world of work.[159]

Single-sex schooling is slowly making inroads in public education. As of 2005, according to the National Association for Single Sex Public Education, there are 36 single-sex public schools and 113 coeducational public schools that offer single-sex classes. The U.S. Department of Education is encouraging "experimentation" and wants to amend Title IX, if necessary, to clear away legal obstacles. Recently I learned about the interest in single-sex education in my own community from an administrator whose middle school is trying all-girls and all-boys classes in science and math, the riskiest turf for girls.[160]

This administrator believes single-sex education is beneficial to boys as well. Reflecting the changing educational climate we will discuss in the next section, he often reminds me that boys have problems, too. In his low-income, all-black middle school, curbing discipline problems is the main goal of single-sex instruction. So far, the evidence he is collecting suggests that both sexes, and especially boys, are less likely to wander off task in single-sex classrooms.

The published research on single-sex schooling is stronger on ideology than empirical evidence. Since 2004, a major study funded by the U.S. Department of Education has been in progress under the direction of sociologist Cornelius Riordan, whom we met earlier in this chapter. Riordan plans to review the literature, little of which focuses on public education, survey existing single-sex public schools, and then study six schools in depth.[161]

What about the Boys?

Reacting to the AAUW reports and others that emphasize the educational obstacles girls face, several studies have argued that boys have a tough time, too. In *The War against Boys: How Misguided Feminism Is Harming Our Young Men* (2000), Christina H. Sommers insists that males are the sex that gets shortchanged socially and academically. To be sure, some of the statistical indicators in the AAUW reports and in *Trends in Educational Equity* show boys are more likely than girls to have behavior problems in school, to repeat a grade, to be identified as learning disabled (LD) or attention deficit/hyperactivity disordered (ADHD), and to drop out of school. Moreover, girls outscore boys on most standardized tests of reading and writing, and girls are more likely to attend and graduate from college.[162]

Sommers is critical of parents, teachers, and others who try to feminize boys by constantly quieting them down, discouraging their sense of competition, and turning them into sensitive little creatures. Boys don't need to be rescued from their masculinity, she says.

To Sommers's charge that feminism, whether misguided or not, has taken over today's schools, most feminists reply, "We only wish." As we saw in Chapters 6 and 7, silence, seatwork, and conformity have ruled the schools for hundreds of years, initially imposed by male school masters and later, after women began to replace men as teachers, reinforced by male administrators. If discipline and order are causing problems for boys, the situation isn't new, and women teachers aren't to blame. Historically, women have been stronger advocates than men of loosening the restrictions of traditional schooling. Sommers's charge that modern feminism is stifling young boys' masculinity misses the mark.

William Pollack also comes to the defense of boys but from a very different point of view. In *Real Boys: Rescuing Our Sons from the Myths of Boyhood* (1999), Pollack argues boys learn very early to put on a "mask of masculinity" to hide their true feelings. Don't cry, people tell them. Hold it in. Take it like a man. At the same time, boys learn they should express affection, love, and other positive emotions. According to Pollack's research, these contradictory social messages help push some boys toward bullying, risk taking, committing violent acts, even committing suicide.[163]

Pollack's work has received a great deal of attention in the aftermath of the 1999 shootings at Columbine High. Parents, teachers, and others should rethink their narrow and restrictive views of masculinity, he says.

The popular media are picking up on the new literature on gnder. The December 3, 2004, issue of *USA Today* urged its editorial page readers to "pay closer attention: Boys are struggling academically."[164] According to the editorial, Michael Gurian's *Boys and Girls Learn Differently!* (2001) may hold part of the solution. Gurian, an educator and family therapist, believes boys are girls are "wired" differently. Based on his study of "brain science," he wants to make teachers more aware of biologically based gender differences so they can teach boys, in particular, more effectively. Gurian's research is fueling the interest in single-sex schooling, but how real and how significant are the differences?[165]

Cognitive Differences between Females and Males

For years, psychologists and sociologists have debated whether girls as a group really have superior verbal skills and whether boys as a group are really better at mathematical and spatial tasks. Synthesizing a complex body of research, the evidence suggests the following:

1. Sex-related cognitive differences standardized tests can measure generally do not appear until adolescence.
2. When differences do appear, they are small. Although females do slightly better on many tests of verbal ability and males slightly better on many tests of mathematical and spatial ability, differences *within* each sex are much greater than differences *between* the sexes. There are greater differences in math ability among boys, for instance, than between boys as a group and girls as a group.
3. The proportion of the differences that seems to be due to biological as opposed to social factors is no more than 5 percent.[166]

Many researchers conclude people make too much of the cognitive differences between males and females. Some students, parents, and educators use gender as a convenient academic excuse: "Of course he doesn't like poetry—he's a boy." "I'm not very good with computers, math, and technical stuff—most girls aren't." The research literature simply does not support such sweeping statements.

Girls still experience subtle but powerful social pressure not to do well in science and math. As children grow up, boys receive more encouragement than girls to investigate electronics and mechanics. Girls who excel in science and math threaten boys on a traditionally masculine turf, and those who want to be popular with the opposite sex had better not be too threatening. Peers, parents, teachers, counselors, textbooks, and other influences may also subtly—often unintentionally—discourage girls from being truly competitive with boys in science and math. We can see the results not only in girls' lower test scores but in the increasingly negative attitudes they develop toward science and math in middle and high school.[167]

Toward the Future: Feminism and Education

I want to place our discussion of gender within the context of three phases of feminism. In the first phase, which we can liken to assimilation, women pursue the goal of equality with men. Striving to prove themselves equal to men in the public sphere—in school, on the job, and elsewhere—women measure themselves against masculine standards. Girls want to prove they can do math as well as boys. Women want to show they can practice medicine as well as men. Given the years of discrimination and exclusion women have faced, these concerns of first-phase feminism are quite understandable.[168]

In the second phase, which is more pluralistic, women recognize their differences from men and try to use their special qualities to enhance society. Carol Gilligan's *In a Different Voice* (1982) helped popularize second-stage feminism. Gilligan concluded women and men see life differently, women through a lens of care and interdependence and men through a lens of rights and independence. In seeking equality with men in the public sphere, women must be careful not to abandon the feminine qualities that are so important at home, in the private sphere.[169]

Gilligan, Jane Roland Martin, Mary F. Belenky, and other feminist scholars urge women to bring such qualities as cooperation and nurturance into schools, work, and the rest of the public sphere, where masculine qualities have traditionally dominated. The goal of second-phase feminist school reform is not educating girls to boys' standards but rather redefining education for all students, so all can hear both the feminine and the masculine voice. Beginning with history and literature, think how the entire curriculum could change if such a reform took place.[170]

Reform this fundamental is exactly what critical theorists advocate, and they urge feminists to move into a third phase, a critical phase, in which women see their struggle as part of the struggle of all oppressed people. Nel Noddings of Stanford University points out that "just as men have dominated, and still dominate, women, so the wealthy and better educated dominate the poor and less educated."[171] The voices of excluded groups will never be heard in schools unless they work together and confront larger issues of power and status. Noddings, like Gilligan, uses an "ethic of care" as the basis of her proposals for social change, as she explains in *Caring: A Feminine Approach to Ethics and Moral Education* (2003). Third-phase feminism, with its call for more attention to the connections among class, race, ethnicity, and gender, makes a fitting conclusion for this chapter.[172]

ACTIVITIES

1. Interview people who have been denied educational opportunities because of their social class, race, ethnicity, or sex.

2. Talk with state or local public school officials about how their schools comply with Title VI of the Civil Rights Act of 1964 and Title IX of the Education Amendments of 1972. Find out which model(s) of second-language instruction they prefer, and why.

3. Conduct your own research on bias in elementary and secondary school textbooks. Locate examples of stereotypes based not only on gender but also on class, race, and ethnicity.

4. Ask teachers and administrators to talk about the causes of the achievement gaps associated with social class, race and ethnicity, proficiency in English, and disability. How much can the schools hope to narrow the gaps? Talk with students and parents about the same issues.

RECOMMENDED READINGS

American Association of University Women. *Gender Gaps: Where Schools Still Fail Our Children* (Washington, DC: AAUW Educational Foundation, 1998). A superb synthesis of research, this progress report surveys the situation six years after *How Schools Shortchange Girls* called attention to issues all too often swept under the rug in the rush to school reform.

Banks, James A., and Cherry A. McGee Banks, eds. *Handbook of Research on Multicultural Education*, 2nd ed. (San Francisco: Jossey-Bass, 2003). Another fine research summary, this volume contains forty-nine chapters on virtually every aspect of multicultural education.

Crawford, James. *Educating English Learners: Language Diversity in the Classroom*, 5th ed. (Los Angeles: Bilingual Educational Service, 2004). The author, an advocate of bilingual education, manages to do justice to all sides in the long-running debate over language issues.

Ogbu, John U., with Astrid Davis. *Black American Students in an Affluent Suburb: A Study of Academic Disengagement* (Mahwah, NJ: Erlbaum, 2003). Culminating Ogbu's thirty-five years of research on minority education, this provocative study offers candid analysis of the causes of the achievement gap.

Payne, Ruby K. *A Framework for Understanding Poverty*, 3rd rev. ed. (Highlands, TX: aha! Process, 2003). Payne has built a solid reputation with classroom teachers with her in-service and staff development workshops. Her approach is now finding its way into university-based teacher education programs.

NOTES

1. Federal Interagency Forum on Child and Family Statistics, *America's Children: Key Indicators of Well-Being 2004* (2004) [Available: www.childstats.gov/ac2004/tables/pop3.asp], Introduction, Tbl. POP3; U.S. Department of Commerce, Bureau of the Census, *Income, Poverty, and Health Insurance Coverage in the United States, 2003* (2004) [Available: www.census.gov/prod/2004pubs/p60-226.pdf], pp. 9–13; U.S. Department of Education, National Center for Education Statistics, *Digest of Education Statistics, 2003* (2004) [Available: nces.ed.gov/programs/digest/d03/tables/dt042.asp], Tbl. 42.

2. U.S. Department of Commerce, Bureau of the Census, *America's Families and Living Arrangements: 2003* (2004) [Available: www.census.gov/prod/2004pubs/p20-553.pdf], Tbls. 2, 5. Federal Interagency Forum, *America's Children*, Fig. 1.

3. Federal Interagency Forum, *America's Children*, Tbl. POP6, Introduction.

4. Daniel U. Levine and Rayna F. Levine, *Society and Education*, 9th ed. (Boston: Allyn & Bacon, 1996), pp. 6–13.

5. George S. Counts, *The Selective Character of American Secondary Education* (Chicago: University of Chicago Press, 1922); Robert S. Lynd and Helen Merrell Lynd, *Middletown: A Study in American Culture* (New York: Harcourt, Brace and World, 1929), Chap. 13.

6. W. Lloyd Warner, Robert J. Havighurst, and Martin B. Loeb, *Who Shall Be Educated: The Challenge of Unequal Opportunity* (New York: Harper and Row, 1944), p. 50.

7. Ibid., p. xi.

8. August B. Hollingshead, *Elmtown's Youth: The Impact of Social Classes on Adolescents* (New York: Wiley, 1949), pp. 168–192, 462.

9. See John Gehring, "Mix of Academics, Technical Skills Heralds a 'New Day' for Vocational Education," *Education Week* (September 27, 2000), pp. 1, 16.

10. Levine and Levine, *Society and Education*, Chap. 2.

11. Ruby K. Payne, *A Framework for Understanding Poverty*, 3rd rev. ed. (Highlands, TX: aha! Process, 2003).

12. Ibid., p. 43.

13. See Joseph W. Newman, "Socioeconomic Class and Education: In What Ways Does Class Affect the Educational Process?" in Joe L. Kincheloe and Shirley R. Steinberg, eds., *Thirteen Questions: Reframing Education's Conversation*, 2nd ed. (New York: Peter Lang, 1995), pp. 195–199, and Sol Adler, *Multicultural Communication Skills in the Classroom: An Interface between Speech-Language Specialists and Educators* (Needham Heights, MA: Allyn & Bacon, 1992).

14. Payne, *A Framework for Understanding Poverty*, p. 100. See also Levine and Levine, *Society and Education*, Chap. 3.

15. Donald A. Hansen, "Family-School Articulations: The Effects of Interaction Rule Mismatch," *American Educational Research Journal* 23 (Winter 1986): 643–659.

16. See Kathleen deMarrais, *The Way Schools Work: A Sociological Analysis of Education*, 3rd ed. (White Plains, NY: Longman Publishing Group, 1998), Chap. 3. The classic study of peer groups in James S. Coleman's *The Adolescent Society* (New York: Free Press, 1971). More recent studies include Philip A. Cusick, *Inside High School: The Student's World* (New York: Holt, Rinehart and Winston, 1973), and Penelope Eckert, *Jocks and Burnouts: Social Categories and Identity in the High School* (New York: Teachers College Press, 1989).

17. Cornelius Riordan, *Equality and Achievement: An Introduction to the Sociology of Education* (Upper Saddle River, NJ: Pearson Prentice Hall, 2004), pp. 117–119, 230–234. For contrasting views of resistance, see Henry A. Giroux, *Theory and Resistance in Education: A Pedagogy for the Opposition* (Westport, CT: Greenwood Publishing Group, 1983), and Paul Willis, *Learning to Labour: How Working Class Kids Get Working Class Jobs* (New York: Columbia University Press, 1981).

18. See Karen L. Kinnear, *Gangs: A Reference Handbook* (Santa Barbara, CA: ABC–CLIO, 1996); and Richard Arthur, *Gangs and Schools* (Holmes Beach, FL: Learning Publications, 1992).

19. "Grappling with Gangs," interview with Mike Knox in *Today's Education* (November 1996), p. 15.

20. Kinnear, *Gangs*, pp. 12–17.

21. Kristen D. Randle, *Breaking Rank* (New York: HarperTempest, 2002), p. 3.

22. U.S. Departments of Education and Justice, National Center for Education Statistics and Bureau of Justice Statistics, *Indicators of School Crime and Safety: 2004* (2004) [Available: nces.ed.gov/pubs2005/2005002.pdf], Executive Summary.

23. Ibid. Regarding zero tolerance, see Richard L. Curwin and Allen N. Mendler, *As Tough as Necessary: Countering Aggression, Violence, and Hostility in Schools* (Washington, DC: Association for Supervision and Career Development, 1999).

24. U.S. Departments of Education and Justice, *Indicators of School Crime and Safety: 2004*, Indicators 17–18.

25. See the nine articles in the May 10, 1999, issue of *Newsweek*, for instance, and the suggestions for teachers in the October 1999 issue of *NEA Today*.

26. For an even-handed discussion of the research, see Debra Viadero, "On the Wrong Track?" *Education Week* (October 14, 1998), pp. 30–31.

27. Jeannie Oakes, *Keeping Track: How Schools Structure Inequality* (New Haven, CT: Yale University Press, 1985); Oakes, *Multiplying Inequalities: The Effects of Race, Social Class, and Tracking on Opportunities to Learn Mathematics and Science* (Santa Monica, CA: Rand Corp., 1990); Oakes, Karen Hunter Quartz, Steve Ryan, and Martin Lipton, *Becoming Good American Schools: The Struggle for Civic Virtue in Education Reform* (San Francisco: Jossey-Bass, 2002); Robert E. Slavin, *Cooperative Learning: Theory, Research, and Practice*, 2nd ed. (Needham Heights, MA: Allyn & Bacon, 1995); Robert E. Slavin and Nancy A. Madden, *One Million Children: Success for All* (Thousand Oaks, CA: Corwin Press, 2000).

28. A study on its way to becoming a classic is Arthur G. Powell, Eleanor Farrar, and David K. Cohen, *The Shopping Mall High School: Winners and Losers in the Educational Marketplace* (Boston: Houghton Mifflin, 1986).

29. Ellen Brantlinger, *Dividing Classes: How the Middle Class Negotiates and Rationalizes School Advantage* (New York: Falmer, 2003); Linda Darling-Hammond, "What Happens to a Dream Deferred? The Continuing Quest for Equal Educational Opportunity," in James A. Banks and Cherry A. McGee Banks, eds., *Handbook of Research on Multicultural Education*, 2nd ed. (San Francisco: Jossey-Bass, 2003), Chap. 29.

30. See the College Board's "Recommended Classes" (2004) [Available: www.collegeboard.com/parents/article/0,3708,703-704-0-21263,00.html]; the ACT's "Recommended College Prep Courses" (2004)

[Available: www.actstudent.org/planning/courses.html]; and Sol H. Pelavin and Michael Kane, *Changing the Odds: Factors Increasing Access to College* (New York: College Entrance Examination Board, 1990).

31. Oakes, *Keeping Track,* and Oakes et al., *Becoming Good American Schools.*

32. Payne, *A Framework for Understanding Poverty,* Chap. 4.

33. Pelavin and Kane, *Changing the Odds,* p. 56.

34. Jeannie Oakes and Martin Lipton, "Detracking Schools: Early Lessons from the Field," *Phi Delta Kappan* 73 (February 1992): 449. Emphasis in the original.

35. Oakes and Lipton, "Detracking Schools," p. 454.

36. Quoted in David Ruenzel, review of Oakes et al., *Becoming Good American Schools, Teacher Magazine* (May 2000), p. 59.

37. Jon Meacham, "The New Face of Race," *Newsweek* (September 18, 2000), pp. 38–41; Clarence Page, "Unspoken Conflicts of Blacks and Latinos," *Mobile Register* (February 10, 2004), p. 11A; Genaro C. Armas, "Census: Half of U.S. Will Be Minorities by 2050," *Mobile Register* (March 18, 2004), p. 7A.

38. Richard T. Shafer, *Racial and Ethnic Groups,* 9th ed. (New York: Prentice Hall, 2003).

39. The discussion in this section is based on Carol Mukhopadhyay and Rosemary C. Henze, "How Real Is Race?" *Phi Delta Kappan* (May 2003): 669–678.

40. This definition comes from Milton M. Gordon's classic study *Assimilation in American Life: The Role of Race, Religion, and National Origins* (New York: Oxford University Press, 1964).

41. See James A. Banks, *Cultural Diversity and Education: Foundations, Curriculum, and Teaching,* 4th ed. (Boston: Allyn and Bacon, 2000), Chaps. 2, 4.

42. Gustav Niebuhr, "Muslims in America: Identity Develops as a Community Grows," *Carnegie Reporter* 4 (Spring 2002): 15–21.

43. For analysis of some of these issues as they relate to whites, see Richard Alba, *Ethnic Identity: The Transformation of White America* (New Haven, CT: Yale University Press, 1992).

44. U.S. Department of Commerce, Bureau of the Census, *Profile of the Foreign-Born Population in the United States: 2000* (2001) [Available: www.census.gov/prod/2002pubs/p23-206.pdf], pp. 8–13; U.S. Immigration and Naturalization Service, "Immigrants, Fiscal Year 1998," *1998 Yearbook of the Immigration and Naturalization Service* (1998) [Available: www.ins.usdoj.gov/graphics/aboutins/statistics/imm98.pdf], pp. 3–15; Lynn Olson, "Mixed Needs of Immigrants Pose Challenges for Schools," *Education Week* (September 27, 2000), pp. 38–39.

45. U.S. Department of Commerce, Bureau of the Census, "Projected Population of the United States, by Race and Hispanic Origin: 2000 to 2050" (2004) [Available: www.census.gov/ipc/www/usinterimproj/natprojtab01a.pdf], Tbl. 1a.

46. Lynn Olson, "Mixed Needs of Immigrants Pose Challenges," p. 38.

47. The discussion in this section is based on Eugene E. Garcia, "Educating Mexican American Students: Past Treatment and Recent Developments in Theory, Research, Policy, and Practice," and Sonia Nieto, "Puerto Rican Students in the United States: A Troubled Past and the Search for a Hopeful Future," in Banks and Banks, eds., *Handbook of Research on Multicultural Education,* Chaps. 24–25.

48. U.S. Department of Commerce, Bureau of the Census, "Hispanic Population Primarily in the West and South" (2004) [Available: factfinder.census.gov/jsp/saff/SAFFInfo.jsp?_pageId=tp9_race_ethnicity].

49. See Amitai Etzioni, "A Diverse Minority Resists Being Labeled," *Brookings Review* (Winter 2002): 10–13.

50. U.S. Department of Commerce, Bureau of the Census, *Statistical Abstract of the United States, 2004–2005* (2004) [Available: www.census.gov/prod/www/statistical-abstract-04.html], Tbls. 665–675; Federal Interagency Forum on Child and Family Statistics, *America's Children,* Education.

51. James D. Anderson, *The Education of Blacks in the South, 1860–1935* (Chapel Hill: University of North Carolina Press, 1988).

52. U.S. Department of Commerce, *Statistical Abstract of the United States, 2004–2005,* Tbls. 665–675, and *Statistical Abstract of the United States, 1999* (1999) [Available: http://www.census.gov/prod/www/statistical-abstract-us.html], Tbl. 747. See William Junius Wilson, *The Truly Disadvantaged: The Inner City, the Underclass, and Public Policy* (Chicago: University of Chicago Press, 1987).

53. Federal Interagency Forum on Child and Family Statistics, *America's Children,* Education.

54. Council for Exceptional Children and National Alliance of Black School Educators, *Addressing Over-Representation of African American Students in Special Education* (2002) [Available: www.cec.sped.org/law_res/doc/resources/files/addressingoverrep.pdf], p. 5.

55. Debra Viadero, "Disparately Disabled," *Quality Counts 2004: Count Me In. Special Education in an Era of Standards*, a special report from *Education Week* (January 8, 2004), pp. 22–26.

56. Valerie Ooka Pang, Peter N. Kiang, and Yoon K. Pak, "Asian Pacific American Students: Challenging a Biased Educational System," in Banks and Banks, eds., *Handbook of Research on Multicultural Education*, Chap. 26, and Jessica L. Sandham, "Educational Needs of Asian Americans Highlighted," *Education Week* (May 21, 1997), p. 8.

57. Noy Thrupkaew, "The Myth of the Model Minority," *The American Prospect* (April 8, 2002): 38–41; Robert C. Johnston, "Who Is 'Asian'? Cultural Differences Defy Simple Categories," *Education Week* (March 15, 2000), p. 21; Peter Schmidt, "After Slow Start, Asian-Americans Beginning to Exert Power on Education-Policy Issues," *Education Week* (February 27, 1991), pp. 1, 18–20.

58. Debra Viadero, "Lags in Minority Achievement Defy Traditional Explanations," *Education Week* (March 22, 2000), p. 19; Levine and Levine, *Society and Education*, pp. 329–334; U.S. Department of Commerce, *Statistical Abstract of the United States, 2004–2005*, Tbls. 665–675.

59. K. Tsianina Lomawaima, "Educating Native Americans," in Banks and Banks, eds., *Handbook of Research on Multicultural Education,* Chap. 22.

60. Lynn Schnaiberg, "Tattered Promise," *Education Week* (March 3, 1999), pp. 1, 40–47.

61. Lomawaima, "Educating Native Americans," p. 332.

62. U.S. Department of Commerce, *Statistical Abstract of the United States, 2004–2005*, Tbl. 35.

63. Levine and Levine, *Society and Education*, pp. 335–341.

64. See the five stories in the special report "Fifty Years after *Brown*: Unequal Education," *U.S. News & World Report* (March 29, 2004), pp. 64–95.

65. Two classic studies of these issues and events are James T. Patterson, *Brown v. Board of Education: A Civil Rights Milestone and Its Troubled Legacy* (New York: Oxford University Press, 2001), and Richard Kluger, *Simple Justice: The History of Brown v. Board of Education and Black America's Struggle for Equality* (New York: Knopf, 1976). For an excellent retrospective, see Forrest R. White, *"Brown Revisited," Phi Delta Kappan* 76 (September 1994): 13–20.

66. The complete text of the *Brown* decision is reprinted in Kluger's *Simple Justice*, pp. 779–785.

67. Gary Orfield, *The Reconstruction of Southern Education: The Schools and the 1964 Civil Rights Act* (New York: Wiley, 1969).

68. Gary Orfield and Susan E. Eaton, *Dismantling Desegregation: The Quiet Reversal of Brown v. Board of Education* (New York: New Press, 1996), Chap. 11.

69. Ibid., Chap. 1.

70. Gary Orfield and John T. Yun, *Resegregation in American Schools* (1999) [Available: www.law.harvard.edu/groups/civilrights/publications.resegregation99.html], p. 6.

71. Orfield and Eaton, *Dismantling Desegregation*, Chap. 3.

72. Ibid.

73. Gary Orfield and Chungmei Lei, Brown *at 50: King's Dream or Plessy's Nightmare?* (2004) [Available: www.civilrightsproject.harvard.edu/research/reseg04/brown50.pdf], p. 2.

74. Ibid., pp. 2–3, 17, 20–21.

75. Ibid., p. 17.

76. Janet Ward Schofield, "Maximizing the Benefits of a Diverse Student Body: Lessons from School Desegregation Research," in Gary Orfield and Michael Kurlaender, eds., *Diversity Challenged: Evidence on the Impact of Affirmative Action* (Cambridge, MA: Harvard Education Publishing Group, 2001), Chap. 4.

77. Rita E. Mahard and Robert L. Crain, "Research on Minority Achievement in Desegregated Schools," in Christine H. Rossell and Willis D. Hawley, eds., *The Consequences of School Desegregation* (Philadelphia: Temple University Press, 1983), pp. 103–125.

78. Orfield and Yun, *Resegregation in American Schools*, p. 16.

79. Ibid.; Orfield and Lei, Brown *at 50,* pp. 21–22.

80. Schofield, "Maximizing the Benefits."

81. Jomills Henry Braddock II and Tamela McNulty Eitle, "The Effects of School Desegregation," in Banks and Banks, eds., *Handbook of Research on Multicultural Education*, Chap. 41.

82. James S. Kunen, "The End of Integration," *Time* (April 29, 1996), p. 44.

83. *USA Today* (May 12, 1994), p. 8A.

84. Orfield and Eaton, *Dismantling Desegregation*, p. 109.

85. Mary Haywood Metz, *Different by Design: The Context and Character of Three Magnet Schools* (New York: Teachers College Press, 2003); Claire Smrekar and Ellen B. Goldring, *School Choice in Urban America: Magnet Schools and the Pursuit of Educational Equity* (New York: Teachers College Press, 1999).

86. Levine and Levine, *Society and Education,* pp. 280–291.

87. See Association for Effective Schools, "What Is Effective Schools Research?" (1996) [Available: www.mes.org/esr.html]. For pioneering studies in this line of research, see Wilbur B. Brookover, *Effective Secondary Schools* (Philadelphia: Research for Better Schools, 1981); Ronald R. Edmonds, "Programs of School Improvement: An Overview," *Educational Leadership* 40 (December 1982): 4–11; and Michael Rutter, Barbara Maughan, Peter Mortimore, and Janet Ouston, *Fifteen Thousand Hours: Secondary Schools and Their Effects on Children* (Cambridge, MA: Harvard University Press, 1979).

88. Carol Ascher, "School Programs for African American Males . . . and Females," *Phi Delta Kappan* 73 (June 1992): 777–782.

89. Viadero, "Lags in Minority Achievement," p. 19; Gerald J. Pine and Asa G. Hilliard III, "Rx for Racism: Imperatives for America's Schools," *Phi Delta Kappan* 71 (April 1990): 593–600.

90. See Vanessa Siddle Walker, *Their Highest Potential: An African American Community in the Segregated South* (Chapel Hill: University of North Carolina Press, 1996).

91. Orfield and Lei, Brown *at 50,* p. 8.

92. John U. Ogbu with Astrid Davis, *Black American Students in an Affluent Suburb: A Study of Academic Disengagement* (Mahwah, NJ: Erlbaum, 2003), p. 281.

93. Brandt Williams, "Roots of Gap Based in Race, Class, Culture Differences," Minnesota Public Radio (2004) [Available: news.minnesota.publicradio.org/features/2004/09/20_williamsb_gapbarriers/].

94. Manny Fernandez, "Actor Defends Better Parenting at Education Forum in D.C.," *Washington Post* (September 9, 2004), p. B3.

95. Signithia Fordham and John U. Ogbu, "Black Students' School Success: Coping with the Burden of 'Acting White,'" *Urban Review* 18 (1986): 176–205. For an insightful discussion of "acting black" as well as "acting white," see Joyce E. King, "Race and Education: In What Ways Does Race Affect the Educational Process?" in Kincheloe and Steinberg, eds., *Thirteen Questions,* pp. 159–179.

96. Levine and Levine, *Society and Education,* pp. 307–310.

97. Caroline Hendrie, "Alienation from High School Is Worst among Black Males, Study Reveals," *Education Week* (January 28, 1998), pp. 1, 11.

98. Abigal Thernstrom and Stephan Thernstrom, *No Excuses: Closing the Racial Gap in Learning* (New York: Simon & Schuster, 2003).

99. Quoted in Fernandez, "Actor Defends Better Parenting," p. B3.

100. Mark Walsh, "Black Private Academies Are Held Up as Filling Void," *Education Week* (March 13, 1991), pp. 1, 28–29.

101. Debra Viadero, "A School of Their Own," *Education Week on the Web* (October 16, 1996) [Available: www.edweek.org/ew/1996/07afro.h16]; Lynn Olson, "Redefining 'Public' Schools," *Education Week* (April 26, 2000), p. 1. On the Afrocentric curriculum, see Joyce Elaine King, "Culture-Centered Knowledge: Black Studies, Curriculum Transformation, and Social Action," in Banks and Banks, eds., *Handbook of Research on Multicultural Education,* Chap. 16, and Molefi Kete Asante, "The Afrocentric Idea in Education," *Journal of Negro Education* 60 (Spring 1991): 170–180.

102. Ascher, "School Programs"; Jawanza Kunjufu, "Detroit's Male Academies: What the Real Issue Is," *Education Week* (November 20, 1991), p. 29.

103. Rosemary C. Salomone, "Sometimes Equal Means Different," *Education Week* (October 8, 1997), pp. 44, 32; Ascher, "School Programs."

104. Donald Leake and Brenda Leake, "African-American Immersion Schools in Milwaukee: A View from the Inside," *Phi Delta Kappan* 73 (June 1992): 783–785.

105. Richard J. Herrnstein and Charles Murray, *The Bell Curve: Intelligence and Class Structure in American Life* (New York: The Free Press, 1994). For a critique of Herrnstein and Murray's position, see Joe L. Kincheloe and Shirley R. Steinberg, eds. *Measured Lies: The Bell Curve Examined* (New York: St. Martin's Press, 1996).

106. W. E. B. Du Bois, "Two Hundred Years of Segregated Schools," in Philip S. Foner, ed., *W. E. B. Du Bois Speaks: Speeches and Addresses, 1920–1963* (New York: Pathfinder Press, 1970), p. 283.

107. Viadero, "Disparately Disabled," pp. 22–26.

108. U.S. Department of Education, National Center for Education Statistics, *English Language Learner Students in U.S. Public Schools: 1994 and 2000* (2004) [Available: nces.ed.gov/pubs2004/2004035.pdf].
109. U.S. Department of Commerce, *Statistical Abstract of the United States, 2004–2005*, Tbl. 48.
110. Joel Spring explores language issues for Mexican Americans and Puerto Ricans in *Deculturalization and the Struggle for Equality: A Brief History of the Education of Dominated Cultures in the United States*, 3rd ed. (New York: McGraw-Hill, 2000), Chaps. 2, 4–5.
111. Schmidt, "After Slow Start"; Sandham, "Educational Needs of Asian Americans."
112. James Crawford's Language Policy Web Site and Emporium, "Language Legislation in the U.S.A." (2003) [Available: ourworld.compuserve.com/homepages/JWCRAWFORD/langleg.htm].
113. James Crawford, *Educating English Learners: Language Diversity in the Classroom*, 5th ed. (Los Angeles: Bilingual Educational Service, 2004).
114. Jonathan Tilove, "Americanization Dulls Values of Inspiration," *Mobile Register* (January 1, 1995), pp. 1C, 4C.
115. "Bilingual Education," *Education Week Research Center* (2004) [Available: www.edweek.org/rc/issues/english-language-learners/].
116. Ibid.
117. Mary Ann Zehr, "Study Gives Advantage to Bilingual Education over Focus on English," *Education Week* (February 4, 2004), p. 10.
118. Quoted in Fernandez, "Actor Defends Better Parenting," p. B3.
119. "Full Text of 'Ebonics' Resolution Adopted by Oakland Board," *Education Week* (January 15, 1997), p. 33.
120. Jack E. White, "Ebonics According to Buckwheat," *Time* (January 13, 1997), p. 62.
121. See, for example, Thomas Sowell, "Teaching of 'Black English' Is More Racial Self-Destruction," *Mobile Register* (December 24, 1996), p. 8A, and Gregory Kane, "Ebonics: An Excuse for Why Black Students Aren't Doing Well," *Mobile Press-Register* (December 29, 1996), p. 1D. One of the few nationally known figures to defend the resolution was Andrew M. Greely in his syndicated editorial "Ebonics Sounds Funny, but It's a Language," *Mobile Register* (January 8, 1997), p. 11A.
122. "Full Text of 'Ebonics' Resolution," p. 33.
123. See Theresa Perry and Lisa Delpit, eds., *The Real Ebonics Debate: Power, Language and the Education of African American Children* (Boston: Beacon Press, 1998); Delpit, *Other People's Children: Cultural Conflict in the Classroom* (New York: New Press, 1996); and Evelyn Baker Dandy, *Black Communications: Breaking Down the Barriers* (Chicago: African American Images, 1991).
124. J. L. Dillard, *Black English: Its History and Usage in the United States* (New York: Vintage, 1973).
125. Ibid.
126. Carlos J. Ovando, "Linguistic Diversity and Education," in James A. Banks and Cherry A. McGee Banks, eds., *Multicultural Education: Issues and Perspectives*, 5th ed. (New York: John Wiley & Sons, 2004), Chap. 12.
127. "Full Text of 'Ebonics' Resolution," p. 33.
128. Kathleen Kennedy Manzo, "Language Lessons," *Education Week* (April 17, 2002), 30–35.
129. Lynn Schnaiberg, "Ebonics' Vote Puts Oakland in Maelstrom," *Education Week* (January 15, 1997), pp. 1, 32–33.
130. Quoted in Ovando, "Language Diversity and Education," p. 298.
131. Lisa Delpit and Joanne Kilgour Dowdy, eds., *The Skin That We Speak: Thoughts on Language and Culture in the Classroom* (New York: W. W. Norton, 2003).
132. Council for Exceptional Children and National Alliance of Black School Educators, *Addressing Over-Representation of African American Students in Special Education*.
133. American Association of University Women, *The AAUW Report: How Schools Shortchange Girls. A Study of Major Findings on Girls and Education* (Washington, DC: AAUW, 1992), pp. v, 2.
134. Myra Sadker, David Sadker, and Lynette Long, "Gender and Educational Equality," in James A. Banks and Cherry A. McGee Banks, eds., *Multicultural Education: Issues and Perspectives*, 3rd ed. (Boston: Allyn and Bacon, 1997), p. 139.
135. American Association of University Women, *Gender Gaps: Where Schools Still Fail Our Children* (Washington, DC: AAUW Educational Foundation, 1998).
136. AAUW Executive Director Janice Weinman quoted in press release "Technology Gender Gap Develops While Gaps in Math and Science Narrow, AAUW Foundation Report Shows" (1998) [Available: www.aauw.org/2000/ggprbd.html].

137. American Association of University Women, *Tech-Savvy: Educating Girls in the New Computer Age* (Washington, DC: AAUW Educational Foundation, 2000).

138. U.S. Department of Education, National Center for Education Statistics, *Trends in Educational Equity of Girls and Women: 2004* (2004) [Available: nces.ed.gov/pubs2005/2005016.pdf], Executive Summary; Christine Hoff Sommers, *The War against Boys: How Misguided Feminism Is Harming Our Young Men* (New York: Simon & Schuster, 2000).

139. American Association of University Women, *Beyond the "Gender Wars": A Conversation about Girls, Boys, and Education* (Washington, DC: AAUW Educational Foundation, 2001).

140. American Association of University Women, *Hostile Hallways: Bullying, Teasing, and Sexual Harassment in Schools* (Washington, DC: AAUW Educational Foundation, 2001), pp. 2–5.

141. Many of these findings are included in the "Report Card" on sexism in David Sadker and Myra Sadker, "Gender Bias: From Colonial America to Today's Classrooms," in Banks and Banks, eds., *Multicultural Education*, pp. 139–144. See also Sadker and Sadker, *Failing at Fairness: How America's Schools Cheat Girls* (New York: Scribner's, 1994), pp. 83–89.

142. Levine and Levine, *Society and Education*, pp. 360–361.

143. Sadker and Sadker, *Failing at Fairness*, pp. 205–209.

144. AAUW, *Hostile Hallways*, pp. 2–5; Donna Eder with Catherine Colleen Evans and Stephen Parker, *School Talk: Gender and Adolescent Culture* (New Brunswick, NJ: Rutgers University Press, 1995), pp. 49–50, Chap. 5; Barrie Thorn, *Gender Play: Girls and Boys in School* (New Brunswick, NJ: Rutgers University Press, 1993), Chap. 7.

145. Rhona Mahony, "Women at Work, Girls at Play," *Ms.* (February 1997), pp. 37–40. For more background, see deMarrais, *The Way Schools Work*, pp. 253–255.

146. Women on Words and Images, *Dick and Jane as Victims: Sex Stereotyping in Children's Readers* (Princeton, NJ: Women on Words and Images, 1975); U.S. Commission on Civil Rights, *Characters in Textbooks: A Review of the Literature* (Washington, DC: Commission on Civil Rights, 1980).

147. Sadker and Sadker, "Gender Bias," pp. 144–148; Gwyneth Britton and Margaret Lumpkin, "Basal Readers: Paltry Progress Pervades," *Interracial Books for Children Bulletin* 14 (1983): 4–7; Sadker and Sadker, *Failing at Fairness*, pp. 69–72.

148. U.S. Department of Commerce, *Statistical Abstract of the United States, 2004–2005*, Tbl. 597; U.S. Department of Education, *Trends in Educational Equity of Girls and Women: 2004*, Tbls. 36–37.

149. James A. Banks, "Multicultural Education: Its Effects on Students' Racial and Gender Role Attitudes," in James P. Shaver, ed., *Handbook of Research on Social Studies Teaching and Learning* (New York: Macmillan, 1991), pp. 459–469.

150. Carol Tavris and Alice R. Baumgartner first reported this research to a popular audience in "How Would Your Life Be Different?" *Redbook* (February 1983), pp. 92–95. Tavris extends the research in *The Mismeasure of Women: Why Women Are Not the Better Sex, the Inferior Sex, or the Opposite Sex* (New York: Touchstone, 1993).

151. Raphaela Best, *We've All Got Scars: What Boys and Girls Learn in Elementary Schools* (Bloomington, IN: Indiana University Press, 1989). See Chapter 2 for a demographic profile of America's teachers.

152. Sadker and Sadker, "Gender Bias," pp. 148–151, and "Sexism in the Schoolroom of the 1980s," *Psychology Today* (March 1985): 54–57.

153. Sadker and Sadker, *Failing at Fairness*, Chap. 3; Marlaine E. Lockheed with Susan S. Klein, "Sex Equity in Classroom Climate and Organization," in Klein, ed., *Handbook for Achieving Sex Equity through Education* (Baltimore, MD: Johns Hopkins University Press, 1989), Chap. 11.

154. Louis Fischer, David Schimmel, and Leslie R. Stellman, *Teachers and the Law*, 6th ed. (Boston: Allyn and Bacon, 2003), Chap. 15.

155. Ibid.; American Association of University Women, *A License for Bias: Sex Discrimination, Schools, and Title IX* (Washington, DC: AAUW Legal Advocacy Group, 2000); Sadker and Sadker, "Gender Bias," pp. 139–144; Erik W. Robelen, "Administration Criticized on Girls' Education Issues," *Education Week* (April 14, 2004), p. 32.

156. U.S. Department of Education, *Trends in Educational Equity*, Tbl. 21.

157. Ibid., Tbl. 29.

158. Sadker and Sadker, "Gender Bias," pp. 153–154.

159. Ibid.

160. Tal Barak, "Number of Single-Sex Schools Growing," *Education Week* (October 20, 2004), p. 33.
161. Michelle R. Davis, "Federal Study Examining Single-Sex Public Schools," *Education Week* (March 24, 2004), pp. 24–28.
162. Sommers, *The War against Boys*.
163. Henry Pollack, *Real Boys: Rescuing Our Sons from the Myths of Boyhood* (New York: Henry Holt, 1999).
164. "Pay Closer Attention: Boys Are Struggling Academically," *USA Today* (December 3, 2004), p. 12A.
165. Michael Gurian and Patricia Henley with Terry Trueman, *Boys and Girls Learn Differently! A Guide for Teachers and Parents* (San Francisco: Jossey-Bass, 2001).
166. Still one of the best and most-cited analyses of these complex issues is Julia A. Sherman's "Sex-Related Cognitive Differences: A Summary of Theory and Practice," *Integrateducation* 16 (January–February 1978): 40–42. See also Levine and Levine, *Society and Education*, pp. 356–360.
167. AAUW, *How Schools Shortchange Girls*, pp. 28–32.
168. Ned Noddings discusses phases similar to these in "Feminist Critiques in the Professions," in Courtney B. Cazden, ed., *Review of Research in Education*, vol. 16 (Washington, DC: American Educational Research Association, 1990), Chap. 8.
169. Carol Gilligan, *In a Different Voice: Psychological Theory and Women's Development* (Cambridge, MA: Harvard University Press, 1982).
170. See Jane Roland Martin, *Reclaiming a Conversation* (New York: Yale University Press, 1985), and Mary Field Belenky, Blythe McVicker Clinchy, Nancy Rule Goldberg, and Fill Mattuck Tarrule, *Women's Ways of Knowing: The Development of Self, Voice, and Mind* (New York: Basic Books, 1988).
171. Noddings, "Feminist Critiques," p. 396.
172. Nel Noddings, *A Feminine Approach to Ethics and Moral Education*, 2nd ed. (Berkeley: University of California Press, 2003).

CHAPTER 9

POLITICS OF EDUCATION

Since 2001, the biggest story in the politics of education has been No Child Left Behind. This federal law mandates such sweeping reform at every level of government, in every public school in the nation, that no other development in education since the 1970s even approaches its significance. The attention we are paying to NCLB throughout this textbook reflects the changes it is making in the real world of the schools. This chapter on the politics of education considers NCLB— and other developments as well—in the context of the political world you are preparing to enter as a teacher.

Think of *politics* as the pursuit of power and influence and the *politics of education* as the quest to control the schools. When a teacher organization stages a public rally for higher salaries, for instance, or when judges order a state legislature to change the way it finances the schools, average citizens who usually show little interest in the schools may stop and take notice. "Those teachers (or judges) have gone too far this time!" one citizen complains. "What do they want—to run the schools?" "No, they don't want complete control," another replies, "but they're willing to use the power they have. Just look at what the local school board (or state legislature) did to force the showdown. Somebody had to call their hand."

Controversies often make the front page of the newspaper, but usually the quest for control of the schools goes on barely noticed by most Americans. It becomes part of the political routine. A local board listens to a parent's concerns about religion in the schools. A state legislature debates alternate routes into teaching. The U.S. Senate's Education Committee holds hearings on the effectiveness of the Title I compensatory education program that provides the legal framework for No Child Left Behind. The results of these deliberations can be just as far reaching as the effects of a union rally or a court order, yet few citizens—including few teachers—pay close attention. This chapter shows what they're missing.

I will organize our discussion of politics around the three levels of government in the United States: *local, state,* and *federal*. At each level, numerous groups compete for control. Major players in the politics of education include elected and appointed officials, ranging from school board members to legislators to judges; education bureaucrats who work in local school districts, state departments of education, and the U.S. Department of Education; teachers and teacher organizations; other education groups, from university teacher educators to parent-teacher organizations; business groups; labor unions; foundations; testing companies; textbook publishers; religious groups; and individual citizens.

This list is long but incomplete. The reason is that so many hands work the controls of American public education. No single level of government and no single group of people are completely in charge. Instead, power is shared, and the balance of power among the levels and the groups is constantly shifting. In order to untangle a fascinating web of political influences, we will begin at the local level, move to the state and then the federal level, and conclude the chapter with a discussion of educational finance.

LOCAL POLITICS OF EDUCATION

Regulations from Above, Pressure from Below

Most Americans believe public schools should be run from the grassroots up. The thirty-sixth annual Phi Delta Kappa/Gallup poll (2004) confirms the findings of the thirty-five preceding polls: The public gives high marks to local control of the schools. Most people believe local actors in the politics of education have the strongest commitment to improving the schools. Local teachers, in fact, get the highest marks for their commitment. Most citizens give the public schools in their immediate area much better ratings than public schools in general. Localism in education, it seems, is an almost unquestioned good thing.[1]

As we saw in Chapter 6, though, local control has been slipping away since the last century, and the trend has only accelerated during the last three decades. Local school board members, traditionally the voice of the public in public education, feel hemmed in by regulations from above and pressure from below. The regulations come from the states and, increasingly under No Child Left Behind, the federal government. The pressure comes from parents, teachers, and other citizens who demand a more direct voice in running the schools.[2]

It is a great political irony that President Ronald Reagan, a strong advocate of decentralization and local control, helped governors and state legislators centralize control over public education in the state capitals. When Reagan came to Washington, the states were already taking on greater financial responsibility for the schools, and his administration handed off even more of the bills—and more of the control—to the states. Under two very different successors, George H. Bush and Bill Clinton, state school reforms inspired by the Reagan administration's report *A Nation at Risk* (1983) generated one regulation after another for local school boards to follow.[3]

The No Child Left Behind Act of 2001 has further increased state control, but with an important political twist. Now the federal government has established broad policies in curriculum and teaching—areas it has always talked about but never regulated—and *required* the states to fill in one regulatory detail after another. Under George W. Bush, NCLB is creating a new chain of educational command with the federal government at the business end. As standards, assessments, and accountability rain down from the federal to the state to the local level, local school boards feel more tightly controlled than ever.

Local boards also feel pressure from below. Teachers, parents, and other local political actors, while not as powerful a force as top-down regulations, are pushing a variety of agendas and competing with local board members for power and influence. Control is also slipping away from local superintendents, the chief administrators who once ran school districts while board members quietly nodded their approval.

Local Boards and Local Superintendents

Operating in a climate of change, some 97,000 board members and 15,000 superintendents are still trying to govern the nation's 15,000 local school districts. These districts are quite diverse, ranging from New York City with its one million students to the 3,000 districts enrolling fewer than 300 students. Most local systems are small—50 percent have fewer than 1,000 students—yet the largest 6 percent, with 10,000 to 1 million students each, educate half the students in the nation.[4]

Americans say they want local governments to become more involved with education, and, in some districts, the voters seem to be paying more attention to school board elections. Why, the candidates in some communities are even running on the issues.[5]

I say this with tongue in cheek because local board elections have traditionally been low-interest, no-issue events. Drive through a community just before a school board election and look for the candidates' signs. Read the local newspapers and check whether the candidates are addressing any issues. Unless a controversy happens to be raging, the candidates may not even bother to campaign. Candidates in about half the districts, in fact, neither take stands nor campaign, and voter turnout is notoriously low.

In other districts, by contrast, the elections are issue oriented and hotly contested. Candidates stake out positions, and large numbers of voters go to the polls to express their preferences. Americans who live in the kind of community I describe in the paragraph above may find it hard to believe how controversial school board politics can become in other communities. Conservative Christian groups, taxpayer organizations, chambers of commerce, and teacher unions—to name four of the most powerful forces—have the dedication and the resources to turn up the heat in local elections. These and other groups square off on such issues as the board's budget, the employment of gay and lesbian teachers, and the content of the science curriculum. In Boston, Chicago, Cleveland, Baltimore, New York City, the District of Columbia, and several other large school districts, local boards have become so controversial and so unpopular with some of their constituents, they have been taken over and restructured by mayors and other political officials.[6]

Community Power Structure.   School board politics vary because communities vary. The power structure of a community has a strong influence on the way it selects people to oversee the public schools. As Joel Spring explains in *Conflict of Interests: The Politics of American Education* (2005), political researchers have developed a number of models to classify community power structures. Most of the models arrange communities on a continuum—from *monolithic* to *pluralistic,* for instance—based on how widely political power is shared. Does a single group of community elites dominate local politics, or do several groups, elite as well as nonelite, compete for control?[7]

Monolithic communities in which one group calls the shots are often rural areas, small towns, or one-industry cities. In these communities, the group in control may appoint the school board. If the members are elected, incumbents usually run without opposition.

At the other end of the continuum, *pluralistic communities* have competitive and often bitterly contested school board elections. In such communities, typically suburbs and diversified cities, candidates campaign on the issues. Although they may state their positions as simply as "against new taxes" or "for school prayer and family values," the candidates speak a language voters seem to understand.

Once elected to a local board, members are responsible for establishing policies for the school district. Local boards make policy within the limits set by the state legislature and state board of education. The state prescribes the minimum course of study required for high school graduation, for instance, but the local board approves the courses that satisfy the requirements. The state sets the

■ ■ ■ ■ ■

BOX 9.1

THE SUPERINTENDENTS' POINT OF VIEW

Get the point of view of superintendents and other administrators from the American Association of School Administrators at www.aasa.org

requirements for teacher licensing, but the local board approves the hiring of teachers. The state sends down state and federal money, but the local board approves the district budget.

Superintendents and Policy Approval.   Traditionally, local board members have relied on the advice of a superintendent of schools, whom they appoint as the district's chief administrator. The superintendent, along with other administrators in the central office and in the schools, is responsible for managing the system on a day-to-day basis. The superintendent recommends policies for the board's approval.

Since the early 1900s, as Chapter 6 points out, superintendents and their staffs have done much more than manage and recommend. Often they have run the show. Superintendents enjoyed the peak of their influence from the 1920s through the 1950s. Although board members held the votes, more often than not they rubber-stamped the superintendent's recommendations. Superintendents positioned themselves as educational experts, the *real* professionals in the school system. Their graduate degrees in school administration and experience in the schools set them apart from everyone else—board members, teachers, parents, other citizens—or so they were able to claim.[8]

During the reign of superintendents and their staffs, school board meetings were typically open-and-shut affairs. The superintendent set the agenda, coached the board through the meeting, and answered questions. At the end, the superintendent thanked the board for approving every recommendation intact. Local board meetings were usually respectable, dull, and poorly attended.

Reinventing Local Control: The Changing Politics of School Districts

There have always been exceptions to this idealized portrait, of course, and in more and more school districts, the exceptions are becoming the rule. Even in rural and small-town America, board members are coming under fire, and superintendents are finding their judgment increasingly called into question.

In a nation with rapidly diversifying demographics, 95 percent of local superintendents are still white, and 87 percent are still male. The superintendency, once a stable job for white males who could play the game and play it well, has become a revolving door. Calling the job stressful is an understatement, as

William Hayes explains from personal experience in *So You Want To Be a Superintendent?* (2001). The average superintendent lasts five or six years on the job, and many districts face a shortage of applicants for a replacement.[9]

Teacher Power and Parent Power.   One reason the superintendency has changed is that teachers have changed. The American Federation of Teachers (AFT) has long advocated teacher power, and superintendents and school boards have had to handle the larger AFT locals with care. The National Education Association (NEA), once little more than a punch-and-cookies society at the local level, is now a formidable union with impressive strength at the grassroots level. Teacher power is a reality, a fact of political life.[10]

Parents have also changed. There have always been a few parents who refused to take no for an answer, who were determined to challenge a textbook, test, or discipline policy. Since the 1960s, activist parents have become more numerous and more insistent, or so it seems to teachers, administrators, and board members. These parents act as if the schools belong to *them.*

Some of the most politically involved parents are fundamentalist Christians. More than willing to stand up for their beliefs, they feel empowered by the results of recent elections that have given George W. Bush a second term as president and increased conservative influence at all three levels of government. We will examine their role in local school politics in a moment.

Assertive Board Members.   Most local boards are jealously guarding the power and influence they have left. Assertive board members, long a fixture in large urban school districts, are now appearing in districts throughout the nation, particularly in the once-complacent suburbs.

Assertive members come to the board with their own agenda. Fed up with high taxes and wasteful spending, they may try to bring sound business principles to the school system. They may poke into detailed financial records other board members never knew existed. They may cross the line into management and invade the superintendent's turf. Assertive board members may try to reform the curriculum, in which case they will almost certainly lock horns with parents, teachers, administrators, and state officials who do not share their views. Or assertive members may be the only representatives of their race or ethnic group on the board, which may lead them to challenge such policies as standardized testing and ability grouping or to push for multicultural education. They can grow frustrated when they find that other players in the politics of education, whether in the same community, the state capital, or Washington, can make it so difficult to reform the schools.[11]

On the other hand, assertive board members can be highly successful when they advance their agenda with the support of activist parents. Conservative Christians, as we will see in the next section, are becoming adept at doing just that.

A Push from the Religious Right.   Fundamentalist Christians take credit for reelecting George W. Bush in 2004, and they are flexing their muscle in numerous political arenas—including the politics of education.[12] Leaders of the Christian Coalition, Eagle Forum, and Family Research Council believe Americans are concerned above all else about "moral issues," which conservative Christians view from the perspective of their own religious faith. Roberta Combs, president of the Christian Coalition, argues that

> the election [of 2004] demonstrates that a majority of Americans are tired of being told they should somehow be ashamed of highlighting their faith in the public square—and yet should accept every ideology, depravity or secular idea that liberals promote. The election results show pro-family Americans stood up and said "enough is enough!"

"Let's take America back," Combs urges.[13]

For activists on the religious right, reforming public education is near the top of the agenda. Ralph Reed, former executive director of the Christian Coalition and now an operative for the Republican Party, maintains that "if we lose our children, our culture, we will have failed ourselves and our God. We cannot fail."[14] For Reed and other politically involved fundamentalists, grassroots action at the local level is the key to reform. "I would exchange the Presidency for 2,000 school board seats," Reed stated.[15]

The Christian Coalition and Eagle Forum distribute voter guides that rate candidates on how closely their views conform to the organizations' views. The "School Board Candidate Questionnaire" (2004) from the Eagle Forum asks such questions as:

- Do you believe schools should give primary emphasis to teaching basic skills (e.g. reading, grammar, spelling, arithmetic) rather than social or psychological matters?
- Do you support the teaching of abstinence as the norm for unmarried teenagers and as the only truly effective way to prevent sexually-transmitted diseases?
- Do you reject classroom instruction that downgrades American sovereignty, limited constitutional government, or private enterprise?
- Do you believe in the fundamental right of parents to direct the upbringing and education of their children?[16]

Churches and other supportive groups circulate the voter guides, which purport to be nonpartisan although they consistently favor Republicans.

A visit to the Web sites of the Christian Coalition, Eagle Forum, and Family Research Council reveals their educational goals are very similar. In addition to the goals you can infer from the candidate questionnaire, the three organizations support government vouchers that give parents a choice between public and private education; home schooling; "Prayer and Pledge"—organized school prayer and daily Pledge of Allegiance to the flag; prominent display of the Ten Commandments; the presentation of creationism alongside evolution in science classes; and a ban on classroom discussions of gays, lesbians, and alternative lifestyles. (See Chapters 5, 8, 10, and 11 for more information on these issues.)

■ ■ ■ ■ ■

BOX 9.2

**THE CHRISTIAN COALITION, THE EAGLE FORUM,
AND THE FAMILY RESEARCH COUNCIL**

Find out more about the Christian Coalition at www.cc.org, Eagle Forum at www.eagleforum.org, and Family Research Council at www.frc.org

No Child Left Behind encourages activism on these issues. Highlighting the emotional issue of school prayer, the federal law requires all local school districts to certify that they have no policies that prevent "constitutionally protected prayer." Guidelines issued by the U.S. Department of Education explain the circumstances under which prayer is legal in public schools. Students can pray quietly before meals in the cafeteria and in other noninstructional settings, for instance, and participate in "Meet you at the flagpole" prayers before school. The Department of Education has also established a Center of Faith-Based and Community Initiatives that awards grants to religious groups that want to conduct moral and character education programs.[17]

Board members and parents who bring a heavy religious agenda to the table know they have to be careful how they pursue their goals. Don't "come across as a crackpot," members of the Christian Coalition advise one another. "Stay in the mainstream of the Main Street of your community."[18] Because the labels *Christian Coalition* and *Eagle Forum* have become so emotionally charged, activists sometimes do not advertise their organizational affiliations.

Estimating the strength of conservative Christians on local boards is difficult. The Christian Coalition claims 2 million members nationwide, the Eagle Forum and Family Research Council fewer than 100,000 members each. But many conservative Christians do not belong to any activist political or educational group. Surveys by the *American School Board Journal* show that although half of local board members describe themselves as religious conservatives and two-thirds as political conservatives, smaller proportions support key items of the religious right agenda. Only one in three board members favors amending the U.S. Constitution to allow organized school prayer, for instance, and only one in three supports government vouchers for private school choice.[19]

Even so, conservative Christians are a force to be reckoned with. They excel at turning out large numbers of their flock in local school board elections—which sometimes attract as few as 5 percent of registered voters.[20]

Local Board Members: Demographics and Representation

"Like Typical Politicians." What kinds of people serve on local school boards? Because Americans cling so strongly to their belief in local control, it seems reasonable to find out more about the board members who represent the people. According to a report prepared in 2002 for the National School Boards Association, the average member is a white male, age 40 to 59, college educated, married, and employed in a managerial or professional position with an annual household income of $75,000 or more. Thirty-seven percent have a household income greater than $100,000. Board members put in long hours of school-related work on top of their regular jobs, and typically for just a few hundred dollars per month.[21]

Of course, people with other demographic characteristics also serve on local boards. Thirty-nine percent of the members are women—an increase over 1978, when only 26 percent were female. Minorities hold approximately 14 percent of board seats. Some 8 percent of the members are African American, 4 percent are Hispanic American, and smaller percentages are Asian American and Native American.[22] Female representation now appears to be holding steady and minority representation to be increasing. Overall, as the *American School Board Journal* observed in 1996, "school board members are an amazingly stable group whose demographics have changed relatively little" since the journal has conducted research.[23]

Discussing this profile, the students in my introductory education classes often say local board members "look like typical politicians." Well, they should. Local board members *are* politicians. Under the broad definition of politics as the pursuit of power and influence, board members are directly involved in the quest for control of the schools—but so are numerous other people, including teachers and parents, whom we usually do not think of as politicians. Perhaps we should, because some of them are as involved as board members in the quest for control.

What my students have in mind, though, is the more traditional view of a politician as an office seeker or office holder. More than 95 percent of local board members are elected to office, and almost all of them run in nonpartisan contests in which they do not declare their affiliation with a political party. The remaining members are appointed by a mayor, city council, county commission, or another governmental body.[24]

How well local school board members represent their constituents is a controversial issue. Demographically, they do not reflect the U.S. population. Females, who make up 51 percent of the population, are still underrepresented on local boards. Hispanic Americans and African Americans, who together account for 27 percent of the population and 36 percent of public school students,

■ ■ ■ ■ ■ ▬▬▬

BOX 9.3

NATIONAL SCHOOL BOARDS ASSOCIATION

The National School Boards Association is the advocacy group for local school board members. Visit the association's Web site at www.nsba.org

are *seriously* underrepresented. And unlike most board members, most Americans are not college educated, nor are most Americans professionals or managers with incomes in excess of $75,000.[25]

The elite makeup of local boards has been a sensitive issue since the rise of common schools, with underrepresented groups complaining board members neglect their children's educational needs. African Americans, Hispanic Americans, other racial and ethnic groups, the poor—their complaints are well documented if not well heeded.

"Do You Have to Be One to Represent One?"   This blunt, provocative question, put several years ago to the board in my community, goes to the heart of the representation controversy.

From one point of view, the answer to the question is a definite *yes*. If a group has been the victim of longstanding discrimination, members of that group have developed insights into critical issues that other people, however sympathetic and well intended, simply lack. African Americans understand segregation as white Americans never can. The very idea of an all-white school board drawing up a desegregation plan for a district that is predominantly black! In a district with a substantial percentage of African American students, black representation on the school board is not just desirable. From this point of view, it is essential. The same reasoning is often applied to Hispanic representation and less frequently to the representation of women, the poor, and other groups.

From another point of view, this kind of reasoning is dangerous. It smacks of quotas. If the courts can order changes in election procedures that virtually ensure the election of blacks to local school boards—as indeed the courts have—what will be next? A decision that, depending on a district's demographic makeup, a certain percentage of board members must be women, or working-class people, or people with no more than a high school education?

Granted that board members and their constituents often come from different backgrounds, the representatives can make an extra effort to stand in other people's shoes. There is no single Hispanic American, African American, female, or working-class perspective; there are many perspectives. Besides, most board members say they regard themselves as trustees who act as their own judgment dictates rather than delegates obligated to do what their constituents want. Thus the idea of demographic representation seems wrongheaded to some Americans.

Local Board Elections: At Large or by Subdistricts?

Although it seems doubtful that court decisions will ever go as far as the previous paragraphs suggest, legal challenges to election procedures could eventually increase the percentage of racial and ethnic minorities on local school boards. Today, 57 percent of board members are elected *at large:* Every voter in the community can cast a ballot for every seat on the board. Candidates campaign throughout the entire school district because they are supposed to represent the whole community rather than particular neighborhoods, wards, or subdistricts.

Many local systems that once elected board members from subdistricts switched to at-large elections in the early 1900s. As we saw in Chapter 6, turn-of-the-century reformers argued that people with the reputation and resources necessary to mount a districtwide campaign had a broader vision than people elected to represent individual subdistricts. Reformers referred to the board members at-large elections produced—successful professionals and businesspeople by and large—as persons of the "better sort."[26]

Racial and Ethnic Bias.   Not only do at-large elections introduce a social class bias into school board politics, in districts where whites compete with others for control of the schools, they also introduce a racial and ethnic bias. I am not exaggerating when I describe the elections as competitions for control. In most at-large elections, voters polarize by race and ethnicity, with whites voting for whites, blacks for blacks, and Hispanics for Hispanics.

Apparently many Americans believe you *do* have to be one to represent one. Except in communities where blacks or Hispanics are in the majority, at-large elections virtually ensure whites will sweep every seat on the school board.[27]

The balance of political power has been shifting, though, and the changes make a fascinating study in the politics of education. In *Bolden v. City of Mobile* (1980), a voting-rights case that originated in my Alabama community, the U.S. Supreme Court ruled against a group of African American voters who challenged Mobile's at-large elections. According to the court, the plaintiffs failed to prove the city had adopted and maintained at-large elections with a discriminatory *intent.* Two years later, in an amendment to the Voting Rights Act of 1965, Congress overrode the decision by stipulating plaintiffs need only show the discriminatory *effect* of election procedures.[28]

Encouraged by this change, African American and Hispanic American voters filed a series of lawsuits against at-large elections. Beginning in the Southeast, spreading to the Southwest, and gradually reaching the rest of the nation, the legal challenges held out the promise of significantly increasing minority representation on local school boards. In Mobile, the change from at-large to by-subdistrict procedures led to the election of two African Americans to a five-person board, mirroring almost exactly the racial composition of the community. In other communities, the results were similar, and now the gains are showing up in the national demographics of board members. The share of local board seats that minorities hold in the 2000s—14 percent—has more than doubled since the 1980s. Looking at the other side of the coin, we can see that more than eight out of ten board members are still white. Minority representation still has a long way to go.[29]

Although the courts have allowed the scope of at-large election suits to broaden from discrimination against African Americans to discrimination against Hispanic Americans and Native Americans, the courts have acted cautiously. In every case, the burden has been on the racial or ethnic group to prove at-large elections have kept members of the group out of office.[30]

Social Class Bias.   The courts have never allowed the scope of voting rights cases to broaden to social class—to discrimination against poor people as a group—even though the evidence is clear that school districts switched to at-large elections in order to ensure the dominance of high-status board members. Could poor people argue at-large elections continue to deny them seats on local boards? That is an intriguing question, certainly, but the courts have consistently refused to consider social class as a factor comparable to race and ethnicity in discrimination suits.[31]

Since the late 1970s, the most striking demographic trend on local school boards has been the election of more female and minority members. There have been no signs of a trend toward poorer board members. Today only 2 percent live in a household that earns less than $25,000—the land of minimum wage—and only about 15 percent have a household income below the national average of $44,000.[32]

The conclusion George S. Counts reached seventy years ago in his pioneering study *The Social Composition of Boards of Education: A Study in the Social Control of Public Education* (1927) still rings true:

> The [typical] board shows a tendency to be narrowly selective. It is composed, for the most part, of college and university men who occupy favored positions in society. The dominant classes of our society dominate the board of education.[33]

STATE POLITICS OF EDUCATION

A varied cast of characters takes the stage as our discussion turns to the state level. Although I will put the spotlight on elected and appointed officials—governors, legislators, state school superintendents, and state school board members—you should be aware many other actors have important roles.

Lobbyists for groups ranging from teacher unions to the chamber of commerce compete for control of the schools. Insiders know restaurants in the state capital are where the real political deals go down. Lobbyists invite legislators to dinner, remind them of campaign contributions, and ask them to take particular stands on key issues. The governor and his or her staff receive the same treatment, and so, to a lesser degree, do the state superintendent of schools, other top officials in the state department of education, and members of the state board of education.

State board meetings, once sleepy affairs, have become lively and controversial. Parents, teachers, and other citizens ask for time to state their views on issues ranging from alleged obscenity in textbooks to teacher licensing standards to high-stakes student tests mandated by No Child Left Behind. The courts also play a role in the politics of education because various actors ask them to referee disputes with other actors. These examples suggest the large number of players and the wide range of issues involved in the state politics of education.[34]

Standing back and taking stock of all this activity, we can safely say the state-level politics of education were already busy before 2001. After NCLB put the states in charge of implementing what longtime observers say is "arguably the most sweeping federal school reform legislation in U.S. history," the activity level *doubled*.[35]

How States Carry Out Their Educational Responsibilities

State Legislatures.   Legally, education is a function of state government. The U.S. Constitution doesn't even mention education; it is a responsibility reserved to the states. Within each state, the ultimate responsibility for public education rests with the legislature.

Much of the legislature's power is financial, because it has the authority to levy taxes and appropriate money to the schools. The state government is often the major source of funding for public education. While the legislature is in session, attention naturally focuses on the education budget, which often accounts for one-third to one-half of all the money the state spends. Legislators who serve on the education committee, finance committee, and other committees with direct influence on the schools play leading roles in the state politics of education.

Since the 1980s, state legislatures have stepped up their involvement in educational policy making, and NCLB has encouraged them to do even more. Pressing well beyond financial matters, legislators have tackled issues ranging from high school graduation requirements to teacher education and licensing standards. Along with governors, they have reasserted their control over the schools. Later in this section, we will focus on the emergence of governors and legislators as school reformers.

State Boards of Education.   State legislatures cannot run the schools alone, and historically they have delegated some of their authority to other groups. In every state but Wisconsin and Minnesota, the legislature authorizes a state board of education to oversee the state school system. Within the limits established by the legislature, state boards of education carry out three major responsibilities:

1. Establishing standards and assessments for elementary and secondary schools.
2. Establishing standards and assessments for teacher education and licensing.
3. Distributing state and federal funds to local school systems.

Although these duties may look dry on paper, they are anything but. Just ask board members who have voted on where to set the cutoff (pass-fail) score on the state high school graduation exam how strongly parents and students feel. Talk about an issue with "high stakes." No Child Left Behind calls public attention to the performance of four subgroups of students: poor, minority, limited English proficient, and disabled. Sensitive to charges of bias and discrimination, boards spend hours analyzing the impact of standardized testing on each subgroup.

How to treat students with disabilities fairly under NCLB has become an especially pressing issue for state boards. Although the federal law permits accommodations in testing procedures for special education students, all students except those with the most severe disabilities must meet the same standards. Special education advocacy groups and parents of children with disabilities regularly appear at state board meetings to make their views—usually their objections—known. As we saw in Chapter 8, the criteria used to classify students as disabled are controversial in themselves because they necessarily involve issues of social class, race and ethnicity, and language and dialect.[36]

For further evidence that board members' lives are anything but dull, ask them how they think the science curriculum should present the origins of the universe. The controversy over evolution versus creationism is heating up again, forcing state boards to referee the many disputes that originate in local school districts. These arguments often pit members of the American Civil Liberties Union against members of the Christian Coalition and Eagle Forum. A 2005 case in a suburban Atlanta school district resulted in a federal court decision ordering a local board to remove stickers it had placed inside biology textbooks—stickers that, according to the court, were intended to cast doubt on evolution.[37]

Demographically, state board of education members are similar to local board members. The average member is a middle-aged white male who is college-educated and professional or managerial, although more women and minorities are gaining seats at the table. In about three-fourths of the states, the governor or legislature appoints the members of the state board. In the remaining states, voters elect the board. The issues of representation we analyzed at the local level also apply to the state level, and minority voters have been challenging at-large elections to state boards of education.[38]

State Superintendents and State Departments of Education.   State board members turn over the management and operation of the state school system to a superintendent and an administrative staff. The state superintendent is often an up-from-the-ranks educator with experience as a teacher, principal, and local superintendent. Many state superintendents still come up through the "good old boy" education network. Make that the good old *person* network, because almost half the state superintendents are now women—a real break with the past—even if the vast majority are still white. Most are appointed by the state board or governor.[39]

Historically, state superintendents have played *the* leading roles in the state politics of education. Horace Mann's official title in Massachusetts was Secretary of the State Board of Education, but in fact he was America's first activist state superintendent. Following in Mann's footsteps, state superintendents have tended to overshadow state board members. Billing themselves, like local superintendents, as educational experts, they have used their influence to shape policy. Since the emergence of reform-minded governors and legislators during the 1980s, however, state superintendents have lost some of their power.

If the state board's chief administrator is the state superintendent, the board's administrative staff is the state department of education. Ranging from secretaries and clerks to experienced educators with doctoral degrees, state department personnel are the bureaucrats who conduct the daily business of the state school system. State departments have grown in size and importance—some of the larger ones employ more than one thousand people. Traditionally, state department personnel have had such responsibilities as conducting research, accrediting local schools, approving teacher education programs, issuing teacher licenses, drawing up curriculum standards, and supervising testing programs. During the 1980s and 1990s, their responsibilities for curriculum and testing increased tremendously.

Now, in the 2000s, No Child Left Behind is increasing their workload to the breaking point. Marc S. Tucker and Thomas S. Toch of the National Center on Education and the Economy vividly describe the situation in the September 2004 *Phi Delta Kappan*: "Like 220 volts of current being forced through a 110-volt kitchen appliance, the system is becoming overloaded, and the smoke is rising."[40]

As if getting state standards and assessments into place were not enough, state department staffers must now monitor the results in each of the nation's 15,000 local school districts. The average state department has 300 districts to keep track of. The thousands of specialists in assessment, evaluation, and statistics who are needed to do the job simply do not exist. The states must hire even larger numbers of specialists in curriculum and supervision to intervene in local schools declared *in need of improvement* for failing to meet their adequate yearly proficiency (AYP) goals for two consecutive years. As Tucker and Toch put it, "these interventions by the state are where the rubber of NCLB will really meet the road."[41]

We will return to this issue at the end of our discussion of state reform. First, though, we will back up and travel the road that led us to No Child Left Behind. The federal law, although pathbreaking in some ways, is in other respects the logical extension of several decades of school reform.

State Politicians Discover School Reform

Jumping on the Bandwagon.   With the release of *A Nation at Risk* (1983) and the flood of education reports that followed, state politicians found an issue they could run with. Who could be opposed to a slogan as positive as "excellence in education"? Governors, legislators, state school superintendents, and state board of education members scrambled to be first in line to make the schools excellent.

Although enthusiasm for state school reform dropped off a bit in the late 1980s and early 1990s, President Clinton helped reenergize the movement during his second administration, and President George W. Bush took it to a new level by requiring every state to jump on the bandwagon. Despite their obvious differences, both Clinton and Bush first attracted attention as education governors, and their views on standards, assessments, and accountability are amazingly similar.

Four Waves of State Reform.   In the era just before *A Nation at Risk,* the major state response to educational problems was climbing aboard the back-to-basics bandwagon that was already rolling through local school districts. Minimum competency tests for students were the most visible result of this first wave of state reform. By 1980, thirty-eight states had mandated the tests, and by 1990, forty-seven states. Some states also raised the grade-point averages and test scores required for admission to teacher education programs. Although the states often copied one another, especially in adopting minimum competency tests, there was little coordination of efforts.[42]

■ ■ ■ ■ ■

BOX 9.4

ABOUT STATE EDUCATIONAL REFORM

Take a look behind the scenes of state educational reform. Visit the National Governors Association at www.nga.org, the Education Commission of the States at www.ecs.org, National Association of State Boards of Education at www.nasbe.org, and the Council of Chief State Officers at www.ccsso.org

Within the states, much of the leadership came from state boards and departments of education. State board members, traditionally among the least important state politicians, were finally beginning to stretch their muscles as if waking up from a long nap. State departments of education, led by state superintendents, stayed busy putting new board policies into effect. But in most states, educational reform still had not attracted the sustained attention of governors and state legislators.

The release of *A Nation at Risk* in 1983, followed by one report after another on the schools, changed the situation. Suddenly almost every state politician wanted to be a school reformer. The result was a second wave of reform, a wave that moved across the states in a surprisingly uniform way. Almost every state raised high school graduation requirements, expanded minimum competency testing into an array of "student performance indicators," and developed new tests for teacher education and licensing.

Governors provided much of the leadership for these second-wave reforms. After 1983, the mark of a politically astute governor was a task force on education and a series of reports with excellence and accountability as their themes. Such education governors as Thomas Kean of New Jersey and Lamar Alexander of Tennessee joined Bill Clinton of Arkansas in making school reform the central goal of their administrations during the 1980s. George W. Bush was an education governor of Texas during the 1990s. For these and other governors, school reform was a state issue that paid off in national prominence. Clinton and Bush followed the road all the way to the White House.

Since the late 1980s, state school reformers have been coordinating their efforts. President George H. Bush held the first education summit conference for governors in 1989, and President Clinton held the second in 1996. Governors exchange ideas on a regular basis in meetings of the National Governors' Association and the Education Commission of the States. The National Association of State Boards of Education provides a similar forum for board members, and state school superintendents work together through the Council of Chief State School Officers. State legislators hold their own caucuses on education.

All this coordinated activity created a third wave of state reform. Spurred on by Clinton's 1996 education summit, one state after another developed standards in the core academic subjects along with a new generation of assessments to measure whether students were meeting the standards. These reforms sent a "let's get tough" message many citizens wanted to hear.

Clinton invited top business executives—the heads of such companies as IBM, AT&T, and Eastman Kodak—to his summit to talk accountability with the governors. The summit took place on business turf, at IBM's conference center in Palisades, New York. *Newsweek*'s reporter characterized the executives as Donald Trump types: "men who actually run the country . . . white-shirted men who look as if they had fired a couple of thousand people before breakfast." Getting serious with the governors about accountability, the CEOs somehow managed to look five years into the future, to the provisions of a federal education law that would be drafted in 2001, when they insisted that "if you hold schools and students responsible for results, you must do the same for teachers."[43]

The fourth wave of state school reform, as mandated by No Child Left Behind, is ushering in that kind of accountability. Joel Spring points out in *Conflict of Interests* that Texas Governor George W. Bush inherited a set of education reforms in 1995 after defeating Ann Richards, another education governor. Claiming credit for working a "Texas miracle" of accountability even though the plan was already in place and test scores were rising before he became governor, Bush took the plan to Washington after his election as president. Bush also took Rod Paige, one of his education advisors and superintendent of schools in Houston, who became U.S. Secretary of Education. With Paige's lobbying and testimony in Congress, the Texas plan became the model for the No Child Left Behind Act of 2001. Margaret Spellings, who replaced Paige as secretary of education in 2005, is another advisor from Bush's days as governor.[44]

The Politics of More of the Same

Measurable Inputs, Measurable Outputs.   Operating at a safe distance from the local schools—above the action, we might say—state reformers have a peculiar perspective on public education. They have a wealth of information at their disposal, and staff members can generate more at a moment's notice. In meeting after meeting, state officials pore over seemingly endless statistics: population, per capita income, school expenditures, dropout rates, and of course test scores. These quantitative data give the officials a quantitative view of schools. They think in terms of measurable inputs and measurable outputs.

BOX 9.5

QUALITY COUNTS

Let me encourage you again to go to *Education Week*'s Web site, www.edweek.org, and browse *Quality Counts* online.

State officials are not the only people with this mindset, of course. Quantitative educational measures have gained wide public acceptance since the early 1970s. *Education Week* is encouraging the trend by publishing *Quality Counts,* a series of annual "report cards on the condition of public education in the 50 states." Although every issue of *Quality Counts* has a different theme, the bottom line of the reports is standards, assessments, and accountability, broken down state by state and presented with eye-catching graphs, tables, and charts. Although *Quality Counts* is hardly a fixture on every American's coffee table, more and more copies are making their way into the hands of reporters who use the data to compare Alaska's curriculum standards to Arizona's or West Virginia's testing program to Wyoming's.

Higher quantitative standards usually call for *more of the same* instead of something different. If one math course is good for high school students, then two courses are better, and three or four are best. If a literacy test for prospective teachers is good, then a literacy test and a teaching field test are better, and so on. State officials seem less concerned with the content of math courses than with the number of courses. They worry less about the content of teacher tests than the number of tests.[45]

What Teachers Think about State Reform.   It is not surprising that classroom teachers, the people closest to the action, have mixed feelings about state school reform. Teachers endorse many of the reformers' glowingly stated goals, such as "We must set higher standards for all students." Who could disagree? But teachers are skeptical of their ability, *given the limitations of the education system,* to help students reach higher standards. Teachers feel they lack the support, the resources, and in some cases the knowledge and skills necessary to make reform work.

As we saw in Chapter 1, research conducted over the last two decades has documented these teacher attitudes again and again. From *The Condition of Teaching* (1990), a Carnegie Foundation survey, to the Public Agenda report *Stand By Me* (2003), polls of teachers show they are far more doubtful than the public that state reform can improve the schools. Many teachers see reform as a public relations show, a parade of one bandwagon after another.[46]

Attitudes about Teaching (2003), a synthesis by Public Agenda of years of survey data, may express it best:

> It is not a question, teachers say, of their needing more accountability or more motivation or more chances for advancement or additional course work in their academic subject. What they need, teachers say, are schools that make teaching and learning the priority—schools that furnish a respectful, civil, orderly environment and demand student effort and responsibility. It would be hard to overstate the depth of teachers' concern about poor student behavior (and lack of parental support when problems occur). Yet this issue rarely seems to make it seriously onto the education reform agenda.[47]

Is This Picture Too Pessimistic?   People who think so should take a careful look at the "performance indicators" state officials swear by. As Chapter 11 points out, the indicators are as mixed as teachers' attitudes toward school reform. On the standardized tests that states use to measure adequate yearly progress for NCLB, some of the scores are indeed up. But teachers explain that the scores are up because they are teaching the tests—not because students are learning more.

Quality Counts 2005 points out big discrepancies between scores on state assessments for NCLB and scores on the National Assessment of Education Progress (NAEP), a battery of tests for which teachers do not rehearse their students—at least not yet. In Mississippi, for instance, 87 percent of fourth graders score proficient in reading on the state test but only 18 percent score proficient on the reading section of the NAEP. In New Mexico, 51 percent of eighth graders are proficient in reading on the state test but only 20 percent on the NAEP. In other states, such as Connecticut and Massachusetts, the discrepancies are smaller. Obviously, the editors of Quality Counts conclude, there is a "range of rigor in tests and performance standards across states."[48]

So why doesn't every state get tough and make its tests as rigorous as the NAEP? Remember that No Child Left Behind requires states to impose sanctions and intervene whenever a school fails to make AYP for two consecutive years. Officials in every state must also consider their public relations situation and how their citizens will react to media reports of failure and success, stories that play differently from one state to another. The result, Marc Tucker and Thomas Toch explain, is a tremendously inconsistent record of state reform.

> Some states chose to set high standards, while others, in an effort to avoid the impact of the sanctions on large numbers of their schools, lowered their standards—sometimes into the basement. Thus the way the law works, states with high standards will soon have to deal with huge numbers of failing schools while states with low standards will have fewer such schools to deal with and so will appear to be doing a better job, when in fact the contrary is true.[49]

At least there is consistency in the nine report cards Quality Counts has issued on state reform since 1997. Although the editors of Education Week are true believers in standards, assessments, and accountability, they conclude that after thirty years of reform, student achievement is about the same, maybe a little better.

FEDERAL POLITICS OF EDUCATION

Federal Money and Federal Influence

When Dwight D. Eisenhower watched John F. Kennedy take the presidential oath of office in 1961, the federal government was providing about 4 percent of the money for the nation's public schools. By the time Lyndon Johnson turned over the executive branch to Richard Nixon in 1969, the federal share had risen to 8 percent. When Ronald Reagan took over from Jimmy Carter in 1981, the federal contribution to the public school budget stood at an all-time high of almost 10 percent. Leaving office in 1989, Reagan felt pleased he had been able to trim

TABLE 9.1   Share of Public School Revenue Contributed by Federal, State, and Local Governments

	PERCENTAGE OF REVENUE				PERCENTAGE OF REVENUE		
SCHOOL YEAR	FEDERAL	STATE	LOCAL	SCHOOL YEAR	FEDERAL	STATE	LOCAL
1919–1920	0.3	16.5	83.2	1985–1986	6.7	49.4	43.9
1929–1930	0.4	16.9	82.7	1987–1988	6.3	49.5	44.1
1939–1940	1.8	30.3	68.0	1989–1990	6.1	47.1	46.8
1949–1950	2.9	39.8	57.3	1991–1992	6.6	46.4	47.0
1959–1960	4.4	39.1	56.5	1993–1994	7.1	45.2	47.8
1969–1970	8.0	39.9	52.1	1995–1996	6.6	47.5	45.9
1979–1980	9.8	46.8	43.4	1997–1998	6.8	48.4	44.8
1981–1982	7.4	47.6	45.0	1999–2000	7.3	49.5	43.2
1983–1984	6.8	47.8	45.4	2001–2002*	7.5	49.5	43.0
				2003–2004*	8.2	49.1	42.7

Note: Some rows do not total 100 due to rounding.

*Figures for 2001–2002 and 2003–2004 are author's estimates.

Source: U.S. Department of Education, National Center for Education Statistics, *Digest of Education Statistics, 2003* (2004) [Available: nces.ed.gov/programs/digest/d03/tables/dt156.asp], Tbl. 156.

the federal portion back to the mid-1960s level of 6 percent. But the federal share drifted upward again in the 1990s under George H. Bush and Bill Clinton, and a larger increase in federal spending has been under way since 2001 courtesy of George W. Bush and No Child Left Behind.

The statistics displayed in Table 9.1 give us a rough sketch of the federal government's involvement in education. Seeing such figures for the first time, many prospective teachers express surprise—not so much at the patterns of increase and decrease but rather at how small *all* the federal percentages are. Compared to state and local funding, federal funding for education has never been great. Yet the federal government has managed to wring a relatively large degree of influence out of a relatively small amount of money.

Understanding Federal Control.   We can explain this phenomenon in three ways. First, federal courts have exercised much of the control. Consider the example of school desegregation. Many legal scholars regard the U.S. Supreme Court's ruling in *Brown v. Board of Education of Topeka* (1954) as the most far-reaching court decision of the twentieth century. The federal government has spent a great deal of money carrying out the mandates of *Brown* and subsequent school desegregation decisions, but state and local governments, businesses, and individual citizens have spent even more. One reason the federal government's control exceeds its funding, then, is that federal courts can order sweeping changes and transfer most of the costs of compliance to other levels of government and other people.

Second, the federal government has increased the impact of its education dollars by earmarking them for particular purposes and insisting state and local school systems spend them according to federal guidelines. *Categorical aid* to education—money provided with strings attached—enables federal officials to maintain control over federal dollars, even after the money has passed through state boards and departments of education and into the hands of local school officials.

During the 1960s and 1970s, Congress justified categorical aid as an essential political safeguard. State and local school officials had consistently neglected the needs of poor, minority, disabled, and female students, the argument went, so how could these same officials be trusted to spend *general aid*—money provided with fewer restrictions—wisely and equitably? While there was more than a little congressional self-righteousness in the argument, there was also an abundance of factual support, as Chapters 6 and 8 of this book demonstrate.

President Reagan tried to change the terms of the argument. Even if categorical aid had been necessary during the sixties and seventies, he contended, it had outlived its usefulness. The people closest to the schools deserve more control over federal aid. As the nation has matured, state and local officials have changed, becoming more sensitive to the needs of all students. Besides, Reagan added, the courts are there to protect students who run into discrimination.

Congress was not convinced. Despite Reagan's efforts, the categorical approach remains a key feature of federal aid to education. Accepted as a given by George H. Bush, Bill Clinton, and George W. Bush, categorical funding offers the federal government a second way to focus and magnify the effects of its spending.

George W. Bush has revived a third way: Making compliance with federal mandates a condition for receiving federal aid. Beginning in the 1960s, Congress told state and local school systems—particularly those in the South—they would lose their federal education funds unless they desegregated. Although conservatives complained about violations of states rights, the strategy worked well. Now Mr. Bush, a conservative president, is using the same strategy. Unless state and local school systems comply with the extensive provisions of NCLB, they lose their Title I funding.

With his track record of increasing federal control along with federal spending, George W. Bush is an unusual conservative. In these respects he is the exact opposite of Ronald Reagan, and he worries traditional conservatives who still favor small federal education budgets and state and local control of education.

Party Politics at the Federal Level.   Keep party politics in mind as you read the rest of this section on the federal government. Remember that Democrats controlled both the House and the Senate for almost all the years between 1954 and 1992. Even with Republican presidents in the White House for most of that time, and even without the support of some southern Democrats during the 1950s and 1960s, the Democratic Party managed to cast the federal government in an activist role in the politics of education.

Since the early 1990s, differences between Democrats and Republicans on education issues have narrowed as both parties have bought into standards, assessments, and accountability. No Child Left Behind passed both houses of Congress with strong bipartisan support. During the presidential campaigns of 2000 and 2004, George Bush and his two Democratic opponents, Al Gore and John Kerry, talked almost the same game when the discussion turned to education.

But as we will see later in this section, genuine differences remain between Republicans and Democrats on private school vouchers and other key education issues. It is possible that Democrats will push these differences during Mr. Bush's second term or that bipartisan support for No Child Left Behind will break up. To understand the situation in Washington and how it will affect your work as a teacher, you need to understand party politics at the federal level.

Cold War, Poverty War, and Other Battles

Historians say America's elementary and secondary school students have marched off to war several times as the federal government has drafted them to fight a variety of enemies. Mixing school children into military metaphors may seem strange, but in this case the imagery is appropriate.

"Happy Warriors" and School Campaigns.   After the Soviet Union orbited the satellite *Sputnik I* in 1957 and added a threatening new dimension to the Cold War, Congress responded by passing the National Defense Education Act (NDEA) of 1958. Believing America's students could help win the war, Congress provided categorical aid to improve math, science, and foreign language instruction in the schools. Through the NDEA, the federal government hoped to gain a scientific, technological, and military edge on the Soviet Union.[50]

During the 1960s, President Johnson declared a War on Poverty, and Congress sent students into action all along the front lines. The Economic Opportunity Act (EOA) of 1964 gave the nation Project Head Start, a program designed to help preschool children compensate for what was then called "cultural deprivation"—in plain English, the negative effects of being poor. Compensatory education became a key weapon in the poverty war, and it remains so today. When Congress passed the Elementary and Secondary Education Act (ESEA) of 1965, the federal government launched its major educational offensive in the poverty war. Congress aimed the act at students who were "disadvantaged," another euphemism for poor. Title I reading and math programs brought compensatory education into the elementary grades. Other titles (sections) of the original ESEA provided money for libraries and instructional materials, for example, and educational research. Initially funded at $1 billion, by 1981 ESEA had provided more than $30 billion in categorical aid to state and local school systems.[51]

The Civil Rights Act of 1964 became a major federal weapon against racial and ethnic discrimination, which Congress regarded as a major cause of poverty. As the federal government channeled more money into public education, it gained powerful leverage over state and local school systems, especially in the South, the nation's poorest region. Making federal dollars contingent on desegregation helped bring southern school systems into line, and the many victories along this front of the poverty war encouraged Congress.[52]

Poverty proved to be an elusive enemy. Congress broadened its attack by expanding the ESEA, adding the Education of Handicapped Children Act (Title VI) in 1966 and the Bilingual Education Act (Title VII) in 1968. By 1972, when Congress was ready to mount a new educational offensive, a president with a different set of priorities sat in the White House. Richard Nixon had less enthusiasm than Lyndon Johnson for fighting a domestic war on poverty, and Nixon was preoccupied with the hot war in Vietnam.[53]

Although Congress shared his preoccupation, it found time to pass the Education Amendments of 1972, which included funds for a variety of categorical programs: desegregation assistance under the Emergency School Aid Act, ethnic studies under the Ethnic Heritage Act, and improved education for Native Americans under the Indian Education Act. The best known of the 1972 amendments is Title IX, which prohibits sex discrimination in all educational institutions—preschool, elementary, secondary, and postsecondary—that receive federal funds.[54]

By the 1970s, poverty was not the only or even the major enemy the federal government was fighting with education. Although the Vietnam War made military metaphors unpopular, it was obvious the legislative and judicial branches of the federal government were still home to many "happy warriors" (as reform-minded politicians and judges were sometimes called) with educational campaigns in mind.

Public Backlash.   The mood of the public, though, was changing, and the media played up the backlash against federal activism. The controversy over school desegregation moved outside the South as federal judges tried to untie the knot of de facto and de jure segregation (Chapter 8). Although desegregation proceeded smoothly and uneventfully in most school districts, whites in a few big-city systems—most notably Boston—made up their minds to fight desegregation in every way possible. Massive resistance was back in the news, and the media paired the words *busing* and *Boston* in the public consciousness. The association was not a pleasant one.[55]

Congress charged into battle on behalf of the disabled with Public Law 94-142 (1975), which affirmed the right of all children to receive an appropriate education at public expense. The media played up the exceptions rather than the rule: teacher complaints about having to draw up Individualized Educational Programs (IEPs) rather than new opportunities for disabled students, and the high cost of educating the most severely disabled rather than the ease with which schools accommodated the majority of exceptional children.[56]

The backlash intensified. Many citizens believed the federal government had gone too far. In the late 1970s, President Jimmy Carter became the symbol of all that was wrong. The first presidential candidate endorsed by the NEA, Carter stuck to the federal educational agenda of the 1960s and early 1970s, just when the word *liberal* was becoming a pejorative in U.S. politics. Federal spending on education reached new heights during the Carter administration, and at the president's insistence, Congress voted narrowly to establish a cabinet-level Department of Education. To head the new department, Carter chose Shirley Hufstedler, a federal judge, judicial activist, and feminist. As Ronald Reagan pointed out on the campaign trail, the symbolism could not have been more appropriate.

Ronald Reagan and the New Federalism: Changing the Politics of Education

Ronald Reagan made short work of Jimmy Carter in 1980 and shorter work of Walter Mondale four years later. Education was not the main issue in either campaign, but the differences between Reagan and his Democratic opponents on the federal role in education mirrored their basic differences. Reagan promised to get the federal government off people's backs. Carter and Mondale promised to use the federal government to solve people's problems. Americans went to the polls and made two clear choices.

Mr. Reagan Leaves His Mark.   More than any other president between Lyndon Johnson and George W. Bush, Ronald Reagan changed the politics of education. Reagan's New Federalism realigned the roles of all three levels of government. The control of public education shifted downward, with state governments gaining most from the transfer. The responsibility for paying for the schools also changed, as federal funding for education dropped dramatically during Reagan's first term in office. By 1984, in inflation-adjusted dollars, the federal government was spending 21 percent less on elementary and secondary education than it had in 1980. And even though the Democratic majority in Congress fought back during Reagan's second term, federal funding remained at that level.[57]

Trying to gain political leverage by using public opinion, Reagan's critics in Congress accused him of being insensitive to the problems of poor, minority, and female students. By cutting the federal education budget and reducing federal scrutiny of state and local school districts, Reagan was turning his back on years of discrimination and neglect, critics charged, allowing vulnerable students to fall through the social "safety net" he often talked about. In the conservative climate of the 1980s, Democrats found it hard to make these charges stick. A large majority of Americans gave the fatherly, affable president a pass on sensitive social issues.[58]

Educational Advocacy: A Nation at Risk.   It may have been "morning in America again," as Reagan often said, but the president had a gloomier outlook on the public schools: They were jeopardizing America's future. Looking back on the Reagan years, historians may see the advocacy role that emerged almost accidentally with the success of *A Nation at Risk* as the most significant part of his educational strategy. No one in the administration expected the report to become an overnight sensation, but it did. No one expected the report to do more than the New Federalism to galvanize the states into action, but it did. *A Nation at Risk* became *the* educational document of the late twentieth century.[59]

The conservative president who had been highly critical of federal involvement in education became an avid practitioner of a certain kind of involvement: advocacy. Without spending much money and without exercising much direct control, the Reagan administration used exhortation and persuasion to advance its educational goals. The U.S. Department of Education, which Reagan came to

Washington promising to close down, became instead a national platform for the advancement of a conservative educational agenda—a "bully pulpit," Secretary of Education William Bennett liked to call it, conjuring memories of Teddy Roosevelt.

Advocacy became a call to arms as once again the federal government sent America's students into battle. *A Nation at Risk* drafted them to fight an international economic war against such friendly enemies as Japan, Korea, and West Germany. Educational historian Joel Spring calls this competition the "Sony War" because *A Nation at Risk* summons up images of a full-scale invasion of Sonys, Hyundais, and Telefunkens:[60]

> Our nation is at risk. Our once unchallenged preeminence in commerce, industry, science, and technological innovation is being overtaken by competitors throughout the world. . . . If an unfriendly foreign power had attempted to impose on America the mediocre educational performance that exists today, we might well have viewed it as an act of war. As it stands, we have allowed this to happen to ourselves. We have even squandered the gains in student achievement made in the wake of the Sputnik challenge. . . . We have, in effect, been committing an act of unthinking, unilateral educational disarmament.

"History is not kind to idlers," the report warned. "We live among determined, well-educated, and strongly motivated competitors."[61]

The result of this kind of advocacy was a new wave of school reform. Almost every state released a report echoing the call to arms of *A Nation at Risk:* Make the schools excellent, or suffer the economic consequences. Then the states went into action, and some local school districts are still wondering what hit them. Although the Reagan administration was not completely satisfied with the way state reform proceeded—it trampled local control in its path—the energy *A Nation at Risk* unleashed was stunning. Gearing students up for economic competition became the educational mission of the era.

A Preacher for the Bully Pulpit.   Although Terrel Bell, Reagan's first secretary of education, supervised production of the big report, it was Bell's successor who strode into the bully pulpit and began to preach with moral fervor. William Bennett quickly became the nation's most visible advocate of educational essentialism (see Chapter 7), educational choice among public *and* private schools (Chapter 10), and such issues as good old-fashioned discipline, sexual abstinence, opposition to abortion, and "Just Saying No" to drugs. With his right-versus-wrong, friends-versus-enemies approach to the politics of education, Bennett also demonized teachers unions, focusing his wrath on the NEA.[62]

Here are the Reagan years' legacies to education: cutbacks in federal spending and control, *A Nation at Risk,* increases in state spending and control, and Bill Bennett. During the 1980s, they turned America's education conversation around, changing the emphasis from *equity* to *excellence,* from *access* to *ability,* from *needs* to *standards of performance.*[63]

George H. Bush and National Education Goals

Although George H. Bush promised during the 1988 campaign "to be the education president . . . to lead a renaissance of quality in our schools," he was unable to talk the reforms he wanted into place. Never matching the results the Reagan administration obtained with its advocacy, the Bush administration at best succeeded in adding a list of national education goals to a conversation that was already going on.[64]

Goals and Governors.   The media paid close attention in 1989 when Bush met with the nation's governors at an Education Summit Conference. The president and the state executives agreed to establish national goals for education and to promote accountability, flexibility, and restructuring. All well and good, most observers said, but the joint statement issued at the summit amounted to little more than a public relations document, a glossary of buzzwords from late-eighties "excellence in education" reforms.

A few months later, Bush and the governors announced the six national goals that would provide the framework for his administration's subsequent efforts in education. By the year 2000:

- All children in America will start school ready to learn.
- The high school graduation rate will increase to at least 90 percent.
- American students will leave grades four, eight, and twelve having demonstrated competency in challenging subject matter including English, mathematics, science, history, and geography.
- U.S. students will be first in the world in science and mathematics achievement.
- Every adult American will be literate and will possess the knowledge and skills necessary to compete in a global economy and exercise the rights and responsibilities of citizenship.
- Every school in America will be free of drugs and violence and will offer a disciplined environment conducive to learning.[65]

Already jockeying with George Bush for the media spotlight was the up-and-coming education governor from Arkansas who cohosted the summit conference. Bill Clinton, a former chair of the National Governors' Association, personally helped draft the six national goals. After defeating Bush in the 1992 election, Clinton would add two more goals and carry them over into his own administration:

- The Nation's teaching force will have access to programs for the continued improvement of their professional skills and the opportunity to acquire the knowledge and skills needed to instruct and prepare all American students for the next century.

- Every school will promote partnerships that will increase parental involvement and participation in promoting the social, emotional, and academic growth of children.[66]

In the early 1990s, when I first discussed the education goals with the prospective teachers in my classes, their reactions were identical to those heard around the nation. The goals are nice, ambitious, and unrealistic, the students said. Funny thing: When my students of the 2000s read about the goals in this textbook, they make the same comments.

Where's the Money?   Above and beyond doubts about whether the nation could ever reach the goals, there was the nagging question of who would pay the bills. Each level of government waited for the others to ante up. Although George H. Bush's education budgets were more generous than Reagan's, they did not fully fund existing programs, much less the plan Bush proposed for reaching the goals, America 2000. Even such long-standing programs as Head Start, which Bush regarded as essential to reaching the first national goal—All children in America will start school ready to learn—came up short. America 2000 got nowhere in Congress.[67]

And so the nation's education conversation continued as President Bush left office in 1993. The conversation stayed focused on terms set by Ronald Reagan during the 1980s—terms that were quite familiar to the education governor of Arkansas who was preparing to move into the White House.

Bill Clinton: An Education Governor but Not Quite an Education President

Mr. Clinton came to Washington talking excellence and accountability, the twin hallmarks of state school reform during the 1980s. But like both Presidents Bush, Clinton quickly discovered that other issues—such as health care, welfare, and national security—made stronger demands on his time and attention. Then, as education emerged as the public's top priority when he was up for reelection in 1996, Clinton began saying he, too, wanted to be remembered as an education president. He might have succeeded if the Monica Lewinsky scandal and the long ordeal over impeachment had not consumed so much of his second term.[68]

Standards and Assessments.   Clinton swore by them. As governor of Arkansas, he helped install minimum competency tests and raise high school graduation requirements. It is not surprising, then, that he pushed national standards and assessments during his first term as president. After running into determined resistance from states-rights conservatives, Clinton made a deft political move. At his 1996 Education Summit Conference for governors and business leaders, he commandeered the standards-and-assessments bandwagon, became its most visible national advocate, and then steered the responsibility for doing the work back to the states.

This strategy defused most of the conservative opposition and set the stage for No Child Left Behind. As we saw earlier in this chapter, George W. Bush has been able to extend federal control of education into curriculum and teaching by claiming he, like Clinton, is leaving the regulatory details to the states. In reality, NCLB contains federal mandates of a magnitude that conservatives would surely have protested had Bill Clinton proposed them.[69]

At War with the Republican Congress.   Clinton came into office stressing his willingness to spend more money on public education, which he certainly did as governor of Arkansas. But he also stressed his commitment to reducing the federal budget deficit, which he certainly did as president. His first two budgets, submitted while Congress was still under Democratic control, disappointed the NEA, AFT, and other education groups that supported him. After Republicans gained control of Congress in 1994, they slashed Clinton's next education budget and then went after him on several other issues right out of Ronald Reagan's playbook from the 1980s: shutting down the U.S. Department of Education, amending the Constitution to allow organized school prayer, and giving parents a tax-subsidized choice between public and private schools.[70]

Republicans also attacked Goals 2000, the plan Clinton proposed for reaching the national education goals. They focused their attack not on the goals themselves but on the federal control they accused Clinton of trying to impose.

Staking Out the Middle of the Road.   Clinton adopted a middle-of-the-road strategy that made his administration look moderate, even conservative, and the Republicans look radical. To counter the drive for a school prayer amendment, Clinton and U.S. Secretary of Education Richard Riley launched a campaign highlighting the religious freedom students already have in public schools. They publicized the Department of Education's antidrug and antiviolence program and accused Republicans of endangering the lives of students and teachers by cutting the program budget and wanting to make even deeper cuts. Clinton reminded Americans he had protected Title I and special education programs from budget cuts, even while Republicans chopped away, and now he needed the voters' help.[71]

During the 1996 presidential campaign, Clinton made sure the public saw a contrast on education issues. Republican candidate Bob Dole sounded shrill and negative when he bashed teacher unions, criticized public education generally, and called for private school choice. Clinton not only staked out the middle of the road, he took the high road, talking in positive if sometimes ambiguous terms about investing in public schools instead of diverting money to private schools.[72]

Clinton won reelection, and throughout his second term he made certain each education budget he submitted was larger than the preceding year's. Congress went along with the increases. Here was a clean break with the budget-cutting mentality of the Reagan years. Out in Texas, education governor George W. Bush watched these events unfold.[73]

Mr. Clinton's Education Legacy.   Although never quite an education president, Clinton left a strong legacy that blends liberal and conservative elements. He left office with Republicans saying they, too, wanted to spend more federal money on education—an attitudinal about-face that carried over into the George W. Bush administration. Clinton's eight-year advocacy of standards and assessments served as a bridge between the "excellence in education" reforms of the 1980s and No Child Left Behind. He and Secretary Riley applied the principles of accountability to teacher preparation (see Chapter 3) by requiring states to issue report cards on all teacher education programs. Clinton supported the National Board of Professional Teaching Standards and, much to the dismay of the NEA, tilted toward merit pay. Finally, Clinton was a promoter of public school choice, especially charter schools, and an opponent of private school choice (Chapter 10).[74]

With the notable exception of the private choice issue, Clinton was able to narrow the differences between Democrats and Republicans on education. His legacy helps explain why elected officials at all three levels of government are in relatively close agreement on standards, assessments, and accountability—the heart of No Child Left Behind—despite the reservations teachers continue to hold.[75]

George W. Bush and No Child Left Behind

> On my second day in office, I sent Congress the boldest plan in a generation to improve our public schools—a plan to raise educational standards and to require accountability from every school. These reforms were entitled No Child Left Behind (NCLB) to reflect my belief that every child can learn. When expectations are high, America's children will rise to meet them. I signed NCLB into law less than one year later, thanks to unprecedented support from members of Congress.[76]

George W. Bush chose these words to begin a review of his education record for the "Election 2004" issue of *Phi Delta Kappan*. Obviously proud of his accomplishments as a school reformer, Bush showed he knew which buttons to push for the public during his successful campaign for a second term: high expectations for all students, success for all—and accountability.

In an unintended tribute to Bush's political skills, John Kerry and other Democrats running for office in 2004 had little to say about either NCLB or other education issues. Opinion polls show Americans have traditionally viewed the Democratic Party as more interested than the Republican Party in improving public schools. But Republicans have been closing the gap, and in 2004—just as in 2000—the public split down the middle on whether Bush or his Democratic opponent would do more for the schools.[77]

Accountability: The Missing Ingredient.   Bush came to Washington in 2001 bragging about the "Texas miracle" he worked as education governor and ready to sell Congress on accountability as the missing ingredient in school reform. Two decades after *A Nation at Risk*, standards and assessments were widely accepted and already in place in most states. But accountability remained more rhetoric than reality.

The law that became known as No Child Left Behind is the 2001 reauthorization of the Elementary and Secondary Education Act, the milestone federal legislation dating back to 1965. Congress had last reauthorized the ESEA in 1994, during the Clinton administration, at a time when conservative Republicans were still waging war over federal control of education. Standards, assessments, and accountability were part of the 1994 reauthorization, but no one took the accountability provisions seriously.[78]

George W. Bush and Rod Paige convinced Congress the time for accountability had come. Texas had tried it, and a miracle had occurred—which meant, quite simply, that scores on the Texas Assessment of Academic Skills (TAAS) had risen. Bush and Paige's optimism that schools could narrow and eventually close test-score gaps associated with social class, race and ethnicity, English language proficiency, and disability had tremendous political appeal. With a "compassionately conservative" president in the White House, Republicans in Congress immediately bought into the plan.[79]

Democrats, suspicious at first, lent their support after becoming "disgusted" with reservations expressed by leaders of the NEA, teacher education associations, and other "interest groups." Their testimony before the Senate and House Education Committees, much of which centered on standardized testing and federal funding, struck members of Congress as a parade of excuses. Why were educators so reluctant to be held accountable? Why were they blaming everybody but themselves for low test scores? When the dust finally settled, Senator Edward Kennedy—hardly a friend of Republicans—was one of the four congressional cosponsors of NCLB, and John Kerry, John Edwards, and most other Democrats lined up in support. The legislation passed the House by a vote of 281 to 41 and the Senate by 87 to 10.[80]

While the legislation worked its way through Congress, Democrats focused their attention on the issue of private school choice: The Bush administration wanted to include private schools in the transfer options of students who attend "failing" public schools. Democrats spent much of their political capital blocking the proposal, investing less of their time and energy examining provisions that would directly affect the classroom.

In the end, Bush pulled off a political hat trick. By reversing the longstanding positions of his own party on federal spending and control, he co-opted Democrats on one of their traditional turfs, public education. That there has been so little resistance to the federal government's new role as national accountability officer is truly amazing.

The Man Who Might Have Been an Education President.   On the road promoting No Child Left Behind, George Bush was reading to children in a Florida elementary school on the morning of September 11, 2001. Some political observers believe he would have enjoyed a comfortable, low-key presidency with NCLB as its signature program if the terrorist attacks had not made national security his top priority.

Even so, education remains close to his heart. First Lady Laura Bush, a former school media specialist, has been a tireless promoter of NCLB and a trusted advisor on education as well as other policy matters. To understand George you must understand his relationship with Laura, their friends say, and you must also understand their religious faith.

The depth of the president's religious convictions delights some Americans and worries others. Stating "I believe God wants me to be president."[81] and referring to his political career as a religious calling, Bush is a born-again Christian whose life was anything but spiritual before he experienced a conversion that began on his fortieth birthday. His belief that people and institutions can change for the better drives his policies. He fully supports the conservative Christian reform agenda we discussed earlier in this chapter, and given a less turbulent first term as president, he might have pushed for more of it.[82]

Considering the margin of votes that fundamentalists provided in his 2004 reelection, Bush may focus on morality and religion during his second term. Renewing the campaign for private school choice would be one way to thank his conservative Christian base. As we will see in Chapter 10, private choice is a "wedge" issue that Bush could use to bring more African Americans into the Republican fold. Other education issues that have bubbled just beneath the political surface during the 2000s—organized school prayer, student morality, and creationism, for instance—could attract Bush's attention as a second-term president who believes he has a mandate for change.

The (Loyal) Opposition.   No Child Left Behind has drawn political opposition, most but not all of it from Democrats. A backlash appeared to be building in 2004 when the Republican-dominated legislatures of Virginia and Utah joined five other states in protesting the costs and regulations of the federal law. For the first time, the law seemed to be in trouble.[83]

In response, Rod Paige and Margaret Spellings have tried to mend fences, and President Bush himself has offered reassurance that NCLB is not an "unfunded mandate": "I have provided the largest increase in federal education funding [in absolute dollars] in our nation's history and the highest percentage gain since President Johnson left office."[84] Table 9.1 supports Bush's claims, and more detailed figures for the years 2001 to 2005 show increases of more than 40 percent for Title I and elementary and secondary education and even greater gains for special education and reading.

The political backlash has subsided—for now—despite the best efforts of the NEA and other "interest groups" to keep it going. But what continues to bother state and local school systems is that federal funding, however much it has increased lately, does not even begin to cover the costs of compliance with NCLB. Recall our discussion of how state departments of education are stretched thin trying to administer their part of NCLB, and remember that federal dollars pay less than 9 percent of all the bills for public education.

When this edition of *America's Teachers* left my word processor and went to the publisher, George W. Bush's second term was before him. The world situation remained perilous. Teachers and administrators were still trying to adjust to NCLB, which is up for renewal in 2007. As you read this textbook, how much have things changed?

EDUCATIONAL FINANCE

Where children live has a powerful effect on the quality of the public schools they attend. Real estate agents are well acquainted with the question "How good are the public schools?" because parents who have the resources to do so shop for homes with the quality of local education in mind. Although public schools differ in many ways, one of the most important variables is *per-pupil expenditure*—the amount of money spent per student. Think of per-pupil expenditure as a financial package put together by local school boards with money received from the local, state, and federal governments.[85]

Table 9.2 ranks the states by their average per-pupil expenditures. As you can see, the annual cost of educating the nation's "average" public school student is $8,724. Variations among the states are wide. In six states the average per-pupil expenditure is more than $12,000, while three states spend less than $6,000.

TABLE 9.2   Average Public School Per-Pupil Expenditures Across the Nation, 2003–2004

1. District of Columbia	$14,621	26. Colorado	8,423
2. Vermont	12,678	27. Kentucky	8,308
3. New York	12,423	28. South Carolina	8,273
4. Connecticut	12,333	29. Hawaii	8,082
5. Massachusetts	12,108	30. California	8,004
6. New Jersey	12,069	31. Nebraska	7,999
7. Alaska	11,423	32. Washington	7,999
8. Delaware	11,386	33. Texas	7,891
9. Rhode Island	10,976	34. Louisiana	7,839
10. Wyoming	10,924	35. South Dakota	7,762
11. Maine	10,517	36. New Mexico	7,643
12. Wisconsin	10,293	37. Missouri	7,548
13. Ohio	10,246	38. Iowa	7,505
14. West Virginia	10,071	39. North Carolina	7,413
15. Illinois	9,997	40. Oklahoma	7,375
16. Minnesota	9,961	41. North Dakota	7,274
17. Georgia	9,352	42. Virginia	7,043
18. Pennsylvania	9,308	43. Nevada	6,953
19. Indiana	9,245	44. Florida	6,873
20. New Hampshire	9,165	45. Idaho	6,779
21. Michigan	9,104	46. Tennessee	6,623
22. Kansas	8,997	47. Mississippi	6,508
23. Montana	8,761	48. Arkansas	6,351
U.S. Average	*8,724*	49. Alabama	5,571
24. Oregon	8,700	50. Utah	5,556
25. Maryland	8,665	51. Arizona	5,548

Source: National Education Association, *Rankings & Estimates: Rankings of the States 2003 and Estimates of School Statistics 2004* (Washington, DC: NEA, 2004), Summary Tbl. K, p. 96. Reprinted with permission of the National Education Association copyright 2004. All rights reserved.

Viewed another way, the differences are even more glaring. In *every classroom* of 25 students, the District of Columbia, Vermont, New York, Connecticut, Massachusetts, and New Jersey spend at least $150,000 more *every school year* than Alabama, Utah, and Arizona. Per-pupil expenditures tend to be highest in the Northeast, followed by the Midwest, the West, and the Southeast—but notice the exceptions to this rule.

In the nation as a whole, total expenditures for public schools have increased by about 39 percent, in real, inflation-adjusted dollars, since 1993–1994. To set the record straight, most of the new money has not been spent raising teacher salaries. Their salaries, as you may recall from Chapter 2, have increased by only 2.6 percent since 1992–1993. Most of the 39 percent increase has gone to pay for other school expenses.[86]

Local Property Taxes: Some School Districts Are More Equal Than Others

Variations within States.   Keep in mind that average state per-pupil expenditures, while useful in making comparisons *between* states, conceal variations *within* states. Per-pupil expenditures tend to be highest in suburban school districts, followed by urban, small-town, and rural districts. Travel around the country and you will almost always find the highest per-pupil expenditures in the suburbs of major cities. Why do the students who live in suburban Shawnee Mission, Kansas, for instance, have more money spent on their public education than students who live in nearby Kansas City, in small-town Mullinville, or on a farm out on the plains? The main reason is that suburban residents are able to raise more money for the schools through local property taxes.

Property Values, Tax Rates, and Financial Effort.   As the major source of local revenue for public schools, local property taxes work to the advantage of wealthier communities and to the disadvantage of poorer communities. In some cases, suburbs with high *property values* can set their *tax rates* low and still rank at the top of the state in per-pupil spending.

Consider the example of two school districts of about the same size, located in the same state. One district serves an upper-middle-class suburb where homes have an average market value of $400,000. The other district serves a less affluent community—a central city, small town, rural area, or working-class suburb—where the market value of property averages $100,000. To keep things straightforward, let's assume property is taxed at full market value in this state.

Residents of the upper-middle-class suburb have set their school tax rate at $1 per $100 of property value. The average home in this suburb, therefore, brings in $4,000 each year for the local schools. With the average family paying school taxes of $4,000, these citizens can truthfully say they are trying hard to support public education.

The residents of the less affluent community have set their tax rate twice as high—at $2 per $100 of assessed value—yet the average home in their community generates only $2,000 each year for the schools. These residents can say they are trying twice as hard, but their *effort*—a technical term in school finance that means exactly what it says—yields only half as much.

You can appreciate the significance of this example if you think again of school finance as a package. In the nation as a whole, local governments contribute over 40 percent of the money that goes into the package, and almost all the local funding comes from property taxes. As Table 9.1 indicates, local governments have historically shouldered most of the financial burden for public education. But Table 9.1 also shows state governments have assumed a progressively larger share of the burden throughout most of this century, motivated in part by the desire to make the quality of education more uniform within each state.

In 1920, when local governments were responsible for raising more than 80 percent of school revenue, the differences in per-pupil expenditures within states were staggering. The amount of wealth in a local community virtually dictated the amount of money spent on the local schools. As we discovered in Chapter 6, race and ethnicity also influenced expenditures: It was standard practice to spend less on African American and Hispanic American students. In the early twentieth century, then, it was not at all unusual for some districts to spend five, ten, even twenty times more per student than other districts within the same state.

State Funds: Reducing the Inequalities

Equalization Programs.   Large gaps have narrowed but not completely closed as the states have increased their spending on public education. Most states have developed *equalization programs* that base the amount of state funding each district receives on such factors as local wealth and effort. By 2005, about half the states were also factoring the percentage of poor and ELL students and of students with disabilities into their equalization formulas.[87]

In our example of the upper-middle-class suburb and the less affluent community, a state equalization program would bring per-pupil expenditures in the two districts closer together. The state department of education would send more state money to the poorer district, and that district would probably receive more federal aid as well because it would be likely to have more students qualifying for categorical federal programs.

***Serrano* and *Rodriguez*.**   Two major 1970s court decisions shaped the trend toward more state funding. In *Serrano v. Priest* (1971), the California Supreme Court considered the complaint of John Serrano, who lived with his family in the working-class suburb of Baldwin Park in Los Angeles. Baldwin Park's property tax rates were twice as high as those in wealthy Beverly Hills, but because of the vastly different property values, the Baldwin Park school district could spend only half as much per student. With class sizes increasing and textbooks in short supply, Serrano felt dissatisfied with the public schools his two children attended.[88]

The California Supreme Court ruled the state's school finance system, heavily dependent on local property taxes, "invidiously discriminates against the poor because it makes the quality of a child's education a function of the wealth of his parents and his neighbors." The court ruled the California system violated the right to equal protection of the laws guaranteed by both the state constitution and the Fourteenth Amendment to the U.S. Constitution. Obviously, said the court, the school laws of California were not protecting the rich and poor citizens equally; the laws were making public schools as unequal as the wealth of the communities where they were located.[89]

The *Serrano* case created a sensation in school finance and precipitated a flood of similar lawsuits in other states. When a case from Texas, *San Antonio Independent School District v. Rodriguez,* reached the U.S. Supreme Court in 1973, many observers predicted a ruling similar to *Serrano*—a national mandate to reform school finance. The cases were virtually identical: unequal per-pupil expenditures, reliance on local property taxes, even a lead plaintiff who was poor and Hispanic.

But the Supreme Court issued no such mandate in *Rodriguez.* Instead, it left the matter up to the states. In a 5-to-4 decision, the majority pointed out the U.S. Constitution does not guarantee the right to an education. The Fourteenth Amendment, therefore, cannot protect citizens from state school finance laws that allow per-pupil expenditures to vary from one district to another. The court suggested, though, that inequitable state laws might well violate state constitutions.

Back to the State Level.   *Rodriguez* shifted the action back to the state level, and in the years since the decision, more than half the nation's state legislatures have overhauled their school finance systems to make them less dependent on local revenue. After the California Supreme Court reaffirmed its earlier decision and reissued its call for reform in *Serrano II* (1976), the state share of the school budget went from less than 40 percent to almost 70 percent. From the late 1970s through the early 1990s, the state share of total spending on public education was greater than the local share for the first time in U.S. history.[90]

Battles over school finance are still raging because differences in local spending persist. Only Hawaii and the District of Columbia, where there are no local school districts, have uniform per-pupil expenditures. In every other state, a gap in per-pupil expenditures—usually a substantial gap—exists between the wealthiest and poorest districts.

Every year *Quality Counts* grades the states on educational equity. The 2005 report, *No Small Change,* uses a sophisticated system that weights a variety of factors including the "wealth-neutrality" of state and local funding and the "coefficient of variation" across local school districts. Hawaii and Nevada get a flat *A*; Utah and Iowa earn an *A−*; and West Virginia, Louisiana, South Dakota, New York, Delaware, Kansas, Minnesota, New Mexico, and Florida receive a *B+*. Down at the other end of the list, Montana and Idaho get a *D*, New Hampshire a *D−*, and Vermont the only *F*.[91]

New York, which raised its grade from an *F* in 2000 to a *B* in 2005, is a school-finance success story. The state has completely revamped its system under court order and now provides *categorical* funding—the same mechanism the federal government uses—to local districts based on their ability to pay for transportation, construction, bilingual education, special education, and an array of other programs. Vermont, which earned an *F* in both 2000 and 2005, could be the next success story because it is implementing a categorical finance system similar to New York's.[92]

Does Money Matter?   To those who argue that money cannot buy everything, the best reply is that money can buy *some* things. To be sure, educators cannot correlate spending with achievement and promise more dollars will produce higher test scores. As we found in Chapter 2, too many factors outside the school influence student achievement for educators to issue that kind of guarantee. What educators can state with confidence, though, is that educational programs and services do not come free. Only money can buy them.[93]

In the wealthiest districts in a given state, high school students have access to a curriculum that offers five or six foreign languages, math and science courses through advanced calculus and second-year physics, challenging courses in other core subjects, and pupil-teacher ratios of 20 or 25 to 1. The cost may run to $15,000 or more per student.

The poorest districts within a state offer their high school students a very different curriculum: one or two foreign languages, no calculus or physics, unexceptional courses in other subjects, and pupil-teacher ratios of 35 or 40 to 1. The price tag may be $5,000 or less per student.

People who believe money doesn't matter should tour schools as different as these. Reading Jonathan Kozol's *Savage Inequalities* is probably the next best thing. With great sensitivity to the human consequences of funding disparities, Kozol provides convincing evidence that only money can buy the programs and services needed to make America's public schools more equal.[94]

For evidence of a more quantitative nature, you can follow the ongoing psychometric debate on the relationship between school spending and student achievement. Educational researchers Rob Greenwald, Larry Hedges, and Richard Laine of the University of Chicago have conducted meta-analyses that show money matters a great deal if we spend it in the right ways—such as to reduce class size or to hire and retain teachers with higher levels of education and experience. Economist Eric Hanushek of Stanford University, on the other hand, concludes that more spending in those areas will never raise student achievement. Hanushek puts his faith in standards, assessments, and accountability instead.[95]

Access, needs, and equality—these issues, downplayed in America's education conversation during the 1980s, have become important once again. Nowhere

---

BOX 9.6

MONEY AND ACHIEVEMENT

The Education Trust conducts ongoing research on the relationship between money and achievement. You can read *The Funding Gap 2004* and other reports at www.edtrust.org

is there greater potential for leveling the playing field than in the educational finance suits working their way through state courts.

Lawsuits, Equity, and Adequacy: Educational Finance in the 2000s

Unless you plan to teach in Hawaii, Nevada, Utah, Mississippi, Delaware, or the District of Columbia, you will work in a state that has been forced to defend its school finance system in court. Since the Kentucky Supreme Court declared the state's entire public education system unconstitutional in the landmark case *Rose v. Council for Better Education* (1989), plaintiffs have won almost two-thirds of the school finance lawsuits filed against 44 other states. Like John Serrano in California, almost all the plaintiffs have been poor, and some have sued on behalf of minority, disabled, and limited English proficient students. The most closely watched litigation since the Kentucky decision has been the long-running *Abbot v. Burke* case in New Jersey, in which the state supreme court has struck down the school finance system four different times.[96]

The Kentucky decision called attention to the concept of a *state school system*. Americans have traditionally thought of public education within a state as a number of local school districts rather than a single school system. But the U.S. Constitution, the Kentucky Constitution, and virtually every other state constitution make public education a function of the state government. Accordingly, the Kentucky Supreme Court ruled that the responsibilities for establishing, maintaining, and funding public schools rest solely with the state. This decision established a precedent for the cases that would soon be filed in other states.[97]

Moreover, the Kentucky court ruled, the legislature must carry out its responsibilities *equitably* and *adequately*. The state school system must provide equal educational opportunities to all students, regardless of who they are, where they live, or how much money their parents and neighbors make. The state school system must also provide an adequate education to all students, one that prepares them to lead productive lives. Concluding that the legislature had failed in its responsibilities, the court declared Kentucky's entire school system unconstitutional and told the legislature to reform it.[98]

A decade and a half later, after many ups and downs, Kentucky's new system is still taking shape. Immediately after the 1989 decision, the legislature passed a 1 cent increase in the state sales tax and a 1 percent hike in corporate taxes. School officials used the new revenue to pay for a variety of curriculum reforms and to narrow the gap between the state's richest and poorest school districts. The first edition of *Quality Counts* (1997) awarded Kentucky's reform efforts a *B+*. But the state rolled back its tax rates in the economic boom of the late 1990s, and now it needs additional revenue to keep the finance gap from widening again. In *Quality Counts 2005*, Kentucky's grade for equity is a *C*.[99]

Adequacy in the Era of No Child Left Behind.   Since the 1990s, the emphasis in state school finance cases has shifted to adequacy, a concept that is much more difficult than equity to define and measure. Equity, as we have seen, involves narrowing the differences in per-pupil expenditures from one district to another. Hard data are readily available to quantify the problem and measure steps toward the solution. Adequacy, by contrast, is necessarily subjective. The editors of *Quality Counts 2005* put the matter this way: "How much does it cost to provide students with a sound basic education? It depends on whom you ask."[100]

The answers vary tremendously in the thirty states that have conducted adequacy studies. But in the era of No Child Left Behind, adequacy increasingly means educating students to the *proficient* level on state standards, paying close attention to student subgroups defined by social class, race/ethnicity, English language proficiency, and disability. *Quality Counts 2005* points out that

> while no consensus exists about how much money is necessary to provide an "adequate" education, it is clear that districts with certain characteristics tend to require more aid. The National Center for Education statistics estimates that students in poverty, for example, need 1.2 times as much funding as other students do. The Center for Special Education finance estimates that students with disabilities need 1.9 times as much money.[101]

New Jersey's *Abbott* case, which has involved ten separate court decisions, is one of the first in the nation to take such factors into account. The state supreme court has singled out 31 poor urban school districts for massive infusions of state assistance. Not only have their per-pupil expenditures risen to a level close to those in the state's wealthiest suburban districts—about $13,000, which as Table 9.2 indicates is an impressive figure in national perspective—the Abbott districts also operate on a whole-school reform model.[102]

In several unusually detailed court orders, the court has mandated "full kindergarten and preschool, broad social-service programs, enhanced school security and technology, high school dropout programs, and smaller class sizes, as well as a major facilities program to overhaul subpar buildings." Students who are the poorest of the poor, the court believes, require an education "beyond the norm."[103]

Robin Hood.   School finance reform has been controversial in New Jersey, to say the least. Unlike Kentucky, where the legislature raised taxes to bring in new revenue, the New Jersey approach to overhauling school finance has created the public perception that the state is taking away money from wealthier districts and redistributing it to the poorest. This "Robin Hood" strategy, as it is fondly known, is a tried-and-true way to provoke resentment. In addition, residents of local districts that are neither rich nor poor are complaining they must raise property taxes to unreasonable levels to provide the educational services their students need. From their point of view, the New Jersey Supreme Court has gone too far, and state support of the Abbott districts looks like a "huge gift."[104]

Accountability for results has also been controversial in New Jersey. "*Abbott* is the poster child for court-run schools," Eric Hanushek observes, and "what is the evidence that any [of the reforms have] impacted student achievement?" To be sure, test scores have risen, especially at the elementary level, but not enough to satisfy the critics. As of 2005, after seven years of near-parity spending, the achievement gap has still not closed completely.[105]

American Dream.   Money can buy some things. Having seen how the infusion of state money can upgrade rundown schools and bring new educational programs to poor communities, the superintendent of one of the Abbott districts feels optimistic: "The American dream is based on good, free education, and the resources of Abbott can make that happen for these kids."[106]

But the resentment and resistance that school finance reform has triggered in many states lends support to Jonathan Kozol's harsher view of the situation. "Equity in education," he contends, "represents a formidable threat to other values held by many affluent Americans": namely, the "right and moral worth of individual advancement at whatever cost to others who may be less favored by accident of birth."[107]

David Berliner and Bruce Biddie, authors of *The Manufactured Crisis: Myths, Frauds, and the Attack on America's Public Schools* (1995), take Kozol's assessment a step further.

> The fundamental goal of public education is defeated when its benefits are unfairly lavished on those who had the happy fate of being born to rich parents. High-quality public education and the opportunity to learn are *rights,* not privileges, in this democracy of ours. And if we do not uphold those rights for *all* our citizens, we can ultimately kiss our affluent democracy good-bye.[108]

Variations between States.   Remember that just as per-pupil expenditures vary *within* states, they also vary *between* states. Notice the vast differences in spending from state to state shown in Table 9.2. The principle of financial effort applies here, too. Poorer states often try harder than wealthier states to raise money for public education—that is, poorer states often spend a greater portion of their total resources on the schools. But their effort yields lower per-pupil expenditures.

In the unlikely event that federal spending on education ever skyrockets, talk of targeting massive federal assistance to poorer states may revive. For years, the NEA has argued the three levels of government should evenly split the total bill for public education, with each level paying about one-third. By varying the exact mix of local, state, and federal funding from district to district and state to state, one-third funding could make per-pupil expenditures relatively equal throughout the nation.

Given the federal deficit, the ups and downs of the national economy, the strong tradition of state and local control, and the take-care-of-your-own values Kozol describes, what are the odds the federal government will increase its share of the public school budget from 8 percent to 33 percent? In the short run, there is no chance at all. In the long run, the odds are still poor, although the NEA would like to make one-third funding a target for the 2000s.

ACTIVITIES

1. Attend a local school board meeting. Ask to interview several board members and the superintendent about local control, representation, and other issues discussed in this chapter.

2. Find out how your state is implementing No Child Left Behind. Ask teachers, administrators, elected or appointed school officials, and state legislators how they feel about the changes.

3. Talk with two members of Congress, one Democrat and one Republican, about how the federal politics of education have evolved from Bill Clinton to George W. Bush.

4. Find out how widely per-pupil expenditures vary from district to district in the state where you plan to teach. How strong is the emphasis on equity and adequacy in your state's school finance formula?

RECOMMENDED READINGS

American School Board Journal. Read this journal, which local school board members receive every month, to keep up with issues and trends the members see as important.

Lewis, Anne C. "Washington Commentary," monthly column in *Phi Delta Kappan*. With a strongly pro–public education spin, Lewis covers the federal politics of education and their impact on the state and local levels.

Quality Counts 2005: No Small Change. Targeting Money toward Student Performance. A special report from *Education Week* (January 6, 2005). Valuable for its insightful articles as well as its state-by-state data, this report reflects the emphasis on adequacy and equity in the era of No Child Left Behind.

U.S. Department of Education, Office of the Under Secretary. *No Child Left Behind: A Toolkit for Teachers* (Washington, DC: USDE, 2003). Here is a positive, teacher-friendly presentation of the federal law and its requirements.

NOTES

1. Lowell C. Rose and Alec M. Gallup, "The 36th Annual Phi Delta Kappa/Gallup Poll of the Public's Attitudes toward the Public Schools," *Phi Delta Kappan* 86 (September 2004): 42–44; Lowell C. Rose and Alec M. Gallup, "The 32nd Annual Phi Delta Kappa/Gallup Poll of the Public's Attitudes toward the Public Schools," *Phi Delta Kappan* 82 (September 2000): 43–44, 55; Stanley M. Elam, Lowell C. Rose, and Alec M. Gallup, "The 28th Annual Phi Delta Kappa/Gallup Poll of the Public's Attitudes toward the Public Schools," *Phi Delta Kappan* 78 (September 1996): 45–46, 50–52.
2. Lynn Olson, "Pulling in Many Directions," *Education Week* (November 17, 1999), pp. 27–30, 32.
3. National Commission on Excellence in Education, *A Nation at Risk: The Imperative for Educational Reform* (Washington, DC: U.S. Department of Education, 1983).
4. U.S. Department of Education, National Center for Education Statistics, *Digest of Education Statistics, 2002* (2003) [Available: nces.ed.gov/programs/digest/d03/tables/dt086.asp], Tbl. 86.
5. James Hinkle, "The Changing Face of School Board Elections," *Updating School Board Policies* (March 1998) [Available: http://www.nsba.org/nepn/newsletter/398.htm].
6. Ibid.; Patrice M. Jones, "Results Mixed in Cities Where Mayors Took Over Schools," *Mobile Register* (January 8, 1997), p. 1D.
7. Joel Spring, *Conflict of Interests: The Politics of American Education*, 5th ed. (New York: McGraw-Hill, 2005), Chap. 8. For various models, see Willis D. Hawley and Frederick M. Wirt, eds., *The Search for Community Power*, 2nd ed. (Englewood Cliffs, NJ: Prentice Hall, 1974); Michael Y. Nunnery and Ralph B. Kimbrough, *Politics, Power, Polls, and School Elections* (Berkeley, CA: McCutchan, 1971); and Donald J.

McCarty, Charles E. Ramsey, and Roald F. Campbell, *The School Managers: Power and Conflict in American Public Education* (Westport, CT: Greenwood Press, 1971).

8. David B. Tyack and Elizabeth Hansot, *Managers of Virtue: Public School Leadership in America, 1820–1980* (New York: Basic Books, 1986); L. Harmon Zeigler and M. Kent Jennings, *Governing American Schools: Political Interaction in Local School Districts* (North Scituate, MA: Duxbury, 1974); Raymond E. Callahan, *Education and the Cult of Efficiency: A Study of the Social Forces That Have Shaped the Administration of the Public Schools* (Chicago: University of Chicago Press, 1962).

9. William Hayes, *So You Want To Be a Superintendent?* (Lanham, MD: Rowman & Littlefield, 2001); "The State of Superintendents," *Education Week* (March 1, 2000); Thomas E. Glass, "The Shrinking Applicant Pool," *Education Week* (November 8, 2000), pp. 68, 50–51; Jackie M. Blount, *Destined to Rule the Schools: Women and the Superintendent, 1873–1995* (Albany, NY: State University of New York Press, 1998).

10. An analysis by a scholar sensitive to teacher power is Susan Moore Johnson's *Leading the Change: The Challenge of the New Superintendent* (San Francisco: Jossey-Bass, 1996).

11. Arthur Blumberg with Phyllis Blumberg, *The School Superintendent: Living with Conflict* (New York: Teachers College Press, 1985), Chaps. 5–6.

12. See Don Melvin and George Edmonson, "Influence of U.S. Religious Right May Remake World Politics," *Mobile Register* (December 5, 2004), p. 28A.

13. Roberta Combs, "Dear Friends," an open letter from the Christian Coalition (2004) [Available: www.cc.org/].

14. Quoted in Kathleen Vail, "Conservatively Speaking: What Does the Christian Coalition Want for U.S. Schools?" *American School Board Journal* 182 (December 1995): 30.

15. Ibid, p. 31. See Ralph Reed's book *Active Faith: How Christians Are Changing the Soul of American Politics* (New York: The Free Press, 1996).

16. Eagle Forum "School Board Candidate Questionnaire" (2004) [Available: www.eagleforum.org/questionnaire/school_board_q.html].

17. U.S. Department of Education, "Guidance on Constitutionally Protected Prayer in Public Elementary and Secondary Schools" (2003) [Available: www.ed.gov/policy/gen/guid/religionandschools/prayer_guidance.htm]; U.S. Department of Education, "Center for Faith-Based and Community Initiatives" (2004) [Available: www.ed.gov/about/inits/list/fbci/index.html].

18. Vail, "Conservatively Speaking," p. 32.

19. Ghassan John Tarazi, Joan L. Curcio, and Jim C. Fortune, "Where You Stand: Do School Board Members' Religious and Political Beliefs Affect Their Board Decisions?" *American School Board Journal* 184 (January 1997): 26–29.

20. George R. Kaplan, "Friends, Foes, and Noncombatants: Notes on Public Education's Pressure Groups," *Phi Delta Kappan* 82 (November 2000): K7–K9.

21. The National School Board Association keeps up with the demographics of local board members and school administrators. See Frederick M. Hess, *School Boards at the Dawn of the 21st Century: Conditions and Challenges of District Governance* (2002) [Available: www.nsba.org/sites/docs/1200/1143.pdf], pp. 25–28.

22. Ibid. For comparisons over time, see Beatrice H. Cameron, Kenneth E. Underwood, and Jim C. Fortune, "It's Ten Years Later, and You've Hardly Changed at All," *American School Board Journal* 175 (January 1988): 20.

23. James E. Upperman, Joan L. Curcio, Jim C. Fortune, and Kenneth E. Underwood, "Who You Are," *American School Board Journal* 183 (January 1996): 34.

24. Hess, *School Boards at the Dawn of the 21st Century*, Chap. 4.

25. Ibid. See Table 8.3.

26. David B. Tyack, *The One Best System: A History of American Urban Education* (Cambridge, MA: Harvard University Press, 1974), part IV.

27. Mark Walsh, "Court Asks Justice Department for Views on School Board Voting Cases," *Education Week* (October 13, 1999), p. 28; Peter Schmidt, "Civil-Rights Lawyers Target School Board Elections," *Education Week* (October 28, 1992).

28. William Montague, "A Vote for Power," *Education Week* (December 9, 1987), pp. 1, 16–17.

29. Ibid.; Walsh, "Court Asks Justice Department," p. 28; Cameron, Underwood, and Fortune, "It's Ten Years Later," p. 20.

30. Mark Walsh, "School Board Voting-Rights Case Accepted," *Education Week* (June 12, 1996), pp. 1, 23; Sean Reilly, "Supreme Court Reverses Lower Court on Racial Redistricting in Alabama," *Mobile Register* (November 28, 2000), p. 4A.

31. Joseph W. Newman, "Socioeconomic Class and Education: In What Ways Does Class Affect the Educational Process?" in Joe L. Kincheloe and Shirley R. Steinberg, eds., *Thirteen Questions: Reframing Education's Conversation,* 2nd ed. (New York: Peter Lang, 1995), p. 193.

32. Hess, *School Boards at the Dawn of the 21st Century,* p. 26.

33. George S. Counts, *The Social Composition of Boards of Education: A Study in the Social Control of Public Education* (Chicago: University of Chicago Press, 1927), p. 81.

34. For helpful overviews of state school politics, see Spring, *Conflict of Interests,* Chap. 7; and Frederick M. Wirt and Michael W. Kirst, *The Political Dynamics of American Education,* 2nd ed. (Richmond, CA: McCutchan, 2001).

35. See Marc S. Tucker and Thomas Toch, "The Secret to Quality Making NCLB Work? More Bureaucrats," *Phi Delta Kappan* 86 (September 2004), p. 28.

36. Lynn Olson, "Enveloping Expectations," *Quality Counts 2004: Count Me In. Special Education in an Era of Standards,* a special report from *Education Week* (January 8, 2004), pp. 8–21.

37. Doug Gross, "Judge Orders Removal of Evolution Stickers," *Mobile Register* (January 14, 2005), p. 5A.

38. The National Association of State Board of Education (NASBE) provides information on state board members at www.nasbe.org. See also NASBE, *State Education Governance at-a-Glance* (Alexandria, VA: NASBE, 2004).

39. Ibid.; Council of Chief State School Officers, "Meet the Chiefs" and "Chiefs' Addresses" (2004) [Available: www.ccsso.org/chief_state_school_officers/meet_the_chiefs/index.cfm].

40. Tucker and Toch, "The Secret to Making NCLB Work," p. 29.

41. Ibid., p. 30.

42. Robert Rothman, *Measuring Up: Standards, Assessment, and School Reform* (San Francisco: Jossey-Bass, 2000), Chap. 4; Richard J. Coley and Margaret E. Goertz, *Educational Standards in the 50 States* (Princeton, NJ: Educational Testing Service, 1990), pp. 3–4.

43. Jonathan Alter, "Busting the Big Blob," *Newsweek* (April 8, 1996), p. 40.

44. Spring, *Conflict of Interests,* pp. 16–21.

45. See Arthur E. Wise, *Legislated Learning: The Bureaucratization of the American Classroom* (Berkeley: University of California Press, 1979), and Wise, "The Two Conflicting Trends in School Reform: Legislated Learning Revisited," *Phi Delta Kappan* 69 (January 1988): 328–333. Michael W. Kirst discusses the quantitative mindset in "Sustaining the Momentum of State Education Reform: The Link between Assessment and Financial Support," *Phi Delta Kappan* 67 (January 1986): 341–345.

46. Carnegie Foundation for the Advancement of Teaching, *The Condition of Teaching: A State-by-State Analysis, 1990* (Lawrenceville, NJ: Princeton University Press, 1990); Public Agenda, *Stand by Me: What Teachers Really Think about Unions, Merit Pay and Other Professional Matters* (New York: Public Agenda, 2003).

47. Public Agenda, *Attitudes about Teaching: Including the Views of Parents, Administrators, Teachers and the General Public* (New York: Public Agenda, 2003), p. 6.

48. Robert A. Skinner, "State of the States," *Quality Counts 2005,* p. 76.

49. Tucker and Toch, "The Secret to Making NCLB Work," p. 30.

50. For contrasting accounts of the federal role since World War II, see Wayne J. Urban and Jennings L. Wagoner, Jr., *American Education: A History,* 2nd ed. (Boston: McGraw-Hill, 2000), Chaps. 10–12; Joel H. Spring, *The Sorting Machine Revisited: National Education Policy since 1945,* rev. ed. (White Plains, NY: Longman, 1989); and Diane Ravitch, *The Troubled Crusade: American Education, 1945–1980* (New York: Basic Books, 1983).

51. Lynn Olson, "Title I Turns 20: A Commemoration and Debate," *Education Week* (May 1, 1985), pp. 1, 12–13; U.S. Department of Education, Center for Education Statistics, *Digest of Education Statistics, 1982* (Washington, DC: U.S. Government Printing Office, 1982), p. 171.

52. Gary Orfield, *The Reconstruction of Southern Education: The Schools and the 1964 Civil Rights Act* (New York: Wiley, 1969).

53. Urban and Wagoner, *American Education,* Chap. 11.

54. Ibid.

55. James T. Patterson, *Brown v. Board of Education: A Civil Rights Milestone and its Troubled Legacy* (New York: Oxford University Press, 2001). For an account of the Boston confrontation, see J. Anthony Lukas, *Common Ground: A Turbulent Decade in the Lives of Three American Families* (New York: Knopf, 1985).

56. Joetta L. Sack, "Bringing Special Education Students into the Classroom," *Education Week* (January 27, 1999), pp. 36–37; Steven Carlson, "'Appropriate' School Programs: Legal vs. Educational Approaches," *Exceptional Parent* 15 (September 1985): 23, 25–26, 28–30.

57. David L. Clark and Terry A. Astuto, "The Significance and Permanence of Changes in Federal Education Policy," *Educational Researcher* 15 (October 1986): 4–13; Dennis P. Doyle and Terry W. Hartle, "Ideology, Pragmatic Politics, and the Education Budget," in John C. Weicher, ed., *Maintaining the Safety Net: Income Redistribution Programs in the Reagan Administration* (Washington, DC: American Enterprise Institute for Public Policy Research, 1984), Chap. 6; Deborah A. Verstegen and David L. Clark, "The Diminution of Federal Expenditures for Education during the Reagan Administration," *Phi Delta Kappa* 70 (October 1988): 134–138.

58. Ibid.

59. Lynn Olson, "Inside 'A Nation at Risk,'" *Education Week* (April 27, 1988), pp. 1, 22–23.

60. Joel Spring, "Education and the Sony War," *Phi Delta Kappan* 65 (April 1984): 534–537.

61. National Commission on Excellence in Education, *A Nation at Risk*, pp. 5, 7.

62. For autobiographical accounts of the two secretaries of education, see Terrel H. Bell, *The Thirteenth Man: A Reagan Cabinet Memoir* (New York: Free Press, 1988), and William J. Bennett, *The Devaluing of America: The Fight for Our Culture and Our Children* (New York: Simon & Schuster, 1994).

63. Clark and Astuto, "The Significance and Permanence of Changes," pp. 10–11.

64. Quoted in Lynn Olson and Julie A. Miller, "The 'Education President' at Midterm: Mismatch between Rhetoric, Results?" *Education Week* (January 9, 1991), p. 1.

65. U.S. Department of Education, *America 2000: An Education Strategy Sourcebook* (Washington, DC: USDE, 1991), p. 19.

66. National Education Goals Panel, *The National Education Goals Report: Building a Nation of Learners* (Washington, DC: U.S. Government Printing Office, 1995), pp. 10–13.

67. See the four evaluations of America 2000 in *Phi Delta Kappan* 73 (November 1991), especially Harold Howe II's essay "A Bumpy Ride on Four Trains," pp. 192–203.

68. Julie A. Miller, "With a Long Track Record on Education, Campaigner Clinton Speaks with Authority," *Education Week* (February 5, 1992), pp. 1, 14–15.

69. David J. Holt, "Taking Stock of Clinton's Spending Record," *Education Week* (October 2, 1996), pp. 21, 24.

70. See Mark Pitsch, "Critics Target Goals 2000 in Schools 'War,'" *Education Week* (October 19, 1994), pp. 1, 21; "Agency: No States Opting Out of Goals 2000," *Mobile Register* (August 29, 1996), p. 2B.

71. See Mark Walsh, "Trace Sought in School Wars over Religion," *Education Week* (March 29, 1995), pp. 1, 10; Holt, "Taking Stock," pp. 21, 24; Pitsch, "Polls Confirm Political Role," pp. 1, 30–31.

72. Mark Pitsch, "GOP Themes Boost Choice, Hamper Dole," *Education Week* (October 30, 1996), pp. 1, 28–29.

73. U.S. Department of Education, "Department of Education Appropriations History" (2000) [Available: www.ed.gov/offices/OUS/History.pdf]; Eric W. Robelen, "Negotiations Continue on Education Department Budget," *Education Week* (December 13, 2000), pp. 31–32.

74. Joetta L. Sack, "Clinton Calls for Emphasis on Teachers," *Education Week* (February 2, 2000), p. 29; Kaplan, "Friends, Foes, and Noncombatants," pp. K11–K12.

75. Dennis P. Doyle, "The Presidential Sweepstakes 2004," *Phi Delta Kappan* 86 (October 2004): 111–113, 121.

76. George W. Bush, "The Essential Work of Democracy," *Phi Delta Kappan* 86 (October 2004): 114.

77. Lowell C. Rose, "The Politicization of K–12 Education," *Phi Delta Kappan* 86 (October 2004): 122–127.

78. Anne C. Lewis, "New ESEA Extends Choice to School Officials," *Phi Delta Kappan* 83 (February 2002): 423–425.

79. Ibid.

80. Ibid.; Eric W. Robelen, "ESEA to Boost Federal Role in Education," *Education Week* (January 9, 2002), pp. 1, 28–31.

81. Quoted in Joan Didion, "Mr. Bush and the Divine," *New York Review of Books* (November 6, 2003), p. 83.

82. Joel Spring, *Conflict of Interests*, pp. 16–21.

83. Tucker and Toch, "The Secret to Making NCLB Work," p. 29; "States Rebel against New Education Law," *Mobile Register* (February 18, 2004), p. 7A.

84. Bush, "The Essential Work of Democracy," p. 120.

85. A useful textbook is Allen R. Odden and Lawrence O. Picus, *School Finance: A Policy Perspective*, 3rd ed. (New York: McGraw-Hill, 2003).

86. National Education Association, *Rankings & Estimates: Rankings of the States 2003 and Estimates of School Statistics 2004* (Washington, DC: NEA), pp. 83–85.

87. Lynn Olson, "Financial Evolution," *Quality Counts 2005*, p. 11; "Resources: Equity," *Quality Counts 2005*, p. 101.

88. Spring, *American Education*, pp. 288–289; Charles A. Tesconi, Jr., and Emanuel Hurwitz, Jr., *Education for Whom?: The Question of Equal Educational Opportunity* (New York: Dodd, Mead, 1974), pp. 50–65.

89. Spring, *American Education*, p. 288.

90. "Resources," *Quality Counts: A Report Card on the Condition of Public Education in the 50 States* (January 22, 1997), p. 54; David L. Kirp and Donald N. Jensen, "The New Federalism Goes to Court," *Phi Delta Kappan* 65 (November 1983): 206–210.

91. "Resources: Equity," *Quality Counts 2005*, pp. 100–101.

92. "Finance Snapshots," *Quality Counts 2005*, pp. 70, 74.

93. Newman, "Socioeconomic Class," p. 203.

94. Jonathan Kozol, *Savage Inequalities: Children in America's Schools* (New York: Crown, 1991).

95. Rob Greenwald, Larry V. Hedges, and Richard D. Laine, "The Effect of School Resources on Student Achievement," *Review of Educational Research* 66 (Fall 1996): 361–396; Eric A. Hanushek, "A More Complete Picture of School Resource Policies," *Review of Educational Research* 66 (Fall 1996): 397–409.

96. Lynn Olson, "Financial Evolution," *Quality Counts 2005*, p. 14; "Financing Better Schools," *Quality Counts 2005*, p. 7.

97. Chris Pipho, "Entire Kentucky Education System Unconstitutional!" *Phi Delta Kappan* 71 (September 1989): 6–7.

98. Ibid.

99. Bess Keller, "After 10 Years, Landmark Kentucky Law Yielding Dividends," *Education Week* (November 17, 1999), p. 18; "Resources," *Quality Counts: A Report on the Condition of Public Education*, p. 57; "Resources: Equity," *Quality Counts 2005*, p. 100.

100. David J. Hoff, "The Bottom Line," *Quality Counts 2005*, p. 29.

101. "Resources: Spending," *Quality Counts 2005*, p. 103.

102. Catherine Gewertz, "A Level Playing Field," *Quality Counts 2005*, pp. 41–48.

103. Ibid., p. 42.

104. Ibid., pp. 47–48.

105. Ibid., p. 47.

106. Ibid., p. 42.

107. Kozol, *Savage Inequalities*, p. 222.

108. David C. Berliner and Bruce J. Biddle, *The Manufactured Crisis: Myths, Fraud, and the Attack on America's Public Schools* (Reading, MA: Addison-Wesley, 1995), pp. 294–295.

PART III

CRITICAL ISSUES
FOR THE 2000S

CHAPTER 10

PRIVATE SCHOOLS VERSUS PUBLIC SCHOOLS

One of the hottest educational issues today is the competition between private schools and public schools. *Competition* is exactly the right word. Historically, advocates of both kinds of schools have been quick to argue the superiority of their particular brand of education, with the arguments always spirited and sometimes bitter.

In this chapter we will hear the ongoing debate. First we will survey the four sectors of private elementary and secondary education—*Roman Catholic schools, other religious schools, independent schools,* and *home schools*—and examine a demographic profile of private schools and their students. Then we will focus on Catholic schools, the largest network of private schools in the United States, and fundamentalist Christian schools, the fastest-growing private schools from the 1970s through the mid-1980s. Catholic schools and fundamentalist schools, as different from each other as they are from public schools, illustrate the diversity of American private education. *Home schools,* the fastest growing sector of private education since the mid-1980s, provide further evidence of this diversity.

This chapter closes with a discussion of *government regulation* and *educational choice,* controversial issues shaping the future of both private and public education. Considered together, these issues can help you understand the climate of *deregulation* that is now affecting education just as it is changing other aspects of life in this nation and much of the world.

Although the distinction between public and private education was hazy in the United States until the middle of the nineteenth century—many church schools, for instance, received public funds and were open to children of all faiths—the common school crusades drew a sharp line between *public* schools controlled by state and local school boards and *private* schools controlled by churches and individuals (see Chapter 6). Since then, Americans have engaged in a running debate on the merits of private schools and public schools. Over the past few decades, as public education has struggled with more than its share of problems, the arguments have intensified.[1]

The debate has always been political in the sense that it reflects disagreements over who should control the education of young people: governments, churches, other groups, or individuals? The arguments are more partisan than they have been in years.

The Republican Party has positioned itself as an advocate of private schools, not necessarily in preference to public schools but certainly as an alternative for those dissatisfied with public schools. According to many Republicans, government should provide money to help people choose the school, public or private, they think best for their children.

The Democratic Party has been trying to defend public education without appearing to defend the status quo. Warming to the idea of choice but only among public schools, many Democrats contend government should work to improve public education rather than siphon off money to subsidize private education.

Reflecting the ongoing sparring between Democrats and Republicans, educational choice has become one of the liveliest issues in education. When Congress passed the No Child Left Behind Act of 2001, for instance, most Republicans supported a provision that would have allowed students in a "failing" public school to transfer to either a public school or private school at government expense. Democrats blocked the provision, insisting that public revenue pay only for transfers to a public school (Chapter 9). In 2002, far more Republicans than Democrats cheered when the U.S. Supreme Court declared constitutional a *voucher* program that allows poor students in Cleveland to attend private schools, including private religious schools, at public expense.

We will examine the debate over private schools and public schools in the context of educational politics in the twenty-first century. If substantial sums of public money begin to flow into schools now considered private, the very definitions of public and private will change, and the most fundamental realignment of American education since the era of common school reform will take place.

FOUR SECTORS OF PRIVATE ELEMENTARY AND SECONDARY EDUCATION

Roman Catholics built this nation's largest system of private schools on their religious objections to common schools. The religious emphasis in Catholic education continues, but now Catholics are calling more attention than ever to the intellectual quality of their schools, touting them as academic alternatives to public schools. Although Catholic schools remain, by far, the largest sector of private education, they are struggling to turn around an enrollment decline that has extended over most of the last forty years. After a brief rally in the mid-1990s, enrollment is decreasing again in the 2000s.

Other religious schools constitute the second-largest sector of private education. Throughout U.S. history, people of many faiths have felt the need to give their children an education grounded in religious doctrine. Fundamentalist Protestants, the most prominent recent example, complain the values they stress at home and in church clash with the values that dominate public education. Their schools were the fastest growing private schools in the nation until home schools took over that title in the late 1980s. Religious schools sponsored by people of other faiths—including Jews, Lutherans, Episcopalians, Seventh-Day Adventists, and Calvinists—offer still other alternatives to public education.

Independent (also called nonsectarian) schools that have no religious affiliation, the third-largest sector of private education, meet the needs of Americans seeking academic and social alternatives to public education—families ranging from those who feel their children are languishing academically in public schools to those who have disabled children to those who insist their children be educated with others from the same socioeconomic background. In the 2000s, independent schools are holding their own in enrollment.

Home schools are the fourth and smallest sector of private education. Until recently they were not categorized separately because so few students went to school at home and because it is difficult to collect accurate information on home schooling. But as more and more families appear to be deciding to educate their children outside *any* formal institutional setting, private or public, home schools are moving into the national spotlight.

Roman Catholic schools, other religious schools, independent schools, and home schools keep the public-versus-private debate alive. Because it is hard to compare public schools and private schools objectively, zealous debaters often get carried away with their arguments and appeal to emotion more than intellect.

The diversity of both kinds of schools should make us wary of such sweeping statements as "private schools are academically superior" and "public schools offer better socialization." Beyond the value judgments embedded in these claims (What constitutes academic quality? What kinds of socialization are desirable?), we must realize that a Catholic school in central-city Chicago, for instance, is likely to be quite different from a Catholic school in the suburbs of Atlanta. Social class, race, ethnicity, and gender—the sociological factors whose influence on public education we examined in Chapter 8—also affect private education,

■ ■ ■ ■ ■

BOX 10.1
COUNCIL FOR AMERICAN PRIVATE EDUCATION

The Council for American Private Education (CAPE) is an advocacy group that tries
to be pro–private schooling without being anti–public schooling. Find out whether it
succeeds by visiting CAPE online at www.capenet.org

although Catholics contend their schools minimize the negative effects of these
factors better than public schools. We would discover even more diversity if we
compared almost any Catholic school with almost any fundamentalist Christian
school, and including independent schools would heighten the contrast even
more. Home schools are also quite diverse, as we will see later in this chapter.

Public schools, of course, vary at least as much. A suburban school in the Silicon Valley of California, a county school in rural Mississippi, and a magnet school
in New York City would strike us as more different than similar, and these are
only three of several hundred thousand public schools. In some communities, virtually all students attend public schools, while in other places public schools have
become just what the common school reformers of the nineteenth century feared:
schools serving only the children of the poor. We must take astonishing diversity
into account when we generalize about public and private education.

PROFILES OF PRIVATE SCHOOLS
AND THEIR STUDENTS

With these words of caution in mind, we can learn a great deal from demographic
profiles of private education. The statistics offer surprises and challenge conventional wisdom.

Throughout the twentieth century, as Table 10.1 indicates, private schools
have enrolled between 7 and 14 percent of the nation's elementary and secondary
school students. Given the massive social changes of this century, what is most striking about these enrollment figures is the stability they reveal. As a share of all K–12
students, the low point of private school enrollment (7.3 percent) came in 1920,
when public schools were key players in the campaign to assimilate immigrant children. Private schools attracted their largest share of students (13.8 percent) in 1959,
when many children and grandchildren of turn-of-the-century immigrants were
choosing Roman Catholic schools for *their* children. Thus the peak for private
schools came, ironically, at the end of the 1950s, a decade that now has a rosy nostalgic reputation for "good public schools."[2]

Trends since 1960 also show more stability than change, calling into question
the popular belief that ever-increasing numbers of students have abandoned public
schools for private schools. In fact, private school enrollment *decreased* during the
social upheavals of the 1960s and early 1970s, falling to a 10 percent share of all

TABLE 10.1   Private School Share of Total Enrollment in Elementary and Secondary Schools, 1890–2005

YEAR	PERCENTAGE OF STUDENTS IN CATHOLIC, OTHER RELIGIOUS, AND INDEPENDENT SCHOOLS	PERCENTAGE OF STUDENTS IN HOME SCHOOLS
1890	11.1	
1900	7.9	
1910	7.8	
1920	7.3	
1930	9.4	
1940	9.3	
1950	11.8	
1959	13.8	
1965	12.9	
1970	10.5	
1975	10.0	
1980	11.5	
1985	12.3	.4
1990	11.2	.6
1995	11.2	1.3
2000	11.2	1.6
2005	10.8	2.2

Sources: Estimates and projections based on U.S. Department of Education, National Center for Education Statistics, *Digest of Education Statistics, 2002* (2003) [Available: nces.ed.gov/programs/digest/d02/tables/dt002.asp], and U.S. Department of Education, National Center for Education Statistics, *1.1 Million Homeschooled Students in the United States in 2003: Issue Brief* (2004) [Available: nces.gov/pubs2004/2004115.pdf]; Patricia M. Lines, *Homeschoolers, Estimating Numbers and Growth,* U.S. Department of Education (1999) [Available: www.ed.gov/offices/OERI/SAI/homeschool/index.html].

K–12 students by 1975. Then private school enrollment rose to a 12.7 percent share in 1985, the first year home schooling attracted enough students to show up in Table 10.1. Notice the two divergent patterns of enrollment since 1985. Although we can see home schooling gaining popularity, we can also see the three main sectors of private education losing their share of total K–12 enrollment.

Into the 2000s, then, trends in enrollment do not show anything like a mass exodus from public schools to private schools or from one sector of private education to another. Once again, the stability of the enrollment balance is more significant than the changes. On the other hand, looking at national demographic data may not change the opinions of true believers in either private or public education because people tend to generalize from their own experience with their local schools.

New Patterns within the Four Sectors

Based on the U.S. Department of Education report *Characteristics of Private Schools in the United States* (2004), Figure 10.1 depicts the world of private education in the

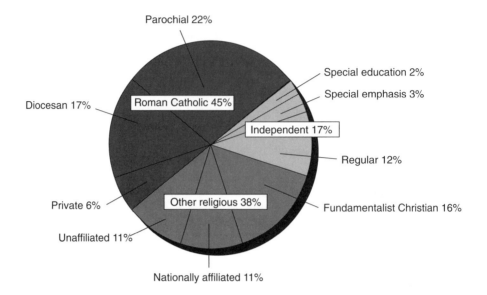

FIGURE 10.1   Private School Enrollment, by Type of Institution, 2005.

Note: This chart does not include home schooled students.

Sources: Estimates and projections based on U.S. Department of Education. National Center for Education Statistics, *Characteristics of Private Schools in the United States: Results from the 2001–2002 Private School Universe Survey* (2004) [Available: nces.ed.gov/pubs2005/2005305.pdf], Tbl 1.

early twenty-first century. Within the largest sector, Roman Catholic, there are three types of schools: parochial, which are governed by individual parishes and enroll about 22 percent of all private school students; diocesan, which are under the control of a larger diocese and enroll about 17 percent; and private order schools sponsored by such groups as the Christian Brothers, Dominicans, and Jesuits, which serve another 6 percent. Altogether, Roman Catholic schools claimed more than 90 percent of private school enrollment during the 1950s and almost two-thirds as late as 1980, but now they have less than half.[3]

The closing of Catholic schools that served their urban parishes for many years is an ongoing reminder of the declining popularity of Catholic education. Many of the Irish, German, Italian, Polish, and other white ethnic families who were the backbone of Catholic schools have moved to the suburbs, and they no longer seem as committed to Catholic education. Across the nation, the story of Catholic education is much the same: Central-city schools are closing, and although schools in some suburban parishes are thriving, overall enrollment continues on a downward course.

Other religious schools now enroll about 38 percent of all private school students, up from 21 percent in 1980. These are the schools that dominate the landscape of private education in suburban, small-town, and rural America. The U.S. Department of Education classifies other religious schools in three groups: those affiliated with a fundamentalist Christian school association (about 16 percent of private school students); those affiliated with a national denomination or another type of national religious school association (about 11 percent); and those with no affiliation (about 11 percent).

Independent private education encompasses a variety of institutions, which the Department of Education also classifies in three groups: regular schools, sometimes called prep schools, which include the selective boarding and day schools that belong to the National Association of Independent Schools (about 12 percent of private school students); special emphasis schools, such as military, Montessori, art, and alternative schools (about 3 percent); and special education schools that serve disabled and other exceptional students (about 2 percent). In all, the independent sector of private education enrolls about 17 percent of private school students, approximately the same percentage as in 1980. This flat pattern disguises a great deal of variation: the rising popularity of institutions affiliated with the National Association of Independent Schools, for instance, contrasts with the near extinction of military academies.[4]

How significant is the growth of home schooling? Home schoolers are independent by nature, and because some do not register with state or local governments, reliable estimates of their numbers are hard to come by. In addition, some researchers believe home schooling associations inflate the size and scope of the movement. Even so, a 2004 report from the U.S. Department of Education estimates that the share of K–12 students who stay at home for their schooling now exceeds 2 percent. That estimate represents more than 1,000,000 young people, a tremendous jump from the 10,000 to 15,000 home-schooled students of the late 1970s and early 1980s.[5]

Who Goes to Private School?

When David Baker and Cornelius Riordan published an article in the September 1998 issue of *Phi Delta Kappan* charging that the "old Catholic common school is fast becoming an elite private school" in which the "proportion of wealthy students has doubled since the early 1970s," many Catholic educators fumed. Father Andrew Greeley, a well-known Catholic scholar and writer, led a hard-hitting counterattack in the pages of the *Kappan*. We will revisit this ongoing debate in the next section, but here it is important to note how sensitive the charge of private school elitism is and how eager many private educators are to shatter the "rich white kid" stereotype.[6]

Social Class.   According to information compiled by the U.S. Census Bureau in 2003, 44 percent of private school students and 51 percent of public school students come from middle-income families (defined as those in the middle half of the nation's income distribution). Roman Catholic schools, the largest sector of private education, are proud of their socioeconomic diversity. Historically, as Father Greeley and other Catholic educators often remind us, their schools have welcomed children from all social classes, often adjusting tuition to match family income. Other private educators make the same kind of claims. Fundamentalist Christian schools appeal primarily to lower-middle class and upper-working class families. Home schoolers appear to be a mostly middle-class group. Even independent schools are more diverse than their prep school image suggests. "Havens for the Rich" is a label that fits very few private schools, their advocates insist.[7]

Public school supporters call attention to major differences between private school and public school enrollment at both ends of the economic ladder. Students from lower-income families (the bottom quarter of the nation) make up 26 percent of the enrollment in public schools but only 10 percent in private schools. Students from upper-income families (the top quarter of the nation) represent 24 percent of the enrollment in public schools but 46 percent in private schools. Said another way, a student is two and a half times as likely to encounter lower-income classmates in a public school and twice as likely to encounter upper-income classmates in a private school.[8]

Race and Ethnicity. With respect to these cultural factors, private schools are much less diverse than public schools. Although the long-term trend has been toward increasing minority enrollment in private education, it now appears that the percentage is stabilizing. According to *Characteristics of Private Schools in the United States* (2004), minority students make up 24 percent of the enrollment in private schools, compared to 42 percent in public schools. Although many of the self-avowed "segregation academies" established from the 1950s through the 1970s to give white students an alternative to desegregated public schools have closed, plenty of segregation remains—in obvious as well as subtle forms—in private education and public education.[9]

Minority students now account for 21 percent of the overall enrollment in other religious schools and 24 percent in the fundamentalist Christian schools many critics once accused of being segregation academies. Today, almost all Christian schools include both minority and white students, and some Christian schools are predominantly African American.[10]

Independent schools, too, have become more diverse. Their overall enrollment is now 26 percent minority. Independent schools established to give black students an alternative to public schools are slowly gaining popularity. Families who choose African American academies often say public schools are only worsening a "desperate situation" for people of their race. As we saw in Chapter 8, several hundred African American academies have opened, and the debate continues over whether the voluntary segregation they promote represents a step forward or a step backward.[11]

Reliable information on the racial and ethnic diversity of the home schooling movement is hard to obtain. Available research, though, suggests more than 90 percent of home-schooled students are white.[12]

For the largest number of minority students who turn to private education, Roman Catholic schools are the alternative. Students from the white ethnic groups that have traditionally dominated Catholic education are being replaced by Hispanic Americans, African Americans, and Asian Americans. These students now represent 26 percent of the enrollment in Catholic schools (Hispanic Americans accounting for 12 percent, African Americans for 8 percent, Asian Americans for 5 percent, and Native Americans for 1 percent). Most of the blacks come from non-Catholic families who, like the families choosing African American academies, believe public schools are miseducating their children. Desegregation remains at lower levels in Catholic elementary schools, which often draw from homogeneous neighborhoods, than in Catholic secondary schools with their broader attendance zones. The racial and ethnic balance of Catholic schools is a major topic of discussion among Catholic educators. It promises to add fuel to the debates about private schools and public schools.[13]

ROMAN CATHOLIC SCHOOLS

Academic Achievement and Socioeconomic Background

The academic quality of Catholic schools versus public schools continues to be another key issue in the debates. Politicians focus national attention on the issue. Popular media sing the praises of Catholic education. The accolades reached a crescendo during the mid-1990s as enrollment trends in Catholic schools turned around and educational choice picked up support in the political arena.

Public schools would do well to emulate Catholic schools, *USA Today* told its readers in a front-page story and six other articles in October 1996. Catholic schools expect more and, yes, *demand* more of students by stressing a "traditional" academic curriculum and "strict-but-fair" discipline policies. Teachers in Catholic schools receive "less pay" but "more respect."[14] Given all this free publicity, a high-powered advertising agency would be hard-pressed to do a better job spreading the word about Catholic education.

Now, in the 2000s, media reports on school closings and allegations of sex abuse threaten to overshadow the praise Catholic schools continue to receive for their academic quality. In 2004 my hometown newspaper ran a front-page series that mixed praise for high academic standards with concerns that the "suburbanization" of Catholic education is depriving poor and minority students of access to private schooling.[15]

With the exception of the abuse issue, which has come to light only recently, all these themes appear prominently in the last two decades of scholarly research on private education. The late James Coleman, a prominent sociologist of education, was the leading voice in this research throughout the 1980s and into the 1990s. Coleman argued that the best high schools—which he defined as the schools whose students have the highest standardized test scores—share a set of characteristics. Their students attend school more regularly, take more academic (as opposed to general and vocational) courses, and do more homework. High-performance schools have a more disciplined and orderly climate.[16]

These findings, which should hardly seem startling by now, are consistent with the research on effective schools we reviewed in Chapter 8. What made Coleman's research so controversial was his insistence that private schools are more likely than public schools to have these characteristics and, as a result, private schools are academically superior.

Coleman and His Critics.   Predictably, these generalizations drew the fire of critics. Public school defenders charged Coleman's conclusions went well beyond his data. Because few of the private schools in his study were non-Catholic religious schools or independent schools, the critics claimed Coleman's findings were valid, at best, for comparing Catholic schools and public schools. But furthermore, the critics continued, Coleman had failed to control adequately for student socioeconomic background. They pointed out private school parents have higher average incomes as well as higher average levels of education, suggesting such factors—which sociologists have found to correlate with student achievement—account for the higher achievement Coleman attributed to private schools. The critics called attention to other studies showing no significant differences in achievement between private school and public school students from the same socioeconomic background.[17]

During the 1980s, these arguments seesawed back and forth. Coleman admitted that his conclusions about non-Catholic private schools were tentative, but he stuck to his guns on Catholic schools.

In the now-classic book *Public and Private High Schools: The Impact of Communities* (1987), Coleman paid more attention to differences between Catholic schools and other private schools and included more data on student socioeconomic background. He also examined *gains* in student achievement over a two-year period instead of measuring achievement at only one point, as he did in his earlier studies.[18]

Focusing on verbal and mathematical skills, Coleman contended students in Catholic high schools show higher gains in achievement than students of comparable socioeconomic status in public schools *and* most other private schools. The evidence on achievement gains in Catholic schools strengthened his earlier conclusion that the schools themselves, not just the socioeconomic background the students bring to the schools, play a major role in academic success. As before, Coleman claimed the academic benefits of a Catholic education are greatest for African Americans, Hispanic Americans, and poor students. He also pointed out that dropout rates are much lower in Catholic schools than in public schools and most other private schools.[19]

A Consensus of Sorts.   As Cornelius Riordan explains in *Equality and Achievement* (2004), the many reanalyses of Coleman's data highlight the difficulties of generalizing about private and public schools. If a consensus is forming at all, it is around the position that while Catholic schools do not offer academic advantages to *every* student, they do to *some* students: in particular, African Americans, Hispanic Americans, and others whose parents are likely to have lower incomes and less education.[20]

Because these are the very students who often get what philosopher Mortimer Adler called "dirty water" in public schools, they have the most to gain from attending a Catholic school. On the other hand, affluent white students—those who fit the private school stereotype—are the students most likely to receive "wine" (or at least "clean water") in public schools. These students have the least to gain from attending a Catholic school. The ongoing debate over Coleman's research is standing much of the conventional wisdom about public and private schools on its head.

Are Private Schools Better?

The academic arguments Coleman touched off continue to fuel a hot political debate. Obviously, a convincing affirmative answer to the question of whether private schools are academically superior to public schools would strengthen the case for educational choice. The debate has heated up since the 1990s as Milwaukee, Cleveland, Florida, and the District of Columbia have launched experimental voucher programs enabling some students to attend private schools at public expense. With popular opinion clearly favoring choice in some form and with some Democratic politicians joining the Republican call for private school vouchers, advocates of public education are stepping forward to attack what they call the "myth" of private school superiority.

We will listen to the debate over choice at the end of this chapter, but here it is important to understand the latest twist in the arguments over academic quality. Are differences in achievement between private and public school students *large enough* to justify the claim that private schools are better?

Clearly Not, Public School Supporters Answer.   On some standardized tests, achievement differences are very small. On the well-respected National Assessment of Educational Progress (NAEP) math tests, for instance, Catholic school students typically score only 7 to 16 points higher *on a 500-point scale* than public school students. In some years this test has been administered, moreover, the gaps between the scores of Catholic schoolers and public schoolers have been smaller in the twelfth grade than in the lower grades. These narrowing gaps cast doubt on Coleman's claim that students make higher achievement gains in Catholic schools than in public schools.[21]

Public school advocates like to call attention to these small and sometimes narrowing achievement differences. "This is amazing," the late Albert Shanker, president of the American Federation of Teachers, often pointed out, "because youngsters in private schools are a far more advantaged group, so they should be leaving public-school students behind in the dust."[22] Gerald Bracey, who regularly defends public schools in the pages of the *Phi Delta Kappan* and in speeches throughout the nation, takes the same position: "People who use private schools tend to be wealthier and better educated than the populace at large. When these advantages are statistically removed, public and private schools look very similar."[23]

Even Small Differences Can Be Significant.   Advocates of private education like to remind their critics that private school students post higher average scores than public school students on almost all standardized tests, and on some tests the differences are larger than those above. On the NAEP's reading assessments, for instance, students in private schools usually outscore those in public schools by 14 to 22 points on a 500-point scale.[24]

And so the arguments continue. Father Greeley and other true believers in Catholic education fall back on the position that Catholic schools offer their greatest benefits to disadvantaged students, particularly those who are minorities. David Baker and Cornelius Riordan, authors of the provocative *Phi Delta Kappan* article I mentioned earlier, retort with evidence on the increasingly "elite" makeup and orientation of Catholic high schools, where almost half of the students are now from families in the top quarter of the nation's income distribution. "Catholic schools are going out of the business of educating the disadvantaged," Baker and Riordan assert.[25]

In this respect, Catholic schools are becoming more like other private schools. As we saw earlier, 46 percent of all private school students are from upper-income families while only 10 percent are from lower-income families.

So how much of the difference in achievement between private and public school students is due to the characteristics of the schools themselves? How much is due to the socioeconomic backgrounds of the students? Statistical analysis may never yield conclusive answers to these questions, but that will not stop debaters on both sides of the issue from throwing empirical data around in the popular media. In the next section, we will see how Coleman, who built his career on quantitative research, tried to reach beyond the numbers to answer these questions.

Functional Communities and Value Communities

In *Public and Private High Schools,* Coleman stressed the importance of communities. He contended a *functional community* surrounds most Catholic and other religious schools. Although the students in these schools may not live in the same neighborhood, their "families attend the same religious services and know one another."[26] The support of the functional community helps families pass their values from one generation to the next.

Independent private schools and a few public schools are surrounded by a different kind of community, a *value community* composed of "people who share similar values about education and childrearing but who are not a functional community."[27] As the name suggests, this kind of community also aids in the intergenerational transmission of values.

Most public schools, by contrast, are grounded in *no* community—or so Coleman argued. Public schools once drew students from rural areas, small towns, and ethnic neighborhoods that constituted functional communities. But no longer. Today's public school attendance zones rarely correspond to either functional or value communities. Thus, according to Coleman, most public schools have lost their base of community support.

Human Capital and Social Capital

Coleman contended that of all schools, Catholic schools are the most effective at increasing *human capital,* which economists define as the skills and capabilities that make people productive. Some students come from families with relatively little human capital—their parents may be poorly educated and unemployed. Yet some families lacking in human capital may have an abundance of *social capital,* which "exists in the *relations* between persons."[28] Families with social capital are close; parents and children share warmth, trust, and support. Some families, of course, lack both human capital and social capital, while other families have both. Still other families have human capital but lack social capital. The parents may be well educated, for instance, but spend precious little time with their children.

Coleman stated social capital exists in communities as well as families. People who attend the same church and share the same religious values can sustain one another. Therefore, he argued, the functional community surrounding Catholic schools can supply social capital to students who lack it at home. Coleman pointed to the remarkable success of Catholic schools with students from single-parent families, families in which both parents work outside the home, and families who rarely talk about school. To a greater degree than any other kind of school, Catholic schools provide the support that can help such students succeed.

The widely quoted book *Catholic Schools and the Common Good* (1995) by Anthony Bryk, Valerie Lee, and Peter Holland builds on Coleman's thesis. "The internal organization of schools as communities fosters, *literally creates*, the engagement of school members in its mission," Bryk and his colleagues conclude.[29] So why are Catholic schools effective? Because their "communal organization" distributes achievement widely among a large group of students, not just a select few, and brings teachers, students, and parents together under an umbrella of shared values, shared activities, and positive social relations.

The *USA Today* stories we discussed earlier, along with many other reports in the media, are bringing a pop version of this research to the American public. Catholic educators offer inner-city students growing up in tough neighborhoods a "haven from mean streets . . . a sanctuary." In Catholic schools, "values and good manners are on the curriculum."[30] Coleman or Bryk could almost have written these stories.

Enough already, other researchers are saying. *Can Public Schools Learn from Private Schools?* (2004), a report from the Economic Policy Institute (EPI), tries to put these glowing claims into perspective. Based on case studies of eight private and eight public schools, EPI researchers conclude that a school's location—more specifically, the socioeconomic status of the community surrounding the school and the families who send their children there—is a more important factor than whether the school is public or private. Inner-city private schools have more in

BOX 10.2
NATIONAL CATHOLIC EDUCATION ASSOCIATION

See Catholic schools through the eyes of their teachers at the Web site of the National Catholic Education Association, www.ncea.org

common with inner-city public schools than with suburban private schools. Teachers in inner-city private schools voice the same complaints as those in inner-city public schools: Parents aren't involved and won't come to meetings. Students won't do their homework. Nor, according to the EPI study, are inner-city private schools more accountable to parents.[31]

Researchers in the Coleman tradition are not convinced. Before Coleman died in 1995, he put the case for private education into the larger context of "two orientations to schooling." Public educators try to keep parents at arm's length, he claimed, while private educators try to keep parents inside a community. Public schools are agents of the larger society and the state, trying to help children transcend the limitations of their family background. Private schools are agents and extensions of families, trying to help one generation transmit its values to the next.

"These two orientations are not in fundamental conflict," Coleman wrote, as long as the values of the family and the society are similar. But when the orientations clash, the families who feel the greatest sense of conflict turn to private schools, hoping to find there the values they miss in public schools. Coleman used this analysis to explain the rise of several different types of private schools. He contended the search for homogeneous values led Roman Catholics to start parochial schools before the Civil War, whites to establish segregation academies in response to the *Brown* decision, and fundamentalist Protestants to open Christian schools after the mid-1960s.[32]

FUNDAMENTALIST CHRISTIAN SCHOOLS

The concept of community is a good point of departure for our discussion of fundamentalist Christian schools. Most parents who send their children to Christian schools are products of the public schools. But public education has changed, fundamentalists insist. Interpreting the Bible literally and approaching their faith evangelically, they believe today's public schools promote secular values that clash with Christian values. Roman Catholics left public schools because they were too Protestant. Now fundamentalists are leaving public schools because they are not Protestant enough. Fundamentalists are opening their own schools and incorporating them into a functional community that also encompasses home and church.[33]

Critics initially dismissed these schools as just another variation on the segregation academy theme, and, to be sure, the early stirrings of the Christian school movement did coincide with the desegregation of public schools in the South. More than 90 percent of Christian schools operating today have been established since the mid-1960s. Without question, the desire to maintain racial homogeneity played a role in the founding of some Christian schools.[34]

By the 1970s, critics began to notice many Christian schools were enrolling both blacks and whites. The schools were growing in parts of the nation where desegregation was simply not an issue. Christian schools are separatist by their very nature, but it now appears the separation their supporters have in mind is not racial—or at least, according to all but their harshest critics, not *primarily* racial. Paraphrasing the New Testament, fundamentalists say they are "in the world but not of the world." They are trying to lead religious lives in the midst of a secular society.[35]

Separation and independence are hallmarks of fundamentalist Christian schools. They do not constitute a distinct system, as Catholic schools do, but instead more than 5,500 locally controlled alternatives to public education. Although Christian schools are becoming more receptive to outside visitors, they continue to resist government regulation. Some schools are controlled by a local congregation of such national denominations as the Baptist Church, Methodist Church, Church of Christ, or Assembly of God. Other schools are under the control of a nondenominational congregation or local foundation. Despite their insistence on local autonomy, many are affiliated with a Christian school association such as the Association of Christian Schools International, Accelerated Christian Education, American Association of Christian Schools, or Oral Roberts University Educational Fellowship.[36]

Inside Christian Schools

Focusing attention on obtaining salvation and preparing for life in the next world, virtually every subject in Christian schools is informed by fundamentalist doctrine. Young children learn to read from textbooks that highlight morality and are strongly reminiscent of the *McGuffey's Readers* that were a staple of nineteenth-century public schools. In some Christian schools, students use the *McGuffey's Readers* themselves. The fundamentalist approach to science stresses God's role as creator, based on a literal interpretation of the book of Genesis and other scriptures. According to the *creationist* view of biology, God made the universe in six days and rested on the seventh; the universe is only about 6,000 years old; and, contrary to the *evolutionist* view, the life forms we know today have not changed significantly since creation. The fundamentalist approach to history emphasizes the story of God's relationship with people on earth. Modern literature fundamentalists often object to in public schools—*Of Mice and Men, Catcher in the Rye, Salem's Lot,* the *Harry Potter* books—is simply excluded from Christian schools. Such literary classics as *Romeo and Juliet* and *Macbeth* may be included but in expurgated editions.

Some Christian schools use a packaged, programmed curriculum that draws a great deal of criticism from nonfundamentalist educators. Produced by such companies as A Beka Book and School of Tomorrow (formerly Accelerated Christian Education), the curriculum features workbooks and other materials designed to let students proceed at their own pace with little or no assistance. A student might take a year-long course in algebra, for instance, working independently in a room—sometimes in an individual cubicle—surrounded by other students taking different courses. Technology makes it possible for students to watch videotaped lessons or go online for part or all of their coursework.

Some developers of these materials downplay the importance of interaction among teachers and students as well as the importance of critical thinking. Instead, according to the publishers of the School of Tomorrow package, the goal is for students to "learn to see life from God's point of view." Such materials allow churches with limited budgets to start their own schools inexpensively, and they are also attractive to the growing ranks of home schoolers.[37]

Critics sometimes generalize the use of programmed materials to all fundamentalist Christian schools. Certainly, from the perspective of any of the theories of education we examined in Chapter 7, the memory-oriented, all-but-teacherless curriculum makes an easy target. Many of the better-established Christian schools, however, have never used programmed materials, and many of the newer ones are discarding them.

Fundamentalist Christian schools, like fundamentalist Christians themselves, are not all alike. I try to stress this point to the prospective teachers in my classes, who are often more curious about Christian schools than any other private schools. Regarding the central matter of religion, I can arrange the Christian schools in my own community on a continuum. At one end of the continuum are a few schools that are so dogmatically Protestant, they are overtly anti-Catholic. At the other end are a few schools that are so ecumenical in their approach to Christianity, Catholics are represented not only in the student body but on the faculty. Most fundamentalist Christian schools fall between these two extremes.

Don't visit a Christian school expecting to find programmed robots working away in cubicles. Visitors to some Christian schools may be surprised at how *essentialist* (see Chapter 7) their approach to education is. Well-groomed and well-disciplined students, enthusiastic teachers, and a familiar core of basic subjects can evoke, on the surface, the atmosphere of suburban public schools of the late 1950s—just as many Catholic schools do.

But visitors who stay for more than a few minutes will find that fundamentalist Christian education, different by design from public education, is also different from Roman Catholic education. When principals of Catholic high schools rank their educational goals, approximately 45 percent put religious development in first place, but a full 30 percent say academic excellence is their most important goal. Among principals of Christian schools, 68 percent put religious development first, and only 12 percent rank academic excellence as their top goal.[38]

BOX 10.3

A BEKA BOOK

To see the complete "scope and sequence" of a Christian school curriculum, visit the Web site of A Beka Book, the largest publisher of fundamentalist Christian textbooks, at www.abeka.com/resources/default.html

Religion informs the academic curriculum to a greater degree in fundamentalist Christian schools than Catholic schools. As the A Beka Book Web site explains, "Our skilled researchers and writers do not paraphrase progressive education textbooks and add Biblical principles; they do primary research in every subject and look at the subject from God's point of view. Of course, the most original source is always the word of God, which is the only foundation for true scholarship in any area of human endeavor."[39] Hearing an English teacher open discussion of a short story by asking "How would Jesus react in that situation?" or seeing a science teacher present evolution as a bogus theory and dismiss Charles Darwin as a mad scientist is sure to remind visitors they are in a fundamentalist environment. For prospective teachers who fill out an application for a teaching position, such questions as "Do you sense that God has called you to be a Christian school teacher?" and "How much time do you spend alone with God, reading the Bible and praying?" make it impossible to miss the fundamentalist orientation.

The Struggle against Secular Humanism

That orientation, fundamentalists insist, offers the best hope for helping their children escape from secularism. Fundamentalists want Christianity to permeate every aspect of their schools because they are firmly convinced *secular humanism*, which they regard as another religion, permeates public education and every other aspect of public life. During the 2000s, recurring controversies over the display of the Ten Commandments and other Judeo-Christian icons in public schools, courthouses, and other government buildings have strengthened the conviction that an organized campaign is under way to crowd out traditional faith and replace it with secular humanism.[40]

Secular Humanism and Public Education.   To fundamentalists, secular humanism is the belief that people are capable of charting their own course through life without divine assistance. In other words, human beings can set moral standards and make their own determination of right and wrong. So defined, secular humanism flies in the face of fundamentalist Christianity, which requires that people look to God for guidance and take their moral standards from the Bible. Fundamentalists argue that because secular humanism deals with ultimate concerns about life and reality, it is indeed a religion. Just as some people seek answers to ultimate questions in Christianity or Judaism, which are *theistic* religions centered on a deity, other people look to secular humanism, which fundamentalists view as a *nontheistic* religion centered on human beings.[41]

They charge that since the 1960s, when the U.S. Supreme Court ruled organized prayer in public schools unconstitutional in the *Engel v. Vitale* (1962) and *Abington v. Schempp* (1963) decisions, public education has been drifting away from its Judeo-Christian moorings. The moral and social revolutions of the sixties and seventies brought "sex, drugs, and rock and roll" into the schools, forcing students to make moral decisions at earlier ages. Just when students needed guidance more than ever, public education abandoned the yes-and-no answers found in a fundamentalist reading of the Bible for a situational morality that encourages students to weigh the consequences of their actions and make their own decisions.[42]

The battle is on, fundamentalists believe, and parents are the first line of defense. In *All about Ethics and Morals* (2004), Robert Sherman alerts parents to the dangers of secular humanism so they can teach their children to tell right from wrong and to "make the right choices when they are out with their friends." Parents must see to it that the schools their children attend do not downgrade the values they have acquired at home and in church, Sherman insists.[43]

Fundamentalists object to the content of many public school textbooks, claiming some social studies texts, for instance, say too little about the role of the Judeo-Christian tradition in U.S. history. Some literature books contain nonjudgmental portrayals of immoral behavior. Textbooks used in a variety of subjects, they say, convey the message "Think for yourself" rather than "Trust in God."

The cumulative effect of public education on students is subtle but powerful, fundamentalists conclude. By persuading students they are in charge of their own destiny, public schools promote the religion of secular humanism. From the fundamentalist point of view, Christian schools teaching submission to God's will offer a clear alternative.

Secular Humanism and the Courts.   In order to understand the kind of education fundamentalists want to foster in Christian schools, we must understand the changes they are trying to make in the public schools. Turning to the judicial system during the 1980s in their quest to reform public education, they won major battles in the lower courts only to encounter setbacks on appeal.

The widely publicized case *Smith v. Board of School Commissioners of Mobile County* (1987) put secular humanism in the national spotlight. The case originated in Alabama, where a federal district court judge sided with more than 600 fundamentalist plaintiffs and not only declared secular humanism a religion but banned forty-four public school textbooks for promoting the religion. If the First Amendment means public schools cannot advance the theistic religions of Judaism and Christianity, the judge reasoned, then neither can public schools advance the nontheistic religion of humanism.[44]

A federal circuit court of appeals rejected most of the district judge's arguments. The appeals court found that while certain passages in the textbooks are consistent with the set of beliefs fundamentalists call secular humanism, other passages are consistent with the doctrines of Christianity, Judaism, and other theistic religions. "Mere consistency with religious tenets," the court of appeals wrote, "is insufficient to constitute unconstitutional advancement of religion." The court pointed out the textbooks expose students to a variety of viewpoints and beliefs, some religious and some nonreligious. The overall "message" the textbooks convey is neither the endorsement nor rejection of any religion. Instead, the books represent a "governmental attempt to instill . . . such values as independent thought, tolerance of diverse views, self-respect, maturity, self-reliance, and logical decision-making."[45]

In *Mozert v. Hawkins County Public Schools* (1987), a case originating in Tennessee, another federal circuit court of appeals considered different issues but reached essentially the same conclusion. In this case, which like *Smith* made national headlines, a group of fundamentalist Christians complained the content of their children's public school readers offended their religious beliefs. A federal district court judge ordered the school board to allow the students to "opt out" of their reading classes and learn to read apart from other students—in the library, the study hall, and the home.[46]

The circuit court of appeals overturned the district judge's decision and concluded that requiring students to read a particular set of books is not the same thing as forcing them to accept a particular set of religious beliefs. "Instead, the record in this case discloses an effort by the school board to offer a reading curriculum designed to acquaint students with a multitude of ideas and concepts, though not in proportions the plaintiffs would like."[47]

The issue is, in part, one of balance and emphasis, although some fundamentalists take a far more adamant stand. On certain matters they simply do not want their children to exercise independent thought. Certain questions, answered by the Bible, are not open to debate. Believing their main responsibility as parents is instilling in children the *one* correct outlook on the world, helping them "see life from God's point of view," some fundamentalists find the clash of ideas in the public schools unacceptable. Because the federal courts of appeal in both the *Smith* and the *Mozert* cases declined to decide what constitutes a religion for purposes of the First Amendment and whether secular humanism is in fact a religion, fundamentalists may take the issue to court again.[48]

Meanwhile, the growth of Christian schools continues, albeit at a slower pace than in the 1970s and 1980s. During the 1840s and 1850s, Roman Catholics became the first major defectors from the common school movement. Early in the twenty-first century, it may be clear whether fundamentalist Protestants are becoming the second.

HOME SCHOOLING

A few Americans are defecting from all institutional schools, public and private. *Home schoolers* want to keep schooling within the family circle. Parents who decide to teach their children at home join a small but enthusiastic movement that now accounts for just over 2 percent of the total K–12 population.[49]

Who Goes to School at Home?   Home schooling has grown in popularity and changed in character since the late 1970s, when it was a radical chic alternative appealing mostly to parents who wanted to give their children an unstructured education. From the few thousand children who went to school at home then, the movement has grown to more than a million students thirty years later. It has also diversified. The neo-hippie family of the late seventies and early eighties, the fundamentalist Christian family of the mid-eighties to mid-nineties, and the socially concerned but institutionally alienated family of the mid-nineties to the present: These popular images of home schoolers reflect ongoing changes in the movement.[50]

According to a 2004 *Issue Brief* from the National Center for Educational Statistics, the two most powerful motives for home schooling are a "concern about the environment of other schools" (the top reason for 31 percent of home schooling parents) and a desire to "provide religious or moral instruction" (the top reason for 30 percent). Other important reasons include "dissatisfaction with academic instruction at other schools" (16 percent) and a desire to meet the physical, mental, or other special needs of children (14 percent).[51]

For many families, these reasons all relate to a larger problem: the perceived breakdown of institutional schooling. According to the Home School Legal Defense Fund, most parents who home school share concerns about widespread sex, drugs, bullying, and violence in America's schools. How can teachers teach and students learn in such an environment?[52] After the shootings at Columbine High School in Littleton, Colorado, saturated the media in 1999 (see Chapter 8), home schooling associations reported a big jump in inquiries. The 9/11 terrorist attacks in the United States and the 2004 massacre of 338 children and adults at a Russian school have heightened the sense of unease and insecurity. "Was Russian School Massacre Preview of Things to Come?" asked an essay posted on numerous conservative Internet sites.[53]

Intertwined with these worldly fears is the conservative Christian faith a majority of home schoolers hold. Like parents in fundamentalist Christian schools, home schoolers are trying to protect their children and fortify them against the negative influences of a secular society. But unlike Christian school parents, they believe the home provides the warmest, richest environment for formal education.

Growing at an annual rate of 7 or 8 percent so far in the 2000s, the home schooling movement shows signs of diversifying, although it continues to attract people with certain demographic and personality characteristics. The majority are white, middle class, religious, and conservative. They are couples in two-parent households where the mother does not work outside the home. They are people who insist on calling their own shots when it comes to raising their children—and who are willing to buck the system, if necessary, to do things their way. Given this last trait, we should not be surprised that some home schoolers are politically liberal, and some are not particularly religious. A few are even "unschoolers" who believe children learn best when they are free to choose their own activities. Whatever their differences, home schoolers are independent people who believe their children can learn more at home than in any public or private institution.[54]

Parents who choose home schooling must enjoy spending time with their children. The mothers who do almost 90 percent of the teaching in home schools say they appreciate the emotional as well as the academic aspects of their work. According to these women, the closeness that develops among family members does not have to be interrupted when children reach five or six years of age and start school. Bonds can continue to grow if families can sit down together, open their books together, and work together on academic studies, just as they do on other tasks.[55]

Criticism and Response.   Although home schooling is now legal in all fifty states and the District of Columbia, opinion polls show it still strikes over half the general public as a bad idea. Home schooling parents are often criticized for depriving their children of peer contact and sheltering them from the real world. Well accustomed to answering these charges, parents say their children spend plenty of time with their peers, especially friends from church, after their lessons are done. Home schooling gives parents more control over peer groups, which is exactly what they want. To an even greater degree than parents in Christian schools, home schoolers feel a sense of moral and religious obligation to shelter their children from certain social influences. Accordingly, most of their children watch one hour or less of television a day. Sheltering children is essential, home schooling parents argue, in this age of drugs, gangs, and AIDS.[56]

Home schooling parents also feel strongly about the academic side of their work. The student-teacher ratio is really low in a home school, they joke, making the more serious point that individual attention is one of the greatest assets of their brand of education. Many home schoolers affiliate with a fundamentalist Christian school association to get access to its packaged, sometimes programmed, curriculum.

Computer technology is transforming home schooling from a single-teacher enterprise—a mother going it alone—to a shared endeavor. When home schooling began to take off during the 1990s, parents and students initially used the Internet as an electronic encyclopedia. Then online magazines and networking became popular, bringing home schooling families into contact and building a sense of community. Now, in the 2000s, distance learning is the thing. A growing number of online schools are moving into the home schooling "market" by providing academic services via the Internet. These schools offer not only interactive instruction but also testing, grading, counseling, and other forms of assistance.

The security of such resources is reassuring to parents who are learning to teach as they go. Few home schoolers have completed a state-approved teacher education program. Fewer still are state licensed. And although the average educational level of home-schooling parents is rising as the movement diversifies, a few hold no more than a high school diploma. Some home schoolers boast their children outscore public school students on standardized achievement tests, while others dismiss standardized testing as one of the wrongheaded practices they hoped to leave behind when they abandoned institutional education.[57]

Visitors who enter home schools full of skepticism often leave with a sense of admiration for the human qualities they find there. It is refreshing to see families whose members function well together. Favorable, even glowing reports in popular media are making a once-exotic alternative seem more acceptable to the public. The Internet is alive with information on home schooling, most of it laudatory. The Republican Party's 1992, 1996, 2000, and 2004 platforms all endorsed home schooling specifically or in principle.

■ ■ ■ ■ ■

BOX 10.4

HELP FOR HOME SCHOOLERS

Browse *Home Education Magazine* at www.homeedmag.com and *Homeschooling Today* at www.homeschooltoday.com. Visit the Calvert School, a leading provider of online support for home schooling, at www.calvertschool.org. The Home School Legal Defense Association maintains a rich Web site with many links at www.hslda.org

But controversies over academic standards surround home schooling. Warm feelings, religious convictions, and political platforms aside, should people who lack state teaching credentials be allowed to teach? How closely should government regulate home schools and other private schools? Church and state come into conflict as home schooling parents and fundamentalist Christian educators continue to test the right of government to set and enforce educational standards.

GOVERNMENT REGULATION OF PRIVATE EDUCATION

Many citizens who strongly disapprove of any religious group's efforts to reshape public education in its own image feel just as strongly that churches and individuals should have the right to control their own private schools. But do they have the right?

Government regulation of private education involves striking a balance between the right of a state to ensure all children an education meeting minimum standards and the right of parents to educate their children as they see fit. Balancing the scales on this issue is a delicate task, judges and politicians have found. In part as a result of determined pressure from fundamentalist Protestants from the 1980s to the 2000s, and in part as a reflection of the nationwide, even worldwide trend toward less government activism, the scales have tipped away from government rights and toward parent rights. *Deregulation* of private education is the order of the day.

Three Broad Approaches to Regulation.   Although school laws vary considerably from one state to another, we can divide the states into three broad groups in their approach to regulating private schools. About one-fifth of the states take a *hands-off* approach to regulation. These states, according to a survey by the Office of Nonpublic Education of the U.S. Department of Education, decline to pass judgment on private schools. Like virtually all states, though, they require private schools to submit attendance reports, comply with health and safety codes, and (in some cases) present student standardized test scores.[58]

At the other end of the continuum are another two-fifths of the states that take a *mandatory* approach to regulation, requiring some form of approval, accreditation, or licensing. Regulations vary greatly from state to state, and several states issue exemptions to religious schools. Although the Office of Nonpublic Education says the states in this group try not to restrict religious freedom, some private educators, as we will see below, dispute that statement.

The remaining two-fifths of the states constitute the third group. Falling between the states that take a hands-off approach and those that take a mandatory approach, these states approve, accredit, or license private schools on a *voluntary* basis.

Reactions to Regulation.   Private schools react to government regulation in different ways. Catholic schools willingly meet the standards of the states where they are located. In states that exempt them from regulations, Catholic educators comply anyway, boasting their teachers and curriculum not only meet but exceed public school standards. Some other religious schools and most independent schools likewise find no problems with compliance.

The controversy over regulation centers on fundamentalist Christian educators and home schoolers, both of whom cite religious reasons for rejecting state standards, especially those applying to teachers and the curriculum. Bitter disputes and legal battles have broken out in some states because fundamentalists regard their schools as ministries of the church. They argue that just as churches are free to select preachers with whatever educational credentials the churches prefer, the choice of teachers should also be free from government interference. Churches should also have the freedom to determine the curriculum for their schools because sensitive issues ranging from sexual morality to the origins of the universe are involved. Many home schooling parents reject government regulation using variations of these same arguments.[59]

Education officials in states that take a mandatory approach to regulation reply requiring private schools to meet minimum academic standards is not only reasonable but essential. Officials often raise the issue of professionalism (see Chapter 4). Just as all states regulate the training and licensing of physicians to ensure quality medical care and protect society from quacks, states must also set standards for teacher education and licensing. State officials point out that some teachers in fundamentalist schools do not even have college degrees, much less state licenses. Few home schoolers, as we have seen, meet state standards for teachers. Would society tolerate such a situation in medicine—or in dentistry, law, or any of the established professions? Certainly not.[60]

According to school officials, state curriculum regulations are broad enough to accommodate religious diversity. State standards often require only that schools teach certain subjects, which leaves private schools a great deal of control over specific content. A course in biology, for instance, could stress creationism and reject evolution—just as fundamentalists insist—but still satisfy state standards. Thus state officials say religious educators and home schoolers should have no objection to meeting minimum curriculum standards.

Naturally the debate does not end there. Fundamentalist Christian educators and home schooling families challenge state officials to prove graduates of state-approved teacher education and licensing programs are measurably better than other teachers. As we have seen, state officials are hard-pressed to do that. Ultimately, fundamentalist educators and home schoolers rest their case on their belief that education is a religious endeavor that government has no right to regulate.[61]

Deregulation: The Trend of the Day.   Since the 1980s, fundamentalists have won major victories in courts and especially in state legislatures. Most legislatures have revised their laws on private schools, and in the process many states have lessened their oversight. Requirements that private school teachers hold state teaching licenses have almost disappeared. Instead, some states now require private school teachers, particularly those without college degrees, to pass state competency tests. States have relaxed curriculum regulations and substituted mandates that private school students demonstrate their ability on standardized achievement tests.[62]

Fundamentalist Christian educators and home schoolers are lobbying to reduce these requirements still further. At the turn of the new century, private schools are operating in a climate of deregulation.

EDUCATIONAL CHOICE

Moving Schools into the Marketplace

The time for choice has come. The idea that parents should have a stronger voice in choosing the schools their children attend enjoys wide approval. Phi Delta Kappan/Gallup polls conducted from the late 1990s through 2004 show support exceeding 60 percent for public school choice: the right to select a public school outside the assigned attendance zone. About 40 percent of Americans favor private school choice: the right to select a private school that a student can attend at public expense, using a government-funded *voucher*.[63]

Political scientists John Chubb and Terry Moe, who along with economist Milton Friedman enjoy the status of gurus in the educational choice movement, are true believers in the reformative power of the free market. In a series of influential studies ranging from *Politics, Markets, and America's Schools* (1990) to *Schools, Vouchers, and the American Public* (2002), Chubb and Moe argue that moving schools into the marketplace will force improvements, empower parents, and make quality education more widely available, especially to students from poor and minority families.[64]

What Makes Some Schools More Effective Than Others?   Chubb and Moe begin with the same question James Coleman and others have asked but conduct a statistical analysis that leads to a different answer. Searching for the key organizational factor that enables some schools to maintain the orderly climate, high expectations, and other characteristics of effective schools, Chubb and Moe isolate the factor of *autonomy*, which they define as freedom from external, bureaucratic control. The more autonomy schools have, the better they can organize themselves for academic achievement. A major reason private schools are generally more effective than public schools is private schools generally have more autonomy.[65]

Chubb and Moe stand back and look at large-scale institutional differences between private schools and public schools. Private schools, they point out, "are controlled by markets—indirectly and from the bottom up." Power flows upward from students and parents, the consumers of educational services, to the teachers and administrators who provide the services. With relatively few external restraints on autonomy, private schools allow providers and consumers to make the educational arrangements they think best.[66]

Public schools, by contrast, "are controlled by politics—directly and from the top down." Power flows downward from a wide array of external agents—including politicians, administrators, teacher unions, and voters—all vying to impose their values on the schools. This is democracy in action, to be sure, but Chubb and Moe believe it has negative effects on the schools. The bureaucratic organizational structure of public education, designed to ensure compliance with political authority, puts shackles on providers and consumers alike. People caught in the system are unable to make changes.[67]

Chubb and Moe have little hope for recent attempts at educational reform. Most are failing because they do not reduce political control and increase market control. They are failing because they are not fundamental enough.

Chubb and Moe place great faith, however, in one particular reform. The ultimate true believers, they come right out and say, "Choice *is* a panacea."

> Choice is a self-contained reform with its own rationale and justification. It has the capacity *all by itself* to bring about the kind of transformation that, for years, reformers have been trying to engineer in myriad other ways. The whole point of a thoroughgoing system of choice is to free the schools from these disabling constraints by sweeping away the old institutions and replacing them with new ones.

With a vision of "better schools through new institutions," they look to choice as a "revolutionary reform that introduces a new system of public education."[68]

Imagine a choice plan that would allow all the students in a given state to choose among all the public schools *and* all the private schools that wish to participate. Suppose the state uses a combination of federal, state, and local funds to pay the schools for every student who attends. Would such a plan, as Chubb and Moe claim, fundamentally reform education in the state?

In the political climate of the 2000s, debates over choice center on equity issues. No Child Left Behind mandates public school choice for students who attend public schools that do not meet their annual yearly progress (AYP) goals for two consecutive years. President George W. Bush, most congressional Republicans, and some congressional Democrats want to give such students the additional option of transferring to a private school. Chubb and Moe believe expanding private school choice depends on convincing Americans that open-market education can help parents and students "who are low in income, minority, and live in low-performing districts: precisely [those] who are the most disadvantaged under the current system."[69] Can choice deliver benefits to the neediest among us?

All advocates of choice believe schools become more responsive to students and parents when schools have to compete for survival in the open market. But even true believers realize markets have their weaknesses. In fact, Chubb and Moe briefly review some of the problems of market control before dismissing them as less significant than the problems of political control.

The Critics Respond.   Listen now as critics of choice join our discussion of education in the marketplace. Three of the best critical studies are *The Great School Debate: Choices, Vouchers, and Charters* (2000) by Thomas L. Good and Jennifer S. Braden; *Who Chooses? Who Loses? Culture, Institutions, and the Unequal Effects of School Choice* (1996), edited by Bruce Fuller et al.; and Jeffrey Henig's *Rethinking School Choice: Limits of the Market Metaphor* (1995). A concise summary of early criticism is *School Choice* (1992), a study directed by the late Ernest Boyer, president of the Carnegie Foundation for the Advancement of Teaching, whom we met briefly in Chapter 7.[70]

"The unequal distribution of income in society may bias certain markets in favor of the rich and against the poor," Chubb and Moe admit. That's quite an admission, critics reply. Although advocates of choice like to talk about helping the students who need help the most, critics question how much choice would improve the education of the poor and minority students who attend the *worst* public schools. How many of the *best* schools participating in a choice program would welcome an influx of these students? Most of the best schools, public and private, are already filled to capacity. Critics charge that throwing public schools completely into the open market might even make them more segregated than they are now, by social class as well as race and ethnicity.[71]

A closely related market problem Chubb and Moe acknowledge is that "consumers may be too poorly informed to make choices that are truly in their best interests."[72] Accurate enough, critics say, pointing to an even more basic problem. Even when people have information, they do not always act in their—or, more important, their *children's*—best interests. Discussing this side of human nature makes economists uncomfortable. Would market forces transform parents who neglect their children today into parents who make thoughtful educational decisions tomorrow? Critics say no.

"Transportation costs may eliminate many options," Chubb and Moe also admit.[73] Critics expand this point into a more comprehensive geographical argument. In many rural school districts, vast distances separate the few public schools. There may well be no private schools at all. In districts with high square mileage and low population density, how many new schools would market forces generate? Even if new private schools somehow sprang up, could we reasonably expect students to make a daily round trip of, say, 100 miles to reach a chosen school? In large urban school districts, some students would have to take long and sometimes dangerous rides on public transportation to attend the schools they choose. How far would we expect these students to travel? Out in the suburbs, where transportation is less of a problem, the quality of public education is higher—sometimes rivaling the many competing private schools, Chubb and Moe admit. Would choice significantly improve the suburban situation? Given these geographical constraints, critics say choice wouldn't be a panacea after all.[74]

And so the arguments continue. Now we will use the arguments we have just considered, pro and con, to evaluate a full range of choice plans.

Choice in Action: Established Options, Controversial Experiments

Choice as a principle, choice in some form, seems here to stay. Figure 10.2 shows how well established it is in the early 2000s. As you can see, about two-thirds of the students in grades 3 through 12 now attend public or private schools that their families played some role in choosing.

But how far will choice go in the future? What directions will it take? Will most parents be content to exercise public choice options? Will private choice become better accepted and begin to transform the educational landscape? As the plans we will review to conclude this chapter suggest, these questions do not have simple answers.

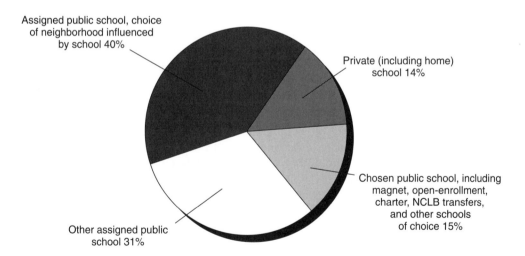

FIGURE 10.2   Students in Grades 3–12, by Family Choice of School Attended, 2006.

Sources: Estimates and projections based on U.S. Department of Education, National Center for Education Statistics, *The Condition of Education 2004* (2004) [Available: nces.ed.gov/pubs2004/2004007_4.pdf], Indicator 25, and U.S. Department of Education, National Center for Education Statistics, *The Condition of Education 1996* (1996) [Available: nces.ed.gov/pubs96/96304.pdf], Indicator 4.

Magnet Schools, Voluntary Transfers, and Other Early Versions of Public Choice

Public school choice has been around for quite some time, only under different names. As we saw in Chapter 8, many school districts trying to facilitate the process of desegregation have opened magnet schools with a variety of academic and vocational themes. Many districts have also developed majority-to-minority (m-to-m) transfer policies allowing students who attend a school where their race or ethnic group is in the majority to transfer to a school where they will be in the minority.

A few public school districts have incorporated magnet schools and voluntary transfers into more comprehensive choice programs. The best-known and most ambitious of these programs is in District No. 4, East Harlem, New York, where choice began in 1974. Consistently ranked at or near the bottom among New York City school districts in student achievement, East Harlem out of desperation encouraged teachers to save the system by designing new schools around innovative themes. By giving teachers more autonomy at the very time most school districts were taking it away, District 4 turned every school into a magnet school with the freedom to pursue its own goals. Here was an early venture in restructuring through school-based management (see Chapter 4) and parent-student choice.[75]

Chubb and Moe praise the East Harlem experiment as an example of how to turn around an urban school system that has failed its poor and minority consumers. Today District 4 ranks near the top on the list of New York's thirty-two districts in student achievement, with test scores 80 percent higher than the system-wide average—nearly twice as high as when choice began. Students now choose among schools with such names as the Academy of Environmental Science, East Harlem Career Academy, Jose Feliciano Performing Arts School, and Isaac Newton School for Math and Science. Having survived a financial scandal in the late 1980s, East Harlem remains a model of public school choice within a local district.[76]

Research on magnet schools can help us understand the larger strengths and weaknesses of educational choice as a reform strategy. On the positive side, magnet schools can compete academically with Roman Catholic schools and other private schools. One study of 4,000 urban high school students, in fact, controlled for socioeconomic background and prior schooling and found higher achievement gains in magnet schools than in private schools. On the negative side, critics point to segregation by social class as a problem in many public and private choice plans. Several studies have concluded that although magnet schools contribute to racial desegregation, "they can also 'cream off' better-educated, more affluent families."[77]

Open Enrollment and Transfers under No Child Left Behind

Well before the era of No Child Left Behind, most states had *open enrollment* options offering students either *statewide* choice of any public school or *limited* choice, usually of any public school within their local district. *Quality Counts 2004* reports that 44 states now provide open enrollment: 14 statewide and 30 on a limited basis. NCLB requires school districts to offer transfers, with transportation included, to students in schools that fail to meet their AYP goals for two consecutive years.[78]

How are these forms of public choice faring? Take another look at Figure 10.2, which shows 15 percent of students enrolled in chosen public schools of all kinds. We can estimate that half these students are in magnet schools while most of the rest attend schools selected under open-enrollment options. A much smaller group, growing but still just over 1 percent of all students, attends charter schools, which we will examine next. The smallest group by far—a mere handful of those eligible—attends schools chosen under No Child Left Behind.

The track record of open enrollment and NCLB, like the one for magnet schools, is a commentary on the larger choice movement. Although students who are using open enrollment to switch schools represent 7 percent of total K–12 enrollment, they are hardly a groundswell, which leads public school defenders to suggest there must not be as many hopelessly bad schools as critics claim.

The tiny group of eligible students who are requesting transfers under NCLB—a fraction of a percent of total enrollment—raises a critical question: If the schools NCLB is identifying through low test scores are really the worst public schools, why aren't more of their students taking advantage of the chance to get out? One answer is that some parents and students aren't aware of their options, while others are aware but choose not to leave. In addition, most big-city school districts have very few seats available in better-performing schools, while rural school districts may have no viable options to offer at all. The Education Commission of the States points out in a 2004 report that even though seat capacity and transportation are not considered valid "excuses" under NCLB, they are in fact holding down the number of transfers.[79]

Charter Schools

The basic concept is simple, the Center for Education Reform explains on its advocacy-oriented Web pages.

> Charter schools are independent public schools, designed and operated by educators, parents, community leaders, educational entrepreneurs and others. They are sponsored by designated local or state educational organizations who monitor their quality and integrity, but allow them to operate freed from the traditional bureaucratic and regulatory red tape that hog-ties public schools. Freed from such micromanagement, charter schools design and deliver programs tailored to educational excellence and community needs. Because they are schools of choice, they are held to the highest level of accountability—consumer demand.[80]

The growth of charter schools is one of the most intriguing educational reform stories of the last two decades. Minnesota, a leader in the choice movement, passed the nation's first charter school law in 1991, and the first charter school opened the next year. By 1995, 19 states had charter laws, and 234 schools were in operation. By 2004, 3,000 charter schools enrolling almost 700,000 students were spread across 37 states and the District of Columbia. To put these figures into perspective, consider that charter schools now enroll several times as many students as all the private school voucher plans combined.[81]

Public Schools with a Difference—that's how advocates describe charter schools. They believe charter schools, like magnet schools, can serve as catalysts for large-scale reform by competing with other schools in the marketplace and developing models to help inferior schools improve. Charter schools can stimulate reform even more effectively than magnet schools, advocates continue. If magnet schools are designed to be different from other public schools, charter schools can be even more different because they are often exempt from all state regulations except those governing health, safety, and discrimination. Like magnet schools, charter schools can offer specialized, innovative programs to attract students and parents, but charters can develop their specializations and innovations in greater depth to the degree they have greater autonomy.

No two states treat charter schools alike. Charter advocates generally regard the Arizona law as the "strongest" in the nation. Arizona allows any individual or group to apply for a charter; permits local school boards, the state board of education, or the state board for charter schools to sponsor the charter; frees charter schools from virtually all academic regulations, including those covering teacher education and licensing; and allows independent private schools to receive charters if they are willing to eliminate their tuition and go public. Despite its small population, Arizona is second only to California in the number of charter schools.

The Center for Education Reform gives Arizona, Minnesota, the District of Columbia, Delaware, Michigan, and Massachusetts a grade of *A* for the most supportive charter laws. California's grade has fallen to a *B* because of the "regulatory fever" that has struck the state. Indeed, the center warns that state boards of education, state departments of education, and local school boards are trying to tighten regulations on charters throughout the nation.

At the other end of the spectrum lie states with laws that are, according to advocates, "weak." Typically they permit only public school faculty or staff to apply for a charter; require the charter to be approved by the local school board and the state board of education; keep charter schools under the authority of the local board and its regulations; and do not permit applications from private schools.

The Center for Education Reform awards Iowa and Mississippi a grade of *F* for having the nation's least supportive charter laws. As of 2004, 9 states had *no* charter school laws on the books: Alabama, Kentucky, Maine, Montana, Nebraska, North Dakota, South Dakota, Vermont, and West Virginia.

Charter advocates count many more successes than failures in the political arena, and even their critics admit the schools have found friends in high places. President George W. Bush is a strong supporter of charter schools, and so was President Clinton. During both administrations, the U.S. Department of Education was a source of charter advocacy. In 2004, for instance, the Department of Education released *Evaluation of the Public Charter Schools Program*, another in its series of glowing reports. Charter schools occupy a kind of middle ground between public and

■ ■ ■ ■ ■

BOX 10.5

ABOUT CHARTER SCHOOLS

Take virtual tours of charter schools, look up their status in your state, and locate a variety of other information on the Web sites maintained by the Center for Education Reform at www.edreform.com/charter_schools and by U.S. Charter Schools at www.uscharterschools.org

private education that makes them attractive to people across the political spectrum. They are public schools, to be sure, but they resemble private schools in their self-governance and relative freedom from government regulation.[82]

Criticism.   Although charter schools are making influential friends and getting good press, they are also getting their share of criticism. Critics issue regular reminders that if something sounds too good to be true, it usually is. The best summary of the criticism is a 2002 study from the American Federation of Teachers: *Do Charter Schools Measure Up? The Charter School Experiment after Ten Years*.[83]

One charge is that charter schools haven't proven to be very innovative. Granted there are all kinds of charters on the map, with themes ranging from Montessori instruction to computer science, from ethnic studies to basic skills. Some charters are controlled by African Americans, Hispanic Americans, or Native Americans who feel other public schools are ill-serving their children. But by and large, critics suggest, families who are looking for genuine innovation had better look elsewhere. The growing body of research on charter schools suggests most of them take a traditional approach to curriculum and instruction. Their originality has been mostly administrative, not academic, and the changes haven't transferred well to other public schools. Moreover, in Arizona and other states with large numbers of charter schools—places where they are indeed competing with other public schools—the trend has been away from charters that try to innovate and toward charters that simply promise a "sound basic education."[84]

What's new here? critics ask. Where are the exciting blueprints for other public schools to follow? Charter supporters, of course, reply that a sound basic education may just be what a majority of families want for their children.

That's the market, supporters say. Learn to live with it. In time, other public schools will feel the pressure and change.

Another charge is that charter schools are contributing to the trends toward *re*segregation we examined in (Chapter 8). Not only are charters more segregated than other public schools by race, ethnicity, and social class, they do not enroll large numbers of English Language Learners (ELLs) or disabled students. Moreover, some studies show charter schools are less likely than public schools to meet their annual yearly progress (AYP) goals under No Child Left Behind.[85]

Although the AFT and NEA have usually backed charter school legislation as a way to direct political support away from private school vouchers, teacher organizations are now joining state and local school boards in their efforts to get more control over charters. School officials and teacher unionists often take opposing sides on educational issues, but in this case they agree the charter school movement could push deregulation too far and wipe out necessary rules along with questionable ones. The unions are especially concerned with teacher qualifications, salaries, and working conditions. As former AFT President Sandra Feldman explains, "I'm for charter schools that are accountable and adhere to the same standards as other public schools [but] not for charter schools that can just go off and do their own thing."[86]

Should the government give public charters—and public money—to people who may lack formal training in education but nevertheless think they can run a public school? Even if the applicants for charters are educated and licensed teachers, should the government allow them to "experiment" on children and, if they choose, ignore academic regulations that have developed over many years of practice? Should charter schools be able to bypass teacher contract provisions negotiated through collective bargaining?

Response to Criticism.   As you try to answer these questions for yourself, remember the arguments over government regulation we heard earlier in this chapter. Think about the controversies over teacher education and licensing we examined in Chapter 3, the issues of professionalism we considered in Chapter 4, and the diversity issues we have encountered throughout this textbook.

Charter advocates frame their answers to these questions by stressing again and again that public education faces deeply entrenched problems and that charter schools must get out of the rut in order to find solutions. Charter schools actually do a better job educating diverse students than other public schools, advocates claim. They like to cite U.S. Department of Education studies suggesting charter schools enroll higher percentages of poor and minority students, especially African Americans, than other public schools. Even if these students find themselves more segregated than in other public schools, charter schools are serving them and serving them well, supporters claim.[87]

Advocates concede some charters are having trouble meeting their AYP goals, but here they borrow a page from the public school scriptbook and attribute the lower scores to the higher enrollment of "at-risk and disadvantaged populations," not to the schools themselves. Advocates point with pride to charter school success stories, some of which have received national media attention. Schools like the Vaughn Next Learning Center in Los Angeles and Houston's KIPP Academy have won praise for their high levels of parental satisfaction as well as their high test scores.[88]

Of course charter schools break the mold in how they hire, treat, and compensate teachers, advocates say. In these areas, charter schools operate more like private schools. Teachers earn less, and fewer of them are state certified, but they choose to work at charters because they appreciate the sense of collegiality and the challenging job.[89]

Privately Managed, For-Profit Public Schools: The Wal-Marts of Education?

The New Education Industry.   Chris Whittle, the media entrepreneur who originated the "Channel One" news and commercial broadcasts beamed into schools since the late 1980s, is the most visible spokesperson for the emerging "education industry." Whittle's Edison Schools Inc. (formerly the Edison Project) are at the forefront of a corporate drive into the "business" of education.

The ventures have been rocky, academically and financially. During the mid-to-late 1990s, Edison and several other companies began contracting with local school boards to take over troubled public schools and turn them around. After several well-publicized failures in such districts as Baltimore, Dade County (FL), Wilkinsburg (PA), Hartford, New York City, and Philadelphia, the companies have increasingly turned their attention elsewhere: to operating charter schools. Edison is the only company that still contracts with districts to run existing public schools.[90]

The trend toward privatization, a small one so far in public education, parallels similar experiments in private management of public institutions such as hospitals, prisons, rehabilitation centers, and housing projects. Educational management organizations are sometimes referred to as *EMOs* because of their similarities to the health maintenance organizations called HMOs.

Whittle, who proudly compares his chain of Edison Schools to McDonald's, Home Depot, and, yes, Wal-Mart, originally wanted to establish for-profit private schools. Under the auspices of the Edison Project, he planned to open 200 private schools in the fall of 1995 and expand his business to 1,000 schools serving 2 million students early in the twenty-first century.[91]

A lukewarm reception and a series of financial disasters forced Whittle to downsize his plans. So he fell back, regrouped, and finally settled for private management of four public schools. Rapid growth followed. By 2000, there were 79 Edison Schools enrolling 38,000 students in 16 states; by 2005, 157 Edison Schools were serving 71,000 students in 20 states and the District of Columbia. Now Edison is building up after-school and summer programs, assisting school districts with raising student test scores, and expanding to the United Kingdom.

And still losing money. Edison has never turned a profit. By 2003 the venture had lost more than $250 million.

Learning or Earnings?   But Edison is hanging on, and its travails have not discouraged other companies from entering the charter school market, which they hope will be lucrative. "Businesses Flock to Charter Frontier," *Education Week* announced in 2002. "Entrepreneurs quickly realized there were business opportunities in charters: Harried teachers or community activists running schools for the first time would need help with the managerial side of the enterprise, and many would elect to hire companies to run every aspect of their schools." *Education Week* wonders whether the bottom line will be "learning or earnings."[92] Or can it be both?

The NEA and AFT have a ready answer: For businesses, the bottom line *has* to be earnings, a harsh fact of life that will either bankrupt companies or force

■ ■ ■ ■ ■ ■

BOX 10.6

FOR-PROFIT PUBLIC EDUCATION

For very different views of privately managed, for-profit public education, visit the Web sites of the Edison Schools at www.edisonschools.com and Corporate Watch ("The Watchdog on the Web") at www.igc.org/trac/feature/education/

them to compromise teaching and learning.[93] While expressing admiration for the Edison Schools, NEA Policy Analyst Heidi Steffens and Teachers College, Columbia University, Professor Peter Cookson conclude that,

> in the end, the market metaphor does not apply to public education. [Public education is] a social commitment that transcends individual interest and corporate gain. It is highly probable that schools designed to meet this responsibility are inherently unprofitable. . . . Public education cannot be squeezed to fit the market model and still meet the needs of a just society.[94]

Chris Whittle and other education entrepreneurs, as we might expect, answer differently. Saying relatively little to the public about profits, losses, and balance sheets, they instead emphasize such things as enrolling poor and minority students, increasing parent involvement, and raising student test scores. To be sure, the Edison Schools have a respectable—in some cases excellent—track record in each of these areas, although the company keeps piling up debt to maintain the record. Entrepreneurs tend to write off the past failures of for-profit education to skeptical school officials and hostile teacher unions. Trying to accentuate the positive, they invite the public to look at what's coming up next: more technology in the classroom![95]

Online education, already making inroads into higher education and home schooling, could prove to be a powerful marketing device in for-profit public education as well. Knowing how appealing computers are to parents, Channel One pioneer Whittle signed an agreement with APEX Online Learning Inc. to bring Advanced Placement courses into Edison Schools over the Internet. Now several other education companies are eyeing online learning to help their schools maintain a competitive edge.

Meanwhile, investors are bringing large sums of money to the table and betting on bright futures for the rapidly expanding *e-services* market, which includes software, Internet education portals, electronic toy, game, and textbook retailers, and "charter school solution providers." An Internet flyer from Eduventures announces "market panels" to help companies "get a leg up" on the charter school market that "accounts for more than $1 billion nationwide in school purchasing and continues to grow at 25% a year. . . . Each part of the event is designed to help your company sharpen its product positioning and sales pitch for the charter school market."[96]

Private School Vouchers in Milwaukee, Cleveland, and Florida

The Controversy Swirls.   *Educational vouchers* are the most controversial vehicle for promoting choice. Actually, vouchers are nothing more than "tickets" redeemable for schooling and issued to parents to cover all or part of their children's educational expenses. Vouchers can come from any of the three levels of government or even from the private sector. Under some plans, vouchers can be redeemed for public as well as private education. But in today's political climate, vouchers are usually government-funded tickets to private schools, and therein lies the controversy.

The voucher programs in Milwaukee, Cleveland, and Florida are often billed as the nation's first *real* experiments with private school choice. We will examine these programs to conclude this chapter. As this edition of *America's Teachers* goes to press, the Florida plan is facing legal roadblocks in state court, and so is a voucher program in Colorado. A newly approved voucher program is just going into effect in the District of Columbia. You should watch all these developments.

Evaluating private school choice, as we have already seen, requires us to answer tough questions. Why do some schools seem to be effective than others at educating students, particularly those from low-income and minority families? What kinds of evidence can we use to judge school effectiveness?

Until recently, another question has often taken center stage in debates over choice: Do private school vouchers violate the First Amendment by giving public money to religious schools? As we will see in more detail in the next section, the U.S. Supreme Court answered that question negatively in a 2002 case involving the Cleveland voucher program, a decision supporters of private school choice hail as a breakthrough. But opponents of private choice, far from giving up, are finding other ways to block vouchers. And so the controversy swirls, thick as ever.

The First Real Experiments.   The Wisconsin legislature started the Milwaukee Parental Choice Program in 1990, agreeing to pay independent schools up to $2,500 (subsequently raised to almost $6,000) per year for each participating low-income student. Beginning with 260 students enrolled in seven schools in the fall of 1990, the program grew to 1,500 students in twenty-three schools by 1997–98. After a pair of 1998 rulings from the Wisconsin Supreme Court and U.S. Supreme Court allowed the plan to include religious schools, it expanded by 1999–2000 to more than 8,000 students enrolled in ninety-one schools, with the largest group in Roman Catholic schools. The demographics of participating students reflect the low-income and heavily African and Hispanic makeup of Milwaukee's public schools. After years of growth, more than 100 private schools are now participating, and the program is expected to reach its enrollment cap of 15,000 students in 2005. School officials seem likely to raise the limit.[97]

The Cleveland plan began in 1995 as a voucher program for 1,500 students, almost all from low-income and minority families even though the program has no income cap. Funded by the Ohio legislature at up to $2,250 per student, a sum that has not increased over the life of the program, the plan initially allowed students to choose independent schools or suburban public schools. But no suburban schools have been willing to accept the vouchers. In its second year, the program grew to 2,000 students and added the controversial option of religious schooling, a move that triggered the lawsuit that worked its way up to the U.S. Supreme Court in 2002. Almost 4,000 voucher students were attending more than fifty private schools by 1999–2000, with Roman Catholic schools leading the list followed by Lutheran, Baptist, Islamic, and Seventh-Day Adventist institutions. Responding to an upsurge in applications after the Supreme Court ruled in favor of the Cleveland program, school officials increased the vouchers available to more than 5,500, virtually all of which are being redeemed at religious schools.[98]

Cleveland's 95 percent black Islamic School of Oasis, where boys dress in kufis (skullcaps) and girls in khimars (scarves), has attracted a great deal of media attention. A *Time* magazine story published before 9/11 vividly describes how the Muslim faith permeates the school, reminding readers of the church-and-state issues behind the lawsuits: "Tuition for more than half its students is paid by Cleveland, Ohio, taxpayers."[99]

More comprehensive than the Milwaukee and Cleveland voucher programs, Florida's statewide plan began in the fall of 1999. Using no income restrictions, the program initially targeted students in public schools the state graded *F* for two consecutive years based on standardized test scores. Sound familiar? Modeled after the Texas school accountability plan and foreshadowing No Child Left Behind, the Florida voucher program found its strongest advocate in Governor Jeb Bush, brother of the soon-to-be-elected president.

The plan now offers three kinds of private school choice: Opportunity Scholarships worth almost $4,000 for students who want to leave Florida's worst performing public schools; McKay Scholarships offering unlimited assistance to special education students who wish to transfer to private schools; and corporate-tax-credit scholarships of $3,500 for other students who want to enroll in private schools. The Florida program is by far the nation's largest voucher experiment, encompassing 700 students who have Opportunity Scholarships, 12,000 with McKay Scholarships, and 16,000 with corporate-tax-credit scholarships.[100]

The Politics of Vouchers.   All three experiments bristle with political intrigue. Chubb and Moe, not surprisingly, endorse them all. The NEA, AFT, and state and local school officials—lumped together as the "education establishment" by advocates of private choice—once again find themselves agreeing on something: They oppose the programs. So do the American Civil Liberties Union, People for the American Way, Anti-Defamation League, and National Association for the Advancement of Colored People. On the other hand, African American politicians are providing support for all three ventures, reflecting the favorable reviews a majority of black people give private school choice in opinion polls. Vouchers are an issue on which African Americans differ from the majority of Democrats. Strong support for vouchers also comes from Roman Catholic educators, who view them as a way to extend the church's outreach and reverse the decline of its central-city schools.

When the Wisconsin legislature voted to extend the Milwaukee plan to private religious schools in 1995, the NEA affiliate in Milwaukee, the ACLU, and People for the American Way filed lawsuits to block the change and brought in high-powered legal counsel. Republican Governor Tommy Thompson hired an equally prominent attorney, a former U.S. solicitor general, to defend the plan. After several years of bouncing back and forth in the judicial system, the litigation finally handed a victory to advocates of private choice. In 1998 the Wisconsin Supreme Court ruled the voucher program constitutional, claiming it aids private schools only "indirectly" and "merely adds religious schools to a range of pre-existing educational choices available to [Milwaukee] children."[101] Later in 1998 the U.S. Supreme Court allowed the ruling to stand by declining to review it.

The *Zelman* Decision (2002).   While voucher advocates celebrated, the legal action shifted to Cleveland. In 2000 a U.S. Circuit Court of Appeals ruled in a lawsuit filed against the Cleveland program that vouchers *do* aid religious groups. This decision ran exactly opposite to the Wisconsin Supreme Court's. Advocates and opponents alike hoped the U.S. Supreme Court would agree to hear an appeal of the Cleveland case, *Zelman v. Simmons-Harris.* The sides were drawn in the usual way, with the newly elected President Bush and his administration supporting the voucher program. In 2001 the Supreme Court accepted the case.

The "establishment clause" of the First Amendment, which the courts have interpreted as banning government aid to religion, was at the heart of the Cleveland voucher case. Advocates argued that vouchers do not have the primary purpose of aiding religion. Vouchers go into the pockets of parents who can then spend them at the private schools they choose, some of which happen to be religious schools. Opponents countered that public money still gets to the same place: the coffers of the churches that sponsor religious schools. How can that be anything but government aid to religion?

In a 5 to 4 decision, the Supreme Court upheld the constitutionality of the Cleveland voucher plan. The program "is entirely neutral with respect to religion," the majority concluded, because it allows all schools, religious or not, to participate. Parents whose students receive vouchers, moreover, "direct government aid to religious schools wholly as a result of their own genuine and independent private choice."[102]

Advocates cheered and renewed the push for voucher programs in other cities and states. The favorable decision helped convince the Colorado legislature to pass a voucher law in 2003 and Congress to approve a program for the District of Columbia in 2004.

Opponents regrouped and turned their attention to the state level. At least thirty-seven states have constitutions that explicitly prohibit state aid to religious schools—language that dates to the school reform campaigns that drew a clean line separating public schools and private schools (Chapter 6). Arguing in state courts on the basis of state constitutions, opponents have won a series of decisions against Florida's voucher program and blocked implementation of a voucher plan in Colorado. Opponents are also building an impressive record of defeating voucher proposals that are subject to approval by voters. At the ballot box, vouchers almost always lose.[103]

Results of the Experiments So Far.   With the media focusing attention on private-school-versus-public-school issues, I almost wish I could end this chapter by giving easy answers to hard questions and declaring a winner in the debate. But by now you must realize arguments over schooling are not so easily settled. What I can do is report the findings of several studies of private choice in Milwaukee and Cleveland, the experiments that have received the most attention from researchers.

John Witte, a University of Wisconsin political scientist who has conducted five annual evaluations of the Milwaukee plan, finds that the standardized test scores of students who attend private schools under the program do not improve significantly, nor are their scores significantly different from the scores of students who remain in public schools. Given the high level of interest in the program and the high political stakes, opponents of private choice are citing Witte's studies for support, even though he gives a qualified endorsement to private school choice as a concept.[104]

Paul Peterson of Harvard's Graduate School of Education reaches very different conclusions about Milwaukee. His studies show the test scores of students in the voucher program *do* improve if they stay in private school for at least three years. Comparing the scores of program students to the scores of students who applied to a private school but were not accepted because all the available seats were taken, Peterson finds program students performing significantly better. Advocates are adding Peterson's studies to their arsenal.[105]

Research on the Cleveland program is just as mixed. A team led by Kim Metcalf at the University of Indiana finds voucher students slightly outperforming Cleveland public school students in language and science skills but doing no better in reading, math, and social studies. These findings do not satisfy Peterson, who has reanalyzed the same data and believes voucher students are also ahead by several percentile points in reading and math.[106]

With the authors of competing studies going for one another's throats over such matters as sample size and skewed data, several conclusions are nevertheless emerging. A point for private choice: Parents of students in the Milwaukee and Cleveland programs seem to be more satisfied than parents of public school students. A point against private choice: The grass may only *look* greener on the private school side of the fence. In both programs and especially in Milwaukee's, a fourth or more of voucher students quit the program every year and return to public schools.

Finally, a point that can go either for or against vouchers, depending on your politics: Private choice advocates clearly would like to loosen eligibility requirements for voucher programs. Although advocates are now focusing the political spotlight on low-income students, most of whom are also minorities, two of the first three major voucher programs have no income restrictions. Chester Finn and other front-line advocates contend *all* Americans deserve public money to help them attend private schools if they wish. Are these first voucher experiments the entering wedge for programs available to just about everyone? If so, is that good or bad?[107]

Whether choice will prove to be *the* educational reform of the early twenty-first century remains to be seen. The trend toward choice in some form is unmistakable, but so far choice seems to be neither panacea nor poison. It may not cure every ill of public education, but neither is it likely to kill the patient. At least it hasn't yet.

ACTIVITIES

1. Visit one school in each of these sectors of private education: Roman Catholic, other religious, and independent. Talk with the teachers and principal in each school about some of the issues discussed in this chapter: demographics of the student body, qualifications and credentials of the teachers, content and academic standards of the curriculum, and state regulations that affect the school. Also ask the teachers and principal why (or if) they prefer to work in a private setting, touching on such things as working conditions, salaries, and intangible rewards.

2. During your visit to each school, request permission to talk with a group of students. Ask them, too, about some of the issues in this chapter, especially their reasons for attending a private rather than a public school.

3. Visit a home school and conduct research similar to the above.

4. Stage a debate in your college class on state regulation of private education.

5. Find out whether your state has an educational choice law and try to interview a family that takes advantage of a public or private choice program.

RECOMMENDED READINGS

Bryk, Anthony S., Valerie E. Lee, and Peter Holland. *Catholic Schools and the Common Good* (Cambridge, MA: Harvard University Press, 1995). This book pulls together the work of James Coleman and other researchers to make a strong case for Catholic schools.

Good, Thomas L., and Jennifer S. Braden. *The Great School Debate: Choice, Vouchers, and Charters* (Mahwah, NJ: Erlbaum, 2000). Good and Braden explore many of the issues the other authors on this recommended list explore—but with a stronger preference for public schools.

Moe, Terry M. *Schools, Vouchers, and the American Public* (Washington, DC: Brookings Institution Press, 2002). Along with the classic *Politics, Markets, and America's Schools* (see note 64), this book offers true-believer testimony on the power of free-market education.

Peshkin, Alan. *God's Choice: The Total World of a Fundamentalist Christian School* (Chicago: University of Chicago Press, 1988). Peshkin wrote this book after spending a year observing in a Christian school.

NOTES

1. For an excellent account of how the line was drawn between public and private schools, see Timothy Walch's recent history *Parish School: American Catholic Parochial Education from Colonial Times to the Present* (New York: Crossroad Publishing, 1996), Chaps. 1–4.

2. For further analysis of these trends, see Joseph W. Newman, "Comparing Public Schools and Private Schools in the 20th Century: History, Demography, and the Debate over Choice," *Educational Foundations* 9 (Summer 1995): 5–18.

3. Estimates and projections based on U.S. Department of Education, National Center for Education Statistics, *Characteristics of Private Schools in the United States: Results from the 2001–2002 Private School Universe Survey* (2004) [Available: nces.ed.gov/pubs2005/2005305.pdf], pp. 1–5, Tbl. 1.

4. For a good discussion of independent prep schools, see Arthur G. Powell, "Reflections on a Century of Independent Schools," *Education Week* (October 20, 1999), pp. 42–44.

5. U.S. Department of Education, National Center for Education Statistics, *1.1 Million Homeschooled Students in the United States in 2003: Issue Brief* (2004) [Available: nces.ed.gov/pubs2004/2004115.pdf]; Patricia M. Lines, "Homeschoolers: Estimating Numbers and Growth," U.S. Department of Education, Office of Educational Research and Improvement (1999) [Available: www.ed. gov/offices/OERI/SAI/homeschool/index.html].

6. David P. Baker and Cornelius Riordan, "The 'Eliting' of the Common American Catholic School and the National Education Crisis," *Phi Delta Kappan* 80 (September 1998): 16–23; Andrew Greeley, "The So-Called Failure of Catholic Schools," *Phi Delta Kappan* 80 (September 1998): 24–25. The arguments continued in letters to the editor and follow-up articles by the same authors in the February 1999 *Kappan.*

7. U.S. Department of Commerce, Bureau of the Census, "School Enrollment—Social and Economic Characteristics of Students: October 2001" (2003) [Available: www.census.gov/population/www/socdemo/school/cps2001.html], Tbl. 6.

8. Ibid.

9. U.S. Department of Education, *Characteristics of Private Schools in the United States*, p. 28, and Table 8.3 in this textbook. See David Nevin and Robert E. Bills, *The Schools that Fear Built: Segregationist Academies in the South* (Washington, DC: Acropolis Books, 1976).

10. U.S. Department of Education, *Characteristics of Private Schools in the United States*, p. 28; U.S. Department of Education, National Center for Education Statistics, *Private Schools in the United States: A Statistical Profile, 1993–94* (1997) [Available: nces.ed.gov/pubs/ps/459t2060.html].

11. Ibid.

12. Lawrence M. Rudner, "Scholastic Achievement and Demographic Characteristics of Home School Students in 1998," *Education Policy Analysis Archives* 7 (March 23, 1999) [Available: epaa.asu.edu/epaa/v7n8].

13. U.S. Department of Education, *Characteristics of Private Schools in the United States*, p. 28; Newman, "Comparing Public Schools and Private Schools," p. 10.

14. Mary Beth Marklein, "Parents and Public School Officials Search for Answers," *USA Today* (October 16, 1996), p. 1A; Nanci Hellmich, "Nuns Have an Aura of Strict but Fair" and "For Teachers, Less Pay, More Respect," *USA Today* (October 16, 1996), p. 7D.

15. See Jeff Amy, "Reading, Writing, Praying, Shrinking," *Mobile Register* (October 10, 2004), pp. 1A, 4A–5A.

16. James S. Coleman, Thomas Hoffer, and Sally Kilgore, *Public and Private Schools* (Washington, DC: National Center for Education Statistics, 1981); Coleman, Hoffer, and Kilgore, *High School Achievement: Public, Catholic, and Private Schools Compared* (New York: Basic Books, 1982).

17. Several journals invited Coleman, his critics, and his defenders to take up these arguments at length in their pages: *Educational Researcher* 10 (August–September 1981); *Harvard Educational Review* 51 (November 1981); *Phi Delta Kappan* 63 (November 1981); and *Sociology of Education* 55 (April–July 1982).

18. James S. Coleman and Thomas Hoffer, *Public and Private High Schools: The Impact of Communities* (New York: Basic Books, 1987).

19. Ibid., Chaps. 3–5. Coleman's studies of private schools led him to conclusions different from those he reached in *Equality of Educational Opportunity* (Washington, DC: U.S. Government Printing Office, 1966), often called "The Coleman Report." There he claimed that achievement is more influenced by the socioeconomic background of students than by the characteristics of the schools they attend.

20. Cornelius Riordan, *Equality and Achievement: An Introduction to the Sociology of Education*, 2nd ed. (Upper Saddle River, NJ: Pearson Prentice Hall, 2004), Chap. 4.

21. U.S. Department of Education, National Center for Education Statistics, *Mathematics: The Nation's Report Card* (2004) [Available: nces.ed.gov/nationsreportcard/mathematics/].

22. Albert Shanker, "What's the Real Score?" *The New York Times* (September 8, 1991), p. E7.

23. Gerald W. Bracey, "The Ninth Bracey Report on the Condition of Public Education," *Phi Delta Kappan* 81 (October 1999): 154.

24. U.S. Department of Education, National Center for Education Statistics, *Reading: The Nation's Report Card* (2004) [Available: nces.ed.gov/nationsreportcard/reading/].

25. David P. Baker and Cornelius Riordan, "It's Not about the Failure of Catholic Schools: It's about Demographic Transformations," *Phi Delta Kappan* 80 (February 1999): 478.

26. Coleman and Hoffer, *Public and Private High Schools*, p. 9.

27. Ibid., p. 10.

28. Ibid., p. 221; emphasis in the original.

29. Anthony S. Bryk, Valerie E. Lee, and Peter B. Holland, *Catholic Schools and the Common Good* (Cambridge, MA: Harvard University Press, 1995), p. 293. Emphasis in the original.

30. Mary Beth Marklein, "Where Class Is a Haven from Mean Streets," *USA Today* (October 16, 1996), p. 8D; Nanci Hellmich "Values and Good Manners Are on the Curriculum," *USA Today* (October 16, 1996), p. 6D.

31. Richard Rothstein, Martin Carnoy, and Luis Benveniste, *Can Public Schools Learn from Private Schools? Case Studies in the Public and Private Nonprofit Sectors* (Washington, DC: Economic Policy Institute, 2004).

32. Coleman and Hoffer, *Public and Private High Schools*, p. 4.

33. For an excellent case study of Christian Education, see Alan Peshkin, *God's Choice: The Total World of a Fundamentalist Christian School* (Chicago: University of Chicago Press, 2004). Another fine account, sympathetic but evenhanded, is James C. Carper, "The Christian Day School," in Carper and Thomas C. Hunt, eds., *Religious Schooling in America* (Birmingham, AL: Religious Education Press, 1984), Chap. 5. Also see Susan D. Rose's *Keeping Them Out of the Hands of Satan: Evangelical Schooling in America* (New York: Routledge, 1990).

34. Nevin and Bills, *The Schools that Fear Built;* U.S. Department of Education, National Center for Education Statistics, *Private Schools in the United States* [Available: nces.ed.gov/pubs/ps/459t1030.html].

35. Virginia D. Nordin and Turner L. Williams, "More than Segregation Academies: The Growing Protestant Fundamentalist Schools," *Phi Delta Kappan* 61 (February 1980): 391–394; William J. Reese, "Soldiers of Christ in the Army of God: The Christian School Movement in America," *Educational Theory* 35 (Spring 1985): 175–194.

36. U.S. Department of Education, *Characteristics of Private Schools in the United States*, p. 9.

37. School of Tomorrow, "School of Tomorrow in a Nutshell" (2004) [Available: www.schooloftomorrow.com/aboutus/index.asp].

38. U.S. Department of Education, National Center for Education Statistics, *How Different, How Similar? Comparing Key Organizational Qualities of American Public and Private Secondary Schools* (Washington, DC: USDE, 1996), p. 9.

39. A Beka Book, "About A Beka Book: Our Foundation" (2004) [Available: www.abeka.com/about/default.html].

40. See Caroline Hendrie, "Justices Accept Two Cases on Ten Commandments," *Education Week* (October 20, 2004), pp. 28, 31.

41. Several chapters in James T. Sears with James C. Carper, eds., *Curriculum, Religion, and Public Education: Conversations for an Enlarging Public Square* (New York: Teachers College Press, 1998), explore the concept of secular humanism. Its very existence is highly controversial, with People for the American Way, American Civil Liberties Union, and similar groups charging the concept is a smoke screen, a catchall for anything fundamentalists dislike.

42. See James W. Fraser, *Between Church and State: Religion and Public Education in a Multicultural America* (New York: Palgrave Macmillan, 2000), Chaps. 6–9, and Robert J. Nash, *Faith, Hype, and Clarity: Teaching about Religion in American Schools and Colleges* (New York: Teachers College Press, 1999), Chaps. 2–3.

43. Robert Sherman's *All about Morals and Ethics* (2004) is an e-book [Available: www.gobob.org/teaching-ethics.htm].

44. Joseph W. Newman, "Organized Prayer and Secular Humanism in Mobile, Alabama's, Public Schools," in Joe L. Kincheloe and William F. Pinar, eds., *Curriculum as Social Psychoanalysis: The Significance of Place* (Albany, NY: State University of New York Press, 1991), pp. 45–74; Kenneth P. Nuger, "The Religion of

Secular Humanism in Public Schools: *Smith v. Board of School Commissioners*," *West's Education Law Reporter* 38 (June 25, 1987): 871–879.

45. Quoted in "Freedom of Religion," *School Law Reporter* 28 (December 1987): 2.

46. Kenneth P. Nuger, "Accommodating Religious Objections to State Reading Programs: *Mozert v. Hawkins County Public Schools*," *West's Education Law Reporter* 36 (February 19, 1987): 255–265.

47. Quoted in "Textbook Religious Matters," *School Law Reporter* 28 (December 1987): 3. For discussions of both *Smith* and *Mozert,* see Kenneth P. Nuger, "Judicial Responses to Religious Challenges Concerning Humanistic Public Education: The Free Exercise and Establishment Debate Continues," *Alabama Law Review* 39 (Fall 1987): 73–101; and Perry A. Zirkel, "The Textbook Cases: Secularism on Appeal," *Phi Delta Kappan* 69 (December 1987): 308–310.

48. Eugene F. Provenzo discusses these and related issues in *Religious Fundamentalism and American Education: The Battle for the Public Schools* (Albany, NY: State University of New York Press, 1990).

49. For introductions to the movement, see John Holt, Patrick Farenga, and Pat Farenga, *Teaching Your Own: The John Holt Handbook of Homeschooling* (New York: Perseus, 2003), and Jane Van Galen and Mary Ann Pittman, eds., *Home Schooling: Political, Historical, and Pedagogical Perspectives* (Norwood, NJ: Ablex, 1991).

50. "Home Schooling," *Education Week*'s "Issues" Web page (April 18, 2000) [Available: www.edweek.org/context/topics/issuespage.cfm?id=37].

51. U.S. Department of Education, *1.1 Million Homeschooled Students.*

52. Home School Legal Defense Association, "About HSLDA" (2004) [Available: www.hslda.org/about/default.asp].

53. Lynn Schnaiberg, "Home Schooling Queries Spike after Shootings," *Education Week* (June 9, 1999), p. 3; Rudner, "Scholastic Achievement and Demographic Characteristics"; Frederick B. Meekins, "Was Russian School Massacre Preview of Things to Come?" (2004) [Available: www.americasvoices.org/archives2004/MeekinsF/MeekinsF_092604.htm].

54. U.S. Department of Education, *1.1 Million Homeschooled Students;* U.S. Department of Education, National Center for Education Statistics, *Homeschooling in the United States: 1999* (2001) [Available: nces.ed.gov/pubs2001/2001033.pdf]; Jay Mathews, "Correcting Misconceptions about Home Schooling," *Washington Post* online (July 27, 2004) [Available: www.washingtonpost.com/wp-dyn/articles/A17676-2004Jul27.html].

55. Mark Walsh, "Home-Schooled Pupils Fare Well on Tests, Survey of Parents Finds," *Education Week* (February 13, 1991), p. 9.

56. Lowell C. Rose, "The 29th Annual Phi Delta Kappa/Gallup Poll of the Public's Attitudes toward the Public Schools," *Phi Delta Kappan* 79 (September 1997): 50; Rudner, "Scholastic Achievement and Demographic Characteristics."

57. Ibid.; Jeff Archer, "Research: Unexplored Territory," *Education Week* (December 8, 1999), pp. 22–25.

58. U.S. Department of Education, Office of Nonpublic Education, *State Regulation of Private Schools* (2000) [Available: www.ed.gov/pubs/regprivschl/title.html].

59. William D. Valente and Christina M. Valente, *Law in the Schools*, 6th ed. (Upper Saddle River, NJ: Pearson Merrill Prentice Hall, 2005), p. 430. James C. Carper and Neal E. Devins give the fundamentalist arguments a favorable review in "Rendering unto Caesar: State Regulation of Christian Day Schools," *Journal of Thought* 20 (Winter 1985): 99–113.

60. Valente and Valente, *Law in the Schools*, pp. 450–452. Michael D. Baker takes the side of state officials in "Regulation of Fundamentalist Christian Schools: Free Exercise of Religion v. the State's Interest in Quality Education," *Kentucky Law Journal* 67 (1978–1979): 415–429.

61. For a good review of the legal arguments on both sides, see Louis Fischer, David Schimmel, and Cynthia Kelly's *Teachers and the Law*, 5th ed. (New York: Addison Wesley Longman, 1999), pp. 215–217, 434–443.

62. Fischer, Schimmel, and Kelly, *Teachers and the Law*, pp. 434–440.

63. Lowell C. Rose and Alex M. Gallup, "The 36th Annual Phi Delta Kappa/Gallup Poll of the Public's Attitudes toward the Public Schools," *Phi Delta Kappan* 86 (September 2004): 50; Rose and Gallup, "The 32nd Annual Phi Delta Kappa/Gallup Poll of the Public's Attitudes toward the Public Schools," *Phi Delta Kappan* 82 (September 2000): 44–45.

64. John E. Chubb and Terry M. Moe, *Politics, Markets, and America's Schools* (Washington, DC: Brookings Institution Press, 1990); Terry M. Moe, *Schools, Vouchers, and the American Public* (Washington, DC: Brookings Institution Press, 2002).

65. Chubb and Moe, *Politics, Markets, and America's Schools*, Chaps. 4–5.

66. Ibid., p. 183.

67. Ibid.

68. Ibid., p. 217.

69. Terry M. Moe, "The Attraction of Private Schools," *Education Next* 1 (Spring 2001) [Available: www.educationnext.org/unabridged/2001sp/moe.html].

70. Bruce Fuller and Richard F. Elmore with Gary Orfield, *Who Chooses? Who Loses? Culture, Institutions, and the Unequal Effects of School Choice* (New York: Teachers College Press, 1996); Jeffrey R. Henig, *Rethinking School Choice: Limits of the Market Metaphor* (Princeton, NJ: Princeton University Press, 1995); Carnegie Foundation for the Advancement of Teaching, *School Choice: A Special Report* (Princeton, NJ: Carnegie Foundation, 1992).

71. Chubb and Moe, *Politics, Markets, and America's Schools*, pp. 34, 220.

72. Ibid., p. 34.

73. Ibid.

74. Ibid., pp. 169, 183–184, 190–191. For an analysis of choice in several different geographical settings, see George Uhlig, "A Question of Choice," *Kappa Delta Pi Record* (Winter 1992): 42–45.

75. Peter W. Cookson, Jr., *School Choice: The Struggle for the Soul of American Education* (New Haven, CT: Yale University Press, 1995), pp. 50–55.

76. Chubb and Moe, *Politics, Markets, and America's Schools*, pp. 212–215; Mark Walsh, "Study Credits Choice with Raising Test Scores," *Education Week* (March 4, 1998), p. 1.

77. Debra Viadero, "Study Highlights Benefits, Shortcomings of Magnet Programs," *Education Week* (May 26, 1999), p. 7. See also Viadero, "Students Learn More in Magnets than Other Schools, Study Finds," *Education Week* (March 6, 1996), p. 6.

78. Ronald A. Skinner and Lisa N. Staresina, "State of the States," *Quality Counts 2004* (January 8, 2004), pp. 99, 116.

79. Eric W. Roebelen, "Few Choosing Public School Choice for This Fall," *Education Week* (August 7, 2002), pp. 1, 38–39; Education Commission of the States, *Bringing to Life the School Choice and Restructuring Requirements of NCLB* (Washington, DC: The Commission, 2004).

80. Center for Education Reform, "Just the FAQs on Charter Schools" (2004) [Available: www.edreform.com/index.cfm?fuseAction=document&documentID=60&sectionID=122&NEWSYEAR=2004].

81. The discussion in this section is based on information from the Center for Education Reform [Available: www.edreform.com].

82. U.S. Department of Education, Office of the Deputy Secretary, Policy and Programs Study Service, *Evaluation of the Public Charter Schools Program: Final Report* (Jessup, MD: Ed Pubs, U.S. Department of Education, 2004).

83. American Federation of Teachers, *Do Charter Schools Measure Up? The Charter School Experiment after Ten Years* (Washington, DC: AFT, 2002).

84. Ibid., Chap. 6; Thomas L. Good and Jennifer S. Braden, "Charter Schools: Another Reform Failure or a Worthwhile Investment?" *Phi Delta Kappan* 10 (June 2000): 745–747; April Gresham, Frederick Hess, Robert Maranto, and Scott Milliman, "Desert Bloom: Arizona's Free Market in Education," *Phi Delta Kappan* 10 (June 2000): 755–756.

85. AFT, *Do Charter Schools Measure Up?* Chap. 1; Thomas L. Good and Jennifer S. Braden, *The Great School Debate: Choice, Vouchers, and Charters* (Mahwah, NJ: Erlbaum, 2000).

86. Quoted in Lynn Olson, "Redefining 'Public' Schools," *Education Week* (April 26, 2000), pp. 1, 24–25, 27.

87. U.S. Department of Education, *Evaluation of the Public Charter Schools Program*, pp. xi–xviii.

88. Center for Education Reform, *Strong Laws Produce Better Results* (2004) [Available: www.edreform.com/_upload/charter_school_laws.pdf].

89. AFT, *Do Charter Schools Measure Up?* Chap. 2.

90. Heidi Steffens and Peter W. Cookson, Jr., "Limitations of the Market Model," *Education Week* (August 7, 2002), pp. 48, 51; Mark Walsh, "Report Card on For-Profit Industry Still Incomplete," *Education Week* (December 15, 1999), pp. 1, 14–16.

91. For the development of Whittle's business, see *The Edison Project* (Knoxville, TN: Edison Project, 1992) and information on the company's Web site at www.edisonschools.com

92. Mark Walsh, "Businesses Flock to Charter Frontier," *Education Week* (May 22, 2002), pp. 1, 12, 15.

93. Walsh, "Report Card on For-Profit Industry," p. 1.

94. Steffens and Cookson, "Limitations of the Market Model."

95. Ibid.

96. Eduventures, "Solutions for Charter Schools" (2004) [Available: www.eduventures.com/pdf/csbpanels.pdf].

97. Linda K. Wertheimer, "A Study on Vouchers," *Dallas Morning News* (July 10, 2000); Jeff Archer, "Positive Voucher Audit Still Raises Questions," *Education Week* (February 16, 2000), p. 3; Caroline Hendrie, "Milwaukee Voucher Schools to See Increased Accountability to State," *Education Week* (March 24, 2004), p. 20.

98. Adam Cohen, "A First Report Card on Vouchers," *Time* (April 26, 1999) [Available: www.cnn.com/ALLPOLITICS/time/1999/04/19/vouchers.html]; Mark Walsh, "Rulings on Voucher Program Cause Turmoil in Cleveland," *Education Week* (September 8, 1999), p. 5; Caroline Hendrie, "Applications for Cleveland Vouchers Soar after High Court Ruling," *Education Week* (September 4, 2002), p. 34.

99. Cohen, "A First Report Card on Vouchers."

100. Alan Richard, "Florida Vouchers Move toward Tighter Rules," *Education Week* (September 17, 2003), pp. 1, 23; Alan Richard, "Florida Weighs Impact of Ruling against Voucher Program," *Education Week* (September 1, 2004), p. 29.

101. Mark Walsh, "Religious School Vouchers Get Day in Court," *Education Week* (March 6, 1996), pp. 1, 14–16; Mark Walsh, "Green Light for School Vouchers?" *Education Week* (November 18, 1998), pp. 1, 10.

102. Cited in Mark Walsh, "Justices Settle Case, Nettle Policy Debate," *Education Week* (July 10, 2002), pp. 1, 18–21.

103. John Gehring, "Voucher Battles Head to State Capitals," *Education Week* (July 10, 2002), pp. 1, 24–25; Joetta L. Sack, "Florida Vouchers Dealt Another Legal Blow," *Education Week* (November 24, 2004), pp. 20, 24; Marianne D. Hurst, "Colorado Vouchers Now Back in Political Arena," *Education Week* (July 14, 2004), pp. 25, 27.

104. John F. Witte, *The Market Approach to Education: An Analysis of America's First Voucher Program* (Princeton, NJ: Princeton University Press, 2001).

105. William G. Howell and Paul E. Peterson, *The Education Gap: Vouchers and Urban Schools* (Washington, DC: Brookings Institution Press, 2002).

106. Kim K. Metcalf, *Evaluation of the Cleveland Scholarship and Tutoring Grant Program, 1996–1999* (Bloomington, IN: Indiana Center for Evaluation, Indiana University, 1999) [Available: www.indiana.edu/~ceep/projects/PDF/199909a_clev_3_exec.pdf].

107. For my answers to these questions, see Joseph W. Newman, "Bribing Students Out of Public Schools: Exodus Metaphors, Market Metaphors, and Vouchers," *Education Week* (January 27, 1999), pp. 53, 76.

CHAPTER 11

TEACHERS AND THE CURRICULUM

Autonomy: the right of the members of an occupation to make their own decisions and use their own judgment. Nearing the end of this book, I want to call attention again to teacher autonomy—the hallmark of professionalism. As autonomy relates to teachers and the curriculum, it is the freedom teachers have to decide what and how to teach. Unfortunately, the prevailing curriculum trends of the last thirty years have reduced teacher autonomy, and this chapter explains how teaching and learning have changed as a result.

Trying to put this chapter in touch with the real world of the schools, I have applied our earlier discussion of theories of education directly to the classroom. In Chapter 7, we examined a wide range of alternatives in search of what ought to be. Here we are more concerned with what has been, what is, and what lies ahead as the twenty-first century unfolds. Our focus is on *essentialism,* the theory that has dominated American education since the mid-1970s. Call it what you will—back to basics; excellence in education; the New Basics; standards, assessments, and accountability; and now No Child Left Behind—essentialism has been in command, even though *progressivism* has been trying to make a comeback.

The chapter opens with a discussion of back to basics and testing, testing, testing. The repetition is intentional. It reflects the nature of the *measurement-driven curriculum.* We will pay special attention to the conflict between standardized testing and teacher autonomy.

Next we will examine the trend toward state standards and high-stakes testing, a trend that built momentum during the 1990s and accelerated with the passage of NCLB in 2001. State politicians and school officials are "getting tough" with accountability measures that put the burden on students and teachers to prove what they have accomplished—a game with high stakes indeed.

Editorials in the nation's newspapers reflect the mixed views the public holds on NCLB.

> It is heavy handed, underfunded, and top-down federal intrusion into local schools. All these flaws flow from one fundamental misconception—that schools alone can fix every child's problem. To really leave no child behind, the act should be replaced with a series of initiatives to improve the lives of children generally—in and out of school [*Des Moines Register*, November 30, 2003].

> In essence, all No Child Left Behind asks is a little accountability, which is just what alarms too much of this country's educational establishment [*Arkansas Democrat Gazette*, June 6, 2004].[1]

When all is said and done, what do Americans need to know? This question goes to the heart of the debate over curriculum reform. Our answer begins with a look at the essentialist curriculum that has moved into place since the release of *A Nation at Risk* in 1983. Then we will study the complex concept of *literacy,* which underlies much of the controversy over the curriculum. The debate over different kinds of literacy, especially *cultural literacy,* reflects the divergent views Americans hold of what they need to know.

BACK TO BASICS AND TESTING, TESTING, TESTING

In the mid-1970s, Americans were convinced public education was in deep trouble. The media gave the nation regular reports on problems in the schools: lax discipline, drug abuse, low standards, and incompetent teachers. As proof positive the schools were in bad shape, many citizens pointed to declining scores on standardized tests, most often to the decline on the Scholastic Aptitude Test (SAT). Although it may be difficult to see from our perspective at the turn of the twenty-first century, a time when standardized testing permeates schools at every level, a significant change occurred when the American public accepted standardized test scores as an important indicator of educational quality.

The president of the College Entrance Examination Board (CEEB) traces the use of the SAT as a quality indicator back to 1974, when "an alert education reporter noticed that the scores had dropped from the previous year. He asked for the figures for earlier years, and was thus able to take public note of the fact that since 1963 there has been a gradual, steady decline." Americans were fascinated. Right there in the numbers was scientific-looking documentation of a nationwide decline in the quality of education. And there, I contend, was a sign that back to basics and testing, testing, testing were just around the corner.[2]

Outputs and Inputs

The alert reporter picked up on the nation's growing interest in judging schools by their outputs rather than their inputs. Since the release of *Equality of Educational Opportunity* (1966), popularly known as the Coleman Report, the *factory model* of schooling we discussed in Chapter 2 had been making a comeback. Average citizens were starting to evaluate schools not by the resources going in but by the products coming out. According to the Coleman Report, there is little or no correlation between school inputs—facilities, programs, and teachers, the things money can buy—and school outputs, *if* the scores of students on standardized achievement tests are used as the outputs.[3]

But *should* test scores be used that way? Ordinary citizens who had never thought much about standardized testing were puzzled at first. Most parents had never even seen their children's test scores. What could a set of numbers tell you that a graded homework assignment, a report card, or a talk with a teacher couldn't?

People who went to elementary and secondary school during the last thirty years may find it hard to believe, but in the not-too-distant past, Americans were just not curious about standardized test scores. In the first place, the complete standardized testing package typically consisted of only one or two IQ tests, several batteries of a nationally normed achievement test, and (for some students) a college entrance examination. That, in most school districts, was the extent of standardized testing.[4]

In the second place, after teachers, counselors, and administrators reviewed the test scores, into the files they went. Case closed. Educators rarely released information on scores to students or parents, nor did the news media publish school-by-school, district-by-district, and state-by-state comparisons.

Before the 1970s, the question "How good are your local schools?" was usually a request for information on facilities, programs, and teachers. As the seventies wore on, though, the question became an invitation to discuss standardized test scores. Local school board members and administrators responded to *Equality of Educational Opportunity* as if James Coleman had insulted them to their faces. A frantic scramble ensued to prove Coleman wrong.

Trying to argue with Coleman on his own terms, dollars against test scores, local officials adopted the factory model as their own. Hoisting the banner of accountability, they set out to prove the schools could deliver the scores for the bucks. Citizens who had never paid attention to standardized testing had a bewildering array of nationally normed assessments paraded in front of them: the California Achievement Tests (CAT), Comprehensive Test of Basic Skills (CTBS), Iowa Tests of Basic Skills (ITBS), Metropolitan Achievement Test (MAT), and Stanford Achievement Test (SAT).

Without fully grasping the magnitude of the change, Americans were learning to think about schooling in a different way. Standardized test scores were becoming *the* measure of educational quality.[5]

By the mid-1970s, with the economy turning sour and a tax revolt brewing, it was obvious the factory model was not providing the evidence school officials needed to make public education look good. In most districts, scores on the national achievement tests were stagnant or declining. Then the media aggravated the situation by playing up the drop in SAT scores. By the time the CEEB and the Educational Testing Service (ETS) issued a report on the causes of the SAT decline, the average composite score had fallen from 980 in 1963 to 899 in 1977. The composite would fall nine more points before bottoming out at 890 in 1980 and 1981.[6]

"Why are SAT scores dropping?" people asked. What they really wanted to know was "What's wrong with the schools?" By the late 1970s, the two questions had become synonymous.

What's Wrong with the Schools?

The CEEB Report *On Further Examination: Report of the Advisory Panel on the Scholastic Aptitude Test Score Decline* (1977) reached several major conclusions, only one of which Americans wanted to hear. According to the CEEB, there were actually *two* declines: one before 1970 and one after. Moreover, the declines had different causes.[7]

The main cause of the initial decline was a change in the pool of test takers. From 1963 to 1970, more students began to take the SAT—in particular, more poor and minority students who in earlier years would have been unable to attend college. Higher education opened its doors to these students, and the federal government eased the way by providing financial assistance. Thus the initial decline was not a sign the schools were in trouble. Americans paid little attention to this conclusion, however. People still cite the "unbroken seventeen-year decline in SAT scores" as evidence something went wrong in the schools in the 1960s, something that did not go right again until the 1980s.[8]

Americans have also ignored repeated warnings from CEEB and ETS that college entrance exams are not valid indicators of the nation's "Gross Educational Product." More than one-third of all graduating seniors take neither the SAT nor its rival, the ACT. College entrance exam scores tell us nothing about this forgotten third, nor do they provide information on the one-fourth of students who drop out of school before graduation. In addition, CEEB and ETS say the SAT is an *aptitude test* measuring the potential for further academic work, not an *achievement test* measuring how much students have learned. Finally, CEEB and ETS caution

■ ■ ■ ■ ■ ■

BOX 11.1

THE COLLEGE BOARD AND EDUCATIONAL TESTING SERVICE

Track trends in SAT scores and locate research on who scores well on the test—and why, according to the board—by going to the College Board's Web site at www. collegeboard.com/splash. Click on www.ets.org to visit the Educational Testing Service, the College Board's parent and the largest testing company in the world.

against using college entrance exam scores to compare the states because the number and the socioeconomic background of test takers varies so widely from state to state.[9]

What people do remember about *On Further Examination* is the conclusion that fit the conventional wisdom: One cause of the decline after 1970 was a "lowering of educational standards" in the schools. According to the report, teachers and administrators had responded to changing times and changing students by making concessions. Teachers and administrators were condoning high rates of student absenteeism. They were practicing grade inflation and social promotion. They were demanding less homework. They were allowing students to take the easy way out, and many students were doing just that, choosing the easiest courses and avoiding critical reading and careful writing. The report also pointed the finger of blame at society—at single-parent homes, television, social and political turmoil, and poorly motivated students—but what the media played up in the report, and what Americans remember, is that the schools had lowered their standards.[10]

Open Season on Teachers

Although *On Further Examination* carefully avoided making teachers the lone villains of the drama, the media and the general public were not so careful. In the late 1970s and early 1980s, the nation declared open season on teachers, engaging in round after round of "teacher bashing." The criticism of this era turned out to be the meanest since the 1950s, but pundits and critics always consider teachers fair game.

The assorted charges leveled against teachers are not so much false as misleading. For instance, the charge that they are to blame for poor student writing skills is accurate enough to graze the target, but it is still a cheap shot. Devoid of context, it ignores the social, political, and institutional influences on teaching and learning. How much writing do students do on their own, outside of school? Have the school board and the central office given teachers a decent writing curriculum to work with? And what about teaching load? As Theodore Sizer would later ask in *Horace's Compromise* (1984) and follow up in *Horace's School* (1992) and *Horace's Hope* (1996), how often can a high school teacher take home a stack of 120 to 175 compositions and do justice to each one? Factors like these limit what teachers can accomplish.[11]

■ ■ ■ ■ ■

BOX 11.2

A SCHOOLYARD BLOG

For heartfelt comebacks to teacher bashing, visit this teacher-maintained Web site at aschoolyardblog.typepad.com/asyb/2004/02/teacher_bashing.html

But in the era before Sizer, John Goodlad, Ernest Boyer, and other progressives came to the defense of teachers, teacher bashers rarely pointed out such constraints. Quite the contrary, the message the public heard was that teachers had too few constraints. Given their weak intellectual ability, teachers had more autonomy than they deserved.

The message got through all too clearly. Robert Rothman, who followed standardized testing for *Education Week,* explains the lingering effects of teacher bashing in *Measuring Up: Standards, Assessment, and School Reform* (2000):

> Many Americans are not ready to trust teachers. . . . Teachers are, unfortunately, not held in very high esteem. They are among the lowest paid of all professionals, and many people do not consider them professionals at all. One of the reasons for the early explosion in popularity of standardized testing was the fact that computer scanners appeared to take teachers' judgment out of the equation.[12]

A major goal of the back-to-basics movement of the late 1970s and early 1980s was telling teachers what and how to teach and then testing their students repeatedly to ensure teachers were following orders. In Chapter 7, I describe the basics movement as grounded in *behavioral essentialism*—a potent combination of behaviorism and essentialism. The desire to cut education down to the essentials led to an emphasis on reading, writing, and arithmetic at the elementary level and on English, social studies, science, and math at the secondary level. Using the tools of behavioral psychology, curriculum specialists reduced each of the 3Rs to a set of skills and the other subjects to a collection of facts and skills.

Because back to basics originated as a grassroots movement, it varied somewhat from one district to the next, but within each district the goal was standardization: getting a uniform curriculum into place. Supervisors distributed curriculum guides that told teachers, in far greater detail than ever before, what to teach and how to teach it. Standardized tests held teachers and students to the prescribed curriculum. The result, according to curriculum theorist Michael Apple, was a step toward the "deskilling" of the teaching force.[13]

To appreciate the significance of this change, consider the example of arithmetic. There are many skills involved in arithmetic and many methods of teaching children to add, subtract, multiply, and divide. Before the back-to-basics movement, teachers in most school districts had considerable freedom to decide which skills to emphasize and which methods to use. Teachers were able to vary their approach, in other words, based on their judgment and expertise.

Anarchy? Not at all. Autonomy. Within certain limits, teachers had individual autonomy. They could help students as they thought best. Their individual autonomy within the classroom allowed teachers to stake their tenuous claim to professionalism—or as we said more precisely in Chapter 4, *semi*professionalism.

The Measurement-Driven Curriculum: From Minimum Competency Testing to No Child Left Behind

Remember the old saying among teachers: "When I close the classroom door, I'm in charge." My mother, a career first-grade teacher, often reassured herself with these words. Central offices have distributed curriculum guides for years, of course, and teachers have generally ignored them. My mother certainly did, preferring to rely instead on her own judgment and the advice of her coworkers. But she retired at the beginning of the back-to-basics era, and since then teachers have been forced to pay more attention to curriculum guides. Standardized tests can now check up on teachers by checking on their students. In the era of No Child Left Behind, teachers feel more pressure than ever to teach by the cookbook.

The *measurement-driven curriculum,* in which tests shape teaching rather than the other way around, enables people outside the classroom to reach in and control instruction. I am not trying to make the process sound sinister. The advocates of measurement-driven instruction claim external control can be quite positive, a "catalyst to improve instruction." The evidence they often cite is higher scores on standardized tests—on the tests for which teachers directly rehearse their students, that is.[14]

The Old Breed of Assessments.   America's teachers discovered what "teaching the test" is all about when they encountered *minimum competency tests,* a breed of standardized tests developed early in the back-to-basics era. These tests, which ran the gamut from districtwide final exams to high school graduation exams, offered school officials a way to monitor the work of teachers in every academic subject.

Minimum competency testing, started at the local level, became a popular state reform in the years just before *A Nation at Risk* and the "excellence" movement it inspired. Before the states took command of the movement, they increased the momentum of back-to-basics by jumping on the minimum-competency-testing bandwagon. By 1980, thirty-eight states required some form of minimum competency testing, and by 1990, forty states were on the bandwagon.[15]

For all their popularity with school officials, minimum competency tests have come under sharp attack since they first appeared. Even the essentialist *A Nation at Risk* brushed them off with the comment they "fall short of what is needed, as the 'minimum' tends to become the 'maximum,' thus lowering educational standards for all." As we saw in Chapter 7, minimum competency testing has usually stressed lower-level rather than higher-level skills, encouraging teachers to emphasize rote learning instead of critical thinking.[16]

Beyond its value to school officials as a classroom monitor, minimum competency testing can be a powerful public relations tool. When school officials were desperately seeking test scores—any test scores—that were rising rather than falling, they hit on minimum competency tests. Soon a pattern appeared in the news media of community after community, state after state. As students and teachers got the knack of the tests, scores rose steadily and impressively. Within two or three years, passing rates climbed well above 90 percent and stayed there.[17] As the Southern Regional Education Board, a cheerleader for higher test scores, explains, "What gets measured gets taught. What gets reported gets taught twice as well."[18]

Until the mid-1990s, minimum competency tests usually brought the public good news. The schools are doing a better job, they announced. Almost everyone's child is minimally competent.

No Child Left Behind and the New Generation of Assessments.   Then the situation changed as the good news grew stale and as state school officials, urged on by the governors and corporate CEO's who attended President Clinton's 1996 Summit Conference on Education, ordered the creation of a new generation of standardized tests keyed to state standards in the core academic subjects of English, mathematics, science, and social studies. Almost every state went right to work. The stage was set for No Child Left Behind.[19]

As we saw in Chapter 7, NCLB requires state content and achievement standards in the four core academic subjects; annual state assessments of basic skills in grades 3 through 8 and at least one state assessment in grades 10 through 12; and accountability for *adequate yearly progress* (AYP), as defined by each state, in local schools and school districts. Moreover, NCLB calls for *disaggregating* student test scores into *subgroups* based on social class, race/ethnicity, proficiency in English, and disability. Educators are now accountable for the achievement of each subgroup of students. The goal is to bring all students up to a *proficient* level of achievement, as defined by the state, by 2014.[20]

How are the states complying with NCLB? The *Education Week* report *Quality Counts 2004* found 48 states and the District of Columbia with standards in place in all four core subjects. The rest have since gone into place. Every state and the District of Columbia now mandate a standardized testing program, and all rate local schools and districts on some measure of adequate yearly progress. Forty-two states use *criterion-referenced* tests that are written directly to state standards; 20 states and the District of Columbia rely on *norm-referenced* tests such as the Stanford or Metropolitan that measure students against a representative national sample; and 12 states use hybrids of the two. NCLB requires every state to issue test score data to the public in the form of a school report card.[21]

The state assessments that carry the highest stakes for individual students are promotion tests and high school graduation exams. These tests are actually holdovers from the minimum competency era. Seven states use standardized promotion tests as a requirement for moving from one grade to the next. Twenty-four states and the District of Columbia either use or are developing standardized graduation exams that cover the knowledge and skills students presumably need to survive in society. Some local districts are even going back to the practice of administering systemwide final exams that determine a percentage of a student's grade in a particular course.[22]

Sensitive to criticism of earlier testing programs, school officials are quick to claim that the new standards-based assessments are different. NCLB requires states to step in and improve local schools and districts that fail to make adequate yearly progress for two consecutive years. No more "hiding" low achievers at test time: Every school must show it has tested at least 95 percent of the students in each subgroup. After a school is identified as *in need of improvement*, the local district must provide transfers and transportation to other public schools for students who want to leave (an option few students and parents have chosen). The state must then use a range of interventions in an effort to turn the school around. On the milder end of the continuum, the state provides special assistance to teachers and remediation for students with low test scores. On the harsher end, the state imposes *sanctions* that range from reconstituting the school with a new faculty and staff to closing the school.[23]

Set Up for Success? Or Failure?   *Quality Counts 2004* found as many as 25,000 schools failing to make adequate yearly progress and more than 5,000 schools identified as needing improvement. These numbers are increasing to astonishing levels in some states as enforcement tightens and thousands of schools fail to make AYP—not because of low scores but because fewer than 95 percent of the students in a particular subgroup showed up to take the tests. Teachers and school officials are crying foul.[24]

Advocates of NCLB are not backing down. Gone are the days when educators could use standardized testing to make schools look good, advocates are saying. No longer can they conceal the low achievement of subgroups of students within schoolwide or systemwide averages. The game has changed.

The new rules call for success for every child. Principals of reconstituted schools—or "transformation schools," as some districts call them—spell out what they hope will be a recipe for success. "There's going to be more homework," the principal of one such school insists. "There's going to be more interaction between teachers and parents to make sure we're all on task. There's going to be very little idle time." Another principal frankly challenges her newly assigned faculty and staff: "You're going to have more time with these children than their parents. People say that it's the parent's fault when these children do not succeed, but I have a problem with that. We're going to have these kids for 150 hours a month, and you're going to tell me that we're not accountable?"[25]

While appreciating the can-do spirit behind these words, critics contend No Child Left Behind is setting up public education for failure. The federal law gives schools the admirable but impossible goal of 100 percent proficiency by 2014. Critics say it is unrealistic to expect public schools to be so successful considering the problems that social class, race/ethnicity, language proficiency, and disability impose on certain students. Teachers put the matter more bluntly: We cannot be accountable for what we cannot control (see Chapter 2).[26]

■ ■ ■ ■ ■

BOX 11.3

NO CHILD LEFT BEHIND: THE OFFICIAL WEB SITE

An A–Z index makes it easy to locate information in this section of the U.S. Department of Education's site: www.ed.gov/nclb/landing.jhtml?src=fb

Surprisingly, a large majority of the general public seems to support this line of criticism. According to the 2003 and 2004 Phi Delta Kappa/Gallup Polls, three-fourths of the public believes the achievement gap between white and minority students is mostly related to factors other than the quality of schooling. The public identifies the most powerful influences as home life, parent involvement, student interest, and community support.[27]

It would be more reasonable, critics say, to set achievement goals based on growth and improvement. James Popham, author of *America's "Failing" Schools: How Parents and Teachers Can Cope with No Child Left Behind* (2004), suggests abandoning absolute proficiency standards that, he predicts, will only stigmatize public education. A specialist in educational testing and measurement, Popham suggests an alternative: States can judge schools and districts based on student progress toward "grade-level expectations." Other researchers point out that technology now makes it possible to establish individual growth targets and measure progress toward goals on a student-by-student basis.[28]

Critics of NCLB also focus on financial support. Despite increases in the federal education budget since 2001, NCLB saddles already cash-strapped state and local school systems with unfunded mandates—requirements that federal dollars do not cover. John Kerry and other Democratic politicians often leveled this charge during the 2004 campaign (see Chapter 9).[29]

Although the general public feels more positively than teachers do about NCLB as a whole, the 2003 and 2004 Phi Delta Kappa/Gallup polls offer evidence that teachers and the public may yet find common ground on the uses and abuses of standardized testing. Two-thirds of the public says using a single test to judge the quality of a school is unfair. Two-thirds believes test-based accountability will encourage "teaching to the test," a practice 60 percent view as a "bad thing." Opinion polls show that even higher percentages of teachers hold these same views. Can teachers help the public take the next logical step and reconsider its support for using student test scores as a factor in teacher evaluation and merit pay?[30]

The National Assessment of Educational Progress: Eventually a National Curriculum Driver?

The National Assessment of Educational Progress (NAEP) is a battery of tests administered at regular intervals since 1969 to a sample of students in the fourth, eighth, and twelfth grades. Educators generally regard the NAEP as the best of the education box scores because it taps a representative sample of the nation's students and because teachers feel no pressure to prepare their students for the test. Or, I should say, teachers *have* felt no pressure, but that could change, as we will find later in this section.

Interpreting trends in NAEP scores is like taking a Rorschach test. What people see in the numbers reveals their feeling about U.S. education, especially the public schools.

Still, observers tend to agree that the most favorable trend over the life of the NAEP is the overall improvement in the scores of minority students. In general, African Americans and Hispanic Americans have increased their scores, while the scores of whites have been relatively stable. The gap between white scores and minority scores has narrowed, then, although large differences in performance remain.[31]

The least favorable trend is in reading, the subject generally regarded as the most basic of the basics. Overall, America's reading scores are stagnant. The NAEP found students reading no better in 2003 than in 1992. Nor have minorities made significant progress toward closing the achievement gap in reading since the early 1990s. With overall math scores improving over the same period and with minority students narrowing the achievement gap in math since 2000, the reading results seem especially disappointing. Figures 8.1 and Figures 8.2 illustrate these trends at the middle school level.[32]

Analyzing NAEP trends in more detail helps reveal the checkered record of the back-to-basics movement. Reading scores of 9- and 13-year-olds improved during the 1970s, before the basics movement really took hold; declined while the movement strengthened during the 1980s; improved again during the early 1990s as the grip of basics weakened somewhat; and have held fairly constant since then. The reading scores of 17-year-olds improved from the 1970s through the early 1990s, declined slightly, and then held steady. On every NAEP reading test administered during the last three decades, students in all three age groups have demonstrated greater mastery of lower-level skills (such as recognizing nouns and verbs) than higher-level skills (such as analyzing challenging passages). And despite the more impressive overall record in math, higher-level skills continue to lag in that subject, too.[33]

The NAEP is certainly a test to watch in the early twenty-first century. During the second Reagan administration, Secretary of Education William Bennett led a successful campaign to turn the NAEP, a high-quality but low-profile standardized test, into "The Nation's Report Card." The NAEP expanded to cover more students and more subjects and, for the first time, began to report scores on a state-by-state basis. Under Presidents George H. Bush and Bill Clinton, the NAEP underwent more refinement and expansion and became the most important indicator for measuring progress toward the National Education Goals we discussed in Chapter 9. Under President George W. Bush, the NAEP became an accountability device, a benchmark for checking state assessments under No Child Left Behind. President Bush also endorsed using the NAEP to measure student readiness for college, military service, and the workplace.[34]

■ ■ ■ ■ ■ ▬▬▬▬▬▬▬▬▬▬▬▬▬▬▬▬▬▬▬▬▬▬▬▬▬▬▬▬▬▬▬▬▬▬▬▬▬▬▬

BOX 11.4

NATIONAL ASSESSMENT OF EDUCATIONAL PROGRESS

The Web site of the National Assessment of Educational Progress contains a wealth of information on trends in student academic performance. Explore it at nces.ed.gov/nationsreportcard/

Raising the stakes on the NAEP by throwing it into the political arena could have negative consequences. Disparities between scores on the NAEP and scores on assessments that the states control make an inviting political target. During the 2000 presidential campaign, for instance, a Rand Corporation study used NAEP trends to cast doubt on the dramatic gains Texas students posted on the Texas Assessment of Academic Skills (TAAS) while George W. Bush was governor. Comparing the students' far more modest gains on the NAEP during the same period, the Rand study suggested Texas teachers had been "devoting a great deal of class time to highly specific TAAS preparation"—in other words, to teaching the state test. NAEP scores are regarded as valid and reliable precisely because teachers do not feel pressure to teach it. That situation could change.[35]

Can Everybody Be above Average? Is Teacher a Cheater?

For a different perspective on raising test scores, we will now examine several controversies that made their way into the news media in the years leading up to No Child Left Behind. West Virginia physician John Jacob Cannell thought the news about test scores sounded a little too good when he heard that, in almost every local school district in his state, the scores of elementary students on the Comprehensive Test of Basic Skills were above the national norm. Because West Virginia, one of the nation's poorest states, ranks low on most other educational indicators, the good doctor was surprised. Checking the data on several neighboring states, he found their students, too, were above average. With surprise turning to suspicion, in 1987 Cannell conducted a now-famous survey of achievement testing across the nation. He discovered state superintendents in every state boasting their students were above average.[36]

In other words, scoring above the norm *was* the norm. In all thirty-two of the states that had statewide testing programs at the time, elementary students scored above average; in the eighteen states with locally selected tests, elementary students in the "vast majority" of the districts scored above average. Across the nation, Cannell estimated about 90 percent of school districts and 70 percent of elementary students were above the national norm.[37]

Two decades later, they are still above the norm. These happy results suggest most Americans have moved to Lake Wobegon, Minnesota, Garrison Keillor's mythical radio community where "the women are strong, the men are handsome, and all the children are above average." Statistically, of course, the results don't add up. It is impossible for 70 percent of the students and 90 percent of the districts to be above average. Friends for Education, a group started by Cannell, filed consumer fraud complaints against the four major publishers of nationally normed achievement tests.

The Lake Wobegon effect confirms what many teachers have been saying since the late 1970s: If the public wants higher scores, school officials will find a way to deliver them. As Cannell put it, "The main purpose of the tests is looking good."[38]

In 1990, the CBS News program *60 Minutes* blew the whistle on the Lake Wobegon effect. A segment featuring Cannell and titled "Teacher Is a Cheater" told the story of a South Carolina teacher who lost her job after admitting she gave her students the answers to a standardized test. She cheated; she acknowledged she was wrong. But instead of blaming the teacher, *60 Minutes* pointed the finger at her principal and state superintendent of schools—indeed, at the entire education establishment—for putting pressure on teachers to teach tests and raise scores. Merit bonuses for teachers as well as grades, promotions, and graduation for students can ride on standardized test scores and, with the new generation of state assessments mandated by NCLB, so can a school's or a district's grades on its state report card. The South Carolina teacher said she was only trying to keep at-risk students from losing a game whose stakes are becoming very high.[39]

Although Cannell's quixotic crusade for honesty in educational testing appears to be over, the few moments he spent in the national spotlight provoked intense reactions. After the *60 Minutes* episode aired, teachers across the nation sent him supportive letters, many of them recounting bad experiences with standardized testing in their schools. Testing companies, as we might expect, reacted negatively and defensively. But when the U.S. Department of Education invited specialists in measurement and evaluation to replicate Cannell's findings, they were able to do just that. The physician may have used questionable methodology and resorted to overstatement, the experts found, but his conclusions are "essentially correct." Even Chester Finn, an ardent defender of standardized testing, conceded Cannell's main points in an *Education Week* article titled "Drowning in Lake Wobegon."[40]

Out in the real world of the schools, though, the situation is worsening, if anything, as politicians and school officials continue to raise the stakes in testing. In the fall of 2000, *60 Minutes* followed up its South Carolina expose with an investigation of the measurement-driven curriculum in Texas. A few months earlier, *Time* and *Newsweek* ran similar stories on how standardized tests are distorting teaching and learning nationwide. *Time* highlighted a backlash against testing, small but apparently gaining strength. *Newsweek* picked up where Cannell left off with a trio of articles titled "When Teachers Are Cheaters," "Bitter Lessons," and "Don't Let Scandals Scuttle Standards."[41]

As No Child Left Behind turns up the heat, more stories are breaking into the news media. In 2002, just after President Bush signed the legislation into law, *Time* reported that although criticizing testing was a "surefire way to commit political suicide a few months ago . . . a change is afoot—the sacred cow of school testing is getting tested itself."[42] In 2003, newspapers throughout the country carried Associated Press accounts of alleged cheating by teachers in New York State and administrators in Texas.[43] A disproportionate share of such stories seems to originate in the Lone Star State, where Houston Superintendent of Schools Rod Paige, who became U.S. secretary of education in 2001, piloted the program that would become No Child Left Behind. People just "do what it takes," one Texas administrator confessed, when accountability by the numbers creates a "pressure-cooker atmosphere."[44]

Running through the media coverage of standardized testing is an undercurrent of sympathy for educators forced to play a game they can't win. In the next section, I take a different position and explain how they *can* win—and without cheating—if the rules continue to define winning as raising standardized test scores.

Curriculum Alignment, Test Teaching, and Data Drilling

No Child Left Behind gives educators a real challenge, to be sure, especially with its insistence on holding them accountable for the achievement of all students regardless of social class, race/ethnicity, English proficiency, and disability. Is the federal law, as some critics charge, setting public schools up for failure?

"Not so fast," one of my graduate students, a school administrator, recently said to me. "This round of the game is just beginning. Watch what happens next."

Consider the advantages school officials bring to the table when they meet to plan their strategies for responding to NCLB. Because national achievement tests are renormed only once every few years, school districts have a chance to *align* their curriculum with the tests, meaning that central-office personnel can change the curriculum to conform to the content of the tests, and teachers can put emphasis on material they know the tests will cover. While the norms stay fixed for several years, scores rise. More students become above average.[45]

Here's a real-world example of how to play the game and win. When the testing company that provides my state's national achievement tests issued a revised and renormed version in the mid-1990s, the initial result was a steep drop in scores. Suddenly Alabama found itself below average. The culturally diverse local school district where I live, Mobile County—the largest in the state and one of the fifty largest in the nation—posted embarrassingly low scores at the 35th percentile, which means 65 percent of the students in the nation scored higher.[46]

Then a miracle happened, or so it seemed. The very next year the state's scores soared above the national average. My school district scored at the 49th percentile, a fourteen-point jump testing experts still cannot completely explain. State and local officials graciously gave teachers much of the credit. Teachers smiled and complimented their students for trying hard, but some teachers confessed that it was no miracle: They were just teaching the test.[47]

Can curriculum alignment work the same wonders with state standards and assessments? The answer is *yes*, and even more easily, because the standards and assessments are completely under state control. That's one reason many states are switching from "off the shelf" nationally normed tests such as the California and Stanford to custom-made criterion-referenced tests that perfectly match the state curriculum. State officials can adjust test item difficulty, cutoff scores, and so forth to produce politically acceptable outcomes.[48]

Do public schools look "tough enough"? Alfie Kohn, the progressive critic we met in Chapter 7, believes the matter boils down to this question. No Child Left Behind has changed the way states try to answer the question. Before NCLB, states made accountability tough on students, and high school graduation exams sometimes had failure rates of 10 or 15 percent. The students who failed were disproportionately poor, minority, limited English proficient, and disabled, but the schools looked rigorous and demanding to the public. Since the passage of NCLB, accountability has become tougher on teachers. Now their job is to help these same subgroups of students attain high *passing* rates.[49]

With the states increasing their control over standards and assessments, it will be possible for teachers—and the schools where they work—to look good under this version of accountability, too. In the short term, large numbers of schools will fail to make adequate yearly progress, and many will be declared in need of improvement. Then a miracle will happen . . .

Are there ethical and unethical ways to teach a test? Obviously, giving students answers to specific questions that will appear on a test is unethical. But what about giving students "practice tests" that include questions from earlier versions of a test they are about to take? Repeated practice, according to specialists in educational testing, "can increase scores without increasing achievement."[50] Is it ethical, moreover, to slant the entire curriculum toward the test to help students get better scores? Is it educationally sound? Students often take ten, fifteen, or more standardized tests each year, and teachers spend large amounts of time prepping their classes to look good.

It is helpful to look back on similar debates in the early days of the back-to-basics movement. Critics warned standardized tests would soon dictate the content of the curriculum. No, defenders of the movement replied. Educators design the curriculum, and testing companies can devise tests to measure whatever educators want. Score one point for the critics.[51]

■ ■ ■ ■ ■ ▬▬▬▬▬▬▬▬▬▬▬▬▬▬▬▬▬▬▬▬▬▬▬▬▬▬▬▬▬▬▬

BOX 11.5

HIGH-STAKES TESTING

The Web sites of Alfie Kohn at www.alfiekohn.org and the National Center for Fair and Open Testing (FairTest) at www.fairtest.org are strongly critical of high-stakes standardized testing. For more positive views, visit the Education Trust at www2. edtrust.org/edtrust and the Educational Testing Service at www.ets.org

The critics also argued there is more to any subject than any test can measure, but given the pressure to raise scores, teachers would narrow their instruction to just the items on the test. Not to worry, back-to-basics advocates said. Good teachers already cover what the test covers, and bad teachers need to start somewhere. Score a point for both sides.

Now, in the 2000s, *data drilling* or *data mining* can allow school officials to manage huge quantities of test score data, tracking, sorting, and analyzing them in almost endless ways. Using powerful (and expensive) Internet-based "warehouses," officials can start with statewide data and then drill down to the district level, school level, and classroom level, finally reaching the scores of individual students. With a few keystrokes, officials can see how African American students, for instance, are doing in third grade reading—across an entire state, within a school district, inside a school, or in a teacher's classroom.

Think of the possibilities. In Ms. Mixon's class at Lincoln Elementary, for instance, what is the noun-recognition proficiency of students who receive a free or reduced-price lunch compared to students who pay full price for their lunch? What about the reading vocabulary skills of the four learning disabled students in Mr. Berg's classroom, just down the hall? How is the English Language Learner (ELL) who was in Ms. Garcia's class last year doing since transferring to the new magnet school across town?

Compliance with No Child Left Behind drives the marketing of this new technology. As one data management company explains on its Web site, NCLB "requires superintendents to continually focus on improving student achievement. However, this is not an easy role. . . . School systems in the past have lacked the tools to analyze test data. Without the ability to analyze, school systems never apply the necessary adjustments in the classroom. We offer a solution with our comprehensive data analysis application."[52]

The teachers I work with in my graduate courses say they know what is involved in "apply[ing] the necessary adjustments."[53] To them, it sounds a lot like teaching the test.

"Teachers don't need creativity," essentialist Diane Ravitch says with amazing bluntness in a *Time* magazine story titled "Sticking to the Script" (March 6, 2000). "Teachers need to use methods that have proved successful." In today's schools, *Time* reminds its readers, the measure of success is test scores.[54]

As the political temperature rises, even excellent teachers are coming under pressure to teach the test. Teachers who work with large numbers of poor and minority students feel the greatest heat. Administrators often tell these teachers to focus at-risk students on the lower-level skills that dominate standardized tests, and that kind of teaching does get their scores up. Sadly, as the results of the more sophisticated NAEP assessments reveal, the students' higher-level skills lag far behind.

In *Measuring Up,* Robert Rothman cites study after study confirming that teachers, administrators, and school officials know they are playing a game with standardized testing. They continue to play because the stakes are so high—for themselves as well as their students.[55]

■ ■ ■ ■ ■

BOX 11.6
SCHOOL REPORT CARDS

You may be able to find a report card on the school or district where you'd like to teach by starting with the links to state departments of education at www.recruitingteachers.org/channels/clearinghouse/deptedu.asp. Click on the appropriate state and then look for information on state report cards.

Pausing to Reconsider Testing, Testing, Testing

Standardized testing is time consuming and expensive. In states and districts that go in for testing in a big way, officials estimate the process consumes a full month—more than 10 percent of the academic year. Time that could be used for other purposes slips away as teachers prepare students, administer tests, analyze results, and take remedial action.[56]

Testing is a multibillion-dollar industry in the United States. Since the beginning of America's latest back-to-basics movement, testing companies have tapped into the elementary and secondary school market as never before. Some states and larger school districts are hiring consultants—"test-score cheerleaders," teachers call them—who fly into town for a few days, meet with school board members and top administrators, deliver pep talks to supervisors and teachers, and develop strategies for aligning curriculum and teaching with standardized tests. Above and beyond fees paid to testing companies and consultants, a little-discussed expense of testing lies in personnel costs. Take the average public school teacher's salary of $46,826; multiply it by the percentage of time the teacher devotes to standardized testing; then multiply that number by 3,051,730 the number of public school teachers in the nation. If the average teacher spends only 5 percent of her or his time on standardized testing, the annual personnel costs amount to more than $7 billion.

In the teacher-bashing era of the late 1970s and early 1980s, politicians, school officials, and the general public dismissed teacher complaints about excessive testing as sour grapes. Teachers who complained obviously had something to hide. Teachers who resisted were afraid of accountability, or so the rationalization went.

Today, the message that teachers have been sending for years is just barely getting through. Louder voices continue to dominate the conversation. The public demand for accountability remains strong.

No Child Left Behind seems to be just what the public wants—or is it? When Americans tell pollsters how they feel about standards and accountability, solid majorities of 60 percent or more say they support them. Raising standards for promotion and graduation gets a rousing vote of confidence. But by the same landslide margins, citizens say standardized tests are not an accurate measure of academic progress and the results of one test should not determine promotion or graduation.[57]

Although some observers chalk these results up to schizophrenia, they seem to indicate instead that Americans can separate standards and testing. They like standards more. Virginians, for instance, cheered on their state's Standards of Learning until they learned about the multiple-choice tests packaged with them. Then, according to *Education Week*, people started booing and hissing the tests at school meetings.[58]

Citizens of Massachusetts and Colorado have challenged their respective governors to take their state's high school graduation exam. One section of the Massachusetts test featured the following item:

What is the rhyme scheme of the first stanza of Robert Herrick's "To Daffodils?"

   A. ABABCDCDEE
   B. ABCDEECDBA
   C. ABCABCDDEE
   D. ABCBDDCEAE[59]

Neither governor could find the time to work the exam into his schedule.[60]

A former teacher who is the father of a Boston tenth grader characterizes the Massachusetts test as "full of trivialities . . . a crapshoot." *Time* says the "questions often resemble those in Trivial Pursuit."[61]

The contributors to *Many Children Left Behind: How the No Child Left Behind Act Is Damaging Our Children and Our Schools* (2004) offer alternatives to the behavioral essentialism that dominates public education today. Theodore Sizer, Deborah Meier, Alfie Kohn, Linda Darling-Hammond, and other progressives we have met throughout this textbook argue for accountability based on limited standardized testing and a wide range of other quantitative and qualitative indicators. For a brief time during the 1990s, for instance, *portfolios* and other *performance assessments* of student work appeared to be catching on. Classroom-based evidence of student work, collected by teachers, enjoyed a moment of popularity. Then the drive to test-based accountability swept it away.[62]

Susan Ohanian, the self-styled "teacher at large" we met in Chapter 3 and author of *One Size Fits Few: The Folly of Educational Standards* (1999), finds parents often praise standardized testing until they discover the negative effects on their children. "It seems to happen when their kids hit the grades where the stakes are very high. . . . It's when their kids come home crying that parents suddenly decide they have to do something."[63] A poignant scene in the *60 Minutes* story on Texas shows a student reduced to tears over his performance on TAAS. In *What Does It Mean To Be Well Educated* (2004) and *The Case Against Standardized Testing* (2000), Alfie Kohn wonders how many students will have to be "burnt at the high stakes" before people come to their senses.[64]

The joy of high-stakes testing.

WHAT DO AMERICANS NEED TO KNOW?

Essentialists, Progressives, and the Basics

In Chapter 7 we studied the ongoing tug-of-war between the educational theories of essentialism and progressivism, a contest essentialists seem to be winning in the 2000s. But even though essentialists have done their best to discredit their rivals, progressives are still trying to get their word out to the public.

A quarter century after the National Commission on Excellence in Education (NCEE) released *A Nation at Risk* (1983), educators are still talking about basics and New Basics. According to the commission, four years of English, three years of mathematics, three years of science, and three years of social studies constitute a core curriculum essential for all high school students. The arts are also important, the commission noted, and college-bound students need at least one more basic, foreign languages. *A Nation at Risk* also called for half a year of computer science, a requirement most students satisfy today by using computers in subject-area courses.[65]

Essentialists still use the NCEE's recommendations as a yardstick to measure the success of curriculum reform. Looking back on curriculum trends since the early 1980s, essentialists have mixed feelings about what the yardstick indicates.

On the one hand, almost every state has raised its coursework requirements for high school graduation. As a result, the percentage of students graduating with the New Basics core curriculum has jumped from 14 percent in 1982 to perhaps 75 percent today.[66]

On the other hand, most states still fall short of NCEE recommendations. The average state requirements are four years of English and three years of social studies but only two to three years of math and three years of science. Figure 11.1 shows that, in the early 2000s, only twenty-two states mandate the full New Basics curriculum for every high school student.[67]

State legislators who love to talk about school reform have shown that their rhetoric and their wallets are in different places. In 1991, Alabama proudly became the first state to exceed the New Basics by requiring four years of study in all four core subjects. At the same time, the Alabama legislature postponed indefinitely enforcing the requirements until the state could pay for them. In 1996, the state board of education finally voted to put the requirements into effect with the class of 2000. These maneuvers reflect the gap between school reform and polit-

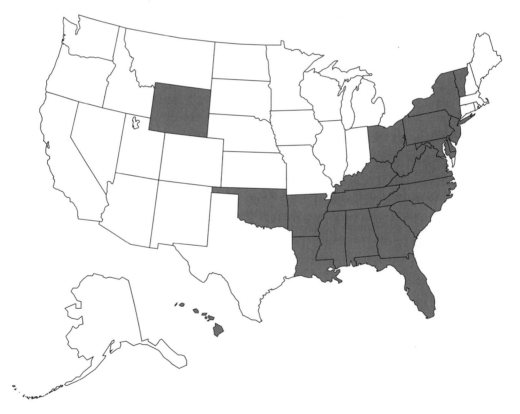

FIGURE 11.1   States that Require the Complete New Basics Cirriculum, 2005.

Source: U.S. Department of Education, National Center for Education Statistics, *Digest of Education Statistics, 2002* (2003) [Available: nces.ed.gov/programs/digest/d02/tables/dt152.asp].

ical reality in other states. Nationwide, it would be an expensive proposition indeed to implement the recommendations of *A Nation at Risk*. Training and hiring the teachers needed to teach the additional math and science courses alone would carry a price tag of several billion dollars.[68]

Progressives fault the last three Republican administrations—Reagan, George H. Bush, and George W. Bush—and the Republican Congress during the Clinton administration for talking up higher standards and passing down the bills to state and local taxpayers. The main strategy Republicans use to increase the supply of teachers, progressives argue, is encouraging state and local school systems to hire almost anybody with a degree in the arts and sciences—a practice No Child Left Behind is certainly promoting (see Chapters 1 and 3). Where is the kind of financial support the federal government provided through the National Defense Education Act of 1958?

According to progressives, essentialists also emphasize quantity over quality. As we saw in Chapter 9, excellence in education often amounts to more of the same, especially for the least able students. One more year of work-sheet science, another required course in skill-'n'-drill math—this is excellence? The quick fix isn't working, perennialist Mortimer Adler, often said, joining progressives in charging that the weakest students are still drinking dirty water.

"If you're in the so-called 'honors' or college-preparatory strand, you're going to read eight or ten books a year," says the vice-president of the Southern Region Education Board. "You're going to have to demonstrate that you understand those materials pretty deeply. You're going to have to write a short paper every week. You're going to have to write major research papers. But if you get stuck in the second-tier language arts curriculum," the vice-president admits, "you're going to read much less, you're going to write less frequently, you're going to have to rewrite your materials less to meet quality."[69]

One reason, as we saw in Chapter 8, is that many educators simply do not believe all students can rise to meet high expectations. After examining the demanding curriculum William Bennett, Chester Finn, and John Cribb outline in *The Educated Child: A Parent's Guide from Preschool through Eighth Grade* (2000), one teacher recently told me, "Average and especially below-average kids just can't meet those standards—at least not in schools set up as they are today."[70]

Bennett, Finn, and other leading essentialists reply that kids will achieve if adults insist on achievement. If adults don't, kids won't. This answer sounds good in political forums—it never fails to score points for President Bush—because it implies that respect for authority, hard work, and other traditional values can cure the ills of American education.

Simplistic and deceptive, counter the progressives. Bennett and company still haven't learned their lessons. *The Educated Child* has the same blind spots Bennett's *Virtues* series and his earlier books have, the same oversights that flaw Finn's and Diane Ravitch's work (see Chapter 7): insensitivity to the problems that keep teachers from reaching more students. Crowded classrooms, different learning styles, outmoded teaching methods—essentialists either ignore or minimize these problems.[71]

When progressives propose their own solutions, essentialists usually reject them. Lower student–teacher ratios? Not cost effective, essentialists claim. Multicultural education? Academically weak and culturally divisive. Cooperative learning? Holds bright kids back. And so the arguments continue.

The Great Literacy Debate

The debate over what Americans need to know often degenerates into shouting matches over why Americans don't know enough and how to reform the schools to make them learn more. The issues are considerably more complex, and underlying all the arguments is the concept of *literacy*. Unfortunately, people often toss the concept around without bothering to define it.

The National Center for Education Statistics (NCES) defines literacy as "using printed information to function in society, to achieve one's goals, and to develop one's knowledge and potential." Literacy is not a single skill, a capacity people either have or don't have. Literacy is a continuum of several different skills.[72]

NCES conducts ongoing studies of literacy, with the most recent National Assessment of Adult Literacy taking place in 2003. This study focuses on three main dimensions of literacy: the *prose* skills necessary for understanding and using information in narrative texts; the *document* skills needed to understand and use graphic and tabular information; and the *numeracy* (or *quantitative)* skills involved in working with numbers, measurements, statistics, shapes, and the like.[73]

Within each literacy dimension, researchers have measured how well Americans perform everyday tasks of varying difficulty. The results are not surprising: the more complex the task, the poorer the performance. While almost 96 percent of young adults can locate a single item of information in a moderately long newspaper article, fewer than 9 percent can state the theme of a poem that uses an unfamiliar metaphor. More than 98 percent can find the expiration date on a driver's license, but only 10 to 30 percent can perform various tasks involving arrival and departure times on a bus schedule. While about 90 percent can add two figures on a bank deposit slip, fewer than 10 percent can use unit pricing to determine the best value at a grocery store.[74]

America is not on the verge of collapse, as some alarmist studies of literacy suggest, nor are people running into walls because of poor reading skills. Indeed, some Americans are well equipped to cope with the changing demands of a technological society. But NCES researchers are convinced that as life becomes

BOX 11.7

ADULT LITERACY AND LIFE SKILLS SURVEY

Find out more about literacy at the Web site of the Adult Literacy and Lifeskills survey: nces.ed.gov/naal/

more and more information-oriented, it is clear that adults will need a broad set of skills in order to participate effectively in the labor market, in political processes, and in their communities. They will need to be literate and numerate; they will need to be capable problem-solvers; and increasingly, they will need to be familiar with information and communications technologies.[75]

Is Literacy Slipping Away?

In the 1991 study *Literacy in the United States: Readers and Reading since 1880,* Carl F. Kaestle of Brown University looks at literacy through the lens of history. Kaestle and his research associates join the debate over "whether students today are performing better than their age- and grade-level counterparts of yesterday."[76]

As we saw earlier, one popular position in the debate is that American education went astray in the late 1960s and 1970s. Advocates of this position claim students' reading skills steadily improved from the early 1900s through the mid-1960s but then went into a tailspin, only to recover somewhat when the schools went back to basics. People who hold this opinion regard the era before the sixties as the golden age of American education. The evidence they cite usually consists of "then-and-now" studies, which involve "giving a group of students today the same test that was given to a comparable group of students years earlier," and trends in standardized test scores.[77]

After evaluating the evidence, Kaestle rejects the golden age view. Then-and-now studies are technically flawed and inconclusive, he states. Kaestle also issues warnings about interpreting trends in college entrance exams and other nationally standardized tests. After cautioning that "the data are sketchy and the trends are murky," Kaestle and his associates nevertheless venture the "educated guess" that "schoolchildren of the same age and socioeconomic status have been performing at similar levels throughout most of the twentieth century."[78]

Kaestle takes an especially close look at trends in standardized test scores from the 1960s to the present. The evidence does not support the popular view that "permissive schools" turned out poor readers during the late sixties and seventies, he maintains, nor that the back-to-basics movement improved reading skills by raising standards and restoring order to the schools.[79]

Kaestle presents studies suggesting that between 20 to 30 percent of adult Americans have difficulty with the reading they do in everyday life. Moreover, there may be a mismatch between "school-reading skills" and "job-literacy skills." The school curriculum focuses mainly on prose literacy, and within that area on stories and poems. Reading in the workplace, by contrast, involves prose of a technical nature (memoranda and advertising copy, for instance) and requires document literacy skills as well.[80]

Finally, Kaestle looks at literacy differences among demographic groups. Although the gender gap has virtually disappeared, differences associated with class, race, and ethnicity persist. "Even if schools today are performing about as well as they have in the past," he reminds us, "they have never excelled at educating minorities and the poor."[81] In *Adult Literacy and Education in America* (2001) and other studies, Kaestle and his colleagues deplore the "constraints" that race/ethnicity, income, age, and parental income continue to impose on educational opportunities and literacy skills in our society. Because some people are able to overcome these constraints, the researchers remain optimistic.[82] But they also caution that as minorities and the poor become a larger part of the school population and labor force, lagging literacy skills will prove costly "to the economy, to the national defense, and to the attainment of economic and social-justice goals."[83]

In the final analysis, we should not base our quest for higher levels of literacy on squiggles in test-score curves or fears about economic competition. "The fundamental threat posed by America's literacy problems today is not that the Japanese will beat us at math tests and computer chips," Kaestle concludes, "but that democracy will wane in the twenty-first century." Faced with the demands lying ahead, an America that continues to reserve higher-level literacy skills for the privileged few cannot survive.[84]

Cultural Literacy

My use of the word *continues* in the last sentence reflects Kaestle's belief that our nation has never done a good job of sharing higher-level literacy. Some Americans strongly disagree, blaming the schools for failing to do today what they once did so well: not only developing literacy skills but transmitting literate culture.

A well-matched pair of essentialist treatises published in 1987 set the tone for a new round in the literacy debate: *Cultural Literacy: What Every American Needs to Know* by E. D. Hirsch, Jr., and *What Do Our 17-Year-Olds Know? A Report on the First National Assessment of History and Literature* by Diane Ravitch and Chester Finn. That year also marked the appearance of the late Allan Bloom's *The Closing of the American Mind,* a perennialist critique of higher education. The books by Hirsch and Bloom were on the best-seller lists for weeks—a testimony to the popularity of traditional theories of education.[85]

To the delight of essentialists, these books—especially Hirsch's—continue to attract public attention. The education shelves of your local bookstore probably hold Hirsch's *Cultural Literacy, The New Dictionary of Cultural Literacy* (2002), and *The Schools We Need: And Why We Don't Have Them* (1999). Go to the children's section and you are likely to find *What Your Kindergartner Needs to Know* (1997), *What Your First Grader Needs to Know* (1998), and other books in the series Hirsch has written for parents of children up through the sixth grade.[86]

Taken together, these works by Hirsch and his colleagues advance the position that some knowledge is so valuable all Americans should possess it. There is indeed a common culture, and the schools are obligated to transmit it. *Cultural literacy,* according to its advocates, is familiarity with the knowledge educated people share. The newsworthy part of debate over cultural literacy is the claim that today's schools, unlike those in the past, are doing a woefully poor job of exposing students to the common culture.

When Hirsch, Ravitch, Finn, and Bloom first went public with the news that the schools are graduating one class of cultural illiterates after another, journalists stopped to listen. Since then, conservative newspaper columnists have had a field day criticizing the curriculum. William F. Buckley, perhaps with tongue in cheek, has proposed solving the problem by requiring students to pass a "common information IQ test" in order to get a driver's license.[87]

Dr. Hirsch's (In)famous List.   Such a test, says Buckley, could be based on the list of nearly 5,000 items "every American needs to know" in the back of Hirsch's book *Cultural Literacy.* Drawn up by Hirsch and his associates, the now well-known list is an attempt to define a cultural knowledge base for the nation and its schools. As a prospective teacher, you should read the list—and the entire book—for yourself. There are many obvious choices on the list: Shakespeare, nuclear energy, California. There are also some curious choices: Fanny Farmer, èminence grise, Marianas Trench.

Trying to validate the list, Hirsch sent a multiple-choice test based on some of the items to 600 lawyers, "on the assumption that lawyers are literate." Those who returned the test correctly identified an average of ninety-two out of one-hundred items. Because cultural literacy is, by definition, familiarity with the knowledge educated people share, Hirsch pronounced his list valid. Then, presumably, he awarded a framed certificate of commendation to every lawyer who scored 92 or above.[88]

My little jest mirrors the more lighthearted criticism of *Cultural Literacy.* Including the list in the book was a stroke of marketing genius—it made lots of people buy the book—but it may have been an intellectual blunder. The list makes for great cocktail party conversation, and that is part of the problem. The message of the book gets lost in jokes about the list.

Teacher-at-large Ohanian, a frequent contributor to the popular education press, calls it a "loony list." Why does it include Babe Ruth and Ty Cobb but not Lou Gehrig or Hank Aaron, she wants to know. Why Gilbert and Sullivan but not Rodgers and Hammerstein? Why the "Rime of the Ancient Mariner" but not *Moby Dick*? Why the trombone but not the tuba?[89]

The list is arbitrary, not in the sense of capricious or whimsical (check your dictionary), but in the sense of discretionary and perhaps even dictatorial. Although Hirsch regards the list as "provisional" and not "definitive," he titles the list "What Literate Americans Know." These 5,000 items are among the things my educated colleagues and I know, he says, and look—some lawyers agree with us. Trying hard not to sound smug, Hirsch includes with every book a card readers can return to suggest items for addition or deletion.[90]

By his very tone, though, Hirsch sets the list up for a fall. And by its very nature, the list turns cultural literacy into a game of Trivial Pursuit™. That's one reason, critics charge, so many of Hirsch's 5,000 factoids are finding their way into the new state standards and assessments. They're a perfect match.

Facts and Skills.   Hirsch makes a stronger case for cultural literacy in the body of the book. "Facts and skills are inseparable," he says. Unless children become familiar with the traditional background information of literate culture, they will never be able to move from lower-level to higher-level academic skills. Content is not neutral. Only a curriculum that teaches reading skills in the context of literate culture can prepare young children to make sense of ever more complex reading.[91]

According to Hirsch, the content of worthwhile, significant reading *is* literate culture. The significant reading materials Americans should whet their minds on are not stories about Dick and Jane and their successors; they are about Ulysses and the Cyclops, George Washington and Abraham Lincoln—and approximately 4,996 other subjects. Unless students acquire this stock of factual information, all the "decoding skills" in the world can take them only so far.

Until the 1940s, Hirsch argues, the schools supplied literate culture to students from all socioeconomic backgrounds. Then, under the influence of John Dewey, William Heard Kilpatrick, and other progressive educators, teachers and administrators overthrew the traditional fact-based curriculum for a curriculum based on broad understandings and general skills.

The new curriculum, harmful to all students, has been disastrous to students from "illiterate homes." Acquiring cultural literacy neither at home nor at school, these students have suffered most from the curriculum revolution. Children from "literate homes" suffered less in the early stages of the revolution, but as these more fortunate students grew up and their children went to school and studied the new curriculum, the decline in literacy from one generation to the next became noticeable. By the 1960s and 1970s, the decline had become so obvious the nation could no longer ignore it.[92]

Diane Ravitch and Chester Finn.   In their book, *What Do Our 17-Year-Olds Know?* Ravitch and Finn maintain that schools got off the track when they shirked their responsibility for transmitting a common culture, and now the nation is suffering the consequences.

To find out what 17-year-olds do know, Ravitch and Finn analyzed the first NAEP assessment of history and literature, which high school juniors took in 1986. In both history and literature, the students answered correctly only a few more than half the multiple-choice questions. Looking forward, perhaps, to the day when the NAEP may drive a national curriculum, Ravitch and Finn offered their own assessment of the situation: "If there were such a thing as a national report card for those studying American history and literature, then we would have to say that this nationally representative sample of eleventh grade students earns failing marks in both subjects."[93]

The media were fascinated. Reporters told the nation that one-third of the students could not place Columbus's landing in North America or the signing of the Declaration of Independence within the correct half-century. Two-thirds could not do the same for the Civil War. Half the students were unable to explain the plot of *Julius Caesar* or *Macbeth*. Two-thirds could not say what the novel *1984* is about—even though the test was administered in 1986. And so the results went.[94]

Like Hirsch, Ravitch and Finn recommend returning to a curriculum that gives every student in every grade a heavy dose of literate culture. "What is needed?" Ravitch and Finn ask. "In a word, more. More knowledge, more teaching, more study, more learning—more history, more geography, and more literature at all grade levels."[95]

Back to the Future.   The Core Knowledge Foundation, which Hirsch heads, is promoting a curriculum designed to give students more. Several hundred public and private schools across the nation are using the Core Knowledge curriculum, which has its strongest appeal to parents who believe schools taught *much* more in their day. These parents want to go "back to the future," as they put it, by sending their children to schools filled with what they remember learning, schools with a curriculum that "spirals upward" so that what is taught in one grade is reinforced in subsequent grades.

The Core Knowledge curriculum is finding a place in the early 2000s cycle of the back-to-basics movement as states incorporate the curriculum into their new standards and assessments. Core Knowledge forms the basis for much of what Bennett, Finn, and Cribb recommend to parents in *The Educated Child*. Hirsch, sensing a chance to score another popular hit like *Cultural Literacy*, has released *Books to Build On: A Grade-by-Grade Resource for Teachers and Parents* (1996) and a multivolume set of readers titled *Realms of Gold* (2000).[96]

The Core Knowledge curriculum, Hirsch claims, is "more multicultural" than his (in)famous list. He has been willing to become "more inclusive," he says, "because I had no political agenda. I had a social-justice agenda."[97]

Sticking to his major points, Hirsch is adamant that students' problems with reading comprehension are due primarily to their lack of background information rather than to inadequate reading skills. In May 2003, Hirsch spoke at a forum on history, civics, and service sponsored by the White House. Sharing the stage with Rod Paige, Laura Bush, and Lynne Cheney, former director of the National Endowment of the Humanities and wife of Vice President Dick Cheney, Hirsch declared that "reading comprehension depends on privileged knowledge that comes from learning about history and science and other areas."[98]

Essentialists are staking out the high ground, positioning themselves as socially concerned activists who want students from all backgrounds to have the very best curriculum the schools can offer. "Conservative curricular content is socially progressive," Hirsch claims.[99] Ravitch and Finn second the point, arguing that cultural literacy is essential for all students, not just those in honors classes. "We cannot settle for an education system that imparts 'passable' amounts of important knowledge to its more fortunate students while the majority learn less than the minimum required for successful participation in the society they are about to enter."[100]

Essentialists surely deserve points for persistence and consistency. Twenty years after Bennett, Finn, Ravitch, and Hirsch won a national audience by promising to save *A Nation at Risk*, they are still elaborating the themes of educational

BOX 11.8

CORE KNOWLEDGE FOUNDATION

Visit the Core Knowledge Foundation online at www.coreknowledge.org

traditionalism. Ravitch's historical study *Left Back: A Century of Failed School Reforms* (2000) clearly identifies progressive education as the archvillain in the drama of twentieth-century American education and poor and minority students as the main victims.[101]

The Critics Respond: *Multi*cultural Literacy and a Better Future

As the debates over curriculum reform continue, those who criticize essentialism have to be careful how they make their rebuttals. Virtually all the critics begin by saying they, too, want to share knowledge widely, that they, too, want the best curriculum for all.

But the best curriculum, some critics contend, is not the one cultural literacy advocates have in mind. Hirsch and his colleagues want schools to transmit a cultural heritage rooted in Great Britain and Western Europe. Some critics, by contrast, want schools to pass along *multiple* heritages, acquainting students not just with Anglo-European culture but with African, Asian, Middle Eastern, and other traditions as well. These critics, led by James Banks of the University of Washington, Seattle, call for *multi*cultural literacy.[102]

Banks, past president of the National Council for the Social Studies and the American Educational Research Association, is a prolific writer who wants to convince teachers they still have *some* control over the curriculum. Regardless of state mandates, he says, teachers can transform course content and make their classrooms more multicultural. His book *Cultural Diversity and Education* (2001) tries to show teachers how.[103]

Other critics emphasize a different argument: Essentialists have misread both the past and the present. There never was a golden age of literacy skills or literate culture, these critics argue. There never was an era when the schools pushed all students to high levels of achievement.[104]

There was an era when only a small group of students entered high school and an even smaller group exited with a diploma (see Table 6.1). In 1900, just 10 percent of the eligible age group went to high school and only 6 percent graduated. In 1920, 31 percent started and 17 percent finished, and in 1940, the percentages were 73 and 51. These statistics are for all 14-to-17-year-olds. The attendance and graduation rates of poor and minority students were much lower.[105]

Throughout these years, moreover, complaints abounded that even those students fortunate enough to get through high school were not acquiring literate culture. As the chair of the education committee of the National Association of Manufacturers grumbled in 1927, "Over forty percent of [high school graduates] cannot accurately express themselves in the English language or cannot write in the mother tongue."[106]

Does this sound like the golden age Hirsch pines for, an age in which literacy was "effectively taught to disadvantaged children under a largely traditional curriculum"? Surely this is not the era essentialists want to recreate in the twenty-first century.[107]

Reanalysis of the NAEP data Ravitch and Finn used in *What Do Our 17-Year-Olds Know?* also makes nostalgia seem unjustified. When another researcher compared the answers of students from the 1930s through the 1960s to questions matching the content of the NAEP questions Ravitch and Finn selected, the researcher found similar performance across the years. Today's students "are not demonstrably different from students in their parents' or grandparents' generation in terms of their knowledge of American history."[108]

Putting together several different strands of criticism, we can see a consensus forming. Instead of looking back to a golden age past, the critics look forward to a better future in which, for the *first* time, America's schools help large numbers of students reach high levels of multicultural literacy. Quite a task!

A Message for Essentialists: Take the Blame along with the Credit

Critics, whether they style themselves progressives or not, also agree it is time to stop flogging the ghost of John Dewey. Essentialism dominated U.S. education from the mid-fifties through the mid-sixties, and since the mid-seventies it has been dominant again. Even if progressivism has been trying to make a modest comeback since the nineties, the schools are hardly packed with disciples of Dewey and Kilpatrick. The critics' point is that essentialists must now accept the blame as well as the credit for educating several distinct "generations" of American students: first the younger half of Generation X, who entered school from the mid-seventies through the early eighties; then all the Generation Y kids, who began reaching school age in the early eighties; and now the students of Generation D, who have started school since the mid-nineties (see Chapter 1).

These students are not the children of general skills, broad understandings, and learning by doing. They are the progeny of back to basics and testing, testing, testing. These are the students whose knowledge of history and literature is shocking; these are the ones whose NAEP scores show no clear benefits from wave after wave of essentialist reform.

Don't blame Dewey, critics say. Blame, most charitably, the gap between essentialism as it is and essentialism as it might be. If the essentialists want to hold Dewey and his disciples responsible for the distortions of progressivism in the schools, then the essentialists must accept the responsibility for the distortions of their theory.

Essentialists must realize their fact-based curriculum is a perfect match for measurement-driven instruction. When they call for "more," what the students get is more of the same. Officers of the National Council of Teachers of English and the National Council for the Social Studies also deserve points for consistency and persistence. For twenty-five years, they have been predicting that the recommendations of Ravitch, Finn, Hirsch, and Bennett—despite their good intentions—will only produce more emphasis on standardized testing and more pressure to teach the test.[109]

They're right. Curriculum alignment is upon us.

It does not reassure teachers when Chester Finn responds to their concerns about teaching the test with such comments as "That's a problem I'd like to see us encounter before we dismiss it"[110] and "Teaching to the test is a grand thing to do so long as the test does a good job of probing the knowledge and skills one wants children to acquire."[111] Finn's attitude strikes teachers as shockingly out of touch with what goes on in classrooms.

So this chapter comes full circle. It ends as it began, on a note of concern for teacher autonomy. The conflict between the mandated, monitored curriculum and the freedom to teach is one of the most pressing educational issues for the new century.

In Closing

I hope my feelings about public education have come through in this textbook. I am critical of the public schools, but for what it is worth, they have won my support.

I hope my feelings about teachers are also clear to you by now. So far, my life has included growing up in a teacher's family, learning from more than forty K–12 teachers, teaching hundreds of high school students, marrying two teachers, teaching thousands of future and in-service teachers, teaching my own children and now grandchildren, and giving support to their teachers.

To express my feelings as simply as possible, teachers have won my respect. I hope they will one day enjoy greater autonomy along with the other privileges and responsibilities of professionalism.

The more time I spend on research and writing, the more complex my justifications of my feelings become. Now they have filled the pages of this textbook. I hope *America's Teachers* has given you useful information and, just as importantly, raised critical questions. As I have said all along, I encourage you to find your own answers.

ACTIVITIES

1. Ask teachers who have been teaching for at least twenty years how the curriculum has changed while they have been in the classroom. Find out their views on standardized testing, teacher autonomy, literacy, and other issues discussed in this chapter.

2. Talk with a public school system's curriculum specialist about the kind of curriculum Hirsch, Bennett, Finn, Ravitch, and other thoughtful essentialists recommend. Then ask the specialist to compare the model essentialist curriculum to the state-mandated curriculum.

3. Interview a state legislator or state school board member about No Child Left Behind and state standards, assessments, and accountability.

4. Invite professors who hold opposing views on literacy, especially cultural literacy, to have a debate or panel discussion in your class.

RECOMMENDED READINGS

Bennett, William J., Chester E. Finn, Jr., and John T. E. Cribb, Jr. *The Educated Child: A Parent's Guide from Preschool through Eighth Grade* (New York: Simon & Schuster, 2000). Drawing on Hirsch's Core Knowledge curriculum, this essentialist guidebook advises parents on how to make their children's elementary and middle schooling more like the schooling they remember.

Hirsch, E. D., Jr. *Cultural Literacy: What Every American Needs to Know* (Boston: Houghton Mifflin, 1987). Still widely read and discussed, Hirsch's best-seller has popularized the concept of cultural literacy.

Kohn, Alfie. *What Does It Mean To Be Well Educated? And More Essays on Standards, Grading, and Other Follies* (Boston: Beacon Press, 2004). The gadfly critic examines many of the issues raised in this chapter from his never-say-die progressive point of view.

Meier, Deborah, and George Wood, eds. *Many Children Left Behind: How the No Child Left Behind Act Is Damaging Our Children and Our Schools* (Boston: Beacon Press, 2004). From Ted Sizer to Linda Darling-Hammond, the well-known contributors to this anthology not only critique NCLB but recommend alternatives with a positive track record.

Rothman, Robert. *Measuring Up: Standards, Assessment, and School Reform* (San Francisco: Jossey-Bass, 2000). Here is a study of the drive to curriculum reform by a former reporter who tracked it for *Education Week*.

NOTES

1. Quoted in "A Matter of Opinion," *Education Week* (June 23, 2004), p. 33.
2. George H. Hanford, "Some Caveats on Comparing S.A.T. Scores," *Education Week* (October 8, 1986), p. 20.
3. James S. Coleman, Ernest Q. Campbell, Carol J. Hobson, James McPartland, Alexander M. Mood, Frederic D. Weinfeld, and Robert L. York, *Equality of Educational Opportunity* (Washington, DC: U.S. Government Printing Office, 1966).
4. Robert Rothman, *Measuring Up: Standards, Assessment, and School Reform* (San Francisco: Jossey-Bass, 2000), Chap. 2.
5. To begin exploring the literature on testing, start with Nicholas Lemann's *The Big Test: The Secret History of the American Meritocracy* (New York: Farrar, Strauss & Giroux, 2000), which despite its title presents a strong case for standardized testing. Examine the other side of the coin with Linda McNeil's *Contradictions of Reform: Educational Costs of Standardized Testing* (New York: Routledge, 2000).
6. U.S. Department of Education, National Center for Education Statistics, *Digest of Education Statistics, 2002* (2003) [Available: nces.ed.gov/programs/digest/d02/tables/dt134.asp], Tbl. 134.
7. College Entrance Examination Board, *On Further Examination: Report of the Advisory Panel on the Scholastic Aptitude Test Score Decline* (New York: CEEB, 1977), p. 3.
8. Ibid. For more analysis of changes in the pool of test takers, see Harold Howe II, "Let's Have Another SAT Score Decline," *Phi Delta Kappan* 66 (May 1985): 599–602.
9. College Entrance Examination Board, *On Further Examination*, p. 3; Hanford, "Some Caveats," p. 20.
10. College Entrance Examination Board, *On Further Examination*, p. 4. The quotation is from p. 31. For a critical discussion of the report, see Ira Shor's *Culture Wars* (Chicago: University of Chicago Press, 1992), Chap. 3.
11. Theodore R. Sizer, *Horace's Compromise: The Dilemma of the American High School* (Boston: Houghton Mifflin, 1984); Sizer, *Horace's School: Redesigning the American High School* (Boston: Houghton Mifflin, 1992); Sizer, *Horace's Hope: What Works for the American High School* (Boston: Houghton Mifflin, 1996).
12. Rothman, *Measuring Up*, p. 149.
13. Michael W. Apple, *Cultural Politics and Education* (New York: Teachers College Press, 1996).
14. Marshall S. Smith and Jessica Levin, "Coherence, Assessment, and Challenging Content," in *Performance-Based Student Assessment: Challenges and Possibilities*, Part I of the *Ninety-fifth Yearbook of the National Society for the Study of Education* (Chicago: NSSE, 1996), pp. 107–108.

15. Richard J. Coley and Margaret E. Goertz, *Educational Standards in the 50 States* (Princeton, NJ: Educational Testing Service, 1990), pp. 3–4; Rothman, *Measuring Up*, Chap. 4. The classic study of the movement is Richard M. Jaeger and Carol K. Tittle, eds., *Minimum Competency Achievement Testing: Motives, Models, Measures, and Consequences* (Berkeley, CA: McCutchan, 1980).

16. National Commission on Excellence in Education, *A Nation at Risk: The Imperative for Educational Reform* (Washington, DC: U.S. Department of Education, 1983), p. 20.

17. Rothman, *Measuring Up*, p. 44; Peter W. Airasian,"The Consequences of High School Graduation Testing Programs," *NASSP Bulletin* 71 (February 1987): 54–67.

18. Southern Regional Education Board, *School Accountability Reports: Lessons Learned in SREB States* (Atlanta: SREB, 1992), p. 16.

19. Lynn Olson, "Rating the Standards," *Quality Counts '99*, a special issue of *Education Week* (January 11, 1999), p. 107; Lynn Olson, "Making Every Test Count," *Quality Counts '99* (January 11, 1999), p. 15.

20. U.S. Department of Education, *Standards and Assessments: Non-Regulatory Draft Guidance. No Child Left Behind* (2003) [Available: http://www.ed.gov/policy/speced/guid/nclb/standassguidance03.pdf]. The Department of Education's *Executive Summary* of the No Child Left Behind Act is available at www.ed.gov/nclb/overview/intro/execsumm.html?exp=0

21. Ronald A. Skinner and Lisa N. Staresina, "State of the States," *Quality Counts 2004: Count Me In*, a special report of *Education Week* (January 8, 2004), pp. 97–109.

22. Ibid., p. 109.

23. Ibid., pp. 98–99.

24. Ibid.

25. Quoted in Rena Havner, "Starting Over: Transformation Restaffs Struggling Schools," *Mobile Register* (August 8, 2004), p. 4A.

26. Center for Education Policy, *From the Capital to the Classroom: Year Two of the No Child Left Behind Act* (2004) [Available: www.cep-dc.org/pubs/nclby2/].

27. Lowell C. Rose and Alec M. Gallup, "The 35th Annual Phi Delta Kappa/Gallup Poll of the Public's Attitudes toward the Public Schools," *Phi Delta Kappan* 85 (September 2003): 48; Rose and Gallup, "The 36th Annual Phi Delta Kappa/Gallup Poll of the Public's Attitudes toward the Public Schools," *Phi Delta Kappan* 86 (September 2004): 49.

28. W. James Popham, *America's "Failing" Schools: How Parents and Teachers Can Cope with No Child Left Behind* (New York: Falmer Press, 2004); Lynn Olson, Critics Float 'No Child' Revisions," *Education Week* (August 11, 2004), pp. 1, 33.

29. William J. Mathis, "No Child Left Behind: Costs and Benefits," *Phi Delta Kappan* 84 (May 2003): 679–686; Erik W. Robelen, "Kerry Softens Rhetoric on 'No Child Left Behind,'" *Education Week on the Web* (August 2, 2004) [Available: www.edweek.org/ew/ewstory.cfm?slug=43kerry_web.h23].

30. Rose and Gallup, "The 35th Annual Phi Delta Kappa/Gallup Poll," p. 46; Rose and Gallup, "The 36th Annual Phi Delta Kappa/Gallup Poll," p. 46.

31. U.S. Department of Education, National Center for Education Statistics, *NAEP 1999 Trends in Academic Progress: Three Decades of Student Performance* (2000) [Available: nces.ed.gov/nationsreportcard/pdf/main1999/2000469.pdf], Chap. 2.

32. U.S. Department of Education, National Center for Education Statistics, *Reading 2003: Major Results* (2003) [Available: nces.ed.gov/nationsreportcard/reading/results2003/]; U.S. Department of Education, National Center for Education Statistics, *Mathematics 2003: Major Results* (2003) [Available: nces.ed.gov/nationsreportcard/mathematics/results2003/].

33. Ibid., U.S. Department of Education, *NAEP 1999 Trends*, Chap. 1.

34. See David J. Hoff, "NAEP Weighed as Measure of Accountability," *Education Week* (March 8, 2000), pp. 1, 20; Sean Cavanagh and Erik W. Roebelen, "Bush Backs Requiring NAEP in 12th Grade," *Education Week* (April 14, 2004), pp. 32, 34.

35. Jim Yardley, "Study Casts Doubt on Texas Test Scores, and Gives the Democrats Ammunition," *New York Times* (October 25, 2000).

36. John J. Cannell, *National Norm-Referenced Elementary Achievement Testing in America's Public Schools: How All Fifty States Are above the National Average* (Charleston, WV: Friends of Education, 1987).

37. Ibid.

38. Robert Rothman, "Normed Tests Skewed to Find Most Pupils 'Above Average,' a Disputed Study Finds," *Education Week* (December 9, 1987), p. 1.

39. CBS News, "Teacher Is a Cheater," *60 Minutes* (1990).

40. Chester E. Finn, Jr., "Drowning in Lake Wobegon," *Education Week* (June 15, 1994), pp. 31, 35.

41. CBS News, "Testing, Testing, Testing," *60 Minutes* (2000); Jodie Morse, "Is That Your Final Answer?" *Time* (June 19, 2000), pp. 34–38; Barbara Kantrowitz and Daniel McGinn, "When Teachers Are Cheaters," *Newsweek* (June 19, 2000), pp. 48–49; Evan Thomas and Pat Wingert, "Bitter Lessons," *Newsweek* (June 19, 2000), pp. 50–52; Nicolas Lemann, "Don't Let Scandals Scuttle Standards," *Newsweek* (June 19, 2000), p. 54.

42. Rebecca Winters, "Getting Testy over Tests," *Time* (June 10, 2002), p. 21.

43. David J. Hoff, "New York Teachers Caught Cheating on State Tests," *Education Week* (November 5, 2003), p. 27.

44. John Gehring, "Principals at the Center of Press for Results," *Education Week* (September 23, 2003), pp. 15, 17.

45. Rothman, *Measuring Up,* Chap. 3.

46. Martha Simmons, "Officials Pleased, Experts Puzzled by Jump in Test Scores," *Mobile Register* (May 29, 1996), p. 1.

47. Ibid.

48. Skinner and Staresina, "State of the States," p. 98.

49. Kerry A. White, "Keeping the Doors Wide Open," *Quality Counts '99* (January 13, 1999), pp. 12–13; Airasian, "The Consequences of High School Graduation Testing Programs."

50. Rothman, *Measuring Up*, p. 60.

51. For early debates on these and other issues, see Jaeger and Tittle, eds., *Minimum Competency Achievement Testing.*

52. See Southwest Learning Resources, "Meeting NCLB" (2004) [Available: bendare1.tripod.com/swlr/id4.html].

53. Ibid.

54. Quoted in Jodie Morse, "Sticking to the Script," *Time* (March 6, 2000), p. 61.

55. Rothman, *Measuring Up,* Chap 3.

56. Gregory R. Anrig, "'A Very American Way': Everybody's Getting into the Act," *Education Week* (June 17, 1992), p. S8.

57. Rose and Gallup, "The 35th Annual Phi Delta Kappa/Gallup Poll," pp. 45–46, 53–54; Rose and Gallup, "The 36th Annual Phi Delta Kappa/Gallup Poll," 45–48, 55. David J. Hoff, "Polls Dispute a 'Backlash' to Standards," *Education Week* (October 11, 2000), pp. 1, 16–17.

58. Hoff, "Polls Dispute a 'Backlash.'"

59. Quoted in "Agora: The Impact of High-Stakes Testing," *Journal of Teacher Education* 51 (September/October 2000): 291.

60. Morse, "Is That Your Final Answer?" pp. 34–35.

61. Quoted in Morse, "Is That Your Final Answer?" p. 35.

62. Deborah Meier and George Wood, eds., *Many Children Left Behind: How the No Child Left Behind Act Is Damaging Our Children and Our Schools* (Boston: Beacon Press, 2004).

63. Quoted in Hoff, "Polls Dispute a 'Backlash,'" p. 17. Susan Ohanian, *One Size Fits Few: The Folly of Educational Standards* (Westport, CT: Heinemann, 1999).

64. Alfie Kohn, *What Does It Mean To Be Well Educated? And More Essays on Standards, Grading, and Other Follies* (Boston: Beacon Press, 2004), and Alfie Kohn, *The Case against Standardized Testing: Raising the Scores, Ruining the Schools* (Portsmouth, NH: Heinemann, 2000).

65. National Commission on Excellence in Education, *A Nation at Risk,* pp. 24–27.

66. I base this estimate on U.S. Department of Education, National Center for Education Statistics, *Digest of Education Statistics, 2002* (2003) [Available: http://nces.ed.gov/programs/digest/d02/tables/dt152.asp], and Lynn Olson, "Quantity of Coursework Rises since 1983," *Education Week* (April 23, 2003), pp. 1, 14–17.

67. U.S. Department of Education, *Digest of Education Statistics, 2002* (2003) [Available: http://nces.ed.gov/programs/digest/d02/tables/dt152.asp].

68. "Graduation Requirements Toughest in Nation," *Mobile Register* (May 7, 1996), p. 5B.

69. Gene Bottoms quoted in Olson, "Quantity of Coursework," p. 14.

70. William J. Bennett, Chester E. Finn, Jr., and John T. E. Cribb, Jr., *The Educated Child: A Parent's Guide from Preschool through Eighth Grade* (New York: The Free Press, 2000).

71. William J. Bennett, *The Book of Virtues: A Treasury of Great Moral Stories* (New York: Simon & Schuster, 1993).

72. U.S. Department of Education, National Center for Education Statistics, "National Assessment of Adult Literacy: Defining Literacy and Sample Items" (2004) [Available: http://nces.ed.gov/naal/defining/defining.asp].

73. Ibid.

74. U.S. Department of Education, National Center for Education Statistics, "1992 National Adult Literacy Survey: Interpreting the Adult Literacy Scales and Literacy Levels" (1999) [Available: nces.ed.gov/pubs99/199909f.pdf].

75. U.S. Department of Education, National Center for Education Statistics, "Adult Literacy and Lifeskills: What Is the Adult Literacy and Lifeskills Survey?" (2004) [Available: http://nces.ed.gov/surveys/all/more.asp].

76. Carl F. Kaestle with Helen Damon-Moore, Lawrence C. Stedman, Katherine Tinsley, and William Vance Trollinger, Jr., *Literacy in the United States: Readers and Reading since 1880* (New Haven, CT: Yale University Press, 1991), p. 80.

77. Ibid.

78. Ibid., pp. 89, 127.

79. Ibid., Chap. 4.

80. Ibid., pp. 121–123, 128.

81. Ibid., p. 128.

82. Carl Kaestle, Anne Campbell, Jeremy D. Finn, Sylvia T. Johnson, and Larry J. Mikulecky, *Adult Literacy and Education in America: Four Studies Based on the National Adult Literacy Survey* (Washington: U.S. Department of Education, 2001).

83. Richard L. Venezky, Carl F. Kaestle, and Andrew M. Sum, *The Subtle Danger: Reflections on the Literacy Abilities of America's Young Adults* (Princeton, NJ: Educational Testing Service, 1987), p. 33.

84. Kaestle et al., *Literacy in the United States*, p. 291.

85. E. D. Hirsch, Jr., *Cultural Literacy: What Every American Needs to Know* (Boston: Houghton Mifflin, 1987); Diane Ravitch and Chester E. Finn, Jr., *What Do Our 17-Year-Olds Know? A Report on the First National Assessment of History and Literature* (New York: Harper & Row, 1987); Allan Bloom, *The Closing of the American Mind* (New York: Simon & Schuster, 1987).

86. James Trefil, E. D. Hirsch, Jr., and Joseph F. Kett, eds., *The New Dictionary of Cultural Literacy: What Every American Needs to Know*, 3rd ed. (Boston: Houghton-Mifflin, 2002); E. D. Hirsch, Jr., *The Schools We Need, and Why We Don't Have Them* (New York: Doubleday, 1999); E. D. Hirsch, Jr., and John Holdren, *What Your Kindergartner Needs to Know: Preparing Your Child for a Lifetime of Learning* (New York: Dell, 1997); E. D. Hirsch, Jr., *What Your First Grader Needs to Know: Fundamentals of a Good First Grade Education* (New York: Dell, 1998).

87. William F. Buckley, Jr., "A Real Driver's Test?" *Mobile Press* (June 10, 1987), p. 8A.

88. "Hirsch Defends Cultural-Literacy List," *Education Week* (April 15, 1987), p. 9.

89. Susan Ohanian, "Finding a 'Loony List' While Searching for Literacy," *Education Week* (May 6, 1987), pp. 21–22.

90. Hirsch, *Cultural Literacy*, p. 146.

91. Ibid., Chap. 5. The quotation is on p. 133.

92. Hirsch, *Cultural Literacy*, Chap. 5. Hirsch elaborates on these views in "Restoring Cultural Literacy in the Early Grades," *Educational Leadership* 45 (December 1987–January 1988): 63–70.

93. Ravitch and Finn, *What Do Our 17-Year-Olds Know?* p. 1.

94. Ibid., Chap. 3.

95. Chester Finn and Diane Ravitch, "Survey Results: U.S. 17-Year-Olds Know Shockingly Little about History and Literature," *American School Board Journal* 174 (October 1987): 33.

96. E. D. Hirsch, Jr., and John Holdren, *Books to Build On: A Grade-by-Grade Resource for Teachers and Parents* (New York: Delta, 1996); Michael J. Marshall and E. D. Hirsch, Jr., eds., *Realms of Gold: A Core Knowledge Reader* (Charlottesville, VA: Core Knowledge Foundation, 2000).

97. David Ruenzel, "By the Book," *Teacher Magazine* (August 1996), pp. 25–29.

98. Kathleen Kennedy Manzo, "Forum Invokes Heroes to Help Students Learn History," *Education Week* (May 7, 2003), p. 28.

99. E. D. Hirsch, Jr., "The Paradox of Traditional Literacy: Response to Tchudi," *Educational Leadership* 45 (December 1987–January 1988): 75.

100. Ravitch and Finn, *What Do Our 17-Year-Olds Know?* p. 252.

101. Diane Ravitch, *Left Back: A Century of Failed School Reforms* (New York: Simon & Schuster, 2000).

102. See James A. Banks, "Approaches to Multicultural Curriculum Reform," in James A. Banks and Cherry A. McGee Banks, eds., *Multicultural Education:Issues and Perspectives,* 4th ed. (New York: John Wiley, 2001), Chap. 10.

103. James A. Banks, *Cultural Diversity and Education: Foundations, Curriculum, and Teaching,* 4th ed. (Boston: Allyn & Bacon, 2001).

104. See Patricia Albjerg Graham, *S. O. S.: Sustain Our Schools* (New York: Hill & Wang, 1992), pp. 16–17, and Stephen Tchudi's "Slogans Indeed: A Reply to Hirsch," *Educational Leadership* 45 (December 1987–January 1988): 72–74. A book that airs arguments on all sides of the debate is *Cultural Literacy and the Idea of General Education,* Part II of *The Eighty-Seventh Yearbook of the National Society for the Study of Education* (Chicago: NSSE, 1988).

105. U.S. Department of Education, *Digest of Education Statistics, 2002* (2003) [Available: nces.ed.gov/pubs2003/2003060.pdf], Tables 56, 103.

106. Quoted in Richard M. Jaeger, "World Class Standards, Choice and Privatization," *Phi Kappan* 74 (October 1992): 124.

107. Hirsch, "Restoring Cultural Literacy," p. 66.

108. Dale Whittington, "What Have 17-Year-Olds Known in the Past?" *American Educational Research Journal* 28 (Winter 1991): 776.

109. Robert Rothman, "Teachers Dispute Studies' Counsel on Humanities," *Education Week* (September 16, 1987), p. 23.

110. Quoted in ibid.

111. Chester E. Finn, Jr., *We Must Take Charge: Our Schools and Our Future* (New York: Free Press, 1991).

INDEX

Italicized page locators indicate a figure; italicized *t* indicates a table.